S0-APM-030

THE OFFICIAL®

2003 BLACKBOOK PRICE GUIDE TO UNITED STATES POSTAGE STAMPS

TWENTY-FIFTH EDITION

BY MARC HUDGEONS, N.L.G., AND TOM HUDGEONS

HOUSE OF COLLECTIBLES

The Crown Publishing Group • New York

Copyright © 2002 by Random House, Inc.

All rights reserved. No part of this book may be reproduced or transmitted in any form or by any means, electronic or mechanical, including photocopying, recording, or by any information storage and retrieval system, without permission in writing from the publisher.

House of Collectibles and colophon are trademarks of Random House, Inc.

Published by: House of Collectibles
The Crown Publishing Group
New York, New York

Distributed by The Crown Publishing Group, a division of Random House, Inc., New York, and simultaneously in Canada by Random House of Canada Limited, Toronto.

www.randomhouse.com

Stamp designs © United States Postal Service

Printed in the United States of America

Buy It • Use It • Become an Expert is a trademark of Random House, Inc.

ISSN: 0195-3559

ISBN: 0-609-80949-0

10 9 8 7 6 5 4 3 2 1

Twenty-fifth Edition: June 2002

TABLE OF CONTENTS

OFFICIAL BOARD OF CONTRIBUTORS

The author would like to express a special thank-you to:

Robert Lamb, Executive Director, Kim Kowalczyk, Education Director, and Frank Sente, Membership Director at THE AMERICAN PHILATELIC SOCIETY, State College, PA, 16803, for directory listings,

Michael Laurence and Donna Houseman at LINN'S STAMP NEWS, Sidney, OH 45365, for their article,

Donald Sundman at Mystic Stamp Company, Camden, NJ, 13316 for their article and pricing information,

Daisy Ridgway, Public Affairs Manager at THE NATIONAL POSTAL MUSEUM, Smithsonian Institution, Washington, D.C, 20560, for articles,

Alex Bereson at UNITED NATIONS PHILATELIST, San Francisco, CA, 94131, for his pricing information,

Barry Newton of THE AMERICAN FIRST DAY COVER SOCIETY, Cleveland, OH, 44120, for his pricing information,

Robert Dumaine of DUCK STAMP COLLECTORS SOCIETY, Houston, TX 77282,

Kelly L. Spinks at THE UNITED STATES POSTAL SERVICE, Washington, D.C., 20260, for permission to reproduce the photography of U.S. stamps. *The designs for the stamps issued from 1978 to date are copyrighted by THE U.S. POSTAL SERVICE and are used with the permission of the U.S. Postal Service.*

NOTE TO READERS

HOW TO FIND YOUR STAMP

This new stamp catalog takes the confusion out of finding and identifying individual stamps. A complete, new FULL-COLOR FAST-FIND PHOTO INDEX is illustrated in the insert in this book. All of the stamp photographs are arranged in Scott numerical order and date of issue. Below each stamp picture is the Scott number.

Scott No.	Date	Page	Scott No.	Date	Page
734–777	1933–1936	A–1	1187–1202	1961–1962	A–22
782–801	1936–1937	A–2	1203–1237	1962–1963	A–23
802–830	1937–1938	A–3	1238–1257	1963–1964	A–24
831–867	1938–1940	A–4	1258–1273	1964–1965	A–25
868–896	1940	A–5	1274-1306	1965–1966	A–26
897–927	1940–1945	A–6	1307–1321	1966	A–27
928–942	1945–1946	A–7	1322–1343	1966–1968	A–28
943–954	1946–1948	A–8	1344–1372	1968–1969	A–29
955–970	1948	A–9	1373–1396	1969–1970	A–30
971–986	1948–1950	A–10	1397–1425	1970–1971	A–31
987–1005	1950–1952	A–11	1426–1447	1971–1972	A–32
1006–1020	1952–1953	A–12	1448–1473	1972	A–33
1021–1037	1953–1954	A–13	1474–1497	1972–1973	A–34
1038–1065	1954–1955	A–14	1498–1531	1973–1974	A–35
1066–1076	1955–1956	A–15	1532–1555	1974–1975	A–36
1077–1093	1956–1957	A–16	1556–1578	1975	A–37
1094–1113	1957–1958	A–17	1579–1623	1975	A–38
1114–1132	1958–1959	A–18	1629–1690	1976	A–39
1133–1149	1959–1960	A–19	1691–1711	1976–1977	A–40
1150–1167	1960	A–20	1712–1730	1977	A–41
1168–1186	1960–1961	A–21	1731–1755	1978	A–42

2003
BLACKBOOK
PRICE GUIDE TO
UNITED STATES
POSTAGE
STAMPS

LINN'S LOOK AT THE NEW STAMP ISSUES

by George Amick,
courtesy of Michael Laurence at
Linn's Stamp News

The size of the United States stamp program took a significant dip in 2001, with the U.S. Postal Service issuing 155 stamps and postal stationery items. It was the Postal Service's lowest output since 1997, when 130 stamps and postal stationery items were released, and it was well below the USPS record of 216 items issued in 2000.

One of the 2001 issues, the 34¢ United We Stand stamp, was planned, designed and printed in near record time in response to the September 11 terrorist attacks on the World Trade Center and Pentagon. To "spread our national message of unity and resolve with every letter we send," as Postmaster General John E. Potter put it, the USPS created definitive booklet and coil stamps depicting an American flag and the words "United We Stand." The Citizens' Stamp Advisory Committee met by e-mail to work on the project, and the stamp was issued October 24, exactly six weeks and a day after the deadly aircraft hijackings. The United We Stand design was issued in panes of 20, coils of 100 and coils of 10,000.

Just 65 commemoratives were issued in 2001, the lowest number in that category since 1991, when 46 were released. Forty of the 2001 commemoratives could be found in three large multiple-stamp panes of 20 or 10. One pane of 20 reproduced the art of 20 notable American illustrators, including several whose work previously appeared on U.S. stamps. The issue is in what the USPS calls its Classic Collection series. The Baseball's Legendary Playing Fields 20-stamp pane featured 10 baseball stadiums of the present and past, with an 11th stadium pictured in the selvage header at the top of the pane. The third entry in the ongoing Nature of America series depicted a Great Plains prairie scene, with 10 self-adhesive stamps that could be peeled out of the design.

The Postal Service acknowledged philatelic history with a souvenir sheet marking the 100th anniversary of the Pan-American Exposition in Buffalo, N.Y. Reproduced on the sheet, through use of the original engraved dies, were the three inverted-center errors from the series of bicolor stamps issued in 1901 to commemorate the exposition: 1¢ Fast Lake Navigation, 2¢ Empire State Express and 4¢ Electric Automobile. It was the first time U.S. postal officials had deliberately recreated a printing error for sale to the public since Postmaster General J. Edward Day's notorious decision in 1962 to order some 40 million 4¢ Dag Hammarskjold commemoratives printed with the yellow background inverted. This was done to destroy the rarity value of a few accidental Hammarskjold inverts that collectors had purchased at post offices. The 2001 Pan-American sheet also included four 80¢ stamps showing a label used in 1901 to promote the exposition. Two separate se-tenant (side-by-side) issues depicted, respectively, four carnivorous plants and four Amish quilts.

The ninth in a projected series of 12 Happy New Year stamps marked the Year of the Snake. Distinguished individuals who were honored on single-design commemoratives included James Madison, fourth president of the United States and author of the Bill of Rights, on the 250th anniversary of his birth; civil rights leader Roy Wilkins, shown on the 24th annual Black Heritage stamp; conductor-composer Leonard Bernstein; Lucille Ball, the 2001 Legends of Hollywood subject; Enrico Fermi, first physicist to split the atom, on his birth centennial; and Alfred Nobel, featured in a joint issue with his native Sweden on the 100th anniversary of the prizes that bear his name. The U.S. and Swedish Nobel Prize stamps were engraved by world-famous craftsman Czeslaw Slania.

The 2001 U.S. stamp honorees included two cartoon personalities. A Porky Pig stamp brought the Looney Tunes series to an end with Porky's signature sign-off, "That's all, folks!" prominent in the design. And Snoopy, the intrepid beagle, was shown in his World War I Flying Ace persona on a stamp honoring the comic strip Peanuts and its creator, Charles M. Schulz, who died in 2001.

By far the most controversial subject, from the point of view of many Linn's readers and other critics, was Mexican artist Frida Kahlo, whose self-portrait was shown on stamps issued simultaneously by the United States and Mexico. Postal Service officials declared the commemorative, the first U.S. stamp to honor directly a Hispanic woman, "a wonderful reflection of [the Postal Service's] commitment to diversity." But critics pointed out that Kahlo was an avowed communist whose final painting—left incomplete on her easel in 1954, when she committed suicide—was a portrait of her idol, Joseph Stalin. U.S. Senator Jesse Helms, ranking Republican on the Senate Foreign Relations Committee, notified Postmaster General Potter that he found the stamp "personally offensive." John J. Miller of National Review wrote in The Wall Street Journal: "By honoring Kahlo, the Postal Service . . . says that not a single Hispanic-American woman, going back to the days of the first Spanish settlers . . . deserves a spot on a stamp before this communist foreigner whose art wasn't especially good. If ever a stamp cried out for cancellation, it is this one."

The public's unhappiness over a U.S. stamp from 1999 was partly responsible for a 2001 commemorative with a photograph of a waving U.S. flag and the inscription "Honoring Veterans Continuing to Serve." In 1999, the USPS tried to honor two disparate groups—U.S. military veterans and police and firefighters who gave their lives in the line of duty—with the 33¢ Honoring Those Who Served stamp. The stamp, which features a highly stylized representation of the U.S. flag, comprising 12 wavy red bars and four blue ones, was the runaway choice for worst-designed commemorative issue in Linn's 1999 U.S. Stamp Popularity Poll. A number of petitioning groups complained that its message was, at best, diluted. "Unfortunately, the majority of people, especially veterans, are literalists," sighed Terrence McCaffrey, USPS manager of stamp development. The design of the 2001 U.S. Veterans stamp, accordingly, was quite literal.

As in past years, the USPS offered its 2001 Classic Collection, Looney Tunes, Nature of America and Legends of Hollywood stamps in uncut press sheets for sale to collectors at face value. Press sheets of the Legendary Playing Fields stamps, the James Madison stamp and the Pan-American Inverts souvenir sheet also were available for sale.

The 2001 stamp program included 42 definitives, a record high for the category. These included a Great Seal Official coil stamp and three airmail stamps in the Scenic American Landscapes series, which USPS previously had called Scenic American Landmarks. With the exception of the United We Stand stamps, each of these definitives was issued in response to two postal rate increases that took place during 2001: an overall set of increases January 7 included raising the first-class letter rate from 33¢ to 34¢, and a targeted hike July 1st included increases in the postcard rate from 20¢ to 21¢, the additional-ounce rate from 21¢ to 23¢, and the basic Express Mail rate from $12.25 to $12.45.

Helping boost the total number of definitives, and complicating life for collectors, was the decision of the USPS to issue many of these rate-change stamps in different formats. And within single formats for both the 20¢ George Washington and the 21¢ Bison, collectible variations exist in the gauge of the die cuts. It was left to the collecting community to discover these varieties, inasmuch as the Postal Service didn't announce them and apparently wasn't even aware of them. Because of the second rate increase at mid-year, the stand-alone life of many of the definitives was short.

In early 2001, the USPS issued a 20¢ George Washington stamp, a 55¢ Art Deco Eagle stamp, a 76¢ Hattie Caraway stamp in the new Distinguished Americans series (it was the first in that series to be self-adhesive), and a $12.25 Express Mail stamp depicting the Washington Monument at sunrise. The subsequent

July 1 increases in the rates for postcards, 2-ounce and 3-ounce first-class letters, and Express Mail made each of these obsolete. Furthermore, the Washington and Art Deco Eagle designs were used again with 23¢ and 57¢ denominations, respectively, and different colors. A 21¢ Bison stamp that was issued February 22 for the additional-ounce rate was retained, however, because it covered the new cost of sending a postcard—21¢—that went into effect July 1.

There were 22 special stamps released in 2001. These included a block of four Santas stamps in three different formats and a religious Christmas stamp reproducing Lorenzo Costa's oil-on-panel Virgin and Child. Two stamps were added to the Holiday Celebrations series, honoring Islamic eids, or festivals, and Thanksgiving. The We Give Thanks stamp, which the USPS said would be the last new design in the holiday series, depicted a needlework with a cornucopia image created by illustrator Margaret Cusack. For the second time since the Hanukkah and Kwanzaa stamps debuted in 1996 and 1997, respectively, their designs were recycled with a new denomination, this time 34¢.

Four new Love stamps were issued: a non-denominated version that sold for 34¢ and covered the first-class rate, a 34¢ denominated version, a 55¢ stamp to meet the cost of sending most wedding invitations with RSVP cards and envelopes enclosed, and, after the July 1st rate increase, a 57¢ stamp featuring the design of the 55¢ stamp. The Love designs featured a rose over a portion of handwritten correspondence between John Adams and his future wife, Abigail Smith, in 1763. It was an appropriate choice in a year in which David McCullough's biography of Adams would become a best-seller.

The USPS issued 22 postal cards in 2001, including 15 that were companions to stamps bearing the same designs: 10 Legendary Playing Fields, four Santa Clauses and one Porky Pig. Also in 2001, the Postal Service doubled the production fee it charges for postal cards above their face value, from 1¢ to 2¢.

Among the year's four postal envelopes was a 34¢ basic envelope depicting a stylized eagle. Late in 2001, this envelope played a central role in the anthrax-by-mail attacks by an unknown person or persons. The attacks killed two postal workers and three other people, caused widespread disruption within the USPS and targeted agencies of the federal government and the media. Because three of the anthrax-laced letters were mailed in 34¢ Federal Eagle envelopes, Postmaster General Potter ordered all postal envelopes taken off sale October 30 for study and re-evaluation of a characteristic that postal officials never before had considered problematic: their degree of porousness.

Encoded text made a return to U.S. stamps after an absence of almost two years. Used as a security measure on high-value stamps, the hidden text is a graphic element that is visible only through a special acrylic decoder lens sold by the USPS. Using the lens, the words "EXPRESS MAIL" can be seen on the $12.25 Washington Monument stamp, while "PRIORITY MAIL" appears on the $3.50 Capitol Dome stamp.

Finally, the Citizens' Stamp Advisory Committee revised its criteria for approving stamp subjects, including one that reflected a de facto policy change. The CSAC previously had banned stamps or postal stationery items "to honor . . . commercial enterprises." That rule didn't deter the USPS from issuing stamps in recent years promoting Ford automobiles, Crayola crayons, Warner Bros. cartoon characters, hit movies, television shows and other business ventures. The new criteria reads, "Stamps or stationery shall not be issued to promote or advertise commercial enterprises or products. Commercial products or enterprises might be used to illustrate more general concepts related to American culture." The loophole in the second sentence appears to be big enough to admit almost any subject under the private-sector sun.

George Amick is the author of *Linn's U.S. Stamp Yearbooks*, 1988 to the present.

MARKET REVIEW
by Donald Sundman

The September 11 attacks on America sent shock waves throughout our society and have directly influenced our hobby and the
stamp market. This story is still unfolding at the time of writing.
The United States quickly released a "United We Stand" stamp picturing the American flag, and 50 other countries have said they
intend to release antiterrorism stamps in support of the United
States.

Anthrax letters, which used the United States mail system to
spread potentially deadly anthrax spores among the very citizens it
serves, had the most dramatic effect on stamp collecting. In total,
37 people were directly exposed to anthrax. Five people died,
including two postal workers employed at the Brentwood, D.C., mail
facility. Postal equipment contaminated. Large amounts of mail
detained. In fact, the combination of recession, terrorist attacks,
and anthrax letters contributed to the USPS delivering 2.8 billion
fewer pieces of mail last fall.

In response to the anthrax attacks, the USPS has eight devices
costing $5 million each that "irradiate" mail. The devices work by
shooting a stream of electrons into the material to be sanitized,
"cooking" the mail. The level of radiation is about 1,000 times
stronger than that used to treat human cancer patients. In layman's
terms, irradiation scrambles the bacteria's DNA, thus killing it.

There's no question that the public needs to know the mail is
safe. However, irradiation is especially bad news for stamp collectors, as it destroys mail. At least two batches of mail burst into
flames and were destroyed during radiation processing. The irradiation process seems to advance the aging of paper, making it gray
and brittle. Irradiated paper may crumble when touched at the
edges. Some reports state it leaves an unpleasant odor. Adhesives
are also damaged. (One report said irradiation sealed reply envelopes.) Also at danger are credit cards, audio and video cas-
settes, magnetic tapes, plants and seeds (or any other living thing),

computer chips, contact lenses, medicines, vitamins, health supplements, food, film, photographs, and anything made of plastic.

Interestingly, this isn't the first time an effort to keep the mail safe has led to its destruction. During the late 1880s, yellow fever spread throughout Florida. (It had not yet been determined that yellow fever was carried by mosquitoes.) Drastic steps were taken in the effort to stop the spread of the disease. Mail was quarantined, placed in special railway box cars, and beaten with spiked paddles so that the envelopes were perforated. The entire box car was then fumigated with sulfur. As you can imagine, the quality of the mail after this process was unsatisfactory. And covers showing the effects of this process are desirable collectibles now, nearly 120 years later.

If you receive any irradiated mail, consider saving the USPS plastic wrapper and the envelope inside. Together, they document a unique time and place in American and U.S. postal history. You'll have an interesting collectible for free. Also consider saving any overseas mail from U.S. soldiers fighting the war against terrorism. Items with APO addresses and markings, or those of foreign nations, will also serve to document special moments in history. Years from now, these items may become very collectible.

Linn's Stamp News, the "World's Largest Weekly Stamp News and Marketplace," features a composite U.S. stamp market index constructed and presented using the same principles as the Dow Jones Industrial Average. In 2001, this index hit its highest levels since 1982.

Continuing the trend from last year, prices paid for 19th-century U.S. stamps are especially on the rise, particularly rare, very high quality, and famous stamps. *Linn's* also releases separate indexes for 19th- and 20th-century stamps. The 19th-century index hit all-time highs during every month of 2001.

As prices are driven higher at the top of the stamp market, they have a tendency to make other stamp prices rise. This trend is positive, as it makes the hobby more exciting for both current collectors and prospective collectors alike. Financially secure baby boomers reaching or approaching retirement are one of the forces driving this "booming" market.

The sale of two important Pony Express covers made headlines in 2001. A Wells Fargo cover, bearing a $4.00 Pony Express stamp considered to be one of the rarest pieces of U.S. postal history, sold at auction for $357,500.00. This set a record for the highest price ever paid for a Pony Express cover. A second cover, which was mailed on the first day of Pony Express service, April 3, 1860, was purchased for $198,000.00. Specialists estimate there are about 200 surviving Pony Express covers today.

The Universal Postal Union (UPU) will launch its own numbering system on January 1, 2002. UPU numbers will help to ensure the authenticity of postage stamps. The sale of illegal and unauthorized stamps has become a growing problem in recent years. In some cases, unscrupulous individuals have even sold stamps from countries that don't exist!

The UPU plan will require nations to register each new stamp issue for a fee of $30.69. (UPU numbers will only be applied to new stamps, older issues will remain unlisted.) In the past, individual catalog publishers, such as Scott, Gibbons, and Michel, have held the responsibility of determining whether to list a stamp or not, thus rendering an opinion on its authenticity. There are many instances when these catalogs disagree in their listings. It's unclear whether the major catalogs will list the additional UPU numbers.

I believe the UPU's efforts will have a positive impact on the hobby. There needs to be some method for protecting poorer nations from those who would take advantage of them, as well as the collectors who acquire these stamps. UPU numbers should accomplish this important task.

In 2001, Scott Publishing Company made portions of its catalogs available on CD-ROM for the first time. The CDs allow collectors to easily page through the catalog. When possible, older stamp images in the catalog that were reproductions have been replaced with color images of the actual stamps, including perforations. Scott's CD-ROM catalogs are useful and cost-effective resources that will have a positive influence on stamp collecting.

Overall, the stamp market is healthy and the future looks promising. A large segment of the American population is at or near retirement age. Some of these people are returning to the hobby they enjoyed in their youth.

As more collectors with sizable disposable incomes enter the stamp market and the supply of U.S. stamps, especially older stamps, dwindles as more are lost to damage, the twin forces of new demand and shrinking supply will continue to drive prices higher.

All 43 U.S. Presidents Postage Stamps

Every American President from Washington to Bush – only $5

Collectors love to see our U.S. Presidents commemorated on postage stamps. And you will too!

This complete set of mint stamps honors every American President from "Father of our Country" George Washington to modern-day George W. Bush. Fun, historical and patriotic!

Save 50% off catalog price on this classic stamp set. A great value for your collection at just $5.

You will also receive special collecting information and other interesting offers on approval. Limit four collections. Send today. Satisfaction guaranteed.

THE NATIONAL POSTAL MUSEUM

On July 30, 1993, the National Postal Museum opened its doors to the public, marking the creation of a new Smithsonian Institution museum, and making way for the nation's first major museum devoted to postal history and philately.

In what is a sophisticated and highly interactive museum, the National Postal Museum features exhibitions that tell the history of the nation's mail service, from the Colonial era and the Pony Express to the art of letters and the beauty and lore of stamps.

"The theme of the museum is 'America's history is in the mail.' We are presenting American history from a new perspective," says James H. Bruns, former director of the National Postal Museum. "The museum is intended to inspire appreciation for a system that affects our lives every day. The history of America's mail service is the history of our success as a nation. The museum tells an upbeat and endearing story of American ingenuity and remarkable progress."

The Postal Museum is located at First Street and Massachusetts Avenue N.E. on the lower level of the former Washington City Post Office Building, which is on Capitol Hill next to Union Station. The museum houses and displays the nation's stamp and postal history collection, the largest and most comprehensive of its kind in the world.

"Not only is America's history in the mail, its future is in the mail, too," says William J. Henderson, former Chief Executive Officer and Postmaster General of the U.S. Postal Service. "We want people to understand the role the Postal Service has played for more than two centuries in helping our nation grow and prosper, and the important social and economic role the mail continues to play for the United States."

The museum occupies approximately 75,000 square feet, with more than 25,000 square feet devoted to exhibit space. It also features a Library Research Center, a Discovery Room for educational programs, a museum shop, and a philatelic sales center. The Library Research Center, available to the public by appointment, is among the largest postal history and philatelic research centers in the world, with more than 40,000 volumes and manuscripts. The museum also houses collections, conservation facilities, and curatorial and administrative offices. A full-service U.S. post office will be accessible from a corridor within the museum.

HISTORY

The National Postal Museum was made possible by an agreement between the Smithsonian and the United States Postal Service. The museum was established after lengthy negotiations about relocating the Smithsonian's vast postal history and philatelic collection of more than 16 million stamps, covers, and artifacts. Previously housed on the third and fourth floors of the National Museum of American History, the collection lacked adequate exhibit, storage, and research space in that location.

On November 6, 1990, the Smithsonian Institution and the U.S. Postal Service signed an agreement in which the Postal Service would provide the site and approximately $15.4 million for start-up and construction costs and the Smithsonian would administer the museum and its staff.

The National Postal Museum is funded by both the Postal Service and the Smithsonian, as well as by money raised from endowments and ongoing fund-raising campaigns. The Smithsonian contribution to the new museum has been the same as that spent on the collection when it was at the Museum of American History. The more than $3 million raised from private organizations through March 1993 went toward the installation of the new and expanding exhibits. Private funds continue to be used to develop and expand exhibits.

THE COLLECTION

The National Philatelic Collection was established at the Smithsonian in 1886 with the donation of a sheet of 10-cent Confederate postage stamps. Generous gifts from individuals and foreign governments, transfers from government agencies and purchases have increased the collection to today's total of more than 16 million items.

From 1908 until 1963, the collection was housed in the Smithsonian's Arts and Industries Building on the National Mall. In 1964, the collection was moved to the National Museum of American History where it was expanded to include postal history and stamp production. In addition to the stamp collection, the museum has postal stationery covers, postal history material that predates stamps, vehicles used to transport the mail, mailboxes, meters, greeting cards, and letters.

EXHIBITIONS

More than 50,000 stamps and objects, and 400 graphics are on display throughout the museum's five major exhibit galleries that explore different facets of mail communication and history. The galleries include:

MOVING THE MAIL

Faced with the challenge of moving the mail quickly, the postal service looked to trains, automobiles, airplanes, and buses to deliver the mail, all of which are the focus of the museum's 90-foot-high Atrium gallery. After the Civil War, postal officials began to take advantage of railway trains for moving and sorting the mail. Sorting the mail while it was being carried between towns was a revolutionary approach to mail delivery, involving generations of devoted postal employees who worked as railway mail clerks.

Airmail service was established between New York, Philadelphia, and Washington, D.C., in 1918 with the remarkable pioneering flights of pilots Torrey Webb, James Edgerton, H. Paul Culver, and George Boyle. Airmail service was the base from which America's commercial aviation industry developed.

Some of the most ambitious movers of the mail were not aviators, railway mail clerks, or even postal employees. They are the star route contractors, who have delivered mail with everything from mules to motorcycles, including the 1850s Concord-style stagecoach on display in the museum.

THE ART OF CARDS AND LETTERS

While other galleries focus on systems of mail service, this gallery emphasizes letters. A cherished art form, letters are windows into history, used throughout museum displays to relate personal stories of survival, success, and tragedy. Through an array of wartime correspondence from World War I to Desert Storm, as well as objects and a video, one section highlights the struggle between soldiers and their loved ones to maintain ties during war. Changing exhibits in this gallery concentrate on the important stories letters tell of families and friends bound by these missives over land and across time.

BINDING THE NATION

The museum's first gallery provides an overview of the events in America from colonial times through the 19th century, stressing the importance of written communication in the young nation. As early as 1673, regular mail was carried between New York and Boston following Indian trails. That route, once known as the King's Best Highway, is now U.S. Route 1.

Benjamin Franklin, a colonial postmaster for the British government, played a key role in establishing mail service in the colonies, as well as in forging a strong link between colonial publishers and the postal service. Many newspapers that relied heavily on information carried in the mail customarily adopted the word "Post" into their title. Newspapers were so important to the dissemination of information to the people that they were granted cheaper postage rates.

By 1800, mail was carried over more than 9,000 miles of postal roads. The challenge of developing mail service over long distances is the central theme of "The Expanding Nation," which features the famed Pony Express. At an interactive video station, visitors can create their own postal route.

CUSTOMERS AND COMMUNITIES

By the turn of the 20th century, nearly 10,000 letter carriers worked in over 400 cities. The nation's population was expanding at top speed, and with it, the nation's mail volume and the need for personal mail delivery. This gallery focuses on the modern changes in mail service introduced at the turn of the century.

Crowded cities inspired postal officials to experiment with a variety of mail delivery systems, such as the impressive but ultimately impractical underground pneumatic tubes. Home delivery of mail began in the cities during the Civil War, when postal officials decided it was inhumane to require soldiers' families to receive death notices at post office windows.

As rural Americans watched city residents receive free home delivery, they began to demand equal treatment. This was the start of Rural Free Delivery. Facets of Rural Free Delivery and its important and often heartwarming role in the fabric of the nation is explored with photographs, mail vehicles, and a variety of rural mailboxes.

The history of the vast direct mail industry is the subject of a special interactive gallery. Through the use of sophisticated technology, the exhibition *What's in the Mail for You!* uses touch screen panels, three-dimensional projections, video workstations, holograms, and computer interactives to tell the story of the mailing industry and its function as a major means of commerce in America. This hands-on exhibit allows visitors to create a mailer and "target" customers; related exhibit topics look at different mail marketing techniques, the key to a successful mail campaign, and the success stories of well-known mail order entrepreneurs like L.L. Bean.

STAMPS AND STORIES

Among some 20 million stamp collectors in the United States, many are casual collectors, while others work at the hobby with a devotion to detail and scholarship unmatched by other pastimes. This gallery is for all collectors, as well as for those who know little about the renowned hobby of philately. The history of the stamp begins in 1840, when Great Britain issued the first gummed postage stamp. Since then stamps of every subject, shape, and design have been produced for consumer use or as collectibles.

Serving not only as proof of postage, stamps are also miniature works of art, keepsakes, and rare treasures—as well as the work-horses of the automated postal system. Some stamps tell stories while others contain secrets and hidden meanings.

Some of the highlights of the gallery are priceless rarities from the museum's vast collection, including inverted stamps and scarce covers. Videos address questions of how and why stamps were invented, and how they are printed. A selection of more than 55,000 stamps is on display, and will be rotated every six months.

Within the exhibit galleries are more than 30 interactive areas, including, for example, video games that invite visitors to choose the best mail route between various cities in the 1800s, or deliver mail in a DeHavilland biplane. The museum features 17 video presentations, with topics ranging from America's railway mail clerks, the star route contractors, early letter carriers, and transportation technology, to stories about mail-train wrecks and robberies, and postal workers.

THE JEANETTE CANTRELL RUDY GALLERY

In this 800-square-foot gallery, a major exhibition devoted to federal duck stamps, entitled "Artistic License: The Duck Stamp Story," opened in Spring 1996. Made possible by a generous donation from Jeanette Cantrell Rudy of Nashville, TN., the exhibition explores the history of duck stamps, their contribution to the conservation of America's water-ways, and the extraordinary craftsmanship that goes into their creation. A selection of rare duck stamps is on display, drawn from the collections of Mrs. Rudy and from the National Postal Museum.

TOURS

One-hour highlights tours are offered daily at 11 A.M. and 1 P.M. The National Postal Museum's Education Office will arrange guided tours for school and camp groups from September through May. Group leaders should call (202) 357-2991 (Voice) or (202) 633-9849 (TTY) for more information.

MUSEUM DESIGNED SPECIFICALLY TO HOUSE UNIQUE COLLECTION

The National Postal Museum was designed by the firm of Flor-ance Eichbaum Esocoff King Architects. Chief among the objectives for designing the museum was the desire to create a maxi-mum-security facility to protect the Smithsonian's priceless stamp collection, while at the same time creating an aesthetically rich setting that will attract visitors and encourage exploration of the museum's themes of postal history and philately.

The new museum's centerpiece is a 90-foot-high atrium that projects through the center of the quadrangle-shaped City Post Office Building. Three airmail planes hang from steel girders inside the atrium, which has a glass ceiling 1.5 inches thick. The entire atrium area houses mail transportation vehicles and related displays; however, enough space on the atrium's marble floor remains for visitors to observe the intricate envelope and stamp design within the floor's tiles.

The museum is equipped with an array of sophisticated surveillance and safety equipment. The museum's research facilities, including the 6,000-square-foot Library Research Center, are meant to enhance the work and study of visiting researchers and scholars. The library features a specimen study room, an audio-visual viewing room, and a separate library of rare books.

HISTORIC BUILDING ENHANCES MUSEUM'S MESSAGE

The Washington City Post Office Building was built between 1911 and 1914 to serve as the District's central post office facility. Designed by architect Daniel Burnham, architect of Union Station, the City Post Office Building was built next door to the elegant train station in order to expedite the distribution of incoming mail to the nation's capital.

Completely renovated and restored to its original appearance, the City Post Office Building houses the National Postal Museum as well as a full-service post office and several federal agencies. The museum is located in what was once the building's mail processing and distribution center. An impressively ornate historic marble lobby, formerly the main service area of the City Post Office Building, will now serve as the foyer to the National Postal Museum. The Beaux Arts–style building is eligible for listing in the National Register of Historic Places.

EDUCATION PROGRAMS AND CHANGING EXHIBITIONS

The National Postal Museum offers a series of educational outreach activities. Through scheduled events in the museum's Discovery Center, individuals from preschool age to adult are invited to participate in events that aim to enhance the information presented in exhibits. Activities range from learning more about the art of stamps, postal transportation, automation, and mail delivery to letter writing and the analysis of historic letters. The museum also engages in school and community collaborative projects.

LIBRARY RESEARCH CENTER

With its more than 40,000 volumes and manuscripts, the museum's Library Research Center is among the world's largest philatelic and postal history research facilities. The 6,000-square-foot library features a rare-book reading room, an audiovisual room, research cubbies, and a workroom for viewing items from the collection. The library also offers current philatelic and postal magazines and newsletters as well as U.S. Postal Service publications and annual reports. The center is operated by the Smithsonian Institution Libraries. It is open to the public by appointment from 10 A.M. to 4 P.M., Monday through Friday. For more information, call (202) 633-9370.

PUBLICATIONS

The official newsletter of the National Postal Museum is a quarterly, titled "EnRoute," and is available by becoming a member of the National Postal Museum for $25.00 annually. A six-month calendar of events and membership information is offered by request by calling (202) 633-9385.

STAFF

The museum staff includes fifty-two full-time professional positions.

FACTORS THAT DETERMINE STAMP VALUES

The collector value (or "market value") of any stamp rests with a variety of factors. Philately becomes a bit less mysterious when one understands the forces at work in the stamp marketplace.

A beginner will normally presume that expensive stamps are expensive because of rarity. Certainly there is a great deal of talk about stamp rarities within the hobby, and so it is natural enough to ascribe high prices to the phenomenon of rarity. In fact, rarity is only one of several factors that influence stamp prices, and the influence it carries is not particularly clear-cut.

In this book you will note some stamps (mostly among the early regular issues) with values of $1,000, $2,000, and even higher. Obviously these stamps are rarer than those selling for $10 or $15. But having said that, we have virtually summed up our useful knowledge of rarity and its effect on prices. A comparison of prices, between stamps in roughly similar ranges of value, does not indicate which is the rarer. A stamp selling for $1,000 is not necessarily rarer than one selling for $500. A $10,000 stamp may actually be more abundant than one which commands $5,000. This hard-to-comprehend fact of philatelic life prevails because of the other factors involved in determining a stamp's price. If rarity were the only factor, one could, of course, easily see which stamps are the rarest by the prices they fetch.

The word "rare" is an elixir to many collectors, not only of stamps but other collectors' items. Sellers are well aware of this, and seldom fail to sprinkle the word liberally in their sales literature. There is no law against calling a stamp rare, as this represents a personal opinion more than anything else and opinions are allowable in advertising. Unfortunately, there is no standard definition for rarity. Does "rare" mean just a handful of specimens in existence, with one reaching the sales portals once in five years? Does it mean 100 in existence, or 1,000, or some other number? Since stamps are—today, at any rate—printed in the multimillions, a thousand surviving specimens might seem a very tiny total to some people. Further complicating this situation is the fact that the specific rarity of most stamps cannot be determined, or even estimated, with any hope of accuracy. The quantities printed are recorded for most of our stamps, going back even into the nineteenth century, but the quantity *surviving* of any particular stamp is anyone's guess. It is obvious that a stamp that goes through the auction rooms once a year is fairly rare, but this provides no sound basis for guessing the number of specimens in existence. That could only be accomplished if some sort of grand census could be taken, and all specimens tallied. This, of course, is nothing but a pipe dream. Some collectors would not participate in such a census; some might be unaware that it was being conducted. Then, too, there are many scarce or rare stamps in hands other than those of collectors, such as dealers and museums. Additionally, there could be (and probably are) existing specimens of rare stamps yet to be discovered, as fresh discoveries are made periodically in the hobby through attic cleaning and the like.

In terms of influence on price, rarity is outdistanced somewhat by *popularity*. Some stamps, for one reason or other, are simply more popular than others. They have a sort of innate appeal for hobbyists, either through reputation, exquisite designing, circumstances of issue, oddity, or various other potential reasons. These stamps sell out rapidly from the stocks of dealers, while some stamps that are supposedly scarcer will linger in stock albums for ages and ages waiting to tempt a customer. It is no wonder, then, that the prices of popular stamps rise more quickly than those that are scarce but not in brisk demand. The Columbian series typifies the effect of popularity on stamp values. If stamp prices were fixed by scarcity alone, none of the Columbians would be selling for nearly as much. Much of their value derives from their overwhelming popularity with collectors of U.S. stamps. It would be safe to say, in fact, that *all* of the Columbians from the lowest face value to the $5, are more plentiful than other U.S. stamps selling for precisely the same sums. Every dealer has Columbians in stock, and quite a few dealers have the high value of the set, too. They are not "hard to get." But they *are* very costly.

Popularity, of course, does not remain constant forever. There are shifts in philatelic popularity, usually slight but occasionally extreme. The popularity of commemoratives as a whole versus regular issues as a whole can change from time to time. Then, too, there are swings of popularity for airmails, first-day covers, blocks, coil pairs, mint sheets, and all other philatelic material. A climb or decline in the price of any philatelic item is often an indication of the forces of popularity at work. Then there are activities of investors to consider, whose buying habits seldom reflect those of the pure collector. A great deal of buying by investors in any short period of time (such as occurred during 1979 and 1980, and to less extent in 1981) can make prices seem well out of balance.

Also on the subject of prices, it is important for the beginner to realize that arithmetic is usually futile when dealing with stamp values. You cannot determine the price of one philatelic item by knowing the value of a similar one. This can best be shown by the relative values of singles and blocks of four. A block of four is, as one would expect, worth *more* than four times as much as single specimens of that stamp. It is not just four specimens of the stamp, but four of them *attached*, which lends added scarcity and appeal. The difficulty lies in trying to use mathematics to determine a block's value. Some blocks are worth five times as much as the single stamp; some six times; some ten times as much or even more. Almost all blocks—except very common ones—will vary somewhat in value, in relation to the value of the individual stamp. There is no satisfactory explanation for this, other than the presumption that some blocks are scarcer than others or just in greater demand than others.

In the case of common philatelic items, the value hinges greatly on the method of sale. If you want to buy one specimen of a common cover, you may have to pay $1.50. But if you were willing to buy a hundred common first-day covers *of the dealer's choice*, you could very likely get them for $75 or 75¢ each. Buying in quantity, and allowing the dealer to make the selections, can save a great deal of money. Of course one may then ask: What is the real value of those covers? Is it $1.50 or 75¢? The only answer is that it depends on how you buy!

If this article seems to raise a great many questions without supplying many answers, it will, hopefully, serve to show that stamp collecting is not bound to rigid formulas. What happens in the stamp market is largely beyond prediction, or precise explanation. This, indeed, is one of the exciting aspects of the hobby.

STAMP COLLECTORS' TERMINOLOGY

Adhesives—A term given to stamps that have gummed backs and are intended to be pasted on articles and items that are to be mailed.

Aerophilately—The collecting of airmail or any form of stamps related to mail carried by air.

Airmail—Any mail carried by air.

Albino—An uncolored embossed impression of a stamp generally found on envelopes.

Approvals—Stamps sent to collectors. They are examined by the collector, who selects stamps to purchase and returns balance with payment for the stamps he retained.

Arrow Block—An arrow-like mark found on blocks of stamps in the selvage. This mark is used as a guide for cutting or perforating stamps.

As-is—A term used when selling a stamp. It means no representation is given as to its condition or authenticity. Buyers should beware.

Backprint—Any printing that may appear on reverse of stamp.

Backstamp—The postmark on the back of a letter indicating what time or date the letter arrived at the post office.

Bantams—A miniature stamp given to a war economy issue of stamps from South Africa.

Batonne—Watermarked paper used in printing stamps.

Bicolored—A two-color printed stamp.

Bisect—A stamp that could be used by cutting in half and at half the face value.

Block—A term used for a series of four or more stamps attached at least two high and two across.

Bourse—A meeting or convention of stamp collectors and dealers where stamps are bought, sold, and traded.

Cachet—A design printed on the face of an envelope, generally celebrating the commemoration of a new postage stamp issue. Generally called a first-day cover.

Cancellation—A marking placed on the face of a stamp to show that it has been used.

Cancelled to Order—A stamp cancelled by the government without being used. Generally remainder stamps or special issues. Common practice of Russian nations.

Centering—The manner in which the design of a stamp is printed and centered upon the stamp blank. A perfectly centered stamp would have equal margins on all sides.

Classic—A popular, unique, highly desired, or very artistic stamp. Not necessarily a rare stamp, but one sought after by the collector. Generally used only for nineteenth-century issues.

Coils—Stamps sold in rolls for use in vending machines.

Commemorative—A stamp issued to commemorate or celebrate a special event.

Crease—A fold or wrinkle in a stamp.

Cut Square—An embossed staple removed from the envelope by cutting.

Dead Country—A country no longer issuing stamps.

Demonetized—A stamp no longer valid for use.

Error—A stamp printed or produced with a major design or color defect.

Essay—Preliminary design for a postage stamp.

Face Value—The value of a stamp indicated on the face or surface of the stamp.

Frank—A marking on the face of an envelope indicating the free and legal use of postage. Generally for government use.

Fugitive Inks—A special ink used to print stamps, which can be rubbed or washed off easily, to eliminate erasures and forgeries.

General Collector—One who collects all kinds of issues and all types of stamps from different countries.

Granite Paper—A type of paper containing colored fibers to prevent forgery.

Gum—The adhesive coating on the back of a stamp.

Handstamped—A stamp that has been handcancelled.

Hinge—A specially gummed piece of glassine paper used to attach a stamp to the album page.

Imperforate—A stamp without perforations.

Inverted—Where one portion of a stamp's design is inverted or upside down from the remainder of the design.

Local Stamps—Stamps that are only valid in a limited area.

Margin—The unprinted area around a stamp.

Miniature Sheet—A smaller-than-usual sheet of stamps.

Mint Condition—A stamp in original condition as it left the postal printing office.

Mirror Print—A stamp error printed in reverse as though looking at a regular stamp reflected in a mirror.

Multicolored—A stamp printed in three or more colors.

Never Hinged—A stamp in original mint condition never hinged in an album.

Off Paper—A used stamp that has been removed from the envelope to which it was attached.

On Paper—A used stamp still attached to the envelope.

Original Gum—A stamp with the same or original adhesive that was applied in the manufacturing process.

Pair—Two stamps unseparated.

Pen Cancellation—A stamp cancelled by pen or pencil.

Perforation Gauge—A printed chart containing various sizes of perforation holes used in determining the type or size of perforation of a stamp.

Perforations—Holes punched along stamp designs allowing stamps to be easily separated.

Philatelist—One who collects stamps.

Pictorial Stamps—Stamps that bear large pictures of animals, birds, flowers, etc.

Plate Block Number—The printing plate number used to identify a block of four or more stamps taken from a sheet of stamps.

Postally Used—A stamp that has been properly used and cancelled.

Precancels—A stamp that has been cancelled in advance. Generally used on bulk mail.

Reissue—A new printing of an old stamp that has been out of circulation.

Revenue Stamp—A label or stamp affixed to an item as evidence of tax payment.

Seals—An adhesive label that looks like a stamp, used for various fund-raising campaigns.

Se-tenant—Two or more stamps joined together, each having a different design or value.

Sheet—A page of stamps as they are printed, usually separated before distribution to post offices.

Soaking—Removing used stamps from paper to which they are attached by soaking in water. *(NOTE: Colored cancels may cause staining to other stamps.)*

Souvenir Sheet—One or more specially designed stamps printed by the government in celebration of a special stamp.

Splice—The splice made between rolls of paper in the printing operation. Stamps printed on this splice are generally discarded.

Tete-Bechs—A pair of stamps printed together so that the images point in opposite vertical directions.

Transit Mark—A mark made by an intermediate post office between the originating and final destination post office.

Typeset Stamp—A stamp printed with regular printer's type, as opposed to engraved, lithographed, etc.

Ungummed—Stamps printed without an adhesive back.

Unhinged—A stamp that has never been mounted with the use of a hinge.

Unperforated—A stamp produced without perforations.

Vignette—The central design portion of a stamp.

Want List—A list of stamps a collector needs to fill gaps in his collection.

Watermark—A mark put into paper by the manufacturer, not readily seen by the naked eye.

Wrapper—A strip of paper with adhesive on one end, used for wrapping bundles of mail. Especially in Britain, it refers to any bit of paper to which a used stamp is still attached.

HOW TO GRADE STAMPS

A person need not be an expert to judge the quality or grade of a stamp. All he needs is a discerning eye, possibly a small linear measuring device, and the grading instructions listed below.

The major catalogs traditionally list stamps simply as "Unused" or "Used." Auction houses, however, will describe the stamps for sale in a more informative manner. The greater the value of the stamp, the more thoroughly it is described.

There is no officially accepted system of grading stamps. What we have done in this book is essentially to set up a system of grading stamps using the suggestions and practices of stamp dealers from all over the country. Total agreement was made to the following categories and grades of stamps that are most frequently traded.

CATEGORIES

Mint—The perfect stamp with superb centering, no faults, and usually with original gum (if issued with gum).

Unused—Although unused, this stamp may have a hinge mark or may have suffered some change in its gum since it was issued.

Used—Basically this will be the normal stamp that passed through the government postal system and will bear an appropriate cancellation.

Cancelled to Order—These are stamps that have not passed through the postal system but have been carefully cancelled by the government usually for a commemoration. These are generally considered undesirable by collectors.

GRADE—STAMP CENTERING

Average—The perforations cut slightly into the design.

Fine—The perforations do not touch the design at all, but the

Average
Centering

Fine
Centering

Very Fine
Centering

Extra Fine
Centering

Superb
Centering

design will be off center by 50 percent or more of a superb centered stamp.

Very Fine—The design will be off center by less than 50 percent of a superb stamp. The off-centered design will be visibly noticeable.

Extra Fine—The design will be almost perfectly centered. The margin will be off by less than 25 percent of a superb stamp.

Superb—This design will be perfectly centered with all four margins exactly the same. On early imperforate issues, superb specimens will have four clear margins that do not touch the design at any point.

GRADE—STAMP GUM

Original Gum—This stamp will have the same gum on it that it had the day it was issued.

Regummed—This stamp will have new gum applied to it as compared to an original gummed stamp. Regummed stamps are worth no more than those with gum missing.

No Gum—This stamp will have had its gum removed or it may have not been issued with gum.

Never Hinged—This stamp has never been hinged so the gum should not have been disturbed in any way.

Lightly Hinged—This stamp has had a hinge applied. A lightly wetted or peelable hinge would do very little damage to the gum when removed.

Heavily Hinged—This stamp has had a hinge applied in such a manner as to secure it to the stamp extremely well. Removal of this hinge usually proves to be disastrous, in most cases, since either part of the hinge remains on the stamp or part of the stamp comes off on the hinge, causing thin spots on the stamp.

GRADE—STAMP FAULTS

Any fault in a stamp such as thin paper, bad perforations, creases, tears, stains, ink marks, pin holes, etc., and depending upon the seriousness of the fault, usually results in grading the stamp to a lower condition.

OTHER STAMP CONSIDERATIONS

CANCELLATIONS

Light Cancel—This stamp has been postally cancelled but the wording and lines are very light and almost unreadable.

Normal Cancel—This stamp has been postally cancelled with just the right amount of pressure. Usually the wording and lines are not distorted and can be made out.

Heavy Cancel—This stamp has been postally cancelled. In the process excessive pressure was used, and the wording and lines are extremely dark and sometimes smeared and in most cases unreadable.

PERFORATIONS

Not to be overlooked in the appearance of a stamp are its perforations. The philatelist might examine these "tear apart" holes with a magnifying glass or microscope to determine the cleanliness of the separations. One must also consider that the different types of paper, upon which the stamp was printed, will sometimes make a difference in the cleanliness of the separations. The term "pulled perf" is used to denote a badly separated stamp in which the perforations are torn or ragged.

COLOR

Other important factors such as color affect the appearance and value of stamps. An expert will have a chart of stamp colors. Chemical changes often occur in inks. Modern printing sometimes uses metallic inks. These "printings" will oxidize upon contact with the natural secretions from human skin.

The color of certain stamps has been deliberately altered by chemicals to produce a rare shade. Overprints can be eliminated. Postmarks may be eradicated. Replacing gum is a simple process. Some stamps have been found to bear forged watermarks. The back of the paper was cut away and then the stamps rebacked with appropriately watermarked paper.

There are stamp experts who earn a living in the business of stamp repairing. They are craftsmen of the first order. A thin spot on a stamp can be repaired by gluing it on a new layer of paper. Missing perforations can be added. Torn stamps can be put back together. Pieces of stamps may be joined.

In some countries it is accepted practice for an expert, upon examination of a stamp, to certify the authenticity by affixing his signature to the back of the stamp. If the stamp is not genuine, it is his right and duty to so designate on the stamp; but these signatures can also be faked.

WHAT IS AN ERROR, FREAK, OR ODDITY?

In an attempt to answer the questions above, an article, *Listing of Existing EFO Variations According to Group,* by Mr. John M. Hotchner, was published originally in the June 1982 issue of *The EFO Collector,* the quarterly journal of the Errors, Freaks, Oddities Collectors Club. Resulting correspondence and experience in the efo field, plus selected portions of Mr. Hotchner's article, are contained herein to attempt to provide some guidance as to what constitutes an error, freak, or oddity.

Nothing makes a philatelist's head turn so fast as an obvious error in an issued stamp. Many of philately's true blue-chip errors are from the early days. The United States 1869 inverts on the fifteen-cent, twenty-four-cent and thirty-cent values, Spain's 1851 two-real value in a six-real blue sheet, New South Wales stamps of the 1850s and '60s with the wrong watermark, etc.

Why? Most stamps of this era had relatively small printings compared to today's. In addition, they were used with little thought given to looking for or saving errors or misprints of lesser significance. Most of the varieties that have been found were used, and exist in very small quantities. Incidentally, this is a very good reason for one to keep one's eye open, for there remains a possibility that classic errors can still be found in old albums or accumulations.

In the early days of philately, collectors gathered efos (errors, freaks, oddities) to dress up their country or topical collections. Many modern collectors continue to collect efos in that fashion. There has, however, been a recent increase in collecting and studying efos as a specialty area.

Modern-day specialization has been fostered by the greatly increased awareness of and search for efo material. This is a search which is often rewarded because of the increasing complexity of modern production equipment and the continuing pressure to reduce cost.

The lack of commonly accepted definitions of efo terms has been an impediment to the growth of efo philately. In the absence of a clear sense of what efos include, philatelists, in large numbers, have found the area complex and difficult. It has been hard to understand how values developed, so collectors merely kept what they came across, but rarely sought out efo material unless it was listed in a catalog.

Catalog listing is, of course, reserved for errors. Catalog-listed errors get space in albums. Thus, recognized errors tend to have an increased value because collectors search for them because they like to fill their empty album spaces. Without a catalog listing, the remainder of efo material tended to wallow in a valley of conflicting and confusing opinion and wildly varying prices. Also, if an item lacks catalog recognition, one might call the item a "freak," "oddity," or "variety."

The answer to an often-asked question regarding efos—"Aren't they expensive?"—is that while some efos are valued in the thousands of dollars, others cost no more than a regular used stamp. In fact, it is quite possible for one to find a spectacular efo item in one's own mailbox. You have probably heard of collectors who bought stamps or postal stationery at their local post office only to find something wrong with the purchase. Think of some of the people who used their find before they realized they had an efo item. *Knowledge* is the key to recognizing efo material when you find it.

The best possible source of information and education can be obtained by becoming a member of a philatelic organization such as the American Philatelic Society (APS), The American Topical Association (ATA), etc.; by joining specialty groups such as the Bureau Issues Association (BIA), The Errors, Freaks, Oddities Collectors Club (EFOCC), etc.; by subscribing to publications such as Linn's, Meekels, Stamp Collector, etc.; by joining libraries such as the Cardinal Spellman Museum, the Western Philatelic Library, etc. Through these organizations and publications, one will obtain knowledge so that one can differentiate between what a postal entity designs and what is the produced product.

The following is the best tool, to date, to attempt to type efo material that is at variance from the intended design.

ERRORS

To be classed as such, an item must be *completely missing* a production step, i.e. the item must be *completely missing* a color, *completely missing* required perforations, contain an inverted design step, etc. Other examples might be:

• Perforations *entirely missing* between stamps—one or more sides.
• Perforations *fully* doubled or tripled.

• Perforations of *wrong gauge* applied.
• Items unintentionally printed on paper watermarked for another issue, or not watermarked at all.

FREAKS

To be classed as such, an item might have a lesser degree of production problem, or problems that are partial and not repeatable. Examples might be:

• Perforations shifted into the design portion of an issue.
• Overinking, underinking, smeared inking.
• Foldovers, foldunders, creases creating crazy perforations.
• Printer's waste (by definition, "Unlawfully Salvaged"). This category would include rejection markings that indicate material that should have been destroyed.
• Gutter snipes (less than a full stamp on one side).

ODDITIES

"Oddities" or, as European collectors seem to favor, "Varieties" include unusual issuances. Examples might be:

• Stamps printed on backs of stamps.
• Usages (bisects).
• Essays, proofs, specimens.
• Cancel/meter varieties.
• Unusual local overprints.
• Double transfers, layout lines, position dots.
• Pre-first-day of issue cancels.

The bottom line is any item, be it freak, error, oddity, or variety, can be collected as a specialty, or a collector can try to obtain an example of each. Some collectors will restrict their collecting to one country, or even one major issue within a country. Others simply accumulate and enjoy anything they come across with no particular rhyme-or-reasoned order.

The Errors, Freaks, Oddities Collectors Club has an international membership, quarterly publication and mail auction, heir's assistance program, study groups, etc. Annual dues are $16 USD North America, Europe $30 USD. Sample copy of *The EFO Collector* is $3 USD, or mint postage. EFOCC, P.O. Box 1126, Kingsland, GA 31548-1126, Phone: (912) 729-1573; FAX: (912) 729-1585; E-mail—cwouscg@aol.com.

REPAIRS, FAKES, AND OTHER UNDESIRABLES

Philately, like most hobbies, is not without its pitfalls. The collector who buys from reputable dealers runs very little risk, as today's stamp pros have high principles and are hard to fool. Buying from auction sales and small dealers, who may not have expert knowledge, is another matter. Here the collector must call into play his own expertise and learn to distinguish the bad from the good.

In the early years of philately, stamps provided a playground for fakers and swindlers. They took advantage of the public's gullibility and the general lack of published information about stamps. Copies were printed of rare stamps, as well as of stamps that never existed in the first place. Cancels were bleached from used specimens to make them appear unused. Fake margins were added to imperforates, to allow ordinary copies to be sold as "superb with jumbo margins." Perforated stamps were reperforated to make them better centered. Thin spots in the paper were filled in, tears closed, missing portions of paper replaced. Stamps were doctored and manipulated in more ways than could be imagined, all in the hope of fooling collectors and making anywhere from a few extra cents to thousands of dollars on them. One of the favorite tricks of fakers was to apply bogus overprints or surcharges. By merely using a rubber handstamp and a pad of ink, they could stamp out a hundred or more "rarities" in a few minutes, turning ordinary British or other issues into varieties not found in any catalog. It was all a great game and proved very profitable, until collectors and the philatelic public at large became wary of such practices. Even though most of these fakes from the hobby's pioneer years have disappeared out of circulation, a few still turn up and must be guarded against.

U.S. stamps have not been faked nearly so extensively as those of many other nations, notably South America and Japan. Still, the collector should learn to watch for fakes and also for repaired specimens.

Total Fake. The counterfeit stamp always varies somewhat from a genuine specimen, though the difference may be very slight.

Detection can usually be made if the suspect stamp is examined alongside one known to be genuine. By using a magnifier, the lines of engraving and paper quality can be compared. The ink on a fake is likely to have a fresher appearance and will lie on the surface as a result of being printed at a later date and on less sophisticated equipment; however, this is not always the case. Experts say that when a stamp appears to be a fake, or a reprint, the odds are very good that it is. Some experience is necessary before anyone can get a first-glance reaction to a stamp. The presence or absence of a cancel has no bearing on the likelihood of a stamp being a fake, as cancels can be faked, too.

Faked Cancel. Faked cancels are very rare on U.S. stamps, as nearly all are worth more unused than used. One notable exception is the 90¢, 1857–1861. These are applied either with a fake hand stamp or simply drawn with pen and ink. Skillfully drawn faked cancels can be very deceptive. Faked cancels are *much more numerous* on covers than loose stamps.

Removed Cancels. So-called cleaned copies of used stamps, sold as unused, were once very plentiful and are still encountered from time to time. The faker, of course, chooses lightly cancelled specimens from which the obliteration can be removed without leaving telltale evidence. In the case of imperforates he may trim down the margins to remove part of the cancel. Rarely will he attempt to clean a stamp whose cancel falls across the face or any important portion of the stamp. Holding the stamp to a strong light may reveal the cancel lines. X-ray examination provides positive proof.

Added Margin(s). When margins have been added to an imperforate stamp, the paper fibers are woven together (after moistening) along the back and at the front where the margin extends beyond the stamp's design. They can usually be detected by looking closely for a seam or joint at the point where the design ends and the margin begins. A magnifying glass will be necessary for this. When held against a light, the reverse side will probably show evidence of the weaving operation. Sometimes the added margins are of a slightly different grade of paper.

Reperforated. A stamp that has been reperforated to improve its centering will usually be slightly smaller than a normal specimen, and this can be revealed by placing it atop an untampered copy.

Filled-in Thin Spots. If held to a light and examined with a good magnifier, filled-in thin spots will normally appear darker than the remainder of the stamp. Such spots are often mistaken for discoloration by beginners. Thin spots are filled in by making a paste of paper pulp and glue and applying it gradually to the injured area. After drying, the stamp is placed in a vise so that no telltale hills or valleys are left. This is not really considered forgery but honest repair work; it becomes forgery only if done with the intent of selling the stamp as undamaged.

Closed Tears. These are almost always visible against a light with a magnifier, even if small. A routine examination of any rare stamp should include a check of its margins for possible closed or open tears.

HOW TO USE THIS BOOK

The main section of this book lists all U.S. stamps with the exception of special issues such as airmail, revenues, etc. Special issues are grouped separately in sections of their own. Please refer to the Table of Contents.

Before pricing your stamps, be sure they are correctly identified. Use the photo section as an aid. In some cases, two or more stamp issues are very similar in appearance and can be distinguished only by minor details. These are always noted in the text. Sometimes the evidence is obvious. If a stamp has perforations, it cannot be earlier than 1857.

Prices are given in columns for used and unused specimens, usually in two grades of condition. You need only refer to the column that applies to your stamp and its condition grade.

Prices shown in this book are actual selling prices, so one should not necessarily expect to receive a discount when buying from dealers.

When a dash (—) appears in place of a price, this indicates that the item is either unavailable in that condition grade or is so seldom available that its price is open to question. It should not be assumed, however, that such items are invariably more valuable than those for which prices are shown.

Prices are given for hinged stamps that have been in collections. In today's stamp market a premium value is placed on stamps that have never been hinged. To determine the premium on any stamp, refer to the premium percentages shown on every page.

The stated values are general guides only and cannot reflect the price of occasional superb specimens, such as imperforates with four wide margins, which may sell considerably higher.

A small box has been provided to the left of each listing for keeping a record of the stamps in your collection.

IMPORTANT

Because of the space limitation on each page we have not been able to include very fine, extra fine, never hinged, or lightly hinged pricing on each stamp. To determine these prices please use the following procedure.

Very Fine Pricing—Prior to 1941: *Double the average price quoted.*

Very Fine Pricing—After 1941: *Add 25 percent to the fine price.*

Extra Fine Pricing—Prior to 1941: *Triple the average price quoted.*

Never Hinged Pricing—Prior to 1941: *Add the percentage indicated at the right of the issue to any price listed. Example: (N-H add 5 percent).*

Never Hinged Pricing—After 1941: *Add 15 percent to any price listed.*

Lightly Hinged Pricing—*Add one half of the N-H percentage indicated for each issue to any price listed.*

DEALER BUYING PRICES

Buying prices will vary greatly depending upon condition, rarity, and existing dealers' stock of a particular stamp. With these facts in mind, a dealer can be expected to buy stamps between 40 percent and 50 percent of their quoted prices; but this will depend upon supply and demand.

THREE TIPS FOR
STAMP COLLECTORS:
Soaking Stamps,
Choosing an Album,
and Using Tongs
Courtesy of the American Philatelic Society.

- **TIP 1: SOAKING STAMPS**

BEFORE SOAKING
Set aside any stamps on colored paper, or on paper with a colored backing. Pick out any stamps with colored cancellations, especially with red or purple ink.

Set aside any dark-colored stamps, stamps on poor-quality paper, or with strange-looking inks that might dissolve in the water and stain other stamps being soaked, etc. Any "problem" stamps must be handled carefully later, one at a time.

Trim the envelope paper close to the stamp, being careful not to cut the perforated edges or otherwise damage the stamp.

SOAKING THE STAMPS
Use a shallow bowl and fill it with several inches of cool-to-lukewarm water. (Never use hot water.) Float the stamps with the picture side up. Make sure the stamps have room to float and do not stick to one another. Don't soak too many at one time.

Let the stamps float until the glue dissolves and the stamps *slide easily* off the paper. Paper is very weak when it is wet and it's easy to tear a wet stamp if you handle it roughly. Be patient, and let the water do its work!

Rinse the back of the stamp gently in fresh water to make sure all the glue is off. Change the water in the soaking bowl often to make sure it is clean.

Place the stamps to dry on paper towels or old newspapers. (Don't use the Sunday comics! The colored inks might stick to the wet stamps.) It's a good idea to use your stamp tongs (see next page!) to lift the wet stamps, instead of using your fingers. Lay the stamps in a single layer, and so they are not touching one another.

Let the stamps dry on their own. They may curl a little or look wrinkled, but don't worry about that. When they are completely dry, lift them with your tongs and put them in a phone book or a dictionary or some other book. (Special "stamp drying books" also can be purchased.) It's important not to put the stamps in a book until they are completely dry. After a few days, they should be nice and flat, and you can put them in your collection.

STAMPS ON COLORED PAPER OR WITH COLORED-INK CANCELS

Cut away all the excess envelope paper without harming the edges of the stamp.

Fill a shallow dish with cool water (cooler than you would usually use for soaking) and float the stamp *face up.* If the water becomes stained before the stamp is free from the paper, empty it out and use clean water, to prevent the stamp from being stained.

Dry as before.

DIRTY OR STAINED STAMPS

These can be soaked carefully in a small amount of undiluted liquid dishwashing detergent (*not* *dishwasher* detergent), then rinsed in clean cool water.

Very badly stained stamps can be washed gently in a weak solution of water and a bit of enzyme laundry detergent. Careful! This can work *too* well and remove the printing ink!

SELF-ADHESIVE STAMPS

Some self-adhesive stamps have a special, water-soluble backing, and they *can* be soaked off envelopes. You just need extra patience, as they may have to soak for an hour or more before they will separate from the backing paper. In general, *U.S. self-adhesive stamps from about 1990 and later can be soaked with water; earlier ones cannot.* If you don't want to try soaking, just trim the paper closely around a self-adhesive stamp on cover, and then mount it in your collection with a stamp mount.

• TIP 2: CHOOSING AN ALBUM

You've raided the mailbox, rummaged in the wastebasket in the post office lobby, and pestered your friends to save their envelopes. Now that you have all these philatelic goodies, where will you put them?

True, an ordinary shoebox gives storage space, but you should want a nicer home for your treasures—a place to *display* your material, not just store it. And, on the practical side, stamps and covers (envelopes with stamps on them, used in the mail) kept in a shoebox or paper folder risk damage from dirt or creases, losing value as well as beauty.

Since the first known commercial stamp album was published in 1862, the stamp hobby has grown tremendously, and many types of albums have become available.

When buying a home for your collection, here are some things to think about:

It may be your first album, but it probably will not be your last or only one. Your first album may be a kind of experiment, unless you already have seen someone else's album and think that kind would be right for you too. You also may have tried homemade pages and got some ideas of what you would want in a standard album.

If you are buying an album in person, rather than by mail, listen to the seller's advice, but don't be fully convinced by claims that one or another album is "the best." An album may be by a famous maker, and expensive, but that doesn't make it "the best" one for you. Be a careful shopper; *consider all the factors—appearance, price, format*— and make the best choice. Good beginners' albums are available that are not too expensive, are fully illustrated to show which stamp goes where, and may even contain extra information, such as maps and facts about the countries.

Certain styles of albums can present problems. For example, if an album is designed for stamps to be mounted on the front and back of each page, when the book is closed, the stamps can become tangled with one another on the facing pages. Opening the book may tear the mounted stamps apart. If you are looking at an album with this page format and don't like that aspect, but do like other things about the album, buy some good-quality plastic sheets to insert between the pages, and prevent the tangles.

You may choose not to buy a top-of-the-line album because of cost, but do *be willing to pay for some quality*. An album with pages of flimsy paper will not stand up to the stress of increasing numbers of stamps as you fill the album. An album with torn, falling-out pages is not much better than the old shoebox.

Homemade pages can be experimented with before album-shopping or may even become your permanent storage choice. Some options include a notebook or looseleaf binder of plain paper, though longtime, safest storage of your stamps should be on acid-free paper. If you have an unusual specialty, or enjoy unique arrangements, no standard album may ever suit your needs, and homemade will be best.

Blank, acid-free album pages punched for three-hole binders are widely available. It is easy to assemble a safe, stable home for your personalized collection, if you don't need or want the kind of structured format that standard albums provide. Makers of custom pages and albums advertise regularly in the philatelic press.

Buying an album is not so different from buying anything else: **Think before and during the purchase;** buy as wisely as you can and not over your budget; and don't be too discouraged if your first acquisition turns out to be less than perfect. You will always need places for temporary storage as you continue in the hobby. Old albums never go to waste!

• TIP 3: USING TONGS

Philatelic tongs (not to be confused with the tweezers in the medicine cabinet) are must-have items for every stamp collector. Get into the habit early of using your tongs every time you work with your stamps. They will act as clean extensions of your fingers and keep dirt, skin oil, and other harmful things from getting on your philatelic paper.

It's important to use tongs correctly and carefully. As with knives, scissors, and other helpful tools, tongs used carelessly are harmful rather than helpful. Cut some plain paper into stamp-sized pieces and practice using your tongs, watching what happens as you change the angle, pressure, and method of using them.

Grip a bit of paper strongly with the pointy-end style of tongs and watch what happens. If that were a favorite stamp, would you have wanted that hole poked in the middle of it? Keep experimenting, and you will find that it's not difficult to hold a stamp firmly but gently with tongs.

There are several common styles of tongs, to suit your preference and for special purposes.

Some have very pointed ends; they touch only a tiny part of the stamp, but there is the risk of poking holes through it. Working with extra-long tongs (five or six inches) with small pointed tips requires a lot of dexterity, and while experts may prefer them, they may not be comfortable or necessary for "everyday" stamp work.

The rounded, spatula-type style known as the "spade" are good, general-purpose tongs. **A squared-off version** of the spade also is commonly available, though the rather sharp corners present the same kind of risk as the thin, pointy tongs. **One handy style is angled,** with a bend near the tips that makes it easier to remove stamps from watermark or soaking trays, or to insert and remove stamps from stockbooks or mounts.

Tongs cost anywhere from a couple of dollars to quite a few for some of the imported, high-quality models. A special gift for a philatelist would be some gold-plated tongs, which are not hard to find, believe it or not! Tongs can be found anywhere stamp supplies are sold; check under "Accessories" in the philatelic press ads.

Tongs are among the least expensive and most essential stamp-hobby needs. You may even want to have several different kinds on hand—instead of your hands! Your stamps will appreciate it.

EQUIPMENT

To collect stamps properly a collector will need some "tools of the trade." These need not be expensive and need not all be bought at the very outset. That might, in fact, be the worst thing to do. Many a beginning collector has spent his budget on equipment, only to have little or nothing left for stamps and then loses interest in the hobby.

It may be economical in the long run to buy the finest quality accessories, but few collectors, just starting out, have a clear idea of what they will and will not be needing. It is just as easy to make impulse purchases of accessories as of stamps and just as unwise. Equipment must be purchased on the basis of what sort of collection is being built *now*, rather than on what the collection may be in the future. There is no shame in working up from an elementary album.

Starter Kits. Starter or beginner outfits are sold in just about every variety shop, drugstore, etc. These come in attractive boxes and contain a juvenile or beginner's album; some stamps, which may be on paper and in need of removal; a packet of gummed hinges; tongs; a pocket stockbook or file; and often other items such as a perforation gauge, booklet on stamp collecting, magnifier, and watermark detector. These kits are specially suited to young collectors and can provide a good philatelic education.

Albums. When the hobby began, more than a century ago, collectors mounted their stamps in whatever albums were at hand. Scrapbooks, school exercise tablets, and diaries all were used, as well as homemade albums. Today a number of firms specialize in printing albums of all kinds for philatelists, ranging from softbounds for the cautious type to huge multi-volume sets that cost hundreds of dollars. There are general worldwide albums, country albums, U.N. albums, and albums for mint sheets, covers, and every other conceivable variety of philatelic material. Choose your album according to the specialty you intend to pursue. It is not necessary, however, to buy a printed album at all. Many collectors feel there is not enough room for creativity in a printed album and prefer to use a binder with unprinted sheets. This allows items to be arranged at will on the page, rather than following the publisher's format, and for a personal write-up to be added. Rod-type binders will prove more durable and satisfactory than ring binders for heavy collections. The pages of an album should not be too thin, unless only one side is used. The presence of tiny crisscrossing lines (quadrilled sheets) is intended as an aid to correct alignment. Once items have been mounted and written up, these lines are scarcely visible and do not interfere with the attractiveness of the page.

Hinges. These are small rectangular pieces of lightweight paper, usually clear or semiopaque, gummed and folded. One side is moistened and affixed to the back of the stamp and the other to the album page. Hinges are sold in packets of 1,000 and are very inexpensive. Though by far the most popular device for mounting stamps, the hobbyist has his choice of a number of other products if hinges are not satisfactory to him. These include cello mounts, which encase the stamp in clear sheeting and have a black background to provide a kind of frame. These are self-sticking. Their cost is much higher than hinges. The chief advantage of cello mounts is that they prevent injuries to the stamp and eliminate the moistening necessary in using hinges; however, they add considerably to the weight of each page, making flipping through an album less convenient, and become detached from the page more readily than hinges.

Glassine Interleaving. These are sheets made of thin semitransparent glassine paper, the same used to make envelopes in which stamps are stored. They come punched to fit albums of standard size and are designed to be placed between each set of sheets, to prevent stamps on one page from becoming entangled with those on the facing page. Glassine interleaving is not necessary if cello mounts are used, but any collection mounted with conventional hinges should be interleaved. The cost is small. Glassine interleaving is sold in packets of 100 sheets.

Magnifier. A magnifier is a necessary tool for *most* stamp collectors, excepting those who specialize in first-day covers or other items that would not likely require study by magnification. There are numerous types and grades on the market, ranging in price from about $1 to more than $20. The quality of magnifier to buy should be governed by the extent to which it is likely to be used, and the collector's dependence upon it for identification and study. A collector of plate varieties ought to have the best magnifier he can afford and carry it whenever visiting dealers, shows, or anywhere that he may wish to examine specimens. A good magnifier is also necessary for a specialist in grilled stamps and for collectors of Civil War and other nineteenth-century covers. Those with built-in illumination are best in these circumstances.

Tongs. Beginners have a habit of picking up stamps with their fingers, which can cause injuries, smudges, and grease stains. Efficient handling of tongs is not difficult to learn, and the sooner the better. Do not resort to ordinary tweezers, but get a pair of philatelic tongs which are specially shaped and of sufficiently large size to be easily manipulated.

Perforation Gauge. A very necessary inexpensive article, as the identification of many stamps depends upon a correct measuring of their perforations.

TEN LOW-COST WAYS TO START COLLECTING STAMPS

Courtesy of the American Philatelic Society.

If you have recently started collecting stamps, or are thinking about starting, you may be wondering if the hobby is expensive. Can you enjoy it with limited financial resources? What if you have no money at all for the hobby?

One of the biggest questions any stamp collector faces is where to find stamps inexpensively. If you intend to save stamps of the United States or the world and want to save used as well as unused stamps, the opportunities are really great. Not all collections consist mainly of unused stamps that you buy in the post office. Used stamps are worth saving, have value, and they may cost you nothing.

Many stamp collectors save only used stamps. Others save both used and unused ones. Others save stamps only from one country or one part of the world. Some collectors save stamps by "topic," for example, stamps that depict horses or trains or birds. There are any number of different types of collections.

1. All postally used stamps started out being received in someone's mailbox, at no cost to the person receiving them. The first place to search for stamps, then, is your own mailbox. Don't be discouraged when you notice that many senders use postage meters or the imprint "Bulk Rate Postage Paid" on their envelopes to enjoy a better postal rate or to keep from affixing stamps. Also, when people do use real stamps, they often use the same common small ones.

You can begin to change this by asking people who write to you to use *commemorative* stamps on their mail. These are normally the larger stamps issued to honor famous people, places, or events. These stamps are printed in lesser quantities than the common smaller *(definitive)* stamps and usually are of much more interest to collectors. Many people will remember to ask for commemorative stamps at the post office when mailing letters to you or your family if you let them know you are a stamp collector. Also, if you write away for offers that require postage or a self-addressed, stamped envelope, you can put commemoratives on your return envelope, knowing that they will come back to you later.

2. Neighbors, friends, and relatives are another good source of stamps. The majority of people just throw away stamps when they receive them on mail and are only too happy to save them for someone who appreciates them. You may even know someone who gets letters from other countries who can save these stamps, too. Always be on the lookout for potentially good stamp contacts, and don't be afraid to ask them to go through their mail for you before they throw away all the envelopes.

3. Office mail may be even better. You may know someone who works in an office that gets a lot of mail. Out of 100 letters a day, there may be ten or twenty good stamps that are being thrown away. Many businesses get a lot of foreign mail and regularly throw away stamps that have interest and/or value to a collector.

4. Ask your parents if they have any old letters, which may have stamps on the envelopes. When taking stamps off envelopes, always tear off the corner so that there is paper all around the stamp, and the stamp and all its perforations are undamaged. Anyone who is saving stamps for you should be told that this is the way to do it; otherwise, he/she may try to peel the stamp off the envelope. This will cause thin spots or tears, both of which will ruin a stamp's appearance and lessen its value to collectors. If you run across envelopes that are very old or have postal markings that may be of particular interest, it is best to save the entire envelope until you can find out if the stamp is worth more attached to the cover.

Now that you have stamps on paper, what do you do with them? The most common way to get stamps off paper is to soak them in cool water, then dry them on paper. To understand more about soaking stamps, it is best to find a handbook on stamp collecting at the library.

There is a lot to learn about stamps as you get more and more of them. For example, different shades of color may exist on stamps with the same design, or they may have different perforation measurements (number of holes per side). Major varieties of stamps and "catalog values" are listed in stamp catalogs, which are available in most libraries. The most common one, the *Scott Standard Postage Stamp Catalogue*, has a very good section in front that explains how stamps are made and how to tell varieties apart, as well as how to use the catalog. Having access to a catalog in a nearby library is very useful until you decide if you want one of your own.

5. Longtime collectors may be another source of stamps. Usually a person who has been a collector for a number of years has developed many sources for stamps. The collector may have thousands of duplicates, some of which may be very inexpensive while others may have more value. Often older collectors are willing to help new philatelists get started by giving them stamps, or at least providing packets of stamps much more cheaply than can be purchased in stores or by mail.

6. Many stamp companies advertise free stamps. However, these ads must be read carefully before you send away for anything. Usually these ads offer "approvals," which means they will send you the free stamps advertised, *plus* an assortment of other stamps which you may either buy or return. By sending for the free stamps, you have already agreed that you will return the other stamps within a reasonable period of time if you do not buy anything. Usually you must pay the return postage. This is a convenient way to buy stamps from your own home.

7. Stamp clubs are another place to get stamps. A club may offer stamps as prizes, or have inexpensive stamps you can afford to buy.

Some stamp clubs sponsor junior clubs that meet at schools or the local YMCA or community center. If you are fortunate enough to have one of these in your area, it can be a great source of both stamps and advice.

8. One way to increase your sources for stamps and also have a lot of fun is to help *start* a local club, if one does not already exist. All it takes are four or five other stamp collectors who are interested in getting together to learn about and trade stamps and ideas.

9. Obtaining a pen pal in another country is a very good way to get stamps from that country. His or her extra stamps may seem really common in that country, but over here they are much scarcer. Your own stamps may look fairly common to you, but he or she is sure to appreciate them.

10. Trading off your duplicate stamps can be a lot of fun. Even if you don't know many collectors where you live, stamps are so light-weight that they can easily be traded by mail. Check out the stamp newspapers and magazines available at your local library for classi-fied ads that list stamp trades. You may find, for example, that another collector will send you 100 large foreign stamps if you send 100 U.S. commemoratives. Usually schools do not subscribe to any of the periodical stamp publications, so you will have to go to your public library. (Many stamp publications also offer to send one free sample issue if you request it, because they are always looking for potential new subscribers.)

Collecting stamps need not be an expensive hobby. Thousands of stamps are issued every year, and while some of them cost many dollars, others cost just a few cents each. Nobody expects you to try to save every stamp that exists, and the key to enjoying philately is to save whatever you enjoy the most! With free stamps and a few inexpensive accessories, such as a small album and a package of stamp hinges, even collectors with little money can have a great time. Don't forget to mention stamps, stamp albums, and hinges before your birthday or Christmas! Also remember that a great many inexpensive stamps in the past have turned into more valuable stamps over the years.

BUYING STAMPS

There are many ways to buy stamps: packets, poundage mixtures, approvals, new issue services, auctions, and a number of others. To buy wisely, a collector must get to know the language of philately and the techniques used by dealers and auctioneers in selling stamps.

Packets of all different worldwide stamps are sold in graduated sizes from 1,000 up to 50,000. True to their word, they contain no duplicates. The stamps come from all parts of the world and date from the 1800s to the present. Both mint and used are included. When you buy larger quantities of most things, a discount is offered; with stamp packets, it works in reverse. The larger the packet, the higher its price per stamp. This is because the smaller packets are filled almost exclusively with low-grade material.

Packets are suitable only as a collection base. A collector should never count on them to build his entire collection. The contents of one worldwide packet are much like that of another. Country jackets are sold in smaller sizes, but there are certain drawbacks with packets.

1. Most packets contain some cancelled-to-order stamps, which are not very desirable for a collection. These are stamps released with postmarks already on them, and are classified as used but have never gone through the mail. Eastern Europe and Russia are responsible for many C.T.O.'s.

2. The advertised value of packets bears little relation to the actual value. Packet makers call attention to the catalog values of their stamps, based on prices listed in standard reference works. The lowest sum at which a stamp can be listed in these books is 2¢, therefore, a packet of 1,000 automatically has a minimum catalog value of $20. If the retail price is $3 this seems like a terrific buy when, in fact, most of those thousand stamps are so common they are almost worthless.

Poundage mixtures are very different than packets. Here the stamps are all postally used (no C.T.O.'s) and still attached to small fragments of envelopes or parcel wrappings. Rather than sold by count, poundage mixtures are priced by the pound or ounce and quite often by kilos. Price varies depending on the grade, and the grade depends on where the mixture was assembled. Bank mixtures are considered the best, as banks receive a steady flow of foreign registered mail. Mission mixtures are also highly rated. Of course, the mixture should be sealed and unpicked. Unless a mixture is advertised as unpicked, the high values have been removed. The best poundage mixtures are sold only by mail. Those available in shops are of medium or low quality. Whatever the grade, poundage mixtures can be counted on to contain duplicates.

If you want to collect the stamps of a certain country, you can leave a standing order for its new releases with a new issue service. Whenever that government puts out stamps, they will be sent to the collector along with a bill. Usually the service will supply only mint copies. The price charged is not the face value, but the face value with a surcharge added to meet the costs of importing, handling, and the like. New issue services are satisfactory only if the collector is positive he wants all the country's stamps, no matter what. Remember that its issues could include semipostals, long and maybe expensive sets, and extra high values.

By far the most popular way to buy stamps is via approvals. There is nothing new about approvals, as they go back to the Victorian era. Not all services are alike, though. Some offer sets, while others sell penny approvals. Then there are remainder approvals, advanced approvals, and seconds on approval. Penny approvals are really a thing of the past, though the term is still used. Before inflation, dealers would send a stockbook containing several thousand stamps, all priced at a penny each. If all the stamps were kept, the collector got a discount plus the book! Today the same sort of service can be found, but instead of 1¢ per stamp, the price is anywhere from 3¢ to 10¢. Remainder approvals are made up from collection remainders. Rather than dismount and sort stamps from incoming collections, the approval merchant saves himself time by sending them out right on the album pages. The collector receives leaves from someone else's collection with stamps mounted just as he arranged them. Seconds on approval are slightly defective specimens of scarce stamps, which would cost more if perfect. Advanced approvals are designed for specialized collectors who know exactly what they want and have a fairly substantial stamp budget.

In choosing an approval service you should know the ground rules of approval buying and not be unduly influenced by promotional offers. Most approval merchants allow the selections to be kept for ten days to two weeks. The unbought stamps are then returned along with payment for those kept. As soon as the selection is received back, another is mailed. This will go on, regardless of how much or how little is bought, until the company is notified to refrain from sending further selections. The reputable services will always stop when told.

Approval ads range from splashy full-pagers in the stamp publications to small three-line classified announcements in magazines and newspapers. Most firms catering to beginners offer loss leaders, or stamps on which they take a loss for the sake of getting new customers. If an approval dealer offers 100 pictorials for a dime, it is obvious he is losing money on that transaction, as 10¢ will not even pay the postage. It is very tempting to order these premiums. Remember that when ordering approvals. What sort of service is it? Will it offer the kind of stamps desired? Will prices be high to pay for the loss leaders? Be careful of confusing advertisements. Sometimes the premium offers seem to promise more than they actually do. A rare, early stamp may be pictured. Of course you do not receive the stamp, but merely a modern commemorative picturing it.

Auction Sales. Stamp auctions are held all over the country and account for millions of dollars in sales annually. Buying at auction is exciting and can be economical. Many sleepers turn up—stamps that can be bought at less than their actual value. To be a good auction buyer, the philatelist must know stamps and their prices pretty well, and know the ropes of auctions. An obvious drawback of auctions is that purchases are not returnable. A dealer will take back a stamp that proves not to a collector's liking, but an auctioneer will not. Also, auctioneers require immediate payment while a dealer may extend credit.

Stamps sold at auction come from private collections and the stocks of dealers; not necessarily defunct dealers, but those who want to get shelf space. Because they were brought together from a variety of sources, the nature and condition will vary. In catalog descriptions the full book value will be given for each stamp, but of course defective stamps will sell for much less than these figures. A bidder must calculate how much less. Other lots which can be difficult for the bidder to evaluate are those containing more than one stamp. Sometimes a superb specimen will be lotted along with a defective one. Then there are bulk lots which contain odds and ends from collections and such. It is usual in auctioning a collection for the better stamps to be removed and sold separately. The remainder is then offered in a single lot, which may consist of thousands or even tens of thousands of stamps. By all means examine lots before bidding. A period of inspection is always allowed before each sale, usually for several days. There may or may not be an inspection on sale day. If the bidder is not able to make a personal examination but must bid on strength of the catalog description, he should scale his bids for bulk lots much lower than for single stamp lots. He might bid $50 on a single stamp lot with a catalog value of $100, if the condition is listed as top-notch, but to bid one-half catalog value on a bulk lot would not be very wise. These lots are not scrutinized very carefully by the auctioneers and some stamps are bound to be disappointing. There may be some heavily canceled, creased, torn, etc. Also, there will very likely be duplication. A bid of one-fifth the catalog value on a bulk lot is considered high. Often a one-tenth bid is successful.

The mechanics of stamp auctions may strike the beginner as complicated. They are run no differently than other auctions. All material to be sold is lotted by the auctioneer; that is, broken down into lots or units and bidding is by lot. Everything in the lot must be bid on, even if just one of the stamps is desired. The motive of bulk lotting is to save time and give each lot a fair sales value.

Before the sale a catalog is published listing all the lots, describing the contents and sometimes picturing the better items. Catalogs are in the mail about 30 days before the sale date. If a bid is to be mailed, it must be sent early. Bids that arrive after the sale are disqualified, even if they would have been successful.

When the bid is received it is entered into a bidbook, along with the bidder's name and address. On sale day each lot opens on the floor at one level above the second-highest mail bid. Say the two highest mail bids are $30 and $20. The floor bidding would begin at $25. If the two highest bids are $100 and $500, the opening bid would probably be $150. The larger the amounts involved, the bigger will be the advances. The auctioneer will not accept an advance of $5 on a $500 lot; but on low-value lots even dollar advances are sometimes made. Then it becomes a contest of floor versus book. The auctioneer acts as an agent, bidding for the absentee until his limit is reached. If the floor tops him, he has lost. If the floor does not get as high as his bid, he wins the lot at one advance over the highest floor bid.

When a collector buys stamps by mail from a dealer, he should choose one who belongs to the American Stamp Dealers' Association or A.S.D.A. The emblem is carried in their ads.

HOW TO ORDER STAMPS "TOLL-FREE" FROM THE USPS

You can now order stamps, toll-free, from the USPS by calling the Philatelic Fulfillment Service Center located in Kansas City, Missouri, 1-800-782-6724. Listening to a computerized voice, you can choose from six options using a touch-tone phone: 1) ordering stamps, 2) catalog requests, subscription programs information, 3) customer assistance, 4) personalized envelopes, post offices and official mail agencies. This is a very useful service. It is recommended that you first order one of the catalogs, "Stamps, Etc." or "Not Just Stamps" in order to correctly place your order for stamps.

SELLING STAMPS

Almost every collector becomes a stamp seller sooner or later. Duplicates are inevitably accumulated, no matter how careful one may be in avoiding them. Then there are the G and VG stamps that have been replaced with F and VF specimens, and have become duplicates by intent. In addition to duplicates, a more advanced collector is likely to have stamps that are not duplicates but for which he has no further use. These will be odds and ends, sometimes quite valuable ones, that once suited the nature of his collection but are now out of place. Collectors' tastes change. The result is a stockpile of stamps that can be converted back to cash.

The alternative to selling the stamps you no longer need or want is trading them with a collector who does want them, and taking his unwanted stamps in return. All stamp clubs hold trading sessions. Larger national stamp societies operate trade-by-mail services for their members. The APS (American Philatelic Society) keeps $8,000,000 worth of stamps constantly circulating in its trading books or "circuit" books. Trading can be an excellent way of disposing of surplus stamps. In most cases it takes a bit longer than selling. Another potential drawback, especially if you are not a club member, is finding the right person with the right stamps.

The nature and value of the material involved may help in deciding whether to sell outright or trade. Also, there are your own personal considerations. If you're not going to continue in the stamp hobby, or need cash for some purpose other than stamp buying, trading is hardly suitable. Likewise, if you have developed an interest in some very exotic group of stamps or other philatelic items it may be impossible to find someone to trade with.

Once you have decided to sell, if indeed you do make that decision, the matter revolves upon how. To a stamp shop? To another collector? Through an auction house? Possibly by running your own advertisements and issuing price lists, if you have enough stamps and spare time to make this worthwhile?

While some individuals have an absolute horror at the prospect of selling anything, stamp collectors tend to enjoy selling. It is difficult to say why. Some enjoy it so much they keep right on selling stamps, as a business, long after their original objective is achieved. Nearly all professional stamp dealers were collectors before entering the trade.

Selling your stamps outright to a dealer, especially a local dealer whom you can personally visit, is not necessarily the most financially rewarding but it is quick and very problem-free. Of course it helps if the dealer knows you and it's even better if he knows some of your stamps. Dealers have no objection to repurchasing stamps they've sold to you. You will find that the dealers encourage their customers to sell to them just as much as they encourage them to buy. The dealers are really anxious to get your stamps if you have good salable material from popular countries. In fact most dealers would prefer buying from the public rather than any other source.

The collector selling stamps to a dealer has to be reasonable in his expectations. A dealer may not be able to use all the stamps you have. It is simply not smart business for a dealer to invest money in something he may not be able to sell. So, if you have esoteric or highly specialized items for sale, it might be necessary to find a specialist who deals in those particular areas rather than selling to a neighborhood stamp shop.

The local stamp shop will almost certainly want to buy anything you can offer in the way of medium-to-better-grade U.S. stamps of all kinds, including the so-called "back of the book" items. He may not want plate blocks or full sheets of commemoratives issued within the past 20 years. Most dealers are well supplied with material of this nature and have opportunities to buy more of it every day. The same is true of first-day covers, with a few exceptions, issued from the 1960s to the present. The dealers either have these items abundantly or can get them from a wholesaler at rock-bottom prices. They would rather buy stamps that are a bit harder to get from the wholesalers, or for which the wholesalers charge higher prices. On the whole you will meet with a favorable reception when offering U.S. stamps to a local dealer. With foreign stamps it becomes another matter: what do you have and how flexible are you in price? Nearly all the stamp shops in this country do stock foreign stamps to one extent or another. They do not, as a rule, attempt to carry comprehensive or specialized stocks of them. In the average shop you will discover that the selection of general foreign consists of a combination of modern mint sets, topicals, souvenir sheets, packets which come from the wholesaler, and a small sprinkling of older material, usually pre-1900. The price range of this older material will be $5 to $50. Non-specialist collectors of foreign stamps buy this type of item and that is essentially who the local shop caters to. When a local dealer buys rare foreign stamps or a large foreign collection, it is not for himself. He buys with the intent of passing them along to another dealer who has the right customers lined up. He acts only as a middleman or go-between. Therefore the price you receive for better-grade foreign stamps tends to be lower than for better-grade U.S., which the dealer buys for his own use.

What is a fair price to get for your stamps? This is always difficult to say, as many variable factors are involved. Consider their condition. Think in terms of what the dealer could reasonably hope to charge for them at retail and stand a good chance of selling them. Some of your stamps may have to be discounted because of no gum, poor centering, bent perfs, hinge remnants, repairs, or other problems. But even if your stamps are primarily F or VF, a dealer cannot pay book values for them. If you check his selling prices on his specimens of those same stamps, you can usually count on receiving from 40 to 50 percent of those prices. Considering the discount made from book values by the dealer in pricing his stock, your payment may work out to about 25 percent of book values. For rare U.S. stamps in top condition you can do better than 25 percent, but on most stamps sold to a dealer this is considered a fair offer. Keep in mind that the difference between a dealer's buying and selling prices is not just "profit margin." Most of the markup goes toward operating costs, for without this markup, there would be no stamp dealers.

PUBLICATIONS—
LINN'S STAMP NEWS

Linn's Stamp News is a tabloid-size newspaper for stamp collectors. It has been published continuously as a weekly since 1928. Both in terms of page count and circulation, *Linn's* is the largest publication in the stamp hobby. Each issue of *Linn's* contains a vast quantity of words and pictures designed to appeal to stamp collectors at every level of interest.

As the dominant publication in the stamp hobby, each weekly issue of *Linn's* is crammed with news and other information stamp collectors need to know, including details on how to order first-day covers directly from the U.S. Postal Service and information on how to order new-issue stamps at face value directly from overseas post offices. Lavishly illustrated features discuss virtually every aspect of the world's most popular collecting hobby, in terms that beginners and newcomers can easily understand. "Trends of Stamp Values" monitors prices (and price changes) for more than 100,000 stamps from every nation of the world. "Linn's U.S. Stamp Market Index" is the stamp equivalent of the Dow Jones Industrial Average. "U.S. Stamp Facts" provides weekly information about classic U.S. stamps in a compact and highly visual format. "Stamp Collecting Made Easy" explains complexities of stamp collecting in an illustrated how-to feature. "Focus on Forgeries" provides visual clues to identify common fake stamps.

One of the most interesting features of *Linn's* is its advertising. Each issue contains fifty or more pages of ads from dealers seeking to buy or sell stamps. *Linn's* classified advertising section consists of fifteen or more pages of small ads from dealers and collectors, all arranged by classification, to help busy collectors locate just what they need.

The publication isn't cheap (current subscription price is $45.95 a year), but stamp collectors say they can't do without it. You can see for yourself, because the publishers of *Linn's* will send a free sample copy to *Blackbook* readers. Write to Linn's Blackbook Offer, P.O. Box 29, Sidney, OH 45365.

Linn's also maintains a Web site for Internet users. *Linn's* Web site at www.linns.com features highlights of the weekly *Linn's Stamp News* as well as "Linn's U.S. Stamp Program," new-issue listings, and an archive of reference material and information on stamp-collecting basics. Look for a complete online version of the weekly print *Linn's* to be available in late 2000.

Linn's also operates an online retail database, *Linn's* Zillions of Stamps, that allows collectors the convenience to shop at one online address for the stamps, covers, and supplies they need any-time, night or day. And Linn's Stampsites.com searchable database has indexed the entire content of more than 20,000 stamp-collecting Web pages worldwide.

THE JUNIOR PHILATELISTS
OF AMERICA

ABOUT THE JPA

There are many stamp organizations in North America today—national, state, and local. The major societies are naturally operated by and for adult collectors. Young people may be allowed to join, but usually are not given an active role.

In the JPA, the situation is different. It is a group run by and for young people, age eighteen and under. Junior members operate services, write for the publication, serve on study groups and committees, and elect their own officers.

The JPA is a dynamic organization; the Officers and Board of the JPA are willing to listen to each and every idea of the membership. Please tell us what you want to see in the JPA. After all, as a member, it is your organization.

Open to Collectors of All Ages—Beginners or Advanced. There's no minimum age for JPA membership. We welcome the youngest and newest collector as well as the advanced philatelist. Everyone can benefit from JPA services and publications!

BENEFITS OF MEMBERSHIP

• You'll be part of an exciting organization that is bringing change and excitement to stamp collecting.

• The opportunity to participate in all of the JPA's activities and our bimonthly magazine, *The Philatelic Observer*.

• Access to the JPA's services, including Pen Pals, Stamp Identification, American Philatelic Research Library access, and periodic stamp auctions.

• The JPA Study Groups are a great way to meet up with other members interested in the same types of stamps as you are interested in.

• As soon as you join you will receive a "Goodie Packet" filled with stamps, a membership card, more information on JPA services, and other great free stuff that varies from month to month.

• Every two months all members receive a copy of *The Philatelic Observer*, which is filled with interesting articles from JPA members as well as prominent stamp collectors.

DUES

All payments must be in U.S. dollars.
Junior Members:
    $9 (one year); $16 (two years)
  Non USA
    $14 (one year); $26 (two years)
Family Memberships:
    Two or more family members 18 and under
    $9 (1st person), $5 (each additional preson)
  Non USA
    $19 (one year); $31 (two years)
Adult Supporting Members:
    19 and above $15 (one year); $28 (two years)
  Non USA
    $20 (one year); $38 (two years)

Don't forget that you can save $2 on your dues if you pay for two years!!

SERVICES AVAILABLE TO MEMBERS OF THE JPA

Awards Committee
  Contact Central Office to request awards for your stamp show/exhibition (JPA, P.O Box 2625, Albany, OR 97321). For more information, contact Central Office.

Educational Projects
  Teachers and Stamp Club Leaders, we have stamps and stamp collecting information available for use in clubs and classrooms.

Library Services
  The American Philatelic Research Library is open to JPA members. Others may browse the library to find books that can be checked out at their local library. Look in the latest *Philatelic Observer* for the person to contact to access the library.

MEMBERSHIP APPLICATION

[ ] Junior 18 and Under
[ ] Family
[ ] Adult Supporting 19 and Older (other organizations may
    join under this category)

PLEASE PRINT ALL INFORMATION

Name _____

Address _____

City, State, & Zip _____

Age (Jr. Members) _____ Date of Birth (Jr. Members) _____

What stamps do you collect? _____

What other stamp clubs do you belong to? _____

Today's Date _____ Applicant's Signature _____

Proposed By: _____ JPA Member Number _____

I am enclosing dues for [ ] 1 year [ ] 2 years (SAVE $2)

NOTICE TO PARENTS OF JUNIOR MEMBERS

Before any application for membership from those under age 18 can be processed, the parent or legal guardian (only) of the applicant must complete the form below. If this is a gift membership, we can contact the parent/legal guardian and obtain the signature for you.

"I agree to act as guarantor of this applicant and hold myself responsible for all debts to the Junior Philatelists of America for this applicant until he/she reaches 18 years of age."

Signature _____

Name and Relationship to Applicant _____

Address (If different from Applicant) _____

City, State, & Zip _____

For Gift Memberships, we will send a gift card if desired.

Gift from _____ Relationship to Applicant _____

Your Address _____

City, State, & Zip _____

Would you like the renewal notice sent to you?

[ ] Yes [ ] No

Fill this out and send with Dues to:
Junior Philatelists of America
PO Box 2625
Albany, OR 97321

Pen Pals Service

Looking for a Pen Pal somewhere in the world? Send your name, JPA No., and what type of Pen Pal you are looking for to the Pen Pal Chairman, Todd Richard.

Recruiting Committee

Help recruit more members to keep the JPA growing! You could even earn next year's dues free! Contact Central Office for Membership Applications and share the JPA's Web site with your friends.

Public Relations

Do you have a Hobbies or Collectibles section in your local paper? Find out how to get the word out about the JPA. Contact Sharolyn Chicoine.

The Philatelic Observer

The JPA's very own award-winning newsletter is sent to all members every two months! It's filled with information, games, and stories from and about other members! For a sample copy of *The Philatelic Observer*, send $1.

Pamphlets

JPA pamphlets are available free of charge from JPA Central Office, P.O. Box 2625, Albany, OR 97321 for members and non-members alike. Please send an SASE.

Stamp Identification

Simply send a photocopy of any stamp you can't identify along with an SASE to the address in the front of the *Observer*.

Welcoming Committee

Do you need help on writing "Welcome Letters" to new JPA members? Look in the front of your *Observer* to see who to contact.

Member E-mail Address Directory

Keep up-to-date with Collin Rickman. Contact him with your JPA No. and e-mail address to be added or removed. Members' e-mail addresses are not included unless they have asked to be included.

Stamp Clusters

About JPA Study Groups Welcome to the Junior Philatelists of America's Stamp Clusters Program! We are glad you've decided to learn more about the program. This handbook has been developed to give you a guided tour into the fun and excitement of participating in one or more JPA study groups. Stamp Clusters are actually a means to learn more about your collecting interests and possible ways to increase your collection through stamp trading and auctions.

There is no actual studying required, just an interest in sharing your knowledge, or a desire to learn more about the stamps you collect, and more fun adventures with your collection. There are no special requirements to join any Stamp Clusters other than being a JPA member. It does not matter how long you have been a member, your age, or your knowledge about a particular subject. Even foreign members can join Stamp Clusters. There are no additional dues required to participate in any Stamp Clusters and you need no special equipment. All you need is an interest in learning more about the stamps you collect. You may even join more than one Cluster. You will be able to explore and participate in such activities as

- Contests and games
- Auctions
- Columnist for *The Philatelic Observer*
- Pen pals
- Adult mentors
- Chairing a Stamp Cluster
- Creating new Stamp Clusters
- Exhibiting your stamps

Many fun opportunities await you when you join a Stamp Cluster. You find that members are excited about the stamps they collect and want to share their enthusiasm and knowledge with other JPA members.

What Stamp Clusters Are Currently Available?

- **Asia Stamp Cluster**—John Tan

Do you have an interest in the Orient? How about the East Indies? Or the Himalayas? Then join the Asian Stamp Cluster! Our purpose is to try and learn what little bits we can of the world's largest land mass, from the Ural Mountains to the Pacific Ocean. It's an open forum about Asia, where we all can talk about the countries, topics, and other things that we want to talk about.

- **Canadian Stamp Cluster**—Tyson Evensen

The Canadian Stamp Cluster is finally out of the grave and back in full motion. If you want to join this fun and informational group, please send me a request! Expect articles, information, and a contest or two. If anyone signing up could write an article on Canadian stamps, that would be great. Look in the *Observer* for Tyson's address.

- **European Stamp Cluster**

Do you collect European stamps and would like to join a free group that gives you the opportunity to participate in contests, quizzes, and write articles for *The Philatelic Observer*? If your answer is yes and you are a JPA member, the European Stamp Cluster is for you.

- **First Day Cover Stamp Cluster**

  If you're a member of the JPA, then why not join the FDCSC? The FDCSC (First Day Cover Stamp Cluster) specializes in the study of First Day Covers. Even if you don't collect FDCs, they're a lot of fun to learn about—why not give it a shot? Who knows . . . you may even learn so much about FDCs that you'll want to start collecting them, too!

- **Historical Stamp Cluster**—Collin Rickman

  Learn about the history of the world in a fun way, the Historical Stamp Cluster! Going back in time by the method of philately, we can see the World War (etc.) all over again, by games, puzzles, a newsletter, and much, much, more! Do you want to join? Or do you have a question or a comment?

    E-mail: collmail@yahoo.com

- **Topical Stamp Cluster**

  If you are a JPA member and enjoy any topic of stamps, then this is the Stamp Cluster for you! In our bimonthly newsletter, the *Variety*, we have a certain topic that the members help decide! There are also contests, prizes, etc., and this is all free!

- **U.S. Stamp Cluster**

  Join the U.S. Stamp Cluster, and see what all the fuss is about! Keep up-to-date on U.S. stamp news with the full-color newsletter *The American Essence*. Participate in group discussions, quizzes, contests. Build your collection with the trading circuit and classified ads, plus take part in activities and earn prizes.

- **Women on Stamps Cluster**

  Do you collect famous women on stamps—or is this a subject that interests you? Join this Stamp Cluster and the fun is just beginning! Learn more about the famous women found on stamps all over the world while having fun with all sorts of games and quizzes.

How Long Can I Stay in a Stamp Cluster?

Participation in any given Stamp Cluster is solely up to the individual JPA member. Not all members will be interested in participating in a Stamp Cluster. There are no time constraints on any member of the JPA. We hope that you'll enjoy the activities provided in the Stamp Cluster program so much that you will participate indefinitely.

How Do I Get More Information About Joining a Study Cluster?

The *Philatelic Observer* contains a listing of current Stamp Clusters along with the name and address of the Chairperson. Simply contact the Chairperson for the Stamp Cluster you are interested in joining. For general information about the Stamp Clusters, contact the JPA Second Vice President.

How Do Stamp Clusters Correspond?

The Stamp Cluster Chair can provide you with a list of names and addresses of the members in your Stamp Cluster. Correspondence is usually carried on directly between members of that particular Stamp Cluster or through articles and columns in the *Observer*. Your Stamp Cluster Chair's address can be found on the inside front cover of the *Observer*. (Please include a #10 SASE.)

How to Start a New Stamp Cluster

While the current Stamp Cluster program covers many popular areas of stamp collecting, there are undoubtedly JPA members who collect stamps that don't fit into any one of the established groups. Any active member may emerge as the leader of the proposed Stamp Cluster. This member should have significant contact with other interested JPA members. A formal request is sent to the President and Second Vice President (Coordinator of the Stamp Clusters) by postal mail. This request should include the proposed name of the cluster; proposed Chairperson's name, age, address, and JPA No.; and the names, addresses, and JPA Nos. of other interested members. A brief statement on how this Stamp Cluster will benefit JPA should be included in your submission. Upon approval for the new Cluster and the appointment of the Chair by the President, a new Cluster can be formed.

What Activities Are Offered in the *Observer*?

Most of the activities of a Stamp Cluster center around the concepts of education, encouragement, and the fellowship of stamp collecting.

The Philatelic Observer—Allows Stamp Cluster members and Adult Supporting Mentors the opportunity to submit articles and columns relating to their Stamp Cluster topic. Through these columns and articles you will be able to participate in such activities as

- Auctions
- Contests
- Educational articles
- Games
- Stamp Cluster quizzes

Columnist for the *Observer*—Ideas for columns and articles may be submitted to the Stamp Cluster Chair or the editor of the

Observer. You should furnish both the Chair and the editor a copy of your article or column. It is not mandatory to write for the newsletter, but if you have an interesting subject to share, why not give it a try? The Stamp Cluster Chairperson can provide you with information for resources relating to your Stamp Cluster topic when participating as a columnist for the *Observer.*

Stamp Cluster Quizzes—Generally follow an article or column pertaining to an individual Stamp Cluster. These quizzes may be submitted to the Stamp Cluster Chairperson either by the writer of an article or by any member of a group. Directions for participation are always included, and usually a philatelic prize is offered to the winner. (Winners of such quizzes and contests are usually listed in Recent Winners.)

Contests—Related to a particular area of study may take any form such as an essay, stamp design, cacheted covers, etc. Ideas for contests may be submitted by members of a Stamp Cluster to the Chairperson. These contests may also be sponsored by a member of the Advisory Council, the Educational Director, an Adult Advisor, or another philatelic society.

Games—Featured on the "Fun Page," may be submitted to the editor of the *Observer* or to the Stamp Cluster Chair. Word search and crossword puzzles, logic problems, cryptograms, and matching games are very popular with many of the readers.

Auctions—Relating to specific Stamp Cluster interests usually take the form of a mini lot auction. These auctions generally contain ten or less items. Auction lots usually consist of donated materials and are generally sponsored by the Educational Director or by an adult advisor to a particular Stamp Cluster. All junior members of JPA may bid on lots featured. The instructions for any type of auction will appear in the *Observer* preceding the auction lots. Money received from the successful bidders of these auctions is used to support and improve the JPA programs.

Newsletters—Many Stamp Clusters have their own newsletters. These newsletters may be circulated by the Stamp Cluster Chair.

What Other Activities Are Offered?

Recruit new members to any Stamp Cluster by writing a welcome letter to new members. Often new members will list their collecting interests, which will give you an opportunity to include them in your Stamp Cluster. If you need more information about recruiting new members to your Stamp Cluster, contact your Stamp Cluster Chairperson.

Pen Pals—Matching your collecting interests may be available through the Pen Pals Service. The coordinator of the Pen Pals Service often receives inquiries from youth groups in other countries requesting pen pals for their youth. To find out more information about JPA's Pen Pal Service, write to the coordinator listed in the Departments and Services Directory.

Contests sponsored by other philatelic societies or periodicals may occasionally appear in *The Philatelic Observer*. These contests may take the form of essays, mini exhibits, or quizzes. All JPA members are encouraged to participate in these contests.

The Stamp Cluster Chair can provide you with a list of names and addresses of the other members of the Stamp Cluster if you wish to establish a pen pal just within the Stamp Cluster you belong to.

Is There Assistance for a Stamp Cluster?

Write to the Second Vice President for assistance with all aspects of your Stamp Cluster. Assistance available to your Cluster and/or individual members can include, but is not limited to, the following:

- Sample letters
- Adult supporting member mentors
- Auctions, contests, and quizzes
- Pen pal service
- Library services, including research support for columnists
- Information about foreign postal administrations
- Information about other societies specializing in your Cluster's interests
- Adult mentors for exhibiting

Additional assistance can be obtained from the Board of Directors and JPA Officers. Their addresses can be found in the Departments and Services Directory located in the *Observer*.

How Do You Become a Stamp Cluster Chair?

The Chairperson of a Stamp Cluster is appointed by the JPA President and works directly with the Second Vice President, who is the coordinator of the Stamp Clusters. Vacancies are announced in the *Observer*. Since JPA members live all over the United States and in other countries, the majority of Stamp Cluster contact will be made through the *Observer* and through letter writing. A candidate for a Chairperson position should have good communication and organizational skills. The Chairperson of each Stamp Cluster is the leader and coordinator of the activities of the Cluster. They are responsible for Clusters' activity updates, recruiting new members, trading programs, and establishing relationships with adult supporting member mentors.

Chairperson Stamp Cluster Kit—Currently in the works for and will be available exclusively to a Stamp Cluster Chair. The kit is a user-friendly tool to help organize and guide Chairs with their responsibilities and Cluster's activities. Each Chair will be responsible for the care and updating of this resource kit.

How Can I Get Exhibiting Help from a Stamp Cluster?

A Stamp Cluster is a great place to start when you are interested in exhibiting. The Stamp Cluster Chair can match you with an adult supporting member mentor who can advise you on the exhibiting process, inform you about the entry process, and even critique your exhibit.

How Can Adult Supporting Members Get Involved with JPA Stamp Clusters?

Adult supporting members are the most valuable resource to any Stamp Cluster. Many adults have many years of expertise and knowledge about philately. They may participate by

- Answering questions of individuals or Stamp Cluster Chairs
- Assisting a Stamp Cluster Chair with mailing lists and updating the Chair's resource kit
- Submitting articles or columns for publication
- Assisting with contests
- Developing and/or coordinating auctions with the Stamp Cluster Chairperson or the Educational Director
- Designing games or puzzles
- Facilitating trading or exchange programs
- Mentoring individual members with an exhibiting project

The best way to support youth in philately is to get involved. The Stamp Cluster Mentorship allows you to actively participate in youth philately within your own boundaries and sharing your expertise in a particular area of philately.

Any adult supporting member interested in getting involved and nurturing future philatelists should contact the Membership Services Department, which coordinates adult supporting member mentorships with the Second Vice President. Their names and addresses can be found in the Departments and Services Directory located in the *Observer*.

THE AMERICAN PHILATELIC SOCIETY

The American Philatelic Society is an internationally recognized association of both stamp experts and enthusiasts that offers a number of services and educational opportunities for stamp collectors. The APS is the national representative to the International Federation of Philately (FIP) and is affiliated with nearly 650 local stamp clubs (APS chapters) and more than 200 "specialty groups" (APS affiliates).

Anyone may browse the 135,000+ items currently offered for sale at www.stampstore.org, the Society's online sales site, but buying and/or selling is a privilege of membership. The online site features some rarities and more expensive stamps, in addition to many modestly priced items.

The services that are available with an APS membership include a monthly subscription to *The American Philatelist*, one of the premier stamp magazines in the world, as well as numerous other brochures and publications that are available at a discount to members. The APS Sales Division provides an opportunity for collectors to buy or sell stamps through the mail. Members may request "circuits" of stamps or covers in more than 160 categories of countries and topics. The items are priced by the submitting members, and most range from under $1 to $20.

The APS also provides an insurance program for members living in the United States, Canada, the United Kingdom, and many other countries. The insurance policy does not require a detailed inventory, only a general description of a collection and a value estimate, and may be applied for along with APS membership.

The APS building includes the American Philatelic Research Library, with a wide range of resource material encompassing thousands of books, journals, auction catalogs, and other material that are loaned or photocopied and available to members by mail for a nominal fee. The APRL also publishes the *Philatelic Literature Review*, a quarterly journal covering literature of interest to collectors. The magazine is available by separate subscription.

The APS offers a weeklong Summer Seminar on Philately that features hands-on instruction by prominent experts. In addition, the APS

Education Department produces many brochures and other materials and answers inquiries from beginner and intermediate collectors on various "how-to" aspects of the hobby.

Other APS services include authentication of members' stamps by the APS Expert Committee, estate advice, a translation service for international trading, and an annual convention-exhibition stamp show.

THE AMERICAN PHILATELIST

The Society's monthly magazine, which is included in the membership fee, features regular columns on U.S. stamps, stamp clubs, exhibitions, topical collecting, and more; articles by experienced philatelists; how-to columns on using the Society's Sales Division; and detailed listings of all new stamps and postal stationery issued by the U.S. Postal Service.

MEMBERSHIP INFORMATION

The APS offers a variety of memberships including special rates for other family members, foreign members, and lifetime memberships. The Society operates on a calendar year. Initial membership fees are pro-rated on a quarterly basis and include a $3 admission fee. The current schedule of membership fees is listed below.

Application received by APS National Headquarters	Membership Fee	U.S.	Other Countries
October, November, December	$28.00	$31.00	$38.00
January, February, March	21.75	24.00	29.25
April, May, June	15.50	17.00	20.50
July, August, September	9.25	10.00	11.75

For more information, call or write the American Philatelic Society at:

APS
PO Box 8000, Dept. HC
State College, PA 16803
(814) 237-3803, Fax (814) 237-6128
E-mail: flsente@stamps.org

For those with access to the Internet, the APS maintains a Web site at http://www.stamps.org. The site contains current APS news, such as minutes of recent official meetings and upcoming events; access to the American Philatelic Research Library; descriptions of member services; online StampStore, listings of books and other items for sale by the APS; educational courses; youth activities; free online stamp review course; and an online membership application form. The page also has links to many other philatelic sites on the Internet.

Members also may sign up for online and correspondence courses on different aspects of the hobby.

NATIONAL STAMP ORGANIZATIONS LISTED ALPHABETICALLY

All of the listed organizations are affiliated with the APS, but each is a separate organization and offers its own services to its members, including, in most cases, a specialized journal. Affiliates that also are affiliated with the American Topical Association are identified by an asterisk (*).

HOW TO BECOME AN APS AFFILIATE

Any organization that is at least national in scope, that was formed for the study of a special phase of philately, and that has objectives and activities compatible with those of the APS may affiliate with the Society upon approval of the APS Board of Directors. Further information may be obtained by contacting APS Headquarters, P.O. Box 8000, State College, PA 16803.

Aerophilatelic Society, Canadian (APS# AF0189)
Journal: The Canadian Aerophilatelist: quarterly.
Dues: Canada $CAN 20; outside Canada $CAN 25.
Services: special awards, library, annual convention.
Contact Person: MAJ R. K. Malott, 16 Harwick Cres., Nepean, ON K2H 6R1 Canada

Air Mail Society, American (APS# AF0077)

Journal: The Airpost Journal: monthly.
Dues: U.S. $23; outside U.S. $28.
Services: local chapters, study groups, sales book circuits, auctions, slide programs, cover service, handbooks, exhibition awards, special awards, annual convention.
Contact Person: Mr. Stephen Reinhard, P. O. Box 110, Mineola, NY 11501
E-mail: SR1501@aol.com
Website: ourworld.compuserve.com/homepages/aams/

Air Post Society, Metropolitan (APS# AF0192)
Journal: MAPS Bulletin: quarterly.
Dues: $8.
Services: auctions (members only), special awards, annual convention.
Contact Person: Mr. Robert B. Spooner, 31 Choate Way, Carlisle, PA 17013
Website: homepage.mac.com/air mails/index.html

Alaska Collectors Club (APS# AF0218)
Journal: The Alaskan Philatelist: quarterly.
Dues: U.S. $15; outside U.S. $20.
Services: directory, auctions.
Contact Person: Mr. Eric R. Knapp, 4201 Folker St., #C102, Anchorage, AK 99508
E-mail: eknapp@gci.com

American First Day Cover Society (APS# UN0033)
Journal: First Days: 8 per year.
Dues: U.S. $20; outside U.S. $28.
Services: local chapters, study groups, auctions, expertizing, slide programs, speakers bureau, handbooks, exhibition awards, special awards, library, annual convention.
Contact Person: Mr. Douglas A. Kelsey, P. O. Box 65960, Tucson, AZ 85728-5960
E-mail: afdcs@aol.com
Website: www.afdcs.org

American Philatelic Congress (APS# AF0139)
Journal: American Congress Book: annually.
Dues: U.S. $30; outside U.S. $35.
Services: directory, exhibition awards, special awards, annual convention.
Contact Person: Mr. David L. Straight, P. O. Box 32858, St. Louis, MO 63132
E-mail: dls@library.wustl.edu
Website: hometown.aol.com/Ton gaJan/APC.html

American Topical Association (APS# AF0177)

Journal: Topical Time: bimonthly.
Dues: U.S. $20; outside U.S. $25.
Services: local chapters, study groups, directory, slide programs, handbooks, exhibition awards, annual convention.
Contact Person: Mr. Paul E. Tyler, P. O. Box 50820, Albuquerque, NM 87181-0820
E-mail: ATAStamps@juno.com
Website: home.prcn.org/~pauld/ata/index.html

Americana Unit (APS# UN0040)
Journal: Americana Philatelic News: quarterly.
Dues: U.S. $6.
Services: auctions, exhibition awards.
Contact Person: Mr. David A. Kent, P. O. Box 127, New Britain, CT 06050
E-mail: ddengel@goti.net
Website: www.americana.org

Arizona-New Mexico Postal History Society (APS# AFO188)
Journal: The Roadrunner: quarterly.
Dues: $10.
Services: local chapters, directory, auctions, speakers bureau, handbooks, annual convention.
Contact Person: Jewell L. Meyer, 20112 Westpoint Dr., Riverside, CA 92507-6608
E-mail: jlmeyer_2000@yahoo.com

Art Cover Exchange Society (APS# AF0243)
Journal: From Cover-to-Cover: monthly
Dues: U.S. $7; outside U.S. $14.
Services: directory, auctions, slide programs, special awards, library, annual convention.
Contact Person: Mr. Robert Fritz, 6108 Saddleback Dr., Oklahoma City, OK 73150
E-mail: rfritz8283@aol.com
Website: www.geocities.com/art-coverexchange

Asociacion Mexicana de Filatelia (APS# AF0194)
Journal: Revista AMEXFIL: bimonthly.

Dues: U.S. $37.
Services: auctions, library.
Contact Person: Mr. Alejandro F. Grossmann, Apartado Postal 18-933, 11800 Mexico DF, Mexico
E-mail: grossman@ragnatela.net.mx

Australasian Specialists/ Oceania, Society of (APS# UN0022)
Journal: The Informer: quarterly.
Dues: U.S. $15; outside U.S. $20.
Services: sales book circuits, auctions, exhibition awards, special awards, library, annual convention.
Contact Person: G. S. Mansfield, P. O. Box 4510, Arlington, VA 22204
Website: members.aol.com/stamp sho/saso.html

Belgian Philatelic Society, American (APS# AF0138)
Journal: The Belgiophile: quarterly.
Dues: U.S. $7.50; Canada $8.50; others $12.50.
Services: directory, auctions, library.
Contact Person: Mr. Ralph Yorio, 1123 Cheyenne Dr., Indian Harbor Beach, FL 32937
E-mail: kcos32@home.com
Website: groups.HamptonRoads.com/ABPS

Bermuda Collectors Society (APS# AF0186)
Journal: Bermuda Post: quarterly.
Dues: U.S. $22; outside U.S. $25–30.
Services: auctions, annual convention.
Contact Person: Mr. Thomas J. McMahon, Villa Del Sol, Apt. 51 11000 S. Ocean Dr., Jensen Beach, FL 34957

Biology Unit* (APS# AF0172)
Journal: Biophilately: quarterly.
Dues: U.S. $15.
Services: special awards, library, annual convention.
Contact Person: Mr. Carl H. Spitzer, Jr., 610 N. Bedford Dr., Tucson, AZ 85710-2620
E-mail: A.Hanks@aci.on.ca

Brazil Philatelic Association (APS# UN0032)
Journal: Bull's Eyes: quarterly.
Dues: U.S. $15; outside U.S. $20.
Services: annual convention.
Contact Person: Mr. Kurt Ottenheimer, 462 W. Walnut St., Long Beach, NY 11561-3133
E-mail: oak462@juno.com

British Caribbean Philatelic Study Group (APS# UN0027)
Journal: Brit Caribbean Phil Journal: quarterly.
Dues: U.S./Canada $18; outside U.S. $21.
Services: local chapters study groups, directory, auctions, slide programs, speakers bureau, handbooks, exhibition awards, special awards, library, annual convention.
Contact Person: Dr. Reuben Ramkissoon, 3011 White Oak Lane, Oak Brook, IL 60523-2513
E-mail: rramkissoon@juno.com
Website: ourworld.compuserve.com/homepages/BCPSG/

British North American Philatelic Society (APS# AF0144)
Journal: BNA TOPICS: quarterly.
Dues: U.S. $18: Canada $24; UK £12.
Services: local chapters, study groups, sales book circuits, speakers bureau, handbooks, exhibition awards, special awards, library, annual convention.
Contact Person: Mr. William W. Radcliffe, III, 500 Colombia Ave., Pitman, NJ 08071-1734
E-mail: bnaps@wep.2b.c2
Website: www.bnaps.org

Bullseye Cancel Collector's Club (APS# AF0108)
Journal: The BCCC Bulletin: quarterly.
Dues: U.S. $10; outside U.S. $15

Services: directory, auctions, round robin trading cricuits.
Contact Person: Mr. Donald Landis, Urb. La Cerca 37, Bajo B, Collado Villalba 28400 (Madrid), Spain
E-mail: donaldj@teleline.es

Canada, Postal History Society of (APS# AF0067)

Journal: PHSC Journal: quarterly.
Dues: $25.
Services: exhibition awards.
Contact Person: F. Narbonne, 216 Mailey Dr., Carleton Place, ON K7C 3X9 Canada

Canadiana Study Unit (APS# AF0213)

Journal: The Canadian Connection: quarterly.
Dues: U.S./Canada $10; others $15.
Services: auctions, slide programs, new issue service.
Contact Person: Mr. Robert A. Haslewood, 2144 Decarie, Apt. 3, Montreal, QC H4A 3J3 Canada
E-mail: john.peebles@odyssey.on.ca

Canal Zone Study Group (APS# UN0042)

Journal: Canal Zone Philatelist: quarterly.
Dues: $8.
Services: local chapters, study group, mail sales, handbooks, exhibition awards, special awards, annual meetings.
Contact Person: Mr. Richard H. Salz, 60 27th Ave., San Francisco, CA 94121-1026
Website: www.czsg.org

Carriers and Locals Society (APS# AF0211)

Journal: The Penny Post: quarterly.
Dues: $35.
Services: directory, annual convention.
Contact Person: Mr. John D. Bowman, P.O. Box 38246, Birmingham, AL 35238
Website: www.pennypost.org

Cats on Stamps Study Unit* (APS# AF0179)

Journal: Cat Mews: quarterly.
Dues: U.S. $6; outside U.S. $8.
Services: new issue service.
Contact Person: Mr. Richard H. Sattinger, 1862 E. 14th St., Apt. 3D, Brooklyn, NY 11229-2847

Censorship Civil, Study Group (APS# AF0086)

Journal: Civil Censorship Study Gp Bul: quarterly
Dues: $14.
Services: auctions, handbooks, exhibition awards, library, annual convention.
Contact Person: COL Charles J. LaBlonde, 2940 Underwood Point, Apt. 5, Colorado Springs, CO 80920
E-mail: clablonde@aol.com
Website: members.aol.com/ww2censor/ccsg.html

Ceremony Program Society, The American (APS# AF0217)

Journal: The Ceremonial: bimonthly.
Dues: $15.
Services: directory, auctions, annual convention.
Contact Person: Monte L. Eiserman, 14359 Chadbourne, Houston, TX 77079
E-mail: litvaks@earthlink.net
Website: webacps.org

Chemistry and Physics on Stamps Study Unit* (APS# AF0123)

Journal: Philatelia Chimica et Physica: quarterly
Dues: U.S. $15; outside U.S. $17.
Services: slide programs, handbooks.
Contact Person: Dr. John B. Sharkey, 1559 Grouse Lane, Mountainside, NJ 07092-1340
E-mail: mmorgan@lausd.k12.ca.us
Website: bravo-med42.lausd.k12.ca.us/chem/chem.html

Chess on Stamps Study Unit* (APS# AF0180)

Journal: Chesstamp Review: quarterly.

Dues: U.S./Canada/Mexico $15; others $25.

Services: directory, auctions.

Contact Person: Mr. Russell E. Ott, P. O. Box 9789, Midland, TX 79708-2789

E-mail: reott@iglobal.net

Website: www.russott.com/stamps1.htm

China Stamp Society (APS# AF0010)

Journal: The China Clipper: bimonthly.

Dues: $18

Services: local chapters, sale book circuits, auctions, expertizing, slide programs, library, annual convention.

Contact Person: Mr. Paul Gault, P. O. Box 20711, Columbus, OH 43220

E-mail: secretary@chinastamp society.org

Website: www.chinastamp society.org

Christmas Philatelic Club* (APS# AF0074)

Journal: Yule Log: bimonthly.

Dues: U.S./Canada $15; outside U.S. $22.

Services: auctions, handbooks, exhibition awards, special awards, library, annual meeting.

Contact Person: Mr. Walton U. Beauvais, 1068 Medhurst Rd., Columbus, OH 43220

E-mail: cpc@hwcn.org

Website: www.hwcn.org/link/cpc/

Christmas Seal & Charity Stamp Society (APS# AF0101)

Journal: Seal News: bimonthly.

Dues: $10.

Services: directory, auctions, handbooks, biannual convention.

Contact Person: Betsy Berry, Jr., 3606 S. Atherton St., State College, PA 16801

E-mail: betsychuck@aol.com

Website: members.aol.com/betsy chuck/cscss.htm

Churchill Society, International* (APS# AF0049)

Journal: Finest Hour: quarterly.

Dues: U.S. $40.

Services: local chapters, cover service, biannual convention.

Contact Person: Sue M. Hefner, 1837 Latham Ave., Lima, OH 45805-1635

E-mail: malakand@conknet.com

Website: www.winstonchurchill.org

Cinderella Stamp Club (APS# AF0091)

Journal: The Cinderella Philatelist: quarterly.

Dues: £16.

Services: study groups, sales book circuits (UK only), auctions, handbooks, special award, library.

Contact Person: Mr. Joseph E. Foley, P. O. Box 183, Riva, MD 21140-0183

Colorado Postal History Society (APS# AF0200)

Journal: Colorado Postal Historian: quarterly.

Dues: $15.

Services: expertizing, slide programs, annual convention.

Contact Person: Mr. Roger Rydberg, 354 S. Nile St., Aurora, CO 80012

E-mail: cphs@att.net

Columbus, Christopher, Philatelic Society* (APS# AF0124)

Journal: Discovery: quarterly.

Dues: $15.

Services: directory.

Contact Person: Mr. James P. Doolin, Suite, 105 11258 Goodnight Lane, Dallas, TX 75229-9828

E-mail: don_ager@conknet.com

Website: home.prcn.org/~pauld/ ata/units/columbus.htm

Confederate Stamp Alliance (APS# AF0073)

Journal: Confederate Philatelist: bimonthly.

Dues: U.S./Canada/Mexico $24; others $32.
Services: directory, expertizing, slide programs, handbooks, exhibition awards, special awards, library, annual convention.
Contact Person: Mr. Richard H. Byne, 7518 Buckskin Lane, San Antonio, TX 78227-2716
E-mail: rhbcsaps@flash.net
Website: www.csalliance.org/

Connecticut Postal History Society (APS# AF0195)
Journal: The Journal;CPHS: quarterly.
Dues: $12.
Services: auctions, slide programs, speakers bureau, handbooks, exhibition awards.
Contact Person: Mr. Stephen W. Ekstrom, P. O. Box 207, Cromwell, CT 06416-0207
E-mail: swekstrom@aol.com
Website: ymug.cs.yale.edu/YMUG/CPHS/info.html

COPAPHIL (Columbia-Panama Philatelic Study Group) (APS# AF0142)
Journal: COPACARTA: quarterly.
Dues: U.S./Canada $8.50; others $12.
Services: study group, directory, auctions, expertizing, exhibition awards, library, biannual convention.
Contact Person: Mr. Lawrence R. Crain, 2919 Aldersgate, Medford, OR 97504
E-mail: lrcrain@mind.net

Costa Rica Collectors, Society of (APS# AF0096)
Journal: Oxcart: quarterly.
Dues: U.S. $12; outside U.S. $15.
Services: study group, directory, auctions, handbooks, exhibition awards, library.
Contact Person: Mr. Raul Hernandez, 4204 Haring Rd., Metairie, LA 70006
E-mail: rherna3870@aol.com
Website: www.socorico.org

Cover Collectors Circuit Club (APS# AF0215)
Journal: CCCC News: 6 per year.
Dues: U.S. $10; outside U.S. $5.
Services: annual convention.
Contact Person: Mr. Thomas M. Fortunato, 42 Maynard St., Rochester, NY 14615-2022
E-mail: stamptmf@frontiernet.net
Website: members.nbci.com/stamptmf/cccc/index.html

Croatian Philatelic Society (APS# AF0053)
Journal: The Trumpeter: quarterly.
Dues: U.S. $22; outside U.S. $25.
Services: local chapters, study groups, directory, auctions, expertizing, slide programs, speakers bureau, exhibition awards, special awards, library, annual convention.
Contact Person: Mr. Eck Spahich, P. O. Box 696, Fritch, TX 79036-0696
E-mail: ou812@arn.net
Website: www.croatianmall./com/cps/

Cuban Philatelic Society of America (APS# AF0173)
Journal: The Cuban Philatelist: 3 times per year.
Dues: U.S. $15: outside U.S. $30.
Services: local chapters, auctions, exhibition awards, special awards, library, annual convention, handbooks.
Contact Person: Mrs. Silvia C. Garcia, P. O. Box 141656, Coral Gables, FL 33114-1656
Website: www.philat.com/cpsa/

Czechoslovak Philately, Society for (APS# UN0018)
Journal: The Czechoslovak Specialist: 6 yearly.
Dues: U.S. $18; outside U.S. $23.
Services: local chapters, expertizing, slide programs, speakers bureau, handbooks, exhibition awards, library, annual convention.
Contact Person: Mr. Henry Hahn, 2936 Rosemoor Lane, Fairfax, VA 22031

E-mail: hhahn25@aol.com
Website: www.erols.com/sibpost/

Dakota Postal History Society (APS# AF0216)
Journal: Dakota Collector: quarterly.
Dues: U.S. $10; outside U.S. $15.
Contact Person: Mr. Gary Anderson, P. O. Box 600039, Saint Paul, MN 55106
E-mail: garyndak@ix.netcom.com

Disabled Collector's Correspondence Club (APS# AF0214)
Journal: Stampabilities: quarterly.
Dues: U.S./Canada $5; outside U.S. $15.
Services: directory.
Contact Person: Mr. Anfelt Albertsen, 31-12 33rd St., Astoria, NY 11106-2442
E-mail: siosal@hotmail.com
Website: members.aol.com/DisabledCC/index.html

Disinfected Mail Study Circle, The (APS# AF0219)
Journal: Pratique: 3 per year.
Dues: U.S. $32; UK£12; others £15.
Services: auctions, expertizing, speakers bureau, annual convention.
Contact Person: Mr. William A. Sandrik, P. O. Box 3277, Arlington, VA 22203

Duck Stamp Collectors Society, National (APS# AF0210)
Journal: Duck Tracks: quarterly.
Dues: U.S. $20.
Services: directory.
Contact Person: June E. Berwald, 1821 Zanzibar Lane, N., Plymouth, MN 55447-2850
E-mail: ndscs@hwcn.org
Website: www.hwcn.org/link/ndscs

Ebony Society of Philatelic Events and Reflections (APS# AF0239)
Journal: Reflections: bimonthly.
Dues: $15.
Services: directory, speakers bureau.

Contact Person: Mr. Sanford L. Byrd, P. O. Box 8888, Corpus Christi, TX 78468-8888
E-mail: esper@attglobal.net
Website: http://www.slsabyrd.com

Eire Philatelic Association (APS# AF0021)
Journal: Revealer: quarterly.
Dues: U.S. $12 Canada/Mexico $15; others $20.
Services: local chapters, directory, auctions, slide programs, handbooks, exhibition awards, special awards, library, annual convention.
Contact Person: Mr. David J. Brennan, P. O. Box 704, Bernardsville, NJ 07924
E-mail: brennan704@aol.com
Website: www.eirephilatelicassoc.org

El Salvador, Associated Collectors of (APS# AF0089)
Journal: El Faro: quarterly.
Dues: $24.
Services: auctions, expertizing.
Contact Person: Mr. Jeff Brasor, P. O. Box 173, Pompano Beach, FL 33061-0173

Empire State Postal History Society (APS# UN0028)
Journal: ESPHS Bulletin: quarterly.
Dues: $10.
Services: directory, auctions, speakers bureau, handbooks, exhibition awards, annual meeting.
Contact Person: Mr. William J. Hart, P. O. Box 167, Shrub Oak, NY 10588
Website: www.westelcom.com/users/gestus/esphs.html

Errors, Freaks & Oddities Collectors Club* (APS# AF0103)
Journal: EFO Collector: quarterly.
Dues: U.S. $16; outside U.S. $30.
Services: study groups, directory, auctions, expertizing, speakers bureau, exhibition awards, annual convention.
Contact Person: James E.

McDevitt, P .O. Box 1126, Kingsland, GA 31548-1126
E-mail: cwouscg@aol.com
Website: www.EFOERS.org

Ethiopian Philatelic Society (APS# AF0145)
Journal: MENELIK'S Journal: quarterly.
Dues: U.S./Canada $7.50; others $12.
Services: directory, auctions, library, expertizing.
Contact Person: Mr. Ulf J. Lindahl, 640 S. Pine Creek Road, Fairfield, CT 06430
E-mail: fbheiser@home.com
Website: members.home.net/ fbheiser/ethiopia5.htm

Europa Study Unit* (APS# AF0017)
Journal: Europa News: bimonthly.
Dues: U.S. $10; Canada $11; others $16.
Services: auctions, handbooks, library.
Contact Person: Mr. Henry S. Klos, P. O. Box 611, Bensenville, IL 60106
E-mail: eunity@aol.com

Exhibitors, Philatelic, American Association of (APS# AF0157)
Journal: The Philatelic Exhibitor: quarterly.
Dues: U.S. $20; outside U.S. $25.
Services: speakers bureau, exhibition awards, special awards convention.
Contact Person: Mr. R. Timothy Bartshe, 13955 W. 30th Ave., Golden, CO 80401
E-mail: vergec@sympatico.ca

Falkland Islands Philatelic Study Group (APS# AF0083)
Journal: The Upland Goose: quarterly.
Dues: U.S./Canada $20; Europe £10; others £15.
Services: study groups, directory, sales book circuits (Great Britain only), auctions, handbooks, exhibition awards, special awards, annual convention.
Contact Person: Mr. Carl J. Faulkner, Williams Inn, On The Green, Williamstown, MA 01267

Federation Quebecquoise de Philatelie (APS# AF0169)
Journal: Philatelie Quebec: 6 per year.
Dues: U.S. $30; outside U.S. $42.
Services: local chapters, study groups, expertizing, speakers bureau, exhibition awards, special awards, library, annual convention.
Contact Person: Mr. Paul Desjardins, 972 Montarville, St. Bruno, QC J3V 5A7 Canada
E-mail: paul.desjardins@ sympatico.ca

Fine Arts Philatelists* (APS# AF0160)
Journal: Jrl Fine/Performing Arts Phil: quarterly.
Dues: U.S. $20; outside U.S. $25.
Services: directory, handbooks.
Contact Person: Mrs. H. Ruth Richards, 10393 Derby Dr., Laurel, MD 20723
Website: www.philately.com/ philately/fap.htm

Fire Service in Philately (APS# AF0080)
Journal: Fire Stamp News: bimonthly.
Dues: $15.
Services: auctions, new issues service, cover service, annual convention.
Contact Person: Mr. Edward Flory, 81 N. Courtland St., East Stroudsburg, PA 18301
E-mail: brenglersr@mail.enter.net

First Issues Collector Club (APS# AF0232)
Journal: First Issues; bimonthly.
Dues: $6.
Services: directory, auctions.
Contact Person: Mr. Robert K. Sylvester, 13 Idlewood Pl., New Orleans, LA 70123

E-mail: bobsyl@prodigy.net
Website:
clubs.yahoo.com/clubs/ficconweb

Florida Postal History Society (APS# AF0227)
Journal: FL Postal History Journal: biannually.
Dues: $10.
Services: directory, slide programs, handbooks, exhibition awards, special awards, library, annual convention.
Contact Person: Dr. Deane R. Briggs, 160 E. Lake Howard Dr., Winter Haven, FL 33881
E-mail: drb@gte.com

France & Colonies Philatelic Society (APS# AF0045)
Journal: France & Colonies Philatelist: quarterly.
Dues: U.S. $15; outside U.S. $20.
Services: expertizing, slide programs, handbooks, special awards, annual convention.
Contact Person: Dr. Edward J. J. Grabowski, 741 Marcellus Dr., Westfield, NJ 07090
E-mail: edjjg@bellatlantic.net

G.B. Overprints Society (APS# AF0072)
Journal: The Overprinter: quarterly.
Dues: U.S. $20; outside U.S. £13.
Services: study groups, sales book circuits, auctions, handbooks, exhibition awards, library, annual convention.
Contact Person: Mr. Francis E. Kiddle, Punch Tree House Reading Road North, Fleet, Hants, GU13 8HS England

Gay & Lesbian History on Stamps Club* (APS# AF0205)
Journal: Lambda Philatelic Journal: quarterly.
Dues: U.S. $8; outside U.S. $10.
Services: directory, slide program, handbooks, annual convention.
Contact Person: Mr. Joe V. Petronie, P. O. Box 515981, Dallas, TX 75251-5981
E-mail: glhsc@aol.com

Website: home.earthlink.net/~glhsc/index.html

Georgia Postal History, Society (APS# AF0224)
Journal: Georgia Post Roads; irregular.
Dues: $10.
Services: directory, handbooks, annual convention.
Contact Person: Mrs. Nancy B.Z. Clark, P. O. Box 427, Marstons Mills, MA 02648-0427
E-mail: nbc@cape.com

German Colonies Collectors (APS# AF0236)
Journal: VORLAUFER: quarterly.
Dues: U.S. $15: outside U.S. $24.
Services: exhibition awards, annual convention, special awards.
Contact Person: Mr. John S. Miller, P. O. Box 27, Newton Upper Falls, MA 02464
E-mail: miller02464@yahoo.com
Website: www.gps.nu/studygroup/colonies/info.html

Germany Philatelic Society (APS# AF0048)
Journal: The German Postal Specialist: monthly.
Dues: U.S. $22; Canada/Mexico $29; others $32.
Services: local chapters, study groups, handbooks, exhibition awards, library, special awards, annual convention.
Contact Person: Mr. Christopher D. Deterding, P. O. Box 779, Arnold, MD 21012-4779
E-mail: germanyphilatelic@juno.com
Website: www.gps.nu/

Golf Society, International Philatelic* (APS# AF0183)
Journal: Tee Time: quarterly.
Dues: $12.
Services: directory, auctions.
Contact Person: Mr. Ron Spiers, 8025 Saddle Run, Powell, OH 43065
E-mail: rwspiers@aol.com
Website: www.ipgsonline.org

Graphics Philately Association*
(APS# AF0133)
Journal: Philateli-Graphics: quarterly.
Dues: U.S. $10; outside U.S. $20.
Contact Person: Mr. Bruce L. Johnson, 2138 Wilshire Road, Indianapolis, IN 46228

Great Britain Collectors Club
(APS# AF0191)
Journal: GBCC Chronicle: quarterly.
Dues: U.S./Canada $18.50; others $27.
Services: directory, sales book circuits, auctions, handbook, exhibition awards, annual convention.
Contact Person: Mr. Parker A. Bailey, 17 Greenwood Road, Merrimack, NH 03054
E-mail: larry@gbstamps.com
Website: www.gbstamps.com/gbcc

Guatemala Collectors, International Society of (APS# UN0036)
Journal: El Quetzal: quarterly.
Dues: U.S. $18, outside U.S. $22.
Services: directory, auctions, new issue service, cover service, handbooks, library.
Contact Person: Mr. Wesley S. Waite, 2818 W. Telegraph Ave., Stockton, CA 95204-2610
E-mail: mjbarie@wwnet.net
Website: www.clubs.yahoo.com/clubs/isgc

Haiti Philatelic Society (APS# AF0081)
Journal: Haiti Philately: quarterly.
Dues: U.S. $15; outside U.S. $23.
Services: directory, auctions, expertizing.
Contact Person: Mr. Carroll L. Lloyd, 2117 Oak Lodge Rd., Baltimore, MD 21228
E-mail: clloyd@bcpl.net
Website: www.waypt.com/users/~glb/

Hawaiian Philatelic Society
(APS# AF0136)
Journal: Po'Oleka O Hawaii: quarterly.
Dues: $12.
Services: auctions, expertizing, handbooks, library.
Contact Person: Mr. Harry A. Foglietta, 1012 Palm Dr., Apt. 1, Honolulu, HI 96814-1926
E-mail: bannan@pixi.com
Website: www.stampshows.com/hps.html

Hellenic Philatelic Society of America (APS# AF0120)
Journal: HPSA News Bulletin: quarterly.
Dues: U.S. $20; Canada $20; others $25.
Services: local chapters, expertizing, handbooks, special awards.
Contact Person: Dr. Nicholas Asimakopulos, 541 Cedar Hill Ave., Wyckoff, NJ 07481
E-mail: nick1821@aol.com

Honduras Collectors Club (APS# AF0229)
Journal: El Hondureno: quarterly.
Dues: $24.
Services: auctions, expertizing, new issue service.
Contact Person: Mr. Jeff Brasor, P. O. Box 143383, Irving, TX 75014
E-mail: jbrasor@aol.com

Hong Kong Stamp Society
(APS# AF0209)
Journal: Hong Kong Philatelist: quarterly.
Dues: U.S. $10; Canada/Mexico $15; others $20.
Services: auctions, expertizing, library, handbooks.
Contact Person: Ming W. Tsang, P. O. Box 206, Glenside, PA 19038
Email: hkstampsoc@yahoo.com
Website: hkss.org

Hungarian Philately, Society for
(APS# UN0034)
Journal: News of Hungarian Philately: quarterly.
Dues: U.S. $15; outside U.S. $20.
Services: directory, sales book circuits, auctions, handbooks, library,

study groups, exhibition awards, annual convention.
Contact Person: Mr. Robert R. Morgan, 2201 Roscomare Rd., Los Angeles, CA 90077-2222
E-mail: info@hungarianphilately.org.
Website: www.hungarianphilately.org

Illinois Postal History Society (APS# AF0112)
Journal: Illinois Postal Historian: quarterly.
Dues: $10.
Services: handbooks, exhibition awards, semi-annual conventions.
Contact Person: Dr. Harvey M. Karlen, 1008 N. Marion St., Oak Park, IL 60302
E-mail: aubreyb@emil.msn.com

India Study Circle (APS# AF0111)
Journal: India Post: quarterly.
Dues: U.S. $32; outside U.S. £18.
Services: auctions, expertizing services, slide programs, handbooks, exhibition awards.
Contact Person: Mr. John Warren, P. O. Box 7326, Washington, DC 20044
E-mail: warren.john@epa.gov

Indiana Postal History Society (APS# AF0241)
Journal: Indiana Postal History Society: quarterly.
Dues: $10.
Services: handbooks, annual convention.
Contact Person: Mr. Vincent A. Ross, R 3, Box 717, Spencer, IN 47460
E-mail: var@bluemarble.net
Website: www.theryles.com/iphs/

Indo-China Philatelists, Society of (APS# AF0038)
Journal: Indo-China Philatelist: quarterly.
Dues: U.S./Canada/Mexico $15; others $20.
Services: directory, auctions, study groups, annual convention.

Contact Person: Mr. Ron Bentley, 2600 N. 24th St., Arlington, VA 22207
E-mail: ronbentley@veridian.com
Website: www.imnahastamps.com/sicp.cfm

Iowa Postal History Society (APS# AF0168)
Journal: IPHS Bulletin: quarterly.
Dues: $16.
Services: directory, auctions, exhibition awards, annual convention.
Contact Person: Mr. Steven J. Bahnsen, Apt. 404, 2921 S. Michigan Ave., Chicago, IL 60616-3255
E-mail: suealmack@home.com

Iran Philatelic Study Circle—No. American Chapter (APS# AF0208)
Journal: I.P.S.C. Bulletin; 5 per year.
Dues: U.S. $15; outside U.S. £8.
Services: directory, sales book circuits (UK only), auctions, handbooks.
Contact Person: Mr. T. P. McDermott, 25 Hillside Ave., White Plains, NY 10601-1111
E-mail: stampstp@msn.com
Website: www.iranphilatelic.org

Israel Philatelists, Society of (APS# AF0105)
Journal: The Israel Philatelist: bimonthly.
Dues: U.S. $20; outside U.S. $33.
Services: local chapters, study groups, slide programs, new issue service, cover service, handbooks, exhibition awards, special awards, library, annual convention.
Contact Person: Mr. Howard S. Chapman, 28650 Settlers Lane, Pepper Pike, OH 44124
Website: www.israelstamps.com

Italian American Stamp Club (APS# AF0175)
Journal: Italian Am Stamp Club Nwlter: monthly.
Dues: U.S. $6; outside U.S. $10.
Services:
Contact Person: Mr. Ralph L.

West, 1135 S. 75th St., West Allis, WI 53214

Italy and Colonies Study Circle (GB) (APS# AF0132)
Journal: Fil-Italia: quarterly.
Dues: U.S. $27; others £17.
Services: sales books circuits, speakers bureau, special awards, library.
Contact Person: Mr. Richard Harlow, 7 Duncombe House 8 Manor Rd., Teddington, Middx., TW11 8BG England
E-mail: L.R.Harlow@btinternet.com

Italy and Colonies Study Circle (USA) (APS# AF0140)
Journal: Mare Nostrum: quarterly.
Dues: $18.
Services: annual convention, directory, auction, handbooks, exhibition awards, special awards, library.
Contact Person: Dr. Robert E. Lana, P. O. Box 7, Narberth, PA 19072
E-mail: ihlana@hotmail.com

Japanese Philately, International Society for (APS# AF0058)
Journal: Japanese Philately: bimonthly.
Dues: $12.
Services: local chapters, directory, expertizing, handbooks, special awards, library, exhibition awards.
Contact Person: Dr. Kenneth Kamholz, P. O. Box 1283, Haddonfield, NJ 08033-0760
E-mail: isjp@home.com
Website: www.isjp.org

JAPOS (Journalists, Authors and Poets on Stamps) Study Group (APS# AF0068)
Journal: JAPOS Bulletin: quarterly.
Dues: U.S. $6; outside U.S. $8.50.
Services: library.
Contact Person: Mr. George Houle, 7260 Beverly Blvd., Los Angeles, CA 90036-2545
E-mail: Houleg@aol.com

Junior Philatelists of America (APS# UN0026)

Journal: Philatelic Observer: bimonthly.
Dues: U.S. $9; outside U.S. $14.
Services: local chapters, study groups, auctions, exhibition awards, special awards.
Contact Person: Mr. Kenneth P. Martin, P. O. Box 8084, State College, PA 16803-8084
E-mail: kpmartin@stamps.org
Website: www.jpastamps.org/

Korea Stamp Society (APS# AF0113)
Journal: Korean Philately: quarterly.
Dues: $25.
Services: directory, expertizing, handbooks, library.
Contact Person: Mr. John E. Talmage, Jr., P. O. Box 6889, Oak Ridge, TN 37831
E-mail: jtalmage@usit.net
Website: www.pennfamily.org/KSS-USA/

Latin American Philatelic Society (APS# AF0104)
Journal: Latin American Post: quarterly.
Dues: U.S./Canada $15; others $17.50.
Services: directory.
Contact Person: Mr. Piet Steen, 197 Pembina Ave., Hinton, AB T7V 2B2 Canada
E-mail: piet.steen@home.com

Liberian Philatelic Society (APS# AF0176)
Journal: Journal of the Liberia Philatelic Society: quarterly.
Dues: U.S. $15; outside U.S. $18.
Services: expertizing, slide programs, annual convention.
Contact Person: Mr. Wm. Thomas Lockard, P. O. Box 106, Wellston, OH 45692-0106
E-mail: tlockard@zoomnet.net
Website: faculty.carlow.edu/trichard/liberia.htm

Lighthouse Stamp Society (APS# AF0221)

Journal: The Philatelic Beacon: bimonthly.
Dues: U.S. $12; outside U.S. $20.
Services: directory, handbooks, exhibition awards, annual convention.
Contact Person: Mrs. Dalene T. Thomas, 8612 W. Warren Lane, Lakewood, CO 80227-2352
E-mail: dalane1@qwest.net
Website: www.lighthousestamp society.homepage.com

Lions International Stamp Club* (APS# AF0153)
Journal: Lions Intl. Philatelist: quarterly.
Dues: U.S. $10; outside U.S. $12.
Services: local chapters, directory, new issue service, cover service, annual conventions.
Contact Person: Mr. Leonard C. Schwab, 400 LeFevre Road, Cumberland, MD

Lithuania Philatelic Society (APS# AF0223)
Journal: Lithuania Phil. Soc. Journal; semiannual.
Dues: U.S. $10; outside U.S. $15.
Services: auctions, annual convention.
Contact Person: Mr. Stanley J. Alsis, P. O. Box 102, Feeding Hills, MA 01030
E-mail: variakojis@earthlink.net
Website: www-public.osf.lt/ ~vasaris/e_bend_0.htm

Local Post Collectors Society (APS# AF0126)
Journal: The Poster: quarterly.
Dues: U.S./Canada $9; others $15.
Services: directory, mail sales, handbook.
Contact Person: Mr. Peter Pierce, 7 Pratt Ave., Oxford, MA 01540-2826
E-mail: p.oxbou@verizon.net

Machine Cancel Society (APS# UN0024)
Journal: Machine Cancel Forum: quarterly.
Dues: U.S. $15; outside U.S. $24.
Services: study groups, auctions, handbooks, exhibition awards, annual convention.
Contact Person: Mr. Gary M. Carlson, 3097 Frobisher Ave., Dublin, OH 43017
E-mail: gcarlson@columbus. rr.com
Website: www.machinecancel.org

Mailer's Postmark Permit Club (APS# AF0100)
Journal: Permit Patter: bimonthly.
Dues: U.S. $7; outside U.S $9.
Services: directory, auctions, expertizing.
Contact Person: Mr. Joseph LoPreiato, 165 Old Farm Dr., Newington, CT 06111-1819
E-mail: EnotriaLP@aol.com

Maritime Postmark Society (APS# UN0037)
Journal: Seaposter: bimonthly.
Dues: U.S. $10; outside U.S. $15.
Services: auctions, handbooks.
Contact Person: Mr. Tom Hirschinger, 415 High Point Dr., Wadsworth, OH 44281

Mask Study Unit of A.T.A. (APS# AF0244)
Journal: Mask Lore: quarterly.
Dues: U.S. $5; Canada $6; others $7.50.
Contact Person: Ms. Hildred Huyssoon, P. O. Box 165, Hubbard, OR 97032-0165
E-mail: kencar@venturalink.net
Website: home.prcn.org/~pauld/ ata/units/masks.htm

Masonic Study Unit* (APS# AF0094)
Journal: The Philatelic Freemason: bimonthly.
Dues: U.S./Canada $8; others $16.
Services: speakers bureau, exhibition awards.
Contact Person: Mr. Stanley R. Longenecker, 930 Wood St., Mount Joy, PA 17552-1926

Massachusetts Postal Research Society (APS# AF0093)
Journal: The Massachusetts Spy: quarterly.
Dues: $8.
Services: handbooks, annual conventions.
Contact Person: H. J. W. Daugherty, P. O. Box 1146, Eastham, MA 02642
E-mail: hjwd@capecod.net

Mathematical Study Unit* (APS# AF0130)
Journal: PHILAMATH: quarterly.
Dues: U.S. $10; outside U.S. $13.
Services: auctions, checklist, quarterly newsletter.
Contact Person: Dr. Monty J. Strauss, 4209 88th St., Lubbock, TX 79423
E-mail: m.strauss@ttu.edu
Website: www.math.ttu.edu/msu/

Maximum Card Study Unit (APS# AF0106)
Journal: Maximaphily USA: quarterly.
Dues: U.S. $15; outside U.S. $20.
Services: auctions, slide programs.
Contact Person: Mr. Daniel Olsen, P. O. Box 9168, Naples, FL 34101
E-mail: olsenaples@att.net

Mesoamerican Archeology Study Unit* (APS# AF0082)
Journal: Codex Filatelica: bimonthly.
Dues: U.S. $8; Canada/Mexico $9; others $16.
Contact Person: Mr. Allen R. Hendricksen, 9111 Raven Oaks Dr., Omaha, NE 68152
E-mail: cmoser@ci.riverside.ca.us
Website: www.masu.web.com

Meter Stamp Society (APS# AF0193)
Journal: Meter Stamp Society Bulletin: quarterly.
Dues: U.S. $20; outside U.S. $24.
Services: handbooks, library.
Contact Person: Mr. Alexander J. Savakis, P. O. Box 609, Warren, OH 44482-0609

E-mail: joel5215@aol.com
Website: www.meterstamp society.org

Mexico-Elmhurst Philatelic Society International (APS# UN0043)
Journal: Mexicana: quarterly.
Dues: $23.
Services: local chapters, study group, directory, sales book circuits, auctions, expertizing, slide programs, speakers bureau, handbooks, exhibition awards, special awards, library, annual convention.
Contact Person: Dr. Mark Banchik, P. O. Box 222125, Great Neck, NY 11022
Website: home.mepsi.org

Military Postal History Society (APS# UN0019)
Journal: M.P.H.S. Bulletin: quarterly.
Dues: U.S. $15; Canada $18; others $22.
Services: study groups, auctions, handbooks, exhibition awards, annual convention.
Contact Person: Mr. Robert T. Kinsley, 5410 Fern Loop, West Richland, WA 99353
E-mail: kinsley@owt.net
Website: homepage.mac.com/mphs/

Minnesota, Postal History Society of (APS# AF0084)
Dues: $4.
Services: auctions.
Contact Person: Mr. John T. Grabowski, P. O. Box 536, Willernie, MN 55090-0536
E-mail: minnjohn@alum.mit.edu

Mobile Post Office Society (APS# AF0064)
Journal: Transit Postmark Collector: bimonthly.
Dues: $18.
Services: directory, auctions, handbooks, exhibition awards, special awards, library, annual convention.
Contact Person: Mr. Douglas N. Clark, P. O. Box 427, Marstons Mills, MA 02648-0427
E-mail: dnc@math.uga.edu

Website: www.eskimo.com/
~rkunz/mposhome.html

Music Circle, Philatelic* (APS# AF0141)
Journal: The Baton: 3 per year.
Dues: U.S. $15; outside U.S. £8.
Services: sales book circuits (UK only), slide programs (UK only), special awards, library, handbooks, exhibition awards, annual convention.
Contact Person: Mrs. Cathleen F. Osborne, P. O. Box 1781, Sequim, WA 98382

Nepal and Tibet Philatelic Study Circle (APS# AF0122)
Journal: Postal Himal: quarterly.
Dues: U.S. $19; outside U.S. £12.
Services: auctions, slide programs, exhibition awards, annual convention.
Contact Person: Mr. Roger D. Skinner, 1020 Covington Rd., Los Altos, CA 94024
Website: www.fuchs-online.com/ntpsc/

Netherlands Philately, American Society of (APS# AF0060)
Journal: Netherlands Philately: 3 per year.
Dues: U.S. $20; outside U.S. $25.
Services: auctions, library.
Contact Person: Mr. J. Enthoven, W6428 Riverview Dr., Onalaska, WI 54650-9312
E-mail: jenthoven@centurytel.net
Website: www.angelfire.com/caz/asnp

New Jersey Postal History Society (APS# AF0095)
Journal: NJPH: 5 per year.
Dues: U.S. $15; outside U.S. $20.
Services: directory, auctions, slide programs, handbooks, exhibition awards, special awards, annual convention.
Contact Person: Mr. Robert G. Rose, P. O. Box 1945, Morristown, NJ 07962

E-mail: Njpostalhistory@aol.com
Website: members.aol.com:/njpostalhistory/phsindex.htm

Nicaragua Study Group (APS# AF0234)
Journal: Nicarao: quarterly.
Dues: $15.
Services: directory, handbooks, exhibition awards, library, annual convention.
Contact Person: Mr. Erick Rodriguez, 11817 S.W. 11th St., Miami, FL 33184-2501
E-mail: nsgsec@yahoo.com
Website: clubs.yahoo.com/clubs/nicaraguastudygroup

North Carolina Postal History Society (APS# AF0155)
Journal: North Carolina Postal Historian: quarterly.
Dues: $15.
Services: special awards, annual convention.
Contact Person: Mr. Tony L. Crumbley, P. O. Box 219, Newell, NC 28126
E-mail: TCrumbley@charlotte chamber.org

Ohio Postal History Society (APS# AF0066)
Journal: Ohio Postal History Journal: quarterly.
Dues: U.S. $15; outside U.S. By Arrangement.
Services: study groups, directory, handbooks, exhibition awards, annual meeting.
Contact Person: James L. Baumann, Ph.D., 5248 Sheila Dr., Toledo, OH 43613-2442

Website: members.aol.com/OPHS3/ophs.html

Old World Archaeological Study Unit (APS# AF0092)
Journal: Old World Archaeologist: quarterly.
Dues: $10.
Services: library.
Contact Person: Mr. Merle Far-

rington, 10 Clark St., Medway, MA 02053

Orange Free State Study Circle (APS# AF0196)
Journal: Orange Free State Bulletin: quarterly.
Dues: U.S. $16; outside U.S. £10.
Services: special awards.
Contact Person: Mr. Alan MacGregor, 'Kinglets', 1 Forder's Close, Woodfalls, Salisburg, Wilts., SP5 20B England
Website: www.ofssc.org

Pacific Islands Study Circle (APS# AF0226)
Journal: Pacifica: quarterly.
Dues: US/Others $20; UK/Europe £7.50.
Services: auctions, speakers bureau, handbooks, exhibition awards, special awards.
Contact Person: Mr. John D. Ray, 24 Woodvale Ave., London, SE25 4AE England
E-mail: jray@dial.pipex.com
Website: dialspace.dial.pipex.com/jray/pisc.html

Pacific Northwest Postal History Society (APS# AF0147)
Journal: Pacific N.W. Journal: quarterly.
Dues: $15.
Services: auctions, study groups, directory.
Contact Person: Mr. William R. Beith, P. O. Box 301263, Portland, OR 97294-9263
E-mail: wrbeith@home.com

Papuan Philatelic Society (APS# AF0228)
Journal: Papua New Guinea Calling: quarterly.
Dues: U.S. $22; outside U.S. £10.
Services: auctions.
Contact Person: Mr. Steven G. Zirinsky, P. O. Box 49, Ansonia Sta., New York, NY 10023
E-mail: szirinsky@cs.com

Pennsylvania Postal History Society (APS# AF0050)
Journal: Pennsylvania Postal Historian: quarterly.
Dues: $17.50
Services: handbooks, exhibition awards, annual convention.
Contact Person: Mr. Norman Shachat, 382 Tall Meadow Lane, Yardley, PA 19067
E-mail: janorm@gateway.net

Perfins Club, The (APS# AF0057)
Journal: The Perfins Bulletin: 10 per year.
Dues: U.S. $15; outside U.S. $20.
Services: directory, sales book circuits, auctions, slide programs, speakers bureau, handbooks, exhibition awards, library, annual convention.
Contact Person: Mr. Kurt Ottenheimer, 462 W. Walnut, Long Beach, NY 11561
E-mail: oak462@juno.com
Website: members.aol.com/perfins/

Petroleum Philatelic Society International* (APS# AF0170)
Journal: The Petro-Philatelist: quarterly.
Dues: U.S. $14; outside U.S. $17.
Services: directory.
Contact Person: Mr. H. Victor Copeland, 615 Orion Dr., Colorado Springs, CO
E-mail: corwin@pdq.net

Philatelic Computing Study Group (APS# AF0212)
Journal: The Compulatelist: quarterly.
Dues: U.S. $10; Canada/Mexico $12; others $15.
Services: library, annual convention
Contact Person: Mr. William F. Sharpe, 455 Lincoln Blvd., Santa Monica, CA 90402
E-mail: dviolini@west.net
Website: www.pcsg.org

Philatelic Pages and Panels, American Society for (APS# AF0165)

Journal: Page & Panel Journal: quarterly.
Dues: U.S. $15; outside U.S. $21.
Services: directory, auctions, handbooks, slide programs, speakers bureau, expertizing, library, annual convention.
Contact Person: Mr. Gerald L. Blankenship, P. O. Box 475, Crosby, TX 77532
E-mail: gblank1941@aol.com

Philatelists and Numismatists, Society of (APS# AF0116)
Journal: ExSPANsion: 3 per year.
Dues: $10.
Services: special award.
Contact Person: Eunice Alter, 19472 Catfish Circle, Huntington Beach, CA 92646-2806
E-mail: span@atsecure.net
Website: spat.atsecure.net

Philaticians, Society of (APS# AF0143)
Journal: The Philatelic Journalist: quarterly.
Dues: $15.
Services: directory, exhibition awards.
Contact Person: Mr. Israel I. Bick, P. O. Box 854, Van Nuys, CA 91408
E-mail: iibick@aol.com
Website: www/bick.net

Philippine Philatelic Society, International (APS# AF0054)
Journal: Philippine Philatelic News: quarterly.
Dues: U.S. $15; outside U.S. $25.
Services: local chapters, study groups, auctions, exhibition awards, special awards.
Contact Person: CAPT David S. Durbin, 3604 Darice Lane, Jefferson City, MO 65109-6812
E-mail: yacano@advi.net

Pitcairn Islands Study Group (APS# AF0046)
Journal: Pitcairn Log: quarterly.
Dues: U.S. $15; outside U.S. £9.
Services: study groups, directory, auctions, handbooks.

Contact Person: Rev. Nelson A. L. Weller, 2940 Wesleyan Lane, Winston-Salem, NC 27106
E-mail: nalweller@aol.com

Plate Number Coil Collectors Club (APS# AF0185)
Journal: Coil Line: monthly.
Dues: U.S. $10; Canada/Mexico $14; others $20.
Services: auctions, directory, slide programs, exhibition awards, annual convention.
Contact Person: Mr. Gene C. Trinks, 3603 Bellows Ct., Troy, MI 48083
E-mail: ron.maifeld@pnc3.org
Website: www.pnc3.org

Plate Number Single Society, American (APS# AF0178)
Journal: Plate Numbers: quarterly.
Dues: U.S. $8, outside U.S. $9.
Services: auctions, study groups. directory, sales book circuits.
Contact Person: Mr. Richard E. Burdsall, 608 S. Bennett Ave., Palatine, IL 60067
E-mail: reb608@attbi.com

Plebiscite-Memel-Saar Study Group, GPS (APS# AF0197)
Journal: PMS Study Group Bulletin: 3 per year.
Dues: U.S. $12; outside U.S. $22.
Services: sales book circuits, auctions, expertizing, library, annual convention.
Contact Person: Mr. Clayton J. Wallace, 100 Lark Ct., Alamo, CA 94507
E-mail: wallacec@earthlink.net

Polar Philatelists, American Society of (APS# UN0031)
Journal: Ice Cap News: quarterly.
Dues: $22.
Services: study groups, auctions, handbooks, exhibition awards, annual convention.
Contact Person: Mr. Alan Warren, P. O. Box 39, Exton, PA 19341-0039
E-mail: alanwar@worldnet.att.net

Website: www.south-pole.com/
p0000010.htm

Polonus Philatelic Society (APS# AF0119)
Journal: Polonus Bulletin: quarterly.
Dues: U.S. $25; outside U.S. $30.
Services: exhibition awards,
Contact Person: Mr. Arkadiusz
Walinski, 7414 Lincoln Ave., #D,
Skokie, IL 60076
E-mail: biistamp@charter.net

Post Mark Collectors Club (APS# AF0062)
Journal: PMCC Bulletin: 11 per
year.
Dues: U.S. $18; outside U.S. $26.
Services: local chapters, directory,
auctions, handbook, exhibition
awards, special awards, library,
annual convention.
Contact Person: Mr. Robert W.
Govern, 404 Rustic Ridge Rd.,
Cary, NC 27511-3752
E-mail: bobgovern@juno.com
Website: www.postmarks.org

Postal History Foundation (APS# AF0148)
Journal: The Heliograph: quarterly.
Dues: U.S. $25; outside U.S. $40.
Services: speakers bureau, library,
annual meeting.
Contact Person: Mrs. Elizabeth G.
Towle, P. O. Box 40725, Tucson,
AZ 85717
E-mail: phf3@mindspring.com

Postal History Society (APS# AF0044)
Journal: Postal History Journal:
3 per year.
Dues: U.S. $30; outside U.S. $40.
Services: exhibition awards, annual
convention.
Contact Person: Mrs. Diane D.
Boehret, P. O. Box 61774, Virginia
Beach, VA 23466-1774
E-mail: dianeb@pinn.net

Postal Label Study Group (APS# AF0207)

Journal: The Bulletin; quarterly.
Dues: U.S./Canada $7; others $10.
Services: auctions, handbooks,
library, study groups, expertizing.
Contact Person: Mr. Charles H.
Smith, 13910-B Rio Hondo Circle,
La Mirada, CA 90638
E-mail: smithplsg@aol.com
Website: wwwplsg.homestead.
com/tomspage.html

Postal Order Society, The (APS# AF0167)
Journal: Postal Order News: quar-
terly.
Dues: U.S. $10; outside U.S. £5.
Services: directory, sales book cir-
cuits, auctions, new issue service,
annual convention.
Contact Person: Mr. Jack Har-
wood, P. O. Box 32015, Sarasota,
FL 34239
E-mail: jharwood@attglobal.net

Postal Stationery Society, United (APS# AF0020)
Journal: Postal Stationery:
bimonthly.
Dues: U.S. $18; outside U.S. $25.
Services: local chapters, study
groups, sales book circuits, slide
programs, handbooks, exhibition
awards, special awards, bi-annual
convention.
Contact Person: Ms. Cora Collins,
P. O. Box 1792, Norfolk, VA 23501-
1792
E-mail: Poststat@juno.com
Website: www.upss.org

Postcard Dealers, International Federation of (APS# AF0174)
Journal: IFPD Newsletter: quarterly.
Dues: $25.
Services: directory, expertizing,
annual convention.
Contact Person: Mr. John H.
McClintock, P. O. Box 1765, Man-
assas, VA 20108

Postcard History Society (APS# AF0187)

Journal: Postcard History Society: quarterly.

Dues: U.S. $6; outside U.S. $8.

Services: auctions, expertizing (postcards only), library, annual convention.

Contact Person: Mr. John H. McClintock, P. O. Box 1765, Manassas, VA 20108

Precancel Stamp Society (APS# AF0065)

Journal: The Precancel Forum: monthly.

Dues: $17.

Services: local chapters, directory, handbooks, exhibition awards, special awards, annual convention.

Contact Person: Arnold H. Selengut, P. O. Box 16681, Temple Terrace, FL 33687

E-mail: arnsel@worldnet.att.net

Website: www.precancels.org

Ration Token Collectors, Society of (APS# AF0230)

Journal: The Ration Board: quarterly.

Dues: $8.

Services: study groups, auctions, handbooks, exhibition awards, library, annual convention.

Contact Person: Mr. Dennis Dillman, North Residence Bldg., Apt. 506, 601 Pennsylvania Ave. N. W., Washington, DC 20004

Religion on Stamps, Collectors of (APS# AF0206)

Journal: The COROS Chronicle: bimonthly.

Dues: U.S. $22; outside U.S. $24.

Services: study group, directory, slide programs, exhibition awards, special awards.

Contact Person: Ms. Verna D. Shackleton, 425 N. Linwood Ave., Apt. 110, Appleton, WI 54914-3476

E-mail: corosec@powernetonline.com

Website: www.powernetonline.com/~corosec/coros1.htm

Revenue Association, American (APS# AF0051)

Journal: The American Revenuer: 6 per year.

Dues: $18.

Services: directory, sales book circuits, auctions, handbooks, exhibition award, library, annual convention.

Contact Person: Mr. Ronald E. Lesher, Sr., P. O. Box 1663, Easton, MD 21601-1663

E-mail: revenuer@dmv.com

Website: www.revenuer.org

Rhodesian Study Circle (APS# AF0107)

Journal: The Journal of the RSC: quarterly.

Dues: £10.

Services: local chapters, study groups, sales book circuits (UK only), auctions, handbooks, exhibition awards, special awards, library, annual convention.

Contact Person: Mr. William R. Wallace, P. O. Box 16381, San Francisco, CA 94116

E-mail: bwall8rscr@earthlink.net

Website: www.rsc.stamps.org.uk/stamps/rsc

Rotary-on-Stamps* (APS# AF0117)

Journal: Rotary on Stamps Bulletin: 6 per year.

Dues: U.S. $20.

Services: directory, video programs, handbooks, exhibition awards, annual convention.

Contact Person: Mr. Donald E. Fiery, P. O. Box 333, Hanover, PA 17331

Russian Philately, Rossica Society of (APS# AF0171)

Journal: Rossica Journal: 2 per year.

Dues: $25

Services: local chapters, handbooks, exhibition awards, special awards, library, annual convention.

Contact Person: Dr. G. Adolph

Ackerman, 629 Sanbridge Circle, E., Worthington, OH 43085
E-mail: gcombs@erols.com
Website: www.rossica.org

Ryukyu Philatelic Specialist Society (APS# AF0047)

Journal: From the Dragon's Den: quarterly.
Dues: U.S. $12.50; outside U.S. $15.
Services: local chapters, directory, expertizing, slide programs, handbooks, exhibition awards, special awards.
Contact Person: Mr. Carmine J. Divincenzo, P. O. Box 381, Clayton, CA 94517-0381
E-mail: Photbob1@aol.com
Website: users.netmdc.com/~rpss/index.htm

Samoa Specialists, Fellowship of (APS# AF0240)

Journal: The Samoa Express: quarterly.
Dues: $15.
Contact Person: Mr. Martin J. Miller, 102-20 67th Dr., Flushing, NY 11375-2809
E-mail: MMiller@LadasParry.com
Website: members.aol.com/TongaJan/foss.html

Sarawak Specialists' Society (APS# AF0110)

Journal: The Sarawak Journal: quarterly.
Dues: $10
Services: sales book circuits, handbooks, exhibition awards, library, study groups, directory, auctions, special awards, annual convention.
Contact Person: Mr. Stuart Leven, P. O. Box 24764, San Jose, CA 95154
E-mail: stulev@ix.netcom.com
Website: http://britbornedstamps.org.uk

Scandinavian Collectors Club (APS# AF0079)

Journal: The Posthorn: quarterly.
Dues: U.S. $15; outside U.S. $21.
Services: local chapters, study groups, sales book circuits, slide programs, exhibition awards, special awards, library, annual convention
Contact Person: Mr. Donald B. Brent, P. O. Box 13196, El Cajon, CA 92020
E-mail: dbrent47@sprynet.com
Website: www.scc-online.org

Scandinavian Philatelic Foundation (APS# AF0137)

Journal: Semi-annual (informal newsletters).
Dues: $10 or greater donation.
Services: handbooks.
Contact Person: Mr. Alan Warren, P. O. Box 39, Exton, PA 19341-0039
E-mail: alanwar@att.net

Scouts on Stamps Society International (APS# AF0202)

Journal: SOSSI Journal: quarterly.
Dues: U.S. $15; outside U.S. $18.
Services: local chapters, auctions, slide programs, special awards, library, directory, expertizing, annual convention.
Contact Person: Mr. Walter M. Creitz, 830 Berkshire Dr., Reading, PA 19601
E-mail: wcreitz@aol.com
Website: www.sossi.org/

Ship Cancellation Society, Universal (APS# AF0098)

Journal: USCS Log: monthly.
Dues: U.S. $16; outside U.S. $21.
Services: local chapters, study groups, directory, sales circuits, slide programs, handbooks, special awards, annual convention.
Contact Person: Mr. David A. Kent, P. O. Box 127, New Britain, CT 06050
Website: www.uscs.org/

Ships on Stamps Unit* (APS# AF0152)

Journal: Watercraft Philately: bimonthly.
Dues: U.S. $10; Canada $14; others $20.
Services: directory, handbooks, exhibition awards, annual convention.
Contact Person: Mr. R. P. Stuckert, 2750 Hwy. 21 East, Paint Lick, KY 40461
Website: personal.palouse.net/hobbies/shipstamps/

Southern Africa, Philatelic Society for Greater (APS# AF0190)
Journal: Forerunners: 3 per year.
Dues: $25.
Services: study group, directory, auctions, expertizing, exhibition awards, library, annual convention.
Contact Person: Dr. Robert F. Taylor, 674 Chelsea Dr., Sanford, NC 27330-8587
E-mail: rtaylor@wave-net.net

Souvenir Card Collectors Society (APS# AF0149)
Journal: The Souvenir Card Journal: quarterly.
Dues: U.S. $20; outside U.S. $25.
Services: local chapters, auctions, annual convention.
Contact Person: Mr. Douglas B. Holl, P. O. Box 234, Annandale, VA 22003

Space Topics Study Group* (APS# AF0029)
Journal: Astrophile: bimonthly.
Dues: $15.
Services: local chapters, directory, auctions, expertizing, cover service, handbooks, exhibition awards, special awards, annual convention.
Contact Person: Mr. Steve Durst, 777 Brushwood Ct., Millersville, MD 21108
Website: stargate.1usa.com/stamps/

Spanish Main, The (APS# AF0162)
Journal: The Mainsheet: quarterly.
Dues: U.S. $22; outside U.S. £10.

Services: study groups, sales books circuits, auctions, handbooks, special awards, annual convention.
Contact Person: Mr. Brian Moorhouse, P. O. Box 105, Peterborough, PE3 8TQ England
E-mail: brian@moorhouse.com
Website: brian.moorhouse.com

Spanish Philatelic Society (APS# AF0201)
Journal: ARANA: quarterly.
Dues: U.S. $15; outside U.S. $22.50.
Services: directory, auction, exhibition awards, library, annual convention.
Contact Person: Mr. Jerry A. Wells, 3313 Melaine, Plano, TX 75023
E-mail: bjwells@flash.net

Spellman Museum of Stamps/Postal History (APS# AF0166)
Dues: Individual $30 (Contact museum for other membership category prices).
Services: library, education programs, free admission to museum.
Contact Person: Mr. George Norton, 235 Wellesley St., Weston, MA 02493
Website: www.spellman.org

Sports Philatelists International* (APS# UN0039)
Journal: Journal of Sports Philately: bimonthly.
Dues: U.S. $20; outside U.S. $30.
Services: directory, auctions, cover service, annual convention.
Contact Person: Mr. Glenn A. Estus, P. O. Box 451, Westport, NY 12993
Website: www.geocities.com/Colosseum/Track/6279/

St. Helena, Ascension, and Tristan da Cunha Philatelic Society (APS# AF0085)
Journal: South Atlantic Chronicle: quarterly.

Dues: U.S. $20; outside U.S. $23–$25.
Services: directory, auctions, handbooks, special awards, library, speakers bureau.
Contact Person: Dr. Everett L. Parker, HC 76, Box 32, Greenville, ME 04441-9727
E-mail: eparker@mooseheadnet
Website: ourworld.compuserve. com/homepages/ST_HELENA_ ASCEN_TDC/

Stamp Dealers Association, National (APS# AF0225)
Journal: NSDA Update.
Dues: $50.
Services: directory, annual convention.
Contact Person: Mr. Edward G. Rosen, P. O. Box 7176, Redwood City, CA 94063-7176
E-mail: NSDAinc@aol.com
Website: www.NSDAinc.org

Stamporama (APS# AF0242)
Journal: The Rambler: monthly.
Dues: Free.
Services: directory, auctions.
Contact Person: Mr. David Teisler, 262 Prospect Pl., Brooklyn, NY 11238-3901
E-mail: teisler@aabt.org
Website: www.stamporama.com

Stamps on Stamps Collectors Club* (APS# AF0127)
Journal: SOS Signal: quarterly.
Dues: U.S. $9; outside U.S. $12.
Contact Person: Mr. William E. Critzer, 1360 Trinity Dr., Menlo Park, CA 94025
E-mail: wcritzer@avenidas.org
Website:
www.stampsonstamps.org

State Revenue Society (APS# AF0164)
Journal: State Revenue News: 4 per year.
Dues: U.S. $12; outside U.S. $18.
Services: directory, auctions, handbooks, library, annual convention.
Contact Person: Mr. Scott M. Troutman, P. O. Box 270184, Oklahoma City, OK 73137-0184
Website: hillcity-mall.com/SRS/

Tannu Tuva Collectors Society (APS# AF0235)
Journal: TbBA: quarterly.
Dues: $5.
Services: auctions, handbooks.
Contact Person: Kenneth R. Simon, 513 6th Ave., S., Lake Worth, FL 33460-4507
E-mail: bigelow9427@cs.com
Website: www.seflin.org/tuva

Texas Postal History Society (APS# AF0076)
Journal: Texas Postal History Journal: quarterly.
Dues: U.S. $10; outside U.S. $15.
Services: directory, auctions, special awards, annual convention.
Contact Person: Mr. Lyle C. Boardman, 3916 Wyldwood Rd., Austin, TX 78739
E-mail: lcboardman@aol.com

Thai Philately, Society for (APS# AF0078)
Journal: Thai Philately: three times yearly.
Dues: $22.
Services: study groups, directory, auctions, exhibition awards, special awards, library.
Contact Person: H. R. Blakeney, P. O. Box 25644, Oklahoma City, OK 73125-0644
E-mail: hrblakeney@mozart.inet. co.th
Website: www.thaiphilately.com

Trans Mississippi Philatelic Society (APS# AF0238)
Journal: Trans Mississippian; quarterly.
Dues: $16
Services: local chapters, bureau speakers, expertizing, exhibition awards, annual convention.

Contact Person: Mr. Alfred E. Mack, Valley View Manor Apt. 210A, 2571 Guthrie Ave., Des Moines, IA 50317-3019
E-mail: suealmack@home.com

U.S. Cancellation Club (APS# AF0075)
Journal: U.S. Cancellation Club News: quarterly.
Dues: U.S. $14; outside U.S. $25.
Services: directory, auctions, exhibition awards, library, annual convention.
Contact Person: Mr. Roger D. Curran, 20 University Ave., Lewisburg, PA 17837
E-mail: rrrhoads@aol.com
Website: www.geocities.com/Athens/2088/uscchome.htm

U.S. Philatelic Classics Society (APS# UN0011)
Journal: U.S. Chronicle: quarterly.
Dues: U.S. $22.50; outside U.S. $30.50.
Services: local chapters, handbooks, study groups, directory, exhibition awards, special awards, library, annual convention.
Contact Person: Mr. Mark D. Rogers, P. O. Box 80708, Austin, TX 78708-0708
E-mail: turgon96@aol.com
Website: www.uspcs.org

U.S. Possessions Philatelic Society (APS# AF0099)
Journal: Possessions: quarterly.
Dues: $15
Services: library.
Contact Person: Mr. Geoffrey Brewster, 141 Lyford Dr., Tiburon, CA 94920

Ukrainian Philatelic and Numismatic Society (APS# AF0134)
Journal: Ukrainian Philatelist: annual.
Dues: U.S. $20; outside U.S. $35.
Services: local chapters, directory, study groups, expertizing, speakers

bureau, handbooks, exhibition awards, special awards, library, annual convention.
Contact Person: Mr. Paul Spiwak, 42 Irving Rd., New Hartford, NY 13413
E-mail: Yurko@warwick.net
Website: www.upns.org

United Nations Philatelists* (APS# AF0071)
Journal: The Journal of the UNP: bimonthly.
Dues: U.S. $15; outside U.S. $25.
Services: local chapters, auctions, handbooks, exhibition awards, special awards, annual convention.
Contact Person: Mr. Alex L. Bereson, 18 Portola Dr., San Francisco, CA 94131
Website: www.unpi.com

United States Stamp Society (APS# AF0150)
Journal: The United States Specialist: monthly.
Dues: U.S. $25; outside U.S. $32.
Services: speakers bureau, handbooks, exhibition award, special awards, annual convention.
Conact Person: Mr. Larry Ballantyne, P. O. Box 6634, Katy, TX, 77491-6634
Website: www.usstamps.org

Universal Postal Union Collectors* (APS# AF0070)
Journal: Goble Union: quarterly
Dues: U.S./Canada $12; others $19.
Services: directory, auctions.
Contact Person: Mr. Charles J. Rejto, P. O. Box 125, Barrington, RI 02806

Vatican Philatelic Society (APS# AF0129)
Journal: Vatican Notes: bimonthly.
Dues: U.S. $9; outside U.S. $16.
Services: local chapters, library.
Contact Person: Mr. Thomas I.

Crimando, 8143 Mill Rd., Bergen, NY 14416
Website: members.tripod.com/~Dcelani/index-VPS.html

Vermont Philatelic Society (APS# AF0156)
Journal: Vermont Philatelist: quarterly.
Dues: U.S. $10; outside U.S. $15.
Services: local chapters, directory, cover service, auctions, handbooks, ibrary, annual convention.
Contact Person: Dr. Paul G. Abajian, P .O. Box 475, Essex Junction, VT 05453-0475
E-mail: pga@surfglobal.net
Website: www.voicenet.com/~vpsoc

Virgina Postal History Society (APS# UN0041)
Journal: Way Markings: quarterly.
Dues: U.S. $15; outside U.S. $35.
Services: auctions, directory, exhibition awards, annual convention.
Contact Person: Mr. Robert L. Lisbeth, P. O. Box 29771, Richmond, VA 23242-0771
E-mail: ael@virginia.edu
Website: www.virginiapostalhistory.com

West Africa Study Circle (APS# AF0231)
Journal: Cameo; twice annually, newsletter; quarterly.
Dues: U.S. $24; Canada $36; UK £12; others £14.
Services: auction, speakers bureau, directory, handbooks, special awards, library, annual convention.
Contact Person: Dr. Peter Newroth, 520 Marsett Pl., #33, Victoria, BC V8Z 7J1 Canada
E-mail: prnew@home.com
Website: ourworld.compuserve.com/homepages/frankwalton/homepage.htm

Western Cover Society (APS# UN0014)
Journal: Western Express: quarterly.

Dues: $20.
Services: directory, handbooks, annual convention.
Contact Person: Mr. John R. Drew, 15370 Skyview Terr., San Jose, CA 95132-3042
E-mail: patera@teleport.com

Wine on Stamps Study Unit (APS# AF0233)
Journal: Enophilatelica; quarterly.
Dues: U.S. $8; outside U.S. $14.
Services: new issue service, directory, annual convention.
Contact Person: Dr. James D. Crum, 816 Kingsbury Ct., Arroyo Grande, CA 93420-4511
E-mail: jdakcrum@aol.com

Wisconsin Postal History Society (APS# AF0061)
Journal: Badger Postal History: quarterly.
Dues: U.S. $10; outside U.S. $15.
Contact Person: Mr. James Maher, 150 Terrace Lane, Hartland, WI 53029

Women on Stamps Study Unit* (APS# AF0118)
Journal: The Topical Woman: quarterly.
Dues: U.S. $8; outside U.S $12.
Services: directory, handbook.
Contact Person: Davida Kristy, 515 Ocean Ave., #608S, Santa Monica, CA 90402
E-mail: dkristy@sprintmail.com

Worldwide Stamp Collectors, International Society of (APS# AF0151)
Journal: The Circuit: bimonthly.
Dues: $12.
Services: directory, sales book circuits, auctions, expertizing exhibition awards.
Contact Person: Dr. Anthony Zollo, P. O. Box 150407, Lufkin, TX 75915-0402
E-mail: stamptmf@frontiernet.net
Website: www.iswsc.org

Writers Unit, APS (APS# UN0030)

Journal: The Philatelic Communicator: quarterly.

Dues: U.S. $15; Canada/Mexico $17.50; others $20.

Services: annual convention.

Contact Person: Mr. George B. Griffenhagen, 2501 Drexel St., Vienna, VA 22180

Zeppelin Collectors Club (APS# AF0135)

Journal: The Zeppelin Collector: quarterly.

Dues: U.S. $23; outside U.S. $28.

Contact Person: Cheryl Ganz, P. O. Box A3843, Chicago, IL 60690-3843

Website: ourworld.compuserve.com/homepages/aams/

NATIONAL STAMP CLUBS LISTED BY GEOGRAPHICAL LOCATION

All of the listed stamp clubs are chapter members of the APS, but each is a separate organization offering its own services to its members. APS Chapters located in the United States are listed alphabetically by state and city. Those outside the United States are listed alphabetically by country and city. The name and APS number of each chapter are given, the time and location of meetings, and, finally, the name and address of a local contact from whom additional information may be obtained.

When communicating with chapters by mail, be sure to use the contact address and *not* the meeting location address. The latter generally is not a valid mailing address.

Clubs that have maintained APS Chapter status for 25, 50, and 75 years are identified as follows:

* = 25 years
** = 50 years
*** = 75 years

SUPPORT FOR CHAPTERS

The APS Chapter Activities Committee serves as the focal point for most services available to APS Chapters. The committee publishes a quarterly newsletter, sponsors a publications contest, and conducts other programs for local clubs. APS Chapters may schedule APS Sales Division circuits and philatelic slide programs produced by the Society exclusively for use by chapters for their meetings through the APS Headquarters.

Local stamp clubs interested in the benefits of APS Chapter membership may obtain detailed information from the APS, P.O. Box 8000, State College, PA 16803; (814) 237-3803.

ALABAMA

Birmingham Philatelic Society (APS# 0485-041050)
Meeting Time and Location: 7:30 p.m., 2nd & 4th Tues., except Dec. Jewish Community Center, 3960 Montclair Rd.
Contact Person: Mr. Charles C. Hancock, P.O. Box 531330, Birmingham, AL 35253
Meeting City: Birmingham

Eastern Shore Stamp Collectors (APS# 1328-142530)
Meeting Time and Location: 7 p.m., 2nd & 4th Tues., 4th Tues. Aug., Nov., & Dec. Contact repr. for info.
Contact Person: Mr. Ian L. Robertson, 117 Kiefer Ave., Fairhope, AL 36532
Meeting City: Fairhope
E-mail: sloloris@earthlink.net

Huntsville Philatelic Club (APS# 0597-047322)
Meeting Time and Location: 7:30 p.m., 1st & 3rd Tues., Trinity Methodist Church, Rm. 265, 607 Airport Road
Contact Person: Mr. Michael C. O'Reilly, P. O. Box 1131, Huntsville, AL 35807-0131
Meeting City: Huntsville
E-mail: mcoreilly@worldnet.att.net

Calhoun County Stamp Club (APS# 0629-049489)
Meeting Time and Location: 7:30 p.m., 2nd & 4th Tues., St. Luke's Church, Campus Ministry Room
Contact Person: Miss Cordelia L. Gray, 703 11th Ave. N.E., Jacksonville, AL 36265
Meeting City: Jacksonville

Stamp Club of Mobile (APS# 0546-044136)
Meeting Time and Location: 7 p.m., 2nd Tues., Saad's Medical Center, Festival Center, Airport Blvd.
Contact Person: Mr. Charles F. Staalmach, P.O. Box 182, Theodore, AL 36590-0182
Meeting City: Mobile
E-mail: kj_snell@yahoo.com

Montgomery Area Stamp Club (APS# 0893-076748)
Meeting Time and Location: 7 p.m., 2nd & 4th Thurs., Nov. & Dec. 2nd Thurs. only, Crump Community Ctr., 1735 Highland Ave.
Contact Person: Mr. Isaacs J. Musgrove, 72 Jeanine Ct., Wetumpka, AL 36093-2007
Meeting City: Montgomery
E-mail: JimMusgrove@excite.com
Website: masc.huntingdon.edu/

Tuscaloosa Stamp Club (APS# 1432-166150)
Meeting Time and Location: 7 p.m., 2nd Thurs, University of Alabama, Chemistry Dept., 103 Lloyd Hall
Contact Person: Mr. Wallace H. Lancaster, P. O. Box 020744, Tuscaloosa, AL 35402
Meeting City: Tuscaloosa

ALASKA

Anchorage Philatelic Society (APS# 0326-029280)
Meeting Time and Location: 7 p.m., 2nd & 4th Wed., Senior Center, 1300 E. 19th St.
Contact Person: Mr. P. Nelson Gnirke, P. O. Box 102214, Anchorage, AK 99510-2214
Meeting City: Anchorage
E-mail: spaugy@micronet.net
Website: home.gci.net/~akphilsoc

Gastineau Philatelic Society (APS# 0863-072342)
Meeting Time and Location: 7 p.m., 3rd Tues., 3025 Clinton Dr.

Contact Person: Mrs. Virginia B. Post, P. O. Box 240363, Douglas, AK 99824-0363
Meeting City: Juneau

ARIZONA

Arizona Federation of Stamp Clubs (APS# 0792-064416)
Meeting Time and Location: Three times a year.
Contact Person: Mr. Carl LeMar John, 5063 E. North Regency Circle, Tucson, AZ 85711-3000
Meeting City: Casa Granda

Flagstaff Stamp Club (APS# 1132-110956)
Meeting Time and Location: 7 p.m., 1st Wed., Adult Center, 245 Thorpe Rd.
Contact Person: Mr. Robert J. Lackner, P. O. Box 43, Flagstaff, AZ 86002
Meeting City: Flagstaff

Mesa Stamp Club (APS# 0938-083978)
Meeting Time and Location: 7 p.m., 4th Wed., members' homes.
Contact Person: Ms. Marsha L. Hunt, 717 E. Halifax St., Mesa, AZ 85203
Meeting City: Mesa

Phoenix Philatelic Association (APS# 0307-028554)
Meeting Time and Location: 6:30 p.m., 2nd Mon. & 4th Wed., 2nd Mon.-Jul/Aug/Nov/Dec, Los Olivos Sr. Center, Rm 1–3, 2802 E. Devonshire
Contact Person: Mr. Harold A. Egy, P. O. Box 15037, Phoenix, AZ 85060-5037
Meeting City: Phoenix
E-mail: haroldegy@aol.com

Prescott Stamp Club (APS# 1008-094275)
Meeting Time and Location: 7 p.m., 1st & 3rd Tues., except Jan., Aug., Dec. Prescott Community Church, 3151 Willow Creek Rd.
Contact Person: Mr. Ethan Davis, 1414 Carlock Dr., Prescott, AZ 86305
Meeting City: Prescott
E-mail: skyridge@northlink.com

Sun City Stamp Club (APS# 0887-076248)
Meeting Time and Location: 7 p.m., 1st Mon. & 3rd, Tues. Marinette Rec. Center, 99th Ave. & Union Hills Dr.
Contact Person: Ms. Margaret Stahl, 19658 N. Willowcreek Circle, Sun City, AZ 85351-2840
Meeting City: Sun City

Sun City West Coin & Stamp Club (APS# 1204-122188)
Meeting Time and Location: 7 p.m., 2nd Tues. (June, July, Aug.), 2 p.m., 4th Tues. (Sept. thru May) 2nd Tues.-Kuentz Recreation Center, Rm. 2; 4th Tues.-Johnson Recreation Center
Contact Person: Mr. Richard J. Scanlon, 15919 Heritage Dr., Sun City West, AZ 85375
Meeting City: Sun City West

Sun Lakes Stamp Club (APS# 1456-172828)
Meeting Time and Location: 7 p.m., 1st Tues., Sun Lakes Ph. I Cty Club, Friendship Rm., 25601 N. Sun Lakes Blvd.
Contact Person: Mr. John R. Storm, 1568 E. Winged Foot Dr., Chandler, AZ 85249
Meeting City: Sun Lakes

Arizona Philatelic Rangers (APS# 0585-046188)
Meeting Time and Location: 6:30 p.m., Fri., Various major stamp shows
Contact Person: Mr. John Birkinbine, II, P. O. Box 36657, Tucson, AZ 85740-6657

Meeting City: Tucson
E-mail: jbirkinbin@aol.com

Tucson Stamp Club (APS# 0059-007566)
Meeting Time and Location: 7 p.m., 1st & 3rd Tues., Armory Park Sr. Ctr., Dining Rm., 220 S. 5th Ave.
Contact Person: Mr. Allen Van Cranebrock, Apt. 3184, 7887 N. LaCholla Blvd., Tucson, AZ 85741
Meeting City: Tucson
E-mail: phf@azstarnet.com

ARKANSAS

Pinnacle Stamp Club of Arkansas (APS# 1300-136599)
Meeting Time and Location: 7 p.m., 4th Thurs., University Mall, Community room, 300 S. University Ave.
Contact Person: Mr. Bill Norton, P.O. Box 55898, Little Rock, AR 72215-5525
Meeting City: Little Rock

Mountain Home Area Stamp Club (APS# 0844-070020)
Meeting Time and Location: 1 p.m., 2nd Sat., Youth Center, 1001 Spring St., #3
Contact Person: Mr. Heinrich Petersen, 296 Westview Rd., #1, Midway, AR 72651-9225
Meeting City: Mountain Home

Razorback Stamp Club (APS# 1111-105688)
Meeting Time and Location: 7 p.m., 2nd Tues., Peace Lutheran Church, 805 W. Olrich St.
Contact Person: Mr. Herbert E. Kauffman, 100 N. Dixieland Rd., Rogers, AR 72756
Meeting City: Rogers

CALIFORNIA

Council N. Calif. Philatelic Society (APS# 0456-039063)
Meeting Time and Location: Quarterly, various affiliated clubs
Contact Person: Mr. Leonard W. Holmsten, 396 Smalley Ave., Hayward, CA 94541
Meeting City: Northern California
E-mail: Lhomsten@aol.com
Website: www.home.earthlink.net/~pennyred/council.html

Fed. Phil. Clubs S. California (APS# 0246-024584)
Meeting Time and Location: Quarterly, various cities
Contact Person: Mr. Robert de Violini, P. O. Box 5025, Oxnard, CA 93031-5025
Meeting City: Southern California
E-mail: dviolini@west.net
Website: www.sescal.org/fed clubs.htm

Alameda Stamp Club (APS# 1517-190547)
Meeting Time and Location: 8 p.m., 1st Tues., Immanuel Lutheran Church, Chestnut & Santa Clara
Contact Person: Mr. Charles A. Kasdorf, P.O. Box 1152, Alameda, CA 94501
Meeting City: Alameda

Arcadia Stamp Club (APS# 1158-114972)
Meeting Time and Location: 7 p.m., 2nd & 4th Tues., Our Saviour Luthern Church, 512 W. Duarte Rd.
Contact Person: Mr. Gerald Delker, 3046 Treefern Dr., Duarte, CA 91010-1517
Meeting City: Arcadia
E-mail: delker@earthlink.net

Bakersfield Stamp Club (APS# 0652-051445)
Meeting Time and Location: 7:30 p.m., 3rd Thurs., except Dec. Jim Burke Ford Confer. Rm. A, 21st & Oak St.
Contact Person: Mr. Robert A. Johnston, 2001 Canter Way, Bakersfield, CA 93309

Meeting City: Bakersfield
E-mail: stamps
@topicalsonstamps.com
Website: www.topicalsonstamps.
com/bakersfield_stamp_club.htm

Santa Cruz County Stamp Club
(APS# 0894-076749)
Meeting Time and Location: 7
p.m., 3rd Tues., City Hall Council
Chambers, 420 Capitola Ave.
Contact Person: Mr. Harold A.
Short, P. O. Box 2864, Santa Cruz,
CA 95063
Meeting City: Capitola

Monterey Peninsula Stamp Club
(APS# 0413-035961)
Meeting Time and Location: 7:30
p.m., 2nd Wed., 3029 Lorca Lane
Contact Person: Mr. Harold
Seyferth, 50 Yankee Point, Carmel,
CA 93923
Meeting City: Carmel
E-mail: mpshuler1@aol.com

Fresno Philatelic Society (APS#
0767-061202)
Meeting Time and Location: 1 p.m.,
1st Sun., 7 p.m. 3rd Thurs. Veterans
Memorial Bldg., 5th @ Hughes
Contact Person: Mr. Gilbert P.
Parent, 5050 E. White, Fresno, CA
93727
Meeting City: Clovis
E-mail: 9pp1927@prodigy.net
Website: www.geocities.com/
~rgh14/frespex

East County Stamp Club (APS#
1154-113999)
Meeting Time and Location: 11
a.m., 2nd & 4th Sat., Westward Ho
Trailer Ct., 12044 Royal Rd.
Contact Person: Mr. Gerhard F.
Lorenzen, 4262 Blackton Dr., La
Mesa, CA 91941
Meeting City: El Cajon

Humboldt Collectors Club (APS#
0978-089465)

Meeting Time and Location: 7:30
p.m., 4th Tues., Senior Resource
Center, 1910 California
Contact Person: Ms. Carolyn
Podratz, 341 Wells Dr., Eureka, CA
95503-6431
Meeting City: Eureka

Mendocino Coast Stamp Club
(APS# 1410-159697)
Meeting Time and Location: 7:30
p.m., 1st Thurs., F.B. Library
Community Room, 499 E. Laurel St.
Contact Person: Dr. Charles A.
Jones, P. O. Box 2910, Fort Bragg,
CA 95437
Meeting City: Fort Bragg
E-mail: drstamps@webtv.net
Website: virtualstampsclub.com/
apsmendocino.html

Fremont Stamp Club (APS# 1120-
107688)
Meeting Time and Location: 7
p.m., 2nd & 5th Thurs., Fremont
Cultural Arts Center, 3375
Country Dr.
Contact Person: Mr. Leonard W.
Holmsten, 396 Smalley Ave.,
Hayward, CA 94541
Meeting City: Fremont
E-mail: lhomlsten@aol.com

Beckman Philatelic Society (APS#
0555-044422)
Meeting Time and Location: 8
p.m., 3rd Mon., various locations
Contact Person: Mrs. Louise
Christian, P. O. Box 369, Placentia,
CA 92870
Meeting City: Fullerton
E-mail: louiseoma@aol.com

Arrowhead Stamp Club (APS#
0340-030432)
Meeting Time and Location: 7
p.m., 2nd Wed., Highland Senior
Center, 3102 E. Highland Ave.
Contact Person: Mr. David M.
Rutherfurd, 166 N. I St., San
Bernardino, CA 92410-1810

Meeting City: Highland
E-mail: drutherfur@cs.com

McDonnell Douglas Philatelic Club
(APS# 0673-052804)
Meeting Time and Location: 7:30
p.m., 1st & 3rd Tues., MDC
Huntington Beach
Contact Person: Mr. Thomas L.
Letto, 40 Seascape Dr., Newport
Beach, CA 92663-2731
Meeting City: Huntington Beach
E-mail: stenhuser@aol.com

Our Saviors Lutheran Church
Stamp Club (APS# 1518-190548)
Meeting Time and Location: 1st
Sat., 1035 Carol Lane
Contact Person: Mr. Richard D.
Jonathan, 1035 Carol Lane,
Lafayette, CA 94549
Meeting City: Lafayette

Saddleback Stamp Club (APS#
0872-073155)
Meeting Time and Location: 7
p.m., 2nd & 4th Wed., Freedom
Village Ret. Comm., Pavilion Rm.,
23442 El Toro Rd.
Contact Person: Mr. Mark R.
Winters, 24721 Paseo Vendaval,
Lake Forest, CA 92630-2136
Meeting City: Lake Forest
E-mail: bigbear7@earthlink.net

A. V. Stamp Club (APS# 1468-
174561)
Meeting Time and Location: 2
p.m., 2nd Sun., Lancaster Estates
Clubhouse, 45465 25th St., E.
Contact Person: Mr. Robert L.
Webb, 4558 Palmdale Hills Dr.,
Palmdale, CA 93552-6226
Meeting City: Lancaster
E-mail: spiderman@qnet.com

Long Beach Stamp Club (APS#
0744-059314)
Meeting Time and Location: 7:30
p.m., 1st & 3rd Tues., Millikan High
Sch., Cafeteria, 2800 Snowden Ave.

Contact Person: Mr. George E.
Franzen, Jr., 14007 Leahy Ave.,
Bellflower, CA 90706
Meeting City: Long Beach
E-mail: westes0380@aol.com

Philatelic Society of Los Angeles
(APS# 0090-010294)
Meeting Time and Location:
7:30 p.m., 2nd & 4th Tues.,
Westside Pavilion, 3rd fl., Pico &
Overland
Contact Person: Mr. Richard S.
Willing, P. O. Box 2217, Culver
City, CA 90230
Meeting City: Los Angeles
E-mail: scribev@aol.com

Scand. Phil. Lib. of S. California
(APS# 0860-071935)
Meeting Time and Location: 7:30
p.m., 1st Wed., except Aug.
Members' home, call for info.
Contact Person: Mr. Paul A. Nel-
son, P.O. Box 310, Claremont, CA
91711
Meeting City: Los Angeles
E-mail: pnels@att.net

Society Israel Phil.-LA Chapter
(APS# 1499-185528)
Meeting Time and Location:
2 p.m., 4th Sun., Institute of
Jewish Education,
8339 W. 3rd St.
Contact Person: Mr. N. Louis
Senensieb, 15032 Acre St.,
Sepulveda, CA 91343
Meeting City: Los Angeles
E-mail: mzsnls@netscape.net

Glendale Stamp Club (APS# 0589-
046674)
Meeting Time and Location: 8
p.m., 4th Mon., except Dec.,
Glendale Federal Savings
Contact Person: Mr. Joseph H.
Mirsky, 4359 Ramsdell Ave., La
Crescenta, CA 91214
Meeting City: Montrose

Conejo Valley Philatelic Society (APS# 1337-145089)
Meeting Time and Location: 7:30 p.m., 2nd Wed., King of Glory Lutheran Church, 2500 Borchard Rd.
Contact Person: Mr. Harlan M. Walker, 637 Paseo Esmeralda, Newbury Park, CA 91320
Meeting City: Newbury Park

West Valley Stamp Club (APS# 1505-187993)
Meeting Time and Location: 7 p.m., 1st Tues./3rd Fri., First Lutheran Church, 18355 Roscoe Blvd.
Contact Person: Mrs. Sally Marx, P.O. Box 227, Canoga Park, CA 91305
Meeting City: Northridge

East Bay Collectors Club (APS# 0220-021297)
Meeting Time and Location: 8 p.m., 1st & 3rd Thurs., Kensington Community Center, The Arlington, Kensington
Contact Person: Mr. William P. Barlow, Jr., P. O. Box 19053, Oakland, CA 94619
Meeting City: Oakland

Tri City Stamp Club (APS# 0592-046968)
Meeting Time and Location: 7 p.m., 1st & 3rd Thurs., Boys/Girls Club of Oceanside, 450 Country Club Lane
Contact Person: CPT Ronald E. Couchot, P. O. Box 1413, Oceanside, CA 92051-1413
Meeting City: Oceanside

Pacific Palisades Stamp Club (APS# 0929-082327)
Meeting Time and Location: 7:30 p.m., 1st & 3rd Tues., Pacific Palisades Library, 861 Alma Real Dr.
Contact Person: Mr. John E. Quinley, Jr., 533 Levering Ave., Los Angeles, CA 90024
Meeting City: Pacific Palisades

J. P. L. Stamp Club (APS# 0948-086293)
Meeting Time and Location: 12 Noon, 2nd Tues., Bldg. 183, Rm. 328, 4800 Oak Grove Dr.
Contact Person: Mr. James R. Rose, P. O. Box 771, La Canada, CA 91012-0771
Meeting City: Pasadena
E-mail: james.r.rose@jpl.nasa.gov

Redwood Empire Collectors Club (APS# 1465-174385)
Meeting Time and Location: 6 p.m., 3rd Wed., River House Restaurant, 10 Weller St.
Contact Person: Mr. Kurt H. Schau, P.O. Box 659, Petaluma, CA 94953
Meeting City: Petaluma

Redding Stamp Club (APS# 1411-160290)
Meeting Time and Location: 2 p.m., 1st & 3rd Sun., River Oaks Retirement Resid., 301 Hartnell Ave.
Contact Person: Mr. G. M. Heminger, 1701 Dana Dr., Apt. 72, Redding, CA 96003-4813
Meeting City: Redding
E-mail: harold@shasta.com

Redlands Stamp Club (APS# 0484-040866)
Meeting Time and Location: 7:30 p.m., 4th Tues., except July Church of Christ, 1000 Roosevelt Rd.
Contact Person: Ms. Sylvia Louise Jay, P.O. Box 226, Redlands, CA 92373
Meeting City: Redlands

TRW Stamp Club (APS# 0979-089466)
Meeting Time and Location: 12 p.m., 2nd & 4th Tues., TRW Complex, R 1 Conference Room
Contact Person: Mr. Allen F. Conrad, 7755 Quimby Ave., West Hills, CA 91304

Meeting City: Redondo Beach
E-mail: allen.conrad@trw.com

Sequoia Stamp Club (APS# 0687-054588)
Meeting Time and Location: 8:15 p.m., 2nd & 4th Tues., Community Activities Center, 1400 Roosevelt Ave.
Contact Person: Mr. William E. Dutcher, 1842 Los Altos Dr., San Mateo, CA 94402-3642
Meeting City: Redwood City
E-mail: wdutchersanmateo@worldnet.att.net
Website: www.biermans.com/sequoia/

Riverside Stamp Club (APS# 0507-042328)
Meeting Time and Location: 7 p.m., 2nd Mon., La Sierra University, Ambs Hall, Room 115
Contact Person: Jewell L. Meyer, 20112 Westpoint Dr., Riverside, CA 92507
E-mail: wclark@lasierra.edu
Meeting City: Riverside
Website: cs.lasierra.edu/~wclarke/RSC.html

Sacramento Philatelic Society (APS# 0390-034230)
Meeting Time and Location: 7 p.m., Wed., Easter Seal Society, 3205 Hurley Way
Contact Person: Mr. David Anderson, P. O. Box 13284, Sacramento, CA 95813
Meeting City: Sacramento

Monterey County Stamp Club (APS# 0598-047341)
Meeting Time and Location: 7:30 p.m., 4th Tues., Seventh Day Adventist Church, Social Hall, 46 Villa St.
Contact Person: Mr. Earl L. Eidson, 741 College Dr., Salinas, CA 93901-1248

Meeting City: Salinas
E-mail: pantry@montereybay.com

San Diego County Philatelic Council (APS# 0930-082328)
Meeting Time and Location: 7:30 p.m., last Mon. of Jan.,, Apr., July, & Oct., San Diego County Phil. Lib., 7403C Princess View Dr.
Contact Person: Ms. Linda Mabin, P. O. Box 80004, San Diego, CA 92138-0004
Meeting City: San Diego
E-mail: ljmsandiego@webtv.net

Collectors Club of San Francisco (APS# 0516-042997)
Meeting Time and Location: 7:30 p.m., 2nd Wed., except July & Dec., Barcelona Restaurant, Spring St.
Contact Person: Mrs. Vesma Grinfelds, 2586 Diamond St., San Francisco, CA 94131
Meeting City: San Francisco
E-mail: dzvesma@sprintmail.com

Golden Gate Stamp Club (APS# 1500-186030)
Meeting Time and Location: 8 p.m., 2nd & 4th Mon., Police Station, 2345 24th Ave.
Contact Person: Mrs. Evelyn Kregar, 2475 17th Ave., San Francisco, CA 94116
Meeting City: San Francisco
E-mail: lundone@worldnet.att.net

San Francisco-Pacific Phil. Society (APS# 0003-003387)
Meeting Time and Location: 7 p.m., 2nd Tues., SFPD-Richmond Station, 461 6th Ave.
Contact Person: Mr. William R. Wallace, P. O. Box 16381, San Francisco, CA 94116
Meeting City: San Francisco
E-mail: bwall8rscr@earthlink.net

San Jose Stamp Club (APS# 0264-025791)

Meeting Time and Location: 7 p.m., 1st & 3rd Wed., Lincoln Glen School
Contact Person: M. R. Renfro, P.O. Box 21429, San Jose, CA 95151
Meeting City: San Jose

West Valley Philatelic Society (APS# 1419-161485)
Meeting Time and Location: 10:30 a.m., every Thurs., Cypress Senior Center, 403 S. Cypress Ave.
Contact Person: Dr. Alvin C. Beckett, c/o Cypress Senior Center, 403 S. Cypress Ave., San Jose, CA 95117-1530
Meeting City: San Jose

Philatelic Society of San Leandro (APS# 0170-015388)
Meeting Time and Location: 8 p.m., 3rd Tues., San Leandro City Hall, Pillar Room
Contact Person: Mr. Mario Pacioretti, P. O. Box 633, San Leandro, CA 94577-0633
Meeting City: San Leandro

San Luis Obispo Philatelic Society (APS# 1484-179443)
Meeting Time and Location: 7:30 p.m., 2nd Weds. & last Fri. Senior Citizen Bldg., 1445 Santa Rosa
Contact Person: Mr. Joe D. Funderburg, 1255 Bay Oaks Dr., Los Osos, CA 93402
Meeting City: San Luis Obispo

Peninsula Stamp Club (APS# 0265-025999)
Meeting Time and Location: 7:30 p.m., 4th Wed., except Dec., The Beresford, Conference Room, 28th Ave. & The Alamenda
Contact Person: Mr. Martin H. Feibusch, P. O. Box 5121, San Mateo, CA 94402
Meeting City: San Mateo
E-mail: dzvesma@sprintmail.com
Website: www.PenStamps@aol.com

Tamalpais Stamp Club (APS# 1170-116381)
Meeting Time and Location: 7:30 p.m., 2nd & 4th Fri., except Nov., 2nd Fri./Dec. 1st Fri. 930 Tamalpais Ave.
Contact Person: Mr. Jay R. Losselyong, 20735 Temelec Dr., Sonoma, CA 95476
Meeting City: San Rafael
E-mail: stampnut@igc.org
Website: www.enw.org/tamalpais/

Santa Barbara Stamp Club (APS# 0236-024016)
Meeting Time and Location: 7 p.m., 1st & 3rd Tues., City Recreation Center, 100 E. Carrillo St.
Contact Person: Mr. David A. Johannsen, 5290 Overpass Rd., Suite 208, Santa Barbara, CA 93111
Meeting City: Santa Barbara

Simi Valley Stamp Club (APS# 1344-145935)
Meeting Time and Location: 7:30 p.m., 1st Mon. & 3rd Thurs., 1st Mon.-Our Redeemer Lutheran Church, 3rd Thurs.-Senior Citizens Center
Contact Person: Mr. Allen Gersh, 2440 Stow St., Simi Valley, CA 93093
Meeting City: Simi Valley
E-mail: namwob@aol.com

Tuolumne County Stamp Club (APS# 1086-103923)
Meeting Time and Location: 7:30 p.m., 2nd Wed., Tuolumne County Library, Greenly Road
Contact Person: Mr. Robert Adam, 17300 Blackbird Lane, Sonora, CA 95370
Meeting City: Sonora

Stockton Stamp Club (APS# 0145-014118)
Meeting Time and Location: 7:30

p.m., 2nd Wed., 2818 W. Telegraph Ave.
Contact Person: Mr. Wesley S. Waite, 2818 W. Telegraph Ave., Stockton, CA 95204
Meeting City: Stockton

Friends Western Philatelic Library (APS# 0836-069388)
Meeting Time and Location: Tues. 11am–5pm, Wed. 6pm–9pm, Fri. 9am–9pm, Sat. Noon–5pm, Raynor Act. Ctr., Bldg. 6,, Rm. 6, 1500 Partridge Ave.
Contact Person: Mr. Roger D. Skinner, P.O. Box 2219, Sunnyvale, CA 94087
Meeting City: Sunnyvale
E-mail: stulev@1×.netcom.com
Website: www.fwpl.org

Sunnyvale Stamp Club (APS# 0460-039214)
Meeting Time and Location: 7 p.m., Tues., Sunnyvale Community Center, Remington Ave.
Contact Person: Mr. Richard Fox, P. O. Box 2909, Sunnyvale, CA 94087
Meeting City: Sunnyvale
E-mail: stampbks@dnai.com
Website: www.fwpl.org/sss.htm

Vallejo Stamp Club (APS# 1289-133895)
Meeting Time and Location: 7 p.m., 1st & 3rd Tues., Holy Trinity Luth. Church, Confer. Rm, 201, Doyle Dr. at Haggertu
Contact Person: Mr. Michael S. Turrini, P. O. Box 121, Vallejo, CA 94590-0012
Meeting City: Vallejo

Burbank Stamp Club (APS# 0257-025176)
Meeting Time and Location: 6:30 p.m., 2nd Tues., 13438 Cantara St.
Contact Person: Mr. Max Bunshaft, P. O. Box 9215, North Hollywood, CA 91609-1215

Meeting City: Van Nuys
E-mail: bunshaftm@hotmail.com

Ventura County Philatelic Society (APS# 0535-043840)
Meeting Time and Location: 8 p.m., 1st & 3rd Mon., Church of the Foothills, 6279 Foothill Road
Contact Person: Mr. John S. Weigle, P. O. Box 6536, Ventura, CA 93006
Meeting City: Ventura
E-mail: jweigle@vcnet.com
Website: www.west.net/~haydn/vcphil.html

Visalia Philatelic Society (APS# 0849-070419)
Meeting Time and Location: 7:30 p.m., 2nd & 4th Tues., Grace Luthern School, 1111 S. Conyer
Contact Person: Mr. Thomas Z. Stillman, 2529 Dartmouth, Visalia, CA 93277
Meeting City: Visalia

Diablo Valley Stamp Club (APS# 0454-038809)
Meeting Time and Location: 7:30 p.m., 2nd & 4th Thurs., except Nov. & Dec., 1st Thurs., Leisure Serv. Bldg., Multi-Purpose Rm., 1650 N. Broadway
Contact Person: Mr. Frank H. Scupero, 418 Beatrice Rd., Pleasant Hill, CA 94523
Meeting City: Walnut Creek
E-mail: fscuders@aol.com

Hughes Stamp Club (APS# 0942-084311)
Meeting Time and Location: 7 p.m., 2nd & 4th Mon., 2nd-Barrington Recreation Center, 4th-Fox Hills Mall Clubroom
Contact Person: Ms. Marjorie Goetz, 11355 Farlin St., Los Angeles, CA 90049
Meeting City: West Los Angeles
E-mail: davestamp@aol.com

COLORADO

Boulder Stamp Club (APS# 0361-031904)
Meeting Time and Location: 7:30 p.m., 4th Thur., except July & Dec., Crossroads Mall Meeting Place, 28th St. & Canyon Blvd.
Contact Person: Mr. James L. Williams, 395 Erie Dr., Boulder, CO 80303
Meeting City: Boulder

North Suburban Stamp Club (APS# 1528-194778)
Meeting Time and Location: 7 p.m., 1st & 3rd Thurs., Friendship Hall, 12205 Perry St.
Contact Person: Mr. L. Donald Koontz, P.O. Box 309, Eastlake, CO 80614
Meeting City: Broomfield

Banana Belt Stamp Club (APS# 1526-193475)
Meeting Time and Location: 1 p.m., 2nd Sat., except July & Aug., Buena Vista Community Center, 715 E. Main St.
Contact Person: Mr. Robert Hitpas, 802 W. 2nd St., Salida, CO 81201
Meeting City: Buena Vista
E-mail: vernrutherford@hotmail.com

Colorado Springs Stamp Club (APS# 0837-069389)
Meeting Time and Location: 7:30 p.m., 1st & 3rd Tues., Aug. 1st Tues. only, Colorado Springs Police Operations Ctr., 705 S. Nevada
Contact Person: Mr. Phillip Zook, P.O. Box 7921, Colorado Springs, CO 80933
Meeting City: Colorado Springs
E-mail: PZook13768@aol.com
Website: www.classicstamps.com/clubs/stampclub.html

Aurora Stamp Club (APS# 0803-066112)
Meeting Time and Location: 7:30 p.m., 1st Wed. & 3rd Mon., Rocky Mountain Phil. Library, 2038 S. Pontiac Way
Contact Person: Mr. Maurice E. Pautz, 3068 S. Pitkin Way, Aurora, CO 80013
Meeting City: Denver

Collectors' Club of Denver (APS# 0176-015797)
Meeting Time and Location: 7:30 p.m., 2nd Tues., BPOE Elk's Lodge #17, 2475 W. 26th Ave.
Contact Person: Mr. Tonny E. Van Loij, 3002 S. Zantia St., Denver, CO 80231
Meeting City: Denver

Denver Germany Stamp Club (APS# 1264-129844)
Meeting Time and Location: 7:30 p.m., 2nd Wed., Rocky Mountain Philatelic Library, 2038 S. Pontiac Way
Contact Person: Mr. Gary H. Gibson, P. O. Box 2371, Englewood, CO 80150-2371
Meeting City: Denver
E-mail: ghgibson@aol.com

Denver Stamp Club (APS# 0022-002554)
Meeting Time and Location: 7:30 p.m., 3rd Mon., Church Of The Ascension, 6th Ave. & Gilpin
Contact Person: COL David C. Snyder, Sr., P. O. Box 94, Evergreen, CO 80437-0094
Meeting City: Denver
E-mail: lwnfo8c@prodigy.com

Rocky Mountain Stamp Show (APS# 1014-094728)
Meeting Time and Location: 7:30 p.m., 4th Tues., except May, July, & Dec., Rocky Mountain Phil. Libr., 2038 S. Pontiac Way
Contact Person: Mr. Stephen A. Schweighofer, 8725 E. Eastman Ave., Denver, CO 80231-4504

Meeting City: Denver
E-mail: info@
rockymountainstampshow.com
Website: www.
rockymountainstampshow.com

Cherrelyn Stamp Club (APS#
0279-026937)
Meeting Time and Location:
7 p.m., 2nd. Mon., except Aug.,
Grace Lutheran Church, 4750 S.
Clarkson
Contact Person: Mr. Robert D.
Gross, 775 S. Alton Way, #3D,
Denver, CO 80231-1861
Meeting City: Englewood

Northern Colorado Philatelic
Society (APS# 1223-123774)
Meeting Time and Location:
7:30 p.m., 3rd Wed.,
St. Luke's Episcopal Church,
2000 Stover
Contact Person: Mr. Ted A.
Beers, P. O. Box 823, Fort Collins,
CO 80522
Meeting City: Fort Collins
E-mail: sohl@ctos.com

Stamp Club of Grand Junction
(APS# 0346-030810)
Meeting Time and Location:
7 p.m., 2nd Wed., Federal Bldg.,
Conf. Rm. 15, 4th & Rood
Contact Person: Mr. Andy Murin,
3095 B½ Rd. Grand Junction, CO
81503
Meeting City: Grand Junction
E-mail: agmurin@wic.net

West Side Stamp Club (APS#
0761-060087)
Meeting Time and Location: 7:30
p.m., 1st & 3rd Tues., First
Presbyterian Church, 8210 W.
10th Ave.
Contact Person: Mr. Donald
McFarland, c/o 1st Presbyterian
Church 8210 W. 10th Ave.,
Lakewood, CO 80215
Meeting City: Lakewood

E-mail: dalene1@uswest.net
Website: www0.delphi.com/
stamps/apslakewood_co.html

Arapahoe Stamp Club (APS#
0596-047269)
Meeting Time and Location: 6:30
p.m., 3rd Wed., Southglenn Public
Library, 7600 S. University Blvd.
Contact Person: Mr. Bob Jackson,
7698 S. Datura Circle, Littleton, CO
80120
Meeting City: Littleton

Pueblo Stamp Club (APS# 0338-
030220)
Meeting Time and Location:
7 p.m., 1st & 3rd Wed., 213 S.
Union
Contact Person: Mr. Richard A.
Tucey, 621 W. Orman Ave.,
Pueblo, CO 81004
Meeting City: Pueblo
E-mail: rk2c@aculink.net

CONNECTICUT

Brookfield Philatelic Society (APS#
1093-104280)
Meeting Time and Location: 7:30
p.m., 2nd Fri., Community Ctr.,
Town Hall, Pocono Road
Contact Person: Mr. Alan Vale, 40
Brittania Dr., Danbury, CT 06811-
2612
Meeting City: Brookfield
E-mail: avg@ct1.nai.net

Cheshire Philatelic Society (APS#
0475-040052)
Meeting Time and Location: 7:30
p.m., 1st & 3rd Thurs., except July
& Aug., Cheshire Convalescent
Hosp.
Contact Person: Mr. Wilson R.
Grime, P. O. Box 206, Cheshire,
CT 06410
Meeting City: Cheshire

Clinton Stamp Club (APS# 0855-
071064)

Meeting Time and Location: 7:30 p.m., 4th Thurs., except July & Aug., Andrews Memorial Town Hall, Boston Post Rd.
Contact Person: Mr. Michael Wells, 14 Overlook Farms Rd., Killingswood, CT 06419
Meeting City: Clinton

Ye Olde King's Highway Stamp Club (APS# 0411-035831)
Meeting Time and Location: 8 p.m., 2nd & 4th Thurs., First Congregational Church of Darien, Corner Post Rd. & Brookside Rd.
Contact Person: Miss Nanette Smith, 21 Ledge Rd., Rowayton, CT 06853-1037
Meeting City: Darien
Website: www.darien.lib.ct.us/philately/

Manchester Philatelic Society (APS# 0626-049353)
Meeting Time and Location: 6 p.m., 2nd & 4th Tues., Hartford Courant Comm. Conf. Rm., 200 Adams St.
Contact Person: Mr. Richard W. Steele, P. O. Box 448, Manchester, CT 06040
Meeting City: Manchester

Middletown Stamp Club (APS# 0733-057917)
Meeting Time and Location: 7:30 p.m., 1st & 3rd Tues., except July & Aug., The Hartford Courant Office, E. Main St.
Contact Person: Mr. Stephen W. Ekstrom, P. O. Box 207, Cromwell, CT 06416
Meeting City: Middletown
E-mail: swekstrom@aol.com

Hardware City Stamp Club (APS# 1009-094276)
Meeting Time and Location: 7:30 p.m., 1st & 3rd Tues., except July & Aug., St. Andrew's Church, Friendship Ctr, 396 Church St.

Contact Person: Mr. David A. Kent, P.O. Box 127, New Britain, CT 06050
Meeting City: New Britain
E-mail: kentdave@aol.com

New Haven Philatelic Society (APS# 0054-025889)
Meeting Time and Location: 7:30 p.m., Tues., except July & Aug., New Haven Colony Hist. Soc., 114 Whitney Ave.
Contact Person: Mr. Robert F. Ford, 2 Green Garden Ct., East Haven, CT 06512
Meeting City: New Haven

Simsbury Stamp Club (APS# 1485-180442)
Meeting Time and Location: 7:30 p.m., 2nd Mon. (September–June), Eno Memorial Hall, 754 Hopmeadow St.
Contact Person: Mr. George Boissard, 15 Simscroft Rd., Simsbury, CT 06070
Meeting City: Simsbury

Nutmeg Stamp Club (APS# 0794-064418)
Meeting Time and Location: 6 p.m., 2nd & 4th Wed., except July & Aug., Baldwin Senior Center, 1000 W. Broad St.
Contact Person: Mr. Ed Cofini, 60 Tremont Ave., Bridgeport CT 06606
Meeting City: Stratford

United Stamp Societies (APS# 1293-135604)
Meeting Time and Location: January-even years, various cities
Contact Person: Mr. Frank R. Fernandez, 25 Tall Timber Dr., Little Egg Harbor, NJ 08087-1822
Meeting City: Various

Waterbury Stamp Club (APS# 1087-103924)
Meeting Time and Location:

7 p.m., 1st & 3rd Mon., Mill Plain Union Church, 242 Southmayd Rd.
Contact Person: Mr. Pat J. Rinaldi, P.O. Box 581, Waterbury, CT 06720
Meeting Time: Waterbury
E-mail: Pestamp@aol.com

Thames Stamp Club (APS# 0784-063332)
Meeting Time and Location: 7:30 p.m., 2nd & 4th Wed., except July & Aug., Clark Lane Middle Sch. Lib., Clark Lane
Contact Person: Mr. Anthony B. Bruno, P. O. Box 624, East Lyme, CT 06333-0624
Meeting City: Waterford
E-mail: tbbee@aol.com
Website: www.collectstamps.com/

DELAWARE

Dover Stamp Club (APS# 1002-093318)
Meeting Time and Location: 7 p.m., 4th Tues., W. Reily Brown Elem. School, 360 Webb's Lane
Contact Person: Mr. Edwin F. Englehart, 1170 E. Lebanon Rd., Dover, DE 19901
Meeting City: Dover

Sussex County Stamp Club (APS# 1413-161195)
Meeting Time and Location: 7:30 p.m., 2nd Tues., Am. Legion Ambulance Garage
Contact Person: Rev. Joseph E. James, P.O. Box 163, Milford, DE 19963
Meeting City: Georgetown

Corbit-Calloway Philatelists (APS# 1387-153677)
Meeting Time and Location: 7:30 p.m., 3rd Mon., Corbit-Calloway Library
Contact Person: Mr. Charles W. Dunham, P.O. Box 176, Odessa, DE 19730
Meeting City: Odessa

Brandywine Valley Stamp Club (APS# 0268-026339)
Meeting Time and Location: 7 p.m., 2nd & 4th Wed, except July & Aug., Hanby Middle School, 2525 Berwyn Rd.
Contact Person: Mr. John A. Harris, 5 Tunison Ct., Devonshire, Wilmington, DE 19810-2020
Meeting City: Wilmington

DISTRICT OF COLUMBIA

Collectors Club of Washington (APS# 1292-135603)
Meeting Time and Location: 7:30 p.m., 1st & 3rd Wed., Christ Methodist Church, 300 Block, I St., S.W.
Contact Person: Mr. Don Peterson, 7408 Alaska Ave., N.W., Washington, DC 20012
Meeting City: Washington

Palisades Stamp Club (APS# 1297-136036)
Meeting Time and Location: 7:30 p.m., 3rd Tues., Palisades Branch Library, 49th & V Sts., N. W.
Contact Person: Mr. Daniel W. Lozier, Jr., 5230 Sherier Pl., N.W., Washington, DC 20016
Meeting City: Washington
E-mail: dlozier@compuserve.com

Philatelic Club, Library of Congress (APS# 0747-059427)
Meeting Time and Location: 11:30 a.m., 1st & 3rd Tues., LOC, James Madison Bldg., Copyright Cataloging Conf. Rm. LM513
Contact Person: Mr. Harry H. Price, 13223 Greenmount Ave., Beltsville, MD 20705-1056
Meeting City: Washington
E-mail: hpri@loc.gov

Washington Philatelic Society (APS# 0169-015412)
Meeting Time and Location: 7:30 p.m., 2nd & 4th Wed., except July &

Aug., Friendship Terr. Apts.-Comm.
Rm., 4201 Butterworth Pl., N.W.
Contact Person: Mr. Brock R.
Covington, P.O. Box 720, Glen
Echo, MD 20812
Meeting City: Washington
E-mail: bbouvier@erols.com
Website: www.philat.com/wps

FLORIDA

Florida Federation of Stamp Clubs
(APS# 0406-035107)
Meeting Time and Location:
Semi-annually, various cities
Contact Person: Mr. Walter
Parker, P. O. Box 532,
Crystal Beach, FL 34681
Meeting City: Various

Highlands Stamp Club (APS#
1452-172490)
Meeting Time and Location: 1:30
p.m., 1st Mon., Union
Congregational Church,
105 N. Forest Ave.
Contact Person: Mr. Paul S.
Hoffman, 99 Rally Rd., Avon Park,
FL 33825-5319
Meeting City: Avon Park

Boca Raton Stamp & Coin Club
(APS# 1511-188747)
Meeting Time and Location: 7
p.m., 2nd & 4th Mon., Spanish
River Community High School,
Yamato & Jog (Powerline) Rds.
Contact Person: Mr. Benjamin
Ladin, P.O. Box 880007, Boca
Raton, FL 33488-0007
Meeting City: Boca Raton

Delray Beach Stamp Club (APS#
1185-118816)
Meeting Time and Location: 7
p.m., 1st & 3rd Wed., Congress
Middle Sch. Library, 101 S.
Congress Ave.
Contact Person: Mr. Arnold
Zenker, 3860 Hidden Cypress
Way, Lake Worth, FL 33467

Meeting City: Boynton Beach
E-mail: barzen@aol.com

Cape Coral Stamp Club (APS#
0741-059033)
Meeting Time and Location: 6:30
p.m., 4th Tues., Epiphany
Episcopal Church, Del Prado Blvd.
at Everest Pkwy.
Contact Person: Mr. Bayard T.
Cowper, 6937 Wittman Dr., S.W.,
Fort Myers, FL 33919
Meeting City: Cape Coral

Clearwater Stamp Club (APS#
0684-054339)
Meeting Time and Location: 7
p.m., 2nd & 4th Mon., Morningside
Recreation Ctr., 2400 Harn Blvd.
Contact Person: Mrs. Suzanne
Yankowski, 15655 Darien Way,
Clearwater, FL 33764-7082
Meeting City: Clearwater

Century Village East S/C Club
(APS# 1201-121747)
Meeting Time and Location: 11 a.m.
to 12:30 p.m.,, every Thurs., Club-
house, General Purpose, Room D
Contact Person: Mr. Samuel
Resnick, 3074 Ventnor Pl., Deer-
field Beach, FL 33442
Meeting City: Deerfield Beach

West Volusia Stamp Club (APS#
1272-131173)
Meeting Time and Location: 2
p.m., Tues. Sept. to May, 1st & 2nd
Tues. June to Aug., Faith Lutheran
Church, 509 E. Penn. Ave.
Contact Person: Mr. William T.
Dure, c/o Faith Lutheran Church,
509 E. Pennsylvania Ave., Deland,
FL 32724
Meeting City: Deland
E-mail: hsellard@bellsouth.net
Website: www0.delphi.com/
stamps/apsvolusia.html

New Port Richey Area Stamp Club
(APS# 1069-100984)

Meeting Time and Location:
1 p.m., 1st & 3rd Sun., Elfers
Senior Center, 3146 Barker St.
Contact Person: Mr. Wilbur
McEvoy, P. O. Box 684, New Port
Richey, FL 34656-0684
Meeting City: Elfers

University City Stamp Club (APS#
0795-064419)
Meeting Time and Location:
8 p.m., 1st & 3rd Tues., Doyle
Connor Bldg., 1911 S.W. 34th St.
Contact Person: Mr. William J.
Creegan, 21011 N.W. 74th Pl.,
Alachua, FL 32615
Meeting City: Gainesville
E-mail: creeganw@
mail.vetmed.ufl.edu

Hollywood Stamp Club (APS#
0665-052140)
Meeting Time and Location: 6:30
p.m., Tues., Senior Citizens
Center, 2030 Polk St.
Contact Person: Mr. Robert L.
Welky, P. O. Box 24474, Fort
Lauderdale, FL 33307-4474
Meeting City: Hollywood

Jacksonville Stamp Collectors Club
(APS# 1052-098565)
Meeting Time and Location: 7:30
p.m., 1st & 3rd Tues., Terry Parker
High School, 7301 Parker School
Rd.
Contact Person: Mr. Charles F.
Winney, 857 S. Edgewood Ave.,
Jacksonville, FL 32205
Meeting City: Jacksonville

Keystone Heights Stamp Club
(APS# 1498-185527)
Meeting Time and Location:
2nd Tues., except June, July, &
Aug., Keystone Hgts. High School,
Bldg. 24
Contact Person: Mr. Robert E.
Havens, 4564 S.E. 3rd Ave.,
Keystone Heights, FL 32656-6287
Meeting City: Keystone Heights

Florida Stamp Dealers' Association
(APS# 1496-184516)
Meeting Time and Location:
Varies, various stamp shows
Contact Person: Mr. Phillip E.
Fettig, P.O. Box 420730,
Kissimmee, FL 34742-0730
Meeting City: Kissimmee
E-mail: annfsda@aol.com

The Villages Philatelic Club (APS#
1525-193261)
Meeting Time and Location:
1 p.m., The Villages, Charlie Chap-
lin Room
Contact Person: Mr. Charles M.
Waff, Jr., P.O. Box 190, Lady Lake,
FL 32158
Meeting City: Lady Lake

Germany Philatelic Society, Chap.
23 (APS# 1377-151683)
Meeting Time and Location:
2 p.m., 2nd Sun., except June,
July, & Aug., St. Paul Lutheran
Church, 3020 S. Florida Ave.
Contact Person: Mr. George E.
Kuhn, P. O. Box 711, Fruitland
Park, FL 34731-0711
Meeting City: Lakeland
E-mail: prebane@tampabay.rr.
com

Ridge Stamp Club of Lakeland
(APS# 1230-124824)
Meeting Time and Location: 7:30
p.m., 1st & 3rd Tues., Magnolia
Bldg., Lake Mirror
Contact Person: Mr. J. Harold
Falls, 1017 Redbud Circle, Plant
City, FL 33566
Meeting City: Lakeland
E-mail: jhfalls1@ix.netcom.com

Missile Stamp Club (APS# 1213-
122933)
Meeting Time and Location:
7 p.m., 1st Wed. & 3rd Tues.,
Eau Gallie Post Office, 681 St.
Clair St.
Contact Person: Ms. Mary F.

Bacco, 608 Citrus Ct., Melbourne, FL 32951
Meeting City: Melbourne
E-mail: fseyboth@iu.net

South Miami Stamp Club (APS# 1149-113285)
Meeting Time and Location:
7 p.m., Thurs., Sunset Congregational Church, 9025 Sunset Dr.
Contact Person: Mr. Kenneth A. Barrus, Sunset Congregational Church, 9025 Sunset Dr., Miami, FL 33173
Meeting City: Miami
E-mail: RonCharles@aol.com
Website: hometown.aol.com/smsc97/index.html

Collier County Stamp Club (APS# 1015-094729)
Meeting Time and Location:
7 p.m., 4th Thur., except Nov. & Dec. 1st, Natl. Bank of Naples, 800 Goodlette Rd.
Contact Person: Mr. Carl A. Hedin, 3562 Antarctic Circle, Naples, FL 33962-5041
Meeting City: Naples
E-mail: cah@naples.net

Fort Lauderdale/Oakland Park S. C. (APS# 1298-136370)
Meeting Time and Location: 2nd & 4th Thurs., Collins Community Centre, 3900 N.W. 3rd Ave.
Contact Person: Mr. William E. Ogden, 248 Utah Ave., Fort Lauderdale, FL 33312
Meeting City: Oakland Park

General Francis Marion Stamp Club (APS# 1422-162111)
Meeting Time and Location:
1 p.m., 1st & 3rd Wed., Friendship Community Bank, 8375 S. W. State Road 200
Contact Person: Mr. Dennis F. Niemira, 6330 S.W. 117th Loop, Ocala, FL 34476
Meeting City: Ocala

E-mail: dniemira5@cs.com

Mid-Florida Philatelic Society (APS# 0699-055178)
Meeting Time and Location:
8 p.m., 1st & 3rd Thurs., doors open at 7 p.m., Oak Room, Marks St. Rec. Complex, 99 E. Marks St.
Contact Person: Mr. Wade H. Beery, Jr., P. O. Box 195006, Winter Springs, FL 32719-5006
Meeting City: Orlando

Bay County Stamp Club (APS# 0740-059032)
Meeting Time and Location: 7:30 p.m., 1st & 3rd Thurs., General Mail Facility
Contact Person: Mrs. Maureen E. Knipper, 303 Alexander Dr., Lynn Haven, FL 32444
Meeting City: Panama City

Pensacola Philatelic Society (APS# 0591-046901)
Meeting Time and Location:
7 p.m., 1st & 3rd Mon., Books-A-Million Store, Davis Highway Store
Contact Person: Mr. Dewey J. Barker, 6411 Myrtle Hill Cir., Pensacola, FL 32506
Meeting City: Pensacola

Port Charlotte Stamp Club (APS# 1088-103925)
Meeting Time and Location:
7 p.m., 2nd Thurs., 2 p.m., 4th Thurs., Port Charlotte Cultural Ctr., Pres. Rm., 2280 Aaron St., N.W.
Contact Person: K. C. Foltuz, P. O. Box 3645, Port Charlotte, FL 33949
Meeting City: Port Charlotte
E-mail: Bigbear@nut_n_but.net

Port St. Lucie Stamp Club (APS# 0866-072805)
Meeting Time and Location: 7:30 p.m., 2nd Tues., Port St. Lucie Community Ctr., 200 S.W. Prima Vista Blvd.

Contact Person: Mr. Michael Rice, 612 S.W. Bayshore Blvd., Port St. Lucie, FL 34983
Meeting City: Port St. Lucie

Sarasota Philatelic Club (APS# 0353-031238)
Meeting Time and Location: 7 p.m., 1st Tues., Selby Public Library, 1331 1st St.
Contact Person: Mr. Jack Harwood, P. O. Box 3553, Sarasota, FL 34239
Meeting City: Sarasota
E-mail: jharwood@attglobal.net

St. Augustine Stamp Club (APS# 1152-113730)
Meeting Time and Location: 7:30 p.m., 1st Tues., except July & Aug., Trinity Episcopal Church, Meeting Rm., 215 St. George
Contact Person: Mrs. Diann Kay, 2443 Hydrangea St., St. Augustine, FL 32084
Meeting City: St. Augustine

St. Petersburg Stamp Club (APS# 0157-014836)
Meeting Time and Location: 7:30 p.m., Wed., Trinity Lutheran Church, 401 5th St., N.
Contact Person: Mr. Raymond H. Murphy, P. O. Box 546, St. Petersburg, FL 33731
Meeting City: St. Petersburg
E-mail: Rayhmurphy@prodigy.net

Tallahassee Stamp/Cover Club (APS# 1414-161196)
Meeting Time and Location: 7:30 p.m., 2nd Tues., Dance Room-Sr. Citizens Center, N. Monroe & 7th St.
Contact Person: Mr. Laurence L. Benson, 1832 Jean Ave., Tallahassee, FL 32308-5227
Meeting City: Tallahassee
E-mail: llbenson@aol.com
Website: www.delphi.com/stamps/apstallahassee.html

Tampa Collectors Club (APS# 0123-013182)
Meeting Time and Location: 7 p.m., 2nd & 4th Mon., Dec. 2nd Mon. only, Piccadilly Cafet., Comm. Rm., 11810 N. Dale Mabry Hwy.
Contact Person: Mr. William H. LaVigne, Sr., P.O. Box 24831, Tampa, FL 33623
E-mail: blavign@tampabay.r.com
Meeting City: Tampa

Titusville-Moonport Stamp Club (APS# 0879-074119)
Meeting Time and Location: 7 pm, 1st Mon., North Brevard Library, 2121 Hopkins Ave.
Contact Person: Mr. Roy L. Whitson, 2875 Armadillo Tr., Titusville, FL 32780
Meeting City: Titusville

Venice Stamp Club (APS# 0653-051446)
Meeting Time and Location: 7 p.m., 3rd Tues., Venice Area Public Library
Contact Person: Mr. George Athens, P. O. Box 1501, Venice, FL 34285
Meeting City: Venice

Indian River Stamp Club (APS# 1503-187690)
Meeting Time and Location: 2nd & 4th Mon., First Presbyterian Church, 520 Royal Palm Blvd.
Contact Person: Mr. Edward D. Oulund, 40 Plantation Dr., Apt. 106, Vero Beach, FL 32966
Meeting City: Vero Beach

Club Cubano De Coleccion (APS# 0951-086296)
Meeting Time and Location: 7 p.m., 2nd & 4th Tues., 901 S.W. 62nd Ave.
Contact Person: Mr. Gerardo Alvarez, 3251 S.W. 21st St., Miami, FL 33145

Meeting City: West Miami

Cuban Philatelic Soc. of America (APS# 0797-064880)
Meeting Time and Location:
7 p.m., 2nd & 4th Tues., West Miami City Hall Bldg., 901 S.W. 62nd Ave.
Contact Person: Mrs. Silvia C. Garcia, 1528 Sevilla Ave., Coral Gables, FL 33114
Meeting City: West Miami

Winter Haven Stamp Club (APS# 1343-145426)
Meeting Time and Location: 7:30 p.m., 2nd & 4th Thurs., Nov. & Dec. 2nd Thurs. only, First Presbyterian Church, 637 6th St., N. W.
Contact Person: L. R. Newkirk, 332 Ave. A S. E., Winter Haven, FL 33880-3026
Meeting City: Winter Haven

GEORGIA
Athens Philatelic Society (APS# 0482-040782)
Meeting Time and Location: 7:30 p.m., 2nd Tues., 1st Presby. Fellowship Hall, Dougherty St. & College Ave.
Contact Person: Mr. Maurice Snook, 160 Plantation Dr., Athens, GA 30605
Meeting City: Athens

Atlanta Stamp Collectors Club (APS# 0357-031583)
Meeting Time and Location:
7 p.m., 2nd & 4th Wed., Dec. 2nd Wed. only, All Saints Episcopal Church/Parish House, 634 W. Peachtree St.
Contact Person: Mr. Robert J. Lewallyn, 2442 Kings Point Dr., Dunwoody, GA 30338-5927
Meeting City: Atlanta
E-mail: lewallyn@mindspring.com
Website: www.gsu.edu/~libpjr/atlstamps.htm

Georgia Federation of Stamp Clubs (APS# 1426-164386)
Meeting Time and Location: Varies, Nov. show Dunwoody Hotel
Contact Person: Mr. John H. Camp, 1766 Austin Dr., Decatur, GA 30032
Meeting City: Atlanta
E-mail: nbc@cape.com

Stone Mountain Philatelic Society (APS# 1178-117707)
Meeting Time and Location: 7:30 p.m., 2nd & 4th Thurs., Central Congregational Church, 2676 Clairmont Road, N.E.
Contact Person: Mr. Frank J. Kana, 723 Windy Dr., S. W., Stone Mountain, GA 30087
Meeting City: Atlanta

Greater Augusta Stamp Club (APS# 0884-075673)
Meeting Time and Location:
7 p.m., 2nd & 4th Thurs., Warren Rd. Community Center, 300 Warren Rd.
Contact Person: Mr. Dwight D. Gray, 527 San Salvador Dr., North Augusta, SC 29841
Meeting City: Augusta
E-mail: petegray@bellsouth.net

Heart of Georgia Philatelic Society (APS# 1398-156218)
Meeting Time and Location:
7 p.m., 3rd Tues., Centerville Public Library, 310 E. Church St.
Contact Person: Mr. Roger J. Wozniak, 303 Forest Hill Dr., Warner Robins, GA 31088
Meeting City: Centerville

Columbus Area Stamp Club (APS# 1470-174902)
Meeting Time and Location:
7 p.m., 2nd Tues., Post Office Conference Room, Milgen Rd.
Contact Person: Mr. Richard F. Sendelbach, Sr., 2941 Florence

Dr., Columbus, GA 31907
Meeting City: Columbus

Camden County Collectors Club
(APS# 1520-191123)
Meeting Time and Location: 1st
Mon., Camden Community Center,
1050 Wildcat Dr.
Contact Person: CW0 Jim
McDevitt, P. O. Box 1126,
Kingsland, GA 31548-1126
Meeting City: Kingsland
E-mail: cwouscg@aol.com

Sweetwater Stamp Society (APS#
1436-166735)
Meeting Time and Location:
2 p.m., last Sun., First Baptist
Church, 3566 Bankhead Hwy.
Contact Person: Mr. Russell
Turner, Jr., 4063 Bearden Lane,
Douglasville, GA 30135-3603
Meeting City: Lithia Springs

Cobb County Stamp Club (APS#
1184-118815)
Meeting Time and Location: 1:30
p.m-3 p.m., 2nd Sun., 1-5 p.m., 4th
Sun. 2nd -Fuller Park Rec. Center,
4th-Mountain View Community
Center
Contact Person: Mr. Jerry Goldoff,
3160 Howell Mill Road #102,
Atlanta, GA 30327
Meeting City: Marietta
E-mail: BJG102@mindspring.com

Coosa Valley Stamp Club (APS#
1393-155609)
Meeting Time and Location:
2 p.m., 3rd Sun., 1st United
Methodist Church, Library
Contact Person: Mr. Horace G.
Edmondson, Jr., 203 Venetian
Way, Rome, GA 30165
Meeting City: Rome

Valdosta Stamp Club (APS# 0940-
083980)
Meeting Time and Location:
7:30 p.m., 2nd Mon., Lowndes-

Valdosta Apts. Comm., 1204 N.
Patterson St.
Contact Person: Mr. Clarence M.
Paine, 406 Mack Dr., Valdosta, GA
31602
Meeting City: Valdosta

HAWAII

Hawaiian Philatelic Society (APS#
0296-027905)
Meeting Time and Location:
7 p.m., 2nd & 4th Mon.,
Nuuanu YMCA, 1441 Pali
Hwy.
Contact Person: Mr. Harry A.
Foglietta, 1012 Palm Dr., Apt. 1,
Honolulu, HI 96814-1926
Meeting City: Honolulu
E-mail: bannan@pixi.com

IDAHO

Snake River Stamp Club (APS#
1070-100985)
Meeting Time and Location:
7:30 p.m., 3rd Tues., Idaho Falls
Public Library, Rm. B, 457
Broadway
Contact Person: Mr. Edwin L.
Reeves, P.O. Box 2622, Idaho
Falls, ID 83403
Meeting City: Idaho Falls

South Central Idaho Stamp Club
(APS# 1395-155611)
Meeting Time and Location: 7:30
p.m., 3rd Mon., 1525 Addison Ave.,
Suite 119
Contact Person: Mr. Philip D.
Furman, 428 6th Ave., W., Jerome,
ID 83338
Meeting City: Twin Falls

ILLINOIS

Roosevelt Philatelic Society (APS#
0231-022504)
Meeting Time and Location:
7 p.m., 1st & 3rd Tues., Worth
Township Hall, 11601 S. Pulaski Rd.
Contact Person: Mr. Stan Urban,

P. O. Box 73, Oak Lawn, IL 60454-0073
Meeting City: Alsip

Belleville Stamp Club (APS# 0587-046632)
Meeting Time and Location:
7 p.m., 2nd & 4th Wed., Governor French Academy, 219 W. Main St.
Contact Person: Mr. William A. Jenner, 307 Alma St., O'Fallon, IL 62269
Meeting City: Belleville

Corn Belt Philatelic Society (APS# 0263-025751)
Meeting Time and Location:
7 p.m., 3rd Tues. & last Wed., National City Bank Bldg., 202 E. Washington St.
Contact Person: Mr. Jack L. Jenkins, P. O. Box 625, Bloomington, IL 61702-0625
Meeting City: Bloomington
E-mail: jackjenk@dave-world.net
Website: www.communityzone.com/community/cbps

Suburban Collectors' Club (APS# 0772-061737)
Meeting Time and Location:
8 p.m., 2nd & 4th Wed., July, Aug., Dec. 2nd Wed. only, Sokol Brookfield Hall, 3909 S. Prairie Ave.
Contact Person: Mr. Stephen Tillotson, P. O. Box 543, Brookfield, IL 60513
Meeting City: Brookfield

Southern Illinois Stamp Club (APS# 0458-039106)
Meeting Time and Location:
5:30–8:30 p.m., 2nd & 4th Thurs, except Nov/Dec 2nd Thur.,- University Mall, Community Rm., 1201 E. Main
Contact Person: Mr. Richard J. Chaklos, 1608 Old US Hwy 51, Makanda, IL 62958-5707
Meeting City: Carbondale
E-mail: rchak@midwest.net

Austin Philatelic Club (APS# 1020-095307)
Meeting Time and Location: 8 p.m., 1st & 3rd Wed., Sts. Cyril and Methodius Hall, 5800 W. Diversey Ave.
Contact Person: Mr. J. Ashby, 7929 W. Sunset Dr., Elmwood Park, IL 60707
Meeting City: Chicago
E-mail: stampman7929@aol .com

Beverly Hills Philatelic Society (APS# 0104-012009)
Meeting Time and Location: 7:30 p.m., 2nd & 4th Tues., except June, July, & Aug., Ridge Park Fieldhouse, 9611 S. Longwood Dr.
Contact Person: Mr. Clarence W. Reiels, 9538 S. Richmond Ave., Evergreen Park, IL 60805-2630
Meeting City: Chicago

Chicago Air Mail Society (APS# 1365-149352)
Meeting Time and Location:
7 p.m., 4th Tues., except July & Dec., Oriole Park Field House, 5430 N. Olcott
Contact Person: Mr. Stephen Neulander, P. O. Box 25, Deerfield, IL 60015-0025
Meeting City: Chicago
E-mail: stepmar@aol.com

Chicago Philatelic Society (APS# 0001-001775)
Meeting Time and Location: 7:30 p.m., 1st & 3rd Thurs., Midland Hotel, 172 W. Adams St.
Contact Person: Dr. Reuben A. Ramkissoon, 3011 White Oak Lane, Oak Brook, IL 60523
Meeting City: Chicago
E-mail: rramkissoon@juno.com
Website: www.mcs.com/~andyo/webbt/splash.html

Chicagoland Chapter, A.T.A. (APS# 1234-125083)
Meeting Time and Location:
8 p.m., 3rd Fri., various locations

Contact Person: Mr. Gary W. Hall, P. O. Box 218, Berwyn, IL 60402-0218
Meeting City: Chicago

Germany Philatelic Society, Chap. 5 (APS# 0690-054878)
Meeting Time and Location: 7:30 p.m., 4th Fri., Holiday Inn, Mart Plaza, 350 N. Orleans
Contact Person: Mr. Austin Dulin, P. O. Box 980, Oak Park, IL 60303
Meeting City: Chicago
E-mail: boblglass@aol.com

North Shore Philatelic Society (APS# 0223-021536)
Meeting Time and Location: 7:30 p.m., 4th Wed., Warren Park Fieldhouse, 6601 N. Western Ave.
Contact Person: Mr. Ronald L. Schloss, P. O. Box 60223, Chicago, IL 60660-0223
Meeting City: Chicago
E-mail: 1stsgt33@megsinet.net

Scandinavian Collectors Club, Chap. 4 (APS# 1119-107014)
Meeting Time and Location: 7:30 p.m., 4th Thurs., except June, July, & Aug., Golden Flame, Foster & Nagle Ave.
Contact Person: Mr. Ronald B. Collin, P. O. Box 63, River Grove, IL 60171
Meeting City: Chicago
E-mail: collin@telocity.com

SOSSI Baden-Powell, Chap. 1 (APS# 1389-154754)
Meeting Time and Location: Meets 6 times per year, various stamp shows & other locations in the Chicago area
Contact Person: Mr. Richard F. Thill, 305 Hillside Pl., North Aurora, IL 60542
Meeting City: Chicago

The Philaterians (APS# 0158-014851)

Meeting Time and Location: When called, members' homes
Contact Person: Mr. Lester E. Winick, 1501 E. Central Rd., Apt. 101, Arlington Heights, IL 60005
Meeting City: Chicago

Decatur Stamp Club (APS# 0293-027772)
Meeting Time and Location: 7 p.m., 1st Wed. & 3rd Thurs., except June, July, Aug., Decatur Stamp & Coin, 104 N. Main
Contact Person: Mr. Ervin Eugene Runion, P. O. Box 114, Decatur, IL 62525
Meeting City: Decatur

Spring Hill Stamp Club (APS# 1373-150545)
Meeting Time and Location: 7 p.m., 2nd & 4th Mon., Elgin Financial Center
Contact Person: Mr. Robert C. Barkhurst, P. O. Box 345, West Dundee, IL 60118-0345
Meeting City: East Dundee

Caterpillar Stamp Club (APS# 0492-041377)
Meeting Time and Location: 7 p.m., 1st & 3rd Tues., Fond du Lac Park Adm. Ctr., 201 Veterans Dr.
Contact Person: Mr. Lawrence J. Miller, Jr., 417 Redbud Dr., Washington, IL 61571-1638
Meeting City: East Peoria
E-mail: chug@bitwisesystems.com

Galesburg Philatelic Society (APS# 1384-153402)
Meeting Time and Location: 7 p.m., 3rd Thurs., 150 E. Simmons St.
Contact Person: Mr. David Nestander, 101 S. Depot St., Galesburg, IL 61401
Meeting City: Galesburg
E-mail: daddona@knoxnet.net

Lake County Philatelic Society (APS# 0423-036864)

Meeting Time and Location:
7 p.m., 4th Tues., except Dec.,
Warren-Newport Library, 221 N.
O'Plaine Rd.
Contact Person: Mr. Howard
Shaughnessy, 6834 W. Monticello
Ct., Gurnee, IL 60031
Meeting City: Gurnee
E-mail: clprr@aol.com

Philatelic Club of Will County
(APS# 1508-188231)
Meeting Time and Location:
7 p.m., 2nd & 4th Thur., Messiah
Lutheran Church, Jefferson St. &
Houbolt Rd.
Contact Person: Mr. Rodney A.
Juell, P. O. Box 3508, Joliet, IL
60434-3508
Meeting City: Joliet
E-mail: rajuell@lycos.com

Naperville Area Stamp Club (APS#
1404-158352)
Meeting Time and Location: 7:30
p.m., 1st & 3rd Wed., Trinity
Lutheran Church, Rm. 201–202,
1101 Kimberly Way (Rte. 53)
Contact Person: Mr. James R.
Garner, 637 Columbine Ave., Lisle,
IL 60532-2711
Meeting City: Lisle
E-mail: philaburn@aol.com

Evanston-New Trier Phil. Society
(APS# 0852-070422)
Meeting Time and Location: 8 p.m.,
1st & 3rd Wed., Norte Dame High
Schools, 7655 Dempster
Contact Person: Mr. Milton J.
Schober, 4032 Lee St., Skokie, IL
60076
Meeting City: Niles

Park Forest Stamp Club (APS#
0522-043135)
Meeting Time and Location: 7:30
p.m., 1st, 3rd, & 5th Tues.,
Freedom Hall, Lakewood Blvd. &
Orchard Dr.
Contact Person: Mr. Paul A.

Larsen, P. O. Box 606, Park
Forest, IL 60466
Meeting City: Park Forest

Peoria Philatelic Society (APS#
0243-024460)
Meeting Time and Location:
7 p.m., 3rd Wed., Lakeview Public
Library, 1137 W. Lake Ave.
Contact Person: Mr. Paul R. King,
104 Montclair Ct., East Peoria, IL
61611
Meeting City: Peoria

Rockford Stamp Club (APS# 0735-
057919)
Meeting Time and Location: 6:30
p.m., 1st Wed., Ken Rock
Community Center, 3218 11th st.
Contact Person: Mr. Dwane T.
Kaplenk, P. O. Box 2301,
Rockford, IL 61131
Meeting City: Rockford
E-mail: rockaires@xta-.com

Midwest Stamp Dealers
Association (APS# 1446-169967)
Meeting Time and Location: 6:30
p.m., meetings as designated
Contact Person: Mr. David Sohn,
P. O. Box 46281, Chicago, IL 60646
Meeting City: Schaumburg
E-mail: drsohn12@juno.com

Northwest Stamp Club (APS#
1054-098567)
Meeting Time and Location:
7 p.m., 2nd Tues & 4th Mon., 2nd
Tues.-Schaumburg Library, 4th
Mon.-Arlington Heights Library
Contact Person: Mr. Peter J.
Zachar, 275 University Dr., Buffalo
Grove, IL 60089
Meeting City: Schaumburg/
Arlington Heights

Smith Center Stamp Club (APS#
1443-168336)
Meeting Time and Location: 1:30
p.m., 1st & 3rd Weds., Smith
Center, 5120 Galitz St.

Contact Person: Mr. Harold M. Stral, 4438 Estes Ave., Lincolnwood, IL 60712
Meeting City: Skokie

Springfield Philatelic Society (APS# 0339-030371)
Meeting Time and Location: 7 p.m., 3rd Mon., Carpenter Union Hall, 211 W. Lawrence
Contact Person: Mr. Larry E. Barregarye, 302 Casson St., Williamsville, IL 62693
Meeting City: Springfield

Champaign-Urbana Stamp Club (APS# 0746-059426)
Meeting Time and Location: 7 p.m., 1st & 3rd Mon., 1st-Urbana Free Library, 3rd-Bevier Hall, Univ. of Ill.
Contact Person: Mr. Robert G. Leigh, 2006 Clover Ct., E., Champaign, IL 61821
Meeting City: Urbana
Website: www.prairienet.org/cusc/

Spring Hill Stamp Club (APS# 1373-150545)
Meeting Time and Location: 7 p.m., 2nd & 4th Mon., Elgin Financial Center
Contact Person: Mr. Robert C. Barkhurst, P. O. Box 345, West Dundee
Meeting City: West Dundee

Glen Ellyn Philatelic Club (APS# 0202-018782)
Meeting Time and Location: 7 p.m., 1st & 3rd Mon., except legal holidays, MidAmerican Bank, SW corner of Roosevelt & Naperville Rds.
Contact Person: Mr. Bob Arundale, III, P. O. Box 1311, Aurora, IL 60507
Meeting City: Wheaton
E-mail: robertkarundaleii@avenew.com

Quad City Stamp Club (APS# 0249-024667)

Meeting Time and Location: 7 p.m., 2nd Thurs., St. Mary's Church, 412 10th St.
Contact Person: Mr. George W. Pettigrew, Jr., P. O. Box 1301, Moline, IL 61266-1301
Meeting City: Moline
E-mail: pmats5@aol.com
Website: embers.aol.com/pmats5/qcsc.html

INDIANA

Madison County Bicentennial S. C. (APS# 0991-091760)
Meeting Time and Location: 7 p.m., 3rd Thurs., Anderson Public Library, Carnegie Room
Contact Person: Mrs. Bonnie L. Lyons, 1732 Mockingbird Lane, Anderson, IN 46013-9646
Meeting City: Anderson
E-mail: mbonlyons@netusa1.net

Bloomington Stamp Club (APS# 1416-161482)
Meeting Time and Location: 7 p.m., 2nd Wed., Monroe Co. Public Library, 303 E. Kirkwood Ave.
Contact Person: Mr. Mark W. Goodson, 202 W. Temperance St., Ellettsville, IN 47429
Meeting City: Bloomington
E-mail: bgoodson@smithville.net

Evansville Stamp Club (APS# 0175-015519)
Meeting Time and Location: 7 p.m., 3rd Tues., North Park Library, 750 N. Park Dr.
Contact Person: Evelyn M. Bosse, P. O. Box 161, Evansville, IN 47702-0161
Meeting City: Evansville

Anthony Wayne Stamp Society (APS# 0186-016444)
Meeting Time and Location: 7 p.m., 2nd Mon., VFW Post, 6814 S. Anthony Blvd.

Contact Person: Mr. James A. Mowrer, 3110 Cannongate, Fort Wayne, IN 46808
Meeting City: Fort Wayne
E-mail: stamp@gte.net

Calumet Stamp Club (APS# 0953-086298)
Meeting Time and Location: 7 p.m., Thurs., Hammond Civic Center, 5825 Sohl Ave.
Contact Person: Mr. Richard Gougeon, 3815 Towle Ave, Highland, IN 46322
Meeting City: Hammond
E-mail: z28468@aol.com
Website: www0.delphi.com/stamps/apscalumet.html

Indiana Stamp Club (APS# 0372-032548)
Meeting Time and Location: 7:30 p.m., 1st Mon., Children's Museum, 30th & Meridian St.
Contact Person: Mrs. Jeanette Knoll Adams, P. O. Box 40792, Indianapolis, IN 46240
Meeting City: Indianapolis
E-mail: info@indianastamp club.org
Website: indianastampclub.org

Centerville Stamp Club (APS# 1094-104281)
Meeting Time and Location: 6:30 p.m., 3rd Fri., The Cabin, Glenn Miller Park
Contact Person: Mr. Wayne Crawford, 228 S. 23rd St., New Castle, IN 47362-3511
Meeting City: Richmond

Northern Indiana Philatelic Society (APS# 1081-102908)
Meeting Time and Location: 6:30 p.m., 2nd & 4th Tues., Centre Township Library, 1150 E. Kern Rd.
Contact Person: Mr. Kenneth Peczkovsky, 121 W. Colfax Ave., South Bend, IN 46601

Meeting City: South Bend
E-mail: grffonb@aol.com

Wabash Valley Stamp Club (APS# 0605-047983)
Meeting Time and Location: 7 p.m., last Thurs., except Nov. & Dec., vigo County Public Library, 7th & Poplar Sts.
Contact Person: Mr. Stephen R. Dawson, 10901 Ole Foxe Rd., Terre Haute, IN 47803
Meeting City: Terre Haute

IOWA

Allison Stamp Club (APS# 0908-079744)
Meeting Time and Location: 7:30 p.m., 2nd Sat., County Extension Office, Meeting Rm., N. Main St.
Contact Person: Mr. Kenneth H. Trettin, P.O. Box 56, Rockford, IA 50468-0056
Meeting City: Allison
E-mail: hogman@omnitelcom. com

Hawkeye Stamp Club (APS# 1339-145091)
Meeting Time and Location: 7 p.m., 3rd Wed., Burlington Public Library, 501 N. 4th
Contact Person: Mr. William E. Saint, 612 N. Cherry St., Mount Pleasant, IA 52641-1412
Meeting City: Burlington

Cedar Rapids Stamp Club (APS# 0106-012487)
Meeting Time and Location: 7 p.m., 1st Mon., 2nd Mon in Sept. only, Mutual Fire Ins. Co. Bldg., 1111 1st Ave., S.E.
Contact Person: Mr. Robert Hulshizer, P. O. Box 2554, Cedar Rapids, IA 52406-2554
Meeting City: Cedar Rapids
E-mail: lynch.dennis@ mcleodusa.net
Website: www0.delphi.com/stamps/apscedarrapids.html

Des Moines Philatelic Society
(APS# 0294-027884)
Meeting Time and Location:
7 p.m., 2nd Fri., except July & Aug.
Staves Memorial Meth. Church, E.
28th St. & Madison Ave.
Contact Person: Mr. John L.
Niehaus, 601 S.E. 2nd St., Ankeny,
IA 50021-3207
Meeting City: Des Moines
E-mail: johnln@ix.netcom.com

Iowa Women's Philatelic Society
(APS# 0427-037027)
Meeting Time and Location: 6:45
p.m., 1st Fri., except July & Aug.,
Baker's Cafeteria, 7400 Hickman
Rd.
Contact Person: Barbara R.
Good, 2804 E. 40th St., Des
Moines, IA 50317
Meeting City: Des Moines

Tri-State Stamp Club (APS# 1434-
166366)
Meeting Time and Location:
7 p.m., 4th Wed., except Jan. &
Feb., Visiting Nurses Assoc. Office
Contact Person: Mr. Merwyn Ellis,
1652 Finley St., Dubuque, IA
52001
Meeting City: Dubuque

Cedar Valley Stamp Club (APS#
0774-062335)
Meeting Time and Location: 7:30
p.m., 2nd & 4th Wed., Nova Carea,
526 Park Lane
Contact Person: Mr. Larry D.
Brownson, 615 1st., Janesville, IA
50647
Meeting City: Waterloo
E-mail: lb11554@cedarnet.org

KANSAS

Lawrence Stamp Club (APS#
1186-118817)
Meeting Time and Location:
7 p.m., 1st Thurs., Watkins Museum, South Door, 11th & Mass.

Contact Person: Mr. Jon W.
Dunham, 2712 Westdale Circle,
Lawrence, KS 66049
Meeting City: Lawrence
E-mail: jondun@lawrence.
ixks.com
Website: community.lawrence.com/
info/StampClub

Lindsborg Stamp Club (APS#
1045-097885)
Meeting Time and Location: 7:30
p.m., 4th Mon., Villa Ro Center
Contact Person: Dr. David C.
Hanson, 1558 Austin Cir., Salw,
KS 67401
Meeting City: Lindsborg
E-mail: djhanson@alltel.net

Collectors Club of Kansas City
(APS# 0839-069391)
Meeting Time and Location:
7 p.m., 2nd Wed., Overland Park
Community Ctr., 87th & Lamar
Contact Person: Mr. Randy L.
Neil, P. O. Box 6552, Leawood, KS
66206-0552
Meeting City: Overland park
E-mail: neilmedia@earthlink.net
Website: www.hpease.com/
cckc.htm

Topeka Stamp Club (APS# 1352-
147411)
Meeting Time and Location: 7:30
p.m., 3rd Thurs., Crestview United
Meth. Church, 2245 S.W.
Eveningside Dr.
Contact Person: Mr. Frank
Thompson, P. O. Box 14, Topeka,
KS 66601
Meeting City: Topeka

Cessna Stamp Club (APS# 1161-
115941)
Meeting Time and Location:
7 p.m., 2nd Thurs., except June,
July, & Aug., Cessna Activity
Center, 2744 Geo. Washington
Blvd.
Contact Person: Mr. Ralph E.

Lott, 914 2nd Circle, Douglass, KS 67039
Meeting City: Wichita

Wichita Stamp Club (APS# 0134-013615)
Meeting Time and Location: 7 p.m., 1st & 3rd Thurs., 3rd July & Aug/1st Dec., Downtown Wichita Public Libr., Patio Room
Contact Person: Mr. Neal E. Danielson, P. O. Box 1427, Wichita, KS, 67201
Meeting City: Wichita
E-mail: ndaniel1525@aol.com

KENTUCKY

Kentucky Stamp Club (APS# 1512-189020)
Meeting Time and Location: 7 p.m., Memorial Baptist Church, 130 Holmes St.
Contact Person: Mr. Ben Wise, 20 Carla Ct., Frankfort, KY 40601
Meeting City: Frankfort

Henry Clay Philatelic Society (APS# 1317-140420)
Meeting Time and Location: 7 p.m., 3rd Mon., Second Presbyterian Church, E. Main at Ransom Ave.
Contact Person: Mrs. Linda L. Lawrence, 312 Northwood Dr., Lexington, KY 40505
Meeting City: Lexington
E-mail: Stamplinda@aol.com
Website: HenryClayPhilatelic.com

Louisville Stamp Society (APS# 0521-043117)
Meeting Time and Location: 8 p.m., 1st & 3rd Fri., except Dec., Crescent Hill Presbyterian, Church, 142 Crescent Ave.
Contact Person: Mr. German P. Dillon, 6103 Norton Ave., Louisville, KY 40213
Meeting City: Louisville

Philatelic Club of Louisville (APS# 0580-045821)

Meeting Time and Location: 7 p.m., 1st Thurs., River Road Country Club, 2930 Upper River Rd.
Contact Person: Mr. Leland G. Bell, 7317 Maria Ave., Louisville, KY 40222
Meeting City: Louisville

Owensboro Area Stamp Club (APS# 1425-163243)
Meeting Time and Location: 7 p.m., 1st Fri., Ky. Wesleyan College's Fine Arts Bldg., corner of College Dr. & S. Griffith Ave.
Contact Person: Mr. Wilfred L. Gorrell, 1025 Peninsula Ct., Maceo, KY 42355
Meeting City: Owensboro
E-mail: DMHBlondie@aol.com

LOUISIANA

Baton Rouge Stamp Club (APS# 0260-025503)
Meeting Time and Location: 7 p.m., 1st & 3rd Wed., Council on Aging Municipal Bldg., 5790 Florida Blvd.
Contact Person: Dr. T. G. (Ron) Snider, III, 743 Bourbon Ave., Baton Rouge, LA 70808
Meeting City: Baton Rouge
E-mail: tsnideriii@aol.com

Red River Stamp Society (APS# 0721-056951)
Meeting Time and Location: 7 p.m., 1st Wed., Aulds Library, 3950 Wayne Ave.
Contact Person: Mr. Charles Atkins, 1718 Shady Lane, Shreveport, LA 71105
Meeting City: Bossier City

Twin City Stamp Club (APS# 0981-090013)
Meeting Time and Location: 10 a.m., 2nd Sat., US Post Office, 2nd fl., 501 Sterlington Rd.
Contact Person: Mr. William H.

Copeland, 1001 McKeen Pl., #807, Monroe, LA 71201
Meeting City: Monroe

MARYLAND

Harford County Stamp Club (APS# 0700-055179)
Meeting Time and Location: 7 p.m., 2nd & 4th Tues., Grace United Meth. Church
Contact Person: Mr. Kenneth F. Kapple, P. O. Box 163, Bel Air, MD 21014
Meeting City: Aberdeen
E-mail: vphilli@erols.com
Website: members.nbci.com/ harfordstampclub/harco~1.htm

Beltway Stamp Club (APS# 1245-127079)
Meeting Time and Location: 7:30 p.m., 2nd & 4th Tues., except Dec., Adelphi Professional Bldg., 8508 Adelphi Rd.
Contact Person: Mr. David H. Elliott, 8508 Adelphi Rd., Adelphi, MD 20783
Meeting City: Adelphi

Annapolis Stamp Club (APS# 0392-034247)
Meeting Time and Location: 6:30 p.m., 1st & 3rd Tues., Eastport-Annapolis Neck, 269 Hillsmere Dr.
Contact Person: Mr. Frank G. Soeder, Jr., 1183 Ramblewood Dr., Annapolis, MD 21401-4667
Meeting City: Annapolis

Baltimore Philatelic Society (APS# 0137-013722)
Meeting Time and Location: 8 p.m., every Wed., 1224 N. Calvert St.
Contact Person: Rev. Edward J. Mullowney, 1224 N. Calvert St., Baltimore, MD 21202
Meeting City: Baltimore
E-mail: balpex@aol.com
Website: www.balpex.org

GPS, Herman L. Halle Chapter16 (APS# 1333-144414)
Meeting Time and Location: 1:30 p.m., 3rd Sun., BPS Clubhouse, 1224 N. Calvert St.
Contact Person: Mr. Christopher D. Deterding, R 10, 741 Holly Dr., N., Annapolis, MD 21401
Meeting City: Baltimore
E-mail: len@iximd.com

Bowie Stamp Club (APS# 0634-049876)
Meeting Time and Location: 6:30 p.m., every Thur., except legal holidays, Bowie City Hall, 2614 Kenhill Dr.
Contact Person: Mr. Allen T. Frank, 12306 Shadow Lane, Bowie, MD 20715
Meeting City: Bowie

Silver Hill Lions Club (APS# 1315-139412)
Meeting Time and Location: Varies
Contact Person: Mr. Earl M. Whitehouse, Jr., 9115 Marlboro Pike, #39, Upper Marlboro, MD 20772
Meeting City: Clinton

Howard County Stamp Club (APS# 0798-064881)
Meeting Time and Location: 7:30 p.m., 1st & 3rd Wed., Harpers Choice Middle School, or East Columbia Library
Contact Person: Mr. Gordon T. Trotter, 10626 Fable Row, Columbia, MD 21044-2203
Meeting City: Columbia

Tri-State Stamp Club (APS# 1467-174387)
Meeting Time and Location: 7 p.m., 2nd Wed., South Cumberland Library
Contact Person: Mr. J. Jeffrey Hutter, Sr., 12212 Bedford Road, N.E., Cumberland, MD 21502

Meeting City: Cumberland
E-mail: jjhsr@hereintown.net
Website: www.tristate.
hereintown.net

Tidewater Stamp Club (APS#
1382-153104)
Meeting Time and Location: 7:30
p.m., 2nd & 4th Tues., City Hall, 14
S. Harrison St.
Contact Person: Mrs. Carol W.
Armstrong, P. O. Box 2000,
Easton, MD 21601
Meeting City: Easton

Waterville Stamp Club (APS#
1323-141243)
Meeting Time and Location: 6:30
p.m., 1st & 3rd Fri., June–Aug. 3rd
Fri. only, Kennebec Valley Tech.
College, Western Ave.
Contact Person: Mr. Richard
Williams, Jr., 20 Ridge Rd., Water-
ville, ME 04901-4121
Meeting City: Fairfield

Rockville-Gaithersburg Stamp Club
(APS# 0905-078421)
Meeting Time and Location: 7:30
p.m., 2nd & 4th Thurs.,
Gaithersburg Sr. High School,
314 S. Frederick Ave.
Contact Person: Mr. Ronald A.
Ward, 15404 Carrolton Rd.,
Rockville, MD 20853
Meeting City: Gaithersburg
E-mail: Anoph2@aol.com
Website: www.rgstampclub.org

Goddard Space Flight Center S. C.
(APS# 1027-095720)
Meeting Time and Location:
11:30 a.m., 2nd Tues., Bldg. 3,
Room 200
Contact Person: Dr. Manfred
Owe, P. O. Box 261, Greenbelt,
MD 20768-0261
Meeting City: Greenbelt
E-mail: owe@hydro4.gsfc.
nasa.gov

Eastern Shore Stamp Club (APS#
1390-154755)
Meeting Time and Location: 7:30
p.m., 1st Wed., except July & Aug.,
Wicomico Co. Youth/Civic Ctr.,
Glen Ave.
Contact Person: Mr. Wayne
Decker, 1302 Taney Ave.,
Salisbury, MD 21801
Meeting City: Salisbury
E-mail: cbrian@bwave.com

York County Stamp Club (APS#
0549-044268)
Meeting Time and Location: 7:30
p.m., 2nd & 4th Thurs., Sanford
Masonic Hall, Elm St.
Contact Person: Mr. C. Rick
Stambaugh, 18 Elmwood Ct.,
North Berwick, ME 03906
Meeting City: Sanford
E-mail: rickstambaugh@cyber-
tours.com

Silver Spring Philatelic Society
(APS# 0595-047100)
Meeting Time and Location:
7:30 p.m., 2nd & 4th Tues.,
M. Schweinhaut Sr. Ctr.,
1000 Forest Glen Rd.
Contact Person: Mr. John F.
Chiusano, 4407 Josephine Ave.,
Beltsville, MD 20705-2536
Meeting City: Silver Spring

MASSACHUSETTS

Northeastern Fed. of Stamp Clubs
(APS# 1131-110585)
Meeting Time and Location:
Varies, Cardinal Spellman Phil.
Mus., Regis College
Contact Person: Dr. Guy R.
Dillaway, P. O. Box 181, Weston,
MA 02193
Meeting City: Massachusetts
E-mail: barbtax@aol.com

Boston Philatelic Society (APS#
0300-028001)
Meeting Time and Location:

7 p.m., 2nd & 4th Tues., except July & Aug., United Parish in Brookline, 210 Harvard St.
Contact Person: Mr. David A. Libby, 300 Oak Hill Circle, Concord, MA 01742
Meeting City: Brookline

Chelmsford Stamp Club (APS# 1021-095308)
Meeting Time and Location: 7:30 p.m., 2nd & 4th Tues., 1st Parish Unitarian Unv. Ch., 2 Westford St.
Contact Person: Mr. Robert Webb, 360 Littleton Rd. #D-18, Chelmsford, MA 01824
Meeting City: Chelmsford

Webster-Dudley Stamp Club (APS# 0620-048795)
Meeting Time and Location: 7 p.m., 1st Tues., except July & Aug., Dudley Town Hall, Schofield Ave. (Rte. 12)
Contact Person: Mrs. Edith C. Ackerman, 156 W. Main St., Dudley, MA 01571
Meeting City: Dudley

Malden Stamp Club (APS# 0379-033586)
Meeting Time and Location: 7:30 p.m., 2nd & 4th Wed., Mystic Side Congregational Church, 420 Main St.
Contact Person: Mr. Philip G. Collins, 97 Central St., Saugus, MA 01906-1277
Meeting City: Everett
Website: www.stampshows.com/msc.html

Fall River Philatelic Society (APS# 1325-142052)
Meeting Time and Location: 7 p.m., 3rd Mon., Super Stop & Shop, Marianno Bishop Blvd.
Contact Person: Mr. Donald F. Craig, 163 New Boston Rd., Fall River, MA 02720-5509

Meeting City: Fall River
E-mail: DFC163@aol.com

Berkshire Stamp Club (APS# 0593-046985)
Meeting Time and Location: 7:30 p.m., 2nd & 4th Tues., Berkshire Mall
Contact Person: Mr. Robert M. Cancilla, 769 Williams St., Pittsfield, MA 01201
Meeting City: Lanesboro
E-mail: rlav615376@aol.com.

Wachusett Philatelic Society (APS# 1082-102909)
Meeting Time and Location: 7:30 p.m., 3rd Tues., except July & Aug., All Saints Chapel Annex, 1469 Main St.
Contact Person: Mr. David Buker, P. O. Box 130, Westminster, MA 01473
Meeting City: Leominster

Pioneer Valley Stamp Club (APS# 1509-188232)
Meeting Time and Location: Every other Tues. (Sept. to June), St. Andrews Church, 385 Longmeadow St., Rt. 5
Contact Person: Mr. David S. Pond, 52 Melwood Ave., East Longmeadow, MA 01028
Meeting City: Longmeadow

Lynn Philatelic Society (APS# 0957-087134)
Meeting Time and Location: 7 p.m., 1st & 3rd Tues., except July & Aug., Marblehead Community Center, 10 Humphrey St.
Contact Person: Mr. Neal G. Frazier, 477 Walnut St., Saugus, MA 01906
Meeting City: Marblehead

Golden Bee Stamp Club (APS# 1159-115324)
Meeting Time and Location:

7 p.m., 2nd Wed., Marshfield Public Library
Contact Person: Mr. Robert J. Martin, P. O. Box 277, Bryantville, MA 02327
Meeting City: Marshfield

Needham Stamp Club (APS# 1472-174904)
Meeting Time and Location: 3rd Fri., Deaconess Glover Hospital
Contact Person: Susanne F. Spatz, 52 Clinton Pl., Newton Center, MA 02459-1141
Meeting City: Needham
E-mail: melvins@aol.com

Whaling City Stamp Club (APS# 1004-093320)
Meeting Time and Location: 7 p.m., 2nd Mon., except July & Aug., New Bedford Boys Club, 166 Jenny St.
Contact Person: Mr. Russell Lizotte, 233 Hersom St., New Bedford, MA 02745
Meeting City: New Bedford
E-mail: baitshoprl@aol.com

Newburyport Stamp Club (APS# 1478-176876)
Meeting Time and Location: 7:15 p.m., 2nd & 4th Wed., Newburyport 5 Cent Savings, 63 State St., Conf. Room
Contact Person: Mr. Neil Foley, P. O. Box 204, Newburyport, MA 01950-1935
Meeting City: Newburyport
E-mail: peetah@mediaone.net

Samuel Osgood Stamp Club (APS# 0640-050725)
Meeting Time and Location: 7 p.m., 1st & 3rd Wed., July & Aug., 3rd Wed. only, The Greenery, 75 Park St.
Contact Person: Mr. Roger G. Brand, 30 Sharon Rd., South Hamilton, MA 01982-1312
Meeting City: North Andover

Clara Barton Stamp Club (APS# 1424-163242)
Meeting Time and Location: 7:30 p.m., 2nd Wed., Zion Lutheran Church, S. Main St.
Contact Person: Mr. Peter V. Pierce, P. O. Box 560, Oxford, MA 01540-0760
Meeting City: Oxford
E-mail: oxbou@aol.com

William C. Stone Chapter (APS# 0028-003305)
Meeting Time and Location: 7:30 p.m., every other Thurs., except July & Aug., members' homes
Contact Person: Mr. Kenneth W. Wise, 65 Allison Lane, West Springfield, MA 01089
Meeting City: Springfield

Stoughton Stamp Club (APS# 0856-071589)
Meeting Time and Location: 7 p.m., 3rd Mon., First Congregational Church, 76 Pierce St.
Contact Person: Mr. Irving Aronson, 702 West St., Stoughton, MA 02072
Meeting City: Stoughton
E-mail: irvinga@mediaone.net

Westfield Stamp Club (APS# 0796-064420)
Meeting Time and Location: 6:30 p.m., 1st & 3rd Tues., except July & Aug., Westfield Anthaneum, 6 Elm St.
Contact Person: Mr. Edmund Bashista, 236 Fowler Rd., Westfield, MA 01085
Meeting City: Westfield

Philatelic Group of Boston (APS# 1400-156220)
Meeting Time and Location: 7:30 p.m., 3rd Wed., except Aug., Spellman Philatelic Museum
Contact Person: Mr. Jeffrey N.

Shapiro, 155-10 Broadmeadow Rd., Marlborough, MA 01752
Meeting City: Weston
E-mail: coverlover1@yahoo.com

Waltham Stamp Club (APS# 0683-054003)
Meeting Time and Location: 8 p.m., 1st & 3rd Tues., July & Aug. 3rd Tues. only, Cardinal Spellman Phil. Mus., Regis College, 235 Wellesley St.
Contact Person: Mr. Jeffrey N. Shapiro, 155-10 Broadmeadow St., Marlborough, MA 01752
Meeting City: Weston

Granite City Stamp Club (APS# 1486-180764)
Meeting Time and Location: 1st & 3rd Wed., except July & Aug., Tufts Library, 46 Broad St.
Contact Person: Dr. Manfred Owe, P. O. Box 261, Greenbelt, MD 20768-0261
E-mail: owe@hydro4.gsfc.nasa.gov

Mohawk Stamp Club (APS# 1288-133894)
Meeting Time and Location: 7 p.m., 3rd Wed., except July, Aug., & Dec., Sweetwood Retirement Home, 1611 Cold Spring Rd.
Contact Person: Mr. Carl Faulkner, The Williams Inn On The Village Green, Williamstown, MA 01267
Meeting City: Williamstown
E-mail: wgraves@aol.com

Worcester County Philatelic Society (APS# 1233-124827)
Meeting Time and Location: 7:30 p.m., 2nd Fri., except July & Aug., Prouty Seminar Room, Goddard Library, Clark Univ., 950 Main St.
Contact Person: Mr. John C. Root, 404 Pleasant St., Paxton, MA 01612-1375
Meeting City: Worcester

MICHIGAN

Peninsular State Philatelic Society (APS# 0226-022015)
Meeting Time and Location: Annually, Chapter Club Host
Contact Person: Mr. Ed Fisher, 1033 Putney, Birmingham, MI 48009
Meeting City: Various
E-mail: efisherco@earthlink.net

Ann Arbor Stamp Club (APS# 0806-066368)
Meeting Time and Location: 7:30 p.m., 2nd Mon. Jan./Feb., 3rd Mon. Mar./, Oct. 1st & 4th Mon. Nov., none Dec., Salvation Army Citadel, 100 Arbana
Contact Person: Mr. Harry C. Winter, P. O. Box 2012, Ann Arbor, MI 48106
Meeting City: Ann Arbor
E-mail: harwin@umich.edu
Website: community.mlive.com/cc/stampclub

Birmingham Stamp Club (APS# 1172-116758)
Meeting Time and Location: 6:30 p.m., 2nd & 4th Tues., BASCC Senior Center
Contact Person: Mr. Michael J. Scivoletti, c/o BASCC Senior Center, 2121 Midvale Ave., Birmingham, MI 48009-4440
E-mail: MScivolett@aol.com

Oakland County Stamp Club (APS# 1513-189123)
Meeting Time and Location: ,TK various club shows
Contact Person: Mr. Stefan Karadian, P. O. Box 0082, Birmingham, MI 48012-0082
Meeting City: Birmingham
E-mail: stefan8bgd@aol.com

West Suburban Stamp Club (APS# 0783-062965)
Meeting Time and Location: 7:30 p.m., 1st & 3rd Fri., Summit

on the Park, 46000 Summit Pkwy.
Contact Person: Mr. Joe Picard, P. O. Box 700049, Plymouth, MI 48170
Meeting City: Canton
E-mail: pnj@oeonline.com
Website: www.oeonline.com/~pnj/wssc.html

Dearborn Stamp Club (APS# 0523-043209)
Meeting Time and Location: 7 p.m., 2nd & 4th Wed., except July & Aug., McFadden-Ross House, 915 Brady St.
Contact Person: Mr. Frederick Levantrosser, 21901 Willoway Rd., Dearborn, MI 48124-1135
Meeting City: Dearborn

Motor City Stamp & Cover Club (APS# 0442-038192)
Meeting Time and Location: Last Sun., 3–6 p.m., Prince of Peace Lutheran Church, 19100 Ford Rd.
Contact Person: Mr. Robert Quintero, 22608 Poplar Ct., Hazel Park, MI 48030
Meeting City: Dearborn
E-mail: qover@ameritech.net

Detroit Philatelic Society (APS# 0025-003219)
Meeting Time and Location: 6 p.m., 1st & 3rd Wed., except July, Aug., & Sept., various locations
Contact Person: Mr. Michael J. Barie, P. O. Box 1445, Detroit, MI 48231
Meeting City: Detroit
E-mail: mjbarie@wwnet.ent

Michigan Stamp Club (APS# 0047-004753)
Meeting Time and Location: 7 p.m., 2nd & 4th Mon., Prince of Peace Lutheran Ch., 19100 Ford Rd.
Contact Person: Mr. Robert F. Rinke, Apt. 204, 51307 Central

Village Rd., New Baltimore, MI 48047-1350
Meeting City: Detroit

Lansing Area Stamp Club (APS# 0780-062751)
Meeting Time and Location: 7 p.m., 2nd Thur., East Lansing Rec. Center, 201 Hillside Ct.
Contact Person: Mr. John N. Nelson, P. O. Box 20242, Lansing, MI 48901-8242
Meeting City: East Lansing

Ferndale Stamp Club (APS# 1175-117291)
Meeting Time and Location: 7 p.m., 1st & 3rd Tues., Zion Lutheran Church, 143 Albany
Contact Person: Mr. Robert K. Helbig, 21624 Jacksonville St., Farmington Hills, MI 48336-5730
Meeting City: Ferndale

Vehicle City Stamp Club (APS# 0660-051908)
Meeting Time and Location: 6:30 p.m., 1st Wed., GMI-Campus Center, 5th fl.
Contact Person: Mr. Roger H. Larman, 132 First St., Mt. Morris, MI 48458
Meeting City: Flint

Kent Philatelic Society (APS# 0476-040322)
Meeting Time and Location: 7 p.m., 2nd & 4th Wed., Kentwood Public Library, 4700 Kalamazoo, S.E.
Contact Person: Mr. Gordon Freeman, P. O. Box 1156, Grand Rapids, MI 49501-1156
Meeting City: Grand Rapids

Northwoods Philatelic Society (APS# 1477-176162)
Meeting Time and Location: 7 p.m., 3rd Tues., First Lutheran Church, 1210 S. Stephenson Ave.

Contact Person: Mr. James D. Stearns, W8071 Old Carney Lake Rd., Iron Mountain, MI 49801
Meeting City: Iron Mountain
E-mail: postcards@bresnanlink.net

Floral City Stamp Club (APS# 0899-077113)
Meeting Time and Location: 7:30 p.m., 2nd Mon., Monroe Senior Center
Contact Person: Adele Rottenbucher, 3785 Heiss Rd., Monroe, MI 48162
Meeting City: Monroe
E-mail: arottenbucher@yahoo.com

Muskegon Stamp Club (APS# 1363-148909)
Meeting Time and Location: 7:30 p.m., McGraft Congregational Church, Activity Room
Contact Person: Andrew Busard, 2361 Westwood Rd., Muskegon, MI 49441
Meeting City: Muskegon

Collectors Club of Michigan (APS# 0883-074901)
Meeting Time and Location: 7:30 p.m., 1st Mon., Oak Park Community Center, 14300 Oak Park Dr.
Contact Person: Dr. Gerald Berks, 138 Pointe West Dr., Amherstburg, ON N9V 3N9 Canada
Meeting City: Oak Park

Kalamazoo Stamp Club (APS# 1247-127323)
Meeting Time and Location: 5 p.m., 3rd Tues., Parchment Community Library, 401 S. Riverview
Contact Person: Mr. George E. McKay, Jr., 170 Frances Dr., Battle Creek, MI 49015-3962
Meeting City: Parchment
E-mail: aspen@net-link.net

Website: www.zenation.com/kazoostamp

Pontiac Stamp Club (APS# 0666-052141)
Meeting Time and Location: 7:30 p.m., 2nd & 4th Tues., Don Tatro Instr. Mat. Ctr., 1325 Crescent Lake Rd.
Contact Person: Mr. Charles Hirchert, 2641 Sun Terrace, Hartland, MI 48353
Meeting City: Pontiac
E-mail: ckhirchert@onemain.com

Saginaw Valley Stamp Society (APS# 0322-029149)
Meeting Time and Location: 7:30 p.m., 1st & 3rd Wed., Chemical Bank, Community Rm., Weiss & M-47
Contact Person: Mr. Richard G. Ebach, 2265 Linda Ave., Saginaw, MI 48603
Meeting City: Saginaw

Southwestern Michigan Stamp Club (APS# 1249-127800)
Meeting Time and Location: 7:30 p.m., 3rd Wed., St. Luke's Lutheran Church, 5020 Cleveland Ave.
Contact Person: Mr. William Kintup, 2802 Willa Dr., St. Joseph, MI 49085
Meeting City: Stevensville
E-mail: hffowler@gtm.net
Website: www.stampshows.com/smsc.html

Greater Grand Rapids Stamp Club (APS# 1527-193476)
Meeting Time and Location: 6 p.m., 1st Wed., Wyoming Senior Center, 2380 DeHoop, S.W.
Contact Person: Dr. Ronald R. Mrozinski, P. O. Box 249, Middleville, MI 49333
Meeting City: Wyoming
E-mail: oldkentstamps@aol.com
Website: ggrsc.homestead.com

MINNESOTA

Arrowhead Stamp Club (APS# 0502-042017)
Meeting Time and Location: 7 p.m., 2nd & 4th Mon., Duluth Rainbow Senior Center, 211 N. 3rd Ave., E.
Contact Person: Mr. Howard J. Pramann, 4072 Haines Rd., #316, Duluth, MN 55811-1723
Meeting City: Duluth

Lake Minnetonka Stamp Club (APS# 1222-123773)
Meeting Time and Location: 7 p.m., 2nd Tues., Excelsior Elementary School, Highways 7 & 19
Contact Person: Mr. Rossmer V. Olson, P. O. Box 23377, Richfield, MN 55423-0377
Meeting City: Excelsior
E-mail: rossvole@aol.com

Lyon County Philatelic Society (APS# 1210-122930)
Meeting Time and Location: 7 p.m., 3rd Mon., except June, July, & Aug., Marshall Middle School Cafeteria, 207 N. 4th St.
Contact Person: Mr. Steve Klein, 401 Charles Ave., Marshall, MN 56258
Meeting City: Marshall

Minnehaha Stamp Club (APS# 0861-071936)
Meeting Time and Location: 7 p.m., 2nd Thurs., except July & Aug., Pearl Park Rec. Center, 414 E. Diamond Lake Rd.
Contact Person: Mr. Frederick E. Dickinson, 1701 James Pl., Burnsville, MN 55337
Meeting City: Minneapolis

Fargo Moorhead Philatelic Society (APS# 0819-067286)
Meeting Time and Location: 6:30 p.m., 2nd & 4th Thurs., June, July, Aug., & Dec. 2nd, Thurs., Lake Agassiz Regional Library, KL Room
Contact Person: Prof. James H. Olsen, 7511 Ellis Lane, Horace, ND 58047-9535
Meeting City: Moorhead

St. Cloud Area Stamp Club (APS# 1336-144703)
Meeting Time and Location: 7:30 p.m., 1st & 3rd Wed., Whitney Senior Center
Contact Person: Mr. Stephen A. Dirksen, 1800 Elkton Rd., Clearwater, MN 55320
Meeting City: St. Cloud

MIPS/ATA (APS# 1260-128886)
Meeting Time and Location: 2:30 p.m., 3rd Sun., except June, July, Aug., & Feb., St Louis Park-Nov.-Dec.-Jan.-Apr., St. Paul-Sept.-Oct.-Mar.-May
Contact Person: Mr. Wayne Hassell, 1765 Juno Ave., Saint Paul, MN 55116-1467
Meeting City: St. Louis Park
E-mail: ray@getsug.com

Twin City Philatelic Society (APS# 0097-011353)
Meeting Time and Location: 7:30 p.m., 1st & 3rd Thurs., except June, July, & Aug., 1st-Bryant Ave. Park, Mpls., 3rd-Christ Lutheran Ch, St. Paul
Contact Person: Mr. Al Sarvi, 3350 Rosewood Lane, Plymouth, MN 55441
Meeting City: St. Paul
E-mail: 105463.2357@compuserve.com

Lake Area Stamp Society (APS# 1445-169652)
Meeting Time and Location: 7 p.m., 1st & 3rd Tues. Apr.–Oct., 1 p.m., 1st Sat. Nov.-Mar., Vergas State Bank, Loon's Nest Cafe
Contact Person: Ms. Ella Sauer,

34718 Big McDonald Lane, Dent, MN 56528
Meeting City: Vergas
E-mail: ersdent@eot.com

Maplewood Stamp Club (APS# 0681-054001)
Meeting Time and Location: 7 p.m., 1st Mon., except holidays-2nd Mon. First Lutheran Church, Hwy 61 & East Co. Road F
Contact Person: Mr. Bryan J. McGinnis, P. O. Box 9073, North St. Paul, MN 55109
Meeting City: White Bear Lake
E-mail: bjmcginnis@mmmpcc.org

West Central Minnesota Stamp Club (APS# 1171-116382)
Meeting Time and Location: 7:30 p.m., 2nd Thurs. & 4th Tues., except June, July, & Aug., Willmar Jr. High
Contact Person: Mr. Elmond D. Ekblad, 501 S.W. 13th Ave., Willmar, MN 56201
Meeting City: Willmar

MISSISSIPPI

Gulf Coast Stamp Club (APS# 0932-082330)
Meeting Time and Location: 7:30 p.m., 1st Sat., except Sept., Knights of Columbus Hall, 717 Water St.
Contact Person: Dr. Robert T. Marousky, 2720 Ocean Springs, Biloxi MS 39564
Meeting City: Biloxi
E-mail: bobm@digiscape.com

Hattiesburg Philatelic Society (APS# 1084-103419)
Meeting Time and Location: 7 p.m., 4th Thur., Garden Center, Hutchinson Ave.
Contact Person: Mr. Alan E. Gould, 38 University Pl., Hattiesburg, MS 39402

Meeting City: Hattiesburg
E-mail: riksstamp@netdoor.com

Jackson Philatelic Society (APS# 0631-049526)
Meeting Time and Location: 7:30 p.m., 2nd Fri., MP & L Auditorium
Contact Person: Mr. Robert C. Munroe, P. O. Box 12369, Jackson, MS 39236
Meeting City: Jackson
E-mail: Jbpettway@aol.com
Website: www0.delphi.com/stamps/apschapjackson.html

MISSOURI

Greater St. Louis Stamp Club (APS# 1011-094278)
Meeting Time and Location: 8 p.m., 4th Mon., Parkway Central High School, 369 N. Woods Mill Rd.
Contact Person: Mr. Gary G. Hendren, 12737 Glenage Dr., Maryland Heights, MO 63043
Meeting City: Chesterfield
E-mail: alan@mophil.org
Website: www.mophil.org/gslsc.htm

Columbia Philatelic Society (APS# 0763-060765)
Meeting Time and Location: 7 p.m., 3rd Tues., Boone Electric, 1413 Rangeline
Contact Person: Dr. Jack R. Horton, 2713 Bayonne Ct., Columbia, MO 65203
Meeting City: Columbia

Kingdom Philatelic Association (APS# 0702-055181)
Meeting Time and Location: 7 p.m., 3rd Thurs., except July & Aug., Methodist Church, Educational, Bldg., 719 Court St.
Contact Person: Mr. Albert E. White, 8175 County Road 403, Fulton, MO 65251
Meeting City: Fulton
E-mail: awhite01@socket.net

Gladstone Philatelic Club (APS# 1351-147410)
Meeting Time and Location: 7 p.m., 2nd Thurs., Gladstone Community Bldg., 69th & N. Holmes
Contact Person: Mr. Howard K. Buhl, III, 002 Frank St., Edgerton, MO 64444
Meeting City: Gladstone

Joplin Stamp Club (APS# 1399-156219)
Meeting Time and Location: 7 p.m., 1st & 3rd Tues., Southwest Missouri Bank, 32nd & Indiana
Contact Person: Mr. John Olson, 3125 Grand Ave., Joplin, MO 64870
Meeting City: Joplin

Midwest Philatelic Society (APS# 0010-000826)
Meeting Time and Location: 1:30 p.m., 1st Sat., Waldo Library, 201 E. 75th
Contact Person: Mr. Tom Poulsen, 7705 Acuff Lane, Lenexa, KS 66216
Meeting City: Kansas City
E-mail: tpoulsen@aol.com

Ozark Mountain Stamp Club (APS# 1207-122462)
Meeting Time and Location: 7 p.m., 3rd Thurs., except Dec., 3731 S. Glenstone (Clubhouse)
Contact Person: Mr. John A. Grant, P. O. Box 651, Nixa, MO 65810
Meeting City: Springfield

St. Joseph Stamp Collectors Club (APS# 0627-049410)
Meeting Time and Location: 1 p.m., 3rd Sat., Senior Citizens Bldg., 10th & Edmond
Contact Person: Mrs. Mary C. Maker, 1901 Jackson St., St. Joseph, MO 64503
Meeting City: St. Joseph
E-mail: mcmaker@ccp.com

Mound City Stamp Club (APS# 0334-029614)
Meeting Time and Location: 7:30 p.m., 1st & 3rd Mon., Olivette Community Center, 9723 Grandview Dr.
Contact Person: Mr. Joseph C. Conti, 1 Royalty Ct., Florissant, MO 63034
Meeting City: St. Louis

St. Louis Branch No. 4 (APS# 0004-000460)
Meeting Time and Location: 1 p.m., 3rd Sat., except July & Aug., members' homes
Contact Person: Mr. David O. Semsrott, 2615 Briar Valley Ct., Des Peres, MO 63122
Meeting City: St. Louis
E-mail: Fixodine@aol.com

Warrensburg Stamp Club (APS# 1415-161197)
Meeting Time and Location: 7 p.m., Methodist Church, 141 E. Gay St.
Contact Person: Mr. Peter L. Viscusi, 328 Jones Ave., Warrensburg, MO 64093
Meeting City: Warrensburg

Webster Groves Stamp Club (APS# 1475-175688)
Meeting Time and Location: 8 p.m., 1st & 3rd Fri., Congregational Church, 10 W. Lockwood
Contact Person: Mr. Hans Stoltz, 34 N. Gore, St. Louis, MO 63119
Meeting City: Webster Groves
Website: www.mophil.org/websterg.htm

MONTANA

Billings Stamp Club (APS# 1346-146241)
Meeting Time and Location: 7:30 p.m., 2nd Tues., Messiah Lutheran Church, 2930 Colton Blvd.
Contact Person: Mr. David L.

Servies, 3115 Zinnia Dr., Billings, MT 59102
Meeting City: Billings

Great Falls Stamp Club (APS# 1287-133893)
Meeting Time and Location: 7 p.m., Last Mon., 1021 Central Ave.
Contact Person: Ms. Shirley Turner, 1625 3rd Ave., S., Great Falls, MT 59405
Meeting City: Great Falls
E-mail: sagebrushslt@prodigy.net

Glacier Stamp Club (APS# 1265-129845)
Meeting Time and Location: 7:30 p.m., 1st Mon., Flathead Co. Library
Contact Person: Mr. J. E. Donald Blais, 90 Miriam Way, Polson, MT 59860
Meeting City: Kalispell
E-mail: donrut@digisys.net

Garden City Stamp Club (APS# 0594-047026)
Meeting Time and Location: 7:30 p.m., 1st Wed. & 3rd Mon., except July & Aug., Western Federal Savings, 2601 Garfield
Contact Person: Mr. James J. Hirstein, 415 Crestline Dr., Missoula, MT 59803
Meeting City: Missoula

NEBRASKA

Central Nebraska Stamp Club (APS# 1058-098569)
Meeting Time and Location: 2 p.m., 2nd Sun., except May, June, & July, Golden Towers, 910 N. Boggs Ave.
Contact Person: Mrs. Doris M. Sundermeier, P. O. Box 248, Cairo, NE 68824
Meeting City: Grand Island

Lincoln Stamp Club (APS# 0799-064882)
Meeting Time and Location:

7 p.m., 1st & 3rd Thurs., Gere Library, 56th & Normal
Contact Person: Mr. Kenneth P. Pruess, 1441 Urbana Lane, Lincoln, NE 68505
Meeting City: Lincoln
E-mail: kppruess@aol.com

Northeast Nebraska Phil. Society (APS# 1451-172097)
Meeting Time and Location: 2 p.m. 3rd Sun., except Dec., Blvd. Village at the Rec Room, 1701 Riverside
Contact Person: Mr. J. Randolph Gilmore, 109 Applewood Dr., Norfolk, NE 68701
Meeting City: Norfolk

Buffalo Bill Stamp Club (APS# 1195-120809)
Meeting Time and Location: 2 p.m., 2nd Sun., Episcopal Church, 203 W. 4th
Contact Person: Dr. John L. Dorwart, 3410 Reagan Ct., North Platte, NE 69101
Meeting City: North Platte
E-mail: htenebr@lakemac.net

Omaha Philatelic Society (APS# 1122-108144)
Meeting Time and Location: 7:30 p.m., 2nd & 4th Fri., Pacific Hills Lutheran Church, 90th & Pacific Sts.
Contact Person: Mr. Richard L. McConnell, Apt. 421, 2235 St. Mary's Ave., Omaha, NE 68102
Meeting City: Omaha
E-mail: Phil8lst@aol.com
Website: www.delphi.com/stamps/apsomaha.html

West Omaha Stamp Club (APS# 1278-132256)
Meeting Time and Location: 7 p.m., 3rd Wed., 721 S. 72nd St., #108
Contact Person: Mr. Maurice (Herb) A. Eveland, Suite 108, 721 S. 72nd, Omaha, NE 68114

Meeting City: Omaha
E-mail: tuvaenterprises@hotmail.com

NEVADA

Southern Nevada Stamp Club
(APS# 0816-067283)
Meeting Time and Location:
7 p.m., 1st & 3rd Fri., except Dec.,
Sutton Terrace Retirement
Community, 3185 E. Flamingo
Rd.
Contact Person: Mrs. Elizabeth O.
Mauck, 3860 San Francisco Ave.,
Las Vegas, NV 89115
Meeting City: Las Vegas
E-mail: bjlvcats@aol.com

Nevada Stamp Study Society
(APS# 0970-088229)
Meeting Time and Location:
10 a.m., 2nd & 4th Sat., Sparks
Heritage Museum
Contact Person: Mr. George N.
Costello, P. O. Box 2907, Sparks,
NV 89432-2907
Meeting City: Sparks
E-mail: lancecom@webtv.net

NEW HAMPSHIRE

White Mountain Stamp Club (APS#
1098-104708)
Meeting Time and Location: 7:30
p.m., 3rd Tues., home of secretary,
Rte. 16 & South End of Bald Hill
Rd.
Contact Person: Mrs. Barbara M.
Savary, P. O. Box 393, Conway,
NH 03818-0393
Meeting City: Conway

Great Bay Stamp Club (APS#
1228-124447)
Meeting Time and Location:
7 p.m., 2nd Tues. & 4th Mon.,
Strafford Lodge Bldg.,
Upper 6th St.
Contact Person: Mr. Edmund H.
Vallery, 5 Thompson Lane,
Durham, NH 03824

Meeting City: Dover
E-mail: ehvalley@aol.com

Manchester Stamp Club (APS#
0805-066114)
Meeting Time and Location: 7:30
p.m., 4th Mon., St. Mary's Bank,
200 McGregor St.
Contact Person: Mr. Robert A.
Dion, P. O. Box 1, North Salem,
NH 03073
Meeting City: Manchester
E-mail: mrzip@mediaone.net

Nashua Philatelic Society (APS#
0825-067623)
Meeting Time and Location:
7 p.m., 1st Mon., Chandler Memorial Library
Contact Person: Mr. T. G. Kudzma,
P. O. Box 1412, Nashua, NH
03061-1412
Meeting City: Nashua

NEW JERSEY

Clifton Stamp Society (APS# 1294-
135605)
Meeting Time and Location: 6:30
P.M., 1st, 3rd, & 5th Mon.,
Community Recreation Center,
1232 Main Ave.
Contact Person: Mr. Thomas
Stidl, 62 Hackberry Pl., Clifton, NJ
07013
Meeting City: Clifton

Middle Forge Philatelic Society
(APS# 0611-048304)
Meeting Time and Location:
7:30 p.m., 2nd & 4th Mon.,
First Memorial Presbyterian
Church
Contact Person: Mr. Willard H.
Hawley, 63 Quaker Church Rd.,
Randolph, NJ 07869
Meeting City: Dover

Molly Pitcher Stamp Club (APS#
0510-042467)
Meeting Time and Location: 7:30
p.m., 1st & 3rd Wed., Grace

Lutheran Church, W. Main St. & Park Ave.
Contact Person: Mr. Harry Shiner, P. O. Box 187, Tennent, NJ 07763
Meeting City: Freehold

Assn. of Bergen County Philatelists (APS# 0903-077911)
Meeting Time and Location: Meets periodically, Lowenthal, 873 Main St., #2F
Contact Person: MAJ Charles Lowenthal, P. O. Box 37, River Edge, NJ 07661-0037
Meeting City: Hackensack

Hamilton Township Philatelic Society (APS# 1095-104282)
Meeting Time and Location: 7:30 p.m., 3rd Tues., except July & Aug., Hamilton Township Library, Whitehouse Mercerville Rd.
Contact Person: Mr. Sherman R. Britton, Jr., 476 S. Olden Ave., Trenton, NJ 08629-1727
Meeting City: Hamilton Township

Hazlet Stamp Club (APS# 0912-080082)
Meeting Time and Location: 8 p.m., 2nd & 4th Tues., July & Aug., 4th Tues. only, James Cullen Rec. Center, 1776 Union Ave.
Contact Person: Mr. Charles M. Rosario, 11 W. Susan St., Hazlet, NJ 07730-1863
Meeting City: Hazlet

Clearbrook Stamp Club (APS# 1290-134656)
Meeting Time and Location: 7:30 p.m., 1st Tues., Clearbrook Club House, Clearbrook Dr.
Contact Person: Mr. Ed Hornichter, 61C Rhus Plaza, Monroe Township, NJ 08831
Meeting City: Monroe Township
E-mail: sared42@aol.com

Jockey Hollow Stamp Club (APS# 0867-072806)

Meeting Time and Location: 8 p.m., 1st & 3rd Mon., Morristown Memorial Hospital, 95 Mt. Kemble Ave. (Rt. 202 S)
Contact Person: Mr. Kurt W. Alstede, P. O. Box 278, Chester, NJ 07930-0278
Meeting City: Morristown
Website: www.eclipse.net/~skitchen/web pages/jhsc.html

Merchantville Stamp Club (APS# 0817-067284)
Meeting Time and Location: 7:30 p.m., 1st Thur. & 3rd Wed., Temple Lutheran Church, Rt. 130 & Merchantville Ave.
Contact Person: Mr. David N. Grayson, P. O. Box 2913, Cherry Hill, NJ 08034
Meeting City: Pennsauken
Website: www.come.to/merpex

Bi-State Stamp Club (APS# 1076-102413)
Meeting Time and Location: 7 p.m., 3rd Thurs., Lopatcong Twsp. Municipal Bldg., 232 S. Third St., Morris Park
Contact Person: Mr. Lloyd E. Foss, 474 Route 173, Stewartsville, NJ 08886
Meeting City: Phillipsburg

North Jersey Stamp Club (APS# 0776-062337)
Meeting Time and Location: 8 p.m., 2nd & 4th Wed., except July & Aug., various members homes
Contact Person: Mr. Stanley F. Rutkowski, 920 Washington Ave., Ho-Ho-Kus, NJ 07423
Meeting City: Ridgewood

Ocean County Stamp Club (APS# 0918-080518)
Meeting Time and Location: 7:30

p.m., 1st & 3rd Wed., Presbyterian Church, R 549, Hooper Ave. & Chestnut St.
Contact Person: Mr. John Karch, 4 Ronda Rd., Toms River, NJ 08755
Meeting City: Toms River

Sussex County Stamp Club (APS# 0778-062339)
Meeting Time and Location: 7 p.m., 2nd Wed., Green Township Municipal Bldg.
Contact Person: Mrs. Joyce A. Storms, 25 Prospect St., Branchville, NJ 07826
Meeting City: Tranquility

West Essex Philatelic Society (APS# 0440-038021)
Meeting Time and Location: 6:30 P.M., 2nd & 4th Mon., Verona Public Library, 17 Gould St.
Contact Person: Mr. Ronald Gollhardt, P. O. Box 223, Cedar Grove, NJ 07009
Meeting City: Verona

Queen City-Warren S. & C. Club (APS# 1198-120812)
Meeting Time and Location: 7:30 p.m., 1st & 3rd Mon., Fleet Bank, 59 Mountain Blvd.
Contact Person: Mr. Edwin W. Lehecka, 217 Hazel Ave., Westfield, NJ 07090
Meeting City: Warren

Westfield Stamp Club (APS# 0540-043965)
Meeting Time and Location: 8 p.m., 4th Thurs., except July & Aug., Westfield Community Room, 425 E. Broad St.
Contact Person: Mr. Henry Laessig, 117 Pearl St., Westfield, NJ 07090
Meeting City: Westfield

North Jersey Federated Stamp Clubs (APS# 0508-042423)
Meeting Time and Location: 8 p.m., 3rd Mon., 117 Pearl St.
Contact Person: Mr. Nathan Zankel, P. O. Box 7449, North Brunswick, NJ 08902
Meeting City: Westfield
E-mail: rrose@phks.com

Coryell's Ferry Stamp Club (APS# 0807-066369)
Meeting Time and Location: 8 p.m., 1st & 3rd Mon., July–Sept. 3rd Mon. only, 1st Mon-Lambertville Baptist Church, 3rd Mon-Washington Crossing Methodist Church
Contact Person: Mrs. Bertha S. Davis, P. O. Box 52, Penns Park, PA 18943
Meeting City: Lambertville NJ or Washington Crossing PA
E-mail: jiwalker@rcn.com

NEW MEXICO

Rocket City Stamp Club (APS# 1449-171911)
Meeting Time and Location: 7 p.m., 2nd Mon., 2300 23rd St.
Contact Person: Ms. Frances Huber, 1207 18th St., Alamogordo, NM 88310-5610
Meeting City: Alamogordo

Albuquerque Philatelic Society (APS# 0250-024690)
Meeting Time and Location: 7 p.m., 2nd & 4th Thurs., except Nov. & Dec., 4th Thurs., Covenant Presbyterian Church, 9315 Candelaria Road
Contact Person: Mr. David Lightle, 10616 Cielo Vista Del Norte, N.W., Corrales, NM 87048
Meeting City: Albuquerque
E-mail: apsstamps@madjac.com

Palo Duro Philatelic Society (APS# 1318-140421)
Meeting Time and Location: Noon, Mon., except holidays, Palo

Duro Senior Center, 5221 Palo Duro Ave., N. E.
Contact Person: Mrs. Dora L. Sylvester, 4935 Skyline View Ct. N.E., Albuquerque, NM 87111
Meeting City: Albuquerque

Animas Valley Stamp Club (APS# 1529-195000)
Meeting Time and Location: 7 p.m., 4th Tues., Farmington Civic Center
Contact Person: Mr. Hubert H. Lesperance, 1801 N. Wagner, Farmington, NM 87401
Meeting City: Farmington

Mesilla Valley Stamp Club (APS# 1157-114549)
Meeting Time and Location: 7:30 p.m., 1st & 3rd Thurs., except Aug., Branigan Library, 200 E. Picacho
Contact Person: Mr. Charles Victor O'Donnell, P. O. Box 546, Mesilla, NM 88046
Meeting City: Las Cruces
E-mail: jtebo@ziant.com

Los Alamos Stamp Collectors Assoc. (APS# 0298-027929)
Meeting Time and Location: 7 p.m., 2nd & 4th Tues., Mesa Public Library, 2400 Central Ave.
Contact Person: Mrs. Eva Lee M. Wentworth, 2161-B 36th St., Los Alamos, NM 87544
Meeting City: Los Alamos

Santa Fe Stamp Club (APS# 0481-040587)
Meeting Time and Location: 7:15 p.m., 3rd Wed., except Dec., LaFarge Branch Library, 1730 Llano St.
Contact Person: Mr. Michael J. Becker, 2592 Camino Chuego, Sante Fe, NM 87505
Meeting City: Santa Fe

NEW YORK

Federation of Central NY Phil. Societies (APS# 0191-016560)
Meeting Time and Location: Bi-annually, various hotel meeting rooms, Greater Utica area
Contact Person: Dr. Louis T. Call, 1284 State Route 169, Little Falls, NY 13365
Meeting City: Central New York
E-mail: rocket@dreamscape.com
Website: www.now.at/fcnyps

Fort Orange Stamp Club (APS# 0138-013745)
Meeting Time and Location: 7 p.m., 2nd & 4th Tues., except June, July, & Aug., Bethany Reformed Church, 760 New Scotland Ave.
Contact Person: Mr. John F. Haefeli, Jr., 57 S. Manning Blvd., Albany, NY 12203-1719
Meeting City: Albany
E-mail: fortorange@hotmail.com
Website: www.virtualstampclub.com/apsftorange.html

Batavia-Genesee County C & S Club (APS# 0698-055177)
Meeting Time and Location: 7:30 p.m., 3rd Thurs., Batavia YMCA, 209 E. Main St.
Contact Person: Mr. Dennis A. Kane, 268 Ross St., Batavia, NY 14020-1642
Meeting City: Batavia

Johnson City Stamp Club (APS# 0359-031785)
Meeting Time and Location: 7:30 p.m., 1st & 3rd Mon., Grand Blvd. Methodist Church, Grand Blvd. & Floral Ave.
Contact Person: Mr. John H. Fiske, 20 McNamara Ave., Binghamton, NY 13903
Meeting City: Binghamton

Polish Philatelic Society (APS# 1510-188233)
Meeting Time and Location: 4th Fri., 612 Fillmore Ave.
Contact Person: Mr. Fred F. Jablonski, 612 Fillmore Ave., Buffalo, NY 14212
Meeting City: Buffalo

Steuben Stamp Club (APS# 1357-148254)
Meeting Time and Location: 7 p.m., 2nd Mon., except July & Aug., Kanestio Historical Soc. Bldg.
Contact Person: Mr. Dan Todd, P. O. Box 64, Canisteo, NY 14823
Meeting City: Canisteo

Putnam Philatelic Society (APS# 1061-099576)
Meeting Time and Location: 7:30 p.m., 1st & 3rd Fri., Guideposts Assoc. Auditorium, Seminary Hill Rd.
Contact Person: Mr. Drew A. Nicholson, 18 Valley Dr., Pawling, NY 12564-1140
Meeting City: Carmel

Buffalo Stamp Club (APS# 0037-003691)
Meeting Time and Location: 7:30 p.m., 1st & 3rd Fri., except June, July, & Aug., Leonard Post, 2450 Walden Ave.
Contact Person: Mr. Tim Carey, 192 N. Union Rd., Buffalo, NY 14221
Meeting City: Cheektowaga
E-mail: careystea@aol.com

Leatherstocking Stamp Club (APS# 1334-144415)
Meeting Time and Location: 6:30 p.m., 1st Tues., Jr. Club., 7:30 p.m. Regular Club, George Tillapaugh Home, 28 Pioneer St.
Contact Person: Mrs. Ellen Tillapaugh, 80 Beaver St., Cooperstown, NY 13326
Meeting City: Cooperstown
E-mail: kuchtill@capital.net

Dansville Area Coin & Stamp Club (APS# 1196-120810)
Meeting Time and Location: 2 p.m., 3rd Sun., Dansville Town Hall, 14 Clara Barton St.
Contact Person: Mr. Robert L. Stickney, P. O. Box 574, Dansville, NY 14437
Meeting City: Dansville

Plewacki Stamp Society (APS# 0609-048166)
Meeting Time and Location: 8 p.m., 2nd & 4th Wed., F.O.E. #2962, 4569 Broadway
Contact Person: Mr. Michael D. Battaglia, 5 Rondelay Ct., Cheektowaga, NY 14227
Meeting City: Depew

Elmira Stamp Club (APS# 0237-024110)
Meeting Time and Location: 8 p.m., 3rd Tues., BSB Bank & Trust, Community Room, 351 N. Main St.
Contact Person: Mr. Alan Parsons, 809 Holley Rd., Elmira, NY 14905
Meeting City: Elmira
E-mail: galerp@lrun.com

Fulton Stamp Club (APS# 1193-120322)
Meeting Time and Location: 7 p.m., 3rd Wed., except July & Aug., Hughes Bldg., 314 Park St.
Contact Person: Mr. John A. Cali, P. O. Box 401, Fulton, NY 13069
Meeting City: Fulton
E-mail: rocket@dreamscape.com

Finger Lakes Stamp Club (APS# 0428-037260)
Meeting Time and Location: 8 p.m., 2nd & 4th Wed., except July & Aug., Sawdust Cafe
Contact Person: Mr. Gary

Chicoine, P. O. Box 31, Hall, NY 14463
Meeting City: Geneva
E-mail: gscz@localnet.com

Chenango Valley Stamp Club (APS# 0781-062616)
Meeting Time and Location: 7:45 p.m., 1st Mon., except July & Aug., ALANA Cultural Center, Colgate Univ.
Contact Person: Mr. R. Braden Houston, Rt. 2, Box 78C, Hamilton, NY 13346
Meeting City: Hamilton
E-mail: bhouston@mail.colgate.edu

Allegany Stamp Club (APS# 1130-110584)
Meeting Time and Location: 7:30 p.m., 1st Thurs. (Apr./July Oct./Dec.), Houghton College, Alumni Dining Room
Contact Person: Dr. Richard A. Gould, P. O. Box 85, Houghton, NY 14744
Meeting City: Houghton

Ithaca Philatelic Society (APS# 0210-019654)
Meeting Time and Location: 7:30 p.m., 2nd & 4th Wed., except 2nd & 3rd Wed. in Nov. & Dec., Cornell University, 348 Morrison Hall
Contact Person: Yoram B. Szekely, 104 Kline Woods Rd., Ithaca, NY 14850
Meeting City: Ithaca
E-mail: yszekely@twcny.rr.com

Reuben E. Fenton Philatelic Society (APS# 0705-055184)
Meeting Time and Location: 7:30 p.m., last Tues., Brooklyn Heights Methodist, Church, 120 Delaware Ave.
Contact Person: Leslie W. Davis, P. O. Box 266, Bemus Point, NY 14712
Meeting City: Jamestown

Stamptrotters Society of Kingston (APS# 0559-044549)
Meeting Time and Location: 7:30 p.m., 2nd & 4th Thurs., except July & Aug., Town Hall, Town of Ulster
Contact Person: Mr. Phil I. Bruno, 4 Willow Dr., Red Hook, NY 12571
Meeting City: Lake Katrine
E-mail: pib39@ulster.net

Lockport Coin and Stamp Club (APS# 1163-115943)
Meeting Time and Location: 7 p.m., 2nd & 4th Tues., Emmanuel Methodist Church, 75 East Ave.
Contact Person: Mr. Burwyn L. Schweigert, 6104 Corwin Ave., Newfane, NY 14108-1119
Meeting City: Lockport

Sperry Stamp Club (APS# 1165-115945)
Meeting Time and Location: 12 Noon, 1st Thur., Lockheed Martin-D.E.S.S., 55 Charles Lindbergh Blvd.
Contact Person: Mr. Michael L. Currie, 1943 Stewart Ave., New Hyde Park, NY 11040-1625
Meeting City: Mitchel Field

Sullivan County Philatelic Society (APS# 0920-080520)
Meeting Time and Location: 7 p.m., 1st Sun., Temple Sholom, East Dillion Rd.
Contact Person: Mr. Arthur Rosenzweig, P. O. Box 230, Monticello, NY 12701
Meeting City: Monticello

Utica Stamp Club (APS# 0066-008021)
Meeting Time and Location: 7 p.m., 1st Tues., except July & Aug., Zion Lutheran Church, 630 French Road
Contact Person: Ms. Janet E. Collmer, P. O. Box 85, Franklin Springs, NY 13341

Meeting City: New Hartford
Website: www0.delphi.com/stamps/apschaputica.html

ATA, New York Chapter (APS# 1383-153401)
Meeting Time and Location: 7:15 p.m., 2nd Thurs., Collectors Club, 22 E. 35th St.
Contact Person: Ms. Caroline Scannell, 14 Dawn Dr., Smithtown, NY 11787
Meeting City: New York
E-mail: philate@ix.netcom.com

International Stamp Club (APS# 1355-148252)
Meeting Time and Location: 12 p.m.-4p.m., Sun., Soldiers', Sailors', & Airmen's Club, Inc., 283 Lexington Ave.
Contact Person: Miss Ruth Gazes, 75 Henry St., Apt. 6D, Brooklyn, NY 11201
Meeting City: New York

Newburgh Stamp Club (APS# 0704-055183)
Meeting Time and Location: 7:30 p.m., 4th Mon., except, May & Dec., 3rd Mon., 1st Baptist Church, South & West Sts.
Contact Person: Mr. William T. McCaw, 368 Grand St., Newburgh, NY 12550-3612
Meeting City: Newburgh

Olean Stamp Club (APS# 1442-168335)
Meeting Time and Location: 7 p.m., 1st Mon., St. Stephens Episcopal Church, 109 S. Barry St.
Contact Person: Mr. Leslie E. Crane, Rt. 1, Box 832, Shinglehouse, PA 16748
Meeting City: Olean
E-mail: searles@eznet.net

Oswego Stamp Club (APS# 0728-057786)
Meeting Time and Location:

6 p.m., 4th Mon., except June, July, & Aug., Faith United Church, 12 Fitzgibbons Rd.
Contact Person: Mr. John Cali, 613 W. 4th St., Fulton, NY 13069
Meeting City: Oswego
E-mail: rocket@dreamscape.com

Dutchess Philatelic Society (APS# 0480-040579)
Meeting Time and Location: 7:30 p.m., 1st & 3rd Tues., except July & Aug., Friends Meeting Hall, Corner, Hooker Ave. & Whittier Blvd.
Contact Person: Mr. Rudy Schaelchli, P. O. Box 515, Millertown, NY 12540
Meeting City: Poughkeepsie

Riverhead Stamp Club (APS# 1341-145424)
Meeting Time and Location: 2nd & last Thurs., Riverhead Free Library, 330 Court St.
Contact Person: Mr. Ted Fredericks, 330 Court St., Riverhead, NY 11901
Meeting City: Riverhead

Kodak Stamp Club (APS# 0655-051448)
Meeting Time and Location: 7:30 p.m., 4th Tues., B-28, Room 151 A & B, Kodak Pk., Ridge Road West at Palm St.
Contact Person: Mr. Joseph K. Doles, 105 Lawson Rd., Rochester, NY 14616-1444
Meeting City: Rochester
E-mail: jkd52@aol.com

Rochester Philatelic Association (APS# 0207-019273)
Meeting Time and Location: 7:45 p.m., 2nd & 4th Thurs., Nov. & Dec. 2nd, Thurs. only, Sept.–June, St. Paul's Episcopal Ch. Hall, East Ave. & Vick Park B
Contact Person: Mr. Norman E.

Wright, Sr., 33 Northumberland Road, Rochester, NY 14618
Meeting City: Rochester
E-mail: normanw2@worldnet.att.net
Website: now.at/rpa/

Fort Stanwix Stamp Club (APS# 1227-124446)
Meeting Time and Location: 7:30 p.m., 2nd & 4th Thurs., except June, July, & Aug., Rome City Hall, 2nd floor, 100 Block of W. Liberty St.
Contact Person: Mr. Joseph O. Christofaro, 201 Maple St., Rome, NY 13440
Meeting City: Rome
E-mail: jozep@borg.com

North Shore Philatelic Society (APS# 0607-048152)
Meeting Time and Location: 8 p.m., 1st & 3rd Wed., Bryant Library
Contact Person: Mr. Adolph H. Stephani, 4 Ann St., Glen Cove, NY 11542
Meeting City: Roslyn

Schenectady Stamp Club (APS# 0153-014474)
Meeting Time and Location: 7:30 p.m., 1st & 3rd Mon., except July & Aug., Union Presbyterian Church, 1068 Park Ave.
Contact Person: Mr. Stephen E. Gray, Apt. C-1 10, Hillcrest Village W., Schenectady, NY 12309
Meeting City: Schenectady
E-mail: nunesnook@aol.com

Community Stamp Club (APS# 1100-104710)
Meeting Time and Location: 7:30 p.m., 3rd Thurs., except June, July, & Aug., CAC Clubhouse, 139 E. Hamilton Ave.
Contact Person: Mr. Ernest L. Lewis, Rt. 2, Box 158, Munnsville, NY 13409-9754
Meeting City: Sherrill

Tri-County Stamp Club (APS# 0292-027733)
Meeting Time and Location: 7 p.m., 3rd Mon., except July & Aug., Sidney Civic Center
Contact Person: Mr. Robert Finnegan, 27 Pearl St. E., Sidney, NY 13838
Meeting City: Sidney
E-mail: rfinnegan@mkl.com

Sodus Stamp Club (APS# 1077-102414)
Meeting Time and Location: 7:30, 3rd Wed., members' homes
Contact Person: Mr. Paul R. Spiers, 54 Orchard Terr., Sodus, NY 14551
Meeting City: Sodus
E-mail: prspiers@rochester.r.r.com

Western Monroe Philatelic Society (APS# 0560-044599)
Meeting Time and Location: 7 p.m., 2nd Tues., except July & Aug., Ogden Farmer's Library, 269 Odgen Center Rd.
Contact Person: Mary W. Gerew, 838 Gallup Rd., Spencerport, NY 14559-9525
Meeting City: Spencerport

Staten Island Philatelic Society (APS# 0814-066935)
Meeting Time and Location: 7:30 p.m., 1st & 3rd Mon., except July & Aug., Rev. Paul Kroon Center, 199 Jefferson Blvd.
Contact Person: Mr. Charles R. Carlson, 30 Hopping Ave., Staten Island, NY 10307-1219
Meeting City: Staten Island
E-mail: kccarlson@aol.com

Syracuse Stamp Club (APS# 0050-005911)
Meeting Time and Location: 8 p.m., 1st & 3rd Fri., Reformed Church of Syracuse, 1228 Teall Ave.

Contact Person: Mr. Michael Ammann, 217 Inwood Dr., Syracuse, NY 13219
Meeting City: Syracuse

Uncle Sam Stamp Club of Troy (APS# 0240-024176)
Meeting Time and Location: 7:30 p.m., 1st & 3rd Wed., Holmes & Watson, Ltd., 450 Broadway, 2nd fl.
Contact Person: Mr. Arnold A. Leiter, 811 2nd Ave., Troy, NY 12182
Meeting City: Troy

Jefferson County Stamp Club (APS# 0579-045718)
Meeting Time and Location: 7:30 p.m., 1st & 3rd Tues., US Postal Facility, Training Room, Commerce Dr.
Contact Person: Mr. Gerald F. Wiley, 921 Mill St., Watertown, NY 13601
Meeting City: Watertown

NORTH CAROLINA

Asheville Stamp Club (APS# 0793-064417)
Meeting Time and Location: 2 p.m., 3rd Sun., North Asheville Comm. Ctr., Larchmont St.
Contact Person: Sonja Richards, P. O. Box 988, Clyde, NC 28721
Meeting City: Asheville
E-mail: sosewtwo@aol.com

Triangle Stamp Club (APS# 0958-087135)
Meeting Time and Location: 7:30 p.m., 2nd Mon., Undercroft, Church of the Holy Family, 200 Hayes Rd.
Contact Person: Dr. Charles Wood, 1910 Glendale Ave., Durham, NC 27701-1326
Meeting City: Chapel Hill

Charlotte Philatelic Society (APS# 0738-058506)

Meeting Time and Location: 2 p.m., 1st Sun., Metrolina Assoc. for Blind, 704 Louise Ave.
Contact Person: Mr. Robert R. Reeves, P. O. Box 30101, Charlotte, NC 28230
Meeting City: Charlotte
Website: www.math.uncc.edu/~hbreiter/clubs/cps.htm

Fortnightly Collectors Club (APS# 0177-015882)
Meeting Time and Location: 8 p.m., every three weeks, members' homes
Contact Person: Mr. John C. Dohmlo, P. O. Box 242053, Charlotte, NC 28224-2053
Meeting City: Charlotte

Thermal Belt Stamp Club (APS# 1179-117708)
Meeting Time and Location: 7:30 p.m., 1st & 3rd Mon., Tryon Federal Savings & Loan, Conference Rm., Mills St.
Contact Person: Mr. Clarke Taube, 108 Laurel Ave., Tryon, NC 28782
Meeting City: Columbus

Emerald Isle Stamp Club (APS# 1489-181643)
Meeting Time and Location: 7 p.m., 2nd & 4th Thurs., Emerald Isle Recreation Ctr., Leasure Dr.
Contact Person: Mr. George A. Kuhhorn, P.O. Box 4486, Emerald Isle, NC 28594
Meeting City: Emerald Isle

Greensboro Stamp Club (APS# 1064-100357)
Meeting Time and Location: 7:30 p.m., 2nd & 4th Thurs., except Nov. & Dec., Lindley Recreation Center, 2907 Springwood Dr.
Contact Person: Mr. Dan R. Beane, 2816 Cyrus Road, Greensboro, NC 27406

Meeting City: Greensboro
E-mail: BeaneDStamps@aol.com

Outer Banks Stamp Club (APS# 1502-187435)
Meeting Time and Location: 3 p.m., 2nd Sun., except July & Aug., Outer Banks Presby. Church, S. Croatan Hwy.
Contact Person: Mr. Kenneth A. Perine, 185 Chicahauk Trl., Kitty Hawk, NC 27949
Meeting City: Kill Devil Hills
E-mail: perine@beachlink.com

Davie County Stamp Club (APS# 1515-189610)
Meeting Time and Location: 1st Thurs., Brock Center, East Room, 622 N. Main
Contact Person: Mr. Fred Whitaker, 830 Country Lane, Mocksville, NC 27028
Meeting City: Mocksville

Raleigh Stamp Club (APS# 0538-043937)
Meeting Time and Location: 7:30 p.m., 1st Mon., Jaycee Center, 2405 Wade Ave.
Contact Person: Mr. Jack C. Scott, P. O. Box 26863, Raleigh, NC 27611
Meeting City: Raleigh
Website: www.mindspring.com/~albumman/RSC/rsc.htm

Wilmington Philatelic Society (APS# 1283-132954)
Meeting Time and Location: 7 p.m., 2nd Tues., UNCW, Room 111
Contact Person: Mr. Peter Jasinski, P. O. Box 2214, Wilmington, NC 28402-2214
Meeting City: Wilmington

Winston-Salem Stamp Club (APS# 1284-132955)
Meeting Time and Location: 7:30 p.m., last Tues., Miller Park Recreation Ctr., 400 Miller Park Circle

Contact Person: Rev. Nelson A. L. Weller, 2940 Wesleyan Lane, Winston-Salem, NC 27106
Meeting City: Winston-Salem
E-mail: nalweller@aol.com

Carolinas Chapter 37, G.P.S. (APS# 1251-128124)
Meeting Time and Location: Varies (Sat.), 11 a.m., various locations in North & South Carolina
Contact Person: Mr. Scott Marusak, P. O. Box 5645, Cary, NC 27512
Meeting City: Various
E-mail: albumman@pobox.com

OHIO

Collectors Club of Akron (APS# 0251-024886)
Meeting Time and Location: 6 p.m., 3rd Tues., Papa Joe's Restaurant
Contact Person: Mr. Roger O. Gilruth, P. O. Box 1721, Akron, OH 44309-1721
Meeting City: Akron

Rubber City Stamp Club (APS# 0051-005912)
Meeting Time and Location: 8 p.m., 1st & 3rd Fri., except July & Aug., Montrose-Zion U. M. Church, 565 N. Cleveland-Massillon Rd.
Contact Person: Mr. Roger O. Gilruth, P. O. Box 1721, Akron, OH 44309-1721
Meeting City: Akron

Athens Stamp Club (APS# 0862-071937)
Meeting Time and Location: 7:30 p.m., 2nd Wed., except July, Aug., & Dec., Community Mental Health Bldg., 8000 Dairy Lane
Contact Person: Mr. Marvin E. Fletcher, 45 Avon Pl., Athens, OH 45701

Meeting City: Athens
E-mail: fletcher@ohio.edu

McKinley Stamp Club (APS# 0078-009294)
Meeting Time and Location: 7:30 p.m., 4th Mon., Mayfield Senior Center, 3825 13th St., S.W.
Contact Person: Dr. Dale Hart, 1730 Coventry Rd., N.E., Massillon, OH 44646-4132
Meeting City: Canton
E-mail: lhartbuf@aol.com

Stark County Stamp Club (APS# 0656-051449)
Meeting Time and Location: 7:30 p.m., 2nd Wed., Sippo Lake Club House, 5300 Tyner Ave., N.W.
Contact Person: Mr. Eugene Swonger, P. O. Box 668, Dover, OH 44622
Meeting City: Canton
E-mail: JRSCEO@aol.com

Greater Cincinnati Phil. Society (APS# 0046-004752)
Meeting Times and Location: 7:30 p.m., 2nd Mon. & 4th Wed., except Sept. & Dec., Mon.-Clifton Comm. Ctr., 320 McAlpine Ave., Wed.-Northside Bank, 9315 Colerain Ave.
Contact Person: Ms. Virginia Fisher, 358 Shiloh St., Apt. 1, Cincinnati, OH 45220-1650
Meeting City: Cincinnati
E-mail: ronmaifeld@juno.com

Cuy-Lor Stamp Club (APS# 0601-047445)
Meeting Time and Location: 8 p.m., 2nd & 4th Fri., July, Aug., & Dec., 2nd Fri. only, West Park United Church of Christ, 3909 Rocky River Dr.
Contact Person: Mr. Stanley M. Fairchild, Jr., P. O. Box 45042, Westlake, OH 44145
Meeting City: Cleveland

E-mail: napoleon@voyager.net

Garfield-Perry Stamp Club (APS# 0030-003208)
Meeting Time and Location: 8 p.m., Fri., Holiday Inn, 1111 Lakeside Ave.
Contact Person: Mr. Richard H. Parker, 1526 Marview Dr., Westlake, OH 44145
Meeting City: Cleveland
Website: members.aol.com/ GPSTAMP/GPSC.html

Columbus Philatelic Club (APS# 0195-017071)
Meeting Time and Location: 7 p.m., 2nd & 4th Mon., Linden Lutheran Church, 1230 Oakland Park Ave.
Contact Person: Dr. Walton U. Beauvais, 1068 Medhurst Rd., Columbus, OH 43220
Meeting City: Columbus
Website: ourworld.compuserve. com/homepages/wbeau/

Nationwide Stamp Club (APS# 0414-036094)
Meeting Time and Location: Currently inactive, Nationwide Ins. Home Office
Contact Person: Mr. Ken Bonvallet, 357 Flour Ct., Westerville, OH 43082-1011
Meeting City: Columbus
E-mail: bonvalk@nationwide.com

Cuyahoga Falls Stamp Club (APS# 0562-044664)
Meeting Time and Location: 7:30 p.m., 1st & 3rd Mon., Rocco's Pizza, Portage Trail & 11th St.
Contact Person: Mr. Hubert W. Kleasen, P. O. Box 104, Cuyahoga Falls, OH 44221-0104
Meeting City: Cuyahoga Falls
E-mail: KIPPY1@prodigy

Dayton Stamp Club (APS# 0913-080083)

Meeting Time and Location: 7:30 p.m., 1st & 3rd Mon., Wegerzyn Garden Center, 1301 E. Siebenthaler Ave.
Contact Person: Mr. L. William Streisel, 2741 Symphony Way, Dayton, OH 45449
Meeting City: Dayton

Black River Stamp Club (APS# 0615-048561)
Meeting Time and Location: 8 p.m., 1st Fri., Elyria Harvest Church, 907 E. Heights Blvd.
Contact Person: Mr. James M. Forbes, 6443 Lake Ave., Elyria, OH 44035
Meeting City: Elyria
E-mail: PREdwardsACE353@aol.com

Euclid Stamp Club (APS# 0657-051450)
Meeting Time and Location: 8 p.m., 2nd & 4th Mon., Euclid Lutheran Church, Forestview & E. 260th St.
Contact Person: Mr. Frank J. Zoretich, Jr., P. O. Box 32211, Euclid, OH 44132
Meeting City: Euclid
E-mail: bonvalk@nation.com

Fort Findlay Stamp Club (APS# 0378-033563)
Meeting Time and Location: 7 p.m., 2nd & 4th Wed., Trinity Lutheran Church, 935 W. Bigelow
Contact Person: Mr. Thomas L. Foust, 5578 State Rt. 186, McComb, OH 45858
Meeting City: Findlay
E-mail: tlfoust@bright.net

Fort Hamilton Philatelic Society (APS# 1362-148908)
Meeting Time and Location: 7:30 p.m., 2nd Thurs., Hamilton West YMCA
Contact Person: Mr. Richard F. Freuler, P. O. Box 224, Hamilton, OH 45012
Meeting City: Hamilton

Ashtabula County Stamp Club (APS# 1429-165211)
Meeting Time and Location: 7:30 p.m., 2nd Mon., Kingsville Public Library, Academy St.
Contact Person: Mr. Douglas J. Gryczan, 1648 S. Denmark Rd., Jefferson, OH 44047
Meeting City: Kingsville

Medina County Stamp Club (APS# 1145-112553)
Meeting Time and Location: 7:30 p.m., 1st Thurs., Sylvester Library, 210 S. Broadway
Contact Person: Mr. Thomas H. Bieniosek, 8020 Spieth Rd., Litchfield, OH 44253
Meeting City: Medina
E-mail: thb@apk.net

Miami Valley Stamp Club (APS# 0614-048457)
Meeting Time and Location: 7 p.m., 4th Thurs., Lebanon Citizens Natl. Bank, 4441 Marie Dr.
Contact Person: Mr. James P. Bruner, 1813 Galway Circle, Middletown, OH 45042
Meeting City: Middletown

Clermont County Stamp Club (APS# 1366-149353)
Meeting Time and Location: 7 p.m., 3rd Thurs., Mulberry Church of Christ, 5857 Highview Dr.
Contact Person: Mrs. Janet R. Klug, 6854 Newtonsville Rd., Pleasant Plain, OH 45162-9616
Meeting City: Milford
E-mail: tongajan@aol.com
Website: hometown.aol.com/TongaJan/ccsc.html

Tuscora Stamp Club (APS# 1433-166151)
Meeting Time and Location: 1st & 3rd Weds., Lutheran Church, 202 E. High Ave.

Contact Person: Mr. Floyd Swinderman, 1113 Sherman Ave., New Philadelphia, OH 44663
Meeting City: New Philadelphia

Firelands Stamp Club (APS# 1488-180986)
Meeting Time and Location: 6:30 p.m., 2nd Tues., Norwalk Public Library, 46 W. Main St.
Contact Person: Dr. Richard P. Germann, Shaker Village, Apt. 11H 333 Cleveland Road, Norwalk, OH 44857-2284
Meeting City: Norwalk

Southwestern Stamp Club (APS# 0706-055185)
Meeting Time and Location: 7:30 p.m., 2nd & 4th Tues., Parma Heights Library, Pearl & Olde York Rds.
Contact Person: Mr. Merlin J. Mason, 6392 Stratford Dr., Cleveland, OH 44130-3173
Meeting City: Parma Heights

Sidney Stamp Club (APS# 1291-135207)
Meeting Time and Location: 7 p.m., 3rd Mon., Dorothy Love Center, Conference Room
Contact Person: Mrs. Susan L. Minniear, P. O. Box 38, Sidney, OH 45365
Meeting City: Sidney
E-mail: susanl@bright.net

Fort Steuben Stamp Club (APS# 0864-072343)
Meeting Time and Location: 7:30 p.m., 1st Mon., Jefferson Community College, 4000 Sunset Blvd.
Contact Person: Mrs. Elsie F. Snyder, P. O. Box 1131, Steubenville, OH 43952
Meeting City: Steubenville

Tiffin Stamp Club (APS# 0754-059698)

Meeting Time and Location: 7:30 p.m., 3rd Thurs., Tiffin Public Library
Contact Person: Mr. Virgil J. Mathias, 30 Gibson Ct., Tiffin, OH 44883
Meeting City: Tiffin

Stamp Collectors Club of Toledo (APS# 0181-016230)
Meeting Time and Location: 7 p.m., 1st & 3rd Thurs., except June, July, & Aug., Wernert's Corner Civic Assn. Hall, 5068 Douglas Rd.
Contact Person: Mr. James L. Baumann, 5248 Sheila Dr., Toledo, OH 43613-2442
Meeting City: Toledo
E-mail: jimbau35@aol.com

Warren Area Stamp Club (APS# 0755-059699)
Meeting Time and Location: 7:30 p.m., 4th Fri., Cortland Bank, Warren Branch, 2935 Elm Rd., N.E.
Contact Person: Mr. Alexander J. Savakis, P. O. Box 609, Warren, OH 44482-0609
Meeting City: Warren
E-mail: WarrenStampClub@aol.com
Website: hometown.aol.com/warrenstampclub

Pike County Stamp Collectors (APS# 1491-182213)
Meeting Time and Location: 7:30 p.m., 2nd Wed., Bristol Village, Activity Center, 625 5th St.
Contact Person: Mrs. June L. Dimmig, 707 E. 3rd St., Waverly, OH 45690-1502
Meeting City: Waverly

Worthington Stamp Club (APS# 0667-052142)
Meeting Time and Location: 7:30 p.m., 1st & 3rd Mon., except July & Aug., Sharon Township Hall, Dublin-, Granville Rd. & Morning St.

Contact Person: Mr. Timothy R. Pusecker, 395 Broadmeadows Blvd., #211, Columbus, OH 43214
Meeting City: Worthington
E-mail: heldforpostage@msn.com

Mahoning Valley Stamp Club (APS# 0072-008537)
Meeting Time and Location: 6:45 p.m., 2nd & 4th Thurs., Bethlehem Lutheran Church, South Ave. & Midlothian Blvd.
Contact Person: Mr. George C. Riebe, Jr., 3139 Sunnybrook Dr., Youngstown, OH 44511-2823
Meeting City: Youngstown

OKLAHOMA

Oklahoma Philatelic Society (APS# 1308-138176)
Meeting Time and Location: Varies, annually
Contact Person: Mr. Lavoy T. Hatchett, P. O. Box 700334, Tulsa, OK 74170
Meeting City: Tulsa
E-mail: lavoyhatch@juno.com

Lawton-Fort Sill Stamp Club (APS# 1066-100359)
Meeting Time and Location: 7:30 p.m., 1st & 3rd Tues., 1st Tues. only in June, July, & Aug., German/American Club, 1410 S.W. Sheridan Rd.
Contact Person: Ms. Sharon V. Loeffler, 415 N.W. 69th St., Lawton, OK 73505-5408
Meeting City: Lawton
E-mail: sloeffle@sirinet.net
Website: www.sirinet.net/~sloeffle/index.htm

Muskogee Stamp Club (APS# 1141-112101)
Meeting Time and Location: 6:30 p.m., 1st Tues., US Post Office, 525 W. Okmulgee
Contact Person: Mr. Gilbert E.

Weisser, 450 Palmer Dr., Muskogee, OK 74401
Meeting City: Muskogee

Norman Stamp Club (APS# 1266-130256)
Meeting Time and Location: Currently inactive, w/o set meeting time. Currently inactive, w/o set meeting place.
Contact Person: Mr. Charles S. Wallis, 480 Elm Ave., Norman, OK 73069-5712
Meeting City: Norman
E-mail: cobweb@telpath.com

Oklahoma City Stamp Club (APS# 0841-069393)
Meeting Time and Location: 7 p.m., 1st & 3rd Tues., except July & Aug.-3rd Tues., Warr Acres Community Center, N.W. 42nd & Ann Arbor
Contact Person: Mr. Scott Troutman, P. O. Box 26542, Oklahoma City, OK 73126
Meeting City: Oklahoma City
Website: members.aol.com/okpex

Tulsa Stamp Club (APS# 0678-053316)
Meeting Time and Location: 7 p.m., 1st & 3rd Thurs., Southern Hills Baptist Church, 5600 S. Lewis
Contact Person: Mr. Lavoy T. Hatchett, P. O. Box 700334, Tulsa, OK 74170
Meeting City: Tulsa

OREGON

Coos Stamp Club (APS# 1012-094279)
Meeting Time and Location: 7:30 p.m., 4th Fri., North Bend Medical Center, 1900 Woodland Dr.
Contact Person: Mrs. Joe Sterrett, 94304 Pleasant Valley Lane, Myrtle Point, OR 97458
Meeting City: Coos Bay

Greater Eugene Stamp Society (APS# 0437-037822)
Meeting Time and Location: 7:30 p.m., 2nd & 4th Wed., 777 Coburg Rd.
Contact Person: Mr. Vern Kilpatrick, P. O. Box 734, Eugene, OR 97440
Meeting City: Eugene
E-mail: bagaaason@rio.com

Rogue Valley Stamp Club (APS# 1480-178924)
Meeting Time and Location: 1st Tues., Valley of the Rogue Bank, N.E. 7th & Midland
Contact Person: Mr. Richard K. Collins, 176 Teel Lane, Grants Pass, OR 97527
Meeting City: Grants Pass

Southern Oregon Philatelic Society (APS# 0526-043418)
Meeting Time and Location: 7 p.m., 1st Thurs., 1st Presbyterian Church, 8th & Holly
Contact Person: Mr. James D. Bryan, 855 Shafer Lane, Medford, OR 97501
Meeting City: Medford
E-mail: jpzen@aol.com

Oregon Stamp Society (APS# 0068-008234)
Meeting Time and Location: 8 p.m., 2nd & 4th Tues., Clubhouse, 4828 N.E. 33rd Ave.
Contact Person: Mr. Thomas G. Current, P. O. Box 18165, Portland, OR 97218-0165
Meeting City: Portland

Umpqua Valley Stamp Club (APS# 1521-191124)
Meeting Time and Location: 7:15 p.m., 3rd Mon., 4388 Old Hwy. 99S
Contact Person: Mr. Phil Black, P. O. Box 175, Umpqua, OR 97486
Meeting City: Roseburg
Website: www.geocities.com/uvsc9/

Salem Stamp Society (APS# 0736-057920)
Meeting Time and Location: 7:30 p.m., 2nd Weds., Fire Hall, Cordon Road at State St.
Contact Person: Mr. Richard J. Abrams, P.O. Box 202, Salem, OR 97308
Meeting City: Salem
E-mail: rabrams2@cs.com

PENNSYLVANIA

Allentown Philatelic Society (APS# 0060-007655)
Meeting Time and Location: 7 p.m., 1st Tues., Sacred Heart Hosp. Conf. Ctr., 4th & Chew Sts.
Contact Person: Mr. David E. Fisher, 909 N. Penn St., Allentown, PA 18102
Meeting City: Allentown
E-mail: epritch@fast.net

Brookhaven Stamp Club (APS# 1437-167085)
Meeting Time and Location: 1:30 p.m., 1st Thurs., Brookhaven Municipal Bldg., 2 Cambridge Rd.
Contact Person: Mr. John Riper, 3617 Victor Ave., Brookhaven, PA 19015
Meeting City: Brookhaven

Cumberland Valley Philatelic Soc. (APS# 0829-067627)
Meeting Time and Location: 6:30 p.m., 4th Tues., Trinity Lutheran Church, Commerce St.
Contact Person: Mr. Paul E. Kolva, Jr., 1101 Hamilton Dr., Chambersburg, PA 17201
Meeting City: Chambersburg

Wilkinsburg Stamp Club (APS# 1214-122934)
Meeting Time and Location: 2 p.m., 2nd & 4th Sun., Borough Bldg., 2300 Wm. Penn Hwy.
Contact Person: Mr. Daid F.

McConaha, 624 Charlotte, Dr., Pittsburgh, PA 15215-1263
Meeting City: Churchill

Blair County Stamp Club (APS# 1378-152207)
Meeting Time and Location: 2 p.m., 3rd Sun., except July & Aug., US Postal Distribution Center
Contact Person: Dr. David W. Bishop, R 4, Box 165A, Altoona, PA 16601
Meeting City: Duncansville
E-mail: dwbishop@earthlink.net

Collectors Club of Philadelphia (APS# 1417-161483)
Meeting Time and Location: 8 p.m., 1st Tues. of Mar./June Sept./Dec., Community Rm., Elkins Park Square, 8080 Old York Rd.
Contact Person: Mr. Alan Warren, P. O. Box 39, Exton, PA 19341-0039
Meeting City: Elkins Park
E-mail: alanwar@att.net

Philadelphia Chapter No. 18 (APS# 0018-001978)
Meeting Time and Location: 7 p.m., 3rd Tues., except July & Aug., Community Rm., Elkins Park Square, 8080 Old York Rd.
Contact Person: Mr. Louis F. Calzi, Sr., 2223 Jenkintown Rd., Glenside, PA 19038-5014
Meeting City: Elkins Park

Erie Stamp Club (APS# 1280-132951)
Meeting Time and Location: 7 p.m., 2nd & 4th Thurs., except June, July, & Aug., First Free Methodist Church, Fellowship Hall
Contact Person: Mr. John J. Pfister, 1808 Manchester Rd., Erie, PA 16505-2632
Meeting City: Erie

Blue And Gray Stamp Club (APS# 1312-139409)
Meeting Time and Location: 7:30 p.m., 4th Wed., North Branch, ACNB, N. Gettysburg Plaza
Contact Person: Mr. Robert G. Zeigler, 175 Gordon Ave., Gettysburg, PA 17325
Meeting City: Gettysburg

Philadelphia Natl. Stamp Exhibition (APS# 0651-051056)
Meeting Time and Location: 7:30 p.m., 1st Mon., Fort Washington Expo Center, 1100 Virginia Dr.
Contact Person: Dr. Robert E. Lana, P. O. Box 43146, Philadelphia, PA 19129
Meeting City: Fort Washington

Capital City Philatelic Society (APS# 0321-029127)
Meeting Time and Location: 7:15 p.m., 1st & 3rd Tues., East Shore Area Library, 4501 Ethel St.
Contact Person: Mr. Roy E. Heller, P. O. Box 61162, Harrisburg, PA 17106
Meeting City: Harrisburg

Havertown Stamp Club (APS# 0463-039274)
Meeting Time and Location: 7:30 p.m., 1st & 3rd Wed., except July & Aug., Union Methodist Church, Brookline Blvd. & Allston Rd.
Contact Person: Dr. Stanley R. Sandler, 221 Hemlock Lane, Springfield, PA 19064-1112
Meeting City: Havertown
E-mail: stanshel@msn.com

Hazleton Stamp Club (APS# 1105-105295)
Meeting Time and Location: 7 p.m., 2nd & 4th Mon., former nurses dorm, across from Hazleton State Hosp.
Contact Person: Mr. David Fink, 10 Deer Run Rd., #2, West Hazleton, PA 18201

Meeting City: Hazleton

Westmoreland County Phil. Society (APS# 0649-051054)
Meeting Time and Location: 2:15 p.m., 2nd Sun., Calvary Baptist Church
Contact Person: Mr. James Vaughn, Rt. 5, Box 549, Mt. Pleasant, PA 15666
Meeting City: Irwin
E-mail: jvaughn@wpa.net
Website: www.wpa.net/~jvaughn/wcps/wcps.htm

Johnstown Stamp Club (APS# 0318-029033)
Meeting Time and Location: 7:30 p.m., 4th Mon., except Sept. & Dec., Seniors Activity Center, 550 Main St., 2nd fl/Conf. Rm.
Contact Person: Mr. Jay W. Hewitt, 443 Corning St., Johnstown, PA 15905-3109
Meeting City: Johnstown
E-mail: jhewitt@charter.net

Lancaster County Philatelic Society (APS# 0173-015492)
Meeting Time and Location: 7:30 p.m., 2nd Wed., except Aug., Lancaster Twp. Community Ctr., Lincoln Hwy. West, Maple Grove
Contact Person: Mr. James G. Boyles, P. O. Box 982, Lancaster, PA 17608-0982
Meeting City: Lancaster

Lebanon Stamp Collectors Club (APS# 0703-055182)
Meeting Time and Location: 7:30 p.m., 2nd Tues., Chamber of Commerce, 250 N. 8th St.
Contact Person: Mr. Richard A. Colberg, 126 Crosswick Lane, Lancaster, PA 17601-5338
Meeting City: Lebanon
E-mail: apraiseart@aol.com

Alle-Kiski Vly Numis/Phil Soc (APS# 1304-137366)
Meeting Time and Location: 8 p.m., 2nd Thurs., except July & Aug., Grace Community Church, 2751 Grant St.
Contact Person: Mr. Glenn E. Nordmark, 331 Claremont Dr., Lower Burrell, PA 15068
Meeting City: Lower Burrell

Butler County Philatelic Society (APS# 1135-111614)
Meeting Time and Location: 7 p.m., 1st & 3rd Wed., except June, July, & Aug., Dunbar Community Center, Hansen Ave. & Pillow St.
Contact Person: Mr. Stanley A. Snyder, 3836 Shepard Rd., Gibsonia, PA 15044
Meeting City: Lyndora

Susq. Valley Stamp/Postcard Club (APS# 1146-112554)
Meeting Time and Location: 7 p.m., 4th Mon., Temple Beth Shalom, 913 Allendale Rd.
Contact Person: Mr. Edward J. Lukanuski, 3809 Conestoga Rd., Camp Hill, PA 17011-1414
Meeting City: Mechanicsburg
E-mail: ejluk@ix.netcom.com

Juniata River Stamp Club (APS# 1495-184237)
Meeting Time and Location: 7:30 p.m., 2nd Thurs., Juniata County Library, Community Room
Contact Person: Mr. John J. Renz, R 1, Box 287, Mifflintown, PA 17059
Meeting City: Mifflintown
E-mail: rkepler@tricountyi.net

Williamsport Stamp Club (APS# 0299-027974)
Meeting Time and Location: 8 p.m., 4th Wed., except July & Aug., Montoursville American Legion, 1312 Broad St.
Contact Person: Mr. Myron H. Shirk, 305 S. Market St. Selinsgrove, PA 17870

Meeting City: Montoursville

Summerseat Stamp Collectors
(APS# 1358-148255)
Meeting Time and Location:
7 p.m., 4th Wed., except Aug.,
Morrisville United Meth. Ch., Ed.
Bldg., Taft & Maples Ave.
Contact Person: Mrs. Doris G.
Burkhardt, 216 Osborne Ave.,
Morrisville, PA 19067-1132
Meeting City: Morrisville
E-mail: fredanddoris@erols.com

Pennswood Village Stamp
Association (APS# 1524-192540)
Meeting Time and Location:
7 p.m., Pennswood Village, 1382
Newtown-Langhorne Rd.
Contact Person: Mr. Heinz J.
Heinemann, Pennswood Village
G103 1382 Newtown-Langhorne
Rd., Newtown, PA 18940-2401
Meeting City: Newtown

Frankford Arsenal Stamp Club
(APS# 0242-024403)
Meeting Time and Location:
Members' homes
Contact Person: Mr. Michael A.
Stefanowicz, 7610 Lexington Ave.,
Philadelphia, PA 19152-3912
Meeting City: Philadelphia

Greater Northeast Stamp Club
(APS# 1368-149723)
Meeting Time and Location:
8 p.m., 3rd Thurs., Rhawnhurt
Recreation Center, Bustleton &
Solly Ave.
Contact Person: Mr. Samuel B.
Rothkoff, 3177 Kensington Ave.,
Philadelphia, PA 19134
Meeting City: Philadelphia

Phoenixville/King Prussia Stamp
Club (APS# 1487-180765)
Meeting Time and Location: 1st
Weds., except July & Aug., Phoe-
nixville Area YMCA, Pothouse Rd.
Contact Person: Mr. Gus Spector,

750 S. Main St., Suite 203,
Phoenixville, PA 19460
Meeting City: Phoenixville

Philatelic Society of Pittsburgh
(APS# 0005-000457)
Meeting Time and Location: 7:30
p.m., 1st & 3rd Mon., First Lutheran
Church, 615 Grant St.
Contact Person: Mr. Ronald G.
Carr, 60 Robinhood Dr., Pittsburgh,
PA 15220-3014
Meeting City: Pittsburgh
E-mail: rgc211215@aol.com

Pottstown Area Stamp Club (APS#
1169-116380)
Meeting Time and Location:
7 p.m., 1st Mon., Leader Nursing &
Rehab. Ctr., basement
Contact Person: Mrs. Barbara M.
Brown, 2020 Harmonyville Rd.,
Pottstown, PA 19465
Meeting City: Pottstown

North Penn Stamp Club (APS#
1206-122461)
Meeting Time and Location:
7 p.m., 1st Tues., James A. Michn-
er Library, California Rd.
Contact Person: Mr. Wolfgang S.
Pohl, 916 W. Broad St.,
Quakertown, PA 18951
Meeting City: Quakertown

Reading Stamp Collectors Club
(APS# 0192-016695)
Meeting Time and Location: 7:30
p.m., 2nd Tues., (Mar., June,
Sept., & Dec. -2nd Mon.) GPU
Service Corp. Bldg., Bernville Road
(Rt. 183)
Contact Person: Mr. Walter M.
Creitz, 830 Berkshire Dr., Reading,
PA 19601
Meeting City: Reading
E-mail: wcreitz@aol.com

Northeastern PA Philatelic Society
(APS# 0360-031880)
Meeting Time and Location:

7 p.m., 1st & 3rd Wed., except July
& Aug., Covenant Presbyterian
Church, Madison & Olive St.
Contact Person: Mr. E. V.
Chadwick, 124 E. Center St.,
Shavertown, PA 18708-1511
Meeting City: Scranton
E-mail: evchad@juno.com
Website: scrantonstampclub.
tripod.com

Spring-Ford Philatelic Society
(APS# 0802-065722)
Meeting Time and Location:
7 p.m., last Thurs., 1st United
Church of Christ, 145 Chestnut St.
Contact Person: Mr. Richard E.
Dehner, 23320 Heather Lane,
Gilbertsville, PA 19525
Meeting City: Spring City
E-mail: dickroslie@aol.com

Mt. Nittany Philatelic Society
(APS# 0199-018536)
Meeting Time and Location: 7:30
p.m., 1st Wed. & 3rd Thurs.,
American Philatelic Building, 100
Oakwood Ave.
Contact Person: Mr. Timothy E.
Kohler, P. O. Box 902, State
College, PA 16804
Meeting City: State College
E-mail: tek5@psu.edu
Website:
richardchunko.tripod.com/mtnit-
tanyphilatelicsociety/

Bux-Mont Stamp Club (APS#
0679-053999)
Meeting Time and Location:
8 p.m., 2nd & 4th Tues., except
Dec., Wilson Senior Citizen Center,
Delmont Ave.
Contact Person: Mr. Michael F.
Matusko, P. O. Box 448, Abington,
PA 19001
Meeting City: Warminster

Germantown-Chestnut Hill Stamp
Club (APS# 0612-048409)
Meeting Time and Location:

8 p.m., 1st Tues. & 3rd Wed.,
Springfield Retirement Home
Contact Person: Mr. Harvey M.
Fleegler, P. O. Box 128, Flourtown,
PA 19031
Meeting City: Wyndmoor

White Rose Phil. Soc. of York, PA
(APS# 0550-044283)
Meeting Time and Location: 7:30
p.m., 1st & 3rd Wed., Aldersgate
Meth. Church, 397 Tyler Run Rd.
Contact Person: Mr. Jerry A. Kotek,
424 Corbin Rd., York, PA 17403
Meeting City: York

RHODE ISLAND

Rhode Island Philatelic Society
(APS# 0370-032462)
Meeting Time and Location:
8 p.m., 1st & 3rd Tues., Meshanti-
cut Pk. Baptist Church, 180 Oak
Lawn Ave.
Contact Person: Mr. Thomas E.
Greene, P. O. Box 40665,
Providence, RI 02940
Meeting City: Cranston
E-mail: Shawn_A_Pease@waters.
com
Website: www.geocities.com/Heart
land/Ranch/7533/

Newport Philatelic Society (APS#
0999-092951)
Meeting Time and Location: 7:30
p.m., 3rd Thurs., 10 Casey Dr.
Contact Person: Mr. Morrie P.
Seiple, 35 Linden St., Middletown,
RI 02842-4924
Meeting City: Middletown

North Kingstown Senior Stamp
Club (APS# 1504-187991)
Meeting Time and Location:
10 a.m., 2nd & 4th Thurs., Wick-
ford Senior Center
Contact Person: Mr. Robert
Benjamin, P. O. Box 160,
Narragansett, RI 02882
Meeting City: North Kingstown

E-mail: ubrocker@aol.com

SOUTH CAROLINA

Columbia Philatelic Society (APS# 0519-043067)
Meeting Time and Location: 7:30 p.m., 2nd Tues. & 4th Thurs., except Nov./Dec., State-Record Newspaper Bldg., Shop Rd.
Contact Person: Mr. Henry B. Kemp, Jr., 2301 Wake Forest Dr., Columbia, SC 29206-1441
Meeting City: Columbia

Greenville Stamp Club (APS# 0890-076251)
Meeting Time and Location: 7 p.m., 3rd Thurs., Sears Shelter, 100 E. Park Ave.
Contact Person: Susan Reshni Whitehead, P. O. Box 2212, Greenville, SC 29602-2212
Meeting City: Greenville
E-mail: stampahlic@aol.com

Hilton Head Island Philatelic Society (APS# 1441-167739)
Meeting Time and Location: 4 p.m., 1st Tues., Palmetto Electric, 111 Mathews Dr.
Contact Person: Mr. Walter Weller, Jr., 14 Pheasant Run, Hilton Head Island, SC 29926
Meeting City: Hilton Head Island
E-mail: whamby1782@aol.com

Myrtle Beach Stamp Club (APS# 1455-172827)
Meeting Time and Location: 7 p.m., 1st Tues., Grand Strand Sr. Center, 1268 21st Ave., N.
Contact Person: Mr. Donn Ebert, 117 Cedar Ridge Lane, Conway, SC 29526
Meeting City: Myrtle Beach
E-mail: lilfort@sccoast.net

SOUTH DAKOTA

Ringneck Stamp Club (APS# 0843-069739)
Meeting Time and Location: 7:30 p.m., 3rd Mon., Aberdeen Area Sr. Center, 1303 7th Ave. S.E.
Contact Person: Ms. Elaine Roth, 118 Elizabeth Dr., Aberdeen, SD 57401
Meeting City: Aberdeen

Sioux Falls Stamp Club (APS# 1212-122932)
Meeting Time and Location: 7 p.m., 1st & 3rd Thurs., McKennan Hospital
Contact Person: Mr. Robert C. Schmidt, 1609 E. 32nd, Sioux Falls, SD 57105
Meeting City: Sioux Falls

TENNESSEE

Brentwood Philatelic Society (APS# 1349-146598)
Meeting Time and Location: 6:30 p.m., 3rd Tues., Brentwood Library, 8109 Concord Rd.
Contact Person: Mr. Donald L. Kotval, P. O. Box 1915, Columbia, TN 38402
Meeting City: Brentwood

Chattanooga Stamp Club (APS# 0731-057915)
Meeting Time and Location: 7:30 p.m., 2nd Thur., except Aug. & Dec., USPS General Mail Facility, Shallowford Rd.
Contact Person: Mr. Ernest F. Seagle, P. O. Box 22022, Chattanooga, TN 37422
Meeting City: Chattanooga
E-mail: mjefseagle@aol.com

Clarksville Stamp Club (APS# 1481-179440)
Meeting Time and Location: 5:30 p.m., alternate Sat., Clarksville Montgomery County Libr. or Gateway Medical Center
Contact Person: Mr. Ladislaus Szilagyi, P. O. Box 251, Clarksville, TN 37041
Meeting City: Clarksville

E-mail: heike@midsouth.net

Sumner County Stamp Club (APS# 1473-175205)
Meeting Time and Location: 6:30 p.m., 3rd Thurs., Hendersonville Public Library, 116 Dunn St.
Contact Person: Mr. Forrest Wise, 104 Greenyards Pl., Hendersonville, TN 37075
Meeting City: Hendersonville
E-mail: mpatrick@mindspring.com

Holston Stamp Club (APS# 0662-051910)
Meeting Time and Location: 7 p.m., 3rd Thurs., Asbury Center, 400 N. Boone St.
Contact Person: Mr. John L. Sanks, 3832 Skyland Dr., Kingsport, TN 37664
Meeting City: Johnson City

Knoxville Philatelic Society (APS# 1189-119261)
Meeting Time and Location: 7 p.m., 1st & 5th Tues., Calvary Baptist Church, 3200 Kingston Pike
Contact Person: Mr. Thomas W. Broadhead, P. O. Box 50422, Knoxville, TN 37950-0422
Meeting City: Knoxville

Memphis Stamp Collectors Society (APS# 0542-044035)
Meeting Time and Location: 7 p.m., 1st & 3rd Thurs., Raleigh Library, 3157 Powers Rd.
Contact Person: Mr. Calvin H. Allen, Jr., 4904 Greenway Ave., Memphis, TN 38117
Meeting City: Memphis
E-mail: challen@memphis.edu

Nashville Philatelic Society (APS# 0431-037461)
Meeting Time and Location: 6:45 p.m., 2nd & 4th Mon., Inglewood Branch Library, 4312 Gallatin Rd.
Contact Person: Mr. Thomas A.

Tribke, 2911 Wingate Ave., Nashville, TN 37211-2523
Meeting City: Nashville
E-mail: ttribke@bellsouth.net

TEXAS

Texas Philatelic Association (APS# 0632-049588)
Meeting Time and Location: Meets annually in Dallas,
Contact Person: Mrs. Jane K. Fohn, 10325 Little Sugar Creek, Converse, TX 78109-2409
Meeting City: Dallas
E-mail: jkfohn1442@aol.com
Website: www.flash.net/~jstamp/

Mid-Cities Stamp Club (APS# 0891-076252)
Meeting Time and Location: 7:30 p.m., 1st & 3rd Wed., 1st-Arlington Community Ctr., 3rd-Irving Ctr. for the Arts
Contact Person: Mr. Steve Magyar, P. O. Box 2158, Arlington, TX 76004
Meeting City: Arlington/Irving
E-mail: bbrads1947@cs.com
Website: www.mid-citiesstamp-club.com/home.htm

Austin Texas Stamp Club (APS# 0462-039231)
Meeting Time and Location: 7:30 p.m., 1st & 3rd Tues., 1st-Howson Br. Library, 3rd-South Austin Sr. Act. Ctr.
Contact Person: COL John G. Karabaic, 9409 Queenswood Dr., Austin, TX 78748
Meeting City: Austin
E-mail: k409queens@aol.com
Website: www.main.org/atsc/

Borger Stamp Club (APS# 1391-155239)
Meeting Time and Location: 7 p.m., 1st Tues., Hutchinson Co. Library, Club Room, 625 Weatherly
Contact Person: Mrs. Ann

Whitesides, 311 Dallas St., Borger, TX 79007-6415
Meeting City: Borger

Texas A&M University Stamp Club (APS# 1096-104283)
Meeting Time and Location: Texas A&M University
Contact Person: Mr. George B. Dresser, 501 Fairview Ave., College Station, TX 77840
Meeting City: College Station
E-mail: g-dresser@tamu.edu

Sea Gull Stamp Club (APS# 0371-032523)
Meeting Time and Location: 7 p.m., 2nd & 4th Wed., Main Library, 805 Comanche
Contact Person: Mr. Stephen R. Powell, P. O. Box 30574, Corpus Christi, TX 78463-0574
Meeting City: Corpus Christi
E-mail: bstever@camdeninc.com

Collectors Club of Dallas (APS# 0909-079745)
Meeting Time and Location: 6:30 p.m., last Wed., members' homes
Contact Person: Mr. Robert I. Benner, 2206 Sutton Pl., Richardson, TX 75080-2543
Meeting City: Dallas
E-mail: rbenner@prodigy.net

Dallas/Park Cities Phil. Soc. (APS# 0835-068806)
Meeting Time and Location: 7:30 p.m., 2nd & 4th Mon., 2nd Mon.-Walnut Hill Rec. Ctr., 4th Mon.-Half-Price Bookstore
Contact Person: Mr. Ronald Sala, 1212 W. Commerce St., Dallas, TX 75208-1616
Meeting City: Dallas
E-mail: salaair@prodigy.net

Denton Stamp Club (APS# 1444-168809)
Meeting Time and Location:
7 p.m., 1st Mon., Senior Citizen Center, 509 N. Bell Ave.
Contact Person: Mr. Jack Baker, 1208 Clover Lane, Denton, TX 76209-1108
Meeting City: Denton

El Paso Philatelic Society (APS# 0301-028021)
Meeting Time and Location: 7:30 p.m., 2nd Tues., Quality Inn, I-10 at Geronimo
Contact Person: Ms. Amy E. Wieting, 2990 Trawood, #11F, El Paso, TX 79936
Meeting City: El Paso
E-mail: awieting@compuserve.com

Panther City Philatelic Society (APS# 0132-013590)
Meeting Time and Location: 7:30 p.m., 2nd Wed., University Christian Church, University & Cantey, Rm. 308
Contact Person: Mr. Herman K. Dallof, 820 Rockledge Dr., Saginaw, TX 76179
Meeting City: Fort Worth
E-mail: dallofs@integrity.com

Twin Lakes Coin & Stamp Club (APS# 1421-162110)
Meeting Time and Location: 7:30 p.m., last Tues., Harker Heights Public Library, 100 E. Beeline
Contact Person: Mr. Bob Pierce, 906 Nola Ruth Blvd., Harker Heights, TX 76548
Meeting City: Harker Heights

Houston Philatelic Society (APS# 0347-030827)
Meeting Time and Location: 7:30 p.m., 1st & 3rd Mon., Central Presbyterian Church, 3788 Richmond Ave.
Contact Person: Mr. Larry F. Ballantyne, P. O. Box 690042, Houston, TX 77269-0042
Meeting City: Houston
E-mail: jctopper@swbell.net

Website: www.houstonphilatelic. org/

Johnson Space Center Stamp Club (APS# 0809-066371)
Meeting Time and Location: 7 p.m., 2nd & 4th Mon., Gilruth Recreation Ctr., JSC, Nasa Rd. 1
Contact Person: Mr. Stan Schmidt, 2105 Butler Dr., Friendswood, TX 77546
Meeting City: Houston
E-mail: stampmn@swbell.net
Website: www0.delphi.com/ stamps/apschapspace.html

Kingwood Stamp Club (APS# 1397-155845)
Meeting Time and Location: 7 p.m., 2nd & 4th Tues., Columbia Kingwood Med. Ctr., 22999 Hwy. 59
Contact Person: Mrs. Myra B. McCain, 2222 Rolling Meadows Dr., Kingwood, TX 77339
Meeting City: Kingwood

Longview Stamp Club (APS# 1237-125515)
Meeting Time and Location: 7:30 p.m., 1st Tues., Trinity Episcopal Church, 906 Padon St.
Contact Person: Mr. Larry Anderson, 1305 Hyacinth Dr., Longview, TX 75601-4144
Meeting City: Longview

South Plains Stamp Club (APS# 0771-061736)
Meeting Time and Location: 7:30 p.m., 1st & 3rd Mon., Lubbock Garden & Arts Center, 4215 University
Contact Person: Mr. J. Keith Young, P. O. Box 68154, Lubbock, TX 79414-8154
Meeting City: Lubbock

Permian Basin Stamp Club (APS# 1330-143239)
Meeting Time and Location: 7:30 p.m., 2nd Tues. & 4th Thurs.,
Midland Airport, General Mail Facility
Contact Person: Mr. Mike Cherrington, P. O. Box 60141, Midland, TX 79711-0141
Meeting City: Midland
E-mail: Lgod1127@aol.com
Website: permianbasinstampclub. homestead.com/Homepage.html

South East Texas Stamp Club (APS# 1501-186356)
Meeting Time and Location: 7 p.m., 3rd Tues., 2748 Viterbo Rd.
Contact Person: Mr. Otis Barnes, 6633 Washington St., Groves, TX 77619
Meeting City: Nederland
E-mail: bwindle@prodigy.net

Paris Stamp Club (APS# 1514-189360)
Meeting Time and Location: 7 p.m., 3rd Mon., Calvary United Methodist Church, 3105 Lamar Ave.
Contact Person: Mr. E. J. Guerrant, Jr., P. O. Box 181, Paris, TX 75460
Meeting City: Paris
E-mail: ejguerrant@prodigy.net

Concho Valley Stamp Club (APS# 1457-173093)
Meeting Time and Location: 7 p.m., 4th Thurs., Norwest Bank
Contact Person: Mr. Gene Hirschfelt, 5229 Beverly Dr., San Angelo, TX 76904-8740
Meeting City: San Angelo
E-mail: hirsch@wcc.net

San Antonio Philatelic Association (APS# 0388-034143)
Meeting Time and Location: 7:30 p.m., Fri., St. Luke's Lutheran Church, 514 Santa Monica
Contact Person: Mr. Manfred Groth, 531 Santa Helena, San Antonio, TX 78232-2787
Meeting City: San Antonio

E-mail: ltc519@aol.com
Website: www.virtualstampclub.
com/aps texas.html

Victoria Stamp Club (APS# 1490-181644)
Meeting Time and Location:
7 p.m., 1st Mon., 1st National
Bank, Town & Country Room
Contact Person: Mr. Gerald
FitzSimmons, 105 Calle Ricardo,
Victoria, TX 77904
Meeting City: Victoria

Heart of Texas Stamp Club (APS# 1062-099577)
Meeting Time and Location:
7 p.m., 1st Thurs., Wiethorn
Visitors Center, University Parks
Dr.
Contact Person: Mr. James B.
Berryhill, Jr., 1700 Plum Circle,
Waco, TX 76706
Meeting City: Waco

Texoma Stamp Club (APS# 1406-158932)
Meeting Time and Location:
7 p.m., 2nd Thurs. & 4th Tues.,
US Post Office, Rm. 312,
1000 Lamar St.
Contact Person: Mr. Raymond E.
Whyborn, 411 Reiman, Seymour,
TX 76380-2439
Meeting City: Wichita Falls
E-mail: rewmjw@worldnet.att.net

UTAH

Utah Philatelic Society (APS# 0352-031236)
Meeting Time and Location:
7 p.m., 1st & 3rd Thurs., 1st Mon.-
Sr. Citizen Rec. Ctr., SLC,
3rd Thurs.-Sandy Sr. Ctr., Sandy,
UT
Contact Person: Mr. Michael A.
Keene, P. O. Box 27742, Salt Lake
City, UT 84127-0742
Meeting City: Salt Lake City
E-mail: mjpenn@aol.com

VERMONT

Green Mountain Stamp Society
(APS# 1375-150943)
Meeting Time and Location: 7:30
p.m., 2nd & 4th Wed., Crescent
Manor Nursing Home, Crescent
Blvd.
Contact Person: Mr. Stuart Libby,
P. O. Box 571, Bennington, VT
05201
Meeting City: Bennington

Brattleboro Stamp Club (APS# 1123-108145)
Meeting Time and Location:
7 p.m., 3rd Mon., Brooks Memorial
Library, Meeting Room, Main St.
Contact Person: Mrs. Janet C.
O'Keefe, 452 Williams St., Brattle-
boro, VT 05301
Meeting City: Brattleboro
E-mail: janet.okeefe@uvm.edu

Washington County Stamp Club
(APS# 0722-056952)
Meeting Time and Location: 7:30
p.m., 3rd Tues., except July &
Aug., 1st Baptist Church School &
St. Paul St.
Contact Person: Mr. William
Lizotte, 98 Brooklyn Heights, Apt.
5, Morrisville, VT 05661-6015
Meeting City: Montpelier

Connecticut Valley Stamp
Collectors (APS# 1519-190728)
Meeting Time and Location:
7 p.m., 2nd Mon., Norwich Public
Library, Main St.
Contact Person: Mr. Peter Jordan,
P. O. Box 10, Washington, VT
05675
Meeting City: Norwich

Rutland County Stamp Club (APS# 0314-028954)
Meeting Time and Location:
7 p.m., every other Thur., except
June, July, & Aug., Pleasant
Manor, 46 Nichols St.
Contact Person: Mr. James P.

Mongeon, P. O. Box 6897, Rutland, VT 05702-6897
Meeting City: Rutland

Chittenden County Stamp Club (APS# 0915-080085)
Meeting Time and Location: 7 p.m., 2nd Mon., Bell Atlantic Bldg., 800 Hinesburg Rd.
Contact Person: Dr. Paul G. Abajian, P. O. Box 475, Essex Junction, VT 05453
Meeting City: South Burlington
E-mail: pga@surfglobal.net

Woodstock Stamp Club (APS# 1494-183679)
Meeting Time and Location: 7 p.m., 3rd Mon., St. James Episcopal Church, On The Green
Contact Person: Mr. John Lutz, 1523 Maple St., Hartford, VT 05047
Meeting City: Woodstock
E-mail: john@vtstamp.com
Website: www.vtstamp.com

VIRGINIA

Virginia Philatelic Federation (APS# 1107-105297)
Meeting Time and Location: Meets quarterly, various locations
Contact Person: Mrs. Joan R. Bleakley, 15906 Crest Dr., Woodbridge, VA 22191-4211
Meeting City: Various
E-mail: jrbleakley@erols.com

Robert C. Graebner Chapter 17 AFDCS (APS# 1523-192390)
Meeting Time and Location: 10 a.m., 2nd Sat., Central United Methodist Church, 4301 N. Fairfax
Contact Person: Mr. Foster E. Miller, III, P. O. Box 44, Annapolis Junction, MD 20701-0044
Meeting City: Arlington
E-mail: fmiller@pobox.com

Charlottesville Stamp Club (APS# 0416-036394)
Meeting Time and Location: 8 p.m., 3rd Mon., Heritage Hall, 505 W. Rio Rd.
Contact Person: Mr. George T. Waaser, Jr., 3835 Graemont Dr., Earlysville, VA 22936
Meeting City: Charlottesville
E-mail: gtwaaser@cstone.net
Website: www0.delphi.com/stamps/apscville.html

Dan River Philatelic Society (APS# 0830-067628)
Meeting Time and Location: 7:30 p.m., 2nd Mon., except Dec., Danville Public Library
Contact Person: Mr. William H. Bogart, Jr., 318 Pendleton Rd., Danville, VA 24541-3339
Meeting City: Danville

Peninsula Stamp Club (APS# 0224-021542)
Meeting Time and Location: 7:15 p.m., 2nd & 4th Wed., phone for information, (757-851-8712)
Contact Person: MAJ N. F. Bretschneider, 4 Riding Path, Hampton, VA 23669
Meeting City: Hampton

Tidewater Stamp Club (APS# 0633-049590)
Meeting Time and Location: 7:30 p.m., 1st & 3rd Wed., Central United Methodist Church, 225 Chapel St.
Contact Person: J. M. Melson, P. O. Box 633, Hampton, VA 23669-0633
Meeting City: Hampton

Lynchburg Stamp Club (APS# 1356-148253)
Meeting Time and Location: 7 p.m., 2nd Tues., except July, US Post Office, 3300 Odd Fellows Rd.
Contact Person: Ms. Vicky M.

Fenimore, 336 Stratford Rd., Concord, VA 24538-3092
Meeting City: Lynchburg
Website: www.hillcity-mall.com/lsc/

Dolley Madison Stamp Club (APS# 0831-067629)
Meeting Time and Location: 7:30 p.m., 1st & 3rd Fri., McLean Governmental Center, 1437 Balls Hill Rd.
Contact Person: Mr. John M. Hotchner, P. O. Box 1125, Falls Church, VA 22041
Meeting City: McLean
E-mail: jmhstamp@ix.netcom.com

Norfolk Philatelic Society (APS# 0345-030753)
Meeting Time and Location: 8 p.m., 1st & 3rd Tues., Life Savings Bank, 7420 Granby St.
Contact Person: Mr. Leroy P. Collins, III, P. O. Box 2183, Norfolk, VA 23501
Meeting City: Norfolk

Potomac Philatelic Society (APS# 1156-114548)
Meeting Time and Location: 8 p.m., 2nd Tues., members' homes
Contact Person: Mr. Robert Stuart Dyer, 6102 Bayliss Pl., Alexandria, VA 22310
Meeting City: Potomac

Richmond Stamp Club (APS# 0218-020653)
Meeting Time and Location: 7:30 p.m., 2nd & 4th Tues., Virginia War Memorial Auditorium, 621 S. Belvedere St.
Contact Person: Mr. George Rosenson, 7400 Cotfield Rd., Richmond, VA 23237
Meeting City: Richmond

Big Lick Stamp Club (APS# 1025-095312)
Meeting Time and Location: 2:30 p.m., 2nd Sun., St. Mark's Lutheran Church, 1008 Franklin Rd.
Contact Person: Mr. Benjamin F. Bennett, 2208 S. Jefferson St., Unit 106, Roanoke, VA 24014
Meeting City: Roanoke
Website: delphia.com/stamps/aps-biglick.html

Springfield Stamp Club (APS# 0993-091762)
Meeting Time and Location: 7:30 p.m., every Wed., Lynbrook Elementary School, 5801 Backlick Rd.
Contact Person: COL Joseph F. Schoen, Jr., P. O. Box 544, Springfield, VA 22150
Meeting City: Springfield

Ayrhill Stamp Club (APS# 0973-088232)
Meeting Time and Location: 7 p.m., 1st & 3rd Thurs., Patrick Henry Library, Maple Ave. & Center St.
Contact Person: Mr. Miles B. Manchester, P. O. Box 162, Vienna, VA 22183
Meeting City: Vienna
E-mail: Richard536@yahoo.com
Website: www.angelfire.com/va2/ayrhill

Tidewater Intl. Topics Society (APS# 1258-128392)
Meeting Time and Location: Irregular, contact society president
Contact Person: Mr. Allen D. Jones, 5113 Greenbrook Dr., Portsmouth, VA 23703
Meeting City: Virginia Beach

Virginia Beach Stamp Club (APS# 0984-090593)
Meeting Time and Location: 7:30 p.m., 2nd & 4th Tues., St. Gregory's School Library, 5345 Virginia Beach Blvd.
Contact Person: Rudolph J. Roy,

Jr., P. O. Box 5367, Virginia Beach, VA 23471-0367
Meeting City: Virginia Beach
E-mail: kcos32@home.com
Website: www.delphi.com/stamps/apschapvbsc.html

Virginia Philatelic Friends (APS# 1458-173371)
Meeting Time and Location: Varies, various locations
Contact Person: Rudolph J. Roy, Jr., P. O. Box 5367, Virginia Beach, VA 23471-0367
Meeting City: Virginia Beach
E-mail: rroyperfin@aol.com

Warrenton Stamp & Coin Club (APS# 1492-182214)
Meeting Time and Location: 7 p.m., 2nd Wed., Warrenton Professional Center, 493 Blackwell Rd.
Contact Person: Mr. Gerald Hoffman, 7290 Hunton St., Warrenton, VA 20187
Meeting City: Warrenton
E-mail: tripi@monumental.com
Website: www0.delphi.com/stamps/apswarrenton.html

Williamsburg Stamp Society (APS# 0610-048228)
Meeting Time and Location: 7 p.m., 3rd Thurs., Ukrop's Monticello Market Place, Community Room
Contact Person: Mr. Carl G. Finstrom, 107 Winter, E., Williamsburg, VA 23188-1655
Meeting City: Williamsburg

Shenandoah Valley Stamp Club (APS# 0748-059428)
Meeting Time and Location: 7:30 p.m., 4th Fri., except Dec., Westminster-Canterbury Comm. Center, Wineberry Dr.
Contact Person: Mr. Willis C. Royall, Jr., 1843 Tilghman Lane, Winchester, VA 22601
Meeting City: Winchester

Eastern Prince William Stamp Club (APS# 0982-090014)
Meeting Time and Location: 7:30 p.m., 1st & 3rd Mon., Potomac Library, Opitz Blvd.
Contact Person: Mrs. Joan R. Bleakley, 15906 Crest Dr., Woodbridge, VA 22191-4211
Meeting City: Woodbridge
E-mail: jrbleakley@erols.com

WASHINGTON

Greater Eastside Stamp Society (APS# 1194-120323)
Meeting Time and Location: 7 p.m., 1st & 3rd Thurs., Knights of Columbus Hall, 14821 S.E. 16th St.
Contact Person: Mr. Eric J. Baker, P. O. Box 7242, Bellevue, WA 98008-1242
Meeting City: Bellevue

Bellingham Stamp Club (APS# 1454-172826)
Meeting Time and Location: 7:30 p.m., 3rd Wed., Bellingham Public Library, 210 Central St.
Contact Person: Mr. Bill Taylor, P. O. Box 6083 Bellingham, WA 98227
Meeting City: Bellingham

Walla Walla Valley Phil. Society (APS# 1097-104284)
Meeting Time and Location: 7 p.m., 2nd Thurs., Walla Walla College, Kretshmar Hall, Room 305
Contact Person: Mr. Larry E. Veverka, 935 University St., Walla Walla, WA 99362-2342
Meeting City: College Place
E-mail: vevela@wwc.edu

Sno King Stamp Club (APS# 0642-050727)
Meeting Time and Location: 7:30 p.m., 2nd & 3rd Wed., 2nd-2320 Calif. St.-Everett, 3rd-220 Railroad Ave.-Edmonds
Contact Person: Mr. Steve

LaVergne, 12726 Palatine Ave., N., Seattle, WA 98133
Meeting City: Everett/Edmonds
E-mail: edkeca@gr.cc.wa.us

Boeing Employees Stamp Club (APS# 0870-072809)
Meeting Time and Location:
6 p.m., 2nd Wed., Boeing Rec. Act. Ctr., Rm A/B, 22649 83rd Ave., S.
Contact Person: Mr. Bruce E. Landry, 12212 Marine View Dr., S.W., Seattle, WA 98146
Meeting City: Kent
E-mail: belandry@earthlink.net

Whidbey Island Stamp Club (APS# 1262-129171)
Meeting Time and Location: 7:30 p.m., 1st & 3rd Tues., Oak Manor Rec. Hall, 640 S.E. 8th Ave.
Contact Person: Mr. Lee R. Dougherty, 563 S. E. 4th Ave., Oak Harbor, WA 98277-3710
Meeting City: Oak Harbor
E-mail: beaglel@whidbey.net

Olympia Philatelic Society (APS# 0895-076750)
Meeting Time and Location:
7:30 p.m., 2nd & 4th Mon., Olympics West Retirement Inn, 929 Trosper Road S.W., Tumwater
Contact Person: Mr. Albert Thirkill, 3482-41 Hwy. 508, Onalaska, WA 98570
Meeting City: Olympia

Palouse Empire Stamp Club (APS# 1394-155610)
Meeting Time and Location:
7 p.m., 2nd Wed., Statesman Recreation Room
Contact Person: Mr. Peter B. Larson, 5301 Robinson Park Rd., Moscow, ID 83843
Meeting City: Pullman
E-mail: plarson@wsu.edu

Tri-City Stamp Club (APS# 0715-056275)

Meeting Time and Location:
7 p.m., 4th Wed., Kramer Senior Center
Contact Person: Mr. Richard A. Evans, 1919 Fairway Dr., Richland, WA 99352
Meeting City: Richland

Collectors Club of Seattle (APS# 0356-031488)
Meeting Time and Location:
11 a.m.-2 p.m., Tues., 7 p.m., Fri., University Christian Church, 4731 15th Ave., N.E.
Contact Person: Mr. James T. Hall, P. O. Box 15205, Seattle, WA 98115
Meeting City: Seattle

Washington State Philatelic Society (APS# 0122-013112)
Meeting Time and Location:
7 p.m., 2nd & 4th Thurs., Gethsemane Lutheran Church Conference Rm., 911 Stewart St.
Contact Person: Mr. Thomas E. Ward, 12250 8th Ave., N.W., Seattle, WA 98177
Meeting City: Seattle
E-mail: wsps@scn.org
Website: www.scn.org/rec/wsps

Strait Stamp Society (APS# 1453-172491)
Meeting Time and Location:
6 p.m., 1st Thurs., Sequim Library, 800 N. Sequim Ave.
Contact Person: Mrs. Cathleen F. Osborne, P. O. Box 1781, Sequim, WA 98382
Meeting City: Sequim

Olympic Philatelic Society (APS# 0985-090594)
Meeting Time and Location:
7 p.m., 2nd & 4th Tues., Silverdale Community Center
Contact Person: Mr. James N. Boyden, P. O. Box 733, Silverdale, WA 98383-0733
Meeting City: Silverdale

E-mail: enzo7@ix.netcom.com
Website: www.delphi.com/
stamps/apschapolympic.html

Inland Empire Philatelic Society
(APS# 0343-030681)
Meeting Time and Location:
7 p.m., 2nd & 4th Tues., Riverview
Terrace, 1801 Up River Dr.
Contact Person: Mr. Charles J.
Rosenstock, E. 11609 12th Ave.,
Spokane, WA 99206
Meeting City: Spokane
E-mail: perfs1@aol.com
Website: home.att.net/~ieps1/
ieps1.html

Tacoma Stamp Club (APS# 0511-
042526)
Meeting Time and Location: 7:30
p.m., 2nd Tues., St. Luke's
Episcopal Church, 3615 N. Gove
St.
Contact Person: Mr. James M.
Coker, P. O. Box 111506, Tacoma,
WA 98411-1506
Meeting City: Tacoma
E-mail: cokej42@gateway.com

Northwest Federation of Stamp
Clubs (APS# 1469-174562)
Meeting Time and Location:
Annual meeting: PIPEX, various
locations, contact APS repr. for
details
Contact Person: Mr. William R.
Geijsbeek, 6616 140th Pl., N.E.,
Redmond, WA 98052-4649
Meeting City: Various cities in
Pacific NW
E-mail: geijsbeek@attglobal.net

Yakima Valley Stamp Club (APS#
0234-023919)
Meeting Time and Location:
7 p.m., 1st Tues., except July &
Aug., 3030 W. Nob Hill-Bank
Contact Person: Mr. Glenn F.
Thiesfeld, 1214 S. 44th Ave.,
Yakima, WA 98908
Meeting City: Yakima

WEST VIRGINIA

Harrison County Stamp Club
(APS# 1244-127078)
Meeting Time and Location: 7:30
p.m., 3rd Mon., Harrison Co.
Senior Center
Contact Person: Mr. Michael
Ravis, P. O. Box 68, Philippi, WV
26416
Meeting City: Clarksburg

Morgantown Area Stamp Club
(APS# 1402-157239)
Meeting Time and Location:
7 p.m., 2nd Thurs., Mileground
Medical Center, 1526 Mileground
Contact Person: Mr. Norval L.
Rasmussen, 1526 Mileground,
Morgantown, WV 26505
Meeting City: Morgantown

Blennerhasset Stamp Society
(APS# 0846-070416)
Meeting Time and Location:
7 p.m., 1st Tues. & 3rd Thurs.,
Trinity Episcopal Church, Trinity
Hall, 430 Juliana St.
Contact Person: Mr. Ronald L.
Jalbert, 61 Canterbury Dr., Park-
ersburg, WV, 26101-8051
Meeting City: Parkersburg
E-mail: rjalber@attglobal.net

WISCONSIN

Wisconsin Federation of Stamp
Clubs (APS# 0350-031025)
Meeting Time and Location:
Annually, various cities
Contact Person: Mrs. Karen L.
Weigt, 4184 Rose Ct., Middleton,
WI 53562
Meeting City: Various
E-mail: karenweigt@cs.com
Website: www0.delphi.com/
stamps/apschapwisconsin.html

Outagamie Philatelic Society
(APS# 0720-056950)
Meeting Time and Location:
7 p.m., 3rd Thurs., except June,

July, & Aug., Thompson Communi-
ty Center, 820 W. College Ave.
Contact Person: Ms. Verna D.
Shackleton, P. O. Box 11, Appleton,
WI 54912-0011
Meeting City: Appleton
E-mail: corosec@powernet
online.com

Baraboo Area Stamp Club (APS#
1316-140419)
Meeting Time and Location:
7 p.m., last Thurs., Univ. of
Wisconsin, Baraboo, Cafeteria,
1006 Connie Dr.
Contact Person: Mr. Robert Jobe,
2125 Surrey Lane, Baraboo, WI
53913
Meeting City: Baraboo

Fond Du Lac Stamp Club (APS#
1331-143810)
Meeting Time and Location:
7 p.m., 1st Tues. & 3rd Thurs.,
Fond du Lac Senior Center,
151 E. 1st
Contact Person: Mr. Fred L.
Ericksen, P. O. Box 821,
Fond du Lac, WI 54936-0821
Meeting City: Fond du Lac

Green Bay Philatelic Society
(APS# 1219-123324)
Meeting Time and Location: 7:30
p.m., 3rd Thurs., Senior Center,
200 S. Adams
Contact Person: Mr. Gordon W.
Lindner, 1002 Amberly Trail, Green
Bay, WI 54311
Meeting City: Green Bay

Janesville Stamp Club (APS#
1371-150543)
Meeting Time and Location:
7 p.m., 3rd Thurs., Senior Center,
69 S. Water St.
Contact Person: Mr. Melbourne
Steil, 1150 Euclid Ave., Beloit, WI
53511
Meeting City: Janesville

Kenosha Stamp & Cover Club
(APS# 1181-118223)
Meeting Time and Location:
7 p.m., 3rd Wed., AmCredit Union
Hall, 6715 Greenbay Rd.
Contact Person: Mr. Dennis R.
Mueller, 7620 10th Ave., Kenosha,
WI 53143
Meeting City: Kenosha

Badger Stamp Club (APS# 1295-
135866)
Meeting Time and Location:
1 p.m., 1st & 3rd Sat., Zimbrick
Buick Community Room, 1601 W.
Belt Line Hwy.
Contact Person: Mr. Curt
Shawkey, 4817 Martha Lane,
Madison, WI 53714
Meeting City: Madison
E-mail: cshawkey@netscape.net
Website: www0.delphi.com/
stamps/apschapbadger.html

Manitowoc Philatelic Society
(APS# 1072-100987)
Meeting Time and Location: 7:30
p.m., 2nd Tues., Sportcard, 731 N.
11th St.
Contact Person: Mr. Ron Tate, P.
O. Box 14, Manitowoc, WI 54221
Meeting City: Manitowoc

Germany Philatelic Society, Chap.
18 (APS# 1252-128125)
Meeting Time and Location:
7 p.m., 4th Sun., except July &
Dec., 8229 W. Capitol Dr.,
Contact Person: Mr. John R.
Fagan, W140N7470 Lilly Rd.,
Menomonee Falls, WI 53051-4608
Meeting City: Milwaukee
E-mail: gbreu@aol.com

Milwaukee Philatelic Society (APS#
0024-002696)
Meeting Time and Location:
7:30 p.m., 3rd Wed., Zablocki
County Park Pavilion, 3716 W.
Howard Ave.
Contact Person: Mr. Arthur A.

Petri, 3754 S. 67th St., Milwaukee, WI 53220-1859
Meeting City: Milwaukee

Oshkosh Philatelic Society (APS# 1238-125516)
Meeting Time and Location: 7 p.m., 1st Tues. & 3rd Mon., Sept. thru May, Oshkosh Post Office Building, 1025 W. 20th Ave.
Contact Person: Mr. Henry J. Schmidt, P. O. Box 3153, Oshkosh, WI 54903-3153
Meeting City: Oshkosh
E-mail: artcoy@vbe.com
Website: www0.delphi.com/stamps/apsoshkosh.html

Northwoods Stamp & Coin Club (APS# 1254-128127)
Meeting Time and Location: 7 p.m., 2nd & 4th Tues., Oneida Cty. Sr. Citizen Ctr.
Contact Person: Mr. Lawrence F. Marten, P. O. Box 126, Rhinelander, WI 54501
Meeting City: Rhinelander

Ripon Philatelic Society (APS# 0101-011633)
Meeting Time and Location: 7:30 p.m., 2nd Thurs., City Hall, All-purpose room
Contact Person: Mrs. Roberta R. Comfort, 564½ Newbury, Ripon, WI 54971
Meeting City: Ripon

Sheboygan Stamp Club (APS# 0124-013296)
Meeting Time and Location: 7:30 p.m., 1st & 3rd Wed., Sheboygan Rehabilition Center, 1305 St. Clair Ave.
Contact Person: Mr. Vern H. Witt, 2422 N. 9th St., Sheboygan, WI 53083
Meeting City: Sheboygan

Central Wisconsin Stamp Club (APS# 1013-094280)
Meeting Time and Location:

7 p.m., 1st & 3rd Thurs., Stevens Point-833 Clark St., Port Edwards-Port Edwards Credit Union
Contact Person: Mr. Gregg Greenwald, 2401 Bluebird Ct., Marshfield, WI 54449-3128
Meeting City: Stevens Point/Port Edwards

Waukesha County Philatelic Society (APS# 0756-059700)
Meeting Time and Location: 7:30 p.m., 2nd & 4th Thurs., except July & Aug., Salvation Army Bldg., 445 Madison St.
Contact Person: Mrs. MaryAnn J. Bowman, P. O. Box 1451, Waukesha, WI 53187
Meeting City: Waukesha

Wisconsin Valley Philatelic Society (APS# 0859-071592)
Meeting Time and Location: 7:15 p.m., 1st Wed., Lydell School, 5205 N. Lydell Ave.
Contact Person: Mr. Robert R. Henak, P. O. Box 17832, Milwaukee, WI 53217-0832
E-mail: henak@compuserve.com
Website: www0.delphi.com/stamps/apsnorthshore.html

Wauwatosa Philatelic Society (APS# 1043-097006)
Meeting Time and Location: 7:30 p.m., 3rd Tues., except Dec., Mayfair Shopping Center, 108th & North Ave., Rm. 110
Contact Person: Mrs. Rosemary J. Jahnke, P. O. Box 13102, Wauwatosa, WI 53213
Meeting City: Wauwatosa

Kettle Moraine Coin & Stamp (APS# 1396-155844)
Meeting Time and Location: 7:30 p.m., 2nd Thurs., except July & Aug., Silverbrook School Library, 724 Elm St.

Contact Person: Mr. Roland D. Essig, P. O. Box 361, West Bend, WI 53095
Meeting City: West Bend
E-mail: essig@hnet.net

WYOMING

Central Wyoming Philatelic Assoc. (APS# 1353-148250)
Meeting Time and Location: 7 p.m., 1st Thurs., Natrona County Library
Contact Person: Mr. Stephen J. Pfaff, 1045 Waterford St., Casper, WY 82609-3231
Meeting City: Casper

Cheyenne Philatelic Society (APS# 0933-082331)
Meeting Time and Location: 7 p.m., 3rd Wed., Cheyenne Municipal Bldg., 2101 Oneil Ave.
Contact Person: Mr. Dennis Bland, 803 Taft, Cheyenne, WY 82001
Meeting City: Cheyenne

CompuServe Stamp Section (APS# 1466-174386)
Meeting Time and Location: 24 hours a day, CompuServe Go Collect Section, 2

Contact Person: Mr. Wolf D. Gohl, 514 McIver St., Nashville, TN 37211
Meeting City: Internet
E-mail: gohl@home.com

eBay Stamp Club (APS# 1522-191441)
Meeting Time and Location: 24 hours a day, 7 days a week, members.tripod.com/ebaystamp/index.html,
Contact Person: Mr. James E. Watson, 3530 Pine Fern Lane, Bonita Springs, FL 34134-1918
Meeting City: Internet
E-mail: nfn05917@naples.net
Website: members.tripod.com/ebaystamp/index.html

Virtual Stamp Club on Delphi (APS# 1461-174150)
Meeting Time and Location: Message Board, 24 hrs./ 7 days a week, Chats every Wed. @ 10 p.m. Eastern Delphi Online Service
Contact Person: Mr. Harry E. Ozmun, PMB 206 14781 Pomerado Rd., Poway, CA 92064
Meeting City: Internet
E-mail: ozmun@home.com
Website: www.virtualstampclub.com

AUSTRALIA

Tasmanian Philatelic Society
(APS# 1430-165212)
Meeting Time and Location: 7:30
p.m., 2nd & 4th Thurs., except Jan.
& Dec., 159 Macquarie
Contact Person: Mrs. E. Genge,
G.P.O. Box 594, Hobart, TAS
7001, Australia
Meeting City: Hobart, Tas.
E-mail: ericagenge@hotmail.com

BRITISH COLUMBIA

British Columbia Philatelic Society
(APS# 1379-152208)
Meeting Time and Location: 7:30
p.m., Wed., Amenity Room,
Grosvenor Bldg.,
1040 W. Georgia St.
Contact Person: Mr. Basil J.
Hunter, 1775 W. 10th Ave., #106,
Vancouver, BC V6J 2A4 Canada
Meeting City: Vancouver, BC

Vancouver Island Philatelic Society
(APS# 1144-112104)
Meeting Time and Location:
8 p.m., 4th Thurs., St. Aidan's
Church Hall
Contact Person: Mr. Walter
Hundleby, P. O. Box 6351, Sta. C,
Victoria, BC V8P 5M3 Canada
Meeting City: Victoria, BC
Website:
members.home.net/pava/vips.htm

Essex County Stamp Club (APS#
1168-116379)
Meeting Time and Location:
7 p.m., 2nd & 4th Wed., Teutonia
Club, 55 Edinborough
Contact Person: Mr. Michael J.
Barie, P. O. Box 1445, Detroit, MI
48231
Meeting City: Windsor, ON

Winnipeg Philatelic Society (APS#
0813-066375)
Meeting Time and Location:
7 p.m., 1st & 3rd Thurs., except

July & Aug., Deaf Centre of Mani-
toba, Meeting Room, 285 Pembina
Hwy.
Contact Person: Mr. Michael
Zacharias, 808 Polson Ave.,
Winnipeg, MB R2X 1M5 Canada
Meeting City: Winnipeg, MB
E-mail: rpenko12@home.com
Website: www.wps.mb.ca

CANADA

Calgary Philatelic Society (APS#
1360-148906)
Meeting Time and Location: 7:30
p.m., 1st Wed., except July & Aug.,
Kerby Centre, 1133 7th Ave.,
S. W., 2nd fl.
Contact Person: Mr. Dale C.
Speirs, P. O. Box 6830, Calgary,
AB T2P 2E7 Canada
Meeting City: Calgary, AB
E-mail: calphilso@home.com
Website: members.home.net/
calphilso/

Soc. Philatelique de Quebec
(APS# 1299-136371)
Meeting Time and Location:
7 p.m., 1st & 3rd Wed., except
July & Aug., Eglise St. Rodrigue,
4760 1 ER Avenue
Contact Person: Mr. Jacques
Poitras, C.P. 2023, Quebec, QC
G1K 7M9 Canada
Meeting City: Charlesbourg, PQ

Lakeshore Stamp Club (APS#
0769-061204)
Meeting Time and Location:
7 p.m., 2nd & 4th Thur., except
July & Aug., Strathmore United
Church, 310 Brookhave Ave.
Contact Person: Mr. Raymond W.
Ireson, 86 Cartier, Roxboro, QC
H8Y 1G8 Canada
Meeting City: Dorval, PQ
E-mail: fsbrisse@videotron.ca
Website: www.geocities.com/
lakeshorestampclub/

Edmonton Stamp Club (APS# 0680-054000)
Meeting Time and Location: 6:30 p.m., 1st & 3rd Mon., St. Joseph High School Cafeteria/Main fl., 109 St. & 108 Ave.
Contact Person: Mr. Keith R. Spencer, P. O. Box 399, Edmonton, AB T5J 2J6 Canada
Meeting City: Edmonton, AB
E-mail: krs2@valberta.ca
Website: www.freenet.edmon ton.ab.ca/stamps

Nova Scotia Stamp Club (APS# 1340-145423)
Meeting Time and Location: 7:30 p.m., 2nd Tues., except July & Aug., Nova Scotia Museum, Summer St.
Contact Person: C. W. Turner, 59 Kearney Lake Rd., Halifax, NS B3M 2S9 Canada
Meeting City: Halifax, NS
E-mail: jjfharvey@hotmail.com

Hamilton Stamp Club (APS# 1049-097889)
Meeting Time and Location: 6 p.m., 2nd, 4th, & 5th Mon., except July & Aug., Bishop Ryan Secondary School, Albright & Quigley Rds.
Contact Person: Mr. John Miller, P. O. Box 60510, 673 Upper James St., Hamilton, ON L9C 7N7 Canada
Meeting City: Hamilton, ON
E-mail: Stamps@hwcn.org
Website: www.hwcn.org/~ip029

Canadian Assn. Israel Phil. (APS# 1403-157892)
Meeting Time and Location: 7:30 p.m., 2nd Tues., except July & Aug., Earl Bales Community Centre, 4169 Bathurst St.
Contact Person: Mr. Joseph Berkovits, 33-260 Adelaide St., E., Toronto, ON M5A 1N1 Canada
Meeting City: North York, ON

Ottawa Philatelic Society (APS# 1182-118224)
Meeting Time and Location: 7:30 p.m., Thurs., except June, July, & Aug., Hintonburg Community Center, 1064 Wellington Ave.
Contact Person: Mr. Bruce Kalbfleisch, P.O. Box 65085, Merivale Postal Outlet, Nepean, ON K2G 5Y3 Canada
Meeting City: Ottawa, ON

Regina Philatelic Club (APS# 1044-097437)
Meeting Time and Location: 7:30 p.m., 1st & 3rd Wed., Library, Sheldon Williams Collegiate, Coronation
Contact Person: Mr. Ken W. Arndt, P.O. Box 1891, Regina, SK S4P 3E1 Canada
Meeting City: Regina, SK

West Toronto Stamp Club (APS# 1462-174151)
Meeting Time and Location: 7:30 p.m., every Tues., Fairfield Seniors' Centre, 80 Lothian Ave.
Contact Person: Mr. F. Alusio, 331 Rathburn Rd., Toronto, ON M9B 2L9 Canada
Meeting City: Toronto, ON

COLOMBIA

Club Filatelico De Bogota (APS# 0351-031126)
Meeting Time and Location: 6:30 p.m., Thurs., 11 a.m., Sat., Calle 121 #9B-27
Contact Person: Mr. Felipe Toro, P. O. Box 5258, Santa Fe de Bogota, Colombia
Meeting City: Santa Fe de Bogota

DOMINICAN REPUBLIC

Soc. Filatelica Dominicana (APS# 1200-121277)
Meeting Time and Location: 8 p.m., last Mon. of month,

Morning, Sun. Arz. Merino No. 358
Contact Person: Dr. Mario Ortiz, P. O. Box 5258, Santa Fe, Columbia
Meeting City: Santa Fe De Bogota

ECUADOR

Club Filatelico Guayaquil (APS# 0832-067630)
Meeting Time and Location: 3–6 p.m., Aguirre 324, 2nd floor, Office #8
Contact Person: Mr. Juan Yela K., P. O. Box 09-01-9615, Guayaquil, Ecuador
Meeting City: Guayaquil
E-mail: clubfilatelico@hotmail.com
Website: clubfg.cjb.net

GERMANY

ARGE USA/CANADA (APS# 1057-098571)
Meeting Time and Location: Various times
Contact Person: Mr. Peter Kuhlhorn, Wormser Str. 36, D-42119 Wuppertal, Germany
Meeting Cities: Hamburg, Cologne, & Mainz

GREAT BRITAIN

American Stamp Club of Great Britain (APS# 0697-055176)
Meeting Time and Location: Various times, various locations
Contact Person: Mr. Michael D. Simons, 42 Owen Gardens, Gwynne Park, Woodford Br., Essex, IG8 8DG England
Meeting City: Great Britain
E-mail: ascofgb@aol.com
Website: www.members.aol.com/ascofgb/asc.html

MEXICO

Sociedad Filatelica Regiomontana (APS# 1448-170642)
Meeting Time and Location: 7:30 p.m., every Mon., Universidad Iberoamericana Campus Monterrey
Contact Person: Mr. Jamie Benavides V., Apartado Postal 244, 66250 Col. Del Valle NL, Mexico
Meeting City: Monterrey, NL
E-mail: jbenavi@mail.giga.com
Website: www.geocities.com/Athens/Pantheon/1985/

NETHERLANDS

USA en Canada Filatelie (APS# 1427-164955)
Meeting Time and Location: Bimonthly meetings, throughout Netherlands
Contact Person: Mr. Victor W. Kuil, Van Deventerlaan 9, 2271 TT Vooburg, Netherlands
Meeting City: Netherlands
E-mail: w.v.kuil@hccnet.nl

NORWAY

Oslo Filatelist Klubb (APS# 0685-054340)
Meeting Time and Location: 7 p.m., Mon., except June & July, Schaftelokken, Solheimsgt 2B
Contact Person: Mr. Sven Anderson, P. O. Box 298, Sentrum, N-0103 Oslo, Norway
Meeting City: Oslo
E-mail: bmuggeru@online.no
Website: www.filatelist.no/klubber/ofk.htm

PUERTO RICO

Puerto Rico Philatelic Society (APS# 0342-030501)
Meeting Time and Location: 9 a.m.–12 p.m., Sun., 773 Andalucia Ave., Puerto Nuevo
Contact Person: Mr. Carlos Hamill, P. O. Box 191500, San Juan, PR 00919-1500
Meeting City: Hato Rey
E-mail: carlosh_22@yahoo.com

SAUDI ARABIA

Arabian Philatelic Association
(APS# 0694-055067)
Meeting Time and Location:
7 p.m., 2nd Sat., ARAMCO Facilities
Contact Person: Mr. David E.
Jessich, ARAMCO, Box 7070,
Udhailiyah 31311, Saudi Arabia
Meeting City: Dhahran
E-mail:
jessicde@mail.aramco.com.sa

VIRGIN ISLANDS

British Virgin Islands Phil. Soc.
(APS# 1506-188229)
Meeting Time and Location:
8 a.m., one Sat. a month, The
Paradise Pub, Road Town
Contact Person: Mr. Roger J.
Downing, P. O. Box 11156, St.
Thomas, VI 00801-1156
Meeting City: Tortola
E-mail: downing@surfbvi.com

IMPORTANT NOTICE: On stamps issued before 1890, prices of unused specimens are for ones without original gum. Specimens with original gum can be expected to command a premium of as much as 50 percent. Beware of regummed specimens.

Scott No.			Fine Unused Each	Ave. Unused Each	Fine Used Each	Ave. Used Each
GENERAL ISSUES						
1847. FIRST ISSUE						
☐1	5¢	Red Brown	4200.00	2600.00	500.00	310.00
☐2	10¢	Black	—	12,500.00	1,100.00	810.00
1875. REPRODUCTIONS OF 1847 ISSUE						
☐3	5¢	Red Brown	800.00	600.00	—	—
☐4	10¢	Black	950.00	625.00	—	—
1851–1856. REGULAR ISSUE—IMPERFORATE						
☐5A	1¢	Blue (1b)	—	—	360.00	240.00
☐6	1¢	Blue (1a)	—	—	640.00	400.00
☐7	1¢	Blue (II)	400.00	300.00	140.00	80.00
☐8	1¢	Blue (III)	—	—	2000.00	1100.00
☐8A	1¢	Blue (IIIa)	200.00	1400.00	700.00	450.00
☐9	1¢	Blue (IV)	400.00	250.00	100.00	60.00
☐10	3¢	Orange Brown (I)	1550.00	1000.00	90.00	50.00
☐11	3¢	Dull Red (I)	170.00	100.00	9.00	6.00
☐12	5¢	Red Brown (I)	—	—	900.00	600.00
☐13	10¢	Green (I)	—	—	680.00	425.00
☐14	10¢	Green (II)	1700.00	950.00	200.00	140.00
☐15	10¢	Green (III)	1500.00	1000.00	200.00	140.00
☐16	10¢	Green (IV)	—	—	1300.00	800.00
☐17	12¢	Black	—	1550.00	310.00	200.00
1857–1861. SAME DESIGNS AS 1851–1856 ISSUE—PERF. 15						
☐18	1¢	Blue (I)	910.00	410.00	400.00	250.00
☐19	1¢	Blue (Ia)	—	—	3300.00	2000.00
☐20	1¢	Blue (II)	500.00	300.00	180.00	140.00
☐21	1¢	Blue (III)	—	360.00	1400.00	700.00
☐22	1¢	Blue (IIIa)	810.00	500.00	340.00	210.00
☐23	1¢	Blue (IV)	2900.00	1750.00	440.00	240.00

Scott No.			Fine Unused Each	Ave. Unused Each	Fine Used Each	Ave. Used Each
☐24	1¢	Blue (V)	82.00	51.00	40.00	25.00
☐25	3¢	Rose (I)	1100.00	610.00	52.00	35.00
☐26	3¢	Dull Red (II)	65.00	40.00	5.00	3.00
☐26A	3¢	Dull Red (IIa)	110.00	60.00	39.00	23.00
☐27	5¢	Brick Red (I)	—	5000.00	800.00	600.00
☐28	5¢	Red Brown (I)	1670.00	1050.00	400.00	240.00
☐28A	5¢	Indian Red (I)	—	—	2000.00	1300.00
☐29	5¢	Brown (I)	800.00	460.00	270.00	175.00
☐30	5¢	Orange Brown (II)	800.00	300.00	800.00	410.00
☐30A	5¢	Brown (II)	760.00	460.00	210.00	140.00
☐31	10¢	Green (I)	—	4000.00	610.00	360.00
☐32	10¢	Green (II)	2200.00	1250.00	200.00	135.00
☐33	10¢	Green (III)	2200.00	1250.00	200.00	135.00
☐34	10¢	Green (IV)	—	—	1800.00	975.00
☐35	10¢	Green (IV)	175.00	100.00	60.00	38.00
☐36	12¢	Black (I)	650.00	360.00	140.00	100.00
☐36b	12¢	Black (II)	360.00	210.00	120.00	85.00
☐37	24¢	Gray Lilac	1500.00	350.00	260.00	190.00
☐38	30¢	Orange	1700.00	400.00	310.00	185.00
☐39	90¢	Blue	2250.00	900.00	—	—

1875. REPRINTS OF 1857–1861 ISSUE

☐40	1¢	Bright Blue	700.00	400.00	—	—
☐41	3¢	Scarlet	2600.00	1800.00	—	—
☐42	5¢	Orange Brown	1200.00	850.00	—	—
☐43	10¢	Blue Green	2500.00	1700.00	—	—
☐44	12¢	Greenish Black	3000.00	2000.00	—	—
☐45	24¢	Blackish Violet	3500.00	2000.00	—	—
☐46	30¢	Yellow Orange	3000.00	2100.00	—	—
☐47	90¢	Deep Blue	4900.00	3000.00	—	—

1861. FIRST DESIGNS—PERF. 12

☐56	3¢	Brown Red	800.00	500.00	—	—
☐62B	10¢	Dark Green	—	—	550.00	410.00

1861–1862. SECOND DESIGNS

☐63	1¢	Blue	130.00	80.00	21.00	13.00
☐63b	1¢	Dark Blue	150.00	90.00	28.00	20.00
☐64	3¢	Pink	—	2150.00	510.00	290.00

Scott No.			Fine Unused Each	Ave. Unused Each	Fine Used Each	Ave. Used Each
☐64	3¢	Rose Pink	4000.00	2400.00	800.00	60.00
☐65	3¢	Rose	120.00	47.00	3.00	2.00
☐66	3¢	Lake	—	1000.00	—	—
☐67	5¢	Buff	—	5500.00	600.00	400.00
☐68	10¢	Yellow Green	500.00	200.00	40.00	28.00
☐69	12¢	Black	900.00	330.00	80.00	45.00
☐70	24¢	Red Lilac	1600.00	550.00	120.00	80.00
☐70b	24¢	Steel Blue	—	4000.00	400.00	200.00
☐70c	24¢	Violet	—	4000.00	900.00	400.00
☐71	30¢	Orange	1600.00	600.00	120.00	75.00
☐72	90¢	Blue	2000.00	820.00	280.00	180.00

1861–1866. NEW VALUES OR NEW COLORS

☐73	2¢	Black	250.00	95.00	60.00	25.00
☐74	3¢	Scarlet	4100.00	3000.00	2000.00	1000.00
☐75	5¢	Red Brown	3000.00	1000.00	400.00	210.00
☐76	5¢	Brown	800.00	300.00	100.00	60.00
☐77	15¢	Black	1200.00	380.00	130.00	62.00
☐78	24¢	Lilac	900.00	250.00	85.00	40.00

1867. SAME DESIGNS AS 1861–1866 ISSUE
GRILL WITH POINTS UP
A. GRILL COVERING ENTIRE STAMP

☐79	3¢	Rose	4000.00	2500.00	1000.00	650.00

C. GRILL ABOUT 13 x 16 MM.

☐83	3¢	Rose	4000.00	1450.00	800.00	480.00

GRILL WITH POINTS DOWN
D. GRILL ABOUT 12 x 14 MM.

☐84	2¢	Black	9000.00	6000.00	2000.00	1300.00
☐85	3¢	Rose	4000.00	1500.00	800.00	45.00

Z. GRILL ABOUT 11 x 14 MM.

☐85B	2¢	Black	4000.00	2300.00	900.00	500.00
☐85C	3¢	Rose	7000.00	2600.00	2000.00	1000.00
☐85E	12¢	Black	8000.00	4000.00	1100.00	600.00

E. GRILL ABOUT 11 x 13 MM.

☐86	1¢	Blue	2000.00	1100.00	410.00	200.00

Scott No.			Fine Unused Each	Ave. Unused Each	Fine Used Each	Ave. Used Each
☐87	2¢	Black	410.00	260.00	95.00	51.00
☐88	3¢	Rose	310.00	160.00	14.00	9.00
☐89	10¢	Green	1710.00	1050.00	215.00	120.00
☐90	12¢	Black	1700.00	1100.00	210.00	140.00
☐91	15¢	Black	3100.00	1900.00	450.00	290.00

F. GRILL ABOUT 9 x 13 MM.

☐92	1¢	Blue	410.00	240.00	125.00	82.00
☐93	2¢	Black	175.00	100.00	37.00	21.00
☐94	3¢	Red	135.00	90.00	5.00	3.50
☐95	5¢	Brown	1200.00	600.00	415.00	310.00
☐96	10¢	Yellow Green	1100.00	600.00	155.00	95.00
☐97	12¢	Black	1300.00	710.00	150.00	96.00
☐98	15¢	Black	1310.00	740.00	210.00	140.00
☐99	24¢	Gray Lilac	1400.00	800.00	300.00	200.00
☐100	30¢	Orange	2400.00	1400.00	500.00	290.00
☐101	90¢	Blue	3800.00	2110.00	900.00	500.00

1875. RE-ISSUE OF 1861–1866 ISSUES

☐102	1¢	Blue	600.00	400.00	1000.00	600.00
☐103	2¢	Black	2000.00	1200.00	4100.00	2700.00
☐104	3¢	Brown Red	2000.00	1800.00	4400.00	300.00
☐105	5¢	Light Brown	1800.00	1200.00	3300.00	2500.00
☐106	10¢	Green	1900.00	1700.00	3600.00	2600.00
☐107	12¢	Black	2200.00	1900.00	4000.00	2900.00
☐108	15¢	Black	3000.00	2200.00	5000.00	3600.00
☐109	24¢	Deep Violet	4100.00	3000.00	4200.00	4000.00
☐110	30¢	Brownish Orange	3000.00	2400.00	8500.00	5000.00
☐111	90¢	Blue	4800.00	4000.00	35,000.00	25,000.00

1869. PICTORIAL ISSUES
GRILL ABOUT 9¹/₂ x 9¹/₂ MM.

☐112	1¢	Buff	310.00	180.00	90.00	61.00
☐113	2¢	Brown	250.00	160.00	39.00	24.00
☐114	3¢	Ultramarine	150.00	90.00	14.00	11.00
☐115	6¢	Ultramarine	1200.00	700.00	160.00	80.00
☐116	10¢	Yellow	875.00	400.00	110.00	60.00
☐117	12¢	Green	810.00	500.00	120.00	75.00
☐118	15¢	Brown & Blue (I)	3000.00	1900.00	450.00	260.00

Scott No.		Fine Unused Each	Ave. Unused Each	Fine Used Each	Ave. Used Each
☐ 119	15¢ Brown & Blue (II)	1400.00	800.00	200.00	110.00
☐ 120	24¢ Green & Violet	2600.00	1650.00	495.00	300.00
☐ 121	30¢ Blue & Carmine	2400.00	1600.00	400.00	200.00
☐ 122	90¢ Carmine & Black	4100.00	2900.00	1500.00	950.00

1875. RE-ISSUE OF 1869 ISSUE, HARD WHITE PAPER—WITHOUT GRILL

☐ 123	1¢ Buff	280.00	180.00	230.00	145.00
☐ 124	2¢ Brown	370.00	200.00	325.00	215.00
☐ 125	3¢ Blue	3100.00	1900.00	1100.00	700.00
☐ 126	6¢ Blue	92.00	600.00	615.00	450.00
☐ 127	10¢ Yellow	1400.00	900.00	1350.00	800.00
☐ 128	12¢ Green	1500.00	900.00	1900.00	1000.00
☐ 129	15¢ Brown & Blue (III)	1200.00	810.00	650.00	450.00
☐ 130	24¢ Green & Violet	1200.00	810.00	710.00	500.00
☐ 131	30¢ Blue & Carmine	1500.00	1200.00	1400.00	850.00
☐ 132	90¢ Carmine & Black	3100.00	3000.00	4100.00	3200.00

1880. SAME AS ABOVE—SOFT POROUS PAPER

☐ 133	1¢ Buff	225.00	140.00	180.00	110.00

1870–1871. PRINTED BY NATIONAL BANK NOTE CO.—GRILLED

☐ 134	1¢ Ultramarine	650.00	410.00	91.00	57.00
☐ 135	2¢ Red Brown	430.00	240.00	50.00	30.00
☐ 136	3¢ Green	310.00	180.00	15.00	10.00
☐ 137	6¢ Carmine	1550.00	1000.00	350.00	190.00
☐ 138	7¢ Vermilion	1300.00	725.00	310.00	210.00
☐ 139	10¢ Brown	2100.00	1210.00	480.00	310.00
☐ 140	12¢ Light Violet	—	—	2000.00	1250.00
☐ 141	15¢ Orange	—	1250.00	800.00	420.00
☐ 142	24¢ Purple	—	—	7100.00	4000.00
☐ 143	30¢ Black	—	3100.00	1400.00	810.00
☐ 144	90¢ Carmine	—	3100.00	1200.00	650.00

1870–1871. SAME AS ABOVE—WITHOUT GRILL

☐ 145	1¢ Ultramarine	210.00	115.00	9.10	6.75
☐ 146	2¢ Red Brown	130.00	80.00	7.00	4.00
☐ 147	3¢ Green	130.00	80.00	1.10	.60

Scott No.		Fine Unused Each	Ave. Unused Each	Fine Used Each	Ave. Used Each
☐148 6¢	Carmine	260.00	150.00	17.00	11.00
☐149 7¢	Vermilion	350.00	200.00	70.00	41.00
☐150 10¢	Brown	280.00	155.00	18.00	10.00
☐151 12¢	Dull Violet	690.00	400.00	95.00	61.00
☐152 15¢	Bright Orange	670.00	350.00	95.00	60.00
☐153 24¢	Purple	675.00	380.00	95.00	60.00
☐154 30¢	Black	1500.00	900.00	115.00	71.00
☐155 90¢	Carmine	1550.00	910.00	210.00	130.00

1873. SAME DESIGNS AS 1870–1871 ISSUE— WITH SECRET MARKS PRINTED BY THE CONTINENTAL BANK NOTE CO. THIN HARD GRAYISH WHITE PAPER

☐156 1¢	Ultramarine	100.00	61.00	3.00	1.90
☐157 2¢	Brown	190.00	100.00	12.00	7.10
☐158 3¢	Green	52.00	30.00	.45	.26
☐159 6¢	Dull Pink	210.00	120.00	13.00	9.00
☐160 7¢	Orange Vermilion	460.00	210.00	52.00	30.00
☐161 10¢	Brown	300.00	180.00	15.00	9.00
☐162 12¢	Black Violet	680.00	400.00	60.00	45.00
☐163 15¢	Yellow Orange	700.00	450.00	72.00	46.00
☐165 30¢	Gray Black	750.00	475.00	80.00	42.00
☐166 90¢	Rose Carmine	1400.00	710.00	180.00	112.00

1875. REGULAR ISSUE

☐178 2¢	Vermilion	165.00	100.00	7.00	4.00
☐179 5¢	Blue	240.00	150.00	13.00	8.00

1879. SAME DESIGNS AS 1870–1875 ISSUES PRINTED BY THE AMERICAN BANK NOTE CO. SOFT POROUS YELLOWISH WHITE PAPER

☐182 1¢	Dark Ultramarine	130.00	72.00	1.80	1.00
☐183 2¢	Vermilion	61.00	38.00	1.75	1.00
☐184 3¢	Green	50.00	29.00	.45	.25
☐185 5¢	Blue	250.00	135.00	10.00	6.00
☐186 6¢	Pink	410.00	240.00	16.00	9.00
☐187 10¢	Brown (no secret mark)	775.00	420.00	18.00	12.00

Scott No.	Fine Unused Each	Ave. Unused Each	Fine Used Each	Ave. Used Each
☐188 10¢ Brown				
(secret mark)	550.00	310.00	20.00	11.00
☐188b 10¢ Black Brown	600.00	320.00	71.00	24.00
☐189 15¢ Red Orange	160.00	110.00	19.00	11.00
☐190 30¢ Full Black	460.00	240.00	42.00	26.00
☐191 90¢ Carmine	1100.00	600.00	185.00	110.00

1882. REGULAR ISSUE

☐205 5¢ Yellow Brown	200.00	160.00	6.00	4.00

1881–1882. DESIGNS OF 1873 ISSUE RE-ENGRAVED (N-H ADD 95%)

☐206 1¢ Gray Blue	40.00	30.00	.80	.60
☐207 3¢ Blue Green	40.00	30.00	.50	.40
☐208 6¢ Rose	300.00	200.00	50.00	33.00
☐208a 6¢ Brown Red	260.00	170.00	70.00	40.00
☐209 10¢ Brown	100.00	65.00	2.90	1.50
☐209b 10¢ Black Brown	210.00	112.00	30.00	15.00

1883. REGULAR ISSUE

☐210 2¢ Red Brown	30.00	18.00	.45	.30
☐211 4¢ Blue Green	150.00	90.00	11.00	4.00

1887. REGULAR ISSUE

☐212 1¢ Ultramarine	70.00	45.00	1.00	.75
☐213 2¢ Green	35.00	16.00	.40	.26
☐214 3¢ Vermilion	57.00	32.00	41.00	22.00

1888. SAME DESIGNS AS 1870–1883 ISSUES

☐215 4¢ Carmine	140.00	85.00	14.00	7.00
☐216 5¢ Indigo	150.00	95.00	9.00	6.00
☐217 30¢ Orange Brown	300.00	192.00	75.00	50.00
☐218 90¢ Purple	750.00	450.00	170.00	95.00

IMPORTANT NOTICE: From this point onward, values of unused stamps and blocks are for specimens with original gum. Prices given for **blocks** are for blocks of 4, **without** plate number.

Scott No.	Fine Unused Block	Ave. Unused Block	Fine Unused Each	Ave. Unused Each	Fine Used Each	Ave. Used Each

1890–1893. SMALL DESIGN (N-H ADD 70%)

☐219 1¢ Dull Blue

	115.00	80.00	28.00	16.00	.36	.21

☐219D 2¢ Lake

| | 750.00 | 600.00 | 200.00 | 125.00 | .60 | .24 |

☐220 2¢ Carmine

| | 90.00 | 75.00 | 23.00 | 15.00 | .36 | .21 |

☐220a 2¢ Carmine (Cap on left 2)

| | 1250.00 | 1000.00 | 54.00 | 40.00 | 2.10 | 1.00 |

☐220c 2¢ Carmine (Cap both 2's)

| | 170.00 | 110.00 | 200.00 | 120.00 | 12.00 | 6.50 |

☐221 3¢ Purple

| | 270.00 | 215.00 | 72.00 | 48.00 | 5.00 | 2.50 |

☐222 4¢ Dark Brown

| | 310.00 | 220.00 | 76.00 | 52.00 | 2.10 | 1.00 |

☐223 5¢ Chocolate

| | 250.00 | 200.00 | 70.00 | 49.00 | 2.10 | 1.00 |

☐224 6¢ Brown Red

| | 310.00 | 240.00 | 81.00 | 52.00 | 15.00 | 8.00 |

☐225 8¢ Lilac

| | 300.00 | 250.00 | 58.00 | 41.00 | 9.00 | 6.00 |

☐226 10¢ Green

| | 480.00 | 400.00 | 170.00 | 90.00 | 3.00 | 1.00 |

☐227 15¢ Indigo

| | 700.00 | 600.00 | 200.00 | 125.00 | 15.00 | 8.00 |

☐228 30¢ Black

| | 900.00 | 750.00 | 340.00 | 210.00 | 20.00 | 9.00 |

☐229 90¢ Orange

| | 1650.00 | 1450.00 | 5.00 | 3.10 | 87.00 | 45.00 |

1893. COLUMBIAN ISSUE (N-H ADD 50%)

☐230 1¢ Blue

| | 120.00 | 90.00 | 30.00 | 19.00 | .45 | .21 |

☐231 2¢ Violet

| | 110.00 | 90.00 | 26.00 | 17.00 | .35 | .20 |

☐231c 2¢ "Broken Hat"

| | 210.00 | 200.00 | 82.00 | 51.00 | .70 | .37 |

☐232 3¢ Green

| | 260.00 | 210.00 | 71.00 | 40.00 | 13.00 | 9.00 |

Scott No.	Fine Unused Block	Ave. Unused Block	Fine Unused Each	Ave. Unused Each	Fine Used Each	Ave. Used Each
☐233 4¢ Ultramarine						
	420.00	300.00	100.00	61.00	7.00	4.00
☐234 5¢ Chocolate						
	490.00	350.00	110.00	74.00	7.00	4.50
☐235 6¢ Purple						
	450.00	340.00	100.00	65.00	18.00	12.00
☐236 8¢ Magenta						
	400.00	290.00	90.00	65.00	10.00	5.00
☐237 10¢ Black Brown						
	610.00	400.00	160.00	110.00	8.00	6.00
☐238 15¢ Dark Green						
	1600.00	900.00	300.00	185.00	60.00	40.00
☐239 30¢ Orange Brown						
	2800.00	2000.00	385.00	245.00	75.00	55.00
☐240 50¢ Slate Blue						
	3100.00	2000.00	700.00	400.00	130.00	85.00
☐241 $1 Salmon						
	—	—	1800.00	1150.00	480.00	400.00
☐242 $2 Brown Red						
	—	—	1820.00	1100.00	450.00	290.00
☐243 $3 Yellow Green						
	—	—	3000.00	1900.00	875.00	550.00
☐244 $4 Crimson Lake						
	—	—	3800.00	2400.00	1050.00	700.00
☐245 $5 Black						
	—	—	4500.00	2800.00	1200.00	900.00

1894. UNWATERMARKED (N-H ADD 60%)

☐246 1¢ Ultramarine						
	90.00	78.00	32.00	21.00	4.00	2.00
☐247 1¢ Blue						
	210.00	190.00	70.00	45.00	3.10	1.50
☐248 2¢ Pink, Type I						
	110.00	76.00	29.00	17.00	3.10	1.10
☐249 2¢ Carmine Lake, Type I						
	600.00	410.00	150.00	115.00	4.00	1.50
☐250 2¢ Carmine, Type I						
	210.00	160.00	30.00	20.00	.45	.20

Scott No.		Fine Unused Block	Ave. Unused Block	Fine Unused Each	Ave. Unused Each	Fine Used Each	Ave. Used Each
☐251	2¢ Carmine, Type II						
		1500.00	1000.00	240.00	150.00	3.75	1.90
☐252	2¢ Carmine, Type III						
		430.00	300.00	120.00	80.00	3.25	1.40
☐253	3¢ Purple						
		410.00	310.00	115.00	70.00	6.50	2.75
☐254	4¢ Dark Brown						
		500.00	400.00	140.00	82.00	4.00	1.40
☐255	5¢ Chocolate						
		510.00	415.00	100.00	70.00	4.10	2.55
☐256	6¢ Dull Brown						
		800.00	620.00	170.00	115.00	11.00	7.50
☐257	8¢ Violet Brown						
		900.00	620.00	150.00	96.00	12.00	5.00
☐258	10¢ Dark Green						
		1400.00	900.00	245.00	160.00	9.00	7.00
☐259	15¢ Dark Blue						
		1700.00	910.00	300.00	190.00	38.00	21.00
☐260	50¢ Orange						
		2100.00	1250.00	450.00	280.00	75.00	40.00
☐261	$1 Black (I)						
		6000.00	3400.00	1000.00	600.00	215.00	120.00
☐261A	$1 Black (II)						
		—	—	2200.00	1400.00	400.00	240.00
☐262	$2 Blue						
		—	—	3300.00	2000.00	610.00	350.00
☐263	$5 Dark Green						
		—	—	4500.00	3000.00	1200.00	710.00

1895. DOUBLE LINE WATERMARKED "U.S.P.S." PERF. 12 (N-H ADD 60%)

☐264	1¢ Blue						
		45.00	30.00	8.00	5.00	.30	.20
☐265	2¢ Carmine, Type I						
		215.00	150.00	33.00	21.00	.90	.40
☐266	2¢ Carmine, Type II						
		265.00	180.00	34.00	21.00	3.00	2.00
☐267	2¢ Carmine, Type III						
		60.00	40.00	6.50	3.90	.30	.22

Scott No.		Fine Unused Block	Ave. Unused Block	Fine Unused Each	Ave. Unused Each	Fine Used Each	Ave. Used Each
☐268	3¢ Purple						
		320.00	175.00	45.00	26.00	1.50	.75
☐269	4¢ Dark Brown						
		310.00	220.00	45.00	27.00	1.50	.70
☐270	5¢ Chocolate						
		300.00	210.00	45.00	28.00	1.70	.70
☐271	6¢ Dull Brown						
		360.00	280.00	95.00	62.00	4.00	1.75
☐272	8¢ Violet Brown						
		230.00	150.00	69.00	46.00	2.00	.75
☐273	10¢ Dark Green						
		320.00	225.00	90.00	60.00	2.00	1.00
☐274	15¢ Dark Blue						
		780.00	540.00	230.00	145.00	8.00	6.00
☐275	50¢ Dull Orange						
		1200.00	810.00	320.00	200.00	18.00	10.00
☐276	$1 Black (I)						
		2600.00	1700.00	650.00	410.00	50.00	30.00
☐276A	$1 Black (II)						
		—	—	1500.00	910.00	115.00	70.00
☐277	$2 Blue						
		—	—	1200.00	750.00	250.00	125.00
☐278	$5 Dark Green						
		—	—	2400.00	1500.00	350.00	220.00

1898. REGULAR ISSUE PERF. (N-H ADD 60%)

Scott No.		Fine Unused Block	Ave. Unused Block	Fine Unused Each	Ave. Unused Each	Fine Used Each	Ave. Used Each
☐279	1¢ Deep Green						
		85.00	52.00	11.50	7.80	.40	.20
☐279B	2¢ Red						
		87.00	52.00	11.50	7.80	.40	.20
☐279C	2¢ Rose Carmine						
		710.00	600.00	210.00	140.00	90.00	50.00
☐279D	2¢ Orange Red						
		750.00	62.00	15.00	10.00	.60	.31
☐280	4¢ Rose Brown						
		220.00	140.00	36.00	24.00	.90	.65
☐281	5¢ Dark Blue						
		230.00	140.00	43.00	26.00	1.00	.50

Scott No.	Fine Unused Block	Ave. Unused Block	Fine Unused Each	Ave. Unused Each	Fine Used Each	Ave. Used Each
☐282 6¢ Lake						
	350.00	240.00	51.00	31.00	2.50	1.10
☐282a 6¢ Purplish Lake						
	460.00	375.00	71.00	44.00	3.10	1.10
☐282C 10¢ Brown (I)						
	810.00	680.00	200.00	130.00	2.00	1.40
☐283 10¢ Orange Brown (III)						
	710.00	506.00	125.00	80.00	2.00	1.00
☐284 15¢ Olive Green						
	750.00	500.00	180.00	100.00	6.00	2.00

1898. TRANS-MISSISSIPPI EXPOSITION ISSUE (N-H ADD 50%)

Scott No.	Fine Unused Block	Ave. Unused Block	Fine Unused Each	Ave. Unused Each	Fine Used Each	Ave. Used Each
☐285 1¢ Yellow Green						
	250.00	110.00	34.00	22.00	5.00	2.50
☐286 2¢ Copper Red						
	260.00	160.00	30.00	21.00	1.50	.90
☐287 4¢ Orange						
	900.00	575.00	180.00	115.00	20.00	10.00
☐288 5¢ Dull Blue						
	910.00	650.00	170.00	100.00	17.00	10.00
☐289 8¢ Violet Brown						
	1250.00	800.00	225.00	140.00	32.00	20.00
☐290 10¢ Gray Violet						
	1000.00	900.00	230.00	140.00	18.00	10.00
☐291 50¢ Sage Green						
	—	—	700.00	510.00	150.00	70.00
☐292 $1 Black						
	—	—	1500.00	950.00	400.00	250.00
☐293 $2 Orange Brown						
	—	—	2500.00	1500.00	680.00	450.00

1901. PAN-AMERICAN ISSUE (N-H ADD 50%)

Scott No.	Fine Unused Block	Ave. Unused Block	Fine Unused Each	Ave. Unused Each	Fine Used Each	Ave. Used Each
☐294 1¢ Green & Black						
	750.00	580.00	25.00	11.00	3.00	2.00
☐295 2¢ Carmine & Black						
	2350.00	2100.00	20.00	12.00	1.00	.75
☐296 4¢ Chocolate & Black						
	2000.00	1500.00	100.00	60.00	15.00	8.00

Scott No.			Fine Unused Block	Ave. Unused Block	Fine Unused Each	Ave. Unused Each	Fine Used Each	Ave. Used Each
□297	5¢	Ultramarine & Black						
			2000.00	1600.00	120.00	80.00	13.00	8.00
□298	8¢	Brown Violet Black						
			2800.00	2000.00	160.00	92.00	50.00	40.00
□299	10¢	Yellow Brown Black						
			4000.00	2500.00	200.00	140.00	20.00	15.00

1902–1903. PERF. 12 (N-H ADD 50%)

Scott No.			Fine Unused Block	Ave. Unused Block	Fine Unused Each	Ave. Unused Each	Fine Used Each	Ave. Used Each
□300	1¢	Blue Green						
			175.00	120.00	13.50	7.50	.30	.20
□301	2¢	Carmine						
			160.00	120.00	16.00	10.00	.30	.20
□302	3¢	Violet						
			500.00	300.00	67.00	39.00	3.00	2.00
□303	4¢	Brown						
			510.00	300.00	65.00	40.00	1.50	.75
□304	5¢	Blue						
			600.00	480.00	65.00	42.00	1.50	.80
□305	6¢	Claret						
			590.00	450.00	70.00	48.00	2.50	1.00
□306	8¢	Violet Black						
			405.00	300.00	50.00	30.00	2.00	1.00
□307	10¢	Red Brown						
			700.00	615.00	70.00	46.00	1.70	.80
□308	13¢	Purple Black						
			420.00	280.00	55.00	40.00	8.00	5.00
□309	15¢	Olive Green						
			1100.00	725.00	180.00	125.00	5.00	3.00
□310	50¢	Orange						
			4000.00	2700.00	500.00	315.00	21.00	12.00
□311	$1	Black						
			4600.00	3400.00	800.00	500.00	42.00	30.00
□312	$2	Dark Blue						
			—	—	1200.00	750.00	160.00	90.00
□313	$5	Dark Green						
			—	—	320.00	2100.00	500.00	340.00

1906–1908. IMPERFORATED (N-H ADD 50%)

Scott No.			Fine Unused Block	Ave. Unused Block	Fine Unused Each	Ave. Unused Each	Fine Used Each	Ave. Used Each
□314	1¢	Blue Green						
			650.00	165.00	25.00	19.00	16.00	10.00

Scott No.	Fine Unused Block	Ave. Unused Block	Fine Unused Each	Ave. Unused Each	Fine Used Each	Ave. Used Each
☐315 5¢ Blue						
	4000.00	3100.00	450.00	310.00	35.00	18.00

1903. PERF. 12 (N-H ADD 50%)

☐319 2¢ Carmine						
	85.00	74.00	8.10	5.00	.40	.20
☐319a 2¢ Lake						
	140.00	90.00	14.00	9.00	.65	.38

1906. IMPERFORATED (N-H ADD 40%)

☐320 2¢ Carmine						
	200.00	160.00	25.00	19.00	15.00	8.00
☐320a 2¢ Lake						
	350.00	300.00	71.00	50.00	39.00	22.00

1904. LOUISIANA PURCHASE ISSUE
PERF. 12 (N-H ADD 50%)

☐323 1¢ Green						
	210.00	160.00	36.00	21.00	5.00	3.00
☐324 2¢ Carmine						
	200.00	140.00	30.00	19.00	2.00	1.10
☐325 3¢ Violet						
	800.00	600.00	100.00	65.00	30.00	20.00
☐326 5¢ Dark Blue						
	850.00	710.00	115.00	72.00	20.00	12.00
☐327 10¢ Red Brown						
	1400.00	1200.00	200.00	132.00	30.00	20.00

1907. JAMESTOWN EXPOSITION ISSUE
(N-H ADD 50%)

☐328 1¢ Green						
	265.00	150.00	35.00	20.00	5.00	2.50
☐329 2¢ Carmine						
	375.00	200.00	40.00	25.00	5.00	2.50
☐330 5¢ Blue						
	2100.00	1400.00	170.00	91.00	25.00	10.00

Scott No.	Fine Unused Block	Ave. Unused Block	Fine Unused Each	Ave. Unused Each	Fine Used Each	Ave. Used Each

1908–1909. DOUBLE LINE WATERMARKED "U.S.P.S." PERF. 12 (N-H ADD 60%)

Scott No.	Fine Unused Block	Ave. Unused Block	Fine Unused Each	Ave. Unused Each	Fine Used Each	Ave. Used Each
☐331 1¢ Green	72.00	50.00	8.00	6.00	.30	.15
☐332 2¢ Carmine	66.00	50.00	7.50	5.10	.30	.10
☐333 3¢ Violet	310.00	250.00	36.00	24.00	3.10	1.50
☐334 4¢ Orange Brown	300.00	250.00	45.00	31.00	1.30	.90
☐335 5¢ Blue	500.00	400.00	56.00	34.00	2.10	1.10
☐336 6¢ Red Orange	425.00	300.00	70.00	45.00	5.00	2.30
☐337 8¢ Olive Green	325.00	210.00	56.00	34.00	2.70	1.50
☐338 10¢ Yellow	600.00	425.00	75.00	50.00	1.40	.90
☐339 13¢ Blue Green	410.00	300.00	51.00	28.00	17.00	10.00
☐340 15¢ Pale Ultramarine	425.00	280.00	68.00	44.00	7.00	3.00
☐341 50¢ Violet	1600.00	800.00	350.00	230.00	18.00	10.00
☐342 $1 Violet Black	2400.00	160.00	550.00	350.00	70.00	40.00

IMPERFORATE (N-H ADD 30%)

Scott No.	Fine Unused Block	Ave. Unused Block	Fine Unused Each	Ave. Unused Each	Fine Used Each	Ave. Used Each
☐343 1¢ Green	64.00	45.00	8.00	6.00	5.00	3.00
☐344 2¢ Carmine	92.00	60.00	12.50	8.00	5.00	2.50
☐345 3¢ Deep Violet	210.00	150.00	26.00	18.00	12.00	9.00
☐346 4¢ Orange Brown	310.00	250.00	34.00	26.00	20.00	12.00
☐347 5¢ Blue	460.00	320.00	58.00	42.00	29.00	20.00

Scott No.	Fine Unused Line Pair	Ave. Unused Line Pair	Fine Unused Each	Ave. Unused Each	Fine Used Each	Ave. Used Each

1908–1910. COIL STAMPS
PERF. 12 HORIZONTALLY (N-H ADD 50%)

☐348 1¢ Green						
	170.00	130.00	35.00	24.00	13.00	8.00
☐349 2¢ Carmine						
	280.00	175.00	52.00	40.00	10.00	6.00
☐350 4¢ Orange Brown						
	640.00	410.00	140.00	90.00	70.00	35.00
☐351 5¢ Blue						
	710.00	400.00	150.00	100.00	80.00	42.00

PERF. 12 VERTICALLY (N-H ADD 40%)

☐352 1¢ Green						
	350.00	280.00	78.00	49.00	31.00	20.00
☐353 2¢ Carmine						
	350.00	260.00	85.00	60.00	9.00	5.00
☐354 4¢ Orange Brown						
	700.00	510.00	200.00	120.00	50.00	28.00
☐355 5¢ Blue						
	750.00	610.00	200.00	120.00	76.00	50.00
☐356 10¢ Yellow						
	—	—	2250.00	1400.00	800.00	400.00

Scott No.	Fine Unused Block	Ave. Unused Block	Fine Unused Each	Ave. Unused Each	Fine Used Each	Ave. Used Each

1909. BLUISH GRAY PAPER
PERF. 12 (N-H ADD 60%)

☐357 1¢ Green						
	670.00	500.00	125.00	78.00	68.00	45.00
☐358 2¢ Carmine						
	710.00	460.00	128.00	78.00	80.00	42.00
☐359 3¢ Violet						
	—	—	2500.00	1400.00	—	—
☐360 4¢ Orange Brown						
	—	—	16,000.00	12,000.00	—	—
☐361 5¢ Blue						
	—	—	3400.00	2800.00	—	—

Scott No.	Fine Unused Block	Ave. Unused Block	Fine Unused Each	Ave. Unused Each	Fine Used Each	Ave. Used Each
□362 6¢ Orange						
	—	—	1800.00	1100.00	1000.00	500.00
□363 8¢ Olive Green						
	—	—	18,500.00	10,000.00	—	—
□364 10¢ Yellow						
	—	—	2000.00	1150.00	1000.00	500.00
□365 13¢ Blue Green						
	—	—	2150.00	1500.00	—	—
□366 15¢ Pale Ultramarine						
	—	—	1600.00	900.00	900.00	400.00

1909. LINCOLN MEMORIAL ISSUE (N-H ADD 50%)

Scott No.	Fine Unused Block	Ave. Unused Block	Fine Unused Each	Ave. Unused Each	Fine Used Each	Ave. Used Each
□367 2¢ Carmine						
	110.00	80.00	6.50	4.50	2.00	1.25
□368 2¢ Carmine, Impf.						
	200.00	160.00	31.00	21.00	16.00	10.00
□369 2¢ Carmine (On B.G. Paper)						
	1000.00	800.00	270.00	200.00	150.00	80.00

1909. ALASKA–YUKON ISSUE (N-H ADD 40%)

Scott No.	Fine Unused Block	Ave. Unused Block	Fine Unused Each	Ave. Unused Each	Fine Used Each	Ave. Used Each
□370 2¢ Carmine						
	200.00	160.00	10.50	7.10	1.60	.70
□371 2¢ Carmine, Impf.						
	200.00	145.00	46.00	35.00	21.00	15.00

1909. HUDSON–FULTON ISSUE (N-H ADD 40%)

Scott No.	Fine Unused Block	Ave. Unused Block	Fine Unused Each	Ave. Unused Each	Fine Used Each	Ave. Used Each
□372 2¢ Carmine						
	220.00	170.00	13.00	11.00	4.00	2.50
□373 2¢ Carmine, Impf.						
	280.00	200.00	42.00	36.00	22.00	16.00

1910–1911. SINGLE LINE WATERMARKED "U.S.P.S." PERF. 12 (N-H ADD 50%)

Scott No.	Fine Unused Block	Ave. Unused Block	Fine Unused Each	Ave. Unused Each	Fine Used Each	Ave. Used Each
□374 1¢ Green						
	72.00	50.00	9.00	6.00	.25	.15
□375 2¢ Carmine						
	73.00	51.00	8.00	7.00	.30	.18
□376 3¢ Deep Violet						
	110.00	85.00	22.00	16.00	1.50	.90

Scott No.	Fine Unused Block	Ave. Unused Block	Fine Unused Each	Ave. Unused Each	Fine Used Each	Ave. Used Each
☐377 4¢ Brown						
	200.00	140.00	36.00	23.00	.85	.40
☐378 5¢ Blue						
	240.00	170.00	34.00	22.00	.70	.40
☐379 6¢ Red Orange						
	285.00	160.00	42.00	27.00	1.00	.60
☐380 8¢ Olive Green						
	65.00	380.00	132.00	82.00	10.00	6.00
☐381 10¢ Yellow						
	410.00	370.00	150.00	85.00	4.10	2.00
☐382 15¢ Ultramarine						
	1150.00	800.00	300.00	210.00	13.50	8.00

IMPERFORATE (N-H ADD 50%)

☐383 1¢ Green						
	55.00	40.00	4.25	3.00	2.10	1.25
☐384 2¢ Carmine						
	50.00	42.00	7.10	6.00	3.25	1.90

Scott No.	Fine Unused Line Pair	Ave. Unused Line Pair	Fine Unused Each	Ave. Unused Each	Fine Used Each	Ave. Used Each
1910–1913. COIL STAMPS						
PERF. 12 HORIZONTALLY (N-H ADD 40%)						
☐385 1¢ Green						
	325.00	200.00	32.00	21.00	12.50	5.00
☐386 2¢ Carmine						
	600.00	400.00	60.00	39.00	15.00	8.00

PERF. 12 VERTICALLY (N-H ADD 50%)

☐387 1¢ Green						
	425.00	300.00	120.00	85.00	38.00	18.00
☐388 2¢ Carmine						
	4400.00	320.00	600.00	400.00	225.00	95.00

PERF. 8½ HORIZONTALLY (N-H ADD 50%)

☐390 1¢ Green						
	3.50	21.00	6.50	5.00	4.00	2.10

Scott No.	Fine Unused Line Pair	Ave. Unused Line Pair	Fine Unused Each	Ave. Unused Each	Fine Used Each	Ave. Used Each
□391 2¢ Carmine						
	215.00	120.00	41.00	27.00	9.10	4.50

PERF. 8½ VERTICALLY (N-H ADD 40%)

Scott No.	Fine Unused Line Pair	Ave. Unused Line Pair	Fine Unused Each	Ave. Unused Each	Fine Used Each	Ave. Used Each
□392 1¢ Green						
	120.00	950.00	28.00	20.00	12.00	8.00
□393 2¢ Carmine						
	175.00	110.00	48.00	30.00	8.00	4.00
□394 3¢ Violet						
	250.00	190.00	60.00	41.00	40.00	25.00
□395 4¢ Brown						
	260.00	210.00	61.00	45.00	40.00	30.00
□396 5¢ Blue						
	275.00	200.00	60.00	51.00	41.00	30.00

Scott No.	Fine Unused Block	Ave. Unused Block	Fine Unused Each	Ave. Unused Each	Fine Used Each	Ave. Used Each

1913–1915. PANAMA–PACIFIC ISSUE
PERF. 12 (N-H ADD 50%)

Scott No.	Fine Unused Block	Ave. Unused Block	Fine Unused Each	Ave. Unused Each	Fine Used Each	Ave. Used Each
□397 1¢ Green						
	140.00	90.00	20.00	12.00	1.70	1.00
□398 2¢ Carmine						
	250.00	210.00	22.00	16.00	.60	.30
□399 5¢ Blue						
	480.00	400.00	80.00	50.00	8.50	4.10
□400 10¢ Orange Yellow						
	850.00	600.00	150.00	120.00	18.00	8.00
□400A 10¢ Orange						
	1250.00	1000.00	300.00	175.00	17.00	9.00

PERF. 10 (N-H ADD 50%)

Scott No.	Fine Unused Block	Ave. Unused Block	Fine Unused Each	Ave. Unused Each	Fine Used Each	Ave. Used Each
□401 1¢ Green						
	250.00	190.00	31.00	21.00	7.00	5.00
□402 2¢ Carmine						
	425.00	300.00	85.00	62.00	2.10	1.00
□403 5¢ Blue						
	1250.00	900.00	200.00	150.00	17.00	9.00

Scott No.	Fine Unused Block	Ave. Unused Block	Fine Unused Each	Ave. Unused Each	Fine Used Each	Ave. Used Each
□404 10¢ Orange						
	6100.00	4100.00	1200.00	750.00	60.00	40.00

1912–1914. REGULAR ISSUE
PERF. 12 (N-H ADD 50%)

Scott No.	Fine Unused Block	Ave. Unused Block	Fine Unused Each	Ave. Unused Each	Fine Used Each	Ave. Used Each
□405 1¢ Green						
	850.00	600.00	7.00	4.75	.21	.15
□406 2¢ Carmine						
	92.00	82.00	6.50	4.50	.21	.15
□407 7¢ Black						
	500.00	375.00	85.00	55.00	9.00	5.00

IMPERFORATE (N-H ADD 50%)

Scott No.	Fine Unused Block	Ave. Unused Block	Fine Unused Each	Ave. Unused Each	Fine Used Each	Ave. Used Each
□408 1¢ Green						
	20.00	12.00	1.50	1.00	.60	.30
□409 2¢ Carmine						
	38.00	30.00	1.70	1.10	.70	.45

Scott No.	Fine Unused Line Pair	Ave. Unused Line Pair	Fine Unused Each	Ave. Unused Each	Fine Used Each	Ave. Used Each

1912. COIL STAMPS
PERF. 8½ HORIZONTALLY (N-H ADD 50%)

Scott No.	Fine Unused Line Pair	Ave. Unused Line Pair	Fine Unused Each	Ave. Unused Each	Fine Used Each	Ave. Used Each
□410 1¢ Green						
	45.00	25.00	8.00	5.00	4.00	2.00
□411 2¢ Carmine						
	50.00	22.00	12.00	8.00	4.00	2.00

PERF. 8½ VERTICALLY (N-H ADD 50%)

Scott No.	Fine Unused Line Pair	Ave. Unused Line Pair	Fine Unused Each	Ave. Unused Each	Fine Used Each	Ave. Used Each
□412 1¢ Green						
	110.00	60.00	31.00	21.00	6.00	3.00
□413 2¢ Carmine						
	220.00	150.00	50.00	31.00	3.00	1.00

Scott No.	Fine Unused Block	Ave. Unused Block	Fine Unused Each	Ave. Unused Each	Fine Used Each	Ave. Used Each

1912–1914. SINGLE LINE WATERMARKED "U.S.P.S." PERF. 12 (N-H ADD 50%)

☐414 8¢ Olive Green

	275.00	180.00	50.00	32.00	1.50	.90

☐415 9¢ Salmon Red

	450.00	300.00	56.00	39.00	11.00	7.00

☐416 10¢ Orange Yellow

	400.00	210.00	50.00	34.00	.40	.25

☐417 12¢ Claret Brown

	350.00	210.00	58.00	38.00	4.00	2.00

☐418 15¢ Gray

	500.00	340.00	110.00	60.00	4.00	2.50

☐419 20¢ Ultramarine

	1150.00	650.00	210.00	140.00	13.00	7.00

☐420 30¢ Orange Red

	700.00	450.00	130.00	90.00	14.00	9.00

☐421 50¢ Violet

	2100.00	1400.00	440.00	320.00	18.00	10.00

1912. DOUBLE LINE WATERMARKED "U.S.P.S." (N-H ADD 50%)

☐422 50¢ Violet

	1100.00	800.00	300.00	210.00	16.00	9.00

☐423 $1 Violet Black

	260.00	190.00	550.00	380.00	58.00	36.00

1914–1915. SINGLE LINE WATERMARKED "U.S.P.S." PERF. 10 (N-H ADD 55%)

☐424 1¢ Green

	31.00	20.00	4.00	3.00	.25	.15

☐425 2¢ Carmine

	25.00	15.00	4.00	2.50	.25	.15

☐426 3¢ Deep Violet

	100.00	65.00	18.00	11.00	1.50	.70

☐427 4¢ Brown

	180.00	140.00	44.00	29.00	.80	.50

☐428 5¢ Blue

	250.00	150.00	40.00	27.00	.65	.40

Scott No.	Fine Unused Block	Ave. Unused Block	Fine Unused Each	Ave. Unused Each	Fine Used Each	Ave. Used Each
□429 6¢ Orange						
	285.00	190.00	62.00	40.00	2.00	1.00
□430 7¢ Black						
	800.00	610.00	90.00	65.00	5.00	2.50
□431 8¢ Olive Green						
	400.00	275.00	45.00	30.00	2.00	1.00
□432 9¢ Salmon Red						
	600.00	350.00	58.00	40.00	10.00	5.00
□433 12¢ Orange Yellow						
	600.00	450.00	56.00	37.00	.50	.15
□434 11¢ Dark Green						
	210.00	125.00	30.00	20.00	8.00	5.00
□435 12¢ Claret Brown						
	230.00	150.00	32.00	20.00	6.75	3.50
□435a 12¢ Copper Red						
	240.00	150.00	46.00	24.00	7.00	4.00
□437 15¢ Gray						
	740.00	550.00	135.00	150.00	7.10	5.00
□438 20¢ Ultramarine						
	2000.00	1300.00	240.00	150.00	5.00	3.00
□439 30¢ Orange Red						
	270.00	1800.00	300.00	200.00	19.00	14.00
□440 50¢ Violet						
	9500.00	6750.00	650.00	450.00	20.00	11.00

Scott No.	Fine Unused Line Pair	Ave. Unused Line Pair	Fine Unused Each	Ave. Unused Each	Fine Used Each	Ave. Used Each
1914. COIL STAMPS						
PERF. 10 HORIZONTALLY (N-H ADD 30%)						
□441 1¢ Green						
	7.50	4.50	1.75	1.00	.90	.50
□442 2¢ Carmine						
	50.00	34.00	12.00	8.00	6.00	4.00
PERF. 10 VERTICALLY (N-H ADD 50%)						
□443 1¢ Green						
	115.00	75.00	31.00	20.00	6.00	4.00

Scott No.		Fine Unused Line Pair	Ave. Unused Line Pair	Fine Unused Each	Ave. Unused Each	Fine Used Each	Ave. Used Each
☐444	2¢ Carmine						
		200.00	150.00	42.00	30.00	1.50	.90
☐445	3¢ Violet						
		850.00	510.00	300.00	190.00	90.00	50.00
☐446	4¢ Brown						
		580.00	400.00	150.00	100.00	41.00	25.00
☐447	5¢ Blue						
		200.00	175.00	65.00	40.00	30.00	15.00

1914–1916. ROTARY PRESS COIL STAMPS PERF. 10 HORIZONTALLY (N-H ADD 50%)

		Fine Unused Line Pair	Ave. Unused Line Pair	Fine Unused Each	Ave. Unused Each	Fine Used Each	Ave. Used Each
☐448	1¢ Green						
		40.00	26.00	9.50	6.50	3.90	2.50
☐449	2¢ Red (I)						
		—	—	2900.00	1900.00	375.00	250.00
☐450	2¢ Carmine (III)						
		50.00	35.00	13.50	9.00	3.00	2.00

PERF. 10 VERTICALLY (N-H ADD 60%)

		Fine Unused Line Pair	Ave. Unused Line Pair	Fine Unused Each	Ave. Unused Each	Fine Used Each	Ave. Used Each
☐452	1¢ Green						
		67.00	43.00	17.00	10.00	2.25	1.00
☐453	2¢ Red (I)						
		470.00	325.00	140.00	90.00	4.00	2.25
☐454	2¢ Carmine (II)						
		420.00	310.00	150.00	80.00	10.00	6.00
☐455	2¢ Carmine (III)						
		50.00	42.00	11.00	9.00	1.25	.65
☐456	3¢ Violet						
		510.00	400.00	350.00	220.00	80.00	60.00
☐457	4¢ Brown						
		125.00	95.00	36.00	26.00	17.00	10.00
☐458	5¢ Blue						
		160.00	90.00	40.00	30.00	18.00	10.00

IMPERFORATE (N-H ADD 50%)

		Fine Unused Line Pair	Ave. Unused Line Pair	Fine Unused Each	Ave. Unused Each	Fine Used Each	Ave. Used Each
☐459	2¢ Carmine						
		1325.00	900.00	475.00	360.00	—	—

Scott No.	Fine Unused Block	Ave. Unused Block	Fine Unused Each	Ave. Unused Each	Fine Used Each	Ave. Used Each

1915. DOUBLE LINE WATERMARKED "U.S.P.S." PERF. 10 (N-H ADD 40%)

☐460 $1 Violet Black

| | 3700.00 | 2800.00 | 1000.00 | 650.00 | 71.00 | 50.00 |

1915. SINGLE LINE WATERMARKED "U.S.P.S." PERF. 11 (N-H ADD 50%)

☐461 2¢ Pale Carmine Rose

| | 300.00 | 200.00 | 185.00 | 100.00 | 80.00 | 65.00 |

1916–1917. UNWATERMARKED PERF. 10 (N-H ADD 60%)

☐462 1¢ Green

| | 100.00 | 72.00 | 10.50 | 8.00 | .45 | .25 |

☐463 2¢ Carmine

| | 100.00 | 70.00 | 6.00 | 3.10 | .20 | .10 |

☐464 3¢ Violet

| | 1100.00 | 700.00 | 90.00 | 60.00 | 11.00 | 7.00 |

☐465 4¢ Orange Brown

| | 490.00 | 380.00 | 60.00 | 40.00 | 2.50 | 1.00 |

☐466 5¢ Blue

| | 800.00 | 500.00 | 95.00 | 62.00 | 2.00 | 1.00 |

☐467 5¢ Carmine (error)

| | — | 1000.00 | 850.00 | 510.00 | — | — |

☐468 6¢ Red Orange

| | 620.00 | 450.00 | 112.00 | 74.00 | 7.00 | 4.00 |

☐469 7¢ Black

| | 500.00 | 410.00 | 140.00 | 90.00 | 12.00 | 6.00 |

☐470 58¢ Olive Green

| | 450.00 | 350.00 | 68.00 | 50.00 | 5.00 | 3.50 |

☐471 9¢ Salmon Red

| | 400.00 | 260.00 | 70.00 | 42.00 | 12.00 | 7.00 |

☐472 12¢ Orange Yellow

| | 1100.00 | 590.00 | 150.00 | 80.00 | 1.25 | .50 |

☐473 11¢ Dark Green

| | 215.00 | 175.00 | 48.00 | 30.00 | 16.00 | 9.00 |

☐474 12¢ Claret Brown

| | 400.00 | 310.00 | 61.00 | 40.00 | 6.00 | 4.00 |

☐475 15¢ Gray

| | 710.00 | 600.00 | 220.00 | 150.00 | 11.00 | 6.50 |

Scott No.	Fine Unused Block	Ave. Unused Block	Fine Unused Each	Ave. Unused Each	Fine Used Each	Ave. Used Each
☐476 20¢ Ultramarine						
	2100.00	1900.00	290.00	180.00	12.00	8.00
☐477 50¢ Light Violet						
	6200.00	4600.00	1200.00	800.00	70.00	44.00
☐478 $1 Violet Black						
	4000.00	2700.00	900.00	610.00	20.00	10.00

1916–1917. DESIGN OF 1902–1903 PERF. 10 (N-H ADD 40%)

☐479 $2 Dark Blue						
	1900.00	1400.00	410.00	280.00	41.00	30.00
☐480 $5 Light Green						
	2100.00	1500.00	350.00	240.00	39.00	35.00

IMPERFORATE (N-H ADD 40%)

☐481 1¢ Green						
	13.00	7.00	1.25	.85	.75	.40
☐482 2¢ Carmine						
	20.00	15.00	1.90	1.60	1.15	.85
☐483 3¢ Violet (I)						
	120.00	90.00	18.00	12.50	8.00	5.00
☐484 3¢ Violet (II)						
	115.00	65.00	13.00	10.50	4.50	2.75

Scott No.	Fine Unused Line Pair	Ave. Unused Line Pair	Fine Unused Each	Ave. Unused Each	Fine Used Each	Ave. Used Each

1916–1922. ROTARY PRESS COIL STAMPS PERF. 10 HORIZONTALLY (N-H ADD 50%)

☐486 1¢ Green						
	4.75	3.00	1.50	1.00	.30	.20
☐487 2¢ Carmine (II)						
	110.00	80.00	20.00	14.00	4.60	2.10
☐488 2¢ Carmine (III)						
	20.00	11.00	4.00	3.00	1.45	.80
☐489 3¢ Violet						
	30.00	24.00	6.50	4.00	1.70	.90

Scott No.		Fine Unused Line Pair	Ave. Unused Line Pair	Fine Unused Each	Ave. Unused Each	Fine Used Each	Ave. Used Each

PERF. 10 VERTICALLY (N-H ADD 50%)

Scott No.		Fine Unused Line Pair	Ave. Unused Line Pair	Fine Unused Each	Ave. Unused Each	Fine Used Each	Ave. Used Each
☐490	1¢ Green	4.00	3.50	.75	.52	.30	.15
☐491	2¢ Carmine (II)	—	—	2200.00	1600.00	460.00	300.00
☐492	2¢ Carmine (III)	30.00	15.00	11.00	7.50	.38	.20
☐493	3¢ Violet (I)	42.00	30.00	20.00	14.00	3.00	1.50
☐494	3¢ Violet (II)	50.00	44.00	13.00	9.00	1.00	.70
☐495	4¢ Orange Brown	65.00	42.00	13.00	9.00	4.00	2.00
☐496	5¢ Blue	24.00	16.00	5.00	3.00	1.00	.65
☐497	10¢ Orange Yellow	130.00	72.00	25.00	16.00	8.50	6.00

Scott No.		Fine Unused Block	Ave. Unused Block	Fine Unused Each	Ave. Unused Each	Fine Used Each	Ave. Used Each

1917–1919. FLAT PLATE PRINTING PERF. 11 (N-H ADD 50%)

Scott No.		Fine Unused Block	Ave. Unused Block	Fine Unused Each	Ave. Unused Each	Fine Used Each	Ave. Used Each
☐498	1¢ Green	16.00	12.00	.60	.45	.25	.18
☐499	2¢ Rose (I)	15.00	13.00	.55	.42	.20	.16
☐500	2¢ Deep Rose (Ia)	100.00	90.00	325.00	200.00	150.00	90.00
☐501	3¢ Violet (I)	140.00	82.00	16.00	10.00	.20	.15
☐502	3¢ Violet (II)	160.00	110.00	21.00	13.00	.45	.20
☐503	4¢ Brown	160.00	110.00	14.00	9.00	.35	.20
☐504	5¢ Blue	125.00	82.00	11.00	8.00	.30	.20
☐505	5¢ Rose (error)	—	—	510.00	360.00	—	—

Scott No.	Fine Unused Block	Ave. Unused Block	Fine Unused Each	Ave. Unused Each	Fine Used Each	Ave. Used Each
☐506 6¢ Red Orange						
	210.00	115.00	16.50	10.00	.45	.25
☐507 7¢ Black						
	360.00	220.00	32.00	24.00	1.50	.80
☐508 8¢ Olive Bistre						
	192.00	120.00	15.00	10.00	1.10	.80
☐509 9¢ Salmon Red						
	180.00	115.00	20.00	12.00	2.10	1.50
☐510 10¢ Orange Yellow						
	250.00	180.00	23.00	15.00	.30	.15
☐511 11¢ Light Green						
	140.00	90.00	11.00	9.00	3.00	1.50
☐512 12¢ Claret Brown						
	150.00	85.00	11.00	8.00	.60	.40
☐513 13¢ Apple Green						
	125.00	78.00	15.00	9.00	6.00	3.00
☐514 15¢ Gray						
	600.00	380.00	50.00	34.00	1.00	.50
☐515 20¢ Ultramarine						
	650.00	410.00	62.00	41.00	.50	.25
☐516 30¢ Orange Red						
	500.00	325.00	51.00	34.00	1.00	.40
☐517 50¢ Red Violet						
	1100.00	610.00	85.00	60.00	.80	.40
☐518 $1 Violet Brown						
	810.00	600.00	84.00	50.00	2.00	1.00
☐518b $1 Deep Brown						
	2600.00	1600.00	1800.00	1250.00	600.00	300.00

1917. DOUBLE LINE WATERMARKED "U.S.P.S." DESIGN OF 1908–1909 PERF. 11 (N-H ADD 50%)

☐519 2¢ Carmine						
	2100.00	1300.00	600.00	329.00	230.00	100.00

1918. UNWATERMARKED PERF. 11 (N-H ADD 40%)

☐523 $2 Orange Red & Black						
	7200.00	5200.00	800.00	500.00	210.00	100.00
☐524 $5 Deep Green & Black						
	3100.00	2100.00	320.00	200.00	30.00	18.00

Scott No.	Fine Unused Block	Ave. Unused Block	Fine Unused Each	Ave. Unused Each	Fine Used Each	Ave. Used Each
1918–1920. OFFSET PRINTING PERF. 11 (N-H ADD 50%)						
☐525 1¢ Gray Green						
	18.00	15.00	3.00	2.00	.85	.40
☐526 2¢ Carmine (IV)						
	175.00	140.00	31.00	20.00	4.00	2.50
☐527 2¢ Carmine (V)						
	150.00	75.00	25.00	17.00	1.30	.70
☐528 2¢ Carmine (Va)						
	56.00	32.00	11.00	7.00	.50	.25
☐528A 2¢ Carmine (VI)						
	250.00	210.00	64.00	41.00	1.30	.70
☐528B 2¢ Carmine (VII)						
	100.00	75.00	25.00	17.00	.30	.20
☐529 3¢ Violet (III)						
	50.00	31.00	4.00	2.50	.30	.15
☐530 3¢ Purple (IV)						
	10.00	5.10	2.50	1.10	.30	.15
1918–1920. IMPERFORATE (N-H ADD 30%)						
☐531 1¢ Gray Green						
	84.00	58.00	20.00	10.00	8.00	5.00
☐532 2¢ Carmine (IV)						
	270.00	210.00	42.00	32.00	29.00	15.00
☐533 2¢ Carmine (V)						
	950.00	800.00	235.00	170.00	80.00	45.00
☐534 2¢ Carmine (Va)						
	100.00	80.00	16.00	12.00	7.00	3.00
☐534A 2¢ Carmine (VI)						
	300.00	210.00	44.00	34.00	25.00	15.00
☐534B 2¢ Carmine (VII)						
	—	—	1800.00	1400.00	650.00	400.00
☐535 3¢ Violet						
	70.00	55.00	11.00	7.00	6.00	4.00
1918–1920. PERF. 12 ½ (N-H ADD 50%)						
☐536 1¢ Gray Green						
	140.00	110.00	23.00	15.00	12.50	7.00

IMPORTANT NOTICE: Beginning here, prices of **blocks** are for blocks of 4 with **plate number attached**. Ordinary blocks of 4 bring lower prices. Plate blocks consisting of more than 4 stamps would sell higher than these sums. Always check the **headings** of price columns to accurately value your stamps.

Scott No.	Fine Unused Plate Blk	Ave. Unused Plate Blk	Fine Unused Each	Ave. Unused Each	Fine Used Each	Ave. Used Each
1919. VICTORY ISSUE (N-H ADD 70%)						
☐537 3¢ Violet						
	95.00	82.00	11.00	8.00	3.50	2.10
1919–1921. REGULAR ISSUE ROTARY PRESS PRINTING PERF. 11 x 10 (N-H ADD 70%)						
☐538 1¢ Green						
	110.00	80.00	15.00	9.00	8.00	4.00
☐538a Same Impf. Horiz. Pair						
	—	—	75.00	60.00	—	—
☐539 2¢ Carmine Rose (II)						
	—	—	3800.00	2650.00	1100.00	600.00
☐540 2¢ Carmine Rose (III)						
	73.00	51.00	16.00	10.00	8.00	5.00
☐540a Same Impf. Horiz. Pair						
	—	—	78.00	50.00	—	—
☐541 3¢ Violet						
	330.00	210.00	49.00	31.00	25.00	18.00
PERF. 10 x 11 (N-H ADD 70%)						
☐542 1¢ Green						
	110.00	82.00	17.00	10.00	1.00	.50
PERF. 10 x 10 (N-H ADD 70%)						
☐543 1¢ Green						
	18.00	12.00	1.10	.75	.28	.15
PERF. 11 x 11 (N-H ADD 70%)						
☐544 1¢ Green						
	—	—	—	—	3000.00	2000.00
☐545 1¢ Green						
	710.00	65.00	190.00	125.00	100.00	81.00

Scott No.		Fine Unused Plate Blk	Ave. Unused Plate Blk	Fine Unused Each	Ave. Unused Each	Fine Used Each	Ave. Used Each
□546	2¢ Carmine Rose						
		520.00	410.00	150.00	100.00	80.00	50.00

FLAT PLATE PRINTING PERF. 11 (N-H ADD 50%)

□547	$2 Carmine & Black						
		—	—	250.00	170.00	38.00	22.00

1920. PILGRIM ISSUE (N-H ADD 50%)

□548	1¢ Green						
		40.00	38.00	5.00	3.50	3.00	1.10
□549	2¢ Carmine Rose						
		63.00	41.00	8.00	6.00	2.50	1.40
□550	5¢ Deep Blue						
		410.00	310.00	51.00	36.00	17.00	12.00

1922–1925. PERF. FLAT PLATE PRINTING PERF. 11 (N-H ADD 50%)

□551	½¢ Olive Brown						
		7.60	6.25	6.00	.35	.20	.15
□552	1¢ Deep Green						
		23.00	15.00	2.00	1.40	.20	.17
□553	1½¢ Yellow Brown						
		30.00	26.00	3.50	2.60	.30	.15
□554	2¢ Carmine						
		20.00	15.00	2.50	2.00	.20	.15
□555	3¢ Violet						
		180.00	140.00	24.00	16.00	1.10	.40
□556	4¢ Yellow Brown						
		175.00	150.00	24.00	16.00	.38	.15
□557	5¢ Dark Blue						
		190.00	170.00	24.00	16.00	.30	.15
□558	6¢ Red Orange						
		300.00	240.00	42.00	31.00	.70	.40
□559	7¢ Black						
		65.00	52.00	10.00	8.00	.75	.40
□560	8¢ Olive Green						
		500.00	400.00	51.00	38.00	.80	.40
□561	9¢ Rose						
		150.00	110.00	20.00	14.00	1.25	.60

Scott No.	Fine Unused Plate Blk	Ave. Unused Plate Blk	Fine Unused Each	Ave. Unused Each	Fine Used Each	Ave. Used Each
☐562 10¢ Orange						
	220.00	180.00	26.00	19.00	.25	.15
☐563 11¢ Blue/Green						
	35.00	22.00	2.10	1.70	.50	.25
☐564 12¢ Brown Violet						
	80.00	70.00	10.00	6.00	.30	.18
☐565 14¢ Dark Blue						
	62.00	42.00	6.50	4.00	1.00	.40
☐566 15¢ Gray						
	260.00	210.00	29.00	21.00	.25	.17
☐567 20¢ Carmine Rose						
	230.00	190.00	28.00	22.00	.25	.17
☐568 25¢ Green						
	210.00	160.00	26.00	18.00	.60	.40
☐569 30¢ Olive Brown						
	330.00	250.00	43.00	29.00	.60	.32
☐570 50¢ Lilac						
	900.00	610.00	72.00	51.00	.40	.21
☐571 $1 Violet Black						
	425.00	310.00	60.00	41.00	.50	.25
☐572 $2 Deep Blue						
	1000.00	850.00	140.00	100.00	9.00	5.00
☐573 $5 Carmine & Blue						
	2000.00	1200.00	280.00	180.00	14.00	6.50

IMPERFORATE (N-H ADD 40%)

Scott No.	Fine Unused Plate Blk	Ave. Unused Plate Blk	Fine Unused Each	Ave. Unused Each	Fine Used Each	Ave. Used Each
☐575 1¢ Green						
	78.00	62.00	10.00	7.00	4.00	1.80
☐576 1½¢ Yellow Brown						
	24.00	18.00	2.00	1.80	1.45	.75
☐577 2¢ Carmine						
	25.00	20.00	2.50	2.10	1.70	.75

1923–1926. ROTARY PRESS PRINTING
PERF. 11 x 10 (N-H ADD 50%)

Scott No.	Fine Unused Plate Blk	Ave. Unused Plate Blk	Fine Unused Each	Ave. Unused Each	Fine Used Each	Ave. Used Each
☐578 1¢ Green						
	615.00	450.00	115.00	70.00	90.00	50.00
☐579 2¢ Carmine						
	450.00	225.00	98.00	60.00	40.00	30.00

Scott No.	Fine Unused Plate Blk	Ave. Unused Plate Blk	Fine Unused Each	Ave. Unused Each	Fine Used Each	Ave. Used Each
1923–1296. PERF. 10 (N-H ADD 50%)						
☐581 1¢ Green						
	95.00	65.00	12.50	8.00	1.10	.50
☐582 1½¢ Brown						
	50.00	35.00	5.50	4.10	.80	.40
☐583 2¢ Carmine						
	26.00	21.00	3.00	1.50	.30	.20
☐584 3¢ Violet						
	190.00	160.00	31.00	21.00	2.50	1.15
☐585 4¢ Yellow Brown						
	150.00	125.00	22.00	14.00	.65	.40
☐586 5¢ Blue						
	150.00	110.00	20.00	15.00	.40	.20
☐587 6¢ Red Orange						
	73.00	61.00	9.00	8.00	.80	.40
☐588 7¢ Black						
	120.00	75.00	13.00	10.00	6.50	3.10
☐589 8¢ Olive Green						
	185.00	150.00	31.00	19.00	3.50	2.00
☐590 9¢ Rose						
	40.00	30.00	5.75	4.00	2.00	1.00
☐591 10¢ Orange						
	600.00	410.00	72.00	48.00	.60	.25

1923–1926. ROTARY PRESS COIL STAMPS PERF. 11 (N-H ADD 50%)

☐595 2¢ Carmine						
	1250.00	810.00	325.00	210.00	240.00	120.00

Scott No.	Fine Unused Line Pair	Ave. Unused Line Pair	Fine Unused Each	Ave. Unused Each	Fine Used Each	Ave. Used Each
1923–1929. ROTARY PRESS COIL STAMPS PERF. 10 VERTICALLY (N-H ADD 50%)						
☐597 1¢ Green						
	2.00	1.50	.50	.35	.25	.15
☐598 1½¢ Deep Brown						
	4.50	3.50	1.05	.75	.25	.15
☐599 2¢ Carmine (I)						
	2.40	1.25	.60	.40	.25	.17

Scott No.	Fine Unused Line Pair	Ave. Unused Line Pair	Fine Unused Each	Ave. Unused Each	Fine Used Each	Ave. Used Each
☐599A 2¢ Carmine (II)						
	510.00	360.00	170.00	105.00	11.00	6.50
☐600 3¢ Deep Violet						
	28.00	21.00	7.50	5.50	.40	.15
☐601 4¢ Yellow Brown						
	31.00	26.00	5.00	4.50	.60	.35
☐602 5¢ Dark Blue						
	13.00	7.50	2.25	1.50	.30	.17
☐603 10¢ Orange						
	24.00	17.00	4.00	3.00	.35	.15

PERF. 10 HORIZONTALLY (N-H ADD 40%)

☐604 1¢ Green						
	3.20	1.50	.45	.28	.25	.15
☐605 1½¢ Yellow Brown						
	3.00	1.50	.45	.28	.25	.15
☐606 2¢ Carmine						
	3.00	1.50	.45	.30	.25	.15

Scott No.	Fine Unused Plate Blk	Ave. Unused Plate Blk	Fine Unused Each	Ave. Unused Each	Fine Used Each	Ave. Used Each

1923. HARDING MEMORIAL ISSUE (N-H ADD 40%)

☐610 2¢ Black, pf. 11						
	24.00	15.00	.80	.55	.25	.16
☐611 2¢ Black, imperf.						
	120.00	80.00	9.00	6.00	5.00	3.00
☐612 2¢ Black, pf. 10 rotary						
	270.00	220.00	21.00	15.00	2.10	1.15

1924. HUGUENOT–WALLOON ISSUE (N-H ADD 40%)

☐614 1¢ Green						
	43.00	24.00	4.00	3.00	2.50	1.75
☐615 2¢ Carmine Rose						
	80.00	65.00	7.00	4.50	2.50	1.75
☐616 5¢ Dark Blue						
	370.00	285.00	38.00	30.00	15.00	9.00

Scott No.	Fine Unused Plate Blk	Ave. Unused Plate Blk	Fine Unused Each	Ave. Unused Each	Fine Used Each	Ave. Used Each

1925. LEXINGTON–CONCORD SESQUICENTENNIAL (N-H ADD 40%)

□617 1¢ Green

| | 43.00 | 32.00 | 4.00 | 3.00 | 2.50 | 1.50 |

□618 2¢ Carmine Rose

| | 70.00 | 55.00 | 6.50 | 4.50 | 4.10 | 2.00 |

□619 5¢ Dark Blue

| | 320.00 | 250.00 | 36.00 | 27.00 | 14.00 | 9.00 |

1925. NORSE–AMERICAN ISSUE (N-H ADD 50%)

□620 2¢ Carmine & Black

| | 172.00 | 120.00 | 6.00 | 4.10 | 3.00 | 2.00 |

□621 5¢ Dark Blue & Black

| | 610.00 | 510.00 | 18.00 | 14.00 | 10.00 | 7.00 |

1925–1926. PERF 11. (N–H ADD 40%)

□622 13¢ Green

| | 150.00 | 90.00 | 19.00 | 14.00 | 1.00 | .60 |

□623 17¢ Black

| | 160.00 | 115.00 | 21.00 | 14.00 | .50 | .25 |

1926–1927. COMMEMORATIVES _____
1926. SESQUICENTENNIAL EXPOSITION (N-H ADD 40%)

□627 2¢ Carmine Rose

| | 44.00 | 30.00 | 4.00 | 2.50 | .60 | .35 |

1926. ERICSSON MEMORIAL ISSUE (N-H ADD 40%)

□628 5¢ Gray Lilac

| | 93.00 | 75.00 | 8.10 | 6.00 | 4.00 | 2.00 |

1926. BATTLE OF WHITE PLAINS (N-H ADD 40%)

□629 2¢ Carmine Rose

| | — | 45.00 | 3.00 | 2.00 | 1.50 | .70 |

□630 2¢ Souvenir Sheet of 25

| | — | — | 510.00 | 450.00 | — | — |

Scott No.	Fine Unused Plate Blk	Ave. Unused Plate Blk	Fine Unused Each	Ave. Unused Each	Fine Used Each	Ave. Used Each

1926 ROTARY PRESS PRINTING IMPERFORATE (N-H ADD 30%)

☐631 1¹/₂¢ Brown

| | 55.00 | 46.00 | 2.50 | 1.75 | 1.40 | .90 |

1926–1928 DESIGNS OF 1926–1928 PERF. 11 x 10¹/₂ (N-H ADD 30%)

☐632 1¢ Green

| | 72.00 | 1.80 | .35 | .21 | .15 | .10 |

☐633 1¹/₂¢ Yellow Brown

| | — | 50.00 | 2.50 | 1.90 | .25 | .15 |

☐634 2¢ Carmine (I)

| | 1.40 | 1.00 | .30 | .21 | .18 | .12 |

☐634A 2¢ Carmine (II)

| | — | — | 375.00 | 230.00 | 18.00 | 9.00 |

☐635 3¢ Violet

| | 7.50 | 6.25 | .60 | .40 | .21 | .12 |

☐636 4¢ Yellow Brown

| | 79.00 | 58.00 | 3.90 | 2.75 | .40 | .20 |

☐637 5¢ Dark Blue

| | 21.00 | 16.00 | 2.50 | 1.80 | .35 | .17 |

☐638 6¢ Red Orange

| | 23.00 | 16.00 | 2.60 | 2.00 | .40 | .17 |

☐639 7¢ Black

| | 22.00 | 16.00 | 2.50 | 2.00 | .40 | .15 |

☐640 8¢ Olive Green

| | 21.00 | 16.00 | 2.75 | 2.00 | .40 | .15 |

☐641 9¢ Orange Red

| | 22.00 | 17.00 | 2.75 | 2.00 | .42 | .15 |

☐642 10¢ Orange

| | 30.00 | 21.00 | 5.00 | 4.10 | .60 | .21 |

1927. VERMONT SESQUICENTENNIAL (N-H ADD 45%)

☐643 2¢ Carmine Rose

| | 41.50 | 36.00 | 2.00 | 1.00 | .80 | .60 |

1927. BURGOYNE CAMPAIGN ISSUE (N-H ADD 45%)

☐644 2¢ Carmine

| | 41.00 | 37.00 | 5.00 | 3.00 | 2.50 | 1.00 |

Scott No.	Fine Unused Plate Blk	Ave. Unused Plate Blk	Fine Unused Each	Ave. Unused Each	Fine Used Each	Ave. Used Each

1928–1929. COMMEMORATIVES
1928. VALLEY FORGE ISSUE (N-H ADD 40%)

□645 2¢ Carmine

| | 30.00 | 23.00 | 1.40 | 1.00 | .60 | .30 |

1928. BATTLE OF MONMOUTH (N-H ADD 40%)

□646 2¢ Carmine

| | 38.00 | 30.00 | 1.60 | 1.10 | 1.00 | .50 |

1928. DISCOVERY OF HAWAII (N-H ADD 30%)

□647 2¢ Carmine Rose

| | 118.00 | 67.00 | 6.50 | 5.00 | 4.00 | 1.25 |

□648 5¢ Blue

| | 230.00 | 160.00 | 18.00 | 12.00 | 8.00 | 4.00 |

1928. AERONAUTICS CONFERENCE (N-H ADD 30%)

□649 2¢ Carmine

| | 12.00 | 9.00 | 2.70 | 1.90 | 1.45 | .60 |

□650 5¢ Blue

| | 60.00 | 45.00 | 6.75 | 5.50 | 3.50 | 2.10 |

1929. GEORGE ROGERS CLARK (N-H ADD 30%)

□651 2¢ Carmine & Black

| | 11.00 | 7.00 | .75 | .50 | .40 | .30 |

1929. DESIGNS OF 1922–1925 ROTARY PRESS PRINTING—PERF. 11 x 10½ (N-H ADD 30%)

□653 ½¢ Olive Brown

| | 1.10 | .65 | .35 | .24 | .20 | .15 |

1929. EDISON COMMEMORATIVE FLAT PLATE PRINTING—PERF. 11 (N-H ADD 30%)

□654 2¢ Carmine Rose

| | 30.00 | 18.00 | 1.10 | .65 | .50 | .30 |

1929. EDISON COMMEMORATIVE ROTARY PRESS PRINTING—PERF. 11 x 10½ (N-H ADD 40%)

□655 2¢ Carmine Rose

| | 47.00 | 30.00 | 1.00 | .65 | .40 | .20 |

Scott No.	Fine Unused Line Pair	Ave. Unused Line Pair	Fine Unused Each	Ave. Unused Each	Fine Used Each	Ave. Used Each

1929. EDISON COMMEMORATIVE ROTARY PRESS COIL STAMPS—PERF. 10 VERTICALLY (N-H ADD 40%)

	Fine Unused Line Pair	Ave. Unused Line Pair	Fine Unused Each	Ave. Unused Each	Fine Used Each	Ave. Used Each
☐656 2¢ Carmine Rose						
	67.00	40.00	16.00	14.00	2.00	1.00

Scott No.	Fine Unused Plate Blk	Ave. Unused Plate Blk	Fine Unused Each	Ave. Unused Each	Fine Used Each	Ave. Used Each

1929. SULLIVAN EXPEDITION (N-H ADD 40%)

	Fine Unused Plate Blk	Ave. Unused Plate Blk	Fine Unused Each	Ave. Unused Each	Fine Used Each	Ave. Used Each
☐657 2¢ Carmine Rose						
	30.00	20.00	.90	.65	.55	.40

1929. 632–42 OVERPRINTED (KANS.) (N-H ADD 30%)

	Fine Unused Plate Blk	Ave. Unused Plate Blk	Fine Unused Each	Ave. Unused Each	Fine Used Each	Ave. Used Each
☐658 1¢ Green						
	30.00	21.00	4.00	2.10	1.50	1.00
☐659 ½¢ Brown						
	48.00	33.00	5.50	3.00	2.20	1.50
☐660 2¢ Carmine						
	40.00	32.00	5.00	4.00	1.25	.80
☐661 3¢ Violet						
	135.00	100.00	30.00	18.00	11.00	6.00
☐662 4¢ Yellow Brown						
	210.00	150.00	26.00	16.00	10.00	5.50
☐663 5¢ Deep Blue						
	130.00	100.00	18.10	12.25	9.00	5.00
☐664 6¢ Red Orange						
	350.00	225.00	36.00	22.00	14.00	9.00
☐665 7¢ Black						
	300.00	200.00	38.00	26.00	19.00	8.00
☐666 8¢ Olive Green						
	850.00	700.00	100.00	74.00	55.00	38.00
☐667 9¢ Light Rose						
	200.00	125.00	20.00	12.00	8.00	6.00
☐668 10¢ Orange Yellow						
	300.00	215.00	32.00	24.00	12.00	7.00

Scott No.	Fine Unused Plate Blk	Ave. Unused Plate Blk	Fine Unused Each	Ave. Unused Each	Fine Used Each	Ave. Used Each

1929. 632–42 OVERPRINTED (NEBR.) (N-H ADD 45%)

	Fine Unused Plate Blk	Ave. Unused Plate Blk	Fine Unused Each	Ave. Unused Each	Fine Used Each	Ave. Used Each
□669 1¢ Green	34.00	24.00	6.00	3.00	2.00	1.00
□670 1½¢ Brown	45.00	32.00	5.00	3.50	2.00	1.00
□671 2¢ Carmine	28.00	21.00	6.00	4.50	2.25	1.00
□672 3¢ Violet	170.00	120.00	22.00	14.00	9.00	4.50
□673 4¢ Brown	170.00	120.00	28.00	16.00	12.00	5.00
□674 5¢ Blue	170.00	125.00	25.00	15.50	13.00	7.00
□675 6¢ Orange	400.00	310.00	58.00	32.00	18.00	9.00
□676 7¢ Black	220.00	180.00	32.00	21.00	14.00	7.50
□677 8¢ Olive Green	300.00	210.00	50.00	28.00	20.00	10.00
□678 9¢ Rose	350.00	200.00	55.00	35.00	24.00	9.00
□679 10¢ Orange Yellow	700.00	510.00	160.00	100.00	18.00	7.00

1929. BATTLE OF FALLEN TIMBERS (N-H ADD 30%)

	Fine Unused Plate Blk	Ave. Unused Plate Blk	Fine Unused Each	Ave. Unused Each	Fine Used Each	Ave. Used Each
□680 2¢ Carmine Rose	25.00	18.00	1.50	1.00	.70	.40

1929. OHIO RIVER CANALIZATION (N-H ADD 30%)

	Fine Unused Plate Blk	Ave. Unused Plate Blk	Fine Unused Each	Ave. Unused Each	Fine Used Each	Ave. Used Each
□681 2¢ Carmine Rose	20.00	12.00	.90	.70	.60	.40

1930–1931. COMMEMORATIVES
1930. MASSACHUSETTS BAY COLONY (N-H ADD 35%)

	Fine Unused Plate Blk	Ave. Unused Plate Blk	Fine Unused Each	Ave. Unused Each	Fine Used Each	Ave. Used Each
□682 2¢ Carmine Rose	29.00	21.00	.80	.70	.50	.30

Scott No.	Fine Unused Plate Blk	Ave. Unused Plate Blk	Fine Unused Each	Ave. Unused Each	Fine Used Each	Ave. Used Each

1930. CAROLINA-CHARLESTON ISSUE (N-H ADD 35%)

☐683 2¢ Carmine Rose						
	45.00	38.00	1.50	1.00	.90	.60

1930. REGULAR ISSUE ROTARY PRESS PRINTING—PERF. 11 x 10½ (N-H ADD 35%)

☐684 1½¢ Brown						
	3.50	2.10	.51	.32	.20	.15
☐685 4¢ Brown						
	11.00	8.10	1.10	.75	.20	.16

Scott No.	Fine Unused Line Pair	Ave. Unused Line Pair	Fine Unused Each	Ave. Unused Each	Fine Used Each	Ave. Used Each

1930. ROTARY PRESS COIL STAMPS PERF. 10 VERTICALLY (N-H ADD 40%)

☐686 1½¢ Brown						
	7.00	5.00	2.10	1.25	.26	.15
☐687 4¢ Brown						
	14.00	11.00	4.00	2.25	.65	.20

Scott No.	Fine Unused Plate Blk	Ave. Unused Plate Blk	Fine Unused Each	Ave. Unused Each	Fine Used Each	Ave. Used Each

1930. BATTLE OF BRADDOCK'S FIELD (N-H ADD 40%)

☐688 2¢ Carmine Rose						
	40.00	28.00	1.50	.80	.60	.30

1930. VON STEUBEN ISSUE (N-H ADD 40%)

☐689 2¢ Carmine Rose						
	20.00	15.00	.65	.50	.40	.20

1931. PULASKI ISSUE (N-H ADD 40%)

☐690 2¢ Carmine Rose						
	18.00	10.00	.38	.25	.21	.15

Scott No.	Fine Unused Plate Blk	Ave. Unused Plate Blk	Fine Unused Each	Ave. Unused Each	Fine Used Each	Ave. Used Each

1931. DESIGNS OF 1922–1926 ROTARY PRESS PRINTING—PERF. 11 x 10½ (N-H ADD 40%)

☐692 11¢ Light Blue

| | 16.00 | 10.00 | 3.50 | 2.10 | .30 | .15 |

☐693 12¢ Brown Violet

| | 30.00 | 20.00 | 7.50 | 5.00 | .30 | .15 |

☐694 13¢ Yellow Green

| | 17.00 | 13.00 | 3.00 | 1.80 | .30 | .15 |

☐695 14¢ Dark Blue

| | 16.00 | 11.00 | 4.00 | 3.00 | .50 | .15 |

☐696 15¢ Gray

| | 45.00 | 29.00 | 11.00 | 7.50 | 3.00 | .50 |

1931. DESIGNS OF 1922–1926 ROTARY PRESS PRINTING—PERF. 10½ x 11 (N-H ADD 40%)

☐697 17¢ Black

| | 26.00 | 20.00 | 6.50 | 5.00 | .60 | .20 |

☐698 20¢ Carmine Rose

| | 42.00 | 24.00 | 12.50 | 11.00 | 1.00 | .50 |

☐699 25¢ Blue Green

| | 43.00 | 26.00 | 12.00 | 11.00 | .30 | .16 |

☐700 30¢ Brown

| | 70.00 | 42.00 | 20.00 | 14.00 | .35 | .16 |

☐701 50¢ Lilac

| | 280.00 | 165.00 | 54.00 | 40.00 | .30 | .16 |

1931. RED CROSS ISSUE (N-H ADD 10%)

☐702 2¢ Black & Red

| | 3.25 | 2.10 | .35 | .25 | .20 | .16 |

1931. SURRENDER OF YORKTOWN (N-H ADD 10%)

☐703 2¢ Carmine Rose & Black

| | 4.00 | 2.50 | .40 | .46 | .35 | .17 |

1932. COMMEMORATIVES
1932. WASHINGTON BICENTENNIAL (N-H ADD 10%)

☐704 ½¢ Olive Brown

| | 4.00 | 3.25 | .40 | .30 | .26 | .15 |

Scott No.	Fine Unused Plate Blk	Ave. Unused Plate Blk	Fine Unused Each	Ave. Unused Each	Fine Used Each	Ave. Used Each
□705 1¢ Green						
	5.00	4.10	.35	.30	.25	.15
□706 1½¢ Brown						
	15.00	12.00	.60	.40	.30	.15
□707 2¢ Carmine						
	2.00	1.50	.40	.30	.25	.15
□708 3¢ Purple						
	15.00	9.00	.70	.50	.30	.15
□709 4¢ Light Brown						
	6.50	5.00	.45	.30	.25	.15
□710 5¢ Blue						
	15.00	12.00	2.20	1.20	.28	.15
□711 6¢ Orange						
	70.00	55.00	5.00	3.00	.25	.15
□712 7¢ Black						
	8.00	6.00	.45	.35	.25	.15
□713 8¢ Olive Bistre						
	70.00	51.00	4.10	3.00	.60	.30
□714 9¢ Pale Red						
	50.00	40.00	3.50	2.20	.47	.15
□715 10¢ Orange Yellow						
	121.00	85.00	16.00	12.00	.35	.15

1932. OLYMPIC WINTER GAMES (N-H ADD 30%)

□716 2¢ Carmine Rose						
	16.00	11.00	.65	.35	.25	.15

1932. ARBOR DAY ISSUE (N-H ADD 30%)

□717 2¢ Carmine Rose						
	8.75	6.50	.35	.30	.25	.15

1932. OLYMPIC SUMMER GAMES (N-H ADD 30%)

□718 3¢ Purple						
	18.00	13.00	2.00	1.20	.30	.15
□719 5¢ Blue						
	24.00	17.00	2.00	1.20	.40	.15

Scott No.	Fine Unused Line Pair	Ave. Unused Line Pair	Fine Unused Each	Ave. Unused Each	Fine Used Each	Ave. Used Each

1932. WASHINGTON ROTARY PRESS (N–H ADD 30%)
☐720 3¢ Deep Violet

	—	—	.30	.25	.20	.15

1932. COIL PERF. 10 VERTICALLY (N-H ADD 30%)
☐721 3¢ Deep Violet

	7.50	3.75	3.50	2.60	.20	.15

1932. COIL PERF. 10 HORIZONTALLY (N-H ADD 30%)
☐722 3¢ Deep Violet

	6.00	4.00	1.70	1.10	.70	.30

1932. COIL DESIGN OF 1922–1925—PERF. 10 VERTICALLY (N-H ADD 30%)
☐723 6¢ Deep Orange

	52.00	39.00	12.00	8.50	.31	.17

Scott No.	Fine Unused Plate Blk	Ave. Unused Plate Blk	Fine Unused Each	Ave. Unused Each	Fine Used Each	Ave. Used Each

1932. WILLIAM PENN ISSUE (N-H ADD 30%)
☐724 3¢ Violet

	18.00	11.00	.46	.32	.26	.15

1932. DANIEL WEBSTER ISSUE (N-H ADD 30%)
☐725 3¢ Violet

	28.00	21.00	.56	.40	.30	.15

1933. COMMEMORATIVES ⸻
1933. GEORGIA BICENTENNIAL (N-H ADD 30%)
☐726 3¢ Violet

	15.00	10.00	.50	.35	.25	.15

1933. PEACE SESQUICENTENNIAL (N-H ADD 30%)
☐727 3¢ Violet

	9.00	4.50	.35	.25	.20	.15

Scott No.	Fine Unused Plate Blk	Ave. Unused Plate Blk	Fine Unused Each	Ave. Unused Each	Fine Used Each	Ave. Used Each

1933. CENTURY OF PROGRESS EXPOSITION (N-H ADD 30%)

☐728 1¢ Yellow Green						
	4.00	3.00	.35	.30	.15	.10
☐729 3¢ Purple						
	4.00	3.50	.35	.30	.15	.10

1933. A.P.S. CONVENTION AND EXHIBITION AT CHICAGO IMPERFORATE—UNGUMMED (N-H ADD 30%)

☐730 1¢ Yellow Green, sheet of 25						
	—	—	42.00	30.00	—	—
☐730a 1¢ Yellow Green, sgl.						
	—	—	.90	.60	.40	.17
☐731 3¢ Violet, sheet of 25						
	—	—	35.00	30.00	—	—
☐731a 3¢ Violet, single						
	—	—	.70	.60	.52	.17

1933. N.R.A. ISSUE (N-H ADD 25%)

☐732 3¢ Violet						
	2.50	2.10	.35	.30	.25	.16

1933. BYRD ANTARCTIC EXPEDITION (N-H ADD 30%)

☐733 3¢ Dark Blue						
	17.00	13.00	.85	.60	.40	.25

1933. KOSCIUSZKO ISSUE (N-H ADD 30%)

☐734 5¢ Blue						
	36.00	30.00	.85	.65	.50	.25

1934. COMMEMORATIVES
1934. NATIONAL PHILATELIC EXHIBITION IMPERFORATE—UNGUMMED (N-H ADD 30%)

☐735 3¢ Dark Blue, sheet of 6						
	—	—	20.00	15.00	12.00	9.00

Scott No.	Fine Unused Plate Blk	Ave. Unused Plate Blk	Fine Unused Each	Ave. Unused Each	Fine Used Each	Ave. Used Each
☐735a 3¢ Dark Blue, sgl.						
	—	—	3.50	3.00	2.50	1.25

1934. MARYLAND TERCENTENARY (N-H ADD 30%)
☐736 3¢ Rose

	12.50	7.50	.35	.25	.20	.15

1934. MOTHER'S DAY ISSUE ROTARY PRESS PRINTING—PERF. 11 x 10½ (N-H ADD 30%)
☐737 3¢ Deep Violet

	2.00	1.50	.40	.30	.24	.15

FLAT PRESS PRINTING—PERF. 11 (N-H ADD 30%)
☐738 3¢ Deep Violet

	5.00	4.10	.35	.30	.22	.15

1934. WISCONSIN TERCENTENARY (N-H ADD 30%)
☐739 3¢ Deep Violet

	5.00	3.25	.40	.28	.22	.15

1934. NATIONAL PARKS ISSUE (N-H ADD 25%)
☐740 1¢ Green

	2.00	1.40	.34	.25	.20	.15

☐741 2¢ Red

	2.00	1.50	.32	.25	.20	.15

☐742 3¢ Purple

	2.00	1.60	.34	.30	.18	.14

☐743 4¢ Brown

	9.00	8.00	.60	.50	.42	.25

☐744 5¢ Blue

	14.00	10.00	1.15	.85	.70	.45

☐745 6¢ Indigo

	16.00	14.00	1.50	1.30	.90	.60

☐746 7¢ Black

	15.00	9.00	1.00	.80	.60	.40

☐747 8¢ Green

	24.00	16.00	2.70	1.90	1.40	.90

☐748 9¢ Salmon

	19.00	16.00	3.00	1.90	.70	.40

☐749 10¢ Gray Black

	28.00	24.00	4.30	3.50	1.20	.80

Scott No.	Fine Unused Plate Blk	Ave. Unused Plate Blk	Fine Unused Each	Ave. Unused Each	Fine Used Each	Ave. Used Each

1934. A.P.S. CONVENTION AND EXHIBITION AT ATLANTIC CITY IMPERFORATE SOUVENIR SHEET (N-H ADD 25%)

☐750 3¢ Purple, sheet of 6						
	—	—	42.00	—	35.00	16.00
☐750a 3¢ Purple, single						
	—	—	5.50	4.50	3.90	2.50

1934. TRANS-MISSISSIPPI PHILATELIC EXPOSITION AND CONVENTION AT OMAHA IMPERFORATE SOUVENIR SHEET (N-H ADD 25%)

☐751 1¢ Green, sheet of 6						
	—	—	16.00	—	12.00	7.50
☐751a 1¢ Green, single						
	—	—	2.25	1.50	1.50	.90

Scott No.	Plate Block	Block Plain	Mint Each	Used Each

1935. "FARLEY SPECIAL PRINTINGS" DESIGNS OF 1933–1934 PERF. 10½ x 11— UNGUMMED (N-H ADD 25%)

☐752 3¢ Violet	17.00	4.50	.25	.15

1935. PERF. 11—GUMMED (N-H ADD 25%)

☐753 3¢ Dark Blue	17.00	2.50	.50	.35

1935. IMPERFORATE—UNGUMMED (N-H ADD 25%)

☐754 3¢ Deep Violet	16.00	3.00	.55	.30
☐755 3¢ Deep Violet	16.00	3.00	.55	.30

1935. NATIONAL PARKS IMPERFORATE—UNGUMMED (N-H ADD 25%)

☐756 1¢ Green	6.00	.50	.25	.15
☐757 2¢ Red	7.00	.50	.20	.20

Scott No.	Plate Block	Block Plain	Mint Each	Used Each
☐758 3¢ Deep Violet	16.00	10.00	.70	.30

Scott No.		Plate Block	Block Plain	Mint Each	Used Each
□759	4¢ Brown	22.00	12.00	1.25	.90
□760	5¢ Blue	28.00	19.00	2.50	1.50
□761	6¢ Dark Blue	45.00	25.00	2.75	1.50
□762	7¢ Black	40.00	25.00	2.00	1.50
□763	8¢ Sage Green	50.00	20.00	2.46	2.00
□764	9¢ Red Orange	52.00	32.00	2.50	1.40
□765	10¢ Gray Black	55.00	32.00	4.40	3.50

1935. IMPERFORATE—UNGUMMED (N–H ADD 25%)

Scott No.		Plate Block	Block Plain	Mint Each	Used Each
□766a	1¢ Yellow Green	—	14.00	1.15	.60
□767a	3¢ Violet	—	16.00	1.15	.60
□768a	3¢ Dark Blue	—	20.00	3.10	2.50
□769a	1¢ Green	—	11.00	2.00	1.50
□770a	3¢ Deep Violet	—	25.00	4.50	2.50

1935. DESIGN OF CE 1 (N–H ADD 30%)

Scott No.		Plate Block	Block Plain	Mint Each	Used Each
□771	16¢ Dark Blue	88.00	41.00	3.00	2.40

1935–1936. COMMEMORATIVES _____

Scott No.		Fine Unused Plate Blk	Ave. Unused Plate Blk	Mint Each	Used Each

1935. CONNECTICUT TERCENTENARY (N-H ADD 25%)

□772	3¢ Red Violet	3.00	2.20	.30	.14

1935. CALIFORNIA PACIFIC EXPOSITION (N-H ADD 25%)

□773	3¢ Purple	3.00	2.00	.20	.15

1935. BOULDER DAM ISSUE (N-H ADD 25%)

□774	3¢ Purple	2.60	2.20	.26	.15

1935. MICHIGAN CENTENARY (N-H ADD 25%)

□775	3¢ Purple	2.50	2.20	.30	.15

1936. TEXAS CENTENNIAL (N-H ADD 25%)

□776	3¢ Purple	2.40	2.10	.30	.15

Scott No.	Plate Block	Block Plain	Mint Each	Used Each

1936. RHODE ISLAND TERCENTENARY (N-H ADD 25%)

☐777 3¢ Purple	2.50	2.00	.40	.17

1936. THIRD INTL. PHILATELIC EXHIBITION "TIPEX" IMPERFORATE SOUVENIR SHEET DESIGNS OF 772, 773, 775, 776 (N-H ADD 25%)

☐778 3¢ Red Violet, sheet of 4	—	—	2.00	1.50
☐778a 3¢ Red Violet, single	—	—	.90	.50
☐778b 3¢ Red Violet, single	—	—	.90	.50
☐778c 3¢ Red Violet, single	—	—	.90	.50
☐778d 3¢ Red Violet, single	—	—	.90	.50

1936. ARKANSAS CENTENNIAL (N-H ADD 25%)

☐782 3¢ Purple	2.10	1.75	.21	.18

Scott No.	Fine Unused Plate Blk	Ave. Unused Plate Blk	Fine Unused Each	Ave. Unused Each	Fine Used Each	Ave. Used Each

1936. OREGON TERRITORY CENTENNIAL (N-H ADD 25%)

☐783 3¢ Purple						
	1.50	1.10	.42	.30	.25	.17

1936. SUFFRAGE FOR WOMEN ISSUE (N-H ADD 25%)

☐784 3¢ Dark Violet						
	1.60	1.00	.44	.30	.25	.17

1936–1937. ARMY AND NAVY ISSUE ARMY COMMEMORATIVES (N-H ADD 20%)

☐785 1¢ Green						
	1.60	1.00	.36	.24	.26	.17
☐786 2¢ Carmine						
	1.60	1.00	.36	.24	.26	.17
☐787 3¢ Purple						
	1.60	1.00	.36	.24	.26	.17

Scott No.	Fine Unused Plate Blk	Ave. Unused Plate Blk	Fine Unused Each	Ave. Unused Each	Fine Used Each	Ave. Used Each
☐788 4¢ Gray						
	12.00	11.00	.70	.40	.30	.20
☐789 5¢ Ultramarine						
	12.00	11.00	.85	.55	.40	.20

NAVY COMMEMORATIVES (N-H ADD 25%)
☐790 1¢ Green						
	—	1.20	.36	.26	.20	.15
☐791 2¢ Carmine						
	1.60	1.40	.36	.26	.20	.15
☐792 3¢ Purple						
	2.00	1.75	.36	.26	.20	.15
☐793 4¢ Gray						
	13.00	11.00	.55	.40	.35	.15
☐794 5¢ Ultramarine						
	16.00	12.00	.75	.50	.40	.15

1937. COMMEMORATIVES ————————
1937. NORTHWEST ORDINANCE ISSUE (N-H ADD 25%)
☐795 3¢ Violet						
	2.00	1.70	.30	.25	.20	.15

1937. VIRGINIA DARE ISSUE (N-H ADD 20%)
☐796 5¢ Gray Blue						
	10.00	9.00	.30	.25	.20	.15

1937. S.P.A. CONVENTION ISSUE (N-H ADD 25%)
DESIGN OF 749 IMPERFORATE SOUVENIR SHEET
☐797 10¢ Blue Green						
	—	—	1.40	.90	.60	.50

1937. CONSTITUTIONAL SESQUICENTENNIAL (N-H ADD 25%)
☐798 3¢ Red Violet						
	2.10	1.40	.40	.30	.26	.15

Scott No.	Fine Unused Plate Blk	Ave. Unused Plate Blk	Fine Unused Each	Ave. Unused Each	Fine Used Each	Ave. Used Each

1937. TERRITORIAL PUBLICITY ISSUE (N-H ADD 25%)

☐799 3¢ Violet

| | 2.50 | 1.60 | .30 | .26 | .20 | .15 |

☐800 3¢ Violet

| | 2.50 | 1.50 | .30 | .26 | .20 | .15 |

☐801 3¢ Bright Violet

| | 3.00 | 1.50 | .30 | .26 | .20 | .15 |

☐802 3¢ Light Violet

| | 3.00 | 1.50 | .30 | .26 | .20 | .15 |

1938. PRESIDENTIAL SERIES ROTARY PRESS PRINTING—PERF. 11 x 10½ (N-H ADD 25%)

☐803 ½¢ Red Orange

| | .75 | .40 | .32 | .25 | .20 | .15 |

☐804 1¢ Green

| | .70 | .40 | .32 | .25 | .20 | .15 |

☐805 1½¢ Bistre Brown

| | .70 | .40 | .32 | .25 | .20 | .15 |

☐806 2¢ Rose Carmine

| | .70 | .40 | .32 | .25 | .20 | .15 |

☐807 3¢ Deep Violet

| | .70 | .40 | .32 | .25 | .20 | .15 |

☐808 4¢ Red Violet

| | 3.80 | 2.10 | 1.50 | .25 | .20 | .15 |

☐809 4½¢ Dark Gray

| | 1.75 | 1.40 | .40 | .25 | .20 | .15 |

☐810 5¢ Bright Blue

| | 1.40 | .90 | .40 | .25 | .20 | .15 |

☐811 6¢ Red Orange

| | 1.80 | 1.50 | .40 | .25 | .20 | .15 |

☐812 7¢ Sepia

| | 2.10 | 1.60 | .45 | .35 | .20 | .15 |

☐813 8¢ Olive Green

| | 2.10 | 1.75 | .45 | .35 | .20 | .15 |

☐814 9¢ Rose Pink

| | 2.30 | 1.80 | .46 | .35 | .20 | .15 |

☐815 10¢ Brown Red

| | 2.00 | 1.80 | .45 | .35 | .20 | .15 |

Scott No.	Fine Unused Plate Blk	Ave. Unused Plate Blk	Fine Unused Each	Ave. Unused Each	Fine Used Each	Ave. Used Each
☐816 11¢ Ultramarine						
	5.50	4.00	.75	.40	.20	.15
☐817 12¢ Bright Violet						
	7.00	5.00	1.45	.70	.20	.15
☐818 13¢ Blue Green						
	10.00	8.50	2.10	.80	.20	.15
☐819 14¢ Blue						
	6.50	6.00	1.40	.75	.20	.15
☐820 15¢ Blue Gray						
	3.00	2.10	1.00	.60	.20	.15
☐821 16¢ Black						
	8.00	7.10	1.35	.70	.60	.41
☐822 17¢ Rose Red						
	7.00	6.00	1.40	.70	.21	.15
☐823 18¢ Brown Carmine						
	11.00	9.50	2.20	1.00	.21	.15
☐824 19¢ Bright Violet						
	10.00	8.00	2.00	1.10	.50	.30
☐825 20¢ Bright Blue Green						
	5.50	4.25	1.10	.80	.20	.15
☐826 21¢ Dull Blue						
	10.00	9.00	2.40	1.80	.20	.15
☐827 22¢ Vermilion						
	14.00	12.00	1.80	.90	.60	.35
☐828 24¢ Gray Black						
	21.00	18.00	4.10	2.60	.36	.15
☐829 25¢ Deep Red Lilac						
	5.50	4.00	1.00	.60	.20	.15
☐830 30¢ Deep Ultramarine						
	24.00	23.00	5.00	3.10	.20	.15
☐831 50¢ Light Red Violet						
	38.00	36.00	8.10	6.00	.20	.15

FLAT PLATE PRINTING—PERF. 11 (N-H ADD 20%)

☐832 $1 Purple & Black						
	45.00	41.00	9.00	6.00	.25	.15
☐832b $1 Watermarked						
	—	—	250.00	200.00	66.00	45.00

Scott No.	Fine Unused Plate Blk	Ave. Unused Plate Blk	Fine Unused Each	Ave. Unused Each	Fine Used Each	Ave. Used Each
☐832c $1 Dry Printing, Thick Paper (1954)						
	43.00	40.00	10.00	7.25	.21	.21
☐833 $2 Green & Black						
	130.00	110.00	26.00	19.00	6.00	4.50
☐834 $5 Carmine & Black						
	490.00	350.00	120.00	80.00	6.50	4.10

1938–1939. COMMEMORATIVES
1938. CONSTITUTION RATIFICATION (N-H ADD 25%)

☐835 3¢ Deep Violet						
	5.00	4.50	.60	.45	.20	.15

1938. SWEDISH-FINNISH TERCENTENARY (N-H ADD 25%)

☐836 3¢ Red Violet						
	6.00	3.00	.40	.40	.20	.15

1938. NORTHWEST COLONIZATION (N-H ADD 25%)

☐837 3¢ Bright Violet						
	12.00	9.00	.40	.40	.20	.15

1938. IOWA TERRITORY CENTENNIAL (N-H ADD 25%)

☐838 3¢ Violet						
	9.75	7.10	.60	.45	.20	.15

Scott No.	Fine Unused Line Pair	Ave. Unused Line Pair	Fine Unused Each	Ave. Unused Each	Fine Used Each	Ave. Used Each

1939. ROTARY PRESS COIL STAMPS PERF. 10 VERTICALLY (N-H ADD 25%)

☐839 1¢ Green						
	1.30	1.20	.60	.30	.20	.15
☐840 1½¢ Bistre Brown						
	1.50	1.25	.60	.30	.20	.15
☐841 2¢ Rose Carmine						
	1.85	1.60	.62	.30	.20	.15
☐842 3¢ Deep Violet						
	1.60	1.30	.65	.40	.20	.15

Scott No.	Fine Unused Line Pair	Ave. Unused Line Pair	Fine Unused Each	Ave. Unused Each	Fine Used Each	Ave. Used Each
☐843 4¢ Red Violet						
	31.00	21.00	7.50	6.00	.60	.20
☐844 4¹/₂¢ Dark Gray						
	5.10	4.00	.90	.60	.50	.21
☐845 5¢ Bright Blue						
	26.00	20.00	6.00	4.50	.48	.20
☐846 6¢ Red Orange						
	7.25	6.50	2.00	1.25	.28	.21
☐847 10¢ Brown Red						
	45.00	30.00	12.00	9.00	.50	.21

PERF. 10 HORIZONTALLY (N-H ADD 25%)

Scott No.	Fine Unused Line Pair	Ave. Unused Line Pair	Fine Unused Each	Ave. Unused Each	Fine Used Each	Ave. Used Each
☐848 1¢ Green						
	3.00	2.50	.90	.60	.30	.15
☐849 1¹/₂¢ Bistre Brown						
	3.75	2.75	1.50	1.10	.50	.21
☐850 2¢ Rose Carmine						
	7.25	5.00	3.50	2.50	.72	.40
☐851 3¢ Deep Violet						
	6.00	4.50	3.00	2.25	.72	.50

Scott No.	Fine Unused Plate Blk	Ave. Unused Plate Blk	Fine Unused Each	Ave. Unused Each	Fine Used Each	Ave. Used Each

1939. GOLDEN GATE INTERNATIONAL EXPOSITION (N-H ADD 25%)

☐852 3¢ Bright Purple						
	2.00	1.50	.40	.30	.20	.15

1939. NEW YORK WORLD'S FAIR (N-H ADD 20%)

☐853 3¢ Deep Purple						
	2.60	1.80	.45	.34	.20	.15

1939. WASHINGTON INAUGURATION SESQUICENTENNIAL (N-H ADD 20%)

☐854 3¢ Bright Red Violet						
	7.75	3.50	.85	.50	.21	.16

Scott No.	Fine Unused Plate Blk	Ave. Unused Plate Blk	Fine Unused Each	Ave. Unused Each	Fine Used Each	Ave. Used Each

1939. BASEBALL CENTENNIAL (N-H ADD 20%)
☐855 3¢ Violet

| | 10.00 | 7.00 | 2.30 | .75 | .30 | .15 |

1939. 25TH ANNIVERSARY PANAMA CANAL (N-H ADD 20%)
☐856 3¢ Deep Red Violet

| | 5.00 | 3.25 | .48 | .30 | .20 | .15 |

1939. COLONIAL PRINTING TERCENTENARY (N-H ADD 20%)
☐857 3¢ Rose Violet

| | 2.00 | 1.50 | .40 | .30 | .20 | .15 |

1939. 50TH ANNIVERSARY OF STATEHOOD (N-H ADD 20%)
☐858 3¢ Rose Violet

| | 1.75 | 1.20 | .30 | .25 | .20 | .15 |

1940. COMMEMORATIVES
1940. FAMOUS AMERICANS SERIES
AMERICAN AUTHORS (N-H ADD 20%)
☐859 1¢ Bright Blue Green

| | 1.80 | 1.40 | .30 | .25 | .23 | .15 |

☐860 2¢ Rose Carmine

| | 1.80 | 1.50 | .30 | .25 | .21 | .15 |

☐861 3¢ Bright Red Violet

| | 1.85 | 1.50 | .30 | .25 | .21 | .15 |

☐862 5¢ Ultramarine

| | 13.00 | 11.50 | .48 | .30 | .25 | .17 |

☐863 10¢ Dark Brown

| | 50.00 | 38.00 | 2.40 | 2.10 | 2.00 | .90 |

1940. AMERICAN POETS (N-H ADD 20%)
☐864 1¢ Bright Blue Green

| | 2.60 | 2.10 | .33 | .25 | .20 | .15 |

☐865 2¢ Rose Carmine

| | 2.50 | 2.10 | .35 | .25 | .20 | .15 |

Scott No.	Fine Unused Plate Blk	Ave. Unused Plate Blk	Fine Unused Each	Ave. Unused Each	Fine Used Each	Ave. Used Each
☐866 3¢ Bright Red Violet						
	3.30	3.10	.40	.30	.21	.15
☐867 5¢ Ultramarine						
	13.00	10.00	.60	.44	.32	.15
☐868 10¢ Dark Brown						
	50.00	37.00	2.50	2.20	1.90	1.45

1940. AMERICAN EDUCATORS (N-H ADD 20%)

☐869 1¢ Bright Blue Green						
	3.00	2.50	.30	.27	.20	.15
☐870 2¢ Rose Carmine						
	2.00	1.80	.30	.27	.20	.15
☐871 3¢ Bright Red Violet						
	4.50	3.00	.30	.27	.20	.15
☐872 5¢ Ultramarine						
	14.00	10.00	.50	.40	.35	.17
☐873 10¢ Dark Brown						
	40.00	30.00	2.50	1.75	1.50	1.00

1940. AMERICAN SCIENTISTS (N-H ADD 20%)

☐874 1¢ Bright Blue Green						
	1.75	1.35	.30	.30	.22	.15
☐875 2¢ Rose Carmine						
	1.75	1.35	.30	.26	.22	.15
☐876 3¢ Bright Red Violet						
	1.60	1.75	.30	.26	.22	.15
☐877 5¢ Ultramarine						
	9.00	7.00	.30	.25	.22	.17
☐878 10¢ Dark Brown						
	30.00	20.00	1.75	1.35	1.10	.90

1940. AMERICAN COMPOSERS (N-H ADD 20%)

☐879 1¢ Bright Blue Green						
	1.80	1.50	.35	.25	.20	.15
☐880 2¢ Rose Carmine						
	1.75	1.50	.35	.25	.20	.15
☐881 3¢ Bright Red Violet						
	1.80	1.50	.35	.25	.20	.15

Scott No.	Fine Unused Plate Blk	Ave. Unused Plate Blk	Fine Unused Each	Ave. Unused Each	Fine Used Each	Ave. Used Each
☐882 5¢ Ultramarine						
	13.50	9.00	.60	.45	.32	.21
☐883 10¢ Dark Brown						
	48.00	32.00	4.75	3.00	2.10	1.25

1940. AMERICAN ARTISTS (N-H ADD 20%)

☐884 1¢ Bright Blue Green						
	1.40	1.10	.30	.24	.21	.15
☐885 2¢ Rose Carmine						
	1.40	1.10	.25	.24	.21	.15
☐886 3¢ Bright Red Violet						
	1.60	1.10	.25	.24	.21	.15
☐887 5¢ Ultramarine						
	11.00	8.50	.70	.60	.35	.20
☐888 10¢ Dark Brown						
	36.00	28.00	2.25	2.00	1.25	.90

1940. AMERICAN INVENTORS (N-H ADD 20%)

☐889 1¢ Bright Blue Green						
	2.75	2.00	.25	.25	.22	.15
☐890 2¢ Rose Carmine						
	1.75	1.25	.32	.25	.22	.15
☐891 3¢ Bright Red Violet						
	2.10	1.50	.40	.25	.22	.15
☐892 5¢ Ultramarine						
	17.00	12.00	1.20	.70	.30	.21
☐893 10¢ Dark Brown						
	90.00	75.00	14.00	11.00	3.00	1.80

1940. 80TH ANNIVERSARY OF PONY EXPRESS (N-H ADD 20%)

☐894 3¢ Henna Brown						
	5.00	4.00	.40	.30	.22	.15

1940. 50TH ANNIVERSARY OF PAN-AMERICAN UNION (N-H ADD 20%)

☐895 3¢ Light Violet						
	5.00	4.00	.45	.30	.22	.15

Scott No.	Fine Unused Plate Blk	Ave. Unused Plate Blk	Fine Unused Each	Ave. Unused Each	Fine Used Each	Ave. Used Each

1940. 50TH ANNIVERSARY OF IDAHO (N-H ADD 20%)

☐896 3¢ Bright Violet

| | 3.00 | 2.60 | .25 | .20 | .15 | .10 |

1940. 50TH ANNIVERSARY OF WYOMING (N-H ADD 20%)

☐897 3¢ Brown Violet

| | 2.00 | 1.50 | .25 | .20 | .15 | .10 |

1940. 400TH ANNIVERSARY OF COLORADO EXPEDITION (N-H ADD 20%)

☐898 3¢ Violet

| | 2.00 | 1.50 | .25 | .20 | .15 | .10 |

1940. NATIONAL DEFENSE ISSUE (N-H ADD 20%)

☐899 1¢ Bright Blue Green

| | .75 | .60 | .25 | .20 | .15 | .10 |

☐900 2¢ Rose Carmine

| | .75 | .60 | .25 | .20 | .15 | .10 |

☐901 3¢ Bright Violet

| | .90 | .60 | .25 | .20 | .15 | .10 |

1940. 75TH ANNIVERSARY EMANCIPATION AMENDMENT (N-H ADD 20%)

☐902 3¢ Deep Violet

| | 4.50 | 3.75 | .30 | .25 | .20 | .15 |

IMPORTANT NOTICE: Values for mint sheets are provided for the following listings. To command the stated prices, sheets must be complete as issued with the plate number (or numbers) intact.

Scott No.	Mint Sheet	Plate Block	Fine Unused Each	Fine Used Each

1941–1943. COMMEMORATIVES
1941. VERMONT STATEHOOD

☐903 3¢ Light Violet

| | 12.00 | 2.40 | .35 | .15 |

Scott No.	Mint Sheet	Plate Block	Fine Unused Each	Fine Used Each
1942. KENTUCKY SESQUICENTENNIAL ISSUE				
☐904 3¢ Violet	11.00	1.70	.30	.16
1942. WIN THE WAR ISSUE				
☐905 3¢ Violet	17.00	1.00	.30	16
1942. CHINA ISSUE				
☐906 5¢ Bright Blue	74.00	18.00	1.00	.25
1943. ALLIED NATIONS ISSUE				
☐907 2¢ Rose Carmine	9.00	.60	.30	.15
1943. FOUR FREEDOMS ISSUE				
☐908 1¢ Green	8.50	.70	.25	.15
1943–1944. OVERRUN COUNTRIES SERIES				
☐909 5¢ (Poland)	16.00	7.50	.25	.15
☐910 5¢ (Czechoslovakia)	15.00	4.00	.25	.15
☐911 5¢ (Norway)	10.00	2.00	.25	.15
☐912 5¢ (Luxembourg)	10.00	1.75	.25	.15
☐913 5¢ (Netherlands)	10.00	1.75	.25	.15
☐914 5¢ (Belgium)	10.00	1.75	.25	.15
☐915 5¢ (France)	10.00	1.75	.35	.15
☐916 5¢ (Greece)	35.00	15.00	.40	.15
☐917 5¢ (Yugoslavia)	23.00	7.00	.30	.15
☐918 5¢ (Albania)	23.00	7.00	.25	.15
☐919 5¢ (Austria)	20.00	7.00	.25	.15
☐920 5¢ (Denmark)	21.00	7.00	.25	.15
☐921 5¢ (Korea)	16.00	7.00	.25	.15
1944. COMMEMORATIVES ———————				
1944. RAILROAD ISSUE				
☐922 3¢ Violet	15.00	2.00	.25	.15
1944. STEAMSHIP ISSUE				
☐923 3¢ Violet	12.00	2.00	.25	.15

*No hinge pricing from 1941 to date is figured at (N-H ADD 10%)

Scott No.	Mint Sheet	Plate Block	Fine Unused Each	Fine Used Each

1944. TELEGRAPH ISSUE
| ☐924 3¢ Bright Red Violet | 10.00 | 1.50 | .25 | .15 |

1944. CORREGIDOR ISSUE
| ☐925 3¢ Deep Violet | 8.00 | 1.40 | .25 | .15 |

1944. MOTION PICTURE ISSUE
| ☐926 3¢ Deep Violet | 9.00 | 1.30 | .25 | .15 |

1945. COMMEMORATIVES _____
1945. FLORIDA ISSUE
| ☐927 3¢ Bright Red Violet | 7.40 | .90 | .24 | .15 |

1945. PEACE CONFERENCE ISSUE
| ☐928 5¢ Ultramarine | 9.00 | .75 | .24 | .15 |

1945. IWO JIMA ISSUE
| ☐929 3¢ Yellow Green | 15.00 | 2.00 | .40 | .15 |

1945–1946. ROOSEVELT MEMORIAL ISSUE
☐930 1¢ Blue Green	3.00	.46	.25	.15
☐931 2¢ Carmine Rose	5.00	.50	.25	.15
☐932 3¢ Purple	7.00	.75	.25	.15
☐933 5¢ Bright Blue	10.00	1.10	.25	.15

1945. ARMY ISSUE
| ☐934 3¢ Olive Gray | 10.00 | .80 | .25 | .15 |

1945. NAVY ISSUE
| ☐935 3¢ Blue | 10.00 | .80 | .25 | .15 |

1945. COAST GUARD ISSUE
| ☐936 3¢ Bright Blue Green | 10.00 | .80 | .25 | .15 |

1945. ALFRED SMITH ISSUE
| ☐937 3¢ Purple | 16.00 | .86 | .25 | .15 |

1945. TEXAS CENTENNIAL ISSUE
| ☐938 3¢ Blue | 10.00 | .80 | .25 | .15 |

*No hinge pricing from 1941 to date is figured at (N-H ADD 10%)

Scott No.	Mint Sheet	Plate Block	Fine Unused Each	Fine Used Each

1946–1947. COMMEMORATIVES

1946. MERCHANT MARINE ISSUE

☐939 3¢ Blue Green	7.00	.75	.25	.15

1946. HONORABLE DISCHARGE EMBLEM ISSUE

☐940 3¢ Dark Violet	13.00	.70	.25	.15

1946. TENNESSEE ISSUE

☐941 3¢ Dark Violet	12.00	.76	.25	.15

1946. IOWA STATEHOOD ISSUE

☐942 3¢ Deep Blue	7.00	.70	.25	.15

1946. SMITHSONIAN INSTITUTION ISSUE

☐943 3¢ Violet Brown	12.00	.75	.25	.15

1946. NEW MEXICO ISSUE

☐944 3¢ Brown Violet	7.25	.75	.25	.15

1947. EDISON ISSUE

☐945 3¢ Bright Red Violet	12.00	1.00	.25	.15

1947. PULITZER PRIZE

☐946 3¢ Purple	12.50	1.10	.25	.15

1947. U.S. POSTAGE STAMP CENTENARY

☐947 3¢ Deep Blue	8.00	.75	.30	.16

1947. "CIPEX" SOUVENIR SHEET

☐948 5¢ & 10¢ Sheet of 2	—	—	.95	.70
☐948a 5¢ Blue, sgl. stp.	—	—	.45	.35
☐948b 10¢ Brown Orange, sgl. stp.				
	—		.55	.35

1947. DOCTORS ISSUE

☐949 3¢ Brown Violet	7.00	.80	.25	.16

1947. UTAH ISSUE

☐950 3¢ Dark Violet	7.00	.80	.25	.16

*No hinge pricing from 1941 to date is figured at (N-H ADD 10%)

Scott No.	Mint Sheet	Plate Block	Fine Unused Each	Fine Used Each

1947. U.S.F. CONSTITUTION ISSUE
☐951 3¢ Blue Green   7.00   .70   .26   .16

1947. EVERGLADES ISSUE
☐952 3¢ Bright Green   7.00   .70   .24   .16

1948. COMMEMORATIVES ————————————
1948. CARVER ISSUE
☐953 3¢ Red Violet   9.00   .70   .24   .16

1948. GOLD RUSH ISSUE
☐954 3¢ Dark Violet   7.00   .70   .24   .16

1948. MISSISSIPPI TERRITORY ISSUE
☐955 3¢ Brown Violet   10.00   .70   .24   .16

1948. FOUR CHAPLAINS ISSUE
☐956 3¢ Gray Black   12.00   .75   .24   .16

1948. WISCONSIN CENTENNIAL ISSUE
☐957 3¢ Dark Violet   7.00   .70   .24   .16

1948. SWEDISH PIONEER ISSUE
☐958 5¢ Deep Blue   8.00   .70   .24   .16

1948. 100 YEARS PROGRESS OF WOMEN
☐959 3¢ Dark Violet   7.00   .72   .24   .16

1948. WILLIAM ALLEN WHITE ISSUE
☐960 3¢ Red Violet   10.00   .72   .24   .16

1948. U.S.-CANADA FRIENDSHIP
☐961 3¢ Blue   7.00   .72   .24   .16

1948. FRANCIS SCOTT KEY ISSUE
☐962 3¢ Rose Pink   10.00   .75   .24   .16

*No hinge pricing from 1941 to date is figured at (N-H ADD 10%)

GENERAL ISSUE—SCOTT NO. 734–777 (1933–1936)

734

736

737, 738, 754

739, 755

740, 751, 756,
769

741, 757

742, 750, 758, 770

743, 759

744, 760

745, 761

746, 762

747, 763

748, 764

749, 765, 797

772, 778A

773, 778B

774

775, 778C

776, 778D

777

782

783

784

785

786

787

788

789

790

791

792

793

794

795

796

798

799

800

801

GENERAL ISSUE—SCOTT NO. 802–830 (1937–1938)

802

803

804, 848

805, 849

806

807

808, 843

809, 844

810, 845

811, 846

812

813

814

815, 847

816

817

818

819

820

821

822

823

824

825

826

827

828

829

830

831

832

833

834

835

836

837

838

852

853

854

855

856

857

858

859

860

861

862

863

864

865

866

867

GENERAL ISSUE—SCOTT NO. 868–896 (1940)

868   869   870   871   872

873   874   875   876   877

878   879   880   881   882

883   884   885   886   887

888   889   890   891   892

893   894   895   896

897

898

899

900

901

902

903

904

905

906

907

908

909

921

922

923

924

925

926

927

GENERAL ISSUE—SCOTT NO. 928–942 (1945–1946)

928

929

930

931

932

933

934

935

936

937

938

939

940

941

942

GENERAL ISSUE—SCOTT NO. 943–954 (1946–1948)

943

944

945

946

947

948

949

950

951

952

953

954

955

956

957

958

959

960

961

962

963

964

965

966

967

968

969

970

GENERAL ISSUE—SCOTT NO. 971–986 (1948–1950)

971

972

973

974

975

976

977

978

979

980

981

982

983

984

985

986

987

988

989

990

991

992

993

994

995

996

997

998

999

1000

1001

1002

1003

1004

1005

1006

1007

1008

1009

1010

1011

1012

1013

1014

1015

1016

1017

1018

1019

1020

1021

1022

1023

1024

1025

1026

1027

1028

1029

1030

1031, 1054

1031A, 1054A

1032

1033, 1055

1034, 1056

1035-1075

1036, 1058

1037, 1059

1038

1039

1040

1041, 1075B

1042A

1043

1044A

1044

1045

1046

1047

1048

1049

1050

1051

1052

1053

1060

1061

1062

1063

1064

1065

1066

1067

1068

1069

1070

1071

1072

1073

1074

1076

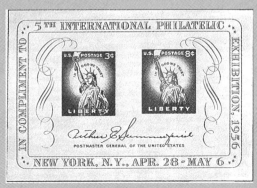

1075

GENERAL ISSUE—SCOTT NO. 1077–1093 (1956–1957)

1077

1078

1079

1080

1081

1082

1083

1084

1085

1086

1087

1088

1089

1090

1091

1092

1093

1094

1095

1096

1097

1098

1099

1100

1104

1105

1106

1107

1108

1109

1110

1111

1112

1113

1114

1115

1116

1117

1118

1119

1120

1121

1122

1123

1124

1125

1126

1127

1128

1129

1130

1131

1132

1133

1134

1135

1136

1137

1138

1139

1140

1141

1142

1143

1144

1145

1146

1147

1148

1149

1150

1151

1152

1153

1154

1155

1156

1157

1158

1159

1160

1161

1162

1163

1164

1165

1166

1167

GENERAL ISSUE—SCOTT NO. 1168–1186 (1960–1961)

1168

1169

1170

1171

1172

1173

1174

1175

1176

1177

1178

1179

1180

1181

1182

1183

1185

1184

1186

1187

1188

1189

1190

1191

1192

1193

1194

1195

1196

1197

1198

1201

1200

1199

1202

GENERAL ISSUE—SCOTT NO. 1203–1237 (1962–1963)

1203

1204

1205

1206

1207

1208

1209, 1225

1213

1230

1231

1232

1233

1234

1235

1236

1237

1238

1239

1240

1241

1243

1244

1245

1242

1247

1248

1246

1249

1250

1251

1252

1253

1254

1255

1256

1257

GENERAL ISSUE—SCOTT NO. 1258–1273 (1964–1965)

1258

1259

1260

1261

1262

1263

1264

1265

1266

1267

1268

1269

1270

1271

1272

1273

GENERAL ISSUE—SCOTT NO. 1274–1306 (1965–1966)

1274

1275

1276

1278

1279

1280

1281, 1297

1282, 1303

1283, 1304

1283B

1284, 1298

1285

1286

1286A

1287

1288

1289

1290

1291

1292

1293

1294, 1305C

1295

1305

1306

GENERAL ISSUE—SCOTT NO. 1307–1321 (1966)

1307

1308

1309

1310

1311

1312

1313

1314

1315

1316

1317

1318

1319

1320

1321

GENERAL ISSUE—SCOTT NO. 1322–1343 (1966–1968)

1322

1323

1324

1325

1326

1327

1328

1329

1330

1333

1334

1331   1332

1336

1335

1337

1338, 1338A

1338F, G

1339

1343

1340

1341

1342

GENERAL ISSUE—SCOTT NO. 1344–1372 (1968–1969)

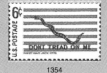

1344

1345

1354

1355

1356

1357

1358

1359

1360

1361

1362

1363

1364

1365-1368

1369

1370

1371

1372

GENERAL ISSUE—SCOTT NO. 1373–1396 (1969–1970)

1373

1374

1376-1379

1380

1375

1381

1382

1383

1385

1386

1384

1391

1393

1387-1390

1392

1393D

1394

1395

1396

A-30

GENERAL ISSUE—SCOTT NO. 1397–1425 (1970–1971)

1397

1398

1399

1400

1405

1406

1407

1408

1409

1410-1413

1414

1415-1418

1419

1420

1421   1422

1423

1424

1425

GENERAL ISSUE—SCOTT NO. 1426–1447 (1971–1972)

1426

1427-1430

1432

1431

1433

1436

1434   1435

1437

1438

1440-1443

1439

1444

1445

1446

1447

A-32

1448-1451

1452

1453

1454

1455

1456-1459

1460

1461

1463

1462

1468

1469

1464-1467

1470

1471

1472

1473

1474

1475

1476

1477

1478

1479

1480–1483

1484

1485

1486

1487

1488

1489

1490

1491

1492

1493

1494

1495

1496

1497

GENERAL ISSUE—SCOTT NO. 1498–1531 (1973–1974)

1498

1499

1500

1501

1502

1503

1504

1506F

1505

1505

1506F

1507

1508

1525

1509, 1519

1510

1511

1518

1526

1527

1528

1529

1530

1531

A-35

GENERAL ISSUE—SCOTT NO. 1532–1555 (1974–1975)

1532

1533

1534

1535

1536

1537

1538-1539
1540-1541

1542

1543-1546

1547

1548

1552

1549

1550

1551

1553

1554

1555

A-36

GENERAL ISSUE—SCOTT NO. 1556–1578 (1975)

1556

1557

1558

Contributes To the Cause
Sybil Ludington — Youthful Heroine
1559

Salem Poor — Gallant Soldier
1560

Contributes To the Cause
Haym Salomon — Financial Hero
1561

Contributes To the Cause...
Peter Francisco — Fighter Extraordinary
1562

Lexington & Concord 1775 by Sandham
US Bicentennial 10cents
1563

Bunker Hill 1775 by Trumbull
US Bicentennial 10c
1564

CONTINENTAL ARMY
1565

CONTINENTAL NAVY
1566

CONTINENTAL MARINES
1567

AMERICAN MILITIA
1568

APOLLO SOYUZ 1975
1569

APOLLO SOYUZ SPACE TEST PROJECT
1570

INTERNATIONAL WOMEN'S YEAR
1571

US10c 200 Years of Postal Service
1572

US10c 200 Years of Postal Service
1573

US10c 200 Years of Postal Service
1574

US10c 200 Years of Postal Service
1575

World Peace through LAW
1576

BANKING   COMMERCE
1577-1578

A-37

1579

1580

1581

1582

1584

1585

1590

1592

1593

1594

1595

1596

1597

1599

1603

1604

1605

1606

1608

1610

1611

1612

1613

1614

1615

1615C

1622

1623

1629-1630-1631

1632

1683

1684

1633-1682

1685

1686

1687

1688

1689

1690

1691-1692-1693-1694

1699

1695

1696

1697

1698

1700

1701

1704

1705

1706

1702-1703

1707

1709

1708

1710

1711

GENERAL ISSUE—SCOTT NO. 1712–1730 (1977)

1712

1713

1714

1715

1716

1717

1718

1719

1720

1721

1722

1723

1724

1725

1726

1727

1728

1729

1730

1731

1732

1733

1734

1735

1737

1738-1739-1740-1741-1742

1744

1745

1746

1747

1748

1749

1750

1751

1752

1753

1754

1755

GENERAL ISSUE—SCOTT NO. 1756–1772 (1978–1979)

1757

1756

1758

1759

1760

1761

1762

1763

1764

1765

1766

1768

1769

1770

1767

1771

1772

1773

1774

1775

1776

1777

1778

1779

1780

1781

1782

1783

1784

1785

1786

1787

1788

1789

1790

1791

1792

1793

GENERAL ISSUE—SCOTT NO. 1794–1824 (1979–1980)

1794

1795

1796

1797

1798

1799

1800

1801

1802

1803

1804

1805–1806

1807–1808

1809–1810

1811

1813

1818

1821

1822

1823

1824

A-45

GENERAL ISSUE—SCOTT NO. 1825–1846 (1980–1983)

1825

1826

1827

1828

1829

1830

1831

1832

1833

1834

1835

1836

1837

1838

1839

1840

1841

1842

1843

1844

1845

1846

1847

1848

1849

1850

1851

1852

1853

1854

1855

1856

1857

1858

1859

1860

1861

1862

1863

1864

1865

1866

1867

1868

1869

1874

1875

1876

1877

1878

1879

1880

1881

1882

1883

1884

GENERAL ISSUE—SCOTT NO. 1885–1923 (1981–1982)

1885

1886

1887

1888

1889

1890

1891

1892

1893

1894

1903

1905

1906

1907

1908

1910

1911

1912-1919

1920

1921

1922

1923

GENERAL ISSUE—SCOTT NO. 1924–1941 (1981)

1924

1925

1926

1927

1928

1929

1930

1931

1932

1933

1934

1935

1937-1938

1936

1939

1940

1941

GENERAL ISSUE—SCOTT NO. 1942–2005 (1981–1982)

1942-1945

1946-1948

1949

1950

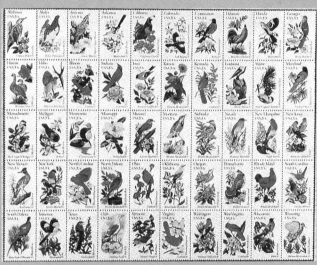

1953-2002

2003

2004

2005

A-50

2006-2009

2010

2012

2011

2013

2014

2015

2016

2017

2018

2023

2019-2022

2024

2025

2026

2027-2030

2031

2032-2035

2036

2037

2038

2039

2040

2041

2042

2043

2044

2045

2046

2047

GENERAL ISSUE—SCOTT NO. 2048–2065 (1983)

2048-2051

2052

2054

2055

2053

2056

2057

2058

2059

2060

2061

2062

2063

2064

2065

A-53

2066

2067-2070

2071

2072

2073

2074

2075

2076-2079

2080

2081

2086

2082-2085

2088

2089

Health Research USA 20c

2087

2090

2091

2092

2093

2094

2095

2096

2097

2098

2099

2100

2101

2102

2103

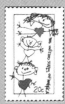

2104

2105

2107

2108

2109

2106

2117-2121

2111-2113

2114-2116

2110

GENERAL ISSUE—SCOTT NO. 2122–2152 (1985)

2122

2123

2124

2125

2126

2128

2130

2131

2132

2133

2134

2135

2136

2137

2138-2141

2142

2143

2144

2145

2146

2147

2149

2150

2152

GENERAL ISSUE—SCOTT NO. 2153–2196 (1985–1990)

2153

2154

2155-2158

2159

2160-2163

2164

2165

2166

2167

2168

2169

2170

2171

2172

2177

2179

2183

2191

2194

2195

2196

2198-2201

2202

2203

2204

2205-2209

2210

2211

2216

2217

2218

GENERAL ISSUE—SCOTT NO. 2219–2250 (1986–1987)

2219

2220-2223

2235-2238

Liberty
1886–1986

USA 22

2224

2240-2243

T.S. Eliot

22 USA

2239

CHRISTMAS
22
USA

Perugino, National Gallery

2244

GREETINGS

2245

Michigan Statehood

2246

2247

LOVE

USA 22

2248

Jean Baptiste
Pointe Du Sable
22

2249

Enrico
Caruso
22 USA

2250

A-59

2251

2275

2276

2336

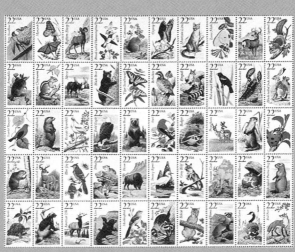

2286-2335

2337

2338

2349

2350

2351-2354

2355-2359

2360

2361

2367

2368

2369

2370

2371

2372-2375

2376

2377

2378

A-61

2379

2380

2386-2389

1928 Locomobile

1929 Pierce Arrow

1931 Cord

1932 Packard

1935 Duesenberg

2381-2385

2390-2393

2394

2395

2396

2397

2398

2399

2400

2401

2402

2403

GENERAL ISSUE—SCOTT NO. 2404–2427 (1989)

2404

2405-2409

2410

2411

2412

2413

2414

2416

2417

2418

2419

2420

2421

2422-2425

2426

2427

2428

2434-2437

2439

2440

2442

2443

2444

2445-2448

2449

2452

2470-2474

2496-2500

2501

2506-2507

2512

2508-2511

2513

2514

2515

2517

2521

2523

2524

2528

2530

2531

2532

2533

2534

2539

2550

2535

2545-2549

2537

2540

2551

2558

2538

2541

2542

2553-2557

2560

2561

2562-2566

2568-2577

2567

2579

2582

2578

2604

2583

2584

2585

2607

2608

2609

2616

2611-2615

2618

2620-2623

2630

2631-2634

2635

2636

2637-2641

2642-2646

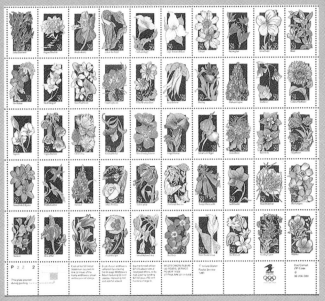

2647-2696

2697

2698

2699

2700-2703

2704

2710

2712

2705-2709

2711

2713

2720

2714

2721

2722

2723

2724

2725

2726

2727

2728

2729

2730

2741-2745

2746

2747

2748

2749

2754

2755

2750-2753

2756-2759

A-71

2760-2764

2765

2766

2767-2770

2779-2782

2804

2805

2806

2812

2813

2814

2807-2811

2815

2829-2833

2818

2834-2837

2838

2840

2841

2843-2847

2848

2849

2850

2851

2852

GENERAL ISSUE—SCOTT NO. 2853–2867 (1995)

2853

2854

2855

2856

2857

2858

2859

2860

2861

2862

2867

2863-2866

GENERAL ISSUE—SCOTT NO. 2868–2905 (1995)

2868

2871

2872

2873

2874

2876

2869

2875

2878

2880

2882

2888

2905

A-76

GENERAL ISSUE—SCOTT NO. 2915–2965 (1995–1998)

2915

2933

2934

2935

2936

2938

2940

2943

2948

2949

2950

2951

2952

2953

2954

2955

2956

2957

2958

2960

2961

2962

2963

2964

2965

2966

2967

2968

2969

2970

2971

2972

2973

2974

2975

2976

2977

2978

2979

2980

1945: Victory at Last

2981

LOUIS ARMSTRONG

2982

COLEMAN HAWKINS

2983

LOUIS ARMSTRONG

2984

JAMES P. JOHNSON

2985

JELLY ROLL MORTON

2986

CHARLIE PARKER

2987

2988

2989

2990

2991

2992

2993

2994

2995

2996

2997

2998

2999

3000

3001

3002

3003

3004

3005

3006

3007

3012

3013

3019

3020

3021

3022

3023

3024

3025-3029

3033

3044

3030

3032

3048

3049

3055

3058

3059

3060

FREDERIC E. IVES (1856-1937) Halftone process

WILLIAM DICKSON (1860-1935) Motion pictures

EADWEARD MUYBRIDGE (1830-1904) Photography

OTTMAR MERGENTHALER (1854-1899) Linotype

3061-3064

3065

3066

3067

GENERAL ISSUE—SCOTT NO. 3068–3081 (1996)

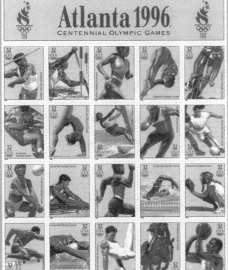

3068

3069

3071

3072-3076

3077-3080

3081

A-85

3082

3083-3086

PAUL BUNYAN

MIGHTY CASEY

PECOS BILL

JOHN HENRY

3087

1846
IOWA

3088

3090

ROBT. E. LEE

SYLVAN DELL

FAR WEST

COUNT BASIE

3096

TOMMY & JIMMY DORSEY

3097

REBECCA EVERINGHAM

GLENN MILLER

3098

BENNY GOODMAN

3099

BAILEY GATZERT

3091-3095

3100

3101

3102

3103

3104

3106

3105

3107 & 3112

3108

3109

3110

3111

3117

3119

3120

3121

3122

3123

GENERAL ISSUE—SCOTT NO. 3124–3138 (1997)

3124

3125

3126, 3128

3127, 3129

3130

3131

3132

3133

3134

3135

3136

3137, 3138

3139

3140

3142

3141

3143

3144

3145

3146

3147

3148

3149

3151

3150

3152

3153

3154

3155

3156

3157

3158

3159

3160

3161

3162

GENERAL ISSUE—SCOTT NO. 3163–3181 (1997–1998)

3163

3164

3165

3166

3167

3168

3169

3170

3171

3172

3173

3174

3175

3176

3177

3179

3180

3181

3182

3183

3184

3185

3192

3193-3197

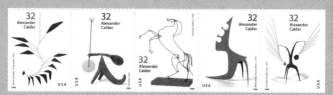

3198-3202

3203

3204

3206

3207

3208

3209–3210

3211

3212

3213

3214

3215

3216

3217

3218

3219

3220

3221

3222–3225

3226

3227

3230

GENERAL ISSUE—SCOTT NO. 3231–3242 (1998)

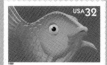

3231

3232

3233

3234

3235

3237

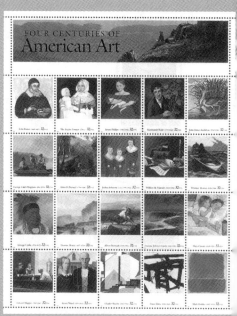

3236

3238–3242

A-96

3243

3244

3244

3245

3246

3247

3248

3257

3259

3260

3261

3262

3270

3273

3272

3274

3275

3276

3277

3283

3286

3306

3287

3288-3292

3293

3308

3309

3314

3315

3316

3321-3324

3310-3313

3317-3320

3325-3328

3329

3331

3330

3332

3338

3333-3337

3339-3344

3345-3350

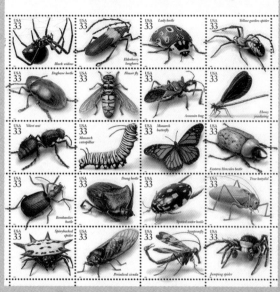

3351a-3351t

3353

3354

3368

3356-3359

3369

3370

3371

3373-3377

3378

3379-3383

3384-3388

3389

3390

3391

3393-3396

3397

3398

3399-3402

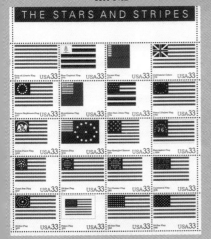

3403

3404-3407

3408

A-105

3409

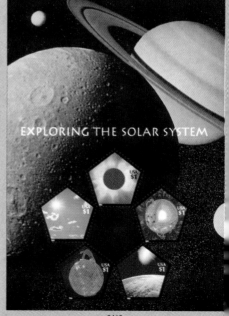

3410

3414-3417

3420

3438

3439-3443

3426

3444

3431

3445

3446

3448

3451

3457

3468

3471

3472

3473

3496

3499

3500

3501

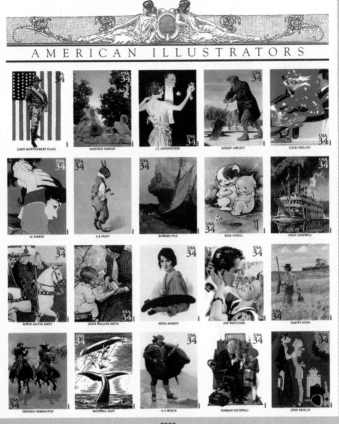

3502

3503

3504

3505

3507

3508

3506

3509

3520

3522

3521

3523

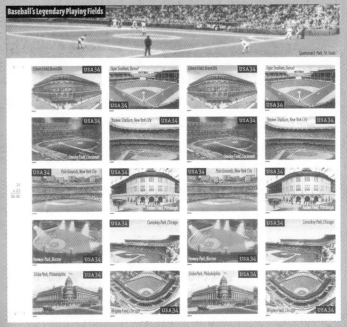

3510-3519

3524-3527

3532

3533

3528-3531

3535

3536

Scott No.	Mint Sheet	Plate Block	Fine Unused Each	Fine Used Each
1948. SALUTE TO YOUTH ISSUE				
☐963 3¢ Deep Blue	8.00	1.10	.21	.16
1948. OREGON TERRITORY ISSUE				
☐964 3¢ Brown Red	7.00	.80	.21	.16
1948. HARLAN FISKE STONE				
☐965 3¢ Bright Red Violet	12.00	1.00	.21	.16
1948. MT. PALOMAR OBSERVATORY				
☐966 3¢ Blue	10.00	1.10	.21	.16
1948. CLARA BARTON ISSUE				
☐967 3¢ Rose Pink	7.00	.75	.21	.16
1948. POULTRY ISSUE				
☐968 3¢ Sepia	10.00	1.10	.21	.16
1948. GOLD STAR MOTHERS				
☐969 3¢ Orange Yellow	8.00	.75	.21	.16
1948. FORT KEARNY ISSUE				
☐970 3¢ Violet	8.00	.75	.21	.16
1948. VOLUNTEER FIREMEN				
☐971 3¢ Bright Rose Carmine	12.00	1.20	.21	.16
1948. INDIAN CENTENNIAL				
☐972 3¢ Dark Brown	7.00	.75	.21	.16
1948. ROUGH RIDERS				
☐973 3¢ Violet Brown	7.00	.75	.21	.16
1948. JULIETTE LOW				
☐974 3¢ Blue Green	10.00	1.00	.21	.16

*No hinge pricing from 1941 to date is figured at (N-H ADD 10%)

Scott No.	Mint Sheet	Plate Block	Fine Unused Each	Fine Used Each
1948. WILL ROGERS				
☐975 3¢ Bright Red Violet	10.00	.65	.21	.16
1948. FORT BLISS				
☐976 3¢ Henna Brown	10.00	.80	.21	.16
1948. MOINA MICHAEL				
☐977 3¢ Rose Pink	11.00	1.10	.21	.16
1948. GETTYSBURG ADDRESS				
☐978 3¢ Bright Blue	7.50	1.10	.21	.16
1948. AMERICAN TURNERS				
☐979 3¢ Carmine	6.50	1.20	.21	.16
1948. JOEL CHANDLER HARRIS				
☐980 3¢ Bright Red Violet	8.00	1.10	.21	.16
1949–1950. COMMEMORATIVES ——————				
1949. MINNESOTA CENTENNIAL				
☐981 3¢ Blue Green	8.00	1.10	.21	.16
1949. WASHINGTON & LEE UNIVERSITY				
☐982 3¢ Ultramarine	10.00	1.10	.21	.16
1949. PUERTO RICO ISSUE				
☐983 3¢ Green	6.50	.70	.21	.16
1949. ANNAPOLIS TERCENTENARY				
☐984 3¢ Aquamarine	10.00	1.00	.21	.16
1949. G.A.R. ISSUE				
☐985 3¢ Bright Rose Carmine	10.00	1.00	.21	.16
1950. EDGAR ALLAN POE				
☐986 3¢ Bright Red Violet	11.00	1.00	.21	.16
1950. BANKERS ASSOCIATION				
☐987 3¢ Yellow Green	12.00	1.00	.21	.16

*No hinge pricing from 1941 to date is figured at (N-H ADD 10%)

Scott No.			Mint Sheet	Plate Block	Fine Unused Each	Fine Used Each

1950. SAMUEL GOMPERS
| ☐988 | 3¢ | Bright Red Violet | 9.00 | .70 | .25 | .16 |

1950. WASHINGTON SESQUICENTENNIAL
☐989	3¢	Bright Blue	8.00	.65	.25	.16
☐990	3¢	Deep Green	8.00	.65	.25	.16
☐991	3¢	Light Violet	10.00	.65	.25	.16
☐992	3¢	Rose Violet	9.00	.65	.25	.16

1950. RAILROAD ENGINEERS
| ☐993 | 3¢ | Violet Brown | 10.00 | .70 | .25 | .16 |

1950. KANSAS CITY CENTENARY
| ☐994 | 3¢ | Violet | 8.00 | .80 | .25 | .16 |

1950. BOY SCOUTS ISSUE
| ☐995 | 3¢ | Sepia | 8.00 | .80 | .25 | .16 |

1950. INDIANA SESQUICENTENNIAL
| ☐996 | 3¢ | Bright Blue | 10.00 | .65 | .25 | .16 |

1950. CALIFORNIA STATEHOOD
| ☐997 | 3¢ | Yellow Orange | 8.00 | .75 | .25 | .16 |

1951–1952. COMMEMORATIVES
1951. UNITED CONFEDERATE VETERANS
| ☐998 | 3¢ | Gray | 10.00 | 1.00 | .25 | .16 |

1951. NEVADA SETTLEMENT
| ☐999 | 3¢ | Light Olive Green | 8.00 | .65 | .25 | .16 |

1951. LANDING OF CADILLAC
| ☐1000 | 3¢ | Bright Blue | 8.00 | .70 | .25 | .16 |

1951. COLORADO STATEHOOD
| ☐1001 | 3¢ | Violet Blue | 8.00 | .75 | .25 | .16 |

*No hinge pricing from 1941 to date is figured at (N-H ADD 10%)

Scott No.	Mint Sheet	Plate Block	Fine Unused Each	Fine Used Each

1951. AMERICAN CHEMICAL SOCIETY
| ☐1002 3¢ Violet Brown | 12.00 | 1.00 | .21 | .16 |

1951. BATTLE OF BROOKLYN ISSUE
| ☐1003 3¢ Violet | 10.00 | 1.00 | .21 | .16 |

1952. BETSY ROSS ISSUE
| ☐1004 3¢ Carmine Rose | 10.00 | 1.00 | .21 | .16 |

1952. 4-H CLUB ISSUE
| ☐1005 3¢ Blue Green | 10.00 | 1.00 | .21 | .16 |

1952. BALTIMORE & OHIO RAILROAD
| ☐1006 3¢ Bright Blue | 8.00 | .65 | .21 | .16 |

1952. AMERICAN AUTOMOBILE ASSOCIATION (AAA)
| ☐1007 3¢ Deep Blue | 8.00 | .65 | .21 | .16 |

1952. NORTH ATLANTIC TREATY ORGANIZATION
| ☐1008 3¢ Deep Violet | 12.00 | .65 | .21 | .16 |

1952. GRAND COULEE DAM ISSUE
| ☐1009 3¢ Blue Green | 8.00 | .65 | .21 | .16 |

1952. ARRIVAL OF LAFAYETTE
| ☐1010 3¢ Ultramarine | 14.00 | 1.10 | .21 | .16 |

1952. MOUNT RUSHMORE
| ☐1011 3¢ Blue Green | 8.00 | .65 | .21 | .16 |

1952. SOCIETY OF CIVIL ENGINEERS
| ☐1012 3¢ Violet Blue | 12.00 | 1.00 | .21 | .16 |

1952. WOMEN IN ARMED FORCES
| ☐1013 3¢ Deep Blue | 8.00 | .65 | .21 | .16 |

*No hinge pricing from 1941 to date is figured at (N-H ADD 10%)

Scott No.	Mint Sheet	Plate Block	Fine Unused Each	Fine Used Each
1952. GUTENBERG PRINTING				
☐ 1014 3¢ Violet	8.00	.65	.21	.16
1952. NEWSPAPERBOYS				
☐ 1015 3¢ Violet	8.00	.65	.21	.16
1952. INTERNATIONAL RED CROSS				
☐ 1016 3¢ Deep Blue & Carmine				
	8.00	.65	.21	.16
1953–1954. COMMEMORATIVES ————				
1953. NATIONAL GUARD				
☐ 1017 3¢ Bright Blue	8.00	.65	.21	.16
1953. OHIO STATEHOOD				
☐ 1018 3¢ Chocolate	18.00	1.00	.21	.16
1953. WASHINGTON TERRITORY				
☐ 1019 3¢ Green	8.00	.65	.21	.16
1953. LOUISIANA PURCHASE				
☐ 1020 3¢ Violet Brown	12.00	1.00	.21	.16
1953. OPENING OF JAPAN				
☐ 1021 3¢ Green	12.00	1.20	.21	.16
1953. AMERICAN BAR ASSOCIATION				
☐ 1022 3¢ Rose Violet	8.00	.90	.21	.16
1953. SAGAMORE HILL				
☐ 1023 3¢ Yellow Green	6.00	.70	.21	.16
1953. FUTURE FARMERS				
☐ 1024 3¢ Deep Blue	6.50	.70	.21	.16
1953. TRUCKING INDUSTRY				
☐ 1025 3¢ Violet	6.00	.70	.21	.16
1953. GENERAL PATTON				
☐ 1026 3¢ Blue Violet	7.50	.70	.21	.16

*No hinge pricing from 1941 to date is figured at (N-H ADD 10%)

Scott No.	Mint Sheet	Plate Block	Fine Unused Each	Fine Used Each

1953. NEW YORK CITY

☐1027 3¢ Bright Red Violet	8.00	1.00	.24	.15

1953. GADSDEN PURCHASE

☐1028 3¢ Copper Brown	7.00	.60	.24	.15

1954. COLUMBIA UNIVERSITY

☐1029 3¢ Blue	9.00	.90	.24	.15

1954–1961. LIBERTY SERIES

☐1030 ¹/₂¢ Red Orange	7.00	.60	.24	.16
☐1031 1¢ Dark Green	6.00	.50	.24	.16
☐1031A 1¹/₄¢ Turquoise	6.00	.50	.24	.16
☐1032 1¹/₂¢ Brown	19.00	1.50	.30	.16
☐1033 2¢ Rose Carmine	9.00	.75	.21	16
☐1034 2¹/₂¢ Dark Blue	18.00	1.00	.30	.16
☐1035 3¢ Deep Violet	10.00	.60	.30	.16
☐1036 4¢ Red Violet	20.00	1.00	.30	.16
☐1037 4¹/₂¢ Green	21.00	1.00	.30	.16
☐1038 5¢ Deep Blue	25.00	1.00	.30	.16
☐1039 6¢ Orange Red	42.00	2.00	.41	.16
☐1040 7¢ Deep Carmine	30.00	1.00	.40	.16
☐1041 8¢ Dark Violet Blue, Carmine	35.00	2.50	.33	.16
☐1042 8¢ Violet Blue, Carmine (Re-engraved)	34.00	1.50	.34	.16
☐1042A 8¢ Brown	35.00	1.60	.34	.16
☐1043 9¢ Rose Lilac	50.00	2.00	.46	.16
☐1044 10¢ Rose Lake	48.00	2.00	.48	.16
☐1044A 11¢ Carmine, Violet Blue	45.00	1.60	.40	.16
☐1045 12¢ Red	60.00	2.10	.45	.16
☐1046 15¢ Maroon	105.00	4.10	.90	.16
☐1047 20¢ Ultramarine	80.00	3.60	.65	.16
☐1048 25¢ Green	180.00	7.50	1.60	.16
☐1049 30¢ Black	200.00	7.00	1.60	.16
☐1050 40¢ Brown Carmine	280.00	12.50	2.60	.16

*No hinge pricing from 1941 to date is figured at (N-H ADD 10%)

Scott No.	Mint Sheet	Plate Block	Fine Unused Each	Fine Used Each
☐1051 50¢ Bright Violet	215.00	9.00	2.00	.16
☐1052 $1 Deep Violet	700.00	30.00	7.00	.24
☐1053 $5 Black	1000.00	475.00	112.00	9.00

1954–1965. ROTARY PRESS COIL STAMPS. PERF. 10 VERTICALLY OR HORIZONTALLY

Scott No.	Fine Unused Line Pair	Ave. Unused Line Pair	Fine Unused Each	Ave. Unused Each	Fine Used Each	Ave. Used Each
☐1054 1¢ Deep Green						
	3.00	1.00	.35	.25	.30	.15
☐1055 2¢ Rose Carmine						
	2.25	1.40	.35	.27	.30	.15
☐1056 2¹/₂¢ Gray Blue						
	4.00	3.00	.41	.28	.30	.15
☐1057 3¢ Deep Violet						
	3.10	.70	.30	.26	.31	.16
☐1058 4¢ Red Violet						
	85.00	.75	.30	.28	.30	.16
☐1059 4¹/₂¢ Green						
	16.00	9.00	2.00	1.60	1.50	.90
☐1059A 25¢ Green						
	3.00	1.75	.80	.50	1.00	.16

Scott No.	Mint Sheet	Plate Block	Fine Unused Each	Fine Used Each

1954. NEBRASKA TERRITORY

☐1060 3¢ Violet	7.00	.70	.26	.16

1954. KANSAS TERRITORY

☐1061 3¢ Brown Orange	7.00	.70	.25	.16

1954. GEORGE EASTMAN ISSUE

☐1062 3¢ Violet Brown	9.00	.70	.26	.16

*No hinge pricing from 1941 to date is figured at (N-H ADD 10%)

Scott No.	Mint Sheet	Plate Block	Fine Unused Each	Fine Used Each

1954. LEWIS & CLARK EXPEDITION
☐1063 3¢ Dark Brown   7.00   .70   .21   .16

1955. COMMEMORATIVES ━━━━━━━
1955. PENNSYLVANIA ACADEMY OF FINE ARTS
☐1064 3¢ Rose Brown   12.00   1.00   .30   .16

1955. LAND GRANT COLLEGES
☐1065 3¢ Green   7.00   .70   .25   .16

1955. ROTARY INTERNATIONAL ISSUE
☐1066 8¢ Deep Blue   14.00   1.60   .26   .16

1955. ARMED FORCES RESERVE
☐1067 3¢ Red Violet   7.00   .75   .21   .16

1955. OLD MAN OF THE MOUNTAINS
☐1068 3¢ Blue Green   12.00   1.00   .30   .16

1955. SOO LOCKS CENTENNIAL
☐1069 3¢ Blue   7.00   .70   .25   .16

1955. ATOMS FOR PEACE
☐1070 3¢ Blue   7.00   .75   .24   .16

1955. FORT TICONDEROGA BICENTENNIAL
☐1071 3¢ Sepia   12.00   1.00   .28   .16

1955. ANDREW MELLON ISSUE
☐1072 3¢ Deep Carmine   19.00   1.10   .28   .16

1956. COMMEMORATIVES ━━━━━━━
1956. 250TH ANNIVERSARY FRANKLIN'S BIRTH
☐1073 3¢ Rose Carmine   10.00   1.00   .26   .16

1956. BOOKER T. WASHINGTON ISSUE
☐1074 3¢ Deep Blue   7.00   .75   .21   .16
*No hinge pricing from 1941 to date is figured at (N-H ADD 10%)

Scott No.	Mint Sheet	Plate Block	Fine Unused Each	Fine Used Each

1956. FIFTH INTL. PHILATELIC EXHIBITION DESIGNS OF 1035 & 1041 IN IMPERF. SOUVENIR SHEET

| ☐ 1075 3¢ & 8¢ Sheet of 2 | — | — | 2.75 | 2.30 |

1956. FIFTH INTL. PHILATELIC EXHIBITION

| ☐ 1076 3¢ Deep Violet | 7.00 | .70 | .24 | .16 |

1956. WILDLIFE CONSERVATION ISSUE

☐ 1077 3¢ Rose Lake	7.00	.72	.21	.16
☐ 1078 3¢ Brown	6.00	.72	.21	.16
☐ 1079 3¢ Green	10.00	1.00	.21	.16

1956. PURE FOOD & DRUG ACT

| ☐ 1080 3¢ Dark Blue Green | 10.00 | 1.00 | .26 | 16 |

1956. HOME OF PRESIDENT BUCHANAN

| ☐ 1081 3¢ Black Brown | 10.00 | .90 | .26 | 16 |

1956. LABOR DAY ISSUE

| ☐ 1082 3¢ Deep Blue | 12.00 | 1.10 | .27 | 16 |

1956. NASSAU HALL—PRINCETON

| ☐ 1083 3¢ Black on Orange | 12.00 | 1.10 | .26 | 16 |

1956. DEVIL'S TOWER

| ☐ 1084 3¢ Purple | 6.00 | .72 | .21 | 16 |

1956. CHILDREN'S ISSUE

| ☐ 1085 3¢ Dark Blue | 6.50 | .72 | .21 | 16 |

1957. COMMEMORATIVES ━━━━━━
1957. ALEXANDER HAMILTON ISSUE

| ☐ 1086 3¢ Rose Red | 7.00 | .82 | .21 | .16 |

1957. POLIO ISSUE

| ☐ 1087 3¢ Light Purple | 7.00 | .65 | .21 | .16 |

*No hinge pricing from 1941 to date is figured at (N-H ADD 10%)

Scott No.	Mint Sheet	Plate Block	Fine Unused Each	Fine Used Each

1957. COAST & GEODETIC SURVEY
☐ 1088 3¢ Dark Blue   7.00   .65   .25   .16

1957. ARCHITECTS ISSUE
☐ 1089 3¢ Red Lilac   7.00   .65   .25   .16

1957. STEEL INDUSTRY CENTENNIAL
☐ 1090 3¢ Bright Ultra   7.00   .65   .25   .16

1957. INTERNATIONAL NAVAL REVIEW
☐ 1091 3¢ Blue Green   7.00   .65   .25   .16

1957. OKLAHOMA STATEHOOD
☐ 1092 3¢ Dark Blue   7.00   .65   .25   .16

1957. SCHOOL TEACHERS
☐ 1093 3¢ Rose Lake   10.00   1.00   .25   .16

1957. U.S. FLAG ISSUE
☐ 1094 4¢ Blue & Red   7.00   .71   .25   .16

1957. 350TH SHIPBUILDING ANNIVERSARY
☐ 1095 3¢ Purple   10.00   .70   .25   .16

1957. PHILIPPINES—CHAMPION OF LIBERTY
☐ 1096 8¢ Red, Blue & Gold   11.00   1.25   .25   .16

1957. BIRTH OF LAFAYETTE
☐ 1097 3¢ Maroon   12.50   1.00   .25   .16

1957. WILDLIFE CONSERVATION ISSUE
☐ 1098 3¢ Blue, Green & Yellow
   10.00   1.00   .25   .16

1957. RELIGIOUS FREEDOM
☐ 1099 3¢ Black   7.00   .70   .25   .16
*No hinge pricing from 1941 to date is figured at (N-H ADD 10%)

Scott No.	Mint Sheet	Plate Block	Fine Unused Each	Fine Used Each

1958. COMMEMORATIVES ─────────

1958. GARDENING & HORTICULTURE

☐1100 3¢ Deep Green	7.00	.68	.21	.16

1958. BRUSSELS EXHIBITION

☐1104 3¢ Deep Claret	7.00	.70	.21	.16

1958. JAMES MONROE BICENTENNIAL

☐1105 3¢ Purple	9.00	.71	.21	.16

1958. MINNESOTA STATEHOOD

☐1106 3¢ Green	7.00	.68	.26	.16

1958. INTERNATIONAL GEOPHYSICAL YEAR

☐1107 3¢ Black & Orange	7.00	.68	.21	.16

1958. GUNSTON HALL BICENTENARY

☐1108 3¢ Light Green	7.00	.66	.21	.16

1958. MACKINAC BRIDGE ISSUE

☐1109 3¢ Bluish Green	7.00	.66	.21	.16

1958. SOUTH AMERICA—CHAMPION OF LIBERTY

☐1110 4¢ Olive Bistre	9.00	.70	.21	.16
☐1111 8¢ Red, Blue & Gold	17.00	1.50	.30	.21

1958. ATLANTIC CABLE CENTENNIAL

☐1112 4¢ Reddish Purple	7.00	.66	.26	.16

1958–1959. LINCOLN COMMEMORATIVE ISSUE

☐1113 1¢ Green	2.50	.50	.21	.16
☐1114 3¢ Rust Brown	12.00	1.00	.21	.16
☐1115 4¢ Sepia	8.00	.70	.21	.16
☐1116 4¢ Blue	12.00	1.10	.26	.16

1958. HUNGARY—CHAMPION OF LIBERTY

☐1117 4¢ Bluish Green	9.50	.72	.26	.16
☐1118 8¢ Red, Blue & Gold	17.00	1.40	.26	.16

*No hinge pricing from 1941 to date is figured at (N-H ADD 10%)

Scott No.	Mint Sheet	Plate Block	Fine Unused Each	Fine Used Each

1958. FREEDOM OF THE PRESS
| ☐1119 4¢ Black | 7.00 | .75 | .26 | .16 |

1958. OVERLAND MAIL CENTENNIAL
| ☐1120 4¢ Crimson Rose | 10.00 | .75 | .26 | .16 |

1958. NOAH WEBSTER
☐1121 4¢ Dark Carmine Rose

| | 12.00 | 1.00 | .26 | .16 |

1958. FOREST CONSERVATION
☐1122 4¢ Yellow, Brown & Green

| | 7.00 | .75 | .26 | .16 |

1958. FORT DUQUESNE BICENTENNIAL
| ☐1123 4¢ Blue | 12.00 | 1.00 | .26 | .16 |

1959. COMMEMORATIVES
1959. OREGON STATEHOOD
| ☐1124 4¢ Blue Green | 7.00 | .75 | .26 | .16 |

1959. ARGENTINA & CHILE—CHAMPION OF LIBERTY
| ☐1125 4¢ Blue | 9.00 | .75 | .26 | .16 |
| ☐1126 8¢ Red, Blue & Gold | 16.00 | 1.30 | .26 | .16 |

1959. 10TH ANNIVERSARY N.A.T.O.
| ☐1127 4¢ Blue | 10.00 | .75 | .26 | .16 |

1959. ARCTIC EXPLORATIONS
| ☐1128 4¢ Blue | 12.00 | 1.00 | .28 | .16 |

1959. WORLD PEACE & TRUST
| ☐1129 8¢ Maroon | 13.00 | 1.25 | .36 | .16 |

1959. SILVER DISCOVERY CENTENNIAL
| ☐1130 4¢ Black | 8.00 | .72 | .28 | .16 |

*No hinge pricing from 1941 to date is figured at (N-H ADD 10%)

Scott No.	Mint Sheet	Plate Block	Fine Unused Each	Fine Used Each

1959. ST. LAWRENCE SEAWAY ISSUE

☐1131 4¢ Red & Blue	10.00	1.00	.26	.16

1959. 49-STAR FLAG ISSUE

☐1132 4¢ Blue, Red & Yellow				
	7.00	.75	.26	.16

1959. SOIL CONSERVATION

☐1133 4¢ Yellow, Green & Blue				
	7.00	.75	.26	.16

1959. PETROLEUM INDUSTRY CENTENNIAL

☐1134 4¢ Brown	12.00	1.00	.26	.16

1959. DENTAL HEALTH ISSUE

☐1135 4¢ Green	10.50	1.10	.26	.16

1959. GERMANY—CHAMPION OF LIBERTY

☐1136 4¢ Gray	10.00	.75	.26	.16
☐1137 8¢ Red, Blue & Gold	18.00	1.40	.26	.16

1959. DR. EPHRAIM McDOWELL

☐1138 4¢ Maroon	16.00	1.00	.26	.16

1960. COMMEMORATIVES ─────────
1960–1961. CREDO OF AMERICA SERIES

☐1139 4¢ Dark Violet, Blue & Carmine				
	10.00	1.00	.26	.16
☐1140 4¢ Olive Bistre & Green				
	10.00	1.00	.26	.16
☐1141 4¢ Gray & Red	10.00	1.00	.26	.16
☐1142 4¢ Red & Blue	12.00	1.00	.26	.16
☐1143 4¢ Violet & Green	10.00	1.00	.26	.16
☐1144 4¢ Green & Brown	10.00	1.00	.26	.16

1960. BOY SCOUTS GOLDEN JUBILEE

☐1145 4¢ Red, Khaki & Blue	12.00	1.15	.26	.17

*No hinge pricing from 1941 to date is figured at (N-H ADD 10%)

Scott No.	Mint Sheet	Plate Block	Fine Unused Each	Fine Used Each

1960. WINTER OLYMPIC GAMES
| ☐ 1146 4¢ Blue | 7.00 | .65 | .26 | .16 |

1960. CZECHOSLOVAKIA—CHAMPION OF LIBERTY
| ☐ 1147 4¢ Blue | 10.00 | .65 | .26 | .16 |
| ☐ 1148 8¢ Yellow, Blue & Red | 18.00 | 1.10 | .26 | .16 |

1960. WORLD REFUGEE YEAR
| ☐ 1149 4¢ Gray Black | 7.00 | .70 | .24 | .16 |

1960. WATER CONSERVATION
| ☐ 1150 4¢ Blue, Green & Orange Brown | | | | |
| | 7.00 | .70 | .24 | .16 |

1960. SOUTHEAST ASIA TREATY ORGANIZATION
| ☐ 1151 4¢ Blue | 10.00 | .70 | .24 | .16 |

1960. HONORING AMERICAN WOMEN
| ☐ 1152 4¢ Violet | 7.00 | .70 | .24 | .16 |

1960. 50-STAR FLAG ISSUE
| ☐ 1153 4¢ Red & Blue | 7.00 | .72 | .24 | .16 |

1960. PONY EXPRESS CENTENNIAL
| ☐ 1154 4¢ Sepia | 9.00 | .90 | .24 | .16 |

1960. EMPLOY THE HANDICAPPED
| ☐ 1155 4¢ Blue | 7.00 | .70 | .24 | .16 |

1960. WORLD FORESTRY CONGRESS
| ☐ 1156 4¢ Green | 7.00 | .80 | .24 | .16 |

1960. MEXICAN INDEPENDENCE SESQUICENTENNIAL
| ☐ 1157 4¢ Red & Green | 7.00 | .65 | .24 | .16 |

1960. UNITED STATES—JAPAN TREATY CENTENNIAL
| ☐ 1158 4¢ Blue & Pink | 7.10 | .75 | .24 | .16 |

*No hinge pricing from 1941 to date is figured at (N-H ADD 10%)

Scott No.	Mint Sheet	Plate Block	Fine Unused Each	Fine Used Each

1960. POLAND—CHAMPION OF LIBERTY
| ☐1159 4¢ Blue | 10.00 | .75 | .24 | .16 |
| ☐1160 8¢ Red, Blue & Gold | 19.00 | 1.50 | .35 | .16 |

1960. ROBERT A. TAFT MEMORIAL ISSUE
| ☐1161 4¢ Dull Violet | 17.00 | 1.00 | .30 | .16 |

1960. WHEELS OF FREEDOM
| ☐1162 4¢ Dark Blue | 7.00 | .75 | .26 | .16 |

1960. BOYS' CLUBS OF AMERICA
| ☐1163 4¢ Indigo, Slate & Red | 12.00 | 1.10 | .25 | .16 |

1960. FIRST AUTOMATED POST OFFICE
| ☐1164 4¢ Dark Blue & Carmine | | | | |
| | 12.50 | 1.15 | .25 | .16 |

1960. FINLAND—CHAMPION OF LIBERTY
| ☐1165 4¢ Blue | 9.00 | .75 | .25 | .16 |
| ☐1166 8¢ Red, Blue & Gold | 17.00 | 1.10 | .25 | .16 |

1960. CAMP FIRE GIRLS
| ☐1167 4¢ Dark Blue & Red | 7.10 | .75 | .24 | .16 |

1960. ITALY—CHAMPION OF LIBERTY
| ☐1168 4¢ Green | 10.00 | .75 | .24 | .16 |
| ☐1169 8¢ Red, Blue & Gold | 17.00 | 1.30 | .36 | .16 |

1960. WALTER F. GEORGE MEMORIAL ISSUE
| ☐1170 4¢ Dull Violet | 18.00 | 1.20 | .31 | .16 |

1960. ANDREW CARNEGIE
| ☐1171 4¢ Deep Claret | 18.00 | 1.20 | .31 | .16 |

1960. JOHN FOSTER DULLES MEMORIAL ISSUE
| ☐1172 4¢ Dull Violet | 18.00 | 1.25 | .32 | .16 |

*No hinge pricing from 1941 to date is figured at (N-H ADD 10%)

Scott No.	Mint Sheet	Plate Block	Fine Unused Each	Fine Used Each
1960. "ECHO I" SATELLITE				
☐ 1173 4¢ Deep Violet	14.00	1.40	.36	.16
1961. COMMEMORATIVES ———————				
1961. INDIA—CHAMPION OF LIBERTY				
☐ 1174 4¢ Red Orange	10.00	.70	.31	.16
☐ 1175 8¢ Red, Blue & Gold	18.00	1.10	.31	.16
1961. RANGE CONSERVATION				
☐ 1176 4¢ Blue, Slate & Brown Orange				
	7.50	.75	.27	.16
1961. HORACE GREELEY				
☐ 1177 4¢ Dull Violet	12.00	1.10	.27	.16
1961–1965. CIVIL WAR CENTENNIAL SERIES				
1961. FORT SUMTER				
☐ 1178 4¢ Light Green	15.00	1.00	.30	.16
1962. BATTLE OF SHILOH				
☐ 1179 4¢ Black on Peach	15.00	1.60	.35	.16
1963. BATTLE OF GETTYSBURG				
☐ 1180 5¢ Blue & Gray	20.00	2.00	.50	.16
1964. BATTLE OF THE WILDERNESS				
☐ 1181 5¢ Dark Red & Black	18.00	1.75	.50	.16
1965. APPOMATTOX				
☐ 1182 5¢ Black & Blue	35.00	4.10	1.00	.16
1961. KANSAS STATEHOOD				
☐ 1183 4¢ Brown, Dark Red & Green on Yellow Paper				
	7.50	.80	.21	16
1961. GEORGE W. NORRIS BIRTH CENTENARY				
☐ 1184 4¢ Blue Green	10.00	1.00	.26	.16

*No hinge pricing from 1941 to date is figured at (N-H ADD 10%)

Scott No.	Mint Sheet	Plate Block	Fine Unused Each	Fine Used Each

1961. NAVAL AVIATION GOLDEN JUBILEE

☐1185 4¢ Blue	7.00	.75	.26	.16

1961. WORKMEN'S COMPENSATION LAW

☐1186 4¢ Ultramarine	7.40	.72	.26	.16

1961. F. REMINGTON BIRTH CENTENNIAL

☐1187 4¢ Blue, Red & Yellow

	12.00	1.10	.35	.16

1961. REPUBLIC OF CHINA ISSUE

☐1188 4¢ Blue	10.00	.90	.26	.16

1961. DR. J. NAISMITH—BASKETBALL FOUNDER

☐1189 4¢ Brown	13.00	1.10	.35	.16

1961. NURSING PROFESSION

☐1190 4¢ Blue, Red, Black & Green

	15.00	1.10	.34	.16

1962. COMMEMORATIVES _____
1962. NEW MEXICO STATEHOOD

☐1191 4¢ Blue, Maroon, Bistre

	7.00	.72	.26	.16

1962. ARIZONA STATEHOOD

☐1192 4¢ Red, Deep Blue, Green

	8.10	.75	.26	.16

1962. PROJECT MERCURY

☐1193 4¢ Dark Blue & Yellow

	11.00	1.15	.26	.16

1962. MALARIA ERADICATION

☐1194 4¢ Blue & Bistre	7.50	.72	.26	.16

*No hinge pricing from 1941 to date is figured at (N-H ADD 10%)

Scott No.	Mint Sheet	Plate Block	Fine Unused Each	Fine Used Each

1962. CHARLES EVANS HUGHES BIRTH CENTENNIAL

☐ 1195 4¢ Black on Buff	7.00	.66	.24	.16

1962. SEATTLE WORLD'S FAIR

☐ 1196 4¢ Red & Dark Blue	7.00	.65	.24	.16

1962. LOUISIANA STATEHOOD

☐ 1197 4¢ Blue, Green, Red	10.50	1.00	.24	.16

1962. THE HOMESTEAD ACT

☐ 1198 4¢ Slate	7.00	.67	.24	.16

1962. GIRL SCOUTS 50TH ANNIVERSARY

☐ 1199 4¢ Red	7.25	.67	.24	.16

1962. BRIEN MCMAHON MEMORIAL ISSUE

☐ 1200 4¢ Purple	10.50	1.00	.24	.16

1962. NATIONAL APPRENTICESHIP ACT

☐ 1201 4¢ Black on Buff	7.75	.65	.24	.16

1962. SAM RAYBURN MEMORIAL ISSUE

☐ 1202 4¢ Brown & Blue	7.00	.65	.24	.16

1962. DAG HAMMARSKJOLD MEMORIAL

☐ 1203 4¢ Yellow, Brown & Black	6.75	.65	.24	.16
☐ 1204 4¢ Yellow Color Inverted	8.00	1.65	.24	.16

1962. CHRISTMAS WREATH

☐ 1205 4¢ Green & Red	14.00	1.00	.24	.16

1962. HIGHER EDUCATION

☐ 1206 4¢ Green & Black	7.10	.80	.24	.16

*No hinge pricing from 1941 to date is figured at (N-H ADD 10%)

Scott No.	Mint Sheet	Plate Block	Fine Unused Each	Fine Used Each

1962. WINSLOW HOMER

Scott No.	Mint Sheet	Plate Block	Fine Unused Each	Fine Used Each
☐ 1207 4¢ Brown & Blue	10.00	1.00	.30	.16

1962–1963. REGULAR ISSUES
1963. 50-STAR FLAG

☐ 1208 5¢ Red & Blue	18.00	1.10	.32	.16

1962–1963. REGULAR ISSUE

☐ 1209 1¢ Green	7.50	.50	.24	.16
☐ 1213 5¢ Dark Blue Gray	18.00	1.00	.24	.16

1962–1963. ROTARY PRESS COIL STAMPS PERF. 10 VERTICALLY

Scott No.	Fine Unused Plate Blk	Ave. Unused Plate Blk	Fine Unused Each	Ave. Unused Each	Fine Used Each	Ave. Used Each
☐ 1225 1¢ Green						
	6.00	3.00	.60	.40	.26	.16
☐ 1229 5¢ Dark Blue Gray						
	6.00	3.00	.60	.40	.26	.16

Scott No.	Mint Sheet	Plate Block	Fine Unused Each	Fine Used Each

1963. COMMEMORATIVES
1963. CAROLINA CHARTER TERCENTENARY

☐ 1230 5¢ Dark Carmine & Brown				
	12.00	1.00	.32	.16

1963. FOOD FOR PEACE—FREEDOM FROM HUNGER

☐ 1231 5¢ Green, Buff & Red				
	7.50	.72	.27	.16

1963. WEST VIRGINIA STATEHOOD

☐ 1232 5¢ Green, Red & Black				
	7.50	.72	.27	.16

*No hinge pricing from 1941 to date is figured at (N-H ADD 10%)

Scott No.	Mint Sheet	Plate Block	Fine Unused Each	Fine Used Each

1963. EMANCIPATION PROCLAMATION
☐ 1233 5¢ Black, Blue & Red   7.75   .80   .26   .16

1963. ALLIANCE FOR PROGRESS
☐ 1234 5¢ Bright Blue & Green
          7.50   .72   .26   .16

1963. CORDELL HULL
☐ 1235 5¢ Blue Green   11.00   1.00   .26   .16

1963. ELEANOR ROOSEVELT
☐ 1236 5¢ Light Purple   12.50   1.10   .26   .16

1963. THE SCIENCES
☐ 1237 5¢ Blue & Black   7.25   .72   .26   .16

1963. CITY MAIL DELIVERY
☐ 1238 5¢ Red, Blue & Gray   7.25   .72   .26   .16

1963. INTERNATIONAL RED CROSS CENTENARY
☐ 1239 5¢ Slate & Carmine   7.25   .72   .26   .16

1963. CHRISTMAS ISSUE
☐ 1240 5¢ Dark Blue, Blue Black & Red
          13.50   .80   .26   .16

1963. JOHN JAMES AUDUBON
☐ 1241 5¢ Blue, Brown, Bistre
          14.00   1.10   .26   .16

1964. COMMEMORATIVES _____
1964. SAM HOUSTON
☐ 1242 5¢ Black   8.00   .85   .26   .16

1964. CHARLES M. RUSSELL
☐ 1243 5¢ Indigo, Red Brown & Olive
          8.00   .85   .26   .16

*No hinge pricing from 1941 to date is figured at (N-H ADD 10%)

Scott No.	Mint Sheet	Plate Block	Fine Unused Each	Fine Used Each
1964. NEW YORK WORLD'S FAIR				
☐1244 5¢ Green	12.00	1.20	.26	.16
1964. JOHN MUIR—CONSERVATIONIST				
☐1245 5¢ Brown, Green & Olive				
	7.00	.90	.26	.16
1964. JOHN F. KENNEDY MEMORIAL				
☐1246 5¢ Blue Gray	20.00	1.90	.40	.16
1964. NEW JERSEY TERCENTENARY				
☐1247 5¢ Ultramarine	14.00	1.40	.36	.16
1964. NEVADA STATEHOOD				
☐1248 5¢ Red, Yellow & Blue				
	7.50	.90	.26	.16
1964. REGISTER AND VOTE				
☐1249 5¢ Dark Blue & Red	7.50	.90	.26	.16
1964. WILLIAM SHAKESPEARE				
☐1250 5¢ Brown on Tan	7.50	.80	.21	.16
1964. DOCTORS MAYO				
☐1251 5¢ Green	14.00	1.30	.32	.16
1964. AMERICAN MUSIC				
☐1252 5¢ Red, Black & Blue	8.00	.80	.26	.16
1964. AMERICAN HOMEMAKERS				
☐1253 5¢ Multicolored	8.00	.80	.26	.16
1964. CHRISTMAS ISSUE				
☐1254 5¢ Red & Green	—	—	1.65	.25
☐1255 5¢ Red & Green	—	—	1.65	.25
☐1256 5¢ Red & Green	—	—	1.30	.25
☐1257 5¢ Red & Green	—	—	1.30	.25

*No hinge pricing from 1941 to date is figured at (N-H ADD 10%)

Scott No.	Mint Sheet	Plate Block	Fine Unused Each	Fine Used Each

1964. VERRAZANO–NARROWS BRIDGE
| ☐1258 5¢ Green | 12.50 | 1.10 | .28 | .16 |

1964. STUART DAVIS—MODERN ART
| ☐1259 5¢ Ultramarine, Black & Red | | | | |
| | 8.25 | .74 | .30 | .16 |

1964. RADIO AMATEURS
| ☐1260 5¢ Red Lilac | 13.00 | 1.20 | .34 | .16 |

1965. COMMEMORATIVES _____
1965. BATTLE OF NEW ORLEANS
| ☐1261 5¢ Carmine, Blue & Gray | | | | |
| | 12.00 | 1.10 | .32 | .16 |

1965. PHYSICAL FITNESS—SOKOL CENTENNIAL
| ☐1262 5¢ Maroon & Black | 7.25 | .72 | .27 | .16 |

1965. CRUSADE AGAINST CANCER
| ☐1263 5¢ Black, Purple, Orange | | | | |
| | 7.25 | .72 | .27 | .16 |

1965. SIR WINSTON CHURCHILL MEMORIAL
| ☐1264 5¢ Black | 9.00 | .72 | .27 | .16 |

1965. MAGNA CARTA 750TH ANNIVERSARY
| ☐1265 5¢ Black, Ochre, Red Lilac | | | | |
| | 7.75 | .72 | .27 | .16 |

1965. INTERNATIONAL COOPERATION YEAR
| ☐1266 5¢ Dull Blue & Black | 7.75 | .72 | .27 | .16 |

1965. SALVATION ARMY
| ☐1267 5¢ Red, Black & Blue | 7.75 | .72 | .27 | .16 |

1965. DANTE ALIGHIERI
| ☐1268 5¢ Maroon on Tan | 7.75 | .72 | .27 | .16 |

*No hinge pricing from 1941 to date is figured at (N-H ADD 10%)

Scott No.	Mint Sheet	Plate Block	Fine Unused Each	Fine Used Each
1965. HERBERT HOOVER				
☐1269 5¢ Red Rose	8.00	.72	.25	.16
1965. ROBERT FULTON BIRTH BICENTENNIAL				
☐1270 5¢ Black & Blue	7.80	.72	.25	.16
1965. FLORIDA SETTLEMENT QUADRICENTENNIAL				
☐1271 5¢ Red, Yellow & Black				
	8.00	.72	.25	.16
1965. TRAFFIC SAFETY				
☐1272 5¢ Green, Black, Red	8.00	.72	.25	.16
1965. JOHN SINGLETON COPLEY—ARTIST				
☐1273 5¢ Black, Brown, Olive				
	13.00	1.10	.25	.16
1965. INTERNATIONAL TELECOMMUNICATION UNION				
☐1274 11¢ Black, Carmine, Bistre				
	27.00	7.00	.60	.45
1965. ADLAI E. STEVENSON MEMORIAL				
☐1275 5¢ Light & Dark Blue, Black & Red				
	7.75	.72	.26	.16
1965. CHRISTMAS ISSUE				
☐1276 5¢ Red, Green & Yellow				
	15.00	.72	.26	.16
1965–1968. PROMINENT AMERICANS SERIES				
☐1278 1¢ Green	7.10	.65	.26	.16
☐1279 1¼¢ Green	15.00	12.00	.26	.16
☐1280 2¢ Slate Blue	7.00	.50	.26	.16
☐1281 3¢ Purple	9.00	.60	.26	.16
☐1282 4¢ Black	30.00	1.25	.36	.16
☐1283 5¢ Blue	19.00	.80	.36	.16

*No hinge pricing from 1941 to date is figured at (N-H ADD 10%)

Scott No.	Mint Sheet	Plate Block	Fine Unused Each	Fine Used Each
☐1283b 5¢ Blue	18.00	.85	.26	.17
☐1284 6¢ Gray Brown	25.00	1.00	.26	.17
☐1285 8¢ Violet	35.00	1.60	.42	.17
☐1286 10¢ Lilac	35.00	1.50	.38	.17
☐1286A 12¢ Black	35.00	1.50	.38	.17
☐1287 13¢ Brown	56.00	2.40	.60	.17
☐1288 15¢ Rose Claret	42.00	2.00	.46	.17
☐1288A 15¢ Rose Claret II	42.00	3.00	.50	.17
☐1289 20¢ Olive Green	74.00	4.00	.80	.17
☐1290 25¢ Rose Lake	100.00	5.00	1.50	.17
☐1291 30¢ Light Purple	150.00	6.00	1.25	.17
☐1292 40¢ Dark Blue	120.00	6.00	1.30	.17
☐1293 50¢ Maroon	160.00	8.00	1.65	.17
☐1294 $1 Purple	315.00	15.00	3.60	.17
☐1295 $5 Gray	1000.00	700.00	15.00	3.10

Scott No.	Fine Unused Line Pair	Ave. Unused Line Pair	Fine Unused Each	Ave. Unused Each	Fine Used Each	Ave. Used Each

1965–1968. PERF. 10 HORIZONTALLY

	Fine Unused Line Pair	Ave. Unused Line Pair	Fine Unused Each	Ave. Unused Each	Fine Used Each	Ave. Used Each
☐1297 3¢ Purple						
	.80	.65	.24	.21	.20	.17
☐1298 6¢ Gray Brown						
	1.85	1.60	.24	.26	.20	.17

1965–1968. PERF. 10 VERTICALLY

	Fine Unused Line Pair	Ave. Unused Line Pair	Fine Unused Each	Ave. Unused Each	Fine Used Each	Ave. Used Each
☐1299 1¢ Green						
	.65	.45	.31	.26	.22	.17
☐1303 4¢ Black						
	.96	.80	.31	.26	.22	.17
☐1304 5¢ Blue						
	.90	.60	.31	.26	.22	.17
☐1305 6¢ Gray Brown						
	.95	.75	.31	.26	.22	.17
☐1305c $1 Purple						
	7.75	4.00	3.10	1.50	1.10	.90

*No hinge pricing from 1941 to date is figured at (N-H ADD 10%)

Scott No.	Mint Sheet	Plate Block	Fine Unused Each	Fine Used Each

1966. COMMEMORATIVES

1966. MIGRATORY BIRD TREATY

| ☐ 1306 5¢ Red, Blue, Black | 8.00 | .72 | .22 | .16 |

1966. HUMANE TREATMENT OF ANIMALS

☐ 1307 5¢ Orange Brown & Black

| | 7.00 | .72 | .22 | .16 |

1966. INDIANA STATEHOOD

☐ 1308 5¢ Ochre, Brown & Violet Blue

| | 9.00 | .72 | .22 | .16 |

1966. AMERICAN CIRCUS

☐ 1309 5¢ Red, Blue, Pink, Black

| | 10.00 | 1.15 | .30 | .16 |

1966. SIXTH INTL. PHILATELIC EXHIBITION "SIPEX"

| ☐ 1310 5¢ Multicolored | 8.00 | .90 | .26 | .16 |

1966. IMPERFORATE SOUVENIR SHEET

| ☐ 1311 5¢ Multicolored | — | .50 | .26 | .16 |

1966. BILL OF RIGHTS

☐ 1312 5¢ Red, Dark & Light Blue

| | 8.00 | .90 | .26 | .16 |

1966. POLISH MILLENNIUM

| ☐ 1313 5¢ Red | 8.00 | .80 | .26 | .16 |

1966. NATIONAL PARK SERVICE

☐ 1314 5¢ Yellow, Black & Green

| | 8.00 | .80 | .26 | .16 |

1966. MARINE CORPS RESERVE

☐ 1315 5¢ Black, Red, Blue, Olive

| | 8.00 | .80 | .26 | .16 |

*No hinge pricing from 1941 to date is figured at (N-H ADD 10%)

Scott No.	Mint Sheet	Plate Block	Fine Unused Each	Fine Used Each

1966. GENERAL FEDERATION OF WOMEN'S CLUBS

| ☐1316 5¢ Blue, Pink, Black | 7.00 | .72 | .26 | .16 |

1966. AMERICAN FOLKLORE—JOHNNY APPLESEED

| ☐1317 5¢ Red, Black, Green | 12.00 | 1.10 | .30 | .16 |

1966. BEAUTIFICATION OF AMERICA

| ☐1318 5¢ Emerald, Pink, Black | 7.25 | .72 | .30 | .16 |

1966. GREAT RIVER ROAD

| ☐1319 5¢ Yellow, Red, Blue, Green | 12.00 | 1.00 | .30 | .16 |

1966. SERVICEMEN & SAVINGS BONDS

| ☐1320 5¢ Red, Light Blue, Dark Blue | 7.25 | .80 | .26 | .16 |

1966. CHRISTMAS ISSUE

| ☐1321 5¢ Multicolored | 15.00 | .80 | .26 | .16 |

1966. MARY CASSATT—ARTIST

| ☐1322 5¢ Multicolored | 8.00 | 1.40 | .26 | .16 |

1967. COMMEMORATIVES ———

1967. NATIONAL GRANGE CENTENARY

| ☐1323 5¢ Orange, Yellow, Black, Brown & Green | 10.00 | 1.00 | .26 | .16 |

1967. CANADA CENTENNIAL

| ☐1324 5¢ Green, Light & Dark Blue, Black | 7.50 | .70 | .26 | .16 |

1967. ERIE CANAL SESQUICENTENNIAL

| ☐1325 5¢ Light & Dark Blue, Red & Black | 13.00 | .80 | .26 | .17 |

*No hinge pricing from 1941 to date is figured at (N-H ADD 10%)

Scott No.	Mint Sheet	Plate Block	Fine Unused Each	Fine Used Each

1967. SEARCH FOR PEACE—LIONS INTL.

☐1326 5¢ Red, Blue & Black	12.00	1.10	.32	.16

1967. HENRY DAVID THOREAU

☐1327 5¢ Black, Red & Green				
	14.00	1.15	.32	.16

1967. NEBRASKA STATEHOOD CENTENNIAL

☐1328 5¢ Yellow Green & Brown				
	14.00	1.25	.32	.16

1967. VOICE OF AMERICA

☐1329 5¢ Red, Blue & Black	7.25	.82	.26	.16

1967. AMERICAN FOLKLORE—DAVY CROCKETT

☐1330 5¢ Green & Black	12.50	1.10	.32	.16

1967. SPACE ACCOMPLISHMENTS

☐1331 5¢ Light & Dark Blue, Red, Black				
	—	4.50	2.10	.16
☐1332 5¢ Light & Dark Blue, Red, Black				
	—	3.00	1.50	.16

1967. URBAN PLANNING

☐1333 5¢ Blue & Black	7.75	.72	.26	.16

1967. FINNISH INDEPENDENCE

☐1334 5¢ Blue	7.25	.72	.26	.16

1967. THOMAS EAKINS—ARTIST

☐1335 5¢ Gold & Multicolored				
	12.00	1.00	.32	.16

1967. CHRISTMAS ISSUE

☐1336 5¢ Multicolored	7.75	.72	.32	.16

1967. MISSISSIPPI STATEHOOD

☐1337 5¢ Multicolored	14.00	1.10	.32	.16

*No hinge pricing from 1941 to date is figured at (N-H ADD 10%)

Scott No.	Mint Sheet	Plate Block	Fine Unused Each	Fine Used Each

1968–1971. REGULAR ISSUES
1968. FLAG ISSUE

Scott No.		Mint Sheet	Plate Block	Fine Unused Each	Fine Used Each
☐1338 6¢	Red, Blue, Green	18.00	.90	.31	.16

1968. COMMEMORATIVES
1968. ILLINOIS STATEHOOD

☐1339 6¢	Black, Gold, Pink	10.00	1.00	.32	.16

1968. HEMISFAIR '68

☐1340 6¢	Indigo, Carmine, White				
		8.00	.90	.26	.16

1968. AIRLIFT TO SERVICEMEN

☐1341 $1	Multicolored	145.00	12.00	3.50	1.50

1968. SUPPORT OUR YOUTH (ELKS)

☐1342 6¢	Blue & Black	8.00	.90	.26	.16

1968. LAW AND ORDER

☐1343 6¢	Blue & Black	16.00	1.40	.40	.16

1968. REGISTER & VOTE

☐1344 6¢	Black & Gold	8.00	.90	.26	.16

1968. HISTORIC AMERICAN FLAGS

☐1345 6¢	Dark Blue	—	—	.50	.32
☐1346 6¢	Red & Dark Blue	—	—	.45	.32
☐1347 6¢	Dark Blue, Olive Green				
		—	—	.41	.26
☐1348 6¢	Dark Blue & Red	—	—	.41	.26
☐1349 6¢	Black, Yellow, Red				
		—	—	.41	.26
☐1350 6¢	Dark Blue & Red	—	—	.41	.26
☐1351 6¢	Blue, Olive Green, Red				
		—	—	.41	.26
☐1352 6¢	Dark Blue & Red	—	—	.41	.26
☐1353 6¢	Blue, Yellow, Red	—	3.00	.41	.26
☐1354 6¢	Blue, Red, Yellow	—	—	.41	.26

*No hinge pricing from 1941 to date is figured at (N-H ADD 10%)

Scott No.	Mint Sheet	Plate Block	Fine Unused Each	Fine Used Each

1968. WALT DISNEY

☐1355 6¢ Multicolored	24.00	2.75	.60	.16

1968. FATHER MARQUETTE—EXPLORATIONS

☐1356 6¢ Black, Brown, Green				
	12.00	1.40	.34	.16

1968. AMERICAN FOLKLORE—DANIEL BOONE

☐1357 6¢ Brown, Yellow, Black, Red				
	10.00	1.00	.26	.16

1968. ARKANSAS RIVER NAVIGATION

☐1358 6¢ Black & Blue	10.00	1.10	.26	.16

1968. LEIF ERIKSON

☐1359 6¢ Dark Brown on Brown				
	10.00	1.00	.26	.16

1968. CHEROKEE STRIP LAND RUSH

☐1360 6¢ Brown	11.00	1.10	.26	.16

1968. JOHN TRUMBULL PAINTING

☐1361 6¢ Yellow Red, Black	17.00	1.50	.26	.16

1968. WILDLIFE CONSERVATION—DUCKS

☐1362 6¢ Multicolored	12.00	1.40	.26	.16

1968. CHRISTMAS ISSUE

☐1363 6¢ Multicolored	9.00	2.00	.26	.16

1968. AMERICAN INDIAN

☐1364 6¢ Multicolored	13.00	1.40	.26	.16

1969. COMMEMORATIVES _____
1969. BEAUTIFICATION OF AMERICA

☐1365 6¢ Multicolored	—	—	1.40	.17
☐1366 6¢ Multicolored	—	—	1.40	.17

*No hinge pricing from 1941 to date is figured at (N-H ADD 10%)

Scott No.	Mint Sheet	Plate Block	Fine Unused Each	Fine Used Each
☐ 1367 6¢ Multicolored	—	—	1.40	.17
☐ 1368 6¢ Multicolored	—	—	1.40	.17

1969. AMERICAN LEGION

| ☐ 1369 6¢ Red, Blue, Black | 7.50 | .80 | .24 | .17 |

1969. GRANDMA MOSES PAINTING

| ☐ 1370 6¢ Multicolored | 7.50 | .80 | .24 | .17 |

1969. APOLLO 8 MOON ORBIT

| ☐ 1371 6¢ Black, Blue, Ochre | 12.50 | 1.30 | .32 | .17 |

1969. W. C. HANDY—MUSICIAN

| ☐ 1372 6¢ Multicolored | 12.00 | 1.15 | .32 | .17 |

1969. SETTLEMENT OF CALIFORNIA

| ☐ 1373 6¢ Multicolored | 8.00 | .80 | .32 | .17 |

1969. MAJOR JOHN WESLEY POWELL— GEOLOGIST

| ☐ 1374 6¢ Multicolored | 8.00 | .80 | .32 | .17 |

1969. ALABAMA STATEHOOD

| ☐ 1375 6¢ Red, Yellow, Brown | 12.00 | 1.00 | .32 | .17 |

1969. XI INTL. BOTANICAL CONGRESS

☐ 1376 6¢ Multicolored	—	—	2.20	.65
☐ 1377 6¢ Multicolored	—	—	2.20	.65
☐ 1378 6¢ Multicolored	—	—	2.20	.65
☐ 1379 6¢ Multicolored	—	—	2.20	.65

1969. DARTMOUTH COLLEGE CASE

| ☐ 1380 6¢ Green | 14.00 | 1.25 | .36 | .17 |

1969. PROFESSIONAL BASEBALL CENTENARY

| ☐ 1381 6¢ Multicolored | 56.00 | 5.00 | 1.50 | .24 |

*No hinge pricing from 1941 to date is figured at (N-H ADD 10%)

Scott No.	Mint Sheet	Plate Block	Fine Unused Each	Fine Used Each
1969. INTERCOLLEGIATE FOOTBALL CENTENARY				
☐1382 6¢ Red & Green	24.00	2.25	.56	.16
1969. DWIGHT D. EISENHOWER MEMORIAL				
☐1383 6¢ Blue, Black & Red	5.50	.80	.25	.16
1969. CHRISTMAS ISSUE				
☐1384 6¢ Multicolored	8.00	1.90	.25	.16
1969. HOPE FOR THE CRIPPLED				
☐1385 6¢ Multicolored	7.25	.80	.25	.16
1969. WILLIAM M. HARNETT PAINTING				
☐1386 6¢ Multicolored	7.00	.80	.26	.16
1970. COMMEMORATIVES				
1970. NATURAL HISTORY				
☐1387 6¢ Multicolored	—	—	.35	.16
☐1388 6¢ Multicolored	—	—	.35	.16
☐1389 6¢ Multicolored	—	—	.35	.16
☐1390 6¢ Multicolored	—	—	.35	.16
1970. MAINE STATEHOOD SESQUICENTENNIAL				
☐1391 6¢ Multicolored	10.00	1.25	.30	.16
1970. WILDLIFE CONSERVATION—BUFFALO				
☐1392 6¢ Black on Tan	12.00	1.40	.31	.16
1970–1974. REGULAR ISSUE				
☐1393 6¢ Blue Gray	18.00	.90	.25	.16
☐1393D 7¢ Light Blue	24.00	1.25	.32	.16
☐1394 8¢ Black, Blue, Red	25.00	1.10	.30	.16
☐1395 8¢ Rose Violet	—	—	.32	.16
☐1396 8¢ Multicolored	22.00	2.75	.30	.16
☐1397 14¢ Brown	36.00	1.75	.42	.16
☐1398 16¢ Orange Brown	50.00	2.40	.50	.16
☐1399 18¢ Purple	60.00	2.50	.50	.16

*No hinge pricing from 1941 to date is figured at (N-H ADD 10%)

Scott No.	Mint Sheet	Plate Block	Fine Unused Each	Fine Used Each
☐1400 21¢ Green	64.00	2.90	.70	.26

Scott No.	Fine Unused Line Pair	Ave. Unused Line Pair	Fine Unused Each	Ave. Unused Each	Fine Used Each	Ave. Used Each

1970–1971. ROTARY PRESS COIL STAMPS— PERF. 10 VERTICALLY

Scott No.	Fine Unused Line Pair	Ave. Unused Line Pair	Fine Unused Each	Ave. Unused Each	Fine Used Each	Ave. Used Each
☐1401 6¢ Blue Gray	.76	—	.42	.32	.24	.16
☐1402 8¢ Rose Violet	.76	—	.42	.32	.24	.16

Scott No.	Mint Sheet	Plate Block	Fine Unused Each	Fine Used Each

1970. COMMEMORATIVES (continued) _____
1970. EDGAR LEE MASTERS—POET

	Mint Sheet	Plate Block	Fine Unused Each	Fine Used Each
☐1405 6¢ Black & Olive Bistre	8.00	.76	.22	.16

1970. 50TH ANNIVERSARY WOMEN'S SUFFRAGE

	Mint Sheet	Plate Block	Fine Unused Each	Fine Used Each
☐1406 6¢ Blue	8.00	.80	.22	.16

1970. SOUTH CAROLINA TERCENTENARY

	Mint Sheet	Plate Block	Fine Unused Each	Fine Used Each
☐1407 6¢ Multicolored	12.00	1.00	.30	.16

1970. STONE MOUNTAIN MEMORIAL

	Mint Sheet	Plate Block	Fine Unused Each	Fine Used Each
☐1408 6¢ Gray Black	14.00	1.00	.30	.16

1970. FORT SNELLING

	Mint Sheet	Plate Block	Fine Unused Each	Fine Used Each
☐1409 6¢ Multicolored	12.00	1.00	.26	.16

1970. ANTI-POLLUTION

	Mint Sheet	Plate Block	Fine Unused Each	Fine Used Each
☐1410 6¢ Multicolored	—	—	.70	.16
☐1411 6¢ Multicolored	—	—	.70	.16
☐1412 6¢ Multicolored	—	—	.70	.16
☐1413 6¢ Multicolored	—	—	.70	.16

*No hinge pricing from 1941 to date is figured at (N-H ADD 10%)

Scott No.	Mint Sheet	Plate Block	Fine Unused Each	Fine Used Each
1970. CHRISTMAS ISSUE				
☐1414 6¢ Multicolored	8.00	1.75	.30	.16
☐1415 6¢ Multicolored	—	—	.60	.16
☐1416 6¢ Multicolored	—	—	.60	.16
☐1417 6¢ Multicolored	—	—	.60	.16
☐1418 6¢ Multicolored	—	—	.60	.16
1970. PRECANCELLED CHRISTMAS ISSUE				
☐1414a 6¢ Multicolored	10.00	3.00	.30	.16
☐1415a 6¢ Multicolored	—	—	1.00	.16
☐1416a 6¢ Multicolored	—	—	1.00	.16
☐1417a 6¢ Multicolored	—	—	1.00	.16
☐1418a 6¢ Multicolored	—	—	1.00	.16
1970. UNITED NATIONS 25TH ANNIVERSARY				
☐1419 6¢ Black, Red, Blue	8.00	.80	.26	.16
1970. PILGRIM LANDING 350TH ANNIVERSARY				
☐1420 6¢ Multicolored	8.00	.80	.26	.16
1970. DISABLED AMERICAN VETERANS AND SERVICEMEN ISSUE				
☐1421 6¢ Blue, Black, Red	—	—	.55	.24
☐1422 6¢ Blue, Black, Red	—	—	.55	.24

1971. COMMEMORATIVES _____

Scott No.	Mint Sheet	Plate Block	Fine Unused Each	Fine Used Each
1971. ADVENT OF SHEEP TO AMERICA				
☐1423 6¢ Multicolored	8.00	.80	.26	.16
1971. GENERAL DOUGLAS MacARTHUR				
☐1424 6¢ Red, Blue, Black	8.00	.80	.26	.16
1971. BLOOD DONORS PROGRAM				
☐1425 6¢ Light Blue, Scarlet, Indigo				
	8.00	.80	.26	.16
1971. MISSOURI STATEHOOD				
☐1426 8¢ Multicolored	13.00	4.15	.32	.16

*No hinge pricing from 1941 to date is figured at (N-H ADD 10%)

Scott No.	Mint Sheet	Plate Block	Fine Unused Each	Fine Used Each
1971. WILDLIFE CONSERVATION				
☐ 1427 8¢ Multicolored	—	—	1.15	.50
☐ 1428 8¢ Multicolored	—	—	1.15	.50
☐ 1429 8¢ Multicolored	—	—	1.15	.50
☐ 1430 8¢ Multicolored	—	—	1.15	.50
1971. ANTARCTIC TREATY				
☐ 1431 8¢ Red & Blue	10.00	1.10	.26	.16
1971. AMERICAN REVOLUTION BICENTENNIAL				
☐ 1432 8¢ Red, Blue, Black	14.00	1.40	.32	.16
1971. JOHN SLOAN PAINTING				
☐ 1433 8¢ Multicolored	11.00	1.10	.26	.16
1971. DECADE OF SPACE ACHIEVEMENTS				
☐ 1434 8¢ Multicolored	—	—	.60	.21
☐ 1435 8¢ Multicolored	—	—	.60	.21
1971. EMILY DICKINSON—POET				
☐ 1436 8¢ Multicolored	14.00	1.40	.32	.16
1971. SAN JUAN 450TH ANNIVERSARY				
☐ 1437 8¢ Brown, Carmine, Blk.	11.00	1.10	.26	.16
1971. DRUG ADDICTION				
☐ 1438 8¢ Blue & Black	11.00	1.40	.27	.16
1971. CARE ANNIVERSARY				
☐ 1439 8¢ Multicolored	12.50	1.90	.30	.16
1971. HISTORIC PRESERVATION				
☐ 1440 8¢ Dark Brown & Ochre	—	—	.40	.16
☐ 1441 8¢ Dark Brown & Ochre	—	—	.40	.16

*No hinge pricing from 1941 to date is figured at (N-H ADD 10%)

Scott No.	Mint Sheet	Plate Block	Fine Unused Each	Fine Used Each
☐1442 8¢ Dark Brown & Ochre				
	—	—	.32	.16
☐1443 8¢ Dark Brown & Ochre				
	—	—	.32	.16

1971. CHRISTMAS
☐1444 8¢ Multicolored	12.00	3.00	.32	.16
☐1445 8¢ Multicolored	12.00	3.00	.32	.16

1972. COMMEMORATIVES
1972. SIDNEY LANIER—POET
☐1446 8¢ Multicolored	16.00	1.50	.38	.16

1972. PEACE CORPS
☐1447 8¢ Red & Blue	12.00	2.00	.30	.16

1972. NATIONAL PARKS CENTENNIAL
☐1448 2¢ Multicolored	—	—	.52	.43
☐1449 2¢ Multicolored	—	—	.52	.43
☐1450 2¢ Multicolored	—	—	.52	.43
☐1451 2¢ Multicolored	—	—	.52	.43
☐1452 6¢ Multicolored	12.00	1.25	.30	.16
☐1453 8¢ Multicolored	8.00	1.10	.26	.16
☐1454 15¢ Multicolored	21.00	1.80	.40	.16

1972. FAMILY PLANNING
☐1455 8¢ Multicolored	11.00	1.25	.30	.16

1972. AMERICAN REVOLUTION BICENTENNIAL—COLONIAL CRAFTSMEN
☐1456 8¢ Deep Brown, Yellow				
	—	—	.56	.16
☐1457 8¢ Deep Brown, Yellow				
	—	—	.56	.16
☐1458 8¢ Deep Brown, Yellow				
	—	—	.56	.16
☐1459 8¢ Deep Brown, Yellow				
	—	—	.56	.16

*No hinge pricing from 1941 to date is figured at (N-H ADD 10%)

Scott No.	Mint Sheet	Plate Block	Fine Unused Each	Fine Used Each

1972. OLYMPIC GAMES

☐1460 6¢ Multicolored	9.00	1.90	.21	.16
☐1461 8¢ Multicolored	11.00	2.00	.26	.16
☐1462 15¢ Multicolored	20.00	4.00	.45	.20

1972. PARENT TEACHER ASSOCIATION

☐1463 8¢ Black & Yellow	11.00	1.10	.26	.16
☐1463a 8¢ Black & Yellow, Reversed Pl. No.				
	—	1.20	—	—

1972. WILDLIFE CONSERVATION

☐1464 8¢ Multicolored	—	—	.60	.35
☐1465 8¢ Multicolored	—	—	.60	.35
☐1466 8¢ Multicolored	—	—	.60	.35
☐1467 8¢ Multicolored	—	—	.60	.35

1972. MAIL ORDER BUSINESS

☐1468 8¢ Multicolored	11.00	3.00	.30	.16

1972. OSTEOPATHIC MEDICINE

☐1469 8¢ Yellow Orange, Brown				
	11.00	1.65	.26	.16

1972. TOM SAWYER—AMERICAN FOLKLORE

☐1470 8¢ Multicolored	14.00	1.50	.32	.16

1972. CHRISTMAS

☐1471 8¢ Multicolored	11.00	3.00	.26	.16
☐1472 8¢ Multicolored	11.00	3.00	.26	.16

1972. PHARMACY

☐1473 8¢ Multicolored	19.00	2.10	.41	.16

1972. STAMP COLLECTING

☐1474 8¢ Multicolored	10.00	1.10	.28	.16

*No hinge pricing from 1941 to date is figured at (N-H ADD 10%)

Scott No.	Mint Sheet	Plate Block	Fine Unused Each	Fine Used Each
1973. COMMEMORATIVES				
1973. LOVE—"FOR SOMEONE SPECIAL"				
☐1475 8¢ Red, Green, Blue	11.00	1.60	.26	.16
1973. COLONIAL COMMUNICATIONS				
☐1476 8¢ Black, Red, Blue	11.00	1.10	.26	.16
☐1477 8¢ Blue, Red, Brown	11.00	1.10	.26	.16
☐1478 8¢ Multicolored	11.00	1.10	.26	.16
☐1479 8¢ Multicolored	11.00	1.10	.26	.16
1973. BOSTON TEA PARTY				
☐1480 8¢ Multicolored	—	—	.40	.16
☐1481 8¢ Multicolored	—	—	.40	.16
☐1482 8¢ Multicolored	—	—	.40	.16
☐1483 8¢ Multicolored	—	—	.40	.16
1973. GEORGE GERSHWIN—COMPOSER				
☐1484 8¢ Multicolored	9.10	3.00	.26	.16
1973. ROBINSON JEFFERS—POET				
☐1485 8¢ Multicolored	9.10	3.15	.26	.16
1973. HENRY OSSAWA TANNER—ARTIST				
☐1486 6¢ Multicolored	9.50	3.15	.26	.16
1973. WILLA CATHER—NOVELIST				
☐1487 8¢ Multicolored	10.00	3.50	.30	.16
1973. NICOLAUS COPERNICUS				
☐1488 8¢ Black & Orange	12.00	1.50	.26	.16
1973. POSTAL PEOPLE				
☐1489 8¢ Multicolored	—	—	.35	.16
☐1490 8¢ Multicolored	—	—	.35	.16
☐1491 8¢ Multicolored	—	—	.35	.16
☐1492 8¢ Multicolored	—	—	.35	.16
☐1493 8¢ Multicolored	—	—	.35	.16
☐1494 8¢ Multicolored	—	—	.35	.16

*No hinge pricing from 1941 to date is figured at (N-H ADD 10%)

Scott No.	Mint Sheet	Plate Block	Fine Unused Each	Fine Used Each
☐1495 8¢ Multicolored	—	—	.40	.16
☐1496 8¢ Multicolored	—	—	.40	.16
☐1497 8¢ Multicolored	—	—	.40	.16
☐1498 8¢ Multicolored	—	—	.40	.16

1973. HARRY S. TRUMAN MEMORIAL

☐1499 8¢ Black, Red, Blue	7.50	1.10	.30	.16

1973. PROGRESS IN ELECTRONICS

☐1500 6¢ Multicolored	8.50	1.00	.25	.16
☐1501 8¢ Multicolored	11.00	1.10	.28	.16
☐1502 15¢ Multicolored	20.00	1.90	.50	.35

1973. LYNDON B. JOHNSON MEMORIAL

☐1503 8¢ Multicolored	8.00	3.15	.30	.16

1973. ANGUS CATTLE—RURAL AMERICA

☐1504 8¢ Multicolored	11.00	1.15	.30	.16

1974. CHAUTAUQUA—RURAL AMERICA

☐1505 10¢ Multicolored	13.00	1.40	.32	.16

1974. WINTER WHEAT—RURAL AMERICA

☐1506 10¢ Multicolored	14.00	1.32	.32	.16

1973. CHRISTMAS

☐1507 8¢ Multicolored	11.00	3.40	.30	.16
☐1508 8¢ Multicolored	11.00	3.40	.30	.16

1973–1974. REGULAR ISSUES

☐1509 10¢ Red & Blue	27.00	6.00	.32	.16
☐1510 10¢ Blue	29.00	1.40	.32	.16
☐1511 10¢ Multicolored	28.00	2.40	.32	.16

Scott No.	Fine Unused Line Pair	Ave. Unused Line Pair	Fine Unused Each	Ave. Unused Each	Fine Used Each	Ave. Used Each

1973–1974. COIL STAMPS—PERF. 10 VERTICALLY

☐1518 63¢ Orange						
	1.00	.80	.50	.32	.26	.16

*No hinge pricing from 1941 to date is figured at (N-H ADD 10%)

Scott No.	Fine Unused Line Pair	Ave. Unused Line Pair	Fine Unused Each	Ave. Unused Each	Fine Used Each	Ave. Used Each
☐1519 10¢ Red & Blue	—	—	.36	.25	.38	.16
☐1520 10¢ Blue	1.30	1.00	.32	.25	.38	.16

Scott No.	Mint Sheet	Plate Block	Fine Unused Each	Fine Used Each

1974. COMMEMORATIVES

1974. VETERANS OF FOREIGN WARS

☐1525 10¢ Carmine & Blue	13.00	1.25	.38	.16

1974. ROBERT FROST—POET

☐1526 10¢ Black	20.00	2.00	.46	.16

1975. EXPO '74—PRESERVE THE ENVIRONMENT

☐1527 10¢ Multicolored	12.00	4.10	.36	.16

1974. HORSE RACING

☐1528 10¢ Multicolored	18.00	4.50	.47	.16

1975. SKYLAB PROJECT

☐152910¢ Multicolored	13.00	1.30	.32	.16

1974. UNIVERSAL POSTAL UNION CENTENARY

☐1530 10¢ Multicolored	—	—	.50	.24
☐1531 10¢ Multicolored	—	—	.50	.24
☐1532 10¢ Multicolored	—	—	.50	.24
☐1533 10¢ Multicolored	—	—	.50	.24
☐1534 10¢ Multicolored	—	—	.50	.24
☐1535 10¢ Multicolored	—	—	.50	.24
☐1536 10¢ Multicolored	—	—	.50	.24
☐1537 10¢ Multicolored	—	—	.50	.24

1974. MINERALS HERITAGE ISSUE

☐1538 10¢ Multicolored	—	—	.42	.16

*No hinge pricing from 1941 to date is figured at (N-H ADD 10%)

Scott No.	Mint Sheet	Plate Block	Fine Unused Each	Fine Used Each
☐1539 10¢ Multicolored	—	—	.40	.16
☐1540 10¢ Multicolored	—	—	.40	.16
☐1541 10¢ Multicolored	—	—	.40	.16

1974. FORT HARROD BICENTENNIAL
| ☐1542 10¢ Multicolored | 16.00 | 1.60 | .42 | .16 |

1974. CONTINENTAL CONGRESS
☐1543 10¢ Red, Blue, Gray	—	—	.50	.16
☐1544 10¢ Red, Blue, Gray	—	—	.50	.16
☐1545 10¢ Red, Blue, Gray	—	—	.50	.16
☐1546 10¢ Red, Blue, Gray	—	—	.50	.16

1974. ENERGY CONSERVATION
| ☐1547 10¢ Multicolored | 14.00 | 1.40 | .32 | .16 |

1974. LEGEND OF SLEEPY HOLLOW
| ☐1548 10¢ Multicolored | 14.00 | 1.40 | .32 | .16 |

1974. RETARDED CHILDREN
| ☐1549 10¢ Light & Dark Brown | | | | |
| | 14.00 | 1.40 | .32 | .16 |

1974. CHRISTMAS
☐1550 10¢ Multicolored	14.00	3.50	.40	.16
☐1551 10¢ Multicolored	14.00	3.50	.40	.16
☐1552 10¢ Multicolored	14.00	6.50	.40	.16
☐1552A 10¢ Multicolored, Plate Block of 12				
	15.00	6.00	.40	.16

1975. COMMEMORATIVES _____
1975. AMERICAN ARTS SERIES
1975. BENJAMIN WEST—ARTIST
| ☐1553 10¢ Multicolored | 20.00 | 4.00 | .42 | .16 |

1975. PAUL LAURENCE DUNBAR—POET
| ☐1554 10¢ Multicolored | 20.00 | 4.00 | .42 | .16 |

*No hinge pricing from 1941 to date is figured at (N-H ADD 10%)

Scott No.	Mint Sheet	Plate Block	Fine Unused Each	Fine Used Each

1975. D.W. GRIFFITH—MOTION PICTURES
| ☐1555 10¢ Multicolored | 20.00 | 2.00 | .40 | .16 |

1975. PIONEER 10 SPACE MISSION
| ☐1556 10¢ Multicolored | 15.00 | 1.60 | .40 | .16 |

1975. MARINER 10 SPACE MISSION
| ☐1557 10¢ Multicolored | 16.00 | 1.65 | .40 | .16 |

1975. COLLECTIVE BARGAINING
☐1558 10¢ Blue, Red, Purple
| | 12.50 | 2.65 | .40 | .16 |

1975. CONTRIBUTORS TO THE CAUSE
☐1559 8¢ Multicolored	13.00	2.50	.40	.16
☐1560 10¢ Multicolored	14.00	2.50	.40	.16
☐1561 10¢ Multicolored	14.00	3.00	.40	.16
☐1562 18¢ Multicolored	24.00	5.00	.50	.16

1975. LEXINGTON AND CONCORD BATTLES BICENTENNIAL
| ☐1563 10¢ Multicolored | 14.00 | 4.00 | .42 | .16 |

1975. BATTLE OF BUNKER HILL
| ☐1564 10¢ Multicolored | 13.00 | 4.00 | .42 | .16 |

1975. CONTINENTAL MILITARY SERVICE UNIFORMS
☐1565 10¢ Multicolored	—	—	.42	.16
☐1566 10¢ Multicolored	—	—	.42	.16
☐1567 10¢ Multicolored	—	—	.42	.16
☐1568 10¢ Multicolored	—	—	.42	.16

1975. U.S.–SOVIET JOINT SPACE MISSION
| ☐1569 10¢ Multicolored | — | — | .50 | .16 |
| ☐1570 10¢ Multicolored | — | — | .50 | .16 |

1975. INTERNATIONAL WOMEN'S YEAR
| ☐1571 10¢ Multicolored | 13.00 | 2.00 | .40 | .16 |

*No hinge pricing from 1941 to date is figured at (N-H ADD 10%)

Scott No.	Mint Sheet	Plate Block	Fine Unused Each	Fine Used Each
1975. U.S. POSTAL SERVICE BICENTENNIAL				
☐1572 10¢ Multicolored	—	—	.45	.16
☐1573 10¢ Multicolored	—	—	.45	.16
☐1574 10¢ Multicolored	—	—	.45	.16
☐1575 10¢ Multicolored	—	—	.45	.16
1975. WORLD PEACE THROUGH LAW				
☐1576 10¢ Blue, Green, Brown				
	15.00	1.70	.40	.16
1975. BANKING AND COMMERCE				
☐1577 10¢ Multicolored	—	—	.42	.16
☐1578 10¢ Multicolored	—	—	.42	.16
1975. CHRISTMAS				
☐1579 10¢ Multicolored	14.00	3.50	.40	.16
☐1580 10¢ Multicolored	16.50	4.10	.40	.16
1975–1980. AMERICANA SERIES				
☐1581 1¢ Blue on Green	6.00	.60	.25	.16
☐1582 2¢ Brown on Green	7.00	1.00	.25	.16
☐1584 3¢ Olive on Green	10.00	.75	.25	.16
☐1585 4¢ Maroon on Green	18.00	1.00	.30	.16
☐1590 9¢ Slate on Green	—	—	.50	.16
☐1591 9¢ Green on Gray	26.00	1.40	.30	.16
☐1592 10¢ Purple	30.00	1.50	.30	.16
☐1593 11¢ Orange on Gray	30.00	2.00	.32	.16
☐1594 12¢ Maroon	32.00	1.80	.32	.16
☐1595 13¢ Brown	—	—	.35	.16
☐1596 13¢ Multicolored	36.00	4.60	.42	.16
☐1597 15¢ Multicolored	45.00	10.00	.45	.16
☐1598 15¢ Multicolored	—	—	.50	.16
☐1599 16¢ Blue & Black	50.00	2.50	.52	.16
☐1603 24¢ Red on Blue	60.00	3.00	.75	.16
☐1604 28¢ Brown & Blue	76.00	4.00	.82	.16
☐1605 29¢ Blue & Blue	84.00	4.00	.80	.30
☐1606 30¢ Green on Blue	87.00	4.00	.90	.16

*No hinge pricing from 1941 to date is figured at (N-H ADD 10%)

Scott No.	Mint Sheet	Plate Block	Fine Unused Each	Fine Used Each
☐1608 50¢ Black & Orange	142.00	7.10	1.60	.20
☐1610 $1 Multicolored	300.00	12.50	2.90	.20
☐1611 $2 Multicolored	5000.00	21.00	5.50	.70
☐1612 $5 Multicolored	1400.00	60.00	13.00	3.00

Scott No.	Fine Unused Line Pair	Ave. Unused Line Pair	Fine Unused Each	Ave. Unused Each	Fine Used Each	Ave. Used Each
1975–1978. AMERICANA COIL STAMPS						
☐1613 3.1¢ Brown on Yellow						
	1.25	.90	.40	.25	.24	.16
☐1614 7.7¢ Gold on Yellow						
	1.25	1.10	.40	.25	.24	.16
☐1615 7.9¢ Red on Yellow						
	1.00	1.10	.40	.25	.24	.16
☐1615 8.4¢ Blue on White						
	2.50	2.15	.40	.25	.24	.16
☐1616 9¢ Green on Gray						
	1.20	1.10	.40	.35	.28	.16
☐1617 10¢ Purple on Gray						
	1.20	1.10	.40	.25	.28	.16
☐1618 13¢ Brown						
	1.15	1.10	.40	.25	.28	.16

Scott No.	Mint Sheet	Plate Block	Fine Unused Each	Fine Used Each
1975–1977. REGULAR ISSUES				
☐1622 13¢ Red, Brown, Blue	36.00	8.50	.40	.16
☐1623 13¢ Blue, Red	—	10.50	.46	.16
☐1623c 13¢ Blue, Red, pf 10	—	—	2.50	.16

Scott No.	Fine Unused Each	Ave. Unused Each	Fine Used Each	Ave. Used Each
1975. COIL STAMPS				
☐1625 13¢ Red, Brown, Blue	1.10	.50	.40	.17

*No hinge pricing from 1941 to date is figured at (N-H ADD 10%)

Scott No.	Mint Sheet	Plate Block	Fine Unused Each	Fine Used Each

1976. COMMEMORATIVES
1976. AMERICAN BICENTENNIAL SERIES
1976. SPIRIT OF '76

☐1629 13¢ Multicolored	—	—	.60	.18
☐1630 13¢ Multicolored	—	—	.60	.18
☐1631 13¢ Multicolored	—	—	.60	.18

1976. INTERPHIL '76

☐1632 13¢ Dark Blue, Red, Ultramarine				
	19.00	1.80	.50	.18

1976. STATE FLAGS

☐ 13¢ Multicolored				
	25.00	7.10	.70	.50

☐1633 Delaware ☐1655 Maine
☐1634 Pennsylvania ☐1656 Missouri
☐1635 New Jersey ☐1657 Arkansas
☐1636 Georgia ☐1658 Michigan
☐1637 Connecticut ☐1659 Florida
☐1638 Massachusetts ☐1660 Texas
☐1639 Maryland ☐1661 Iowa
☐1640 South Carolina ☐1662 Wisconsin
☐1641 New Hampshire ☐1663 California
☐1642 Virginia ☐1664 Minnesota
☐1643 New York ☐1665 Oregon
☐1644 North Carolina ☐1666 Kansas
☐1645 Rhode Island ☐1667 West Virginia
☐1646 Vermont ☐1668 Nevada
☐1647 Kentucky ☐1669 Nebraska
☐1648 Tennessee ☐1670 Colorado
☐1649 Ohio ☐1671 North Dakota
☐1650 Louisiana ☐1672 South Dakota
☐1651 Indiana ☐1673 Montana
☐1652 Mississippi ☐1674 Washington
☐1653 Illinois ☐1675 Idaho
☐1654 Alabama ☐1676 Wyoming

*No hinge pricing from 1941 to date is figured at (N-H ADD 10%)

☐1677 Utah   ☐1680 Arizona
☐1678 Oklahoma   ☐1681 Alaska
☐1679 New Mexico   ☐1682 Hawaii

Scott No.	Mint Sheet	Plate Block	Fine Unused Each	Fine Used Each

1976. TELEPHONE CENTENNIAL
☐1683 13¢ Black, Purple, Red

	21.00	1.80	.52	.16

1976. COMMERCIAL AVIATION

☐1684 13¢ Multicolored	16.00	4.50	.45	.16

1976. CHEMISTRY

☐1685 13¢ Multicolored	22.00	5.00	.55	.16

1976. BICENTENNIAL SOUVENIR SHEETS

Scott No.	Mint Sheet	Plate Block	Fine Unused Each	Fine Used Each
☐1686 65¢ Sheet of 5	—	—	5.00	1.00
☐1686a 13¢ Multicolored	—	—	1.00	.90
☐1686b 13¢ Multicolored	—	—	—	.90
☐1686c 13¢ Multicolored	—	—	—	.90
☐1686d 13¢ Multicolored	—	—	—	.90
☐1686e 13¢ Multicolored	—	—	—	.90
☐1687 90¢ Sheet of 5	—	—	6.80	5.10
☐1687a 18¢ Multicolored	—	—	1.40	1.25
☐1687b 18¢ Multicolored	—	—	1.40	1.25
☐1687c 18¢ Multicolored	—	—	1.40	1.25
☐1687d 18¢ Multicolored	—	—	1.40	1.25
☐1687e 18¢ Multicolored	—	—	1.40	1.25
☐1688 1.20 Sheet of 5	—	—	9.00	9.00
☐1688a 24¢ Multicolored	—	—	1.10	1.40
☐1688b 24¢ Multicolored	—	—	1.10	1.40
☐1688c 24¢ Multicolored	—	—	1.10	1.40
☐1688d 24¢ Multicolored	—	—	1.10	1.40
☐1688e 24¢ Multicolored	—	—	1.10	1.40
☐1689 1.55 Sheet of 5	—	—	11.00	9.00

*No hinge pricing from 1941 to date is figured at (N-H ADD 10%)

Scott No.	Mint Sheet	Plate Block	Fine Unused Each	Fine Used Each
☐1689a 31¢ Multicolored	—	—	2.40	—
☐1689b 31¢ Multicolored	—	—	2.40	—
☐1689c 31¢ Multicolored	—	—	2.40	—
☐1689d 31¢ Multicolored	—	—	2.40	—
☐1689e 31¢ Multicolored	—	—	2.40	—

1976. BENJAMIN FRANKLIN

☐1690 13¢ Blue & Multicolored				
	17.00	1.70	.45	.16

1976. DECLARATION OF INDEPENDENCE

☐1691 13¢ Multicolored	—	—	1.00	.30
☐1692 13¢ Multicolored	—	—	1.00	.30
☐1693 13¢ Multicolored	—	—	1.00	.30
☐1694 13¢ Multicolored	—	—	1.00	.30

1976. OLYMPIC GAMES

☐1695 13¢ Multicolored	—	—	.90	.25
☐1696 13¢ Multicolored	—	—	.90	.25
☐1697 13¢ Multicolored	—	—	.90	.25
☐1698 13¢ Multicolored	—	—	.90	.25

1976. CLARA MAASS

☐1699 13¢ Multicolored	17.50	6.00	.48	.16

1976. ADOLPH S. OCHS

☐1700 13¢ Black, Green & White				
	14.00	2.00	.50	.16

1976. CHRISTMAS

☐1701 13¢ Multicolored	13.00	5.00	.45	.16
☐1702 13¢ Multicolored	13.00	4.00	.45	.16
☐1703 13¢ Multicolored	13.00	6.00	.45	.16

1977. COMMEMORATIVES
1977. WASHINGTON

☐1704 13¢ Multicolored	15.00	4.10	.55	.16

*No hinge pricing from 1941 to date is figured at (N-H ADD 10%)

Scott No.	Mint Sheet	Plate Block	Fine Unused Each	Fine Used Each
1977. SOUND RECORDING CENTENARY				
☐1705 13¢ Multicolored	20.00	2.00	.48	.16
1977. PUEBLO ART				
☐1706 13¢ Multicolored	—	—	.52	.16
☐1707 13¢ Multicolored	—	—	.52	.16
☐1708 13¢ Multicolored	—	—	.52	.16
☐1709 13¢ Multicolored	—	—	.52	.16
1977. TRANSATLANTIC FLIGHT				
☐1710 13¢ Multicolored	18.50	4.50	.45	.16
1977. COLORADO				
☐1711 13¢ Multicolored	17.00	4.50	.45	.16
1977. BUTTERFLIES				
☐1712 13¢ Multicolored	—	—	.45	.16
☐1713 13¢ Multicolored	—	—	.45	.16
☐1714 13¢ Multicolored	—	—	.45	.16
☐1715 13¢ Multicolored	—	—	.45	.16
1977. LAFAYETTE				
☐1716 13¢ Multicolored	17.00	2.00	.52	.16
1977. SKILLED HANDS				
☐1717 13¢ Multicolored	—	—	.45	.16
☐1718 13¢ Multicolored	—	—	.45	.16
☐1719 13¢ Multicolored	—	—	.45	.16
☐1720 13¢ Multicolored	—	—	.45	.16
1977. PEACE BRIDGE				
☐1721 13¢ Blue & White	20.00	1.90	.50	.16
1977. BATTLE OF ORISKANY				
☐1722 13¢ Multicolored	15.00	4.00	.45	.16

*No hinge pricing from 1941 to date is figured at (N-H ADD 10%)

Scott No.	Mint Sheet	Plate Block	Fine Unused Each	Fine Used Each
1977. ENERGY CONSERVATION AND DEVELOPMENT				
☐1723 13¢ Multicolored	—	—	.45	.17
☐1724 13¢ Multicolored	—	—	.45	.17
1977. ALTA, CALIFORNIA BICENTENNIAL				
☐1725 13¢ Multicolored	17.00	1.65	.42	.16
1977. ARTICLES OF CONFEDERATION				
☐1726 13¢ Red & Brown on Tan				
	18.50	1.80	.46	.16
1977. TALKING PICTURES				
☐1727 13¢ Multicolored	17.00	1.75	.42	.16
1977. SURRENDER AT SARATOGA				
☐1728 13¢ Multicolored	14.50	4.10	.42	.16
1977. CHRISTMAS				
☐1729 13¢ Multicolored	34.00	8.10	.42	.16
☐1730 13¢ Multicolored	36.00	4.10	.42	.16
1978. COMMEMORATIVES				
1978. CARL SANDBURG				
☐1731 13¢ Brown, Black, White				
	18.00	1.75	.42	.16
1978. CAPTAIN COOK ISSUES				
☐1732 13¢ Dark Blue	—	1.65	.42	.16
☐1733 13¢ Green	—	1.65	.42	.16
1978–1980. REGULAR ISSUES				
1978. INDIAN HEAD PENNY				
☐1734 13¢ Brown & Blue Green				
	54.00	1.90	.42	.16
1978. NONDENOMINATED "A"				
☐1735 15¢ Orange	43.00	2.00	.47	.16
1978. ROSES				
☐1737 15¢ Multicolored	—	—	.42	.16

*No hinge pricing from 1941 to date is figured at (N-H ADD 10%)

Scott No.	Mint Sheet	Plate Block	Fine Unused Each	Fine Used Each

1980. WINDMILL—VIRGINIA

☐1738 15¢ Black	—	—	.90	.16

1980. WINDMILL—RHODE ISLAND

☐1739 15¢ Black	—	—	.60	.16

1980. WINDMILL—MASSACHUSETTS

☐1740 15¢ Black	—	—	.62	.16

1980. WINDMILL—ILLINOIS

☐1741 15¢ Black	—	—	.62	.16

1980. WINDMILL—TEXAS

☐1742 15¢ Black	—	—	.62	.16

1978. COMMEMORATIVES (CONTINUED) ———

1978. HARRIET TUBMAN

☐1744 13¢ Multicolored	24.00	6.50	.52	.16

1978. AMERICAN FOLK ART ISSUE

☐1745 13¢ Multicolored	—	—	.45	.16
☐1746 13¢ Multicolored	—	—	.45	.16
☐1747 13¢ Multicolored	—	—	.45	.16
☐1748 13¢ Multicolored	—	—	.45	.16

1978. AMERICAN DANCE ISSUE

☐1749 13¢ Multicolored	—	—	.45	.16
☐1750 13¢ Multicolored	—	—	.45	.16
☐1751 13¢ Multicolored	—	—	.45	.16
☐1752 13¢ Multicolored	—	—	.45	.16

1978. FRENCH ALLIANCE

☐1753 13¢ Blue, Black & Red				
	13.00	1.65	.45	.16

1978. EARLY CANCER DETECTION

☐1754 13¢ Brown	19.00	1.90	.46	.16

*No hinge pricing from 1941 to date is figured at (N-H ADD 10%)

Scott No.	Mint Sheet	Plate Block	Fine Unused Each	Fine Used Each

1978. JIMMIE RODGERS
| ☐1755 13¢ Multicolored | 21.00 | 6.00 | .50 | .16 |

1978. GEORGE M. COHAN
| ☐1756 15¢ Multicolored | 25.00 | 6.50 | .52 | .16 |

1978. "CAPAX" '78 SOUVENIR SHEET
| ☐1757 13¢ Multicolored, set of 6 | | | | |
| | 16.50 | — | 3.10 | 2.60 |

1978. PHOTOGRAPHY
| ☐1758 15¢ Multicolored | 16.00 | 6.00 | .46 | .16 |

1978. VIKING MISSION TO MARS
| ☐1759 15¢ Multicolored | 19.00 | 1.90 | .46 | .16 |

1978. AMERICAN OWL ISSUE
☐1760 15¢ Multicolored	—	—	.70	.16
☐1761 15¢ Multicolored	—	—	.70	.16
☐1762 15¢ Multicolored	—	—	.70	.16
☐1763 15¢ Multicolored	—	—	.70	.16

1978. AMERICAN TREES ISSUE
☐1764 15¢ Multicolored	—		.60	.16
☐1765 15¢ Multicolored	—		.60	.16
☐1766 15¢ Multicolored	—		.60	.16
☐1767 15¢ Multicolored	—		.60	.16

1978. CHRISTMAS ISSUES
| ☐1768 15¢ Multicolored | 40.50 | 6.50 | .50 | .16 |
| ☐1769 15¢ Multicolored | 40.50 | 6.50 | .50 | .16 |

1979. ROBERT F. KENNEDY ISSUE
| ☐1770 15¢ Blue | 23.00 | 4.50 | .52 | .16 |

1979. COMMEMORATIVES ⎯⎯⎯⎯⎯⎯
1979. MARTIN LUTHER KING ISSUE
| ☐1771 15¢ Multicolored | 23.00 | 6.50 | .52 | .16 |

*No hinge pricing from 1941 to date is figured at (N-H ADD 10%)

Scott No.	Mint Sheet	Plate Block	Fine Unused Each	Fine Used Each
1979. INTERNATIONAL YEAR OF THE CHILD				
☐1772 15¢ Light Brown	20.00	1.90	.46	.16
1979. JOHN STEINBECK ISSUE				
☐1773 15¢ Dark Blue	18.00	1.90	.46	.16
1979. ALBERT EINSTEIN ISSUE				
☐1774 15¢ Brown	24.00	1.90	.46	.16
1979. PENNSYLVANIA TOLEWARE ISSUE				
☐1775 15¢ Multicolored	—	—	.48	.16
☐1776 15¢ Multicolored	—	—	.48	.16
☐1777 15¢ Multicolored	—	—	.48	.16
☐1778 15¢ Multicolored	—	—	.48	.16
1979. ARCHITECTURE U.S.A. ISSUE				
☐1779 15¢ Light Blue & Brown	—	—	.55	.16
☐1780 15¢ Light Blue & Brown	—	—	.55	.16
☐1781 15¢ Light Blue & Brown	—	—	.55	.16
☐1782 15¢ Light Blue & Brown	—	—	.55	.16
1979. ENDANGERED FLORA ISSUE				
☐1783 15¢ Multicolored	—	—	.46	.16
☐1784 15¢ Multicolored	—	—	.46	.16
☐1785 15¢ Multicolored	—	—	.46	.16
☐1786 15¢ Multicolored	—	—	.46	.16
1979. SEEING FOR ME ISSUE				
☐1787 15¢ Multicolored	25.00	11.00	.50	.16
1979. SPECIAL OLYMPICS				
☐1788 15¢ Multicolored	20.00	5.00	.46	.16

*No hinge pricing from 1941 to date is figured at (N-H ADD 10%)

Scott No.	Mint Sheet	Plate Block	Fine Unused Each	Fine Used Each

1979. JOHN PAUL JONES

☐1789 15¢ Multicolored	20.00	5.10	.42	.16

1979. OLYMPIC DECATHALON

☐1790 10¢ Multicolored	15.00	4.75	.42	.16

1979. OLYMPIC RUNNERS

☐1791 15¢ Multicolored	—	—	.42	.16

1979. OLYMPIC SWIMMERS

☐1792 15¢ Multicolored	—	—	.45	.16

1979. OLYMPIC ROWERS

☐1793 15¢ Multicolored	—	—	.45	.16

1979. OLYMPIC EQUESTRIAN

☐1794 15¢ Multicolored	—	—	.45	.16

1979. OLYMPIC SKATER

☐1795 15¢ Multicolored	—	—	.45	.16

1979. OLYMPIC SKIER

☐1796 15¢ Multicolored	—	—	.45	.16

1979. OLYMPIC SKI JUMPER

☐1797 15¢ Multicolored	—	—	.45	.16

1979. OLYMPIC GOALTENDER

☐1798 15¢ Multicolored	—	—	.45	.16

1979. MADONNA

☐1799 15¢ Multicolored	40.00	6.00	.45	.16

1979. CHRISTMAS

☐1800 15¢ Multicolored	40.00	6.00	.46	.16

1979. WILL ROGERS

☐1801 15¢ Multicolored	22.00	6.00	.46	.16

*No hinge pricing from 1941 to date is figured at (N-H ADD 10%)

Scott No.	Mint Sheet	Plate Block	Fine Unused Each	Fine Used Each

1979. VIETNAM VETERANS
☐1802 15¢ Multicolored	26.00	6.10	.50	.16

1980. COMMEMORATIVES _____
1980. W. C. FIELDS
☐1803 15¢ Multicolored	20.00	6.10	.50	.16

1980. BENJAMIN BANNEKER
☐1804 15¢ Multicolored	23.00	6.50	.45	.16

1980. LETTERS PRESERVE MEMORIES
☐1805 15¢ Violet & Bistre	—	—	.45	.16

1980. PRESERVE MEMORIES—P.S. WRITE SOON
☐1806 15¢ Violet & Pink	—	—	.45	.16

1980. LETTERS LIFT SPIRITS
☐1807 15¢ Green, Pink & Orange				
	—	—	.55	.16

1980. LIFT SPIRITS—P.S. WRITE SOON
☐1808 15¢ Green & Yellow Green				
	—	—	.55	.16

1980. LETTERS SHAPE OPINIONS
☐1809 15¢ Scarlet & Blue	—	—	.55	.16

1980. SHAPE OPINIONS—P.S. WRITE SOON
☐1810 15¢ Scarlet & Blue	—	—	.55	.16

1980. AMERICANA SERIES
☐1811 1¢ Dark Blue & Green				
	—	.90	.25	.16
☐1813 3.5¢ Purple & Yellow	—	1.25	.25	.16
☐1816 12¢ Green	—	1.50	.32	.16

1980. NONDENOMINATED "B"
☐1818 18¢ Purple	—	2.75	.55	.16

*No hinge pricing from 1941 to date is figured at (N-H ADD 10%)

Scott No.	Mint Sheet	Plate Block	Fine Unused Each	Fine Used Each
1980. FRANCIS PERKINS				
☐1821 15¢ Blue	20.00	2.00	.46	.16
1980. DOLLY MADISON				
☐1822 15¢ Multicolored	60.00	2.15	.48	.16
1980. EMILY BISSELL				
☐1823 15¢ Scarlet & Black	26.00	2.10	.52	.16
1980. HELLEN KELLER—ANNE SULLIVAN				
☐1824 15¢ Multicolored	20.00	1.85	.46	.16
1980. VETERANS ADMINISTRATION				
☐1825 15¢ Carmine & Blue	20.00	—	.46	.16
1980. GENERAL BERNARDO de GALVEZ				
☐1826 15¢ Multicolored	20.50	—	.46	.16
1980. CORAL REEFS—VIRGIN ISLANDS				
☐1827 15¢ Multicolored	21.00	—	.51	.16
1980. CORAL REEFS—FLORIDA				
☐1828 15¢ Multicolored	20.00	—	.51	.16
1980. CORAL REEFS—AMERICAN SAMOA				
☐1829 15¢ Multicolored	20.00	—	.48	.16
1980. CORAL REEFS—HAWAII				
☐1830 15¢ Multicolored	20.00	—	.48	.16
1980. ORGANIZED LABOR				
☐1831 15¢ Multicolored	20.00	5.75	.48	.16
1980. EDITH WHARTON				
☐1832 15¢ Violet	22.00	4.00	.48	.16
1980. EDUCATION				
☐1833 15¢ Multicolored	25.00	4.00	.48	.16

*No hinge pricing from 1941 to date is figured at (N-H ADD 10%)

Scott No.	Mint Sheet	Plate Block	Fine Unused Each	Fine Used Each

1980. INDIAN ARTS
☐1834 15¢ Multicolored	—	—	.65	.19
☐1835 15¢ Multicolored	—	—	.65	.19
☐1836 15¢ Multicolored	—	—	.65	.19
☐1837 15¢ Multicolored	—	—	.65	.19

1980. ARCHITECTURE
☐1838 15¢ Black & Red	—	—	.65	.19
☐1839 15¢ Black & Red	—	—	.65	.19
☐1840 15¢ Black & Red	—	—	.65	.19
☐1841 15¢ Black & Red	—	—	.65	.19

1980. CHRISTMAS ISSUE
☐1842 15¢ Multicolored	19.00	5.50	.46	.17
☐1843 15¢ Multicolored	20.00	9.50	.46	.17

1980–1985. GREAT AMERICANS

1982. DOROTHEA DIX
☐1844 1¢ Black	8.50	2.10	.22	.17

1983. IGOR STRAVINSKY
☐1845 2¢ Brown	7.00	.90	.22	.17

1983. HENRY CLAY
☐1846 3¢ Green	10.00	.75	.22	.17

1983. CARL SCHURZ
☐1847 4¢ Purple	12.00	.80	.22	.17

1985. PEARL BUCK
☐1848 5¢ Reddish Brown	16.00	.75	.22	.17

1985. WALTER LIPPMANN
☐1849 6¢ Orange	17.00	4.00	.22	.17

1985. ABRAHAM BALDWIN
☐1850 7¢ Red	26.00	6.00	.22	.17

1985. HENRY KNOX
☐1851 8¢ Black	22.00	1.50	.22	.17

*No hinge pricing from 1941 to date is figured at (N-H ADD 10%)

Scott No.	Mint Sheet	Plate Block	Fine Unused Each	Fine Used Each
1985. SYLVANUS THAYER				
☐ 1852 9¢ Green	30.00	7.00	.40	.21
1984. RICHARD RUSSELL				
☐ 1853 10¢ Blue	34.00	8.00	.40	.21
1985. ALDEN PARTRIDGE				
☐ 1854 11¢ Blue	38.00	2.00	.40	.21
1982. CRAZY HORSE				
☐ 1855 13¢ Brown	41.00	3.00	.46	.32
1985. SINCLAIR LEWIS				
☐ 1856 14¢ Green	41.00	9.00	.46	.17
1981. RACHEL CARSON				
☐ 1857 17¢ Blue Green	48.00	2.50	.52	.17
1981. GEORGE MASON				
☐ 1858 18¢ Dark Blue	46.00	3.00	.55	.17
1980. SEQUOYAH				
☐ 1859 19¢ Light Brown	59.00	3.10	.68	.24
1982. RALPH BUNCHE				
☐ 1860 20¢ Carmine	63.00	3.75	.68	.17
1983. THOMAS H. GALLAUDET				
☐ 1861 20¢ Green	65.00	4.00	.72	.17
1984. HARRY S TRUMAN				
☐ 1862 20¢ Black & White	65.00	14.00	.72	.17
1985. JOHN J. AUDUBON				
☐ 1863 22¢ Blue	74.00	16.00	.85	.17
1984. FRANK C. LAUBACH				
☐ 1864 30¢ Dark Green	82.00	20.00	.95	.17

*No hinge pricing from 1941 to date is figured at (N-H ADD 10%)

Scott No.	Mint Sheet	Plate Block	Fine Unused Each	Fine Used Each
1981. CHARLES DREW				
☐1865 35¢ Gray	105.00	6.00	1.50	.21
1982. ROBERT MILLIKAN				
☐1866 37¢ Blue	106.00	5.00	1.15	.21
1985. GRENVILLE CLARK				
☐1867 39¢ Reddish Purple	105.00	25.00	1.15	.21
1984. LILLIAN M. GILBRETH				
☐1868 40¢ Green	115.00	24.50	1.20	.21
1985. CHESTER W. NIMITZ				
☐1869 50¢ Dark Brown	155.00	10.50	1.45	.21
1981. COMMEMORATIVES				
1981. EVERETT M. DIRKSEN				
☐1874 15¢ Dark Green	19.00	1.85	.46	.16
1981. WHITNEY M. YOUNG				
☐1875 15¢ Multicolored	21.50	1.90	.46	.16
1981. FLOWERS				
☐1876 18¢ Multicolored	—	—	.70	.18
☐1877 18¢ Multicolored	—	—	.70	.18
☐1878 18¢ Multicolored	—	—	.70	.18
☐1879 18¢ Multicolored	—	—	.70	.18
1981–1982. REGULAR ISSUES				
1981. AMERICAN WILDLIFE				
☐1880 18¢ Light Brown	—	—	.80	.17
☐1881 18¢ Light Brown	—	—	.80	.17
☐1882 18¢ Light Brown	—	—	.80	.17
☐1883 18¢ Light Brown	—	—	.80	.17
☐1884 18¢ Light Brown	—	—	.80	.17
☐1885 18¢ Light Brown	—	—	.80	.17
☐1886 18¢ Light Brown	—	—	.80	.17
☐1887 18¢ Light Brown	—	—	.80	.17
☐1888 18¢ Light Brown	—	—	.80	.17
☐1889 18¢ Light Brown	—	—	.80	.17

*No hinge pricing from 1941 to date is figured at (N-H ADD 10%)

Scott No.	Mint Sheet	Plate Block	Fine Unused Each	Fine Used Each

1981. FLAG—FOR AMBER WAVES OF GRAIN

| ☐1890 18¢ Multicolored | 51.00 | 11.75 | .60 | .16 |

1981. FLAG—FROM SEA TO SHINING SEA

| ☐1891 18¢ Multicolored | — | 6.00 | .65 | .16 |

1981. U.S.A.
☐1892 6¢ Carmine & Dark Blue

| | — | — | .75 | .16 |

1981. FLAG—FOR PURPLE MOUNTAIN MAJESTIES

| ☐1893 18¢ Multicolored | — | — | .61 | .19 |

1981. FLAG OVER SUPREME COURT
☐1894 20¢ Carmine & Dark Blue

| | 90.00 | 20.00 | 1.10 | .28 |

1981–1984. TRANSPORTATION ————
1983. OMNIBUS

| ☐1897 1¢ Violet | — | — | .28 | .17 |

1982. LOCOMOTIVE

| ☐1897a 2¢ Black | — | — | .28 | .17 |

1983. HANDCAR

| ☐1898 3¢ Dark Green | — | — | .28 | .17 |

1982. STAGECOACH

| ☐1898a 4¢ Red Brown | — | — | .28 | .17 |

1983. MOTORCYCLE

| ☐1899 5¢ Gray Green | — | — | .28 | .17 |

1983. SLEIGH

| ☐1900 5.2¢ Carmine | — | — | .28 | .17 |

1982. BICYCLE

| ☐1901 5.9¢ Blue | — | — | .28 | .17 |

*No hinge pricing from 1941 to date is figured at (N-H ADD 10%)

Scott No.	Mint Sheet	Plate Block	Fine Unused Each	Fine Used Each
1984. BABY BUGGY				
☐1902 7.4¢ Brown	—	—	.32	.17
1982. MAIL WAGON				
☐1903 9.3¢ Carmine	—	—	.32	.17
1982. HANSOM CAB				
☐1904 10.9¢ Purple	—	—	.55	.17
1984. RAILROAD CABOOSE				
☐1905 11¢ Red	—	—	.40	.17
1981. ELECTRIC CAR				
☐1906 17¢ Ultramarine	—LP.	4.50	.52	.17
1981. SURREY				
☐1907 18¢ Brown	—LP.	4.50	.55	.17
1982. FIRE PUMPER				
☐1908 20¢ Vermilion	—	—	.65	.17
1981. COMMEMORATIVES (CONTINUED)				
1981. AMERICAN RED CROSS				
☐1910 18¢ Multicolored	—	3.00	.60	.16
1981. SAVINGS AND LOAN				
☐1911 19¢ Multicolored	—	2.75	.60	.16
1981. COMMEMORATIVES				
1981. SPACE ACHIEVEMENT				
☐1912 18¢ Multicolored	—	—	.72	.17
☐1913 18¢ Multicolored	—	—	.72	.17
☐1914 18¢ Multicolored	—	—	.72	.17
☐1915 18¢ Multicolored	—	—	.72	.17
☐1916 18¢ Multicolored	—	—	.72	.17
☐1917 18¢ Multicolored	—	—	.72	.17
☐1918 18¢ Multicolored	—	—	.72	.17
☐1919 18¢ Multicolored	—	—	.72	.17

*No hinge pricing from 1941 to date is figured at (N-H ADD 10%)

Scott No.	Mint Sheet	Plate Block	Fine Unused Each	Fine Used Each

1981. PROFESSIONAL MANAGEMENT

☐1920 18¢ Dark Blue & Black	26.00	2.50	.60	.16

1981. PRESERVATION OF WILDLIFE HABITATS

☐1921 18¢ Multicolored	—	—	.72	.17
☐1922 18¢ Multicolored	—	—	.72	.17
☐1923 18¢ Multicolored	—	—	.72	.17
☐1924 18¢ Multicolored	—	—	.72	.17

1981. DISABLED PERSONS

☐1925 18¢ Multicolored	24.50	2.50	.62	.16

1981. EDNA ST. VINCENT MILLAY

☐1926 18¢ Multicolored	25.50	2.40	.62	.16

1981. ALCOHOLISM

☐1927 18¢ Dark Blue	62.00	41.00	.80	.16

1981. ARCHITECTURE

☐1928 18¢ Brown & Black	—	—	.78	.17
☐1929 18¢ Brown & Black	—	—	.78	.17
☐1930 18¢ Brown & Black	—	—	.78	.17
☐1931 18¢ Brown & Black	—	—	.78	.17

1981. BABE ZAHARIAS

☐1932 18¢ Purple	—	4.25	.90	.17

1981. BOBBY JONES

☐1933 18¢ Dark Green	—	8.75	1.50	.17

1981. FREDERIC REMINGTON

☐1934 18¢ Light Brown & Green				
	24.50	2.75	.65	.16

1981. JAMES HOBAN

☐1935 18¢ Multicolored	24.50	2.50	.65	.16

*No hinge pricing from 1941 to date is figured at (N-H ADD 10%)

Scott No.	Mint Sheet	Plate Block	Fine Unused Each	Fine Used Each

1981. JAMES HOBAN
| ☐1936 20¢ Multicolored | 26.00 | 2.60 | .70 | .16 |

1981. YORKTOWN MAP
| ☐1937 18¢ Multicolored | — | — | .70 | .16 |

1981. VIRGINIA CAPES MAP
| ☐1938 18¢ Multicolored | — | — | .70 | .16 |

1981. CHRISTMAS—BOTTICELLI
| ☐1939 20¢ Multicolored | 51.00 | 2.40 | .60 | .16 |

1981. SEASONS GREETINGS
| ☐1940 20¢ Multicolored | 27.00 | 2.55 | .70 | .16 |

1981. JOHN HANSON
| ☐1941 20¢ Multicolored | 28.00 | 2.70 | .72 | .16 |

1981. DESERT PLANTS
☐1942 20¢ Multicolored	—	—	.72	.17
☐1943 20¢ Multicolored	—	—	.72	.17
☐1944 20¢ Multicolored	—	—	.72	.17
☐1945 20¢ Multicolored	—	—	.72	.17

1981–1982. REGULAR ISSUES _____
1981. "C" EAGLE—SINGLE
| ☐1946 20¢ Light Brown | 52.00 | 2.60 | .65 | .16 |

1981. "C" EAGLE—COIL SINGLE
| ☐1947 20¢ Light Brown | — | — | .76 | .16 |

1981. "C" EAGLE—BOOKLET SINGLE
| ☐1948 20¢ Light Brown | — | — | .68 | .16 |

1981. BIGHORN SHEEP
| ☐1949 20¢ Dark Blue | — | — | .75 | .16 |

1982. COMMEMORATIVES _____
1982. FRANKLIN ROOSEVELT
| ☐1950 20¢ Dark Blue | 26.00 | 4.00 | .60 | .16 |

*No hinge pricing from 1941 to date is figured at (N-H ADD 10%)

Scott No.	Mint Sheet	Plate Block	Fine Unused Each	Fine Used Each

1982. "LOVE" FLOWERS

| □1951 20¢ Multicolored | 31.00 | 3.00 | .65 | .16 |

1982. GEORGE WASHINGTON

| □1952 20¢ Multicolored | 29.00 | 3.10 | .75 | .16 |

1982. STATE BIRDS AND FLOWERS
□1953–2002 20¢ Multicolored

| | 41.00 | — | .80 | .18 |

1982. THE NETHERLANDS

| □2003 20¢ Dark Blue & Red | 32.00 | 15.00 | .70 | .16 |

1982. LIBRARY OF CONGRESS

| □2004 20¢ Rose & Dark Gray | 28.00 | 3.00 | .65 | .16 |

1982. CONSUMER EDUCATION
□2005 20¢ Light Blue & Dark Blue

| | — | 35.00 | 1.30 | .16 |

1982. KNOXVILLE WORLD'S FAIR

□2006 20¢ Multicolored	34.00	3.25	.90	.19
□2007 20¢ Multicolored	34.00	3.25	.90	.19
□2008 20¢ Multicolored	34.00	3.25	.90	.19
□2009 20¢ Multicolored	34.00	3.25	.90	.19

1982. HORATIO ALGER

| □2010 20¢ Carmine & Black | 27.00 | 2.80 | .55 | .16 |

1982. AGING TOGETHER

| □2011 20¢ Light Rose | 27.00 | 2.75 | .65 | .16 |

1982. THE BARRYMORES

| □2012 20¢ Multicolored | 27.00 | 2.75 | .65 | .16 |

1982. DR. MARY WALKER

| □2013 20¢ Multicolored | 29.00 | 2.90 | .65 | .16 |

*No hinge pricing from 1941 to date is figured at (N-H ADD 10%)

Scott No.	Mint Sheet	Plate Block	Fine Unused Each	Fine Used Each

1982. INTERNATIONAL PEACE GARDEN
| ☐ 2014 20¢ Multicolored | 29.00 | 2.80 | .70 | .17 |

1982. AMERICA'S LIBRARIES
| ☐ 2015 20¢ Orange Red & Black | | | | |
| | 27.00 | 2.75 | .70 | .17 |

1982. JACKIE ROBINSON
| ☐ 2016 20¢ Multicolored | 98.00 | 9.10 | 2.10 | .17 |

1982. TOURO SYNAGOGUE
| ☐ 2017 20¢ Multicolored | 37.00 | 16.00 | .75 | .17 |

1982. WOLF TRAP FARM PARK
| ☐ 2018 20¢ Multicolored | 27.00 | 2.60 | .70 | .17 |

1982. ARCHITECTURE—WRIGHT
| ☐ 2019 20¢ Black and Brown | — | — | .90 | .17 |

1982. ARCHITECTURE—VAN DER ROHE
| ☐ 2020 20¢ Black and Brown | — | — | .90 | .17 |

1982. ARCHITECTURE—GROPIUS
| ☐ 2021 20¢ Black and Brown | — | — | .90 | .17 |

1982. ARCHITECTURE—SAARINEN
☐ 2022 20¢ Black and Brown	—	—	.90	.17
☐ Architecture, above four attached				
	34.00	—	—	—

1982. FRANCIS OF ASSISI
| ☐ 2023 20¢ Multicolored | 31.00 | 3.00 | .80 | .17 |

1982. PONCE DE LEON
| ☐ 2024 20¢ Multicolored | 36.00 | 17.00 | .85 | .17 |

1982. CHRISTMAS ISSUE—CAT AND DOG
| ☐ 2025 13¢ Multicolored | 22.00 | 2.10 | .55 | .17 |

*No hinge pricing from 1941 to date is figured at (N-H ADD 10%)

Scott No.	Mint Sheet	Plate Block	Fine Unused Each	Fine Used Each

1982. CHRISTMAS ISSUE—TIEPOLO'S "MADONNA AND CHILD"

| ☐2026 20¢ Multicolored | 30.00 | 13.00 | .70 | .17 |

1982. SEASON'S GREETINGS—SLEDDING

| ☐2027 20¢ Multicolored | — | — | .85 | .17 |

1982. SEASON'S GREETINGS—BUILDING SNOWMAN

| ☐2028 20¢ Multicolored | — | — | .85 | .17 |

1982. SEASON'S GREETINGS—ICE SKATING

| ☐2029 20¢ Multicolored | — | — | .85 | .17 |

1982. SEASON'S GREETINGS—TRIMMING TREE

| ☐2030 20¢ Multicolored | — | — | .85 | .17 |
| ☐Season's Greetings, above four attached | 36.00 | — | — | — |

1982. SCIENCE AND INDUSTRY

| ☐2031 20¢ Multicolored | 27.00 | 2.40 | .75 | .17 |

1983. BALLOONING—INTREPID

| ☐2032 20¢ Multicolored | — | — | .75 | .17 |

1982. BALLOONING—RED, WHITE & BLUE

| ☐2033 20¢ Multicolored | — | — | .75 | .17 |

1982. BALLOONING—YELLOW & GOLD

| ☐2034 20¢ Multicolored | — | — | .75 | .17 |

1982. BALLOONING—EXPLORER II

| ☐2035 20¢ Multicolored | — | — | .75 | .17 |
| ☐Ballooning, above four attached | 27.00 | — | — | — |

1983. COMMEMORATIVES
1983. TREATY OF AMITY

| ☐2036 20¢ Blue and Black | 27.00 | 2.30 | .60 | .17 |

*No hinge pricing from 1941 to date is figured at (N-H ADD 10%)

Scott No.	Mint Sheet	Plate Block	Fine Unused Each	Fine Used Each

1983. CIVILIAN CONSERVATION CORPS

☐2037 20¢ Multicolored	27.00	2.40	.60	.16

1983. JOSEPH PRIESTLEY

☐2038 20¢ Rust Brown	30.00	2.65	.60	.16

1983. VOLUNTEER—LEND A HAND

☐2039 20¢ Black and Red	30.00	14.00	.65	.16

1983. CONCORD 1683

☐2040 20¢ Beige	27.00	2.45	.65	.16

1983. BROOKLYN BRIDGE

☐2041 20¢ Blue	27.00	2.45	.65	.16

1983. TENNESSEE VALLEY AUTHORITY

☐2042 20¢ Multicolored	31.00	14.00	.70	.16

1983. PHYSICAL FITNESS

☐2043 20¢ Multicolored	29.00	14.00	.70	.16

1982. SCOTT JOPLIN

☐2044 20¢ Multicolored	31.00	3.00	.65	.16

1983. MEDAL OF HONOR

☐2045 20¢ Multicolored	29.00	3.10	.80	.16

1983. BABE RUTH

☐2046 20¢ Blue	110.00	10.00	2.50	.16

1983. NATHANIEL HAWTHORNE

☐2047 20¢ Multicolored	30.00	2.80	.70	.16

1983. SUMMER OLYMPICS 1984—DISCUS

☐2048 13¢ Multicolored	—	—	.70	.16

1983. SUMMER OLYMPICS 1984—HIGH JUMP

☐2049 13¢ Multicolored	—	—	.70	.16

*No hinge pricing from 1941 to date is figured at (N-H ADD 10%)

Scott No.	Mint Sheet	Plate Block	Fine Unused Each	Fine Used Each

1983. SUMMER OLYMPICS 1984—ARCHERY

☐2050 13¢ Multicolored	—	—	.55	.17

1983. SUMMER OLYMPICS 1984—BOXING

☐2051 13¢ Multicolored	—	—	.55	.17

1983. TREATY OF PARIS

☐2052 20¢ Multicolored	24.00	3.00	.65	.17

1983. CIVIL SERVICE

☐2053 20¢ Multicolored	30.00	14.00 (20)	.65	.17

1983. METROPOLITAN OPERA

☐2054 20¢ Yellow & Brown	30.00	2.80	.65	.17

1983. INVENTORS—CHARLES STEINMETZ

☐2055 20¢ Multicolored	38.00	4.30	.90	.17

1983. INVENTORS—EDWIN ARMSTRONG

☐2056 20¢ Multicolored	32.00	4.10	.90	.17

1983. INVENTORS—NIKOLA TESLA

☐2057 20¢ Multicolored	32.00	4.10	.90	.17

1983. INVENTORS—PHILO T. FARNSWORTH

☐2058 20¢ Multicolored	32.00	4.10	.90	.17

1983. STREETCARS—FIRST

☐2059 20¢ Multicolored	32.00	4.00	.90	.17

1983. STREETCARS—ELECTRIC TROLLEY

☐2060 20¢ Multicolored	31.00	2.50	.90	.17

1983. STREETCARS—BOBTAIL HORSECAR

☐2061 20¢ Multicolored	31.00	2.50	.90	.17

1983. STREETCARS—ST. CHARLES

☐2061 20¢ Multicolored	31.00	2.50	.90	.17

*No hinge pricing from 1941 to date is figured at (N-H ADD 10%)

Scott No.	Mint Sheet	Plate Block	Fine Unused Each	Fine Used Each

1983. CHRISTMAS—MADONNA

| ☐2063 20¢ Multicolored | 27.00 | 2.60 | .65 | .17 |

1983. CHRISTMAS—SEASON'S GREETINGS

| ☐2064 20¢ Multicolored | 31.00 | 14.00 | .65 | .17 |

1983. MARTIN LUTHER

| ☐2065 20¢ Multicolored | 27.00 | 2.30 | .65 | .17 |

1984. COMMEMORATIVES _____
1984. ALASKA STATEHOOD

| ☐2066 20¢ Multicolored | 27.00 | 3.00 | .65 | .17 |

1984. WINTER OLYMPICS 1984—ICE DANCING

| ☐2067 20¢ Multicolored | 30.00 | 4.00 | .70 | .17 |

1984. WINTER OLYMPICS 1984—DOWNHILL SKIING

| ☐2068 20¢ Multicolored | 30.00 | 4.00 | .70 | .17 |

1984. WINTER OLYMPICS 1984—CROSS COUNTRY CLINIC

| ☐2069 20¢ Multicolored | 31.00 | 4.00 | .70 | .17 |

1984. WINTER OLYMPICS 1984—HOCKEY

| ☐2070 20¢ Multicolored | 30.00 | 4.00 | .70 | .17 |

1984. FEDERAL DEPOSIT INSURANCE CORPORATION

| ☐2071 20¢ Red & Yellow | 30.00 | 2.00 | .65 | .17 |

1984. LOVE

| ☐2072 20¢ Multicolored | 31.00 | 15.00 (20) | .65 | .17 |

1984. CARTER G. WOODSON

| ☐2073 20¢ Multicolored | 30.00 | 2.65 | .65 | .17 |

1984. SOIL AND WATER CONSERVATION

| ☐2074 20¢ Multicolored | 27.00 | 2.60 | .65 | .17 |

1984. CREDIT UNION

| ☐2075 20¢ Multicolored | 27.00 | 2.60 | .65 | .17 |

*No hinge pricing from 1941 to date is figured at (N-H ADD 10%)

Scott No.	Mint Sheet	Plate Block	Fine Unused Each	Fine Used Each

1984. ORCHIDS—WILD PINK
| ☐2076 20¢ Multicolored | 31.00 | 3.50 | .70 | .17 |

1984. ORCHIDS—YELLOW LADY SLIPPER
| ☐2077 20¢ Multicolored | 32.00 | 3.50 | .70 | .17 |

1984. ORCHIDS—SPREADING POGONIA
| ☐2078 20¢ Multicolored | 32.00 | 3.50 | .70 | .17 |

1984. ORCHIDS—PACIFIC CALYPSO
| ☐2079 20¢ Multicolored | 31.00 | 3.20 | .70 | .17 |

1984. HAWAII STATEHOOD
| ☐2080 20¢ Blue & Yellow | 30.00 | 3.10 | .70 | .17 |

1984. NATIONAL ARCHIVES
| ☐2081 20¢ Brown & Black | 30.00 | 2.80 | .70 | .17 |

1984. SUMMER OLYMPICS 1984—MEN'S DIVING
| ☐2082 20¢ Multicolored | 48.00 | 6.00 | 2.00 | .17 |

1984. SUMMER OLYMPICS 1984—LONG JUMP
| ☐2083 20¢ Multicolored | 48.00 | 6.00 | 2.00 | .17 |

1984. SUMMER OLYMPICS 1984—WRESTLING
| ☐2084 20¢ Multicolored | 48.00 | 6.00 | 1.75 | .17 |

1984. SUMMER OLYMPICS 1984—WOMEN'S KAYAK
| ☐2085 20¢ Multicolored | 47.00 | 4.00 | 1.50 | .17 |

1984. LOUISIANA WORLD'S EXPOSITION
| ☐2086 20¢ Multicolored | 26.00 | 3.00 | .75 | .17 |

1984. HEALTH RESEARCH—USA
| ☐2087 20¢ Multicolored | 32.00 | 3.10 | .70 | .17 |

1984. DOUGLAS FAIRBANKS
| ☐2088 20¢ Black & White | 34.00 | 18.00 | .68 | .17 |

*No hinge pricing from 1941 to date is figured at (N-H ADD 10%)

Scott No.	Mint Sheet	Plate Block	Fine Unused Each	Fine Used Each
1984. JIM THORPE				
☐2089 20¢ Black & White	36.00	3.20	.81	.17
1984. JOHN McCORMACK				
☐2090 20¢ Multicolored	27.00	2.60	.70	.17
1984. ST. LAWRENCE SEAWAY				
☐2091 20¢ Multicolored	27.00	2.60	.70	.17
1984. PRESERVING WETLANDS				
☐2092 20¢ Multicolored	40.00	4.00	1.00	.17
1984. ROANOKE VOYAGES 1584				
☐2093 20¢ Multicolored	34.00	3.10	.78	.17
1984. HERMAN MELVILLE				
☐2094 20¢ Green	27.00	2.65	.60	.17
1984. HORACE MOSES				
☐2095 20¢ Orange & Brown	41.00	19.00	.90	.17
1984. SMOKEY THE BEAR				
☐2096 20¢ Multicolored	31.00	3.10	.68	.17
1984. ROBERTO CLEMENTE				
☐2097 20¢ Multicolored	132.00	12.50	2.70	.17
1984. DOGS: BEAGLE & BOSTON TERRIER				
☐2098 20¢ Multicolored	30.00	3.60	1.00	.17
1984. DOGS: RETRIEVER & COCKER SPANIEL				
☐2099 20¢ Multicolored	32.00	3.50	.85	.17
1984. DOGS: MALAMUTE & COLLIE				
☐2100 20¢ Multicolored	32.00	3.60	.70	.17
1984. DOGS: COONHOUND & FOXHOUND				
☐2101 20¢ Multicolored	32.00	3.50	.70	.17

*No hinge pricing from 1941 to date is figured at (N-H ADD 10%)

Scott No.	Mint Sheet	Plate Block	Fine Unused Each	Fine Used Each
1984. CRIME PREVENTION				
☐2102 20¢ Multicolored	26.00	2.40	.60	.17
1984. HISPANIC AMERICANS				
☐2103 20¢ Multicolored	21.00	2.40	.60	.17
1984. FAMILY UNITY				
☐2104 20¢ Multicolored	41.00	18.00 (20)	.90	.17
1984. ELEANOR ROOSEVELT				
☐2105 20¢ Blue	27.00	2.80	.65	.17
1984. NATION OF READERS				
☐2106 20¢ Brown & Maroon	32.00	2.75	.72	.17
1984. MADONNA AND CHILD				
☐2107 20¢ Multicolored	27.00	2.60	.65	.17
1984. SANTA CLAUS				
☐2108 20¢ Multicolored	27.00	2.40	.65	.17
1984. VIETNAM VETERANS MEMORIAL				
☐2109 20¢ Multicolored	34.00	4.30	.95	.17
1985. COMMEMORATIVES ———				
1985. JEROME KERN				
☐2110 22¢ Multicolored	32.00	3.10	.75	.17
1985. REGULAR ISSUES ———				
1985. "D" NON-DENOMINATIONAL				
☐2111 22¢ Green	110.00	34.00 (20)	.86	.17
1985. "D" NON-DENOMINATIONAL COIL				
☐2112 22¢ Green	—	7.00	.80	.17
1985. "D" NON-DENOMINATIONAL BOOKLET				
☐2113 22¢ Green	—	—	.85	.17
1985. FLAG OVER DOME				
☐2114 22¢ Multicolored	62.00	3.10	.65	.17

*No hinge pricing from 1941 to date is figured at (N-H ADD 10%)

Scott No.	Mint Sheet	Plate Block	Fine Unused Each	Fine Used Each

1985. FLAG OVER DOME COIL
☐2115 22¢ Multicolored	—	—	.85	.17

1985. FLAG OVER DOME BOOKLET
☐2116 22¢ Multicolored	—	—	.90	.17

1985. SEASHELLS: FRILLED DOGWINKLE
☐2117 22¢ Brown	—	—	1.00	.17

1985. SEASHELLS: RETICULATED HELMET
☐2118 22¢ Brown	—	—	.85	.17

1985. SEASHELLS: NEW ENGLAND NEPTUNE
☐2119 22¢ Brown	—	—	.85	.17

1985. SEASHELLS: CALICO SCALLOP
☐2120 22¢ Pink	—	—	.85	.17

1985. SEASHELLS: LIGHTNING WHELK
☐2121 22¢ Brown	—	—	.85	.17

1985. EXPRESS MAIL U.S.A.
☐2122 $10.75 Multicolored	—	—	26.00	11.00

1985. SCHOOL BUS 1920s
☐2123 3.4¢ Dark Brown	—	—	.26	.17

1985. BUCKBOARD 1880s
☐2124 4.9¢ Dark Brown	—	—	.26	.17

1986. STAR ROUTE TRUCK 1910s
☐2125 5.5¢ Carmine	—	—	.26	.17

1985. TRICYCLE 1880s
☐2126 6¢ Red	—	—	.26	.17

1985. TRACTOR 1920s
☐2127 71¢ Lake	—	—	.26	.17

*No hinge pricing from 1941 to date is figured at (N-H ADD 10%)

Scott No.	Mint Sheet	Plate Block	Fine Unused Each	Fine Used Each

1985. AMBULANCE 1860s

☐2128 8.3¢ Green	—	—	.35	.19

1985. TOW TRUCK 1920s

☐2129 8.5¢ Dark Green	—	—	.35	.19

1985. OIL WAGON 1890s

☐2130 10.1¢ Black	—	—	.35	.19

1985. STUTZ BEARCAT 1933

☐2131 11¢ Blue	—	—	.42	.19

1985. STANLEY STEAMER 1909

☐2132 12¢ Blue	—	—	.54	.19

1985. PUSHCART 1880s

☐2133 12.5¢ Black	—	—	.54	.19

1985. ICEBOAT 1880s

☐2134 14¢ Blue	—	—	.54	.19

1986. DOG SLED 1920s

☐2135 17¢ Blue	—	—	.72	.19

1986. BREAD WAGON 1880s

☐2136 25¢ Brown	—	—	.82	.19

1985.COMMEMORATIVES (CONTINUED) _____
1985. MARY McCLEOD BETHUNE

☐2137 22¢ Multicolored	38.00	4.00	.82	.19

1985. DUCKS: BROADBILL

☐2138 22¢ Multicolored	90.00	12.00	.90	.19

1985. DUCKS: MALLARD

☐2139 22¢ Multicolored	90.00	12.00	.90	.19

1985. DUCKS: CANVASBACK

☐2140 22¢ Multicolored	90.00	12.00	.90	.19

*No hinge pricing from 1941 to date is figured at (N-H ADD 10%)

Scott No.	Mint Sheet	Plate Block	Fine Unused Each	Fine Used Each

1985. DUCKS: REDHEAD
☐2141 22¢ Multicolored   90.00   11.00   .90   .18

1985. WINTER SPECIAL OLYMPICS
☐2142 22¢ Multicolored   26.00   3.00   .75   .18

1985. LOVE
☐2143 22¢ Multicolored   34.00   3.15   .75   .18

1985. RURAL ELECTRIFICATION ADMINISTRATION
☐2144 22¢ Multicolored   62.00   34.00 (20)   .85   .18

1985. AMERIPEX SHOW
☐2145 22¢ Multicolored   29.00   3.00   .65   .18

1985. ABIGAIL ADAMS
☐2146 22¢ Multicolored   28.00   3.25   .75   .18

1985. BARTHOLDI—STATUE OF LIBERTY
☐2147 22¢ Multicolored   28.00   3.00   .70   .18

1985. REGULAR ISSUES ───────
1985. GEORGE WASHINGTON
☐2149 18¢ Multicolored   —   —   .80   .18

1985. ENVELOPES
☐2150 2.1¢ Multicolored   —   —   .65   .18

1985. COMMEMORATIVES (CONTINUED) ───────
1985. KOREAN VETERANS
☐2152 22¢ Red & Green   38.00   4.00   .86   .18

1985. SOCIAL SECURITY
☐2153 22¢ Blue   30.00   3.00   .70   .18

1985. WORLD WAR I VETERANS
☐2154 22¢ Red & Green   40.00   3.85   .86   .18

1985. HORSES: QUARTER HORSE
☐2155 22¢ Multicolored   116.00   16.00   6.00   .18

*No hinge pricing from 1941 to date is figured at (N-H ADD 10%)

Scott No.	Mint Sheet	Plate Block	Fine Unused Each	Fine Used Each
1985. HORSES: MORGAN				
☐2156 22¢ Multicolored	116.00	15.50	6.00	.18
1985. HORSES: SADDLEBRED				
☐2157 22¢ Multicolored	116.00	15.50	6.00	.18
1985. HORSES: APPALOOSA				
☐2158 22¢ Multicolored	116.00	15.50	6.00	.18
1985. PUBLIC EDUCATION				
☐2159 22¢ Multicolored	68.00	6.00	1.00	.18
1985. YOUTH YEAR: Y.M.C.A.				
☐2160 22¢ Multicolored	61.00	8.10	6.00	.18
1985. YOUTH YEAR: BOY SCOUTS				
☐2161 22¢ Multicolored	61.00	8.10	6.00	.18
1985. YOUTH YEAR: BIG BROTHERS				
☐2162 22¢ Multicolored	61.00	8.10	6.00	.18
1985. YOUTH YEAR: CAMPFIRE				
☐2163 22¢ Multicolored	61.00	8.10	6.00	.18
1985. HELP END HUNGER				
☐2164 22¢ Multicolored	32.00	3.10	.70	.18
1985. MADONNA AND CHILD				
☐2165 22¢ Multicolored	28.00	3.00	.70	.18
1985. SEASON'S GREETINGS—POINSETTIA				
☐2166 22¢ Multicolored	28.00	3.00	.70	.18
1986. COMMEMORATIVES ━━━━━━━				
1986. ARKANSAS—STATEHOOD				
☐2167 22¢ Multicolored	30.00	3.10	.70	.18
1986–1993 GREAT AMERICANS **1986. MARGARET MITCHELL**				
☐2168 1¢ Brown	10.00	—	.30	.18

*No hinge pricing from 1941 to date is figured at (N-H ADD 10%)

Scott No.	Mint Sheet	Plate Block	Fine Unused Each	Fine Used Each
1987. MARY LYON				
☐2169 2¢ Blue	7.00	.52	.25	.17
1986. DR. PAUL DUDLEY WHITE M.D.				
☐2170 3¢ Blue	10.50	.65	.25	.17
1986. FATHER FLANAGAN				
☐2171 4¢ Blue	11.00	.78	.25	.17
1986. HUGO L. BLACK				
☐2172 5¢ Olive Green	14.00	.80	.25	.17
1990. LUIS MUÑOZ MARIN				
☐2173 5¢ Carmine	16.00	.92	.25	.17
1988. RED CLOUD				
☐2175 10¢ Lake	40.50	2.10	.48	.17
1987. JULIA WARD HOWE				
☐2176 14¢ Red	39.00	2.00	.42	.17
1988. BUFFALO BILL CODY				
☐2177 15¢ Claret	70.00	4.00	.70	.17
1986. BELVA ANN LOCKWOOD				
☐2178 17¢ Blue Green	49.00	2.75	.60	.17
1986. VIRGINIA APGAR				
☐2179 20¢ Multicolored	46.00	3.00	.60	.17
1988. CHESTER CARLSON				
☐2180 21¢ Blue Violet	58.00	4.00	.62	.17
1988. MARY CASSATT				
☐2181 23¢ Purple	61.00	3.75	.65	.17
1986. JACK LONDON				
☐2182 25¢ Blue	61.00	4.00	.65	.17
1989. SITTING BULL				
☐2183 28¢ Myrtle Green	76.00	4.10	.75	.17

*No hinge pricing from 1941 to date is figured at (N-H ADD 10%)

Scott No.	Mint Sheet	Plate Block	Fine Unused Each	Fine Used Each
1992. EARL WARREN				
☐2184 29¢ Blue	76.00	4.10	.80	.19
1993. THOMAS JEFFERSON				
☐2185 29¢ Black	76.00	4.10 (4)	.82	.19
1986. DENNIS CHAVEZ				
☐2186 35¢ Black	90.00	4.75	.90	.24
1990. CLAIRE CHENAULT				
☐2187 40¢ Dark Blue	94.00	6.00	.95	.20
1988. DR. HARVEY CUSHING				
☐2188 45¢ Blue	100.00	6.00	1.10	.26
1991. HUBERT HUMPHREY				
☐2189 52¢ Purple	200.00	11.00	2.10	.60
1986. JOHN HARVARD				
☐2190 56¢ Brown	160.00	8.00	1.70	.25
1988. H. H. ARNOLD				
☐2191 65¢ Blue/Gray	165.00	9.00	1.80	.26
1992. WENDELL WILKIE				
☐2192 75¢ Magenta	180.00	9.50	1.90	.22
1986. BERNARD REVEL				
☐2193 $1.00 Green	360.00	17.00	4.10	.32
1989. JOHNS HOPKINS				
☐2194 $1.00 Dark Green	54.00	13.00	3.00	.26
1986. WILLIAM JENNINGS BRYAN				
☐2195 $2.00 Violet	490.00	24.00	6.00	.60
1987. BRET HARTE				
☐2196 $5.00 Brown	240.00	54.00	12.00	2.00
1988. JACK LONDON				
☐2197 25¢ Black	—	—	.75	.20

1986. COMMEMORATIVES (CONTINUED) ⎯⎯⎯
1986. STAMP COLLECTING: AMERICAN PHILATELIC ASSOC.

☐2198 22¢ Multicolored	—	—	1.00	.20

*No hinge pricing from 1941 to date is figured at (N-H ADD 10%)

Scott No.	Mint Sheet	Plate Block	Fine Unused Each	Fine Used Each

1986. STAMP COLLECTING: LITTLE BOY

| ☐2199 22¢ Multicolored | — | — | 1.00 | .21 |

1986. STAMP COLLECTING: MAGNIFIER

| ☐2200 22¢ Multicolored | — | — | 1.00 | .21 |

1986. STAMP COLLECTING: RUBBER STAMP

| ☐2201 22¢ Multicolored | — | — | 1.00 | .21 |

1986. LOVE

| ☐2202 22¢ Multicolored | 33.00 | 3.00 | .75 | .17 |

1986. SOJOURNER TRUTH

| ☐2203 22¢ Multicolored | 36.00 | 3.60 | .85 | .17 |

1986. TEXAS—SAN JACINTO 1836

| ☐2204 22¢ Multicolored | 33.00 | 3.00 | .75 | .17 |

1986. FISH: MUSKELLUNGE

| ☐2205 22¢ Multicolored | — | — | 3.25 | .17 |

1986. FISH: ATLANTIC COD

| ☐2206 22¢ Multicolored | — | — | 3.25 | .17 |

1986. FISH: LARGEMOUTH BASS

| ☐2207 22¢ Multicolored | — | — | 3.25 | .17 |

1986. FISH: BLUEFIN TUNA

| ☐2208 22¢ Multicolored | — | — | 3.25 | .17 |

1986. FISH: CATFISH

| ☐2209 22¢ Multicolored | — | — | 3.25 | .17 |

1986. PUBLIC HOSPITALS

| ☐2210 22¢ Multicolored | 33.00 | 3.00 | .90 | .17 |

1986. DUKE ELLINGTON

| ☐2211 22¢ Multicolored | 30.00 | 2.90 | .75 | .17 |

*No hinge pricing from 1941 to date is figured at (N-H ADD 10%)

Scott No.	Mint Sheet	Plate Block	Fine Unused Each	Fine Used Each
1986. AMERIPEX '86-PRESIDENTS I				
☐2216 22¢ Brown & Black	—	7.00 (9)	1.00	.45
1986. AMERIPEX '86-PRESIDENTS II				
☐2217 22¢ Brown & Black	—	7.00 (9)	1.00	.45
1986. AMERIPEX '86-PRESIDENTS III				
☐2218 22¢ Brown & Black	—	7.00 (9)	1.00	.45
1986. AMERIPEX '86-PRESIDENTS IV				
☐2219 22¢ Brown & Black	—	7.00 (9)	1.00	.45
1986. POLAR EXPLORERS: ELISHA KANE KENT				
☐2220 22¢ Multicolored	—	—	2.00	.55
1986. POLAR EXPLORERS: ADOLPHUS W. GREELY				
☐2221 22¢ Multicolored	—	—	2.00	.55
1986. POLAR EXPLORERS: VILHJALMUR STEFANSSON				
☐2222 22¢ Multicolored	—	—	2.00	.55
1986. POLAR EXPLORERS: ROBERT PERRY & MATTHEW HENSON				
☐2223 22¢ Multicolored	—	—	2.00	.45
1986. STATUE OF LIBERTY				
☐2224 22¢ Carmine & Blue	34.00	3.50	1.20	.17
1986. NAVAJO ART				
☐2235 22¢ Multicolored	40.00	4.00	1.10	.17
1986. NAVAJO ART				
☐2236 22¢ Multicolored	38.00	4.00	1.10	.17
1986. NAVAJO ART				
☐2237 22¢ Multicolored	38.00	4.00	1.10	.17
1986. NAVAJO ART				
☐2238 22¢ Multicolored	38.00	4.00	1.10	.17

*No hinge pricing from 1941 to date is figured at (N-H ADD 10%)

Scott No.	Mint Sheet	Plate Block	Fine Unused Each	Fine Used Each

1986. T.S. ELIOT

☐2239 22¢ Brown	29.00	3.00	.65	.17

1986. FOLK ART: HIGHLANDER

☐2240 22¢ Multicolored	40.00	4.20	.75	.18

1986. FOLK ART: SHIP

☐2241 22¢ Multicolored	40.00	4.20	.75	.18

1986. FOLK ART: NAUTICAL

☐2242 22¢ Multicolored	39.00	4.10	.75	.18

1986. FOLK ART: CIGAR STORE

☐2243 22¢ Multicolored	39.00	4.10	.75	.18

1986. CHRISTMAS: PEROGINO GALLERY

☐2244 22¢ Multicolored	58.00	3.00	.75	.17

1986. CHRISTMAS: GREETINGS—VILLAGE

☐2245 22¢ Multicolored	58.00	3.00	.75	.17

1987. COMMEMORATIVES ─────────
1987. MICHIGAN STATEHOOD

☐2246 22¢ Multicolored	30.00	3.00	.70	.17

1987. PAN AMERICAN GAMES

☐2247 22¢ Multicolored	29.00	3.00	.70	.17

1987. LOVE

☐2248 22¢ Multicolored	56.00	3.00	.70	.17

1987. JEAN BAPTISTE POINTE DU SABLE

☐2249 22¢ Multicolored	31.00	3.10	.75	.17

1987. ENRICO CARUSO

☐2250 22¢ Multicolored	28.00	3.00	.70	.17

1987. GIRL SCOUTS

☐2251 22¢ Multicolored	32.00	3.15	.75	.17

*No hinge pricing from 1941 to date is figured at (N-H ADD 10%)

Scott No.	Mint Sheet	Plate Strip	Fine Unused Each	Fine Used Each

1987–1993. TRANSPORTATION COILS ———

1988. CONESTOGA WAGON

| ☐2252 3¢ Claret | — | 1.50 | .21 | .17 |

1988. MILK WAGON

| ☐2253 5¢ Black | — | 1.60 | .21 | .17 |

1988. ELEVATOR

| ☐2254 5.3¢ Black | — | 2.75 | .32 | .17 |

1988. CARRETA

| ☐2255 7.6¢ Brown | — | 3.25 | .32 | .17 |

1988. WHEELCHAIR

| ☐2256 8.4¢ Claret | — | 3.10 | .35 | .17 |

1988. CANAL BOAT

| ☐2257 10¢ Sky Blue | — | 2.70 | .40 | .17 |

1988. POLICE WAGON

| ☐2258 13¢ Black | — | 5.00 | .65 | .17 |

1988. RAILROAD COALCAR

| ☐2259 13.2¢ Slate Green | — | 4.50 | .45 | .17 |

1988. TUG BOAT

| ☐2260 15¢ Violet | — | 3.50 | .50 | .17 |

1988. POPCORN WAGON

| ☐2261 16.7¢ Rose | — | 4.10 | .55 | .17 |

1988. RACING CAR

| ☐2262 17.5¢ Violet | — | 6.00 | .65 | .17 |

1988. CABLE CAR

| ☐2263 20¢ Blue Violet | — | 5.00 | .65 | .17 |

1988. FIRE ENGINE

| ☐2264 20.5¢ Rose | — | 8.00 | 1.25 | .35 |

*No hinge pricing from 1941 to date is figured at (N-H ADD 10%)

Scott No.	Mint Sheet	Plate Strip	Fine Unused Each	Fine Used Each
1988. RAILROAD MAILCAR				
☐ 2265 21¢ Green	—	5.50	.75	.40
1988. TANDEM BICYCLE				
☐ 2266 24.1¢ Ultramarine	—	7.00	.76	.40
1987. COMMEMORATIVES (CONTINUED) ———				
1987. SPECIAL OCCASIONS				
☐ 2267– b 2274 22¢ Multicolored	—	—	2.50	.19
1987. UNITED WAY UNITING COMMUNITIES				
☐ 2275 22¢ Multicolored	28.00	3.00	.65	.17
1987–1989. REGULAR ISSUES ———				
1987. AMERICAN FLAG				
☐ 2276 22¢ Multicolored	58.00	3.10	.65	.17
1987. "E" EARTH				
☐ 2277 25¢ Multicolored	78.00	4.00	.90	.17
1987. FLAG ON CLOUDS				
☐ 2278 25¢ Multicolored	72.00	3.30	.75	.17
1987. "E" EARTH				
☐ 2279 25¢ Multicolored	—	4.00	.75	.17
1987. FLAG YOSEMITE				
☐ 2280 25¢ Multicolored	—	5.10	.75	.17
1987. HONEY BEE				
☐ 2281 25¢ Multicolored	—	4.60	.75	.17
1987. "E" EARTH				
☐ 2282 25¢ Multicolored	—	—	.75	.17
1987. PHEASANT				
☐ 2283 25¢ Multicolored	—	—	.75	.17
1987. GROSBEAK				
☐ 2284 25¢ Multicolored	—	—	.75	.17

*No hinge pricing from 1941 to date is figured at (N-H ADD 10%)

Scott No.	Mint Sheet	Plate Block	Fine Unused Each	Fine Used Each

1987. OWL

| ☐2285 25¢ Multicolored | — | — | .75 | .21 |

1987. COMMEMORATIVES (CONTINUED) ————
1987. AMERICAN WILDLIFE SERIES

| ☐2286–2335 22¢ Multicolored | | | | |
| | 71.00 | — | — | .40 |

1987. DELAWARE

| ☐2336 22¢ Multicolored | 32.00 | 4.00 | .75 | .20 |

1987. PENNSYLVANIA

| ☐2337 22¢ Multicolored | 41.00 | 4.00 | .85 | .20 |

1987. BICENTENNIAL SERIES

| ☐2338–2348 22¢ Multicolored | | | | |
| | 38.00 | 3.50 | .85 | .20 |

1987. FRIENDSHIP WITH MOROCCO

| ☐2349 22¢ Multicolored | 28.00 | 3.00 | .75 | .17 |

1987. WILLIAM FAULKNER

| ☐2350 22¢ Green | 35.00 | 3.40 | .75 | .17 |

1987. LACEMAKING

| ☐2351–2354 22¢ Blue | | | | |
| | 36.00 | 4.50 | 1.50 | .19 |

1987. CONSTITUTION (BICENTENNIAL)

| ☐2355 22¢ Multicolored | — | — | 2.00 | .17 |

1987. CONSTITUTION (WE THE PEOPLE)

| ☐2356 22¢ Multicolored | — | — | 1.10 | .17 |

1987. CONSTITUTION (ESTABLISH JUSTICE)

| ☐2357 22¢ Multicolored | — | — | 1.10 | .17 |

1987. CONSTITUTION (AND SECURE)

| ☐2358 22¢ Multicolored | — | — | 1.10 | .17 |

*No hinge pricing from 1941 to date is figured at (N-H ADD 10%)

Scott No.	Mint Sheet	Plate Block	Fine Unused Each	Fine Used Each
1987. CONSTITUTION (DO ORDAIN)				
☐2359 22¢ Multicolored	—	—	1.10	.17
1987. U.S. CONSTITUTION				
☐2360 22¢ Multicolored	38.00	4.10	.90	.17
1987. C.P.A. CERTIFIED PUBLIC ACCOUNTANTS				
☐2361 22¢ Multicolored	165.00	15.00	3.50	.17
1987. LOCOMOTIVES				
☐2362–2366 22¢ Multicolored				
	—	—	3.50	.25
1987. CHRISTMAS: MARONI, NATIONAL GALLERY				
☐2367 22¢ Multicolored	56.00	3.00	.75	.17
1987. GREETINGS				
☐2368 22¢ Multicolored	56.00	3.00	.75	.17
1988. COMMEMORATIVES				
1988. OLYMPICS (WINTER)				
☐2369 22¢ Multicolored	32.00	3.50	.90	.17
1988. AUSTRALIA BICENTENNIAL				
☐2370 22¢ Multicolored	25.00	3.00	.65	.17
1988. J. W. JOHNSON				
☐2371 22¢ Multicolored	31.00	3.50	.72	.17
1988. CATS (SHORT HAIR)				
☐2372 22¢ Multicolored	37.00	6.00	1.50	.17
1988. CATS (HIMALAYAN)				
☐2373 22¢ Multicolored	37.00	6.00	1.50	.17
1988. CATS (BURMESE)				
☐2374 22¢ Multicolored	37.00	6.00	1.50	.17
1988. CATS (PERSIAN)				
☐2375 22¢ Multicolored	37.00	6.00	1.50	.17

*No hinge pricing from 1941 to date is figured at (N-H ADD 10%)

Scott No.	Mint Sheet	Plate Block	Fine Unused Each	Fine Used Each
1988. KNUTE ROCKNE				
☐2376 22¢ Multicolored	39.00	4.10	.85	.17
1988. FRANCIS OUIMET				
☐2377 25¢ Multicolored	51.00	6.00	1.15	.22
1988. LOVE				
☐2378 25¢ Multicolored	68.00	3.50	.75	.17
1988. LOVE				
☐2379 45¢ Multicolored	64.00	5.75	1.40	.22
1988. OLYMPICS (SUMMER)				
☐2380 25¢ Multicolored	38.00	4.00	.90	.17
1988. CARS (LOCOMOBILE)				
☐2381 25¢ Multicolored	—	—	2.10	.17
1988. CARS (PIERCE-ARROW)				
☐2382 25¢ Multicolored	—	—	2.10	.17
1988. CARS (CORD)				
☐2383 25¢ Multicolored	—	—	2.10	.17
1988. CARS (PACKARD)				
☐2384 25¢ Multicolored	—	—	2.20	.17
1988. CARS (DUESENBERG)				
☐2385 25¢ Multicolored	—	—	2.20	.17
1988. ANTARCTIC: NATHANIEL PALMER				
☐2386 25¢ Multicolored	56.00	8.00	2.00	.17
1988. ANTARCTIC: LT. CHARLES WILKES				
☐2387 25¢ Multicolored	56.00	8.00	2.00	.17
1988. ANTARCTIC: RICHARD E. BYRD				
☐2388 25¢ Multicolored	56.00	8.00	2.00	.17
1988. ANTARCTIC: LINCOLN ELLSWORTH				
☐2389 25¢ Multicolored	56.00	8.00	2.00	.17

*No hinge pricing from 1941 to date is figured at (N-H ADD 10%)

Scott No.	Mint Sheet	Plate Block	Fine Unused Each	Fine Used Each

1988. CAROUSEL: DEER

Scott No.	Mint Sheet	Plate Block	Fine Unused Each	Fine Used Each
☐2390 25¢ Multicolored	56.00	6.00	1.40	.17

1988. CAROUSEL: HORSE

☐2391 25¢ Multicolored	56.00	6.00	1.40	.17

1988. CAROUSEL: CAMEL

☐2392 25¢ Multicolored	56.00	6.00	1.40	.17

1988. CAROUSEL: GOAT

☐2393 25¢ Multicolored	56.00	6.00	1.40	.17

1988. EXPRESS MAIL

☐2394 $8.75 Multicolored	510.00	116.00	26.00	9.00

1988. OCCASIONS: HAPPY BIRTHDAY

☐2395 25¢ Multicolored	—	—	.95	.17

1988. OCCASIONS: BEST WISHES

☐2396 25¢ Multicolored	—	—	.95	.17

1988. OCCASIONS: THINKING OF YOU

☐2397 25¢ Multicolored	—	—	.90	.17

1988. OCCASIONS: LOVE YOU

☐2398 25¢ Multicolored	—	—	.90	.17

1988. CHRISTMAS (BOTTICELLI)

☐2399 25¢ Multicolored	31.00	3.25	.90	.17

1988. GREETINGS (CHRISTMAS)

☐2400 25¢ Multicolored	31.00	3.25	.90	.17

1989. COMMEMORATIVES ——————
1989. MONTANA

☐2401 25¢ Multicolored	40.50	4.10	.92	.17

1989. A. PHILIPP RANDOLPH

☐2402 25¢ Multicolored	39.00	4.10	.92	.17

*No hinge pricing from 1941 to date is figured at (N-H ADD 10%)

Scott No.	Mint Sheet	Plate Block	Fine Unused Each	Fine Used Each
1989. NORTH DAKOTA				
☐2403 25¢ Multicolored	38.00	4.00	.86	.17
1989. WASHINGTON				
☐2404 25¢ Multicolored	34.00	4.00	.86	.17
1989. STEAMBOATS: EXPERIMENT				
☐2405 25¢ Multicolored	—	—	.86	.17
1989. STEAMBOATS: PHOENIX				
☐2406 25¢ Multicolored	—	—	.86	.17
1989. STEAMBOATS: NEW ORLEANS				
☐2407 25¢ Multicolored	—	—	.86	.17
1989. STEAMBOATS: WASHINGTON				
☐2408 25¢ Multicolored	—	—	.86	.17
1989. STEAMBOATS: WALK IN THE WATER				
☐2409 25¢ Multicolored	—	—	.86	.17
1989. WORLD STAMP EXPO '89				
☐2410 25¢ Black & Carmine	34.00	3.75	.85	.17
1989. ARTURO TOSCANINI				
☐2411 25¢ Multicolored	37.00	4.10	.85	.17
1989. BICENTENNIAL: HOUSE OF REPRESENTATIVES				
☐2412 25¢ Multicolored	41.00	4.00	.87	.17
1989. BICENTENNIAL: UNITED STATES SENATE				
☐2413 25¢ Multicolored	42.00	4.10	.90	.17
1989. BICENTENNIAL: EXECUTIVE BRANCH				
☐2414 25¢ Multicolored	41.00	4.00	.92	.17
1989. U.S. SUPREME COURT				
☐2415 25¢ Multicolored	38.00	4.10	.90	.17

*No hinge pricing from 1941 to date is figured at (N-H ADD 10%)

Scott No.	Mint Sheet	Plate Block	Fine Unused Each	Fine Used Each
1989. SOUTH DAKOTA 1889: STATEHOOD				
☐2416 25¢ Multicolored	34.00	3.70	.80	.17
1989. LOU GEHRIG				
☐2417 25¢ Multicolored	52.00	5.00	1.20	.22
1989. ERNEST HEMINGWAY				
☐2418 25¢ Multicolored	36.00	3.90	.82	.17
1989. MOON LANDING				
☐2419 $2.40 Multicolored	140.00	32.00	7.00	.25
1989. LETTER CARRIERS				
☐2420 25¢ Multicolored	26.00	3.50	.75	.17
1989. BILL OF RIGHTS				
☐2421 25¢ Multicolored	46.00	5.00	1.00	.17
1989. DINOSAURS: TYRANNOSAURUS				
☐2422 25¢ Multicolored	52.00	6.50	1.60	.18
1989. DINOSAURS: PTERANODON				
☐2423 25¢ Multicolored	52.00	6.50	1.60	.18
1989. DINOSAURS: STEGOSAURUS				
☐2424 25¢ Multicolored	52.00	6.50	1.60	.18
1989. DINOSAURS: BRONTOSAURUS				
☐2425 25¢ Multicolored	52.00	6.50	1.60	.18
1989. COLUMBIAN ARTIFACTS				
☐2426 25¢ Multicolored	31.00	3.10	.70	.17
1989. CHRISTMAS: MADONNA				
☐2427 25¢ Multicolored	31.00	3.10	.70	.17
1989. CHRISTMAS: SLEIGH				
☐2428 25¢ Multicolored	31.00	3.10	.70	.17

*No hinge pricing from 1941 to date is figured at (N-H ADD 10%)

Scott No.	Mint Sheet	Plate Block	Fine Unused Each	Fine Used Each

1989. MAIL DELIVERY: STAGECOACH

| ☐2434 25¢ Multicolored | 44.00 | 6.10 | 1.45 | .20 |

1989. MAIL DELIVERY: PADDLEWHEEL

| ☐2435 25¢ Multicolored | 44.00 | 6.10 | 1.45 | .20 |

1989. MAIL DELIVERY: BIPLANE

| ☐2436 25¢ Multicolored | 44.00 | 6.10 | 1.45 | .20 |

1989. MAIL DELIVERY: AUTOMOBILE

| ☐2437 25¢ Multicolored | 44.00 | 6.10 | 1.45 | .20 |

1990. COMMEMORATIVES _____
1990. IDAHO CENTENARY: BLUEBIRD

| ☐2439 25¢ Multicolored | 31.00 | 3.10 | .70 | .17 |

1990. LOVE

| ☐2440 25¢ Multicolored | 31.00 | 3.10 | .70 | .17 |

1990. BLACK HERITAGE: IDA B. WELLS

| ☐2442 25¢ Multicolored | 31.00 | 3.10 | .70 | .17 |

1990. BEACH UMBRELLA

| ☐2443 25¢ Multicolored | — | — | .70 | .17 |

1990. WYOMING CENTENARY—MOUNTAIN

| ☐2444 25¢ Multicolored | 35.00 | 3.75 | .80 | .17 |

1990. CLASSIC FILMS: WIZARD OF OZ

| ☐2445 25¢ Multicolored | 86.00 | 9.50 | 4.00 | .17 |

1990. CLASSIC FILMS: GONE WITH THE WIND

| ☐2446 25¢ Multicolored | 86.00 | 9.50 | 4.00 | .17 |

1990. CLASSIC FILMS: BEAU GESTE

| ☐2447 25¢ Multicolored | 86.00 | 9.50 | 4.00 | .17 |

1990. CLASSIC FILMS: STAGECOACH

| ☐2448 25¢ Multicolored | 86.00 | 9.50 | 4.00 | .17 |

*No hinge pricing from 1941 to date is figured at (N-H ADD 10%)

Scott No.	Mint Sheet	Plate Block	Fine Unused Each	Fine Used Each

1990. LITERARY ARTS: MARIANNE MOORE
☐ 2449 25¢ Multicolored	31.00	3.10	.75	.17

1990. TRANSPORTATION
☐ 2451–2464 4¢, 5¢, 10¢, 23¢ Multicolored

	—	3.00	.85	.17

1990. LIGHTHOUSES: ADMIRALTY HEAD
☐ 2470 25¢ Multicolored	—	—	1.25	.17

1990. LIGHTHOUSES: CAPE HATTERAS
☐ 2471 25¢ Multicolored	—	—	1.25	.17

1990. LIGHTHOUSES: WEST QUODDY HEAD
☐ 2472 25¢ Multicolored	—	—	1.25	.17

1990. LIGHTHOUSES: AMERICAN SHOALS
☐ 2473 25¢ Multicolored	—	—	1.25	.17

1990. LIGHTHOUSES: SANDY HOOK
☐ 2474 25¢ Multicolored	—	—	1.25	.17

1990. KESTRAL
☐ 2476 1¢ Multicolored	6.00	.70	.30	.17

1990. BLUEBIRD
☐ 2478 3¢ Multicolored	9.00	.70	.30	.17

1990. FAWN
☐ 2479 19¢ Multicolored	46.00	3.00	.65	.17

1990. CARDINAL
☐ 2480 30¢ Multicolored	65.00	4.00	.70	.17

1990. BOBCAT
☐ 2482 $2.00 Multicolored	84.00	19.10	4.75	.17

1990. WOOD DUCK
☐ 2484–2495 29¢ Black & Multicolored	—		.80	.17

*No hinge pricing from 1941 to date is figured at (N-H ADD 10%)

Scott No.	Mint Sheet	Plate Block	Fine Unused Each	Fine Used Each

1990. OLYMPIANS: JESSE OWENS
| ☐2496 25¢ Multicolored | 38.00 | 12.00 | 1.50 | .35 |

1990. OLYMPIANS: RAY EWRY
| ☐2497 25¢ Multicolored | 38.00 | 12.00 | 1.50 | .35 |

1990. OLYMPIANS: HAZEL WIGHTMAN
| ☐2498 25¢ Multicolored | 38.00 | 12.00 | 1.50 | .35 |

1990. OLYMPIANS: EDDIE EAGAN
| ☐2499 25¢ Multicolored | 38.00 | 12.00 | 1.50 | .35 |

1990. OLYMPIANS: HELENE MADISON
| ☐2500 25¢ Multicolored | 38.00 | 12.00 | 1.50 | .35 |

1990. INDIAN: ASSINIBOINE
| ☐2501 25¢ Multicolored | — | — | 1.00 | .20 |

1990. INDIAN: CHEYENNE
| ☐2502 25¢ Multicolored | — | — | 1.00 | .20 |

1990. INDIAN: COMANCHE
| ☐2503 25¢ Multicolored | — | — | 1.00 | .20 |

1990. INDIAN: FLATHEAD
| ☐2504 25¢ Multicolored | — | — | 1.00 | .20 |

1990. INDIAN: SHOSHONE
| ☐2505 25¢ Multicolored | — | — | 1.00 | .20 |

1990. MICRONESIA
| ☐2506 25¢ Multicolored | 39.00 | 4.10 | 1.00 | .20 |

1990. MARSHALL ISLANDS
| ☐2507 25¢ Multicolored | 39.00 | 4.10 | 1.00 | .20 |

1990. SEA CREATURES: KILLER WHALE
| ☐2508 25¢ Multicolored | 38.00 | 4.20 | 1.00 | .17 |

*No hinge pricing from 1941 to date is figured at (N-H ADD 10%)

Scott No.	Mint Sheet	Plate Block	Fine Unused Each	Fine Used Each

1990. SEA CREATURES: NORTHERN SEA LION

| ☐2509 25¢ Multicolored | 35.00 | 4.25 | 1.25 | .17 |

1990. SEA CREATURES: SEA OTTER

| ☐2510 25¢ Multicolored | 35.00 | 4.25 | 1.25 | .17 |

1990. SEA CREATURES: DOLPHIN

| ☐2511 25¢ Multicolored | 36.00 | 4.25 | 1.25 | .17 |

1990. GRAND CANYON

| ☐2512 25¢ Multicolored | 36.00 | 3.50 | 1.00 | .17 |

1990. DWIGHT D. EISENHOWER

| ☐2513 25¢ Multicolored | 43.00 | 5.10 | 1.00 | .17 |

1990. CHRISTMAS: MADONNA

| ☐2514 25¢ Multicolored | 31.00 | 3.10 | .75 | .17 |

1990. CHRISTMAS: CHRISTMAS TREE

| ☐2515 25¢ Multicolored | 33.00 | 3.40 | .75 | .17 |

1991. "F" FLOWER: TULIP

| ☐2517 29¢ Multicolored | 78.00 | 4.10 | .86 | .17 |

1991. "F" STAMP RATE: EXTRA POSTAGE

| ☐2521 4¢ Multicolored | 12.00 | .80 | .30 | .17 |

1991. FLAG: MT. RUSHMORE

| ☐2523 29¢ Multicolored | — | 6.10 | .80 | .17 |

1991. FLOWER: TULIP

| ☐2524 29¢ Multicolored | 76.00 | 4.10 | .82 | .17 |

1991. FLAG: OLYMPIC RINGS

| ☐2528 29¢ Multicolored | — | — | .82 | .17 |

1991. FISHING BOAT

| ☐2529 19¢ Multicolored | — | 5.50 | .70 | .17 |

*No hinge pricing from 1941 to date is figured at (N-H ADD 10%)

Scott No.	Mint Sheet	Plate Block	Fine Unused Each	Fine Used Each
1991. BALLOONING				
☐2530 19¢ Multicolored	—	—	.72	.21
1991. FLAGS: ON PARADE				
☐2531 29¢ Multicolored	78.00	4.10	.90	.21
1991. COMMEMORATIVES ▬▬▬▬▬▬				
1991. SWITZERLAND: 700TH ANNIVERSARY				
☐2532 50¢ Multicolored	58.00	7.00	1.50	.34
1991. VERMONT: BICENTENNIAL				
☐2533 29¢ Multicolored	42.00	4.00	.90	.25
1991. SAVINGS BONDS: 50TH ANNIVERSARY				
☐2534 29¢ Multicolored	39.00	4.00	.82	.24
1991. LOVE: HEART				
☐2535 29¢ Multicolored	36.00	4.00	.82	.17
1991. LOVE				
☐2536 29¢ Multicolored	—	—	.90	.24
1991. LOVE: LOVE BIRDS				
☐2537 52¢ Multicolored	68.00	6.00	1.50	.38
1991. LITERARY ARTS: WILLIAM SAROYAN				
☐2538 29¢ Multicolored	36.00	3.40	.70	.21
1991. USPS: OLYMPIC RINGS				
☐2539 $1.00 Multicolored	51.00	12.00	3.10	.60
1991. EAGLE: OLYMPIC RINGS				
☐2540 $2.90 Multicolored	155.00	36.00	8.40	2.75
1991. DOMESTIC: EXPRESS MAIL				
☐2541 $9.95 Multicolored	500.00	120.00	24.00	10.00
1991. INTERNATIONAL: EXPRESS MAIL				
☐2542 $14.00 Multicolored	650.00	140.00	34.00	21.00
1991. SPACE VEHICLE				
☐2543 $2.90 Multicolored	280.00	34.00	7.50	2.60
1991. SPACE SHUTTLE				
☐2544 $3.00 Multicolored	140.00	30.00	7.60	3.00
1991. FISHING FLIES				
☐2545 29¢ Multicolored	—	—	1.50	.29
☐2546 29¢ Multicolored	—	—	1.50	.29

*No hinge pricing from 1941 to date is figured at (N-H ADD 10%)

Scott No.	Mint Sheet	Plate Block	Fine Unused Each	Fine Used Each
☐2547 29¢ Multicolored	—	—	1.50	.25
☐2548 29¢ Multicolored	—	—	1.50	.25
☐2549 29¢ Multicolored	—	—	1.50	.25

1991. PERFORMING ARTS: COLE PORTER

☐2550 29¢ Multicolored	42.00	4.10	.92	.25

1991. DESERT STORM: SOUTHWEST ASIA

☐2551 29¢ Multicolored	36.00	3.75	.80	.25

1991. 1992 SUMMER OLYMPICS: BARCELONA

☐2553 29¢ Multicolored	36.00	10.00	4.50	1.00
☐2554 29¢ Multicolored	36.00	10.00	4.50	1.00
☐2555 29¢ Multicolored	36.00	10.00	4.50	1.00
☐2556 29¢ Multicolored	36.00	10.00	4.50	1.00
☐2557 29¢ Multicolored	36.00	10.00	4.50	1.00

1991. NUMISMATICS: COINS AND NOTES

☐2558 29¢ Multicolored	46.00	4.60	1.10	.25

1991. WORLD WAR II

☐2559 29¢ Multicolored	20.00	6.00	1.10	.75

1991. BASKETBALL: 100TH ANNIVERSARY

☐2560 29¢ Multicolored	48.00	4.40	1.10	.25

1991. DISTRICT OF COLUMBIA: BICENTENNIAL

☐2561 29¢ Multicolored	34.00	3.50	.80	.25

1991. COMEDIANS

☐2562 29¢ Multicolored	—	—	.80	.25
☐2563 29¢ Multicolored	—	—	.80	.25
☐2564 29¢ Multicolored	—	—	.80	.25
☐2565 29¢ Multicolored	—	—	.80	.25
☐2566 29¢ Multicolored	—	—	.80	.25

1991. BLACK HERITAGE

☐2567 29¢ Multicolored	41.00	4.50	.90	.25

*No hinge pricing from 1941 to date is figured at (N-H ADD 10%)

Scott No.	Mint Sheet	Plate Block	Fine Unused Each	Fine Used Each
1991. SPACE EXPLORATION				
☐2568 29¢ Multicolored	—	—	1.00	.25
☐2569 29¢ Multicolored	—	—	1.00	.25
☐2570 29¢ Multicolored	—	—	1.00	.25
☐2571 29¢ Multicolored	—	—	1.00	.25
☐2572 29¢ Multicolored	—	—	1.00	.25
☐2573 29¢ Multicolored	—	—	1.00	.25
☐2574 29¢ Multicolored	—	—	1.00	.25
☐2575 29¢ Multicolored	—	—	1.00	.25
☐2576 29¢ Multicolored	—	—	1.00	.25
☐2577 29¢ Multicolored	—	—	1.00	.25
1991. CHRISTMAS				
☐2578 29¢ Multicolored	34.50	3.75	.85	.20
☐2579 29¢ Multicolored	34.50	3.75	.85	.20
☐2582 29¢ Multicolored	34.50	3.75	.85	.20
☐2583 29¢ Multicolored	34.50	3.75	.85	.20
☐2584 29¢ Multicolored	34.50	3.75	.85	.20
☐2585 29¢ Multicolored	34.50	3.75	.85	.20
1991–1993. COIL ISSUES				
1992. BULK RATE				
☐2604 10¢ Multicolored	—	3.75	.60	.21
☐2607 23¢ Multicolored	—	5.00	.70	.21
☐2608 23¢ Multicolored	—	5.00	.70	.21
☐2609 29¢ Multicolored	—	5.00	.75	.21
1992. COMMEMORATIVES				
1992. WINTER OLYMPICS				
☐2611 29¢ Multicolored	34.00	9.00	1.00	.21
☐2612 29¢ Multicolored	—	—	1.00	.21
☐2613 29¢ Multicolored	—	—	1.00	.21
☐2614 29¢ Multicolored	—	—	1.00	.21
☐2615 29¢ Multicolored	—	—	1.00	.21
1992. WORLD COLUMBIAN STAMP EXPO				
☐2616 29¢ Multicolored	34.00	4.00	.80	.21

*No hinge pricing from 1941 to date is figured at (N-H ADD 10%)

Scott No.	Mint Sheet	Plate Block	Fine Unused Each	Fine Used Each

1992. BLACK HERITAGE
| ☐2617 29¢ Multicolored | 40.00 | 4.75 | .90 | .22 |

1992. LOVE
| ☐2618 29¢ Multicolored | 34.00 | 3.75 | .80 | .22 |

1992. OLYMPIC BASEBALL
| ☐2619 29¢ Multicolored | 56.00 | 5.50 | 1.25 | .22 |

1992. VOYAGES OF COLUMBUS
☐2620 29¢ Multicolored	35.50	4.40	3.00	.28
☐2621 29¢ Multicolored	35.50	—	3.00	.28
☐2622 29¢ Multicolored	35.50	—	3.00	.28
☐2623 29¢ Multicolored	35.50	—	3.00	.28

1992. NEW YORK STOCK EXCHANGE BICENTENNIAL
| ☐2630 29¢ Green, Red & Black | 27.00 | 4.00 | .80 | .22 |

1992. SPACE ACCOMPLISHMENTS
☐2631 29¢ Multicolored	45.00	4.75	1.50	.21
☐2632 29¢ Multicolored	—	—	1.50	.21
☐2633 29¢ Multicolored	—	—	1.50	.21
☐2634 29¢ Multicolored	—	—	1.50	.21

1992. ALASKA HIGHWAY—50TH ANNIVERSARY
| ☐2635 29¢ Multicolored | 34.00 | 3.75 | .80 | .22 |

1992. KENTUCKY STATEHOOD BICENTENNIAL
| ☐2636 29¢ Multicolored | 36.00 | 3.60 | .80 | .22 |

1992. SUMMER OLYMPICS
☐2637 29¢ Multicolored	32.00	10.50	2.00	.22
☐2638 29¢ Multicolored	32.00	10.50	2.00	.22
☐2639 29¢ Multicolored	32.00	10.50	2.00	.22
☐2640 29¢ Multicolored	32.00	10.50	2.00	.22
☐2641 29¢ Multicolored	32.00	10.50	2.00	.22

*No hinge pricing from 1941 to date is figured at (N-H ADD 10%)

Scott No.	Mint Sheet	Plate Block	Fine Unused Each	Fine Used Each

1992. HUMMINGBIRDS

☐ 2642 29¢ Multicolored	—	—	1.00	.22
☐ 2643 29¢ Multicolored	—	—	1.00	.22
☐ 2644 29¢ Multicolored	—	—	1.00	.22
☐ 2645 29¢ Multicolored	—	—	1.00	.22
☐ 2646 29¢ Multicolored	—	—	1.00	.22

1992. WILD FLOWERS

☐ 29¢ Multicolored	47.00	38.00 (50)	1.30	.45

☐ 2647 Indian Paintbrush
☐ 2648 Fragrant Water Lily
☐ 2649 Meadow Beauty
☐ 2650 Jack-in-the-Pulpit
☐ 2651 California Poppy
☐ 2652 Large Flower Trillium
☐ 2653 Tickseed
☐ 2654 Shooting Star
☐ 2655 Stream Violet
☐ 2656 Bluets
☐ 2657 Herb Robert
☐ 2658 Marsh Marigold
☐ 2659 Sweet White Violet
☐ 2660 Claret Cup Cactus
☐ 2661 White Mountain Avens
☐ 2662 Sessile Bellwort
☐ 2663 Blue Flag
☐ 2664 Harlequin Lupine
☐ 2665 Twin Flower
☐ 2666 Common Sunflower
☐ 2667 Sego Lily
☐ 2668 Virginia Bluebells
☐ 2669 Ohi'a Lehua
☐ 2670 Rosebud Orchid
☐ 2671 Showy Evening Primrose
☐ 2672 Fringed Gentian
☐ 2673 Yellow Lady's Slipper
☐ 2674 Passion Flower
☐ 2675 Bunch Berry
☐ 2676 Pasque Flower
☐ 2677 Round-Lobed Hepatica
☐ 2678 Wild Columbine
☐ 2679 Firewood
☐ 2680 Indian Pond Lily
☐ 2681 Turk's Cap Lily
☐ 2682 Dutchman's Breeches
☐ 2683 Trumpet Honeysuckle
☐ 2684 Jacob's Ladder
☐ 2685 Plains Prickly Pear
☐ 2686 Mots Campion
☐ 2687 Bearberry
☐ 2688 Mexican Hat
☐ 2689 Harebell
☐ 2690 Desert Five Spot
☐ 2691 Smooth Solomon's Seal
☐ 2692 Red Maids

*No hinge pricing from 1941 to date is figured at (N-H ADD 10%)

☐2693 Yellow Skunk Cabbage ☐2695 Standing Cypress
☐2694 Rue Anemone ☐2696 Wild Flax

Scott No.	Mint Sheet	Plate Block	Fine Unused Each	Fine Used Each
1992. WORLD WAR II				
☐2697 29¢ Multicolored	20.00	—	.90	.46
1992. LITERARY ART SERIES				
☐2698 29¢ Multicolored	34.50	3.60	.72	.21
1992. THEODORE VON KÁRMÁN				
☐2699 29¢ Multicolored	35.00	3.60	.80	.21
1992. MINERALS				
☐2700 29¢ Multicolored	37.00	4.60	.80	.21
☐2701 29¢ Multicolored	37.00	4.60	.80	.21
☐2702 29¢ Multicolored	37.00	4.60	.80	.21
☐2703 29¢ Multicolored	37.00	4.60	.80	.21
1992. JUAN RODRÍGUEZ CABRILLO				
☐2704 29¢ Multicolored	34.00	3.60	.70	.21
1992. WILD ANIMALS				
☐2705 29¢ Multicolored	—	—	1.10	.21
☐2706 29¢ Multicolored	—	—	1.10	.21
☐2707 29¢ Multicolored	—	—	1.10	.21
☐2708 29¢ Multicolored	—	—	1.10	.21
☐2709 29¢ Multicolored	—	—	1.10	.21
☐2709a 29¢ Multicolored Five Above Attached				
	—	—	4.90	.21
1992. MADONNA AND CHILD				
☐2710 29¢ Multicolored	35.00	3.60	.85	.21
1992. GREETINGS—HORSE AND RIDER				
☐2711 29¢ Multicolored	41.00	4.50	1.10	.21

*No hinge pricing from 1941 to date is figured at (N-H ADD 10%)

Scott No.	Mint Sheet	Plate Block	Fine Unused Each	Fine Used Each

1992. GREETINGS—TOY LOCOMOTIVE
☐2712 29¢ Multicolored 44.00 4.60 1.00 .18

1992. GREETINGS—TOY FIRE PUMPER
☐2713 29¢ Multicolored 44.00 4.60 1.00 .18

1992. GREETINGS—RIVERBOAT ON WHEELS
☐2714 29¢ Multicolored 44.00 4.60 1.00 .18

1992. HAPPY NEW YEAR
☐2720 29¢ Multicolored 19.00 4.00 .95 .18

1993. COMMEMORATIVES ————————
1993. ELVIS
☐2721 29¢ Multicolored 32.00 4.50 1.00 .18

1993. OKLAHOMA
☐2722 29¢ Multicolored 28.00 3.75 .80 .18

1993. HANK WILLIAMS
☐2723 29¢ Multicolored 28.00 3.75 .80 .18

1993. AMERICAN MUSIC—ELVIS PRESLEY
☐2724 29¢ Multicolored 38.00 10.00 (10) .80 .18

1993. AMERICAN MUSIC—BILL HALEY
☐2725 29¢ Multicolored 38.00 10.00 (10) .80 .18

1993. AMERICAN MUSIC—CLYDE McPHATTER
☐2726 29¢ Multicolored 38.00 10.00 (10) .80 .18

1993. AMERICAN MUSIC—RITCHIE VALENS
☐2727 29¢ Multicolored 38.00 10.00 (10) .80 .18

1993. AMERICAN MUSIC—OTIS REDDING
☐2728 29¢ Multicolored 38.00 10.00 (10) .80 .18

1993. AMERICAN MUSIC—BUDDY HOLLY
☐2729 29¢ Multicolored 38.00 10.00 (10) .80 .18

*No hinge pricing from 1941 to date is figured at (N-H ADD 10%)

Scott No.	Mint Sheet	Plate Block	Fine Unused Each	Fine Used Each
1993. AMERICAN MUSIC—DINAH WASHINGTON				
☐2730 29¢ Multicolored	36.00	9.00 (10)	.90	.25
1993. SPACE FANTASY				
☐2741 29¢ Multicolored	—	—	.90	.25
☐2742 29¢ Multicolored	—	—	.90	.25
☐2743 29¢ Multicolored	—	—	.90	.25
☐2744 29¢ Multicolored	—	—	.90	.25
☐2745 29¢ Multicolored	—	—	.90	.25
1993. PERCY LAVON JULIAN				
☐2746 29¢ Multicolored	37.00	3.80	.85	.25
1993. OREGON TRAIL				
☐2747 29¢ Multicolored	36.00	3.40	.70	.25
1993. WORLD UNIVERSITY GAMES				
☐2748 29¢ Multicolored	38.00	3.90	.80	.25
1993. GRACE KELLY				
☐2749 29¢ Multicolored	36.00	3.50	.70	.25
1993. CIRCUS				
☐2750 29¢ Multicolored	39.00	7.00 (6)	.90	.25
☐2751 29¢ Multicolored	39.00	7.00 (6)	.90	.25
☐2752 29¢ Multicolored	39.00	7.00 (6)	.90	.25
☐2753 29¢ Multicolored	39.00	7.00 (6)	.90	.25
1993. CHEROKEE STRIP LAND RUN				
☐2754 29¢ Multicolored	17.00	3.75	.82	.25
1993. DEAN ACHESON				
☐2755 29¢ Multicolored	34.00	3.50	.70	.25
1993. SPORTING HORSES				
☐2756 29¢ Multicolored	38.00	4.90	1.25	.32
☐2757 29¢ Multicolored	38.00	4.90	1.25	.32

*No hinge pricing from 1941 to date is figured at (N-H ADD 10%)

Scott No.	Mint Sheet	Plate Block	Fine Unused Each	Fine Used Each
☐2758 29¢ Multicolored	38.00	4.90	1.25	.32
☐2759 29¢ Multicolored	38.00	4.90	1.25	.32

1993. GARDEN FLOWERS
☐2760 29¢ Multicolored	—	—	1.00	.25
☐2761 29¢ Multicolored	—	—	1.00	.25
☐2762 29¢ Multicolored	—	—	1.00	.25
☐2763 29¢ Multicolored	—	—	1.00	.25
☐2764 29¢ Multicolored	—	—	1.00	.25

1993. WORLD WAR II 1943
☐2765 29¢ Multicolored	20.00	—	1.00	.50

1993. JOE LOUIS
☐2766 Multicolored	48.00	5.00	.95	.35

1993. BROADWAY MUSICALS
☐2767 29¢ Multicolored	—	4.00	1.00	.25
☐2768 29¢ Multicolored	—	4.00	1.00	.25
☐2769 29¢ Multicolored	—	4.00	1.00	.25
☐2770 29¢ Multicolored	—	4.00	1.00	.25

1993. NATIONAL POSTAL MUSEUM
☐2779 29¢ Multicolored	21.00	4.50	.90	.24
☐2780 29¢ Multicolored	21.00	4.50	.90	.24
☐2781 29¢ Multicolored	21.00	4.50	.90	.24
☐2782 29¢ Multicolored	21.00	4.50	.90	.24

1993. MARIANA ISLANDS
☐2804 29¢ Multicolored	16.50	4.00	.80	.24

1993. COLUMBUS LANDING
☐2805 29¢ Multicolored	37.00	3.75	1.00	.24

1993. AIDS AWARENESS
☐2806 29¢ Multicolored	41.00	4.00	1.00	.24

*No hinge pricing from 1941 to date is figured at (N-H ADD 10%)

Scott No.	Mint Sheet	Plate Block	Fine Unused Each	Fine Used Each

1994. COMMEMORATIVES _____

1994. WINTER OLYMPICS
☐2807 29¢ Multicolored	16.50	10.00	.90	.27
☐2808 29¢ Multicolored	16.50	10.00	.90	.27
☐2809 29¢ Multicolored	16.50	10.00	.90	.27
☐2810 29¢ Multicolored	16.50	10.00	.90	.27
☐2811 29¢ Multicolored	16.50	10.00	.90	.27

1994. EDWARD R. MURROW
☐2812 29¢ Brown	37.00	3.60	.85	.27

1994. LOVE
☐2813 29¢ Multicolored	—	—	.75	.25
☐2814 29¢ Multicolored	—	—	.75	.25
☐2815 52¢ Multicolored	70.00	7.40	1.40	.25

1994. BLACK HERITAGE
☐2816 29¢ Multicolored	15.00	3.90	.90	.25

1994. CHINESE NEW YEAR
☐2817 29¢ Multicolored	28.00	5.00	1.10	.25

1994. BUFFALO SOLDIERS
☐2818 29¢ Multicolored	16.00	3.90	.88	.25

1994. SILENT SCREEN STARS
☐2819 29¢ Multicolored	—	—	1.00	.28
☐2820 29¢ Multicolored	—	—	1.00	.28
☐2821 29¢ Multicolored	—	—	1.00	.28
☐2822 29¢ Multicolored	—	—	1.00	.28
☐2823 29¢ Multicolored	—	—	1.00	.28
☐2824 29¢ Multicolored	—	—	1.00	.28
☐2825 29¢ Multicolored	—	—	1.00	.28
☐2826 29¢ Multicolored	—	—	1.00	.28
☐2827 29¢ Multicolored	—	—	1.00	.28
☐2828 29¢ Multicolored	—	—	1.00	.28
☐2828a 29¢ Multicolored	30.00	7.00	1.00	.28

1994. GARDEN FLOWERS
☐2829 29¢ Multicolored	—	—	1.00	.28

*No hinge pricing from 1941 to date is figured at (N-H ADD 10%)

Scott No.	Mint Sheet	Plate Block	Fine Unused Each	Fine Used Each
☐2830 29¢ Multicolored	—	—	1.00	.28
☐2831 29¢ Multicolored	—	—	1.00	.28
☐2832 29¢ Multicolored	—	—	1.00	.28
☐2833 29¢ Multicolored	—	—	1.00	.28

1994. WORLD CUP SOCCER

☐2834 29¢ Multicolored	17.00	4.50	.91	.28
☐2835 40¢ Multicolored	21.00	5.50	.91	.28
☐2836 50¢ Multicolored	27.00	6.25	1.50	.28
☐2837 29¢ -40¢ -50¢ Souvenir Sheet				
	—	—	5.00	3.50

1994. WORLD WAR II

☐2838 29¢ Multicolored	20.00	10.00	1.00	.40

1994. NORMAN ROCKWELL

☐2839 29¢ Multicolored	40.00	4.30	1.00	.36
☐2840 50¢ Multicolored	—	—	6.00	3.75

1994. MOON LANDING ANNIVERSARY

☐2841 29¢ Multicolored	—	—	1.25	.75
☐2842 $9.95 Multicolored	485.00	120.00	27.00	12.00

1994. LOCOMOTIVES

☐2843 29¢ Multicolored	—	—	1.00	.30
☐2844 29¢ Multicolored	—	—	1.00	.30
☐2845 29¢ Multicolored	—	—	1.00	.30
☐2846 29¢ Multicolored	—	—	1.00	.30
☐2847 29¢ Multicolored	—	—	1.00	.30

1994. GEORGE MEANY

☐2848 29¢ Multicolored	38.00	4.00	.80	.30

1995. COMMEMORATIVES_____
1995. POPULAR SINGERS

☐2849–53 29¢ Multicolored	22.00	6.50 (10)	1.00	.30

1995. JAZZ/BLUES SINGERS

☐2854–61 29¢ Multicolored	40.00	12.00 (10)	1.00	.30

1995. JAMES THURBER

☐2862 29¢ Red, Blue, Black	36.00	4.00	1.00	.30

*No hinge pricing from 1941 to date is figured at (N-H ADD 10%)

Scott No.	Mint Sheet	Plate Block	Fine Unused Each	Fine Used Each

1995. WONDERS OF THE SEA
| ☐ 2863–66 29¢ Multicolored | 26.00 | 4.10 | .90 | .28 |

1995. CRANES
| ☐ 2867–68 29¢ Multicolored | 18.00 | 4.10 | .90 | .28 |

1995. LEGENDS OF THE WEST (SHEET OF 20)
☐ 2869 29¢ Multicolored	115.00	—	13.50	10.00
Single Stamps			1.00	.60
☐ 2870* 29¢ Multicolored	345.00	—	34.00	18.00

*error sheet Bill Picket recalled.

1995. CHRISTMAS
☐ 2871 29¢ "Elisabetta Sirani," Multicolored				
	36.00	4.00	.80	.30
☐ 2872 29¢ Teddy bear stocking, Multicolored				
	36.00	4.00	.80	.30
☐ 2873 Self-adhesive, 29¢ Santa	—	—	.80	.30
☐ 2874 Self-adhesive, 29¢ Cardinal	—	—	.80	.30

1995. BUREAU OF PRINTING AND ENGRAVING (SHEET OF 4)
| ☐ 2875 2¢ Multicolored | — | — | 20.00 | 13.00 |
| Single Stamps | — | — | 5.00 | 2.40 |

1995. YEAR OF THE BOAR
| ☐ 2876 29¢ Multicolored | 17.00 | 4.50 | .90 | .30 |

1995. REGULAR ISSUES
1995. DOVES
☐ 2877 4¢ Tan, Bright Blue, Red G, Make up rate				
	9.00	.80	.33	.20
☐ 2878 4¢ Tan, Dark Blue, Red G, Make up rate				
	11.00	1.00	.33	.20

1995. SERIES G STAMP FLAGS
☐ 2879 20¢ Black G, Yellow, Multicolored				
	55.00	6.00	.75	.20
☐ 2880 20¢ Red G, Yellow, Multicolored				
	55.00	8.00	.90	.20

*No hinge pricing from 1941 to date is figured at (N-H ADD 10%)

Scott No.	Mint Sheet	Plate Block	Fine Unused Each	Fine Used Each
☐2881 32¢ Black G, White, Multicolored				
	90.00	7.50	.90	.25
☐2882 32¢ Red G, White, Multicolored				
	84.00	5.00	.90	.25
☐2883 Booklet 32¢ Black G, White, Multicolored				
	—	—	.90	.25
☐2884 Booklet 32¢ Blue G, White, Multicolored				
	—	—	.90	.25
☐2885 Booklet 32¢ Red G, White, Multicolored				
	—	—	.90	.25
☐2886 Booklet, Self adhesive 32¢ Black G, White, Multicolored				
	—	—	.90	.25
☐2887 Self adhesive 32¢ Black G, White, Multicolored				
	—	—	.90	.25
☐2888 Coil 25¢ Black G, First class presort, Blue, Multicolored				
	—	6.20	.90	.25
☐2889 Coil 32¢ Black G, White, Multicolored				
	—	6.25	.90	.25
☐2890 Coil 32¢ Blue G, White, Multicolored				
	—	6.40	.90	.25
☐2891 Coil 32¢ Red G, White, Multicolored				
	—	6.40	.90	.25
☐2892 Coil, Rouletted, 32¢ Red G, White, Multicolored				
	—	6.40	.90	.25
☐2893 Coil 5¢ Black G, Non-profit, Green, Multicolored				
	—	3.00	.40	.25
☐2894–96 NOT ISSUED				
☐2897 32¢ Flag over porch, Multicolored				
	78.00	4.50	.90	.25
☐2898–01 NOT ISSUED				
☐2902 Coil 5¢ Butte, Non-Profit, Multicolored				
	—	3.00	.40	.25
☐2903–04 NOT ISSUED				
☐2905 Coil 10¢ Automobile, Bulk rate, Black Orange				
	—	3.50	.40	.25
☐2906–07 NOT ISSUED				
☐2908–09 Coil 15¢ Auto Tailfin, First class presort, Multicolored				
	—	4.50	.70	.25

☐2910 NOT ISSUED

*No hinge pricing from 1941 to date is figured at (N-H ADD 10%)

Scott No.	Mint Sheet	Plate Block	Fine Unused Each	Fine Used Each
☐2911–12 Coil 25¢ Juke Box, First class presort, Multicolored				
	—	5.40	.90	.50
☐2913–14 Coil 25¢ Flag over porch, Presort, Multicolored				
	—	6.50	.90	.50
☐2915 Self-adhesive, 25¢ Flag over porch, Presort, Multicolored				
	—	7.50	.90	.50
☐2916 Booklet, 25¢ Flag over porch, Presort, Multicolored				
	—	—	.90	.32
☐2917–18 NOT ISSUED				
☐2919 Booklet, Self-adhesive 32¢ Flag over field				
	—	—	.90	.32
☐2920 Booklet, Self-adhesive 32¢ Flag over porch				
	—	—	.90	.32
☐2921–32 NOT ISSUED				

1995. COMMEMORATIVES (CONTINUED)
1995. GREAT AMERICAN ISSUE—MILTON HERSHEY

☐2933 32¢ Brown	70.00	4.20	.90	.32

1996. HUMANITARY—FARLEY

☐2934 32¢ Green	70.00	4.20	.90	.32

1998. HENRY R. LUCE

☐2935 32¢ Multicolored	15.00 (20)	4.20 (4)	.90	.25

1998. LILA & DEWITT WALLACE

☐2936 32¢ Multicolored	15.00 (20)	4.20 (4)	.90	.25

1995. GREAT AMERICAN ISSUE—RUTH BENEDICT

☐2938 46¢ Red	110.00	6.50	1.25	.32
☐2939 NOT ISSUED				

1995. GREAT AMERICAN ISSUE—ALICE HAMILTON, MD

☐2940 55¢ Green	120.00	6.50	1.25	.32
☐2941–42 NOT ISSUED				

1995. GREAT AMERICAN ISSUE—ALICE PAUL

☐2943 78¢ Purple	170.00	6.00	1.90	.32
☐2944–47 NOT ISSUED				

*No hinge pricing from 1941 to date is figured at (N-H ADD 10%)

Scott No.	Mint Sheet	Plate Block	Fine Unused Each	Fine Used Each

1995. NON-DENOMINATIONAL LOVE
☐2948 32¢ Multicolored	37.00	4.10	.80	.28
☐2949 Booklet self-adhesive	—	—	.80	.28

1995. FLORIDA STATEHOOD
☐2950 32¢ Multicolored	18.00	4.00	.80	.28

1995. KID'S CARE (EARTH DAY)
☐2951–54 32¢ Multicolored	16.00	4.80	2.00	1.25

1995. RICHARD NIXON
☐2955 32¢ Multicolored	37.00	3.90	.80	.32

1995. BESSIE COLEMAN
☐2956 32¢ Black, Red	37.00	4.00	.85	.32

1995. LOVE CHERUB
☐2957 32¢ Multicolored	37.00	7.00	1.00	.30
☐2958 55¢ Multicolored	74.00	—	1.20	.30
☐2959 Booklet 32¢ Multicolored	—	—	1.00	.27
☐2960 Self-adhesive 55¢ Multicolored	—	—	1.30	.46

1995. RECREATIONAL SPORTS
☐2961–65 32¢ Multicolored	19.00	10.00 (10)	1.00	.26

1995. POWs/MIAs
☐2966 32¢ Multicolored	16.00	4.00	.85	.26

1995. MARILYN MONROE
☐2967 32¢ Multicolored	30.00	5.50	.90	.26

1995. TEXAS STATEHOOD
☐2968 32¢ Multicolored	17.00	4.10	.90	.26

1995. GREAT LAKES LIGHTHOUSES
☐2969–73 Booklet 32¢ Multicolored	—	—	4.50	2.00
Single Stamps			1.00	.26

1995. UNITED NATIONS
☐2974 32¢ Light Blue	14.50	4.10	.90	.26

*No hinge pricing from 1941 to date is figured at (N-H ADD 10%)

Scott No.	Mint Sheet	Plate Block	Fine Unused Each	Fine Used Each
1995. CIVIL WAR (SHEET OF 20 DIFFERENT)				
☐2975 32¢ Multicolored	30.00	—	4.00	1.00
1995. CAROUSEL HORSES				
☐2976–79 32¢ Multicolored	18.00	4.10	1.00	.26
1995. WOMEN'S SUFFERAGE				
☐2980 32¢ Multicolored	31.00	4.00	.90	.26
1995. 1945: WW II VICTORY AT LAST (SHEET OF 10)				
☐2981 32¢ Multicolored	20.00	—	.90	.50
1995. LOUIS ARMSTRONG				
☐2982 32¢ (White 32¢) Multicolored				
	18.00	4.10	1.00	.28
1995. JAZZ MUSICIANS				
☐2983–92 32¢ Multicolored	15.00	10.00 (10)	.90	.47
1995. FALL GARDEN FLOWERS				
☐2993–97 32¢ Multicolored	—	—	1.00	.26
1995. EDDIE RICKENBACKER				
☐2998 60¢ Multicolored	80.00	8.00	1.80	.50
1995. REPUBLIC OF PALAU				
☐2999 32¢ Multicolored	40.00	4.10	.85	.26
1995. COMIC STRIP CLASSICS (SHEET OF 20)				
☐3000 32¢ Multicolored	20.00	—	15.00	9.00
Single Stamps			.90	.65
1995. U.S. NAVAL ACADEMY				
☐3001 32¢ Multicolored	15.50	3.60	.85	.27
1995. TENNESSEE WILLIAMS				
☐3002 32¢ Multicolored	17.00	4.00	1.00	.27
1995. HOLIDAY MADONNA AND CHILD				
☐3003 32¢ Multicolored	37.00	4.00	.85	.27

*No hinge pricing from 1941 to date is figured at (N-H ADD 10%)

Scott No.	Mint Sheet	Plate Block	Fine Unused Each	Fine Used Each

1995. HOLIDAY CHILDREN AND SANTA

| ☐3004–07 32¢ Multicolored | 41.00 | 4.00 | .70 | .28 |
| ☐3008–11 Self-adhesive | — | — | .70 | .28 |

1995. MIDNIGHT ANGEL

☐3012 Self-adhesive, 32¢ Multicolored

| | | | .70 | .28 |

1995. CHILDREN SLEDDING

| ☐3013 32¢ Multicolored | — | — | .70 | .28 |
| ☐3014–18 NOT ISSUED |

1995. ANTIQUE AUTOMOBILES

| ☐3019–23 32¢ Multicolored | 21.00 | 9.00 (10) | .70 | .30 |

1996. COMMEMORATIVES ———————
1996. UTAH 1896

| ☐3024 32¢ Multicolored | 36.00 | 4.00 | .70 | .28 |

1996. FLOWER—CROCUS

| ☐3025 32¢ Multicolored | — | — | .70 | .28 |

1996. FLOWER—WINTER ACONITE

| ☐3026 32¢ Multicolored | — | — | .70 | .28 |

1996. FLOWER—PANSY

| ☐3027 32¢ Multicolored | — | — | .70 | .28 |

1996. FLOWER—SNOWDROP

| ☐3028 32¢ Multicolored | — | — | .70 | .28 |

1996. FLOWER—ANEMONE

| ☐3029 32¢ Multicolored | — | — | .70 | .28 |

1996. LOVE ANGEL

☐3030 Self-adhesive 32¢ Multicolored

| | | | .70 | .28 |

1996 WOODPECKER

| ☐3032 2¢ Multicolored | 6.50 | .90 | .40 | .28 |

1996. EASTERN BLUEBIRD

| ☐3033 3¢ Multicolored | 7.00 | .90 | .52 | .28 |

*No hinge pricing from 1941 to date is figured at (N-H ADD 10%)

Scott No.	Mint Sheet	Plate Block	Fine Unused Each	Fine Used Each

1996. AMERICAN KESTREL
| ☐3044 1¢ Multicolored | — | 1.00 | .40 | .27 |

1996. BLUE JAY
☐3048 Self-adhesive 20¢ Multicolored
| | — | — | .40 | .27 |

1996. YELLOW ROSE
☐3049 Self-adhesive 32¢ Multicolored
| | — | — | .75 | .27 |

1998. RING-NECKED PHEASANT
| ☐3055 20¢ Multicolored | — | — | .65 | .27 |

1996. BLACK HERITAGE—ERNEST E. JUST: BIOLOGIST
| ☐3058 32¢ Multicolored | 17.00 | 4.00 | .85 | .27 |

1996. SMITHSONIAN INSTITUTION 1846–1996
| ☐3059 32¢ Multicolored | 15.00 | 3.40 | .65 | .27 |

1996. HAPPY NEW YEAR—RAT
| ☐3060 32¢ Multicolored | 18.00 | 4.00 | .90 | .27 |

1996. COMMUNICATION—EADWEARD MUYBRIDGE
| ☐3061 32¢ Multicolored | 16.50 | 4.10 | .90 | .27 |

1996. COMMUNICATION—OTTMAR MERGENTHALER
| ☐3062 32¢ Multicolored | 15.00 | 4.00 | .85 | .27 |

1996. COMMUNICATION—FREDRICK E. IVES
| ☐3063 32¢ Multicolored | 15.00 | 4.00 | .85 | .27 |

1996. COMMUNICATION—WILLIAM DICKSON
| ☐3064 32¢ Multicolored | 15.00 | 4.00 | .85 | .27 |

1996. FULBRIGHT SCHOLARSHIPS
| ☐3065 32¢ Multicolored | 37.00 | 3.80 | .85 | .27 |

*No hinge pricing from 1941 to date is figured at (N-H ADD 10%)

Scott No.	Mint Sheet	Plate Block	Fine Unused Each	Fine Used Each

1996. PIONEER PILOT—JACQUELINE COCHRAN
| ☐3066 50¢ Multicolored | 62.00 | 6.00 | 1.40 | .38 |

1996. MARATHON
| ☐3067 32¢ Multicolored | 15.00 | 4.00 | .85 | .30 |

1996. ATLANTA OLYMPIC GAMES (SHEET OF 20)
| ☐3068 32¢ Multicolored | 18.00 | — | 12.00 | 9.00 |
| Single Stamps | — | — | .90 | .50 |

1996. GEORGIA O'KEEFFE
| ☐3069 32¢ Multicolored | 13.50 | — | .88 | .30 |

1996. TENNESSEE—1796
☐3070 32¢ Multicolored	37.00	4.10	.85	.30
☐3071 Self-adhesive 32¢ Multicolored				
	—	—	.90	.30

1996. INDIAN—FANCY DANCE
| ☐3072 32¢ Multicolored | 17.00 | 10.00 (10) | .90 | .30 |

1996. INDIAN—BUTTERFLY DANCE
| ☐3073 32¢ Multicolored | 17.00 | 10.00 (10) | .90 | .30 |

1996. INDIAN—TRADITIONAL DANCE
| ☐3074 32¢ Multicolored | 17.00 | 10.00 (10) | .90 | .30 |

1996. INDIAN—RAVEN DANCE
| ☐3075 32¢ Multicolored | 17.00 | 10.00 (10) | .90 | .30 |

1996. INDIAN—HOOP DANCE
| ☐3076 32¢ Multicolored | 17.00 | 10.00 (10) | .90 | .30 |

1996. PREHISTORIC ANIMALS—EOHIPPUS
| ☐3077 32¢ Multicolored | 18.00 | 4.00 | .90 | .30 |

1996. PREHISTORIC ANIMALS—WOOLY MAMMOTH
| ☐3078 32¢ Multicolored | 17.00 | 4.00 | .90 | .30 |

1996. PREHISTORIC ANIMALS—MASTODON
| ☐3079 32¢ Multicolored | 17.00 | 4.00 | .90 | .30 |

*No hinge pricing from 1941 to date is figured at (N-H ADD 10%)

Scott No.	Mint Sheet	Plate Block	Fine Unused Each	Fine Used Each

1996. PREHISTORIC ANIMALS—SABER-TOOTH CAT
☐3080 32¢ Multicolored | 17.00 | 4.50 | .90 | .26

1996. BREAST CANCER AWARENESS
☐3082 32¢ Multicolored | 18.00 | 4.50 | .90 | .26

1996. JAMES DEAN
☐3082 32¢ Multicolored | 18.00 | 4.50 | .90 | .26

1996. FOLK HEROES—MIGHTY CASEY
☐3083 32¢ Multicolored | 18.00 | 4.50 | .90 | .26

1996. FOLK HEROES—PAUL BUNYAN
☐3084 32¢ Multicolored | 17.00 | 4.60 | .90 | .26

1996. FOLK HEROES—JOHN HENRY
☐3085 32¢ Multicolored | 17.00 | 4.50 | .90 | .26

1996. FOLK HEROES—PECOS BILL
☐3086 32¢ Multicolored | 17.00 | 4.50 | .90 | .26

1996. CENTENNIAL OLYMPIC GAMES—DISCUS THROWER
☐3087 32¢ Brown/Black | 17.50 | 4.50 | .90 | .26

1996. IOWA—1846
☐3088 Water-adhesive 32¢ Multicolored
| | 37.00 | 4.50 | .90 | .26 |
☐3089 Self-adhesive 32¢ Multicolored
| | — | — | .90 | .26 |

1996. RURAL FREE DELIVERY—RFD
☐3090 32¢ Multicolored | 17.00 | 4.00 | .90 | .26

1996. RIVERBOATS—ROBT. E. LEE
☐3091 Self-adhesive 32¢ Multicolored
| | 17.00 | 10.00 (10) | .90 | .26 |

1996. RIVERBOATS—SYLVAN DELL
☐3092 Self-adhesive 32¢ Multicolored
| | 16.50 | 10.00 (10) | .90 | .26 |

*No hinge pricing from 1941 to date is figured at (N-H ADD 10%)

Scott No.	Mint Sheet	Plate Block	Fine Unused Each	Fine Used Each

1996. RIVERBOATS—FAR WEST
☐3093 Self-adhesive 32¢ Multicolored

| | 17.00 | 10.00 (10) | .85 | .27 |

1996. RIVERBOATS—REBECCA EVERINGHAM
☐3094 Self-adhesive 32¢ Multicolored

| | 17.00 | — | .85 | .27 |

1996. RIVERBOATS—BAILEY GATZERT
☐3095 Self-adhesive 32¢ Multicolored

| | 17.00 | — | .85 | .27 |

1996. BIG BAND LEADERS—COUNT BASIE: PIANIST AND BANDLEADER
☐3096 32¢ Multicolored

| | 17.00 | 4.00 | .85 | .27 |

1996. BIG BAND LEADERS—TOMMY & JIMMY DORSEY: BANDLEADERS
☐3097 32¢ Multicolored

| | 17.00 | 4.00 | .85 | .27 |

1996. BIG BAND LEADERS—GLEN MILLER: TROMBONIST AND BANDLEADER
☐3098 32¢ Multicolored

| | 17.00 | 4.00 | .85 | .27 |

1996. BIG BAND LEADERS—BENNY GOODMAN: CLARINETIST AND BANDLEADER
☐3099 32¢ Multicolored

| | 17.00 | 4.00 | .85 | .27 |

1996. SONGWRITERS—HAROLD ARLEN: COMPOSER
☐3100 32¢ Multicolored

| | 17.00 | 4.00 | .85 | .27 |

1996. SONGWRITERS—JOHNNY MERCER: LYRICIST
☐3101 32¢ Multicolored

| | 17.00 | 4.00 | .85 | .27 |

1996. SONGWRITERS—DOROTHY FIELDS: LYRICIST
☐3102 32¢ Multicolored

| | 17.00 | 4.00 | .85 | .27 |

*No hinge pricing from 1941 to date is figured at (N-H ADD 10%)

Scott No.	Mint Sheet	Plate Block	Fine Unused Each	Fine Used Each

1996. SONGWRITERS—HOAGY CARMICHAEL: COMPOSER

☐3103 32¢ Multicolored	17.00	4.10	.90	.27

1996. F. SCOTT FITZGERALD

☐3104 23¢ Multicolored	30.00	4.10	.90	.27

1996. ENDANGERED SPECIES (SHEET OF 15)

☐3105 32¢ Multicolored	13.00	—	4.00	—
Single Stamps	—	—	1.10	.40

1996. COMPUTER TECHNOLOGY

☐3106 32¢ Multicolored	31.00	4.00	.84	.27

1996. MADONNA AND CHILD

☐3107 Water-adhesive 32¢ Multicolored

	36.00	4.00	.82	.27

1996. CHRISTMAS FAMILY SCENES—FIREPLACE

☐3108 Self-adhesive 32¢ Multicolored

	46.00	4.50	.82	.27

1996. CHRISTMAS FAMILY SCENES—TREE

☐3109 Self-adhesive 32¢ Multicolored

	36.00	3.75	.82	.27

1996. CHRISTMAS FAMILY SCENES—DREAMING

☐3110 Self-adhesive 32¢ Multicolored

	36.00	3.75	.82	.27

1996. CHRISTMAS FAMILY SCENES—SHOPPING

☐3111 Self-adhesive 32¢ Multicolored

	36.00	3.75	.82	.27

1996. MADONNA AND CHILD

☐3112 Self-adhesive 32¢ Multicolored

	—	—	.82	.27

☐3113–3116 NOT ISSUED

*No hinge pricing from 1941 to date is figured at (N-H ADD 10%)

Scott No.	Mint Sheet	Plate Block	Fine Unused Each	Fine Used Each

1996. SKATERS
☐3117 32¢ Multicolored   —   —   .90   .27

1996. HANUKKAH
☐3118 Self-adhesive 32¢ Multicolored

    16.00   —   .90   .27

1996. CYCLING (SHEET OF 2)
☐3119 32¢ Multicolored   —   —   2.70   .50

1997. COMMEMORATIVES ▬▬▬▬▬▬
1997. YEAR OF THE OX
☐3120 32¢ Multicolored   16.00 (20)   4.00 (4)   .90   .27

1997. BENJAMIN O. DAVIS, SR.
☐3121 Self-adhesive 32¢ Multicolored

    16.00 (20)   4.00 (4)   .90   .27

1997. STATUE OF LIBERTY
☐3122 Self-adhesive 32¢ Multicolored

    —   —   .90   .27

1997. SWANS
☐3123 Self-adhesive 32¢ Multicolored

    —   —   .90   .27

1997. SWANS
☐3124 Self-adhesive 55¢ Multicolored

    —   —   1.40   .45

1997. HELPING CHILDREN LEARN
☐3125 Self-adhesive 32¢ Multicolored

    17.00 (20)   4.50 (4)   1.00   .27

1997. MERIAN BOTANICAL PRINT—CITRON (FROM PANE OF 20)
☐3126 Self-adhesive 32¢ Multicolored

    —   —   1.00   .27

*No hinge pricing from 1941 to date is figured at (N-H ADD 10%)

Scott No.	Mint Sheet	Plate Block	Fine Unused Each	Fine Used Each

1997. MERIAN BOTANICAL PRINT—FLOWERING PINEAPPLE (PANE OF 20)
☐3127 Self-adhesive 32¢ Multicolored

	—	—	.93	.27

1997. MERIAN BOTANICAL PRINT—CITRON (FROM BOOK OF 15)
☐3128 Self-adhesive 32¢ Multicolored

	—	—	.93	.27

1997. MERIAN BOTANICAL PRINT—FLOWERING PINEAPPLE (FROM BOOK OF 15)
☐3129 Self-adhesive 32¢ Multicolored

	—	—	.93	.27

1997. SHIP PACIFIC 1997
☐3130 32¢ Blue — — .93 .27

1997. STAGECOACH PACIFIC 1997
☐3131 32¢ Red — — .93 .27

1997. JUKEBOX (EXPERIMENTAL LINERLESS COIL)
☐3132 Self-adhesive 25¢ Multicolored

	—	—	.70	.36

1997. FLAG OVER PORCH (EXPERIMENTAL LINERLESS COIL)
☐3133 Self-adhesive 32¢ Multicolored

	—	—	.85	.28

1997. THORNTON WILDER
☐3134 32¢ Multicolored 14.50 (20) 3.50 (4) .85 .28

1997. RAOUL WALLENBERG
☐3135 32¢ Multicolored 14.50 (20) 3.50 (4) .85 .28

*No hinge pricing from 1941 to date is figured at (N-H ADD 10%)

Scott No.	Mint Sheet	Plate Block	Fine Unused Each	Fine Used Each

1997. DINOSAURS (15 VARIETIES)

☐3136 32¢ Multicolored 30.00 (15) — 4.00 .85
(a) Ceratosaurus, (b) Camptosaurus, (c) Camarasaurus,
(d) Brachiosaurus, (e) Goniopholis, (f) Stegosaurus, (g) Allosaurus,
(h) Ophisthias, (i) Edmontonia, (j) Einiosaurus,
(k) Daspletosaurus, (l) Palaeosaniwa, (m) Corythosaurus,
(n) Ornithomimus, (o) Parasaurolophus

1997. BUGS BUNNY

☐3137 Self-adhesive 32¢ Multicolored
45.00 — 1.00 .30

1997. BUGS BUNNY (DIE-CUT)

☐3138 Self-adhesive 32¢ Multicolored
12.00 — 1.00 .30

1997. BENJAMIN FRANKLIN

☐3139 50¢ Multicolored 15.00 (12) — 1.80 .82

1997. GEORGE WASHINGTON

☐3140 60¢ Multicolored 18.00 (12) — 1.80 .82

1997. MARSHALL PLAN

☐3141 32¢ Multicolored 18.00 (20) 4.00 (4) .92 .30

1997. CLASSIC AMERICAN AIRCRAFT (20 VARIETIES)

☐3142 32¢ Multicolored 60.00 (20) — .92 .32
(a) Mustang, (b) Model B, (c) Cub, (d) Vega, (e) Alpha, (f) B-10,
(g) Corsair, (h) Stratojet, (i) GeeBee, (j) Staggerwing, (k) Flying Fortress, (l) Stearman, (m) Constellation, (n) Lightning, (o) Peashotter,
(p) Tri-Motor, (q) DC-3, (r) Clipper, (s) Jenny, (t) Wildcat

1997. PAUL "BEAR" BRYANT

☐3143 32¢ Multicolored 13.50 — .92 .30

1997. GLEN "POP" WARNER

☐3144 32¢ Multicolored — — .92 .30
*No hinge pricing from 1941 to date is figured at (N-H ADD 10%)

Scott No.	Mint Sheet	Plate Block	Fine Unused Each	Fine Used Each

1997. VINCE LOMBARDI
☐3145 32¢ Multicolored — 15.00 — 4.00 — .70 — .33

1997. GEORGE HALAS
☐3146 32¢ Multicolored — 15.00 — 4.00 — .70 — —

1997. VINCE LOMBARDI (RED STRIPE)
☐3147 32¢ Multicolored — 15.00 — 4.00 — .70 — .32

1997. PAUL "BEAR" BRYANT (RED STRIPE)
☐3148 32¢ Multicolored — 15.00 — 4.00 — .70 — .32

1997. GLEN "POP" WARNER
☐3149 32¢ Multicolored — 15.00 — 4.00 — .70 — .32

1997. GEORGE HALAS
☐3150 32¢ Multicolored — 15.00 — 4.00 — .70 — .32

1997. CLASSIC AMERICAN DOLLS (15 VARIETIES)
☐3151 32¢ Multicolored — 18.00 (15) — — — 1.00 — .30
(a) "Alabama Baby" and Martha Chase, (b) "The Columbian Doll,"
(c) Johnny Gruelle's "Raggedy Ann," (d) Martha Chase,
(e) "American Child," (f) "Baby Coos," (g) Plains Indian, (h) Izannah Walker, (i) "Babyland Rag," (j) "Scooties," (k) Ludwig Greiner, (l) "Betsy McCall," (m) Percy Cosby's "Skippy," (n) "Maggie Mix-up," (o) Albert Schoenhut.

1997. HUMPHREY BOGART
☐3152 32¢ Multicolored — 16.00 (20) — 4.50 (4) — 1.00 — .30

1997. THE STARS AND STRIPES FOREVER
☐3153 32¢ Multicolored — 38.00 (50) — 4.00 (4) — 1.00 — .30

1997. OPERA SINGERS—LILY PONS
☐3154 32¢ Multicolored — 21.00 (20) — 4.00 (4) — 1.00 — .30

1997. OPERA SINGERS—RICHARD TUCKER
☐3155 32¢ Multicolored — 21.00 (20) — 4.00 (4) — 1.00 — .30
*No hinge pricing from 1941 to date is figured at (N-H ADD 10%)

Scott No.	Mint Sheet	Plate Block	Fine Unused Each	Fine Used Each

1997. OPERA SINGERS—LAWRENCE TIBBETT
| ☐3156 32¢ Multicolored | 17.00 (20) | 4.10 (4) | .85 | .28 |

1997. OPERA SINGERS—ROSA PONSELLE
| ☐3157 32¢ Multicolored | 17.00 (20) | 4.10 (4) | .85 | .28 |

1997. COMPOSERS AND CONDUCTORS— LEOPOLD STOKOWSKI
| ☐3158 32¢ Multicolored | 17.00 (20) | 8.00 (8) | .85 | .28 |

1997. COMPOSERS AND CONDUCTORS— ARTHUR FIEDLER
| ☐3159 32¢ Multicolored | 17.00 (20) | 8.00 (8) | .85 | .28 |

1997. COMPOSERS AND CONDUCTORS— GEORGE SZELL
| ☐3160 32¢ Multicolored | 17.00 (20) | 8.00 (8) | .85 | .28 |

1997. COMPOSERS AND CONDUCTORS— EUGENE ORMANDY
| ☐3161 32¢ Multicolored | 17.00 (20) | 8.00 (8) | .85 | .28 |

1997. COMPOSERS AND CONDUCTORS— SAMUEL BARBER
| ☐3162 32¢ Multicolored | 17.00 (20) | 8.00 (8) | .85 | .28 |

1997. COMPOSERS AND CONDUCTORS— FERDE GROFÉ
| ☐3163 32¢ Multicolored | — | — | .85 | .25 |

1997. COMPOSERS AND CONDUCTORS— CHARLES IVES
| ☐3164 32¢ Multicolored | — | — | .85 | .25 |

1997. COMPOSERS AND CONDUCTORS— LOUIS MOREAU GOTTSCHALK
| ☐3165 32¢ Multicolored | — | — | .85 | .25 |

1997. PADRE FÉLIX VARELA
| ☐3166 32¢ Multicolored | 16.00 (20) | 4.00 (4) | .85 | .25 |

*No hinge pricing from 1941 to date is figured at (N-H ADD 10%)

Scott No.	Mint Sheet	Plate Block	Fine Unused Each	Fine Used Each

1997. U. S. DEPARTMENT OF AIR FORCE (1947–1997)
| ☐3167 32¢ Multicolored | 16.00 (20) | 4.00 (4) | .82 | .27 |

1997. CLASSIC MOVIE MONSTERS—PHANTOM OF THE OPERA
| ☐3168 32¢ Multicolored | 16.00 (20) | 4.00 (4) | .82 | .28 |

1997. CLASSIC MOVIE MONSTERS—DRACULA
| ☐3169 32¢ Multicolored | 16.00 (20) | 4.00 (4) | .82 | .27 |

1997. CLASSIC MOVIE MONSTERS—FRANKENSTEIN
| ☐3170 32¢ Multicolored | 16.00 (20) | 4.00 (4) | .82 | .27 |

1997. CLASSIC MOVIE MONSTERS—THE MUMMY
| ☐3171 32¢ Multicolored | 16.00 (20) | 4.00 (4) | .82 | .27 |

1997. CLASSIC MOVIE MONSTERS—WOLF MAN
| ☐3172 32¢ Multicolored | 16.00 (20) | 4.00 (4) | .82 | .27 |

1997. SUPERSONIC FLIGHT
| ☐3173 Self-adhesive 32¢ Multicolored | | | | |
| | 16.00 (20) | 4.00 (4) | .82 | .27 |

1997. WOMEN IN MILITARY
| ☐3174 32¢ Multicolored | 16.00 (20) | 4.00 (4) | .82 | .27 |

1997. KWANZAA
| ☐3175 Self-adhesive 32¢ Multicolored | | | | |
| | 37.00 (50) | 4.00 (4) | .82 | .27 |

1997. MADONNA AND CHILD
| ☐3176 Self-adhesive 32¢ Multicolored | | | | |
| | 18.00 (20) | — | .82 | .27 |

1997. AMERICAN HOLLY
| ☐3177 Self-adhesive 32¢ Multicolored | | | | |
| | 16.00 (20) | — | .82 | .26 |

1998. COMMEMORATIVES ━━━━━━
1998. HAPPY NEW YEAR—YEAR OF THE TIGER
| ☐3179 32¢ Multicolored | 16.00 (20) | 4.00 (4) | .82 | .27 |

*No hinge pricing from 1941 to date is figured at (N-H ADD 10%)

Scott No.	Mint Sheet	Plate Block	Fine Unused Each	Fine Used Each

1998. ALPINE SKIING
☐3180 32¢ Multicolored   17.00 (20)   4.10 (4)   .92   .28

1998. BLACK HERITAGE—MADAM C.J. WALKER
☐3181 Self-adhesive 32¢ Multicolored

   17.00 (20)   4.10 (4)   .92   .28

1998. CELEBRATE THE CENTURIES 1900s (15 VARIETIES)
☐3182 32¢ Multicolored, commemorative sheet

   13.00 (15)   —   1.50   .85

(a) Model T Ford, (b) President Theodore Roosevelt, (c) The Great Train Robbery, (d) Crayola Crayons, (e) 1904 St. Louis World's Fair, (f) Pure Food and Drug Act, (g) Kitty Hawk, (h) Ash Can Painters, (i) Immigrants Arrive, (j) Preservationist—John Muir, (k) Teddy Bear Was Created, (l) W.E.B. DuBois, Social Activist, (m) Gibson Girl, (n) First World Series, (o) Robie House, Chicago

1998. CELEBRATE THE CENTURIES 1910s
☐3183 32¢ Multicolored, commemorative sheet

   12.00 (15)   —   1.50   .70

(a) Charlie Chaplin's Little Tramp, (b) Federal Reserve System, (c) George Washington Carver, (d) Armory Show, (e) Telephone Spans the Nation, (f) Panama Canel Opens, (g) Jim Thorpe, (h) Grand Canyon National Park, (i) U.S. Enters WWI, (j) Boy & Girl Scouts Begins, (k) President Wilson, (l) First Crossword Puzzle, (m) Jack Dempsey Wins Title, (n) Construction Toys, (o) Child Labor Reform

1998. CELEBRATE THE CENTURIES 1920s
☐3184 32¢ Multicolored, commemorative sheet

   11.00 (15)   —   1.10   .75

(a) Babe Ruth, (b) The Gatsby Style, (c) 18th Amendment, (d) Electric Toy Trains, (e) 19th Amendment, (f) Emily Post, (g) Margaret Mead, (h) Flappers Do the Charleston, (i) Radio Entertains America, (j) Art Deco Style (Chrysler Building), (k) Jazz Flourishes, (l) Four Horsemen of Notre Dame, (m) Lindbergh Flies the Atlantic, (n) American Realism, (o) Stock Market Crash

*No hinge pricing from 1941 to date is figured at (N-H ADD 10%)

Scott No.	Mint Sheet	Plate Block	Fine Unused Each	Fine Used Each

1998. CELEBRATE THE CENTURIES 1930s
☐3185 32¢ Multicolored, commemorative sheet

| | 12.00 (15) | — | 1.50 | .75 |

(a) President Franklin Roosevelt, (b) Empire State Building, (c) *Life* Magazine, (d) First Lady Eleanor Roosevelt, (e) FDR's New Deal, (f) Superman, (g) Household Conveniences, (h) Walt Disney's Snow White, (i) Gone With the Wind, (j) Jesse Owens, (k) Streamline Design, (l) Golden Gate Bridge, (m) America Survives the Depression, (n) Bobby Jones, (o) The Monopoly Game
☐3186–3191 NOT ISSUED

1998. REMEMBER THE MAINE (PANE OF 20)
☐3192 32¢ Red & Black | 17.00 (20) | 4.10 (4) | .85 | .26

1998. FLOWERING TREES—SOUTHERN MAGNOLIA
☐3193 Self-adhesive 32¢ Multicolored

| | 16.00 (20) | 9.00 (10) | .82 | .28 |

1998. FLOWERING TREES—BLUE PALOVERDE
☐3194 Self-adhesive 32¢ Multicolored

| | 16.00 (20) | 9.00 (10) | .82 | .28 |

1998. FLOWERING TREES—YELLOW POPLAR
☐3195 Self-adhesive 32¢ Multicolored

| | 16.00 (20) | 9.00 (10) | .82 | .28 |

1998. FLOWERING TREES—PRAIRIE CRAB APPLE
☐3196 Self-adhesive 32¢ Multicolored

| | 16.00 (20) | 9.00 (10) | .82 | .28 |

1998. FLOWERING TREES—PACIFIC DOGWOOD
☐3197 Self-adhesive 32¢ Multicolored

| | 16.00 (20) | 9.00 (10) | .82 | .28 |

1998. ALEXANDER CALDER—BLACK CASCADE
☐3198 32¢ Multicolored | 16.00 (20) | 9.00 (10) | .82 | .28

1998. ALEXANDER CALDER—UNTITLED
☐3199 32¢ Multicolored | 16.00 (20) | 9.00 (10) | .82 | .28

*No hinge pricing from 1941 to date is figured at (N-H ADD 10%)

Scott No.	Mint Sheet	Plate Block	Fine Unused Each	Fine Used Each

1998. ALEXANDER CALDER—REARING STALLION
| ☐3200 32¢ Multicolored | 17.00 (20) | 9.00 (10) | .82 | .28 |

1998. ALEXANDER CALDER—PORTRAIT OF A YOUNG MAN
| ☐3201 32¢ Multicolored | 17.00 (20) | 9.00 (10) | .82 | .28 |

1998. ALEXANDER CALDER—UN EFFET DU JAPONAIS
| ☐3202 32¢ Multicolored | 17.00 (20) | 9.00 (10) | .82 | .28 |

1998. CINCO DE MAYO
| ☐3203 32¢ Multicolored | 17.00 (20) | 4.20 (4) | .82 | .28 |

1998. SYLVESTER & TWEETY (PANE OF 10)
☐3204 Self-adhesive 32¢ Multicolored
| | — | — | .82 | .28 |

1998. SYLVESTER & TWEETY (PANE OF 10, & 1 IMPERFORATE)
☐3205 Self-adhesive 32¢ Multicolored
| | — | — | 12.00 | — |

1998. WISCONSIN
☐3206 Self-adhesive 32¢ Multicolored
| | 16.00 (20) | 4.50 (4) | .75 | .28 |

1998 REGULAR ISSUE
1998. WETLANDS—NON-PROFIT COIL
| ☐3207 5¢ Multicolored | — | — | .40 | .28 |

1998. DINER—PRESORTED FIRST-CLASS COIL
| ☐3208 25¢ Multicolored | — | — | .70 | .31 |

1998. COMMEMORATIVES (CONTINUED)
1998. BI-COLOR REISSUE OF THE 1898 TRANS-MISSISSIPPI DESIGN (SHEET OF 9)
| ☐3209 1C $2 Red & Black | — | — | 9.50 | — |

*No hinge pricing from 1941 to date is figured at (N-H ADD 10%)

Scott No.	Mint Sheet	Plate Block	Fine Unused Each	Fine Used Each

1998. BI-COLOR REISSUE OF THE 1898 TRANS-MISSISSIPPI DESIGN (SHEET OF 9) CATTLE IN STORM

☐3210 $1 Red & Black	—	—	22.00	—

1998. BERLIN AIRLIFT 1948–49

☐3211 32¢ Multicolored	16.00 (20)	3.75 (4)	.82	.28

1998. FOLK MUSICIANS—LEADBELLY

☐3212 32¢ Multicolored	17.00 (20)	4.40 (4)	.82	.28

1998. FOLK MUSICIANS—WOODY GUTHRIE

☐3213 32¢ Multicolored	17.00 (20)	4.40 (4)	.82	.28

1998. FOLK MUSICIANS—SONNY TERRY

☐3214 32¢ Multicolored	17.00 (20)	4.40 (4)	.82	.28

1998. FOLK MUSICIANS—JOSH WHITE

☐3215 32¢ Multicolored	17.00 (20)	4.40 (4)	.82	.28

1998. GOSPEL SINGERS—MAHALIA JACKSON

☐3216 32¢ Multicolored	17.00 (20)	4.40 (4)	.82	.28

1998. GOSPEL SINGERS—ROBERTA MARTIN

☐3217 32¢ Multicolored	17.00 (20)	4.40 (4)	.82	.28

1998. GOSPEL SINGERS—CLARA WARD

☐3218 32¢ Multicolored	17.00 (20)	4.40 (4)	.82	.28

1998. GOSPEL SINGERS—SISTER ROSETTA

☐3219 32¢ Multicolored	17.00 (20)	4.40 (4)	.82	.28

1998. SPANISH SETTLEMENT OF THE SOUTHWEST

☐3220 32¢ Multicolored	17.00 (20)	4.40 (4)	.82	.28

1998. STEPHEN VINCENT BENÉT

☐3221 32¢ Multicolored	17.00 (20)	4.40 (4)	.82	.28

*No hinge pricing from 1941 to date is figured at (N-H ADD 10%)

Scott No.	Mint Sheet	Plate Block	Fine Unused Each	Fine Used Each

1998. TROPICAL BIRDS—ANTILLEAN EUPHONIA

☐ 3222 32¢ Multicolored	16.00 (20)	4.10 (4)	.80	.27

1998. TROPICAL BIRDS—GREEN-THROATED CARIB

☐ 3223 32¢ Multicolored	16.00 (20)	4.10 (4)	.80	.27

1998. TROPICAL BIRDS—CRESTED HONEYCREEPER

☐ 3224 32¢ Multicolored	16.00 (20)	4.10 (4)	.80	.27

1998. TROPICAL BIRDS—CARDINAL HONEYEATER

☐ 3225 32¢ Multicolored	16.00 (20)	4.10 (4)	.80	.27

1998. ALFRED HITCHCOCK

☐ 3226 32¢ Multicolored	16.00 (20)	4.10 (4)	.80	.27

1998. ORGAN & TISSUE DONATION "SHARE YOUR LIFE"

☐ 3227 32¢ Self-adhesive Multicolored

	16.00 (20)	4.10 (4)	.80	.27

☐ 3228–3229 NOT ISSUED

1998. BRIGHT EYES—DOG

☐ 3230 32¢ Self-adhesive Multicolored

	16.00 (20)	8.40 (10)	.80	.27

1998. BRIGHT EYES—FISH

☐ 3231 32¢ Self-adhesive Multicolored

	16.00 (20)	8.40 (10)	.80	.27

1998. BRIGHT EYES—CAT

☐ 3232 32¢ Self-adhesive Multicolored

	16.00 (20)	8.40 (10)	.80	.27

1998. BRIGHT EYES—PARAKEET

☐ 3233 32¢ Self-adhesive Multicolored

	16.00 (20)	8.40 (10)	.80	.27

*No hinge pricing from 1941 to date is figured at (N-H ADD 10%)

Scott No.	Mint Sheet	Plate Block	Fine Unused Each	Fine Used Each

1998. BRIGHT EYES—HAMSTER
☐3234 32¢ Self-adhesive Multicolored

	16.00 (20)	9.00 (10)	.82	.28

1998. KLONDIKE GOLD RUSH 1898
☐3235 32¢ Multicolored | 16.00 (20) | 4.00 (4) | .82 | .28 |

1998. FOUR CENTURIES OF AMERICAN ART (20 VARIETIES)
☐3236 32¢ Multicolored | 17.00 (20) | — | .82 | .27 |

(a) John Foster, (b) The Freake Limmer, (c) Ammi Phillips, (d) Rembrandt Peale, (e) John James Audubon, (f) George Caleb Bingham, (g) Asher B. Durand, (h) Joshua Johnson, (i) William Hamett, (j) Winslow Homer, (k) George Catlin, (l) Thomas Moran, (m) Alfred Bierstadt, (n) Frederic Edwin Church, (o), Mary Cassatt, (p) Edward Hopper, (q) Grant Wood, (r) Charles Sheeler, (s) Franz Kline, (t) Mark Rothko

1998. BALLET
☐3237 32¢ Multicolored | 17.00 (20) | 4.00 (4) | .82 | .26 |

1998. SPACE DISCOVERY—SPACE VEHICLE
☐3238 32¢ Multicolored | 17.00 (20) | 9.00 (10) | .82 | .26 |

1998. SPACE DISCOVERY—SPACE SHIP
☐3239 32¢ Multicolored | 17.00 (20) | 9.00 (10) | .82 | .26 |

1998. SPACE DISCOVERY—ASTRONAUT
☐3240 32¢ Multicolored | 17.00 (20) | 9.00 (4) | .82 | .26 |

1998. SPACE DISCOVERY—SPACE SHIP TAKING OFF
☐3241 32¢ Multicolored | 17.00 (20) | 9.00 (4) | .82 | .26 |

1998. SPACE DISCOVERY—SPACE CITY
☐3242 32¢ Multicolored | 17.00 (20) | 9.00 (4) | .82 | .26 |

*No hinge pricing from 1941 to date is figured at (N-H ADD 10%)

Scott No.	Mint Sheet	Plate Block	Fine Unused Each	Fine Used Each

1998. GIVING & SHARING

| ☐3243 32¢ Multicolored | 16.00 | 4.00 | .82 | .26 |

1998. MADONNA & CHILD

| ☐3244 32¢ Multicolored | — | — | .82 | .26 |

1998. EVERGREEN WREATH

| ☐3245 32¢ Multicolored | — | — | .82 | .26 |

1998. VICTORIAN WREATH

| ☐3246 32¢ Multicolored | — | — | .82 | .26 |

1998. CHILI PEPPER WREATH

| ☐3247 32¢ Multicolored | — | — | .82 | .26 |

1998. TROPICAL WREATH

| ☐3248 32¢ Multicolored | — | — | .82 | .26 |

1998. EVERGREEN WREATH—LARGE

☐3249 32¢ Self-adhesive Multicolored

| | 14.00 (20) | 3.00 (4) | .82 | .26 |

1998. VICTORIAN WREATH—LARGE

☐3250 32¢ Self-adhesive Multicolored

| | 14.00(20) | 3.00(4) | .82 | .26 |

1998. CHILI PEPPER WREATH—LARGE

☐3251 32¢ Self-adhesive Multicolored

| | 14.00(20) | 3.00(4) | .82 | .26 |

1998. TROPICAL WREATH—LARGE

☐3252 32¢ Self-adhesive Multicolored

| | 14.00(20) | 3.00(4) | .82 | .26 |

☐3253–56 NOT ISSUED

1998. WEATHER VANE

| ☐3257 1¢ White U.S.A. | 3.50 | .55 | .25 | .21 |

1998. WEATHER VANE

| ☐3258 1¢ Blue U.S.A. | 3.50 | .55 | .25 | .21 |

*No hinge pricing from 1941 to date is figured at (N-H ADD 10%)

Scott No.	Mint Sheet	Plate Block	Fine Unused Each	Fine Used Each
1998. UNCLE SAM				
☐3259 22¢ Multicolored	9.00	3.00	.55	.22
1998. UNCLE SAM'S HAT				
☐3260 33¢ Multicolored	38.00	4.00	.82	.21
1998. SPACE SHUTTLE				
☐3261 $3.20 Multicolored	140.00	30.00	7.00	3.50
1998. PIGGYBACK SPACE				
☐3262 $11.75	480.00	112.00	26.00	9.00
1998. UNCLE SAM				
☐3263 22¢ Self-adhesive Coil Multicolored			.55	.35
1998. UNCLE SAM'S HAT				
☐3264 33¢ Coil Multicolored		—	.75	.35
1998. UNCLE SAM'S HAT				
☐3265 33¢ Self-adhesive Coil Multicolored Square			.75	.35
1998. UNCLE SAM'S HAT				
☐3266 33¢ Self-adhesive Coil Multicolored Round			.75	.35
1998. UNCLE SAM'S HAT				
☐3267 33¢ Self-adhesive Multicolored		—	.75	.35
1998. UNCLE SAM'S HAT				
☐3268 33¢ Self-adhesive Multicolored	14.00(20)	—	.75	.35
1998. UNCLE SAM'S HAT				
☐3269 33¢ Self-adhesive Multicolored	12.50(18)	—	.75	.35

*No hinge pricing from 1941 to date is figured at (N-H ADD 10%)

Scott No.	Mint Sheet	Plate Block	Fine Unused Each	Fine Used Each

1998. EAGLE & SHIELD
| ☐ 3270-3271 10¢ Multicolored | — | 3.00 | .30 | .24 |

1998. EAGLE & SHIELD
| ☐ 3271 10¢ Self-adhesive Coil Multicolored | | | .30 | .24 |

1999. YEAR OF THE RABBIT
| ☐ 3272 33¢ Multicolored | 18.00 | 4.50 | 1.50 | .27 |

1999. MALCOLM X CIVIL RIGHTS
| ☐ 3273 33¢ Multicolored | 17.00 | 4.50 | .90 | .27 |

1999. LOVE
| ☐ 3274 33¢ Multicolored | — | — | .82 | .26 |

1999. LOVE LACE
| ☐ 3275 55¢ Multicolored | — | — | 1.50 | .48 |

1999. HOSPICE CARE
| ☐ 3276 33¢ Multicolored | 14.00 | 3.50 | .80 | .26 |

1999. FLAG & CITY
| ☐ 3277 33¢ Multicolored | 70.00 | 4.50 | .82 | .24 |

1999. FLAG & CITY
| ☐ 3278 33¢ Self-adhesive Multicolored | — | | .82 | .24 |

1999. FLAG & CITY
| ☐ 3279 33¢ Self-adhesive Multicolored | — | | .82 | .24 |

1999. FLAG & CITY
| ☐ 3280 33¢ Self-adhesive Coil Multicolored Small Date | | | .82 | .24 |

1999. FLAG & CITY
| ☐ 3281 33¢ Self-adhesive Coil Multicolored Large Date | | | .82 | .24 |

1999. FLAG & CITY
| ☐ 3282 33¢ Self-adhesive Multicolored Round | | | .82 | .24 |

*No hinge pricing from 1941 to date is figured at (N-H ADD 10%)

Scott No.	Mint Sheet	Plate Block	Fine Unused Each	Fine Used Each
1999. FLAG & CHALKBOARD				
☐3283 33¢ Multicolored	—	—	.82	.24
☐3284-85 NOT ISSUED				
1999. IRISH IMMIGRATION				
☐3286 33¢ Multicolored	15.00	4.00	.82	.24
1999. ALFRED LUNT & LYNN FONTANNE				
☐3287 33¢ Multicolored	15.00	—	.82	.24
1999. ARCTIC HARE				
☐3288 33¢ Multicolored	—	—	.85	.30
1999. ARCTIC FOX				
☐3289 33¢ Multicolored	—	—	.85	.30
1999. SNOWY OWL				
☐3290 33¢ Multicolored	—	—	.90	.36
1999. POLAR BEAR				
☐3291 33¢ Multicolored	—	—	.90	.36
1999. GRAY WOLF				
☐3292 33¢ Multicolored	—	—	.90	.36
1999. SONORAN DESERT				
☐3293 33¢ Self-adhesive Multicolored	7.00(10)	—	.82	.27
1999. BLUEBERRIES				
☐3294 33¢ Self-adhesive Multicolored	—	—	.82	.27
1999. RASPBERRIES				
☐3295 33¢ Self-adhesive Multicolored	—	—	.82	.27
1999. STRAWBERRIES				
☐3296 33¢ Self-adhesive Multicolored	—	—	.82	.27

*No hinge pricing from 1941 to date is figured at (N-H ADD 10%)

Scott No.	Mint Sheet	Plate Block	Fine Unused Each	Fine Used Each

1999. BLACKBERRIES
☐3297 33¢ Self-adhesive Multicolored — .82 .27

1999. BLUEBERRIES
☐3298 33¢ Self-adhesive Multicolored — .82 .27

1999. RASPBERRIES
☐3299 33¢ Self-adhesive Multicolored — .82 .27

1999. STRAWBERRIES
☐3300 33¢ Self-adhesive Multicolored — .82 .27

1999. BLACKBERRIES
☐3301 33¢ Self-adhesive Multicolored — .82 .27

1999. BLUEBERRIES
☐3302 33¢ Self-adhesive Coil Multicolored .82 .27

1999. RASPBERRIES
☐3303 33¢ Self-adhesive Coil Multicolored .82 .27

1999. STRAWBERRIES
☐3304 33¢ Self-adhesive Coil Multicolored .82 .27

1999. BLACKBERRIES
☐3305 33¢ Self-adhesive Coil Multicolored .82 .27

1999. DAFFY DUCK
☐3306–3307 33¢ Self-Adhesive Multicolored
7.00 (10) — .82 .27

1999. AYN RAND—LITERARY ARTS
☐3308 33¢ Multicolored 16.00 4.00 .82 .27

1999. CINCO DE MAYO
☐3309 33¢ Self-Adhesive Multicolored
16.00 4.00 .82 .27

*No hinge pricing from 1941 to date is figured at (N-H ADD 10%)

Scott No.	Mint Sheet	Plate Block	Fine Unused Each	Fine Used Each

1999. TROPICAL FLOWERS—BIRD OF PARADISE
☐3310 33¢ Self-Adhesive Multicolored

			.82	.27
—	—			

1999. TROPICAL FLOWERS—ROYAL POINCIANA
☐3311 33¢ Self-Adhesive Multicolored

—	—	.82	.27

1999. TROPICAL FLOWERS—GLORIOSA
☐3312 33¢ Self-Adhesive Multicolored

—	—	.78	.26

1999. TROPICAL FLOWERS—CHINESE HIBISCUS
☐3313 33¢ Self-Adhesive Multicolored

—	—	.78	.26

1999. JOHN & WILLIAM BARTRAM—BOTANISTS
☐3314 33¢ Self-Adhesive Multicolored

14.00	3.90	.82	.24

1999. PROSTATE CANCER AWARENESS
☐3315 33¢ Self-Adhesive Multicolored

14.00	3.90	.82	.24

1999. CALIFORNIA GOLD RUSH—150TH ANNIVERSARY
☐3316 33¢ Multicolored

14.00	3.90	.82	.24

1999. AQUARIUM FISH—YELLOW & RED FISH
☐3317 33¢ Self-Adhesive Multicolored

—	—	.82	.28

1999. AQUARIUM FISH—FISH THERMOMETER
☐3318 33¢ Self-Adhesive Multicolored

—	—	.82	.28

*No hinge pricing from 1941 to date is figured at (N-H ADD 10%)

Scott No.	Mint Sheet	Plate Block	Fine Unused Each	Fine Used Each

1999. AQUARIUM FISH—RED & BLUE FISH
☐3319 33¢ Self-Adhesive Multicolored

| | — | — | .82 | .28 |

1999. AQUARIUM FISH—SHELL FISH
☐3320 33¢ Self-Adhesive Multicolored

| | — | — | .82 | .28 |

1999. EXTREME SPORTS—SKATEBOARDING
☐3321 33¢ Self-Adhesive Multicolored

| | — | — | .82 | .28 |

1999. EXTREME SPORTS—BMX BIKING
☐3322 33¢ Self-Adhesive Multicolored

| | — | — | .82 | .28 |

1999. EXTREME SPORTS—SNOW BOARDING
☐3323 33¢ Self-Adhesive Multicolored

| | — | — | .82 | .28 |

1999. EXTREME SPORTS—INLINE SKATING
☐3324 33¢ Self-Adhesive Multicolored

| | — | — | .82 | .21 |

1999. AMERICAN GLASS—FREE-BLOWN GLASS
☐3325 33¢ Multicolored — — .82 .21

1999. AMERICAN GLASS—MOLD-BLOWN GLASS
☐3326 33¢ Multicolored — — .82 .21

1999. AMERICAN GLASS—PRESSED GLASS
☐3327 33¢ Multicolored — — .82 .21

1999. AMERICAN GLASS—ART GLASS
☐3328 33¢ Multicolored — — .82 .21

*No hinge pricing from 1941 to date is figured at (N-H ADD 10%)

Scott No.	Mint Sheet	Plate Block	Fine Unused Each	Fine Used Each

1999. LEGENDS OF HOLLYWOOD—JAMES CAGNEY

| ☐3329 33¢ Multicolored | 14.00 | 4.10 | .80 | .21 |

1999. GENERAL BILLY MITCHELL

| ☐3330 33¢ Multicolored | 22.00 | 6.00 | .90 | .26 |

1999. HONORING THOSE WHO SERVED

| ☐3331 33¢ Multicolored | 16.00 | 4.10 | .82 | .26 |

1999. FAMOUS TRAINS—UNIVERSAL POSTAL UNION

| ☐3332 45¢ Multicolored | 22.00 | 6.10 | 1.00 | .28 |

1999. FAMOUS TRAINS—DAYLIGHT TRAIN

| ☐3333 33¢ Multicolored | — | — | .82 | .21 |

1999. FAMOUS TRAINS—CONGRESSIONAL TRAIN

| ☐3334 33¢ Multicolored | — | — | .82 | .21 |

1999. FAMOUS TRAINS—20TH-CENTURY LIMITED TRAIN

| ☐3335 33¢ Multicolored | — | — | .82 | .21 |

1999. FAMOUS TRAINS—HIAWATHA TRAIN

| ☐3336 33¢ Multicolored | — | — | .82 | .27 |

1999. FAMOUS TRAINS—SUPER CHIEF TRAIN

| ☐3337 33¢ Multicolored | — | — | .82 | .27 |

1999. FREDERICK LAW OLMSTED

| ☐3338 33¢ Multicolored | 14.50 | 4.00 | .82 | .27 |

1999. MAX STEINER

| ☐3339 33¢ Multicolored | — | — | .82 | .27 |

*No hinge pricing from 1941 to date is figured at (N-H ADD 10%)

Scott No.	Mint Sheet	Plate Block	Fine Unused Each	Fine Used Each

1999. DMITRI TIOMKIN

| ☐3340 33¢ Multicolored | — | — | .82 | .27 |

1999. BERNARD HERRMANN

| ☐3341 33¢ Multicolored | — | — | .82 | .27 |

1999. FRANZ WAXMAN

| ☐3342 33¢ Multicolored | — | — | .82 | .27 |

1999. ALFRED NEWMAN

| ☐3343 33¢ Multicolored | — | — | .82 | .27 |

1999. ERICH WOLFGANG KORNGOLD

| ☐3344 33¢ Multicolored | — | — | .82 | .27 |

1999. IRA & GEORGE GERSHWIN

| ☐3345 33¢ Multicolored | — | — | .82 | .27 |

1999. LERNER & LOEWE

| ☐3346 33¢ Multicolored | — | — | .82 | .27 |

1999. LORENZ HART

| ☐3347 33¢ Multicolored | — | — | .82 | .27 |

1999. RODGERS & HAMMERSTEIN II

| ☐3348 33¢ Multicolored | — | — | .76 | .24 |

1999. MEREDITH WILLSON

| ☐3349 33¢ Multicolored | — | — | .76 | .24 |

1999. FRANK LOESSER

| ☐3350 33¢ Multicolored | — | — | .76 | .24 |

1999. INSECTS & SPIDERS (20 VARIATIONS)

| ☐3351 Multicolored | 14.00(10) | — | .76 | .24 |

1999. HANUKKAH

| ☐3352 33¢ Multicolored | 14.50 | 3.50 | .76 | .24 |

*No hinge pricing from 1941 to date is figured at (N-H ADD 10%)

Scott No.	Mint Sheet	Plate Block	Fine Unused Each	Fine Used Each
1999. UNCLE SAM				
☐3353 22¢ Multicolored	—	3.50	.76	.22
1999. NATO—50TH ANNIVERSARY				
☐3354 33¢ Multicolored	14.50	3.50	.76	.24
1999. MADONNA & CHILD				
☐3355 33¢ Multicolored	—	—	.76	.22
1999. CHRISTMAS DEER				
☐3356-3367 33¢ Multicolored	14.50	3.00	.76	.22
1999. KWANZAA				
☐3368 33¢ Multicolored	14.50	3.00	.76	.22
1999. YEAR 2000—BABY NEW YEAR				
☐3369 33¢ Multicolored	14.50	3.00	.76	.22
2000. CHINESE NEW YEAR—YEAR OF THE DRAGON				
☐3370 33¢ Multicolored	14.50	3.00	.76	.24
2000. PATRICIA ROBERTS HARRIS				
☐3371 33¢ Multicolored	14.50	3.00	.76	.24
2000. LOS ANGELES CLASS SUBMARINE				
☐3372 33¢ Multicolored	14.00	3.00	.78	.28
2000. S CLASS SUBMARINE				
☐3373 22¢ Multicolored	—	—	.78	.28
2000. OHIO CLASS SUBMARINE				
☐3375 55¢ Multicolored	—	—	1.40	.45
2000. USS HOLLAND SUBMARINE				
☐3376 60¢ Multicolored	—	—	1.40	.45

*No hinge pricing from 1941 to date is figured at (N-H ADD 10%)

Scott No.	Mint Sheet	Plate Block	Fine Unused Each	Fine Used Each

2000. GATO CLASS SUBMARINE
☐3377 $3.20 Multicolored — — 7.80 6.00

2000. PACIFIC COAST RAIN FOREST
☐3378 Multicolored 7.00(10) — .75 .25

2000. LOUISE NEVELSON—SILENT MUSIC #1
☐3379 33¢ Multicolored — — .76 .28

2000. LOUISE NEVELSON—ROYAL TIDE #1
☐3380 33¢ Multicolored — — .76 .28

2000. LOUISE NEVELSON—BLACK CHORD
☐3381 33¢ Multicolored — — .76 .28

2000. LOUISE NEVELSON—NIGHTSPHERE LIGHT
☐3382 33¢ Multicolored — — .76 .28

2000. LOUISE NEVELSON—DAWN'S WEDDING CHAPEL 1
☐3383 33¢ Multicolored — — .76 .28

2000. HUBBLE IMAGES—EAGLE NEBULA
☐3384 33¢ Multicolored — — .76 .28

2000. HUBBLE IMAGES—RING NEBULA
☐3385 33¢ Multicolored — — .76 .28

2000. HUBBLE IMAGES—LAGOON NEBULA
☐3386 33¢ Multicolored — — .75 .27

2000. HUBBLE IMAGES—EGG NEBULA
☐3387 33¢ Multicolored — — .75 .27

2000. HUBBLE IMAGES—GALAXY NGC1316
☐3388 33¢ Multicolored — — .75 .27

*No hinge pricing from 1941 to date is figured at (N-H ADD 10%)

Scott No.	Mint Sheet	Plate Block	Fine Unused Each	Fine Used Each
2000. AMERICAN SAMOA				
☐3389 33¢ Multicolored	14.00	3.50	.75	.27
2000. LIBRARY OF CONGRESS				
☐3390 33¢ Multicolored	14.00	3.50	.75	.27
2000. ROAD RUNNER & WILE E. COYOTE				
☐3391-3392 33¢ Multicolored				
	7.00(10)	6.00(9)	.75	.27
2000. MAJOR GENERAL JOHN HINES				
☐3393 33¢ Multicolored	—	—	.75	.27
2000. GENERAL OMAR BRADLEY				
☐3394 33¢ Multicolored	—	—	.75	.27
2000. SERGEANT ALVIN YORK				
☐3395 33¢ Multicolored	—	—	.75	.27
2000. SECOND LIEUTENANT AUDIE MURPHY				
☐3396 Multicolored	—	3.00(4)	.75	.27
2000. SUMMER SPORTS—RUNNERS				
☐3397 33¢ Multicolored	—	—	.70	.25
2000. ADOPTION				
☐3398 33¢ Self-adhesive Multicolored	—		.70	.25
2000. YOUTH TEAM SPORTS—BASKETBALL				
☐3399 33¢ Multicolored	—	—	.70	.25
2000. YOUTH TEAM SPORTS—FOOTBALL				
☐3400 33¢ Multicolored	—	—	.70	.25
2000. YOUTH TEAM SPORTS—SOCCER				
☐3401 33¢ Multicolored	—	—	.70	.25

*No hinge pricing from 1941 to date is figured at (N-H ADD 10%)

Scott No.	Mint Sheet	Plate Block	Fine Unused Each	Fine Used Each

2000. YOUTH TEAM SPORTS—BASEBALL

☐3402 33¢ Multicolored	—	—	.70	.25

2000. HISTORIC AMERICAN FLAGS (20 VARIETIES)

☐3403 (a–t) 33¢ Multicolored

	15.00(20)	4.00	.70	.25

(a) Sons of Liberty, (b) New England, (c) Forester, (d) Continental, (e) Francis Hopkins, (f) Brandywine, (g) John Paul Jones, (h) Pierre L'Enfant, (i) Indian Peace, (j) Easter, (k) Star Spangled Banner, (l) Bennington, (m) Great Seal, (n) Star, (o) Fort Sumter, (p) Centennial, (q) 38 Star, (r) Peace, (s) 48 Star, (t) 50 Stars

2000. BLUEBERRIES

☐3404 33¢ Self-adhesive Multicolored	—	.70	.25

2000. STRAWBERRIES

☐3405 33¢ Self-adhesive Multicolored	—	.70	.25

2000. BLACKBERRIES

☐3406 33¢ Self-adhesive Multicolored	—	.70	.25

2000. RASPBERRIES

☐3407 33¢ Self-adhesive Multicolored	—	.70	.25

2000. LEGENDS OF BASEBALL (20 VARIETIES)

☐3408 (a–t) 33¢ Self-adhesive Multicolored

	14.00(20)	—	.70	.25

(a) Jackie Robinson, (b) Eddie Collins, (c) Christy Mathewson, (d) Ty Cobb, (e) George Sisler, (f) Roger Hornsby, (g) Mickey Cochrane, (h) Babe Ruth, (i) Walter Johnson, (j) Roberto Clemente, (k) Lefty Grove, (l) Tris Speaker, (m) Cy Young, (n) Jimmie Fox, (o) Pie Traynor, (p) Satchel Page, (q) Honus Wagner, (r) Josh Gibson, (s) Dizzy Dean, (t) Lou Gherig

2000. PROBING THE VASTNESS OF SPACE (6 VARIATIONS)

☐3409 33¢ Multicolored	9.00(6)	—	1.30	.70

*No hinge pricing from 1941 to date is figured at (N-H ADD 10%)

Scott No.	Mint Sheet	Plate Block	Fine Unused Each	Fine Used Each

2000. EXPLORING THE SOLAR SYSTEM
☐3410 $1.00 Multicolored	11.00(5)	—	2.25	1.10

2000. ESCAPING THE GRAVITY OF EARTH
☐3411 $3.20 Multicolored	12.50(2)	—	6.50	3.25

2000. SPACE ACHIEVEMENT AND EXPLORATION
☐3412 $11.75 Multicolored	25.00	—	6.50	3.10

2000. LANDING ON THE MOON
☐3413 $11.75 Multicolored	25.00	—	6.00	3.00

2000. SPACE FIGURES BY ZACHARY CANTER
☐3414 33¢ Self-adhesive Multicolored		—	.70	.25

2000. HEART BY SARAH LIPSEY
☐3415 33¢ Self-adhesive Multicolored		—	.70	.25

2000. MOMMY ARE WE THERE YET BY MORGAN HILL
☐3416 33¢ Self-adhesive Multicolored		—	.70	.25

2000. SPACE DOG BY ASHLEY YOUNG
☐3417 33¢ Self-adhesive Multicolored		—	.70	.25
☐3418–19 NOT ISSUED				

2000. DISTINGUISHED AMERICANS—GENERAL JOSEPH W. STILLWELL
☐3420 10¢ Multicolored	—	—	.30	.25
☐3421–25 NOT ISSUED				

2000. DISTINGUISHED AMERICANS—CLAUDE PEPPER
☐3426 33¢ Multicolored	—	—	.70	.25
☐3427–30 NOT ISSUED				

*No hinge pricing from 1941 to date is figured at (N-H ADD 10%)

Scott No.	Mint Sheet	Plate Block	Fine Unused Each	Fine Used Each

2000. DISTINGUISHED AMERICANS—HATTIE W. CARAWAY

| ☐3431 76¢ Multicolored | — | — | 1.60 | .25 |

☐3432–37 NOT ISSUED

2000. CALIFORNIA STATEHOOD—150TH ANNIVERSARY

| ☐3438 33¢ Multicolored | — | — | .70 | .25 |

2000. SEA CREATURES—FANFIN ANGLERFISH

| ☐3439 33¢ Multicolored | — | — | .70 | .25 |

2000. SEA CREATURES—SEA CUCUMBER

| ☐3440 33¢ Multicolored | — | — | .70 | .25 |

2000. SEA CREATURES—FANGTOOTH

| ☐3441 33¢ Multicolored | — | — | .70 | .25 |

2000. SEA CREATURES—AMPHIPOD

| ☐3442 33¢ Multicolored | — | — | .70 | .25 |

2000. SEA CREATURES—MEDUSA

| ☐3443 33¢ Multicolored | — | — | .70 | .25 |

2000. LITERARY ARTIST—THOMAS WOLFE

| ☐3444 33¢ Multicolored | — | — | .70 | .25 |

2000. WHITE HOUSE—200TH ANNIVERSARY

| ☐3445 33¢ Multicolored | — | — | .70 | .25 |

2000. LEDGENDS OF HOLLYWOOD—EDWARD G. ROBINSON

| ☐3446 33¢ Multicolored | — | — | .70 | .25 |

2000. NEW YORK LIBRARY LION

| ☐3447 10¢ Multicolored | — | — | .50 | .25 |

*No hinge pricing from 1941 to date is figured at (N-H ADD 10%)

Scott No.	Mint Sheet	Plate Block	Fine Unused Each	Fine Used Each
2000. FLAG OVER FARM				
☐3448–3450 34¢ Self-adhesive Multicolored				
	13.00(18)	3.00	.70	.25
2000. STATUE OF LIBERTY				
☐3451 34¢ Self-adhesive Multicolored			.70	.25
☐3452 34¢ Coil Multicolored			.70	.25
☐3453 34¢ Self-adhesive Coil Multicolored			.70	.25
☐3454 34¢ Self-adhesive Purple			.70	.25
☐3455 34¢ Self-adhesive Tan			.70	.25
☐3456 34¢ Self-adhesive Green			.70	.25
☐3457 34¢ Self-adhesive Red			.70	.25
☐3458 34¢ Purple			.70	.25
☐3459 34¢ Tan			.70	.25
☐3460 34¢ Green			.70	.25
☐3461 34¢ Red			.70	.25
☐3462 34¢ Coil Purple			.70	.25
☐3463 34¢ Coil Tan			.70	.25
☐3464 34¢ Coil Green			.70	.25
☐3465 34¢ Coil Red			.70	.25
2000. STATUE OF LIBERTY				
☐3466 34¢ Self-adhesive Multicolored		—	.70	.25
☐3467 NOT ISSUED				
2001. AMERICAN BUFFALO				
☐3468 21¢ Multicolored	—	—	.40	.20
2001. FLAG OVER FARM				
☐3469 34¢ Multicolored			.70	.25
☐3470 34¢ Self-adhesive Multicolored			.70	.25
2001. ART DECO EAGLE				
☐3471 55¢ Self-adhesive Multicolored		—	1.20	.25
2001. U.S. CAPITOL DOME				
☐3472 $3.50 Multicolored		—	7.10	3.75

*No hinge pricing from 1941 to date is figured at (N-H ADD 10%)

Scott No.	Mint Sheet	Plate Block	Fine Unused Each	Fine Used Each

2001. WASHINGTON MONUMENT
☐3473 $12.25 Multicolored 400.00 120.00 24.00 11.00
☐3474 NOT ISSUED

2001. AMERICAN BUFFALO
☐3475 21¢ Self-adhesive Coil Multicolored
8.00 2.00 .40 .20

2001. STATUE OF LIBERTY
☐3476 34¢ Coil Multicolored — — .70 .25

2001. STATUE OF LIBERTY
☐3477 34¢ Self-adhesive Coil Multicolored
.70 .25

2001. FLOWER
☐3478 34¢ Self-adhesive Coil Multicolored
.70 .25

2001. FLOWER
☐3479 34¢ Self-adhesive Coil Multicolored
.70 .25

2001. PEANUTS COMIC STRIP
☐3507 34¢ Multicolored — — .70 .25

2001. U.S. VETERANS
☐3508 34¢ Self-adhesive Multicolored — — .70 .25

2001. FRIDA KAHLO—PAINTER
☐3509 34¢ Multicolored — — .70 .25

2001. LEDGENDARY PLAYING FIELDS—EBBETS FIELD
☐3510 34¢ Self-adhesive Multicolored
8.00(10) — .70 .25

2001. LEDGENDARY PLAYING FIELDS—TIGER STADIUM
☐3511 34¢ Self-adhesive Multicolored
8.00(10) — .70 .25

*No hinge pricing from 1941 to date is figured at (N-H ADD 10%)

Scott No.	Mint Sheet	Plate Block	Fine Unused Each	Fine Used Each

2001. LEDGENDARY PLAYING FIELDS—CROSLEY FIELD
☐3512 34¢ Self-adhesive Multicolored

| | 8.00(10) | — | .70 | .25 |

2001. LEDGENDARY PLAYING FIELDS—YANKEE STADIUM
☐3513 34¢ Self-adhesive Multicolored

| | 8.00(10) | — | .70 | .25 |

2001. LEDGENDARY PLAYING FIELDS—POLO GROUNDS
☐3514 34¢ Self-adhesive Multicolored

| | 8.00(10) | — | .70 | .25 |

2001. LEDGENDARY PLAYING FIELDS—FORBES FIELD
☐3515 34¢ Self-adhesive Multicolored

| | 8.00(10) | — | .70 | .25 |

2001. LEDGENDARY PLAYING FIELDS—FENNWAY FIELD
☐3516 34¢ Self-adhesive Multicolored

| | 8.00(10) | — | .70 | .25 |

2001. LEDGENDARY PLAYING FIELDS—COMINSKY PARK
☐3517 Self-adhesive Multicolored

| | 8.00(10) | — | .70 | .25 |

2001. FLOWER
☐3480 34¢ Self-adhesive Coil Multicolored

| | | | .70 | .25 |

2001. FLOWER
☐3481 34¢ Self-adhesive Coil Multicolored

| | | | .70 | .25 |

*No hinge pricing from 1941 to date is figured at (N-H ADD 10%)

Scott No.	Mint Sheet	Plate Block	Fine Unused Each	Fine Used Each

2001. GEORGE WASHINGTON
☐3482 20¢ Self-adhesive Multicolored

| | 6.00(10) | 2.00(4) | .50 | .25 |

2001. GEORGE WASHINGTON
☐3483 20¢ Self-adhesive Multicolored

| | 12.00(10) | 9.00(6) | .50 | .25 |

☐3484 NOT ISSUED

2001. STATUE OF LIBERTY
☐3485 34¢ Self-adhesive Multicolored

| | 14.00(20) | 4.50(6) | .70 | .25 |

☐3486 NOT ISSUED

2001. FLOWER
☐3487 34¢ Self-adhesive Multicolored

| | — | | .70 | .25 |

2001. FLOWER
☐3488 34¢ Self-adhesive Multicolored

| | — | | .70 | .25 |

2001. FLOWER
☐3489 34¢ Self-adhesive Multicolored

| | — | | .70 | .25 |

2001. FLOWER
☐3490 34¢ Self-adhesive Multicolored

| | — | | .70 | .25 |

2001. APPLE
☐3491 34¢ Self-adhesive Multicolored

| | — | | .70 | .25 |

2001. ORANGE
☐3492 34¢ Self-adhesive Multicolored

| | — | | .70 | .25 |

2001. APPLE
☐3493 34¢ Self-adhesive Multicolored

| | — | | .70 | .25 |

*No hinge pricing from 1941 to date is figured at (N-H ADD 10%)

Scott No.	Mint Sheet	Plate Block	Fine Unused Each	Fine Used Each

2001. ORANGE
☐3494 34¢ Self-adhesive Multicolored — .70 .25
☐3495 NOT ISSUED

2001. ROSE AND LOVE
☐3496 34¢ Multicolored 14.00(20) — .70 .25

2001. ROSE AND LOVE
☐3497 34¢ Multicolored 14.00(20) — .90 .40

2001. ROSE AND LOVE
☐3498 34¢ Multicolored — 3.00(4) .90 .40

2001. ROSE AND LOVE
☐3499 55¢ Multicolored — — 1.25 .40

2001. CHINESE NEW YEAR—YEAR OF THE SNAKE
☐3500 34¢ Multicolored 13.00 — .70 .25

2001. BLACK HERITAGE—ROY WILKINS
☐3501 34¢ Multicolored — — .70 .25

2001. AMERICAN ILLUSTRATORS (20 VARIETIES)
☐3502 (a–t) 34¢ Multicolored
                14.00(20) — .70 .25
(a) James Montgomery Flagg, (b) Maxfield Parrish, (c) J.C. Leyen-decker, (d) Robert Fawcett, (e) Coles Phillips, (f) Al Parker, (g) A. B Frost, (h) Howard Pyle, (i) Rose O'Neil, (j) Dean Cornwell, (k) Edwin Austin Abbey, (l) Jessie Wilcox Smith, (m) Neysa McMein, (n) John Whitcomb, (o) Havey Dunn, (p) Frederrick Remington, (q) Rockwell Kent, (r) N.C. Wyeth, (s) Norman Rockwell, (t) John Held, Jr.

2001. DIABETES AWARENESS
☐3503 34¢ Multicolored — — .70 .25

*No hinge pricing from 1941 to date is figured at (N-H ADD 10%)

Scott No.	Mint Sheet	Plate Block	Fine Unused Each	Fine Used Each

2001. NOBEL PRIZE—CENTENARY
☐3504 34¢ Multicolored — — .70 .25

2001. PAN AMERICAN EXPO
☐3505A 1¢ Multicolored — — .25 .25

2001. PAN AMERICAN EXPO
☐3505B 2¢ Multicolored — — .25 .25

2001. PAN AMERICAN EXPO
☐3505C 4¢ Multicolored — — .25 .25

2001. PAN AMERICAN EXPO
☐3505D 80¢ Multicolored — — 2.00 1.00

2001. GREAT PLAINS—PRAIRIE (10 VARIETIES)
☐3506 34¢ Multicolored 8.00(10) — .70 .25

2001. LEDGENDARY PLAYING FIELDS—SHIBE PARK
☐3518 34¢ Self-adhesive Multicolored
8.00(10) — .70 .25

2001. LEDGENDARY PLAYING FIELDS—WRIGLEY FIELD
☐3519 34¢ Self-adhesive Multicolored
8.00(10) — .70 .25

2001. ATLAS STATUE—NEW YORK CITY
☐3520 34¢ Self-adhesive Coil Multicolored .25 .25

2001. LEONARD BERNSTEIN
☐3521 34¢ Multicolored — — .70 .25

2001. WOODY WAGON
☐3522 15¢ Self-adhesive Coil Multicolored .40 .25

*No hinge pricing from 1941 to date is figured at (N-H ADD 10%)

Scott No.	Mint Sheet	Plate Block	Fine Unused Each	Fine Used Each

2001. LEDGENDS OF HOLLYWOOD—LUCILLE BALL

☐3523 34¢ Self-adhesive Multicolored	—		.70	.25

2001. AMERICAN TREASURES SERIES AMISH QUILTS—DIAMOND IN THE SQUARE

☐3524 34¢ Self-adhesive Multicolored

	3.00(4)	—	.70	.25

2001. AMERICAN TREASURES SERIES AMISH QUILTS—LONE STAR

☐3525 34¢ Self-adhesive Multicolored

	3.00(4)	—	.70	.25

2001. AMERICAN TREASURES SERIES AMISH QUILTS—SUNSHINE $ SHADOWS

☐3526 34¢ Multicolored	3.00(4)	—	.70	.25

2001. AMERICAN TREASURES SERIES AMISH QUILTS—DOUBLE NINEPATCH VARIATION

☐3427 34¢ Self-adhesive Multicolored

	3.00(4)	—	.70	.25

2001. CARNIVOROUS PLANTS—VENUS FLYTRAP

☐3528 34¢ Self-adhesive Multicolored

	3.00(4)	—	.70	.25

2001. CARNIVOROUS PLANTS—YELLOW TRUMPET

☐3529 34¢ Self-adhesive Multicolored

	3.00(4)	—	.70	.25

2001. CARNIVOROUS PLANTS—COBRA LILLY

☐3530 34¢ Self-adhesive Multicolored

	3.00(4)	—	.70	.25

*No hinge pricing from 1941 to date is figured at (N-H ADD 10%)

Scott No.	Mint Sheet	Plate Block	Fine Unused Each	Fine Used Each

2001. CARNIVOROUS PLANTS—ENGLISH SUNDEW

☐3531 34¢ Self-adhesive Multicolored				
	3.00(4)	—	.70	.25

2001. EID MUBARAK

☐3532 34¢ Self-adhesive Multicolored	—		.70	.25

2001. ENRICO FERMI

☐3533 34¢ Multicolored	—	—	.70	.25

2001. PORKY PIG "THAT'S ALL FOLKS"

☐3535 34¢ Multicolored	—	—	.70	.25

2001. MADONNA & CHILD

☐3536 34¢ Multicolored	—	—	.70	.25

*No hinge pricing from 1941 to date is figured at (N-H ADD 10%)

AIRMAIL STAMPS

THE AMERICAN AIR MAIL SOCIETY

The American Air Mail Society, organized in 1923, is one of the oldest and largest aerophilatelic societies in existence. The dues are as low as possible; privileges and services to members are many. It is not necessary that a person be an advanced collector or a wealthy specialist to attain membership—or to enjoy aerophilately to its fullest extent. Over twenty AAMS chapters and study units offer members a chance to interact either by mail or at regular meetings held throughout the United States. With two national meetings per year, the AAMS makes it possible for members and friends to meet each year in different parts of the United States. For three days or more the subject is always airmail stamps and covers, as well as the plans and progress of the AAMS itself.

The Airpost Journal (APJ) has been supported and published by the AAMS since October 1931. The *APJ* is a generously illustrated magazine covering a wide range of aerophilately. AAMS news appears regularly to keep members apprised of the organization. Feature articles, written by leading scholars in each field, are published each month covering areas of worldwide interest. Regular columns of a continuing interest include areas such as astrophilately, air postal stationery, auction results, first flight cover news, new airmail stamp issues, show news, Zeppelin posts, book reviews, and members exchange ads.

The *Jack Knight Air Log (JKAL)* became an AAMS publication after the 1995 merger of the AAMS and the Aerophilatelic Federation of the Americas. This diverse 100-page publication includes an auction of airmail material, reports and research studies by various airmail specialty groups, and member exchange ads. AAMS study units on Canadian

Air Mails, Lindbergh, 1934 Emergency Air Mail, Pan American Airlines, Rocket Mail, and Zeppelin posts publish regular sections in the *JKAL.*

The AAMS is one of the world's largest and most successful publishers of airmail literature. The *American Air Mail Catalogue (AAMC)* has been published since 1935. Other AAMS handbooks and monographs treat a variety of specialist U.S. and foreign airmail topics, from pioneer airmails worldwide to specialty topics. Members receive a discount on many of these handbooks. To receive a list of current publications for sale, write the AAMS Publications Sales Manager, 1978 Fox Burrow Court, Neenah, WI 54956.

Please join with us to bring airmail into the 21st century as a continuing, exciting hobby! For a membership application, write to: The American Air Mail Society, P.O. Box 110, Mineola, NY 11501-0110.

COLLECTING AIRMAIL STAMPS
by Kent Kobersteen

Airmail stamps can provide a fascinating, aesthetically pleasing, historically informative topic for the collector. You can build a collection of airmail stamps which is as broad as a single copy of every airmail stamp which has been issued worldwide, or as narrow as a specialized look at a single series or a single issue. Airmail postcards, stationery, and aerogrammes provide yet another area of specialization.

A collection of worldwide airmail stamps will show not only the development of aircraft and air-related events, but also will show how the airmail service developed worldwide. So, too, will the collection of a single country's airmail issues tell the story of the development of airmail in that country. In the case of the United States, for instance, the development of the airmail both domestically and internationally, and the rates for this service, can be traced through a collection of U.S. airmail stamps.

You can also specialize in a single series, such as the U.S. Transport issue of the early 1940s, or a single stamp such as the Beacon airmail stamp of 1928. At first glance you might assume such specialization would limit your collecting options. Quite the contrary. After avidly collecting the Beacon airmail stamp for over fifteen years, one continually finds new material in usages on covers and in an extensive representation of the stamps.

A first step in building such a specialized collection of a single issue or series is to consult catalogs and specialized literature. *The American Air Mail Catalogue, Scott's Specialized U.S. Stamp Catalogue,* and Max. G. Johl's *The United States Postage Stamp of the Twentieth Century, Volume III,* will indicate plate positions, recuts, varieties, and errors which have been found by other specialists. Many aerophilatelists have published works based on their research; a search of the philatelic literature will reveal new information in a variety of areas. It is extremely gratifying to make a discovery that has been overlooked by earlier experts.

You might begin with the design itself, researching its origins. Essays of some stamps may be on the market, others exist only in the archives of the Bureau of Engraving and Printing in Washington, D.C.

Mint stamps can be obtained showing various plate positions, guide lines, plate numbers, and other marginal markings, as well as sideographer and plate finisher's initials—if they occur on the issue being studied.

It is also important to learn about the appropriate printing and perforating processes to analyze production varieties of the stamp or stamps in question. As you look at more copies of the stamp, you will find slight variations due to production differences. The archives of the Bureau of Engraving and Printing contain a wealth of information about the production of United States issues.

Used copies of airmail stamps offer unusual and interesting cancellations with numerous possibilities: fancy cancels, slogan cancels, socked-on-the-nose cancels, numeral cancels, paquebot and foreign cancels—the list is nearly endless. You can also search for stamps with perforated insignia or perfins and precancels. Many pleasant hours can be had poring over dealers' stocks or large lots of relatively common stamps. And, when mounted, the display of various cancellation varieties can be impressive.

Once you feel you have exhausted the possibilities of your stamp study, keep looking, and examine other stamp exhibits for ideas of new directions to pursue. You can always find more fascinating material to add to your stamp collection, and through study and scholarship you can contribute to the overall body of knowledge of your specialty.

Scott No.	Fine Unused Plate Blk	Ave. Unused Plate Blk	Fine Unused Each	Ave. Unused Each	Fine Used Each	Ave. Used Each

AIRMAIL STAMPS
1918. FIRST ISSUE—(N-H ADD 45%)

☐C1 6¢ Orange

| | 900.00 | 600.00 | 800.00 | 72.00 | 32.00 | 23.00 |

☐C2 16¢ Green

| | 1500.00 | 1200.00 | 110.00 | 95.00 | 36.00 | 26.00 |

☐C3 24¢ Carmine & Blue

| | 1800.00 | 1400.00 | 110.00 | 85.00 | 40.00 | 26.00 |

1923. SECOND ISSUE—(N-H ADD 35%)

☐C4 8¢ Dark Green

| | 400.00 | 280.00 | 32.00 | 24.00 | 15.00 | 13.00 |

☐C5 16¢ Dark Blue

| | 2400.00 | 1800.00 | 100.00 | 76.00 | 38.00 | 25.00 |

☐C6 24¢ Carmine

| | 3000.00 | 2200.00 | 115.00 | 80.00 | 32.00 | 25.00 |

1926–1927. LONG MAP (N-H ADD 35%)

☐C7 10¢ Dark Blue

| | 60.00 | 40.00 | 3.00 | 2.50 | 40.00 | .25 |

☐C8 15¢ Olive Brown

| | 70.00 | 50.00 | 3.75 | 2.50 | 2.30 | 1.75 |

☐C9 20¢ Yellow Green

| | 110.00 | 80.00 | 10.00 | 8.00 | 1.90 | 1.60 |

1927. LINDBERGH TRIBUTE ISSUE (N-H ADD 25%)

☐C10 10¢ Dark Blue

| | 180.00 | 120.00 | 8.00 | 6.00 | 2.30 | 1.25 |

1928. BEACON (N-H ADD 20%)

☐C11 5¢ Carmine & Blue

| | 60.00 | 35.00 | 5.00 | 3.00 | .80 | .30 |

1930. WINGED GLOBE—FLAT PRESS (N-H ADD 35%)

☐C12 5¢ Violet

| | 200.00 | 140.00 | 10.00 | 8.00 | .45 | .30 |

1930. GRAF ZEPPELIN ISSUE (N-H ADD 20%)

☐C13 65¢ Green

| | 2300.00 | 2000.00 | 260.00 | 240.00 | 200.00 | 140.00 |

Scott No.	Fine Unused Plate Blk	Ave. Unused Plate Blk	Fine Unused Each	Ave. Unused Each	Fine Used Each	Ave. Used Each
☐C14 $1.30 Brown						
	6200.00	4800.00	700.00	600.00	400.00	300.00
☐C15 $2.60 Blue						
	10,000.00	8000.00	1000.00	850.00	600.00	450.00

1931–1932.
WINGED GLOBE—ROTARY PRESS (N-H ADD 25%)

☐C16 5¢ Violet						
	150.00	100.00	6.00	3.80	.65	.40
☐C17 8¢ Olive Bistre						
	50.00	36.00	2.50	1.90	.42	.25

1933. CENTURY OF PROGRESS ISSUE
(N-H ADD 25%)

☐C18 50¢ Green						
	900.00	800.00	80.00	70.00	74.00	40.00

1934. DESIGN OF 1930 (N-H ADD 25%)

☐C19 6¢ Orange						
	35.00	25.00	3.00	2.10	.25	.15

1935–1937. TRANS-PACIFIC ISSUE
(N-H ADD 10%)

☐C20 25¢ Blue						
	30.00	22.00	1.45	1.00	1.00	.75
☐C21 20¢ Green						
	135.00	100.00	10.00	7.00	1.65	1.25
☐C22 50¢ Carmine						
	130.00	100.00	11.00	9.00	6.00	3.00

1938. EAGLE (N-H ADD 20%)

☐C23 6¢ Blue & Carmine						
	8.00	7.00	.52	.36	.23	.16

1939. TRANS-ATLANTIC (N-H ADD 20%)

☐C24 30¢ Dull Blue						
	170.00	130.00	11.00	8.50	1.45	.90

Scott No.	Mint Sheet	Plate Block	Fine Unused Each	Fine Used Each

1941–1944. TRANSPORT PLANE*

Scott No.	Mint Sheet	Plate Block	Fine Unused Each	Fine Used Each
☐C25 6¢ Carmine	8.50	1.00	.20	.15
☐C26 8¢ Olive Green	12.00	2.10	.19	.15
☐C27 10¢ Violet	85.00	10.00	1.20	.16
☐C28 15¢ Brown Carmine	160.00	12.00	3.00	.40
☐C29 20¢ Bright Green	120.00	100.00	2.75	.35
☐C30 30¢ Blue	150.00	13.00	3.00	.40
☐C31 50¢ Orange	650.00	75.00	12.00	3.50

1946–1947. DC-4 SKYMASTER*

Scott No.	Mint Sheet	Plate Block	Fine Unused Each	Fine Used Each
☐C32 5¢ Carmine	7.50	.75	.22	.16
☐C33 5¢ Carmine	15.00	.75	.25	.15

1947. REGULAR ISSUE*

Scott No.	Mint Sheet	Plate Block	Fine Unused Each	Fine Used Each
☐C34 10¢ Black	12.00	1.50	.25	.17
☐C35 15¢ Bright Blue Green	20.00	1.75	.40	.15
☐C36 25¢ Blue	55.00	5.00	1.00	.15

Scott No.	Fine Unused Line Pair	Ave. Unused Line Pair	Fine Unused Each	Ave. Unused Each	Fine Used Each	Ave. Used Each

1948. DESIGN OF 1947*

Scott No.	Fine Unused Line Pair	Ave. Unused Line Pair	Fine Unused Each	Ave. Unused Each	Fine Used Each	Ave. Used Each
☐C37 5¢ Carmine	10.00	8.50	1.00	.85	.86	.40

Scott No.	Mint Sheet	Plate Block	Fine Unused Each	Fine Used Each

1948. NEW YORK CITY JUBILEE ISSUE*

Scott No.	Mint Sheet	Plate Block	Fine Unused Each	Fine Used Each
☐C38 5¢ Red	19.00	5.00	.22	.16

*No hinge pricing from 1941 to date is figured at (N-H ADD 10%)

Scott No.	Mint Sheet	Plate Block	Fine Unused Each	Fine Used Each

1949. DESIGN OF 1947*

Scott No.	Mint Sheet	Plate Block	Fine Unused Each	Fine Used Each
☐C39 6¢ Carmine	14.00	.80	.22	.18

1949. ALEXANDRIA BICENTENNIAL*

☐C40 6¢ Carmine	7.50	.75	.21	.16

Scott No.	Fine Unused Line Pair	Ave. Unused Line Pair	Fine Unused Each	Ave. Unused Each	Fine Used Each	Ave. Used Each

1949. DESIGN OF 1947*

☐C41 6¢ Carmine						
	14.00	10.00	3.40	3.00	.24	.17

Scott No.	Mint Sheet	Plate Block	Fine Unused Each	Fine Used Each

1949. U.P.U.—UNIVERSAL POSTAL UNION ISSUE*

☐C42 10¢ Purple	15.00	2.00	.30	.24
☐C43 15¢ Ultramarine	20.00	2.00	.35	.25
☐C44 25¢ Carmine	40.00	6.50	.50	.30

1949. WRIGHT BROTHERS ISSUE*

☐C45 6¢ Magenta	10.00	.65	.22	.17

1952. HAWAII—DIAMOND HEAD*

☐C46 80¢ Bright Red Violet	410.00	32.00	6.00	1.40

1953. 50TH ANNIVERSARY POWERED FLIGHT*

☐C47 6¢ Carmine	8.00	.70	.21	.16

1954. EAGLE IN FLIGHT*

☐C48 4¢ Bright Blue	14.00	1.90	.21	.16

1957. 50TH ANNIVERSARY AIR FORCE*

☐C49 6¢ Blue	8.00	.80	.21	.16

*No hinge pricing from 1941 to date is figured at (N-H ADD 10%)

Scott No.	Mint Sheet	Plate Block	Fine Unused Each	Fine Used Each

1958. DESIGN OF 1954*
| ☐C50 5¢ Red | 14.00 | 1.50 | .21 | .16 |

1958. JETLINER SILHOUETTE*
| ☐C51 7¢ Blue | 18.00 | .80 | .21 | .16 |

Scott No.	Fine Unused Line Pair	Ave. Unused Line Pair	Fine Unused Each	Ave. Unused Each	Fine Used Each	Ave. Used Each
☐C52 7¢ Blue						
	18.00	15.00	2.15	1.80	.25	.16

1959. COMMEMORATIVES*

Scott No.	Mint Sheet	Plate Block	Fine Unused Each	Fine Used Each

1959. ALASKA STATEHOOD*
| ☐C53 7¢ Dark Blue | 8.00 | .70 | .21 | .16 |

1959. BALLOON JUPITER FLIGHT*
| ☐C54 7¢ Dark Blue & Red | 8.00 | .70 | .21 | .16 |

1959. HAWAII STATEHOOD*
| ☐C55 7¢ Rose Red | 8.00 | .70 | .21 | .16 |

1959. PAN AMERICAN GAMES*
| ☐C56 10¢ Red & Blue | 14.00 | 1.60 | .28 | .17 |

1959–1961. REGULAR ISSUE*
☐C57 10¢ Black & Green	90.00	7.00	1.25	.65
☐C58 15¢ Black & Orange	28.00	1.80	.36	.17
☐C59 25¢ Black & Maroon	32.00	2.00	.50	.17

1960. DESIGN OF 1958*
| ☐C60 7¢ Carmine | 17.00 | .70 | .22 | .17 |

*No hinge pricing from 1941 to date is figured at (N-H ADD 10%)

Scott No.		Fine Unused Line Pair	Ave. Unused Line Pair	Fine Unused Each	Ave. Unused Each	Fine Used Each	Ave. Used Each
☐C61	7¢ Carmine						
		42.00	34.00	5.50	4.10	.26	.24

Scott No.		Mint Sheet	Plate Block	Fine Unused Each	Fine Used Each

1961. DESIGNS OF 1959–1960*

Scott No.		Mint Sheet	Plate Block	Fine Unused Each	Fine Used Each
☐C62	13¢ Black & Red	22.00	2.10	.41	.16
☐C63	15¢ Black & Orange	18.00	1.40	.35	.16

1962. JETLINER OVER CAPITOL*

☐C64	8¢ Carmine	21.00	1.00	.21	.16

Scott No.		Fine Unused Line Pair	Ave. Unused Line Pair	Fine Unused Each	Ave. Unused Each	Fine Used Each	Ave. Used Each
☐C65	8¢ Carmine						
		7.00	6.00	.45	.36	.21	.15

Scott No.		Mint Sheet	Plate Block	Fine Unused Each	Fine Used Each

1963. FIRST INTERNATIONAL POSTAL CONFERENCE CENTENARY*

☐C66	15¢ Dull Red, Dark Brown & Blue				
		36.00	4.00	.61	.50

1963. POSTAL CARD RATE*

☐C67	6¢ Red	22.00	2.00	.22	.17

1963. AMELIA EARHART*

☐C68	8¢ Carmine & Maroon				
		11.00	1.00	.22	.17

1964. DR. ROBERT H. GODDARD*

☐C69	8¢ Blue, Red, Bistre	24.00	2.30	.50	.20

1967. ALASKA PURCHASE CENTENARY*

☐C70	8¢ Dark Brown	15.00	2.10	.25	.18

*No hinge pricing from 1941 to date is figured at (N-H ADD 10%)

Scott No.	Mint Sheet	Plate Block	Fine Unused Each	Fine Used Each

1967. COLUMBIA JAYS*
☐C71 20¢ Blue, Brown, Bistre

	52.00	5.00	1.00	.16

1967. 50 STARS*
☐C72 10¢ Carmine

	28.00	1.40	.22	.16

Scott No.	Fine Unused Line Pair	Ave. Unused Line Pair	Fine Unused Each	Ave. Unused Each	Fine Used Each	Ave. Used Each

1968. 50 STARS*
☐C73 10¢ Carmine

	2.45	2.10	.46	.32	.28	.18

1968. 50TH ANNIVERSARY AIRMAIL SERVICE*
☐C74 10¢ Black, Blue, Red

	20.00		3.00		.30	.17

1968. U.S.A.*
☐C75 20¢ Red, Blue, Black

	30.00		3.10		.40	.17

1969. FIRST MAN ON THE MOON*
☐C76 10¢ Red, Blue, Brown

	10.50		2.10		.30	.17

1971–1973.
☐C77 9¢ Red
☐C78 11¢ Carmine
☐C79 13¢ Carmine
☐C80 17¢ Green, Blue, Red
☐C81 21¢ Blue, Red, Black
☐C82 11¢ Carmine
☐C83 13¢ Carmine

C77 9¢ Red	20.00		1.25		.25	.20
C78 11¢ Carmine	28.00		1.50		.25	.17
C79 13¢ Carmine	40.00		1.70		.30	.17
C80 17¢ Green, Blue, Red	28.00		2.70		.40	.17
C81 21¢ Blue, Red, Black	27.00		2.10		.50	.17
C82 11¢ Carmine	1.25	1.20	.43	.33	.30	.17
C83 13¢ Carmine	1.30	1.20	.47	.35	.31	.17

Scott No.	Mint Sheet	Plate Block	Fine Unused Each	Fine Used Each

1972. NATIONAL PARKS CENTENNIAL*
☐C84 11¢ Multicolored

	14.00	1.00	.30	.17

*No hinge pricing from 1941 to date is figured at (N-H ADD 10%)

Scott No.	Mint Sheet	Plate Block	Fine Unused Each	Fine Used Each
1972. OLYMPIC GAMES*				
☐C85 11¢ Multicolored	14.00	3.10	.50	.17
1973. PROGRESS IN ELECTRONICS*				
☐C86 11¢ Multicolored	14.00	1.50	.30	.17
1974. STATUE OF LIBERTY*				
☐C87 18¢ Red, Blue, Black	30.00	2.50	.40	.25
1974. MOUNT RUSHMORE*				
☐C88 26¢ Red, Blue, Black	40.00	3.10	.60	.17
1976. PLANE*				
☐C89 25¢ Red, Blue, Black	38.00	3.00	.55	.17
☐C90 31¢ Red, Blue, Black	45.00	4.00	.65	.17
1979. WRIGHT BROTHERS*				
☐C91 31¢ Blue, Brown, Red	100.00	5.00	.75	.20
☐C92 31¢ Blue, Brown, Red	100.00	5.00	.75	.20
1979. CHANUTE & PLANE*				
☐C93 21¢ Blue, Brown, Red	98.00	5.00	.80	.30
☐C94 21¢ Blue, Brown, Red	98.00	5.00	.80	.30
1980. PLANE & WILEY POST*				
☐C95 25¢ Multicolored	180.00	13.00	1.50	.30
☐C96 25¢ Multicolored	180.00	13.00	1.00	.30
1980. HIGH JUMPER*				
☐C97 31¢ Multicolored	39.00	13.00	.75	.31
1981. PHILIP MAZZEI*				
☐C98 40¢ Multicolored	55.00	12.50	.90	.18
1981. BLANCHE SCOTT*				
☐C99 28¢ Multicolored	42.00	8.00	.75	.19
1981. GLENN CURTIS*				
☐C100 35¢ Multicolored	55.00	90.00	.75	.18
1983. SUMMER OLYMPICS*				
☐C101 28¢ Multicolored	60.00	6.00	1.10	.26
☐C102 28¢ Multicolored	60.00	6.00	1.10	.26
☐C103 28¢ Multicolored	60.00	6.00	1.10	.26

*No hinge pricing from 1941 to date is figured at (N-H ADD 10%)

Scott No.	Mint Sheet	Plate Block	Fine Unused Each	Fine Used Each
☐ C104 28¢ Multicolored	60.00	6.00	1.10	.26
☐ C105 40¢ Multicolored	70.00	7.00	1.10	.26
☐ C106 40¢ Multicolored	70.00	7.00	1.10	.26
☐ C107 40¢ Multicolored	70.00	7.00	1.10	.26
☐ C108 40¢ Multicolored	70.00	7.00	1.10	.26
☐ C109 35¢ Multicolored	60.00	7.50	1.10	.30
☐ C110 35¢ Multicolored	60.00	7.50	1.10	.30
☐ C111 35¢ Multicolored	60.00	7.50	1.10	.30
☐ C112 35¢ Multicolored	60.00	7.50	1.10	.30

1985. ALFRED VERVILLE*
☐ C113 33¢ Multicolored	50.00	4.90	.75	.24

1985. LAWRENCE & ELMER SPERRY*
☐ C114 39¢ Multicolored	50.00	6.00	.90	.24

1985. TRANSPACIFIC*
☐ C115 44¢ Multicolored	65.00	6.00	.90	.26

1985. JUNIPERO SERRA*
☐ C116 44¢ Multicolored	70.00	9.00	1.20	.26

1988. NEW SWEDEN*
☐ C117 44¢ Multicolored	60.00	9.00	1.10	.26

1988. SAMUEL LANGLEY*
☐ C118 45¢ Multicolored	65.00	6.00	1.00	.24

1988. IGOR SIKORSKY*
☐ C119 36¢ Multicolored	55.00	5.00	.80	.24

1989. FRENCH REVOLUTION*
☐ C120 45¢ Multicolored	40.00	6.00	1.10	.25

1989. AMERICA*
☐ C121 45¢ Multicolored	65.00	6.00	1.10	.25

1989. SPACE SHUTTLE*
☐ C122 45¢ Multicolored	70.00	7.00	1.25	.32

1989. SPACE MAIL DELIVERY*
☐ C123 45¢ Multicolored	70.00	7.00	1.25	.32

1989. MOON ROVER*
☐ C124 45¢ Multicolored	75.00	7.00	1.25	.32

*No hinge pricing from 1941 to date is figured at (N-H ADD 10%)

Scott No.	Mint Sheet	Plate Block	Fine Unused Each	Fine Used Each
1989. SPACE SHUTTLE STATION*				
☐C125 45¢ Multicolored	75.00	7.00	1.10	.30
1989. SPACE MAIL*				
☐C126 1.80 Multicolored	—	—	5.00	3.00
1990. AMERICA*				
☐C127 45¢ Multicolored	60.00	6.00	1.10	.25
1991. HARRIET QUIMBY*				
☐C128 50¢ Multicolored	62.00	7.00	1.25	.27
1991. WILLIAM PIPER*				
☐C129 40¢ Multicolored	56.00	6.00	1.00	.27
1991. ANTARCTIC TREATY*				
☐C130 50¢ Multicolored	66.00	7.00	1.00	.27
1991. AMERICA*				
☐C131 50¢ Multicolored	70.00	7.00	1.10	.26
1993. WILLIAM PIPER				
☐C132 40¢ Multicolored	62.00	6.00	1.25	.26

Scott No.	Fine Unused Plate Blk	Ave. Unused Plate Blk	Fine Unused Each	Ave. Unused Each	Fine Used Each	Ave. Used Each
AIRMAIL SPECIAL DELIVERY						
☐CE1 16¢ Dark Blue						
	20.00	15.00	.91	.50	.65	.40
☐CE2 16¢ Red & Blue						
	7.00	6.00	.60	.50	.42	.17
SPECIAL DELIVERY STAMPS						
1885.						
☐E1 10¢ Blue—	—	230.00	150.00		32.00	20.00
1888.						
☐E2 10¢ Blue—	—	230.00	130.00		10.00	6.50

*No hinge pricing from 1941 to date is figured at (N-H ADD 10%)

Scott No.	Fine Unused Plate Blk	Ave. Unused Plate Blk	Fine Unused Each	Ave. Unused Each	Fine Used Each	Ave. Used Each
1893. (N-H ADD 60%)						
☐E3 10¢ Orange						
	—	—	175.00	90.00	15.00	9.00
1894. (N-H ADD 40%)						
☐E4 10¢ Blue	—	—	700.00	350.00	26.00	12.00
1895. (N-H ADD 50%)						
☐E5 10¢ Blue						
	—	—	140.00	82.00	3.00	1.75
1902. (N-H ADD 40%)						
☐E6 10¢ Ultramarine						
	—	—	100.00	60.00	3.50	2.00
1908. (N-H ADD 20%)						
☐E7 10¢ Green						
	—	—	62.00	38.00	35.00	14.00
1911. (N-H ADD 40%)						
☐E8 10¢ Ultramarine						
	—	—	80.00	61.00	4.50	2.60
1914. (N-H ADD 40%)						
☐E9 10¢ Ultramarine						
	—	—	150.00	100.00	6.00	3.00
1916. (N-H ADD 40%)						
☐E10 10¢ Pale Ultramarine						
	—	—	250.00	190.00	26.00	12.00
1917. (N-H ADD 50%)						
☐E11 10¢ Ultramarine						
	—	—	19.00	10.00	.51	.30
1922–1925. (N-H ADD 30%)						
☐E12 10¢ Deep Ultramarine						
	260.00	200.00	40.00	14.00	.28	.21

Scott No.	Fine Unused Plate Blk	Ave. Unused Plate Blk	Fine Unused Each	Ave. Unused Each	Fine Used Each	Ave. Used Each
☐E13 10¢ Deep Orange						
	210.00	160.00	23.00	16.00	1.00	.45
☐E14 20¢ Black						
	50.00	35.00	3.10	2.00	1.10	.65

1927–1951. (N-H ADD 30%)

Scott No.	Fine Unused Plate Blk	Ave. Unused Plate Blk	Fine Unused Each	Ave. Unused Each	Fine Used Each	Ave. Used Each
☐E15 10¢ Gray Violet						
	9.00	7.00	.70	.50	.23	.16
☐E16 15¢ Orange						
	7.00	6.00	.80	.75	.20	.16
☐E17 13¢ Blue						
	6.00	5.00	.70	.45	.22	.16
☐E18 17¢ Yellow						
	36.00	28.00	3.00	2.60	1.60	1.40
☐E19 20¢ Black						
	12.00	9.00	2.00	1.50	.20	.14

Scott No.	Mint Sheet	Plate Block	Fine Unused Each	Fine Used Each
1954. (N–H ADD 10%)				
☐E20 20¢ Blue	32.00	2.50	.42	.20
1957. (N–H ADD 20%)				
☐E21 30¢ Maroon	36.00	2.50	.60	.20
1969. (N–H ADD 30%)				
☐E22 45¢ Red & Blue	70.00	7.50	1.25	.20
1971.				
☐E23 60¢ Blue & Red	60.00	7.00	1.25	.20

THE UNITED NATIONS PHILATELISTS, INC.

UNPI is an organization of philatelists devoted to the collection, study, and exhibition of the issues of the United Nations Postal Administration, the postal history of the U.N., the issues and postal history of its branches, specialized agencies and forerunners, as well as worldwide topical issues that call attention to the U.N., its agencies and programs. The annual domestic dues of the UNPI are U.S. $15, of which U.S. $14 applies to the subscription to *The Journal*.

The Journal (ISSN 0164-6842) is published bimonthly by United Nations Philatelists, Inc. (UNPI), 18 Portola Drive, San Francisco, CA 94131. First-class postage is paid at the United Nations, New York.

Please make your check payable to: "UNPI." Please send payment to the UNPI Secretary: Blanton Clement, Jr., UNPI Secretary, 292 Springdale Terrace, Yardley, PA 19067-3421

Scott No.		Name Block 4	Plain Block 4	Unused Each	Used Each
UNITED NATIONS STAMPS					
1951.					
☐1	1¢ Magenta	.65	.40	.10	.10
☐2	1½¢ Blue Green	.65	.40	.10	.10
☐2a	1½¢ Precancelled	—	—	20.00	25.00
☐3	2¢ Purple	.65	.40	.10	.10
☐4	3¢ Magenta & Blue	.65	.40	.10	.10
☐5	5¢ Blue	.65	.40	.10	.10
☐6	10¢ Chocolate	1.40	1.50	.40	.22
☐7	15¢ Violet & Blue	1.50	1.00	.25	.22
☐8	20¢ Dark Brown	5.00	3.75	1.00	.50
☐9	25¢ Olive Gray & Blue	4.00	2.00	.50	.40
☐10	50¢ Indigo	24.00	16.00	4.00	1.50
☐11	$1 Red	10.00	8.00	2.00	1.20

Scott No.		Name Block 4	Plain Block 4	Unused Each	Used Each
☐1–11	First Postage Set Complete				
		40.00	24.00	6.00	4.00

1952.

☐12	5¢ War Memorial Bldg.	2.50	1.00	.26	.16
☐13–14	3¢, 5¢ Fourth H.R. Day	4.00	2.50	.50	.30

1953.

☐15–16	3¢, 5¢ Refugees	6.00	3.50	.80	.50
☐17–18	3¢, 5¢ U.P.U.	9.00	5.00	1.25	.50
☐19–20	3¢, 5¢ Technical Assist	6.00	4.00	.90	.50
☐21–22	3¢, 5¢ Human Rights	11.00	8.00	1.70	.50

1954.

☐23–24	3¢, FAO (Agriculture)	7.00	5.25	1.50	1.00
☐25–26	3¢, 8¢ OIT (Labor Org.)	13.00	10.00	2.50	1.30
☐27–28	3¢, 8¢ UN Day	15.00	12.00	3.00	2.00
☐29–30	3¢, 8¢ H.R. Day	35.00	27.50	7.00	3.00

1955.

☐31–32	3¢, 8¢ I.C.A.O	16.00	13.00	3.25	1.50
☐33–34	3¢, 8¢ UNESCO	4.00	3.00	.70	.40
☐35–37	3¢, 4¢, 8¢ UN Day	13.00	11.00	2.75	1.50
☐38	3¢, 4¢, 8¢ UN Day Sheet	—	—	80.00	35.00
☐39–40	3¢, 8¢ Human Rights	4.00	3.50	.80	.80

1956.

☐41–42	3¢, 8¢ Telecommunication	4.50	3.50	.80	.40
☐43–44	3¢, 8¢ World Health	4.50	3.00	.90	.40
☐45–46	3¢, 8¢ UN Day	1.00	.60	.18	.15
☐47–48	3¢, 8¢ Human Rights	1.00	.60	.18	.15

1957.

☐49–50	3¢, 8¢ W.M.O. Meteorological				
		1.00	.60	.18	.15
☐51–52	3¢, 8¢ U.N.E.F. 1st Printing				
		1.10	.60	.18	.15
☐53–54	3¢, 8¢ U.N.E.F. 2nd Printing	1.10	.60	.18	.15
☐55–56	3¢, 8¢ Security Council	.90	.60	.18	.15
☐57–58	3¢, 8¢ Human Rights	.90	.60	.18	.15

*No hinge pricing from 1941 to date is figured at (N-H ADD 15%)

Scott No.	Name Block 4	Plain Block 4	Unused Each	Used Each
1958.				
☐59–60 3¢, 8¢ Atomic Energy	.90	.60	.18	.10
☐61–62 3¢, 8¢ General Assembly	.90	.60	.18	.10
☐63–64 4¢, 8¢ Regular Issues	.90	.60	.18	.10
☐65–66 4¢, 8¢ Economic Council	.90	.60	.18	.10
☐67–68 4¢, 8¢ Human Rights	.90	.60	.18	.10
☐69–70 4¢, 8¢ Flushing Meadows	.90	.60	.18	.10
☐71–72 4¢, 8¢ E.C.E.	.90	1.25	.25	.20
☐73–74 4¢, 8¢ Trusteeship	.90	.60	.18	.10
☐75–76 4¢, 8¢ World Refugee Year				
	.90	.60	.18	.10
1960.				
☐77–78 4¢, 8¢ Palais de Chaillot				
	1.00	.80	.20	.10
☐79–80 4¢, 8¢ Forestry Congress				
	1.00	.80	.20	.10
☐83–84 4¢, 8¢ 15th Anniv.	1.00	.80	.20	.10
☐85 4¢, 8¢ 15th Anniv. Souv. Sheet				
	—	—	1.00	.75
☐86–87 4¢, 8¢ International	1.00	.80	.22	.15
1961.				
☐88–89 4¢, 8¢ Court of Justice	1.00	.80	.22	.10
☐90–91 4¢, 7¢ Monetary Fund	1.00	.80	.22	.10
☐92 30¢ Regular Issue	1.00	1.60	.40	.15
☐93–94 4¢, 11¢ E.C. for Latin Am.				
	2.00	1.60	.40	.15
☐95–96 4¢,11¢ E.C. for Africa	1.30	1.00	.25	.15
☐97–99 3¢,4¢,13¢ Children's Fund				
	1.50	1.20	.30	.15
1962.				
☐100–01 4¢, 7¢ Housing	1.00	.80	.22	.15
☐102–03 4¢, 11¢ Malaria	1.20	1.00	.25	.15
☐104–07 1¢, 3¢, 5¢, 11¢ Reg. Issue				
	1.80	1.60	.40	.25

*No hinge pricing from 1941 to date is figured at (N-H ADD 15%)

Scott No.	Name Block 4	Plain Block 4	Unused Each	Used Each
☐108–09 5¢, 15¢ Hammarskjold 9.50	1.80	1.60	.40	.25
☐110–11 4¢, 11¢ UN Congo	1.80	1.40	.35	.25
☐112–13 4¢, 11¢ Peaceful Space Use				
	1.25	1.00	.26	.20

1963.

☐114–15 5¢, 11¢ Econ. Development				
	1.30	1.00	.26	.20
☐116–17 5¢, 11¢ Freedom—Hunger				
	1.25	1.00	.26	.20
☐118 25¢, UNTEA W. Irian	1.80	1.20	.30	.20
☐119–20 5¢, 11¢, 10th Hdqrs. Anniv.				
	1.25	1.00	.26	.20
☐121–22 5¢, 11¢, 15th Anniv. H. Rights				
	1.50	1.20	.30	.20

1964.

☐123–24 5¢, 11¢ Maritime	1.00	.75	.24	.20
☐125–27 2¢, 7¢, 10¢ Reg. Issue	1.50	1.40	.35	.30
☐128 50¢ New Regular	4.00	3.00	.70	.60
☐129–30 5¢, 11¢ Trade & Develop				
	1.75	1.25	.35	.20
☐131–32 5¢, 11¢ Narcotics Control				
	1.75	1.20	.30	.20
☐133 5¢ Nuclear Tests End	.90	.60	.15	.10
☐134–36 4¢, 5¢, 11¢ Education	1.25	1.00	.28	.20

1965.

☐137–38 5¢, 11¢ Special Fund	1.25	1.00	.28	.20
☐139–40 5¢, 11¢ UN in Cyprus	1.25	1.00	.28	.20
☐141–42 5¢, 11¢ I.T.U. (Satellite)				
	1.25	1.00	.26	.20
☐143–44 5¢, 15¢ Co-operation	1.40	1.20	.30	.30
☐145 5¢, 15¢ Min. Sheet	—	—	.40	.25
☐146–49 1¢, 15¢, 20¢, 25¢ Regular				
	5.50	4.75	1.20	.90
☐150 $1 Regular Issue (1966)				
	6.00	5.00	1.25	.80
☐151–53 4¢, 5¢, 11¢ Population Trends				
	1.25	1.00	.26	.20

Scott No.	Name Block 4	Plain Block 4	Unused Each	Used Each
1966.				
☐154–55 5¢, 15¢ World Federation				
	1.10	.85	.22	.20
☐156–57 5¢, 11¢ W.H.O. Building				
	1.10	.85	.22	.20
☐158–59 5¢, 11¢ Coffee Agreement				
	1.10	.85	.22	.20
☐160 15¢ Peacekeeping	1.10	.85	.22	.20
☐161–63 4¢, 5¢, 11¢ UNICEF Anniv.				
	1.10	.85	.22	.20
1967.				
☐164–65 5¢, 11¢ Development	1.25	1.00	.25	.21
☐166–67 1½¢, 5¢ Regular Issue	1.25	1.00	.25	.21
☐168–69 5¢, 11¢ Independence	1.25	1.00	.25	.21
1967.				
☐170–74 4¢, 5¢, 8¢, 10¢, 15¢ EXPO				
	2.75	2.50	.65	.40
☐175–76 5¢, 15¢ Int'l. Tourist Year				
	1.50	1.20	.30	.20
☐177–78 6¢, 13¢ Toward Disarm	1.50	1.20	.30	.20
☐179 6¢ Chagall Sheet of Six	—	—	.45	.35
☐180 6¢ Chagall Window	.75	.60	.15	.10
1968.				
☐181–82 6¢, 13¢, Secretariat	1.25	1.00	.25	.20
☐183–84 6¢, 75¢ Starcke Statue	6.00	4.50	1.25	1.00
☐185–86 6¢, 13¢ ONUDI	1.50	1.20	.30	.20
☐187 6¢ Regular Issue	.80	.60	.15	.10
☐188–89 6¢, 20¢ Weather Watch	1.25	1.00	.24	.20
☐190–91 6¢, 13¢ Int'l. Year Human Rts.				
	1.25	1.00	.24	.20
1969.				
☐192–93 6¢, 13¢ UNITAR	1.25	1.00	.25	.20
☐194–95 6¢, 15¢ ECLA Bldg	1.25	1.00	.25	.20
☐196 13¢, Regular Issue	1.20	1.00	.25	.20
☐197–98 6¢, 13¢ Peace thru Law	1.25	1.00	.24	.20
☐199–00 6¢, 20¢ Labor & Devl	1.50	1.20	.30	.22

Scott No.		Name Block 4	Plain Block 4	Unused Each	Used Each
☐201–02 6¢, 13¢ Art Series		1.25	1.00	.25	.20
☐203–04 6¢, 25¢ Japan Peace Bell					
		1.50	1.20	.30	.20
☐205–06 6¢, 13¢ Mekong Basin		1.50	1.00	.25	.20
☐207–08 6¢, 13¢ Cancer		1.25	1.00	.25	.20
☐209–11 6¢, 13¢, 25¢ 25th UN Anniv.					
		2.75	2.40	.60	.45
☐212	Same, Souvenir Sheet				
		—	—	.50	.35
☐213–14 6¢, 13¢ Peace, Just. Prog.					
		1.50	1.20	.40	.35

1971.

Scott No.		Name Block 4	Plain Block 4	Unused Each	Used Each
☐215	6¢ Sea Bed	.50	.40	.15	.10
☐216–17 6¢, 13¢ Refugees		1.50	1.25	.25	.20
☐218	13¢ World Food Prog.	1.50	1.25	.25	.20
☐219	20¢ U.P.U. Building	1.50	1.25	.25	.20
☐220–21 3¢, 13¢ Anti-Discrim.		1.50	1.25	.25	.20
☐222–23 8¢, 60¢ Regular Issue		3.50	3.25	.82	.70
☐224–25 8¢, 21¢ Int'l. Schools		1.50	1.20	.34	.30

1972.

Scott No.		Name Block 4	Plain Block 4	Unused Each	Used Each
☐226	95¢ Regular Issue	7.00	6.00	1.40	.70
☐227	8¢ Non-Proliferation	.60	.50	.15	.10
☐228	15¢ World Health	1.25	1.00	.25	.20
☐229–30 8¢, 15¢ Environment		1.60	1.40	.35	.20
☐231	21¢ E.C. Europe	1.60	1.40	.35	.20
☐232–33 8¢, 15¢ UN Art Sert.		1.60	1.40	.35	.20

1973.

Scott No.		Name Block 4	Plain Block 4	Unused Each	Used Each
☐234–35 8¢, 15¢ Disarmament		1.60	1.30	.30	.20
☐236–37 8¢, 15¢ Drug Abuse		1.60	1.30	.35	.20
☐238–39 8¢, 21¢ UN Volunteers		1.60	1.50	.40	.20
☐240–41 8¢, 15¢ Namibia		1.60	1.50	.40	.20
☐242–43 8¢, 21¢ Human Rights		1.60	1.30	.30	.20

1974.

Scott No.		Name Block 4	Plain Block 4	Unused Each	Used Each
☐244–45 10¢, 21¢ ILO Hdqr.		1.80	1.60	.40	.30
☐246	10¢ UPU Centenary	.80	.60	.15	.10
☐247–48 10¢, 18¢ Brazil Mural		2.00	1.80	.45	.30

Scott No.	Name Block 4	Plain Block 4	Unused Each	Used Each
☐249–51 2¢, 10¢, 18¢ Regular	2.00	1.75	.38	.30
☐252–53 10¢, 18¢ Population	2.00	1.75	.50	.35
☐254–55 10¢, 26¢ Law of Sea	2.25	2.00	.50	.35

1975.

☐256–57 10¢, 26¢ Space Usage	2.25	2.00	.50	.35
☐258–59 10¢, 18¢ Women's Year	2.25	2.00	.50	.30
☐260–61 10¢, 26¢ UN 30th Anniv	2.25	2.00	.50	.35
☐262 36¢ Same Souv. Sheet	—	—	.65	.30
☐263–64 10¢, 18¢ Namibia	1.80	1.60	.40	.30
☐265–66 13¢, 26¢ Peacekeeping	2.50	1.90	.50	.35

1976.

☐267–71 3¢, 4¢, 9¢, 30¢, 50¢ Regular				
	6.50	5.25	1.30	.80
☐272–73 13¢, 26¢ WFUNA	2.25	2.00	.60	.40
☐274–75 13¢, 31¢ UNCTAD	2.25	2.00	.60	.40
☐276–77 13¢, 25¢ HABITAT	2.25	2.00	.60	.40
☐278–79 13¢, 31¢ 25th Postal Anniv.				
	13.00	11.00	2.75	2.00
☐280 13¢ Food Council	1.25	1.00	.25	.15

1977.

☐281–82 13¢, 31¢ WIPO	2.25	2.00	.50	.35
☐283–84 13¢, 25¢ Water Conf.	2.25	2.00	.50	.35
☐285–86 13¢, 31¢ Security Council				
	2.25	2.00	.50	.35
☐287–88 13¢, 25¢ Combat Racism				
	2.25	2.00	.50	.35
☐289–90 13¢,18¢ Atomic Energy	2.00	1.60	.50	.35

1978.

☐291–93 1¢, 25¢, $1 Regular	7.50	6.25	1.60	.90
☐294–95 13¢, 31¢ Small Pox	2.50	2.40	.60	.40
☐296–97 13¢, 18¢ Namibia	2.25	1.90	.60	.40
☐298–99 13¢, 25¢ ICAO-Air Safety				
	2.25	2.00	.60	.40
☐300–01 13¢, 18¢ General Assembly	2.25	2.00	.50	.40
☐302–03 13¢, 31¢ Technical Cooperation				
	2.75	2.40	.60	.40

Scott No.	Name Block 4	Plain Block 4	Unused Each	Used Each

1979.

☐304–07 5¢, 14¢, 15¢, 20¢ Regular Issues

	3.50	2.75	.75	.40
☐308–09 15¢, 20¢ UNDRO	2.25	2.00	.60	.40

☐310–11 15¢, 31¢ Int'l. Year of Child

	3.50	3.00	.75	.40
☐312–13 15¢, 31¢ Namibia	2.50	2.00	.60	.40

☐314–15 15¢, 31¢ Court of Justice

	2.78	2.50	.60	.40

1980.

☐316–17 15¢, 31¢ Economic Order	3.25	2.60	.70	.40

☐318–19 15¢, 20¢ Women's Decade

	2.75	2.50	.60	.40
☐320–21 15¢, 31¢ Peacekeeping	6.00	4.00	1.00	.40

☐322–23 15¢, 31¢ 35th Anniversary

	2.25	2.00	.65	.40

☐324　　15¢ Same, Souvenir Sheet

	—	—	.65	.50
☐325–40 15¢ World Flags	10.50	—	2.25	2.00

☐341–42 15¢, 20¢ Economic and Social Council

	2.80	2.50	.70	.50

1981.

☐343　　15¢ Palestinian People	1.50	1.10	.36	.25

☐344–45 20¢, 35¢ Disabled Persons

	3.75	3.20	.85	.60
☐346–47 20¢, 31¢ Fresco	3.75	3.20	.90	.70

☐348–49 20¢, 40¢ Sources of Energy

	4.50	4.00	.95	.70
☐350–65　　1981 World Flags	17.50	—	3.50	3.50

☐366–67 18¢, 28¢ Volunteers Program

	3.50	3.00	.80	.60

1982.

☐368–70 17¢, 28¢, 40¢ Definitives

	5.00	4.75	1.20	.90

☐371–72 20¢, 40¢ Human Environment

	5.50	4.75	1.20	.80
☐373　　20¢ Space Exploration	2.75	2.50	.60	.40
☐374–89　　World Flags	21.00	16.00	5.00	.35

Scott No.		Name Block 4	Plain Block 4	Unused Each	Used Each
☐390–91	20¢, 28¢ Nature Conservation				
		4.50	4.00	1.00	.80

1983.

☐392–93	20¢, 40¢ Communication				
		4.50	4.00	1.00	.80
☐394–95	20¢, 37¢ Safety at Sea				
		5.00	4.40	1.25	1.00
☐396	20¢ World Food	2.50	2.00	.50	.45
☐397–98	20¢, 28¢ Trade	4.60	4.00	1.00	.80
☐399–14	World Flags	22.00	19.00	4.50	3.00
☐415–16	20¢, 40¢ Human Rights	8.00	6.75	1.75	1.30

1984.

☐417–18	20¢, 40¢ Population Conference				
		6.00	5.25	1.30	1.00
☐419–20	20¢, 40¢ World Food Day				
		7.00	6.80	1.70	1.00
☐421–22	20¢, 50¢ Heritage	10.00	9.00	2.25	1.00
☐423–24	20¢, 50¢ Refugees	8.50	7.25	1.80	1.00
☐425–40	World Flags	38.50	36.00	8.75	5.00
☐441–42	20¢, 35¢ Youth Year	9.00	8.00	2.00	1.00

1985.

☐443	23¢ Turin Centre	3.10	2.80	.70	.45
☐444	50¢ UN University	6.00	5.20	1.30	.95
☐445–46	22¢, $3.00 People of the World				
		18.00	15.00	3.75	2.00
☐447–48	22¢, 45¢ 40th UN Anniversary	7.50	6.50	1.60	1.25
☐449	22¢, 45¢ 40th Anniversary Souvenir Sheet				
		—	—	2.00	1.00
☐450–65	22¢ World Flags	39.00	36.00	9.50	2.50
☐466–67	22¢, 33¢ UNICEF	7.50	6.00	1.50	1.00

1986.

☐468	22¢ Africa in Crisis	3.80	3.20	.80	.40
☐469–72	22¢ UN Resources	8.00	6.00	—	4.00
☐473–74	22¢, 44¢ Philately	8.50	7.50	1.80	1.25
☐475–76	22¢, 33¢ Peace Year	8.50	7.50	1.80	1.25
☐477–92	22¢ World Flags	35.00	32.00	8.00	4.00
☐493	22¢, 44¢ WFUNA Souvenir Sheet				
		—	—	5.00	4.00

Scott No.		Name Block 4	Plain Block 4	Unused Each	Used Each
1987.					
☐494	22¢ Trygve H. Lie	3.10	2.60	.65	.38
☐495–96	22¢, 44¢ Shelter Homeless				
		7.00	6.50	1.65	.90
☐497–98	22¢, 33¢ Fight Drugs	6.00	5.20	1.30	.65
☐499–514	22¢ World Flags	35.00	33.00	8.75	4.00
☐515–16	22¢, 39¢ United Nations Day				
		6.50	5.60	1.50	1.00
☐517–518	22¢, 44¢ Child Immunizations				
		6.50	5.50	1.50	1.00
1988.					
☐519–20	22¢, 33¢ World Hunger				
		6.50	5.50	1.40	.88
☐521	3¢ UN A Better World				
		.60	.40	.15	.10
☐522–23	25¢, 44¢ Forest Survival				
		32.00	28.00	2.10	1.25
☐524–25	25¢, 50¢ Int. Volunteers				
		7.00	6.25	2.00	1.10
☐526–27	25¢, 38¢ Health Sports				
		8.00	7.00	1.80	1.00
☐528–43	25¢ World Flags	36.00	33.00	9.00	3.75
☐544	25¢ Human Rights	—	—	.40	—
☐545	25¢ Human Rights Souvenir Sheet				
		—	—	1.50	1.00
1989.					
☐546–47	25¢, 45¢ World Bank	6.00	4.50	1.10	.90
☐548	25¢ Nobel Peace Prize	2.50	2.00	.60	.30
☐549	45¢ UN Building	2.60	2.10	.60	.30
☐550–51	25¢, 36¢ World Weather				
		5.50	5.00	1.20	1.00
☐552–53	25¢, 90¢ UN Vienna	9.00	8.00	2.00	1.00
☐554–69	World Flags	35.00	32.00	8.00	3.50
☐570–71	Human Rights	5.50	4.90	1.25	1.00
1990.					
☐572	25¢ Int'l Trade Center	2.50	2.00	.50	.30
☐573–74	25¢, 40¢ AIDS	6.00	5.00	1.25	.75

Scott No.	Name Block 4	Plain Block 4	Unused Each	Used Each
☐575–76 25¢, 90¢ Medicinal Plants				
	8.00	7.00	1.80	1.40
☐577–78 25¢,45¢ UN 45th Anniversary				
	5.25	4.80	1.20	.90
☐579 25¢, 45¢ UN 45th Anniversary Souvenir Sheet				
	—	—	1.40	.80
☐580–81 25¢, 96¢ Crime Prevention				
	6.10	5.10	1.40	.80
☐582–83 25¢, 45¢ Human Rights				
	6.00	5.00	1.35	.80

1991.

Scott No.	Name Block 4	Plain Block 4	Unused Each	Used Each
☐584–87 30¢ Economic Comm. Europe				
	3.00	2.00	2.00	1.40
☐588–89 30¢, 36¢ Namibia	6.00	4.50	1.25	.90
☐590–91 30¢, 50¢ UN Golden Rule				
	6.00	5.60	1.40	1.00
☐592 $2 UN Building	11.00	9.50	2.50	1.40
☐593–94 30¢, 70¢ Children's Rights	7.00	6.50	1.60	1.00
☐595–96 30¢, 90¢ Banning Chem. Weapons				
	8.00	6.50	1.80	1.50
☐597–98 30¢, 40¢ UNPA 40th Anniversary				
	8.00	6.50	1.20	1.00
☐599–600 30¢, 50¢ Human Rights	—	—	1.45	.90

1992.

Scott No.	Name Block 4	Plain Block 4	Unused Each	Used Each
☐601–02 29¢, 50¢ UNESCO Heritage				
	5.50	4.50	1.20	.90
☐603–04 29¢ Clean Oceans	5.50	4.50	1.25	.60
☐605–08 29¢ UNICEF Summit	9.00	8.00	2.00	1.25
☐609–10 29¢ Mission to Earth	10.00	8.00	3.00	1.50
☐611–12 29¢, 59¢ Science and Technology				
	5.50	4.50	1.20	.90
☐613–15 4¢, 40¢ Definitives	3.00	2.80	.80	.50
☐616–17 29¢, 50¢ Human Rights				
	5.00	4.40	1.20	.90

1993.

Scott No.	Name Block 4	Plain Block 4	Unused Each	Used Each
☐618–19 29¢, 52¢ Aging	—	8.00	2.00	.90
☐620–23 29¢ Endangered Species				
	—	11.00	2.75	1.50

Scott No.	Name Block 4	Plain Block 4	Unused Each	Used Each
☐624–25 29¢, 50¢ Health Environment				
	—	8.00	2.00	1.00
☐626 5¢ Definitive	—	8.00	.20	.18
☐627–28 29¢, 30¢ Human Rights				
	—	15.00	4.00	1.50
☐629–32 29¢ Peace	—	3.50	3.00	1.50
☐633–36 29¢ Environment	—	6.25	3.00	1.30

1994.

☐637–38 29¢, 45¢ Year of the Family	—	8.00	2.00	1.00
☐639–42 29¢ Endangered Species	—	4.00	2.50	1.20
☐643 50¢ Refugees	—	5.00	1.50	.75
☐644–46 10¢, $1 Definitives	—	11.00	2.50	1.25
☐647–50 29¢ Natural Disaster	—	10.50	3.00	1.50
☐651–52 29¢, 52¢ Population Development				
	—	8.00	2.00	1.00
☐653–54 29¢, 50¢ Development Partnership				
	—	8.00	2.00	1.00

1995.

☐655 32¢ 50th Anniversary of the UN				
	—	4.00	1.00	.55
☐656 50¢ Social Summit	—	5.00	1.50	.55
☐657–60 29¢ Endangered Species				
	—	4.00	3.00	1.50

UNITED NATIONS AIRMAILS
1951–1957.

☐C1 6¢ Airmail (1951)	1.75	1.50	.35	.25
☐C2 10¢ Airmail	3.00	1.50	.35	.25
☐C3 15¢ Airmail	3.50	1.90	.45	.30
☐C4 25¢ Airmail	4.00	2.50	.60	.40
☐C1–4 First Issue Airmails				
	10.00	6.00	1.50	1.00
☐C5–7 4¢, 5¢, 7¢ Airmail (1957)				
	1.75	1.25	.30	.20

1963–1964.

☐C8–10 6¢, 8¢, 13¢ Airmail (1963)				
	2.00	1.60	.40	.30
☐C11–12 15¢, 25¢ Airmail (1964)	4.50	4.00	1.00	.60

Scott No.	Name Block 4	Plain Block 4	Unused Each	Used Each
1968–1972.				
☐C13 20¢ Airmail (1968)	1.25	1.00	.25	.20
☐C14 10¢ Airmail (1969)	1.25	1.00	.25	.20
☐C15–18 9¢, 11¢, 17¢, 21¢ (1972)	3.50	3.00	.75	.50
1974–1977.				
☐C19–21 13¢, 18¢, 26¢ (1974)	3.00	2.75	.80	.60
☐C22–23 25¢, 31¢ (1977)	3.00	2.75	.80	.60

	Unused Each	Used Each

UNITED NATIONS SOUVENIR CARDS

		Unused Each	Used Each
☐1	WHO, First Printing	.75	—
☐1a	WHO, Second Printing	5.50	—
☐2	Art at UN	.60	—
☐3	Disarmament	.50	—
☐4	Human Rights	1.50	—
☐5	Universal Postal Union	1.50	—
☐6	World Population	7.00	—
☐7	Outer Space	3.00	—
☐8	Peacekeeping	2.50	—
☐9	World Federation of UN	4.75	—
☐10	World Food Council	2.50	—
☐11	World Intellectual Property	1.50	—
☐12	Combat Racism	1.60	—
☐13	Namibia	1.00	—
☐14	ICAO-Air Safety	1.25	—
☐15	International Year of the Child	.70	—
☐16	Court of Justice	1.50	—
☐17	Women's Decade	8.00	—
☐18	Economic and Social Council	1.30	—
☐19	Disabled Persons	1.30	—
☐20	Energy Sources	1.50	—
☐21	Human Environment	2.75	—
☐22	Outer Space	2.00	—
☐23	Safety at Sea	2.25	—
☐24	Trade & Development	3.00	—
☐25	Intl. Population Year	3.00	—
☐26	Intl. Youth Year	3.00	—

☐27	Intl. Labor Org.		3.25	—
☐28	Child Survival		5.00	—
☐29	Philately		9.75	—
☐30.	Intl. Peace Year		5.00	—

Scott No.	Name Block 4	Plain Block 4	Unused Each	Used Each

UNITED NATIONS—GENEVA, SWITZERLAND ISSUES. DENOMINATIONS ARE GIVEN IN SWISS CURRENCY, DESIGNS ARE SIMILAR TO U.N. NEW YORK ISSUES

1969–1970.

☐1–14	5¢ to 10 franc	30.00	28.00	7.00	5.00

1971.

☐15	30¢ Sea Bed	.75	.60	.18	.15
☐16	50¢ Refugees	1.25	1.00	.26	.20
☐17	50¢ World Food Prog.	1.50	1.20	.35	.25
☐18	75¢ U.P.U. Building	3.50	3.00	.80	.60
☐19–20	30¢,50¢ Anti-Discrim.	4.00	3.00	.60	.50
☐21	1.10fr Int'l. Schools	4.50	4.00	.90	.70

1972.

☐22	40¢ Regular Issue	1.50	1.25	.30	.25
☐23	40¢ Non-Proliferation	2.50	2.00	.55	.45
☐24	80¢ World Health	3.75	2.50	.60	.45
☐25–26	40¢,80¢ Environment	6.00	4.50	1.10	.90
☐27	1.10fr E.C. Europe	6.00	4.50	1.10	.90
☐28–29	40¢,80¢ UN Art-Sert	6.50	4.50	1.20	.90

1973.

☐30–31	60¢,1.10fr Disarm.	6.00	5.00	1.20	.90
☐32	60¢ Drug Abuse	2.50	2.00	.60	.40
☐33	80¢ UN Volunteers	2.50	2.00	.60	.40
☐34	60¢ Namibia	2.50	2.00	.60	.40
☐35–36	40¢, 80¢ Human Rights	4.10	3.50	.85	.60

1974.

☐37–38	60¢, 80¢ ILO Hdqrs.	4.50	4.00	1.00	.90
☐39–40	30¢, 60¢ UPU Centenary	3.50	3.00	.75	.60
☐41–42	60¢, 1fr Brazil Mural	4.25	3.60	.90	.60

Scott No.	Name Block 4	Plain Block 4	Unused Each	Used Each
☐43–44 60¢, 80¢ Population	4.25	3.60	.90	.70
☐45 1.30fr Law of Sea	4.25	3.50	.90	.70

1975.

☐46–47 60¢, 80¢ Space Usage	4.00	3.25	.80	.60
☐48–49 60¢, 90¢ Women's Year	4.50	4.00	1.10	.85
☐50–51 60¢, 90¢ UN Anniv.	4.00	3.50	.90	.70
☐52 1.50fr Same, Souv. Sheet	—	—	.90	.70
☐53–54 50¢, 1.30fr Namibia	4.00	3.50	1.00	.70
☐55–56 60¢, 70¢ Peacekeeping	4.00	3.10	1.00	.70

1976.

☐57 90¢ WFUNA	3.50	3.00	.80	.60
☐58 .10fr UNCTAD	3.50	3.00	.80	.60
☐59–60 40¢ 1.50fr HABITAT	4.50	4.00	1.10	.90
☐61–62 80¢, 1.10fr UN Postal Anniv.	14.00	12.00	3.00	2.10
☐63 70¢ World Food Council	2.25	2.00	.60	.40

1977.

☐64 80¢ WIPO	2.50	2.00	.60	.40
☐65–66 80¢, 1.10fr Water Conf.	5.50	5.00	1.25	1.00
☐67–68 80¢, 1.10fr Security Council	6.00	5.00	1.25	1.00
☐69–70 40¢, 1.10fr Combat Racism	4.50	4.00	1.25	1.00
☐71–72 80¢, 1.10fr Atomic Energy	6.00	5.00	1.20	1.00
☐73 35¢ Doves	1.25	1.00	.30	.20
☐74–75 80¢, 1.10fr Smallpox	6.00	5.00	1.25	1.00
☐76 80¢ Namibia	3.50	3.00	.85	.70
☐77–78 70¢, 80¢ ICAO-Air Safety	4.50	4.00	1.00	.75
☐79–80 70¢, 1.10fr General Assembly	4.50	4.00	1.50	1.20
☐81 80¢ Technical Cooperation	2.50	2.00	.50	.45

1979.

☐82–83 80¢, 1.50fr UNDRO	7.00	6.00	1.50	1.20
☐84–85 80¢, 1.10fr Int'l. Year of the Child				
	4.50	4.00	1.00	.70
☐86 1.10fr Namibia	4.00	3.00	.80	.70
☐87–88 80¢, 1.10fr Court of Justice	6.00	5.00	1.25	.80

1980.

☐89 80¢ Economic Order	3.35	3.00	.75	.50

Scott No.	Name Block 4	Plain Block 4	Unused Each	Used Each
☐90–91 40¢, 70¢ Women's Decade	3.50	3.00	.80	.60
☐92 1.10fr Peacekeeping	3.50	3.00	.80	.60
☐93–94 40¢, 70¢ 35th Anniversary	3.50	3.00	.80	.60
☐95 40¢, 70¢ Sheet	—	—	.85	.60
☐96–97 40¢, 70¢ Economic and Social Council				
	3.50	3.00	1.10	.90

1981.

☐98 80¢ Palestinian People	4.00	2.50	.70	.50
☐99–100 40¢, 1.50fr Disabled Persons	6.00	5.50	1.30	.90
☐101 80¢ Bulgarian Mural	3.10	2.50	.60	.40
☐102 1.10fr Energy Sources	5.00	4.00	1.20	.90
☐103–04 40¢, 70¢ Volunteers	5.00	4.00	1.00	.80

1982.

☐105–06 1fr Definitives	6.00	4.00	1.00	.80
☐107–08 40¢, 1.20fr Human Environment				
	6.00	4.00	1.25	.75
☐109–10 80¢, 1fr Space	—	7.00	1.40	.80
☐111–12 40¢, 1. 50fr Nature Conservation				
	8.50	7.50	1.80	.90

1983.

☐113 1.20fr Communications	6.00	5.00	1.40	1.25
☐114–15 40¢, 80¢ Safety at Sea	4.50	4.00	1.60	1.25
☐116 1.50fr World Food Program	6.50	6.00	1.60	1.25
☐117–18 80¢, 1.10fr Trade & Development				
	7.00	6.50	1.60	1.25
☐119–20 40¢, 1.20fr Human Rights	8.00	7.00	1.70	1.25

1984.

☐121 1.20fr Population Conference	8.50	8.00	1.75	1.25
☐122–23 50¢, 80¢ Food Day	8.50	8.00	1.75	1.25
☐124–25 50¢, 70¢ UNESCO	8.50	8.00	1.75	1.25
☐126–27 35¢, 1.50fr Refugees	8.50	8.00	2.10	1.50
☐128 1.20fr Youth Year	8.00	7.00	2.10	1.50

1985.

☐129–30 80¢, 1.20fr Turin Centre	10.00	9.00	2.15	1.50

Scott No.	Name Block 4	Plain Block 4	Unused Each	Used Each
☐131–32 50¢, 80¢ UN University of Japan				
	9.00	7.00	1.60	.90
☐133–34 20¢, 1.20fr Definitives	9.00	7.50	1.60	.90
☐135–36 50¢, 70¢ 40th Anniversary	9.00	7.00	1.60	.90
☐137 same, souvenir sheet			2.50	1.10
☐138–39 50¢, 4fr UNICEF	15.00	13.00	3.10	1.50

1986.

☐140 1.40fr Africa	10.00	8.00	2.00	1.00
☐141–44 35¢ UN Development	—	9.00	6.00	4.50
☐145 5¢ Definitive	.80	.65	.25	.15
☐146–47 50¢, 80¢ Philately	9.00	8.00	2.00	1.00
☐148–49 45¢, 1.40fr Peace	11.00	10.00	2.50	1.25
☐150 35¢, 70¢ WFUNA, souv. sheet	—	—	5.00	3.00

1987.

☐151 1.40fr Trygve Lie	9.00	8.00	1.75	1.00
☐152–53 90¢, 1.40fr Definitive	10.00	9.00	2.00	1.50
☐154–55 50¢, 90¢ Homeless Shelter	9.00	8.00	2.00	1.00
☐156–57 70¢, 1.20fr Anti-Drug	13.00	11.00	3.00	2.00
☐158–59 35¢, 50¢ United Nations	8.00	7.00	1.40	.80
☐160–61 Immunization	16.00	13.00	3.25	1.75

1988.

☐162–63 35¢, 1.40fr UN Better World	10.00	8.00	2.00	1.50
☐164 50¢ For a Better World	4.00	3.50	.80	.60
☐165–66 50¢, 1.10fr Forest Conservation		26.00	6.50	4.50
☐167–68 80¢, 90¢ International Volunteers Day				
	9.00	2.00	1.25	
☐169–70 50¢, 1.40fr Health in Sports		9.00	2.00	1.25
☐171 90¢ Human Rights 40th Anniversary		4.50	1.20	.80
☐172 2fr Human Rights 40th Anniversary souvenir sheet				
		—	3.10	2.50

1989.

☐173–74 80¢, 1.40fr World Bank				
		9.25	2.30	1.50
☐175 90¢ Peace Nobel Prize		5.00	1.10	.60
☐176–77 90¢, 1.10fr Weather Watch		9.00	2.00	1.50
☐178–79 50¢ & 2fr UN Offices in Vienna		10.00	2.50	1.75
☐180–81 35¢, 80¢ Human Rights 40th Ann.		6.00	1.25	.75

Scott No.	Name Block 4	Plain Block 4	Unused Each	Used Each

1990.

☐182 1.50fr International Trade Center	6.00	1.75	.90
☐183 5fr Definitive	18.00	4.50	3.00
☐184–85 35¢, 80¢ Fight Against AIDS	6.00	1.40	.90
☐186–87 90¢, 1.40fr Plants	10.00	2.50	1.50
☐188–89 90¢, 1.10fr 45th Anniversary of UN	8.75	2.00	1.50
☐190 same, souvenir sheet	—	2.00	2.50
☐191–92 50¢, 2fr Crime Prevention	11.50	2.75	1.50
☐193–94 35¢, 90¢ Declarations of Human Rights			
	16.00	3.75	1.25

1991.

☐195–98 90¢ Economy Commission	16.00	4.50	2.75
☐199–200 70¢, 90¢ Namibia	9.00	2.10	1.50
☐201–02 80¢, 1.50fr Definitives	13.00	3.00	1.50
☐203–04 80¢, 1.10fr Children's Rights	10.00	2.50	1.50
☐205–06 80¢, 1.40fr Chemical Weapons Ban	11.00	2.75	1.50
☐207–08 50¢, 1.60fr UNPA 40th Anniversary	11.00	2.75	1.50
☐209–10 50¢, 90¢ Human Rights	8.00	2.00	1.50

1992.

☐211–12 50¢, 1.10fr World Heritage			
	7.00	1.60	1.25
☐213 3fr Definitive	12.00	2.10	1.50
☐214–15 80¢ Clean Oceans	8.50	2.00	1.40
☐216–19 75¢ Earth Summit	10.00	3.00	1.50
☐220–21 1.10fr Plant Earth	10.00	2.50	1.50
☐222–23 90¢, 1.60fr Science and Technology	11.00	2.50	1.50
☐224–25 50¢, 90¢ Human Rights	28.50	7.00	1.50

1993.

☐226–27 50¢, 1.60fr Aging	25.00	6.50	2.00
☐228–31 80¢ Endangered Species	5.50	4.50	2.00
☐232–33 6¢, 1fr Healthy Environment	12.00	3.00	1.50
☐234–35 50¢, 90¢ Declaration of Human Rights			
	28.00	6.00	1.50
☐236–39 60¢ Peace	6.00	5.00	2.00
☐240–43 1.10fr Environment	21.00	6.00	3.00
☐244–45 80¢, 1fr Int'l Year of the Family	12.00	3.00	1.50

Scott No.	Plain Block 4	Unused Each	Used Each
☐246–49 80¢ Endangered Species	19.00	5.00	2.50
☐250 1.20fr Refugees	11.00	2.50	1.20
☐251–254 60¢ Natural Disaster	14.00	3.50	2.50
☐255–56 60¢, 80¢ Population and Development			
	12.00	3.00	1.75
☐257–59 60¢, 1.80fr Definitives	18.00	4.50	1.75

1995.

☐262 80¢ UN 50th Anniversary	8.00	1.80	.90
☐263 1fr. Social Summit	8.00	2.00	.90
☐264–67 80¢ Endangered Species			
	8.00	3.00	2.00
☐268 80¢, 1fr Youth	11.00	3.00	1.50
☐269–70 60¢, 80fr UN 50th Anniversary	16.00	4.00	1.80
☐271 2.40fr UN 50th Anniversary souvenir sheet			
	—	4.00	2.00
☐272–73 60¢, 1fr 4th Conference on Women	12.00	3.00	1.80
☐274 25¢ UN 50th Anniversary booklet single	6.00	1.50	.90

SOUVENIR CARDS

Scott No.		Fine	Scott No.		Fine
☐1	Truck w/gum	80.00	☐	ANA 1973	7.50
☐	Truck w/o gum	15.00	☐31	PLOSKA	2.40
☐2	Barcelona	430.00	☐32	NAPEX '73	2.40
☐3	SIPEX Scenes	180.00	☐33	ASDA '73	2.10
☐3a	SIPEX Miner	13.00	☐34	Stamps Expo '73	2.50
☐4	EFIMEX	4.50	☐35	Hobby Show	
☐5	SANDIPEX	75.00		Chicago	3.00
☐	Ana '69	75.00	☐36	MILCOPEX '72	3.00
☐	FRESNO	510.00	☐37	INTERNABA 1974	2.75
☐6	ASDA '69	25.00	☐	ANA 1974	12.00
☐7	INTERPEX '70	56.00	☐38	STOCKHOLMIA	
☐8	COMPEX '70	18.00		'74	4.50
☐	ANA 1970	120.00	☐39	EXFILMEX '74	2.60
☐9	PHILYMPIA	3.50	☐40	ESPANA '75	2.70
☐10	HAPEX	18.00	☐41	NAPEX '75	9.50
☐11	INTERPEX '71	3.00	☐42	ARPHILA '75	3.20
☐12	WESTPEX	3.00	☐43	Women's Year	24.00
☐13	NAPEX '71	3.00	☐	ANA 1975	14.00
☐	ANA 1971	4.50	☐44	ASDA '75	38.00
☐14	TEXANEX	3.00	☐45	WERABA '76	4.50
☐15	EXFILIMA	3.00	☐46	INTERPHIL '76	8.00
☐16	ASDA '71	2.75	☐	INTERPHIL Program	
☐17	ANPHILEX	2.50		with BEP Card.	12.50
☐18	INTERPEX '72	2.50	☐47	Science BEP	9.00
☐19	NOPEX	2.00	☐48	Science U.S.P.S.	4.50
☐20	BELGICA	2.00	☐49	Stamp Expo '76	8.50
☐	ANA 1972	4.25	☐50	Colorado	
☐21	Olympia Phil.			Statehood	4.00
	Munchen	2.00	☐51	HAFNIA '76	4.00
☐22	EXFILBRA	2.00	☐	ANA 1976	9.00
☐23	Postal Forum	2.15	☐52	ITALIA '76	4.50
☐24	SEPAD '72	2.15	☐53	NORDPOSTA '76	4.10
☐25	ASDA '72	2.15	☐54	MILCOPEX '77	3.75
☐26	Stamp Expo '75	2.15	☐55	ROMPEX '77	3.00
☐27	INTERPEX '73	2.15	☐56	AMPHILEX '77	4.60
☐28	IBRA	2.40	☐	ANA 1977	4.00
☐29	COMPEX '73	2.20	☐57	SAN MARCO	4.20
☐30	APEX	2.30	☐58	Puripex	3.50
			☐59	ASDA '77	4.00

Scott No.		Fine	Scott No.		Fine
☐60	ROPEX '78	6.00	☐69	ESSEN '80	6.50
☐	Paper Money Show	4.50	☐70	STAMP EXPO '81	19.00
☐61	NAPOSTA '78	4.50	☐	Visitor Center	8.50
☐62	CENTEX '78	6.00	☐71	WIPA '81	6.00
☐63	BRASILIANA '79	7.00	☐	Paper Money	18.00
☐64	JAPEX '79	7.00	☐	ANA '81	18.00
☐	ANA '80	21.00	☐72	STAMP COLLECTORS MONTH	6.50
☐65	LONDON '80	8.00	☐73	PHILATOKYO '81	6.50
☐	Money Show '80	12.00			
☐66	NORWEX '80	6.00	☐74	NORD POSKTA '81	6.50
☐67	NAPEX '80	14.00			
☐	Visitor Center	10.00			
☐68	ASDA STAMP FESTIVAL '80	19.00			

Scott No.		Fine Unused Each	Ave. Unused Each	Fine Used Each	Ave. Used Each

POSTAGE DUE STAMPS—1879.
PERFORATED 12 (N-H ADD 20%)

Scott No.		Fine Unused Each	Ave. Unused Each	Fine Used Each	Ave. Used Each
☐J1	1¢ Brown	45.00	21.00	7.00	4.50
☐J2	2¢ Brown	250.00	100.00	7.00	4.00
☐J3	3¢ Brown	30.00	18.00	4.00	3.00
☐J4	5¢ Brown	400.00	200.00	41.00	20.00
☐J5	10¢ Brown	450.00	200.00	20.00	12.00
☐J6	30¢ Brown	200.00	100.00	40.00	20.00
☐J7	50¢ Brown	300.00	130.00	50.00	22.00

POSTAGE DUE STAMPS—1884–1889.
SAME DESIGN—PERF. 12 (N-H ADD 20%)

Scott No.		Fine Unused Each	Ave. Unused Each	Fine Used Each	Ave. Used Each
☐J15	1¢ Red Brown	40.00	20.00	4.00	2.10
☐J16	2¢ Red Brown	60.00	30.00	4.00	2.10
☐J17	3¢ Red Brown	800.00	500.00	100.00	60.00
☐J18	5¢ Red Brown	400.00	200.00	20.00	10.00
☐J19	10¢ Red Brown	300.00	200.00	15.00	8.00
☐J20	30¢ Red Brown	150.00	70.00	40.00	20.00
☐J21	50¢ Red Brown	1200.00	800.00	160.00	75.00

Scott No.		Fine Unused Each	Ave. Unused Each	Fine Used Each	Ave. Used Each

POSTAGE DUE STAMPS—1891–1893.
SAME DESIGN—PERF. 12 (N-H ADD 20%)

☐J22	1¢ Bright Claret	20.00	10.00	.75	.60
☐J23	2¢ Bright Claret	30.00	9.00	.75	.60
☐J24	3¢ Bright Claret	40.00	20.00	7.00	3.00
☐J25	5¢ Bright Claret	50.00	21.00	7.00	3.00
☐J26	10¢ Bright Claret	85.00	40.00	16.00	7.00
☐J27	30¢ Bright Claret	405.00	200.00	120.00	50.00
☐J28	50¢ Bright Claret	400.00	200.00	140.00	50.00

1894. POSTAGE DUE STAMPS—NEW SMALL
DESIGN—NO WTMK.—PERF. 12 (N-H ADD 20%)

☐J29	1¢ Vermilion	1000.00	600.00	200.00	90.00
☐J30	2¢ Vermilion	600.00	400.00	100.00	40.00
☐J31	1¢ Claret	45.00	20.00	6.00	4.10
☐J32	2¢ Claret	35.00	15.00	3.00	2.00
☐J33	3¢ Claret	100.00	60.00	21.00	13.00
☐J34	5¢ Claret	200.00	100.00	30.00	20.00
☐J35	10¢ Claret	200.00	100.00	20.00	12.00
☐J36	30¢ Claret	300.00	200.00	80.00	60.00
☐J37	50¢ Claret	800.00	500.00	200.00	1200.00

1895. POSTAGE DUE STAMPS—SAME NEW SMALL
DESIGN—D.L. WTMK.—PERF. 12 (N-H ADD 70%)

☐J38	1¢ Claret	7.00	4.00	.60	.36
☐J39	2¢ Claret	7.00	3.00	.30	.22
☐J40	3¢ Claret	50.00	24.00	1.50	1.00
☐J41	5¢ Claret	60.00	30.00	2.00	1.20
☐J42	10¢ Claret	60.00	30.00	3.00	2.00
☐J43	30¢ Claret	500.00	300.00	40.00	14.00
☐J44	50¢ Claret	310.00	210.00	30.00	20.00

1910–1912. POSTAGE DUE STAMPS—SMALL
DESIGN—S.L. WTMK.—PERF. 12 (N-H ADD 50%)

☐J45	1¢ Claret	30.00	15.00	2.50	2.00
☐J46	2¢ Claret	30.00	15.00	1.00	.50
☐J47	3¢ Claret	500.00	300.00	21.00	12.00
☐J48	5¢ Claret	80.00	40.00	5.00	2.00

Scott No.	Fine Unused Each	Ave. Unused Each	Fine Used Each	Ave. Used Each
☐J49 10¢ Claret	100.00	60.00	10.00	6.00
☐J50 50¢ Claret	800.00	500.00	100.00	55.00

1914–1916. POSTAGE DUE STAMPS—SAME SMALL DESIGN—S.L. WTMK.—PERF. 10. (N-H ADD 50%)

Scott No.	Fine Unused Each	Ave. Unused Each	Fine Used Each	Ave. Used Each
☐J52 1¢ Carmine	50.00	30.00	10.00	6.00
☐J53 2¢ Carmine	50.00	30.00	.30	.19
☐J54 3¢ Carmine	750.00	400.00	30.00	20.00
☐J55 5¢ Carmine	40.00	250.00	2.10	1.50

Scott No.	Fine Unused Each	Ave. Unused Each	Fine Used Each	Ave. Used Each
☐J56 10¢ Carmine	50.00	30.00	1.50	1.00
☐J57 30¢ Carmine	200.00	100.00	15.00	12.00
☐J58 50¢ Carmine	8000.00	5000.00	700.00	400.00
☐J59 1¢ Rose (No Wtmk.)	2000.00	1200.00	300.00	200.00
☐J60 2¢ Rose (No Wtmk.)	150.00	90.00	18.00	9.00

Scott No.	Fine Unused Plate Blk	Ave. Unused Plate Blk	Fine Unused Each	Ave. Unused Each	Fine Used Each	Ave. Used Each

1917–1926. POSTAGE DUE STAMPS—SAME SMALL DESIGN—NO WTMK.—PERF. 11(N-H ADD 40%)

Scott No.	Fine Unused Plate Blk	Ave. Unused Plate Blk	Fine Unused Each	Ave. Unused Each	Fine Used Each	Ave. Used Each
☐J61 1¢ Carmine Rose	40.00	26.00	2.00	1.50	.24	.16
☐J62 2¢ Carmine Rose	34.00	26.00	2.00	1.50	.24	.16
☐J63 3¢ Carmine Rose .	100.00	75.00	18.00	9.00	.24	.16
☐J64 5¢ Carmine Rose	98.00	75.00	10.00	8.00	.24	.16
☐J65 10¢ Carmine Rose	140.00	90.00	15.00	9.00	.24	.16

Scott No.	Fine Unused Plate Blk	Ave. Unused Plate Blk	Fine Unused Each	Ave. Unused Each	Fine Used Each	Ave. Used Each
☐J66 30¢ Carmine Rose						
	415.00	310.00	70.00	40.00	.70	.50
☐J67 50¢ Carmine Rose						
	700.00	510.00	100.00	60.00	.28	.17
☐J68 ½¢ Dull Red						
	12.00	9.00	.90	.60	.24	.17

1930–1931. POSTAGE DUE STAMPS— NEW DESIGN FLAT PRESS— PERF. 11 x 11 (N-H ADD 30%)

Scott No.	Fine Unused Plate Blk	Ave. Unused Plate Blk	Fine Unused Each	Ave. Unused Each	Fine Used Each	Ave. Used Each
☐J69 ½¢ Carmine						
	36.00	25.00	4.00	1.80	1.00	.65
☐J70 1¢ Carmine						
	30.00	26.00	3.00	2.00	.24	.16
☐J71 2¢ Carmine						
	40.00	30.00	3.50	2.50	.22	.16
☐J72 3¢ Carmine						
	260.00	210.00	24.00	15.00	1.50	.90
☐J73 5¢ Carmine						
	225.00	175.00	18.00	11.00	2.00	1.50
☐J74 10¢ Carmine						
	450.00	310.00	40.00	30.00	.90	.50
☐J75 30¢ Carmine						
	1300.00	900.00	125.00	78.00	1.50	1.00
☐J76 50¢ Carmine						
	1400.00	140.00	130.00	85.00	.60	.40
☐J77 $1 Carmine						
	250.00	190.00	29.00	19.00	.22	.16
☐J78 $5 Carmine						
	360.00	300.00	36.00	23.00	.22	.16

1931–1956. POSTAGE DUE STAMPS— SAME DESIGN—ROTARY PRESS— PERF. 10 x 10½ (N-H ADD 20%)

Scott No.	Fine Unused Plate Blk	Ave. Unused Plate Blk	Fine Unused Each	Ave. Unused Each	Fine Used Each	Ave. Used Each
☐J79 ½¢ Carmine						
	25.00	12.00	1.00	.75	.25	.17
☐J80 1¢ Carmine						
	3.00	1.60	.24	.20	.25	.17

Scott No.			Fine Unused Plate Blk	Ave. Unused Plate Blk	Fine Unused Each	Ave. Unused Each	Fine Used Each	Ave. Used Each
☐J81	2¢	Carmine						
			2.15	1.50	.26	.20	.25	.17
☐J82	3¢	Carmine						
			3.50	1.60	.26	.24	.25	.17
☐J83	5¢	Carmine						
			4.75	2.00	.40	.26	.25	.17
☐J84	10¢	Carmine						
			10.00	6.00	1.10	.72	.25	.17
☐J85	30¢	Carmine						
			40.00	250.00	7.50	5.00	.25	.17
☐J86	50¢	Carmine						
			62.00	35.00	8.00	5.00	.25	.17
☐J87	$1	Red (10½ x 11)						
			250.00	220.00	38.00	29.00	.25	.17

Scott No.			Mint Sheet	Plate Block	Fine Unused Each	Fine Used Each
1959. POSTAGE DUE STAMPS— NEW SERIES—NEW DESIGN— ROTARY PRESS—PERF. 11 x 10½ (N-H ADD 20%)						
☐J88	½¢	Red & Black	375.00	220.00	1.50	.90
☐J89	1¢	Red & Black	3.50	.40	.23	.17
☐J90	2¢	Red & Black	6.00	.46	.23	.17
☐J91	3¢	Red & Black	7.00	.50	.23	.17
☐J92	4¢	Red & Black	9.00	.86	.23	.17
☐J93	5¢	Red & Black	11.00	.80	.23	.17
☐J94	6¢	Red & Black	15.00	1.00	.23	.17
☐J95	7¢	Red & Black	20.00	2.10	.23	.17
☐J96	8¢	Red & Black	20.00	1.70	.23	.17
☐J97	10¢	Red & Black	26.00	1.70	.23	.17
☐J98	30¢	Red & Black	62.00	5.00	.60	.17
☐J99	50¢	Red & Black	110.00	6.00	1.00	.20
☐J100	$1	Red & Black	200.00	10.00	2.00	.20
☐J101	$5	Red & Black	1000.00	55.00	10.00	.21

Scott No.		Mint Sheet	Plate Block	Fine Unused Each	Fine Used Each

1978. POSTAGE DUE STAMPS—
SAME DESIGN, NEW VALUES

☐J102 11¢	Red & Black	28.00	4.00	.36	.21
☐J103 13¢	Red & Black	30.00	3.00	.38	.21
☐J104 17¢	Red & Black	90.00	25.00	.40	.21

1985. POSTAGE DUE STAMPS—
SAME DESIGN, NEW VALUES

| ☐J104 17¢ | Red & Black | 80.00 | 50.00 | .75 | .45 |

Scott No.		Fine

1927–1940. MINT SHEETS

☐643	2¢ Vermont	210.00
☐644	2¢ Burgoyne	275.00
☐645	2¢ Valley Forge	200.00
☐646	2¢ Molly Pitcher	190.00
☐647	2¢ Hawaii	700.00
☐648	5¢ Hawaii	1900.00
☐649	2¢ Aeronautics	95.00
☐650	5¢ Aeronautics	400.00
☐651	2¢ George R. Clark	50.00
☐653	½¢ Hale	25.00
☐654	2¢ Edison-Flat	130.00
☐655	2¢ Edison-Rotary	135.00
☐657	2¢ Sullivan	150.00
☐680	2¢ Fallen Timbers	150.00
☐681	2¢ Ohio River Canal	135.00
☐682	2¢ Mass. Bay	140.00
☐683	2¢ Carolina-Charleston	200.00
☐684	1½¢ Harding	40.00
☐685	4¢ Taft	140.00
☐688	2¢ Braddock	140.00
☐689	2¢ Von Steuben	80.00
☐690	2¢ Pulaski	50.00
☐702	2¢ Red Cross	25.00
☐703	2¢ Yorktown	27.00
☐704	½¢ Wash. Bicent'l	17.00
☐705	1¢ Wash. Bicent'l	20.00
☐706	1½¢ Wash. Bicent'l	70.00
☐707	2¢ Wash. Bicent'l	15.00
☐708	3¢ Wash. Bicent'l	100.00
☐709	4¢ Wash. Bicent'l	42.00
☐710	5¢ Wash. Bicent'l	250.00
☐711	6¢ Wash. Bicent'l	620.00
☐712	7¢ Wash. Bicent'l	43.00
☐713	8¢ Wash. Bicent'l	600.00
☐714	9¢ Wash. Bicent'l	450.00
☐715	10¢ Wash. Bicent'l	1800.00
☐716	2¢ Lake Placid	70.00
☐717	2¢ Arbor Day	30.00
☐718	2¢ Olympics	210.00
☐719	5¢ Olympics	300.00
☐720	3¢ Washington	35.00
☐724	3¢ Penn	52.00
☐725	3¢ Webster	90.00
☐726	3¢ Oglethorpe	52.00
☐727	3¢ Newburgh	28.00
☐728	1¢ Chicago	25.00
☐729	3¢ Chicago	25.00
☐732	3¢ N.R.A.	22.00
☐733	3¢ Byrd	60.00
☐734	5¢ Kosciuszko	125.00
☐736	3¢ Maryland	35.00
☐737	3¢ Mother's Day Rotary	15.00
☐738	3¢ Mother's Day Flat	14.00
☐739	3¢ Wisconsin	16.00
☐740	1¢ Nat'l. Parks	15.00
☐741	2¢ Nat'l. Parks	14.00
☐742	3¢ Nat'l. Parks	14.00
☐743	4¢ Nat'l. Parks	40.00
☐744	5¢ Nat'l. Parks	60.00
☐745	6¢ Nat'l. Parks	100.00
☐746	7¢ Nat'l. Parks	60.00
☐747	8¢ Nat'l. Parks	135.00
☐748	9¢ Nat'l. Parks	115.00
☐749	10¢ Nat'l. Parks	225.00
☐752	3¢ Newburg	390.00
☐753	3¢ Byrd	550.00
☐754	3¢ Mother's Day	210.00
☐755	3¢ Wisconsin	210.00

Scott No.		Fine
☐756	1¢ Park	75.00
☐757	2¢ Park	80.00
☐758	3¢ Park	210.00
☐759	4¢ Park	300.00
☐760	5¢ Park	600.00
☐761	6¢ Park	650.00
☐762	7¢ Park	600.00
☐763	8¢ Park	625.00
☐764	9¢ Park	625.00
☐765	10¢ Park	1000.00
☐766a	1¢ Chicago	600.00
☐767a	3¢ Chicago	600.00
☐768a	3¢ Byrd	600.00
☐769	1¢ Park	350.00
☐770	3¢ Park	600.00
☐771	16¢ Air Spec. Deal	800.00
☐772	3¢ Connecticut	15.00
☐773	3¢ San Diego	7.00
☐774	3¢ Boulder Dam	12.00
☐775	3¢ Michigan	11.00
☐776	3¢ Texas	12.00
☐777	3¢ Rhode Island	10.00
☐782	3¢ Arkansas	9.00
☐783	3¢ Oregon	9.00
☐784	3¢ Susan B. Anthony	15.00
☐785	1¢ Army	10.00
☐786	2¢ Army	10.00
☐787	3¢ Army	14.00
☐788	4¢ Army	32.00
☐789	5¢ Army	50.00
☐790	1¢ Navy	12.00
☐791	2¢ Navy	12.00
☐792	3¢ Navy	12.00
☐793	4¢ Navy	32.00
☐794	5¢ Navy	60.00
☐795	3¢ N.W. Territory	8.00
☐796	5¢ Virginia Dare	16.00
☐798	3¢ Constitution	12.00
☐799	3¢ Hawaii	13.00

Scott No.		Fine
☐800	3¢ Alaska	10.00
☐801	3¢ Puerto Rico	10.00
☐802	3¢ Virgin Islands	10.00
☐835	3¢ Ratification	20.00
☐836	3¢ Swede-Finn	10.00
☐837	3¢ N.W. Territory	25.00
☐838	3¢ Iowa	16.00
☐852	3¢ Golden Gate	8.50
☐853	3¢ N.Y. Fair	10.00
☐854	3¢ Inauguration	27.00
☐855	3¢ Baseball	110.00
☐856	3¢ Canal Zone	13.00
☐857	3¢ Printing	9.00
☐858	3¢ Four States	9.00
☐859	1¢ Irving	7.00
☐860	2¢ Cooper	7.00
☐861	3¢ Emerson	8.50
☐862	5¢ Alcott	35.00
☐863	10¢ Clemens	180.00
☐864	1¢ Longfellow	8.00
☐865	2¢ Whittier	9.00
☐866	3¢ Lowell	10.00
☐867	5¢ Whitman	40.00
☐868	10¢ Riley	250.00
☐869	1¢ Mann	8.50
☐870	2¢ Hopkins	7.80
☐871	3¢ Elliot	20.00
☐872	5¢ Willard	50.00
☐873	10¢ B.T. Washington	180.00
☐874	1¢ Audubon	6.50
☐875	2¢ Long	7.00
☐876	3¢ Burbank	9.00
☐877	5¢ Reed	35.00
☐878	10¢ Addams	130.00
☐879	1¢ Fosters	6.00
☐880	2¢ Sousa	12.00
☐881	3¢ Herbert	10.00
☐882	5¢ MacDowell	44.00
☐883	10¢ Nevin	400.00
☐884	1¢ Sturat	5.50

Scott No.		Fine	Scott No.		Fine
☐885	2¢ Whistler	7.50	☐894	3¢ Pony Express	22.00
☐886	3¢ St. Gaudens	9.00	☐895	3¢ Pan American	20.00
☐887	5¢ French	48.00	☐896	3¢ Idaho	12.00
☐888	10¢ Remington	200.00	☐897	3¢ Wyoming	10.00
☐889	1¢ Whitney	10.00	☐898	3¢ Coronado	10.00
☐890	2¢ Morse	9.00	☐899	1¢ Defense	8.00
☐891	3¢ McCormick	26.00	☐900	2¢ Defense	10.00
☐892	5¢ Howe	90.00	☐901	3¢ Defense	11.00
☐893	10¢ Bell	1200.00	☐902	3¢ Emancipation	15.00

Scott No.		Fine Unused Each	Ave. Unused Each	Fine Used Each	Ave. Used Each

OFFICIAL STAMPS—
1873. CONTINENTAL PRINTING AGRICULTURAL DEPARMENT (N-H ADD 70%)

Scott No.		Fine Unused Each	Ave. Unused Each	Fine Used Each	Ave. Used Each
☐O1	1¢ Yellow	90.00	60.00	80.00	50.00
☐O2	2¢ Yellow	80.00	50.00	50.00	22.00
☐O3	3¢ Yellow	80.00	60.00	50.00	4.00
☐O4	6¢ Yellow	80.00	60.00	30.00	14.00
☐O5	10¢ Yellow	100.00	90.00	80.00	50.00
☐O6	12¢ Yellow	250.00	150.00	150.00	60.00
☐O7	15¢ Yellow	250.00	150.00	100.00	60.00
☐O8	24¢ Yellow	200.00	125.00	100.00	60.00
☐O9	30¢ Yellow	250.00	150.00	120.00	80.00

1873. OFFICIAL STAMPS—EXECUTIVE DEPARTMENT

Scott No.		Fine Unused Each	Ave. Unused Each	Fine Used Each	Ave. Used Each
☐O10	1¢ Carmine	500.00	300.00	250.00	140.00
☐O11	2¢ Carmine	300.00	200.00	150.00	80.00
☐O12	3¢ Carmine	300.00	180.00	120.00	90.00
☐O13	6¢ Carmine	500.00	300.00	350.00	180.00
☐O14	10¢ Carmine	600.00	400.00	300.00	150.00

1873. OFFICIAL STAMPS—INTERIOR DEPARTMENT

Scott No.		Fine Unused Each	Ave. Unused Each	Fine Used Each	Ave. Used Each
☐O15	1¢ Vermillion	30.00	15.00	7.00	4.10
☐O16	2¢ Vermillion	30.00	15.00	6.00	2.40
☐O17	3¢ Vermillion	40.00	20.00	4.00	2.40
☐O18	6¢ Vermillion	30.00	15.00	4.00	2.40

Scott No.			Fine Unused Each	Ave. Unused Each	Fine Used Each	Ave. Used Each
☐019	10¢	Vermillion	30.00	16.00	12.00	6.00
☐020	12¢	Vermillion	40.00	25.00	7.00	4.00
☐021	15¢	Vermillion	60.00	40.00	15.00	7.00
☐022	24¢	Vermillion	60.00	40.00	10.00	6.00
☐023	30¢	Vermillion	70.00	50.00	12.00	7.00
☐024	90¢	Vermillion	150.00	100.00	20.00	16.00

1873. OFFICIAL STAMPS—JUSTICE DEPARTMENT

☐025	1¢	Purple	80.00	60.00	60.00	40.00
☐026	2¢	Purple	150.00	90.00	60.00	30.00
☐027	3¢	Purple	150.00	100.00	15.00	10.00
☐028	6¢	Purple	120.00	90.00	20.00	12.00
☐029	10¢	Purple	150.00	90.00	60.00	30.00
☐030	12¢	Purple	110.00	60.00	46.00	15.00
☐031	15¢	Purple	200.00	120.00	90.00	50.00
☐032	24¢	Purple	600.00	400.00	210.00	100.00
☐033	30¢	Purple	600.00	400.00	200.00	100.00
☐034	90¢	Purple	800.00	600.00	300.00	175.00

1873. OFFICIAL STAMPS—NAVY DEPARTMENT

☐035	1¢	Ultra Marine	60.00	40.00	20.00	12.00
☐036	2¢	Ultra Marine	50.00	40.00	20.00	12.00
☐037	3¢	Ultra Marine	50.00	40.00	8.00	6.00
☐038	6¢	Ultra Marine	50.00	40.00	8.00	5.00
☐039	7¢	Ultra Marine	300.00	200.00	125.00	70.00
☐040	10¢	Ultra Marine	70.00	40.00	20.00	12.00
☐041	12¢	Ultra Marine	90.00	50.00	15.00	10.00
☐042	15¢	Ultra Marine	150.00	100.00	50.00	30.00
☐043	24¢	Ultra Marine	150.00	100.00	50.00	30.00
☐044	30¢	Ultra Marine	100.00	60.00	30.00	15.00
☐045	90¢	Ultra Marine	600.00	400.00	150.00	80.00

1873. OFFICIAL STAMPS—POST OFFICE DEPARTMENT

☐047	1¢	Black	11.00	8.00	6.00	3.00
☐048	2¢	Black	14.00	10.00	6.00	2.70
☐049	3¢	Black	5.00	3.00	1.00	.70
☐050	6¢	Black	15.00	11.00	5.00	2.00
☐051	10¢	Black	60.00	40.00	30.00	16.00
☐052	12¢	Black	30.00	20.00	7.00	4.00
☐053	15¢	Black	45.00	30.00	12.00	5.00

Scott No.			Fine Unused Each	Ave. Unused Each	Fine Used Each	Ave. Used Each
☐O54	24¢	Black	45.00	25.00	15.00	9.00
☐O55	30¢	Black	50.00	25.00	15.00	8.00
☐O56	90¢	Black	60.00	30.00	16.00	9.00

1873. OFFICIAL STAMPS—STATE DEPARTMENT

☐O57	1¢	Green	100.00	80.00	40.00	25.00
☐O58	2¢	Green	200.00	125.00	60.00	40.00
☐O59	3¢	Green	70.00	50.00	16.00	12.00
☐O60	6¢	Green	70.00	50.00	20.00	15.00
☐O61	7¢	Green	140.00	100.00	40.00	25.00
☐O62	10¢	Green	100.00	700.00	30.00	25.00
☐O63	12¢	Green	175.00	100.00	70.00	50.00
☐O64	15¢	Green	200.00	125.00	50.00	40.00
☐O65	24¢	Green	350.00	250.00	150.00	110.00
☐O66	30¢	Green	350.00	300.00	120.00	100.00
☐O67	90¢	Green	600.00	450.00	200.00	150.00
☐O68	$2	Green	750.00	500.00	600.00	500.00
☐O69	$5	Green & Black	5000.00	4000.00	3000.00	2000.00
☐O70	$10	Green & Black	3000.00	2500.00	2000.00	1500.00
☐O71	$20	Green & Black	3000.00	2500.00	1500.00	1000.00

1873. OFFICIAL STAMPS—TREASURY DEPARTMENT

☐O72	1¢	Brown	30.00	20.00	4.00	2.00
☐O73	2¢	Brown	40.00	22.00	4.00	2.00
☐O74	3¢	Brown	30.00	20.00	2.00	1.00
☐O75	6¢	Brown	40.00	22.00	2.00	1.25
☐O76	7¢	Brown	80.00	50.00	18.00	15.00
☐O77	10¢	Brown	80.00	50.00	8.00	4.40
☐O78	12¢	Brown	80.00	50.00	5.00	3.00
☐O79	15¢	Brown	75.00	50.00	7.00	5.00
☐O80	24¢	Brown	400.00	250.00	60.00	30.00
☐O81	30¢	Brown	120.00	100.00	8.00	5.00
☐O82	90¢	Brown	120.00	100.00	8.00	5.00

1873. OFFICIAL STAMPS—WAR DEPARTMENT

☐O83	1¢	Rose	120.00	100.00	6.00	4.00
☐O84	2¢	Rose	100.00	90.00	8.00	4.00
☐O85	3¢	Rose	115.00	90.00	2.00	1.00
☐O86	6¢	Rose	400.00	300.00	5.00	3.00

Scott No.		Fine Unused Each	Ave. Unused Each	Fine Used Each	Ave. Used Each
☐087	7¢ Rose	100.00	80.00	70.00	30.00
☐088	10¢ Rose	40.00	30.00	12.00	3.00
☐089	12¢ Rose	100.00	90.00	9.00	3.20
☐090	15¢ Rose	40.00	30.00	10.00	3.00
☐091	24¢ Rose	35.00	25.00	5.00	2.00
☐092	30¢ Rose	35.00	30.00	6.00	2.00
☐093	90¢ Rose	80.00	60.00	30.00	20.00

1879. OFFICIAL STAMPS—AMERICAN PRINTING—SOFT POROUS PAPER AGRICULTURAL DEPARTMENT (N-H ADD 80%)

☐094	1¢ Yellow	3500.00	—	—	—
☐095	3¢ Yellow	250.00	200.00	60.00	30.00

1879. OFFICIAL STAMPS—INTERIOR DEPARTMENT

☐096	1¢ Vermillion	210.00	150.00	190.00	70.00
☐097	2¢ Vermillion	400.00	2.00	1.10	.75
☐098	3¢ Vermillion	3.00	2.00	1.10	.75
☐099	6¢ Vermillion	5.00	3.00	2.00	1.20
☐0100	10¢ Vermillion	50.00	40.00	40.00	20.00
☐0101	12¢ Vermillion	100.00	60.00	50.00	30.00
☐0102	15¢ Vermillion	250.00	200.00	200.00	100.00
☐0103	24¢ Vermillion	2500.00	2000.00	—	—

1879. OFFICIAL STAMPS—JUSTICE DEPARTMENT

☐0106	3¢ Purple	90.00	70.00	50.00	30.00
☐0107	6¢ Purple	200.00	150.00	125.00	60.00

1879. OFFICIAL STAMPS—POST OFFICE DEPARTMENT

☐0108	3¢ Black	13.00	9.00	4.00	1.85

1879. OFFICIAL STAMPS—TREASURY DEPARTMENT

☐0109	3¢ Brown	40.00	16.00	5.00	3.00
☐0110	6¢ Brown	70.00	40.00	20.00	15.00
☐0111	10¢ Brown	100.00	600.00	40.00	12.00
☐0112	30¢ Brown	1000.00	600.00	200.00	100.00
☐0113	90¢ Brown	1500.00	1000.00	200.00	100.00

Scott No.		Fine Unused Each	Ave. Unused Each	Fine Used Each	Ave. Used Each

1879. OFFICIAL STAMPS—WAR DEPARTMENT

Scott No.		Fine Unused Each	Ave. Unused Each	Fine Used Each	Ave. Used Each
☐0114	1¢ Rose	3.00	2.00	2.50	.90
☐0115	2¢ Rose	4.50	2.00	3.00	.90
☐0116	3¢ Rose	4.00	2.00	1.00	.85
☐0117	6¢ Rose	4.50	2.00	1.00	.85
☐0118	10¢ Rose	35.00	20.00	20.00	12.00
☐0119	12¢ Rose	25.00	15.00	9.00	4.00
☐0120	30¢ Rose	75.00	40.00	60.00	40.00

1910–1911. POSTAL SAVINGS STAMPS (N-H ADD 50%)

Scott No.		Fine Unused Each	Ave. Unused Each	Fine Used Each	Ave. Used Each
☐0121	2¢ Black, D.L. Wmk	11.00	5.00	1.40	.90
☐0122	50¢ Dark Green, D.L. Wmk	115.00	70.00	40.00	20.00
☐0123	$1 Ultramarine, D.L. Wmk	115.00	70.00	40.00	10.00
☐0124	1¢ Dark Violet, S.L. Wmk	4.00	3.00	1.50	1.00
☐0125	2¢ Black, S.L. Wmk	42.00	20.00	6.00	3.00
☐0126	10¢ Carmine, S.L. Wmk1	15.00	1.30	1.20	

1983–1989. OFFICIAL STAMPS—GREAT SEAL SERIES

Scott No.		Mint Sheet	Plate Block	Fine Used Each	Fine Used Each
☐0127	1¢	12.00	1.50	.25	.20
☐0128	4¢	12.00	1.50	.25	.20
☐0129	13¢	30.00	2.00	.80	.60
☐0130	17¢	35.00	2.00	.80	.50
☐0132	$1	225.00	15.00	2.50	1.75
☐0133	$5	800.00	60.00	12.00	7.00
☐0135	20¢	—	—	1.25	.90
☐0136	22¢	—	—	1.00	.80
☐0138	14¢	350.00	—	3.75	2.00
☐0139	22¢	—	—	3.50	2.25
☐0140	25¢	—	—	1.00	.75
☐0141	25¢	—	—	1.00	.70

Scott No.		Mint Sheet	Plate Block	Fine Used Each	Fine Used Each
☐ O143	1¢	12.00	—	.30	.22
☐ O144	29¢	—	—	2.00	1.50
☐ O145	29¢	—	—	1.00	.50
☐ O146	4¢	12.00	—	.50	.35
☐ O147	19¢	43.00	—	.75	.50
☐ O148	23¢	52.00	—	.75	.50
☐ O151	$1	210.00	—	2.50	2.00
☐ O152	32¢	—	—	1.50	.60
☐ O153	32¢	—	—	1.50	.60
☐ O154	1¢	12.00	—	.50	.26
☐ O155	20¢	45.00	—	1.00	.45
☐ O156	23¢	50.00	—	1.00	.45

Scott No.	Fine Unused Block	Ave. Unused Block	Fine Unused Each	Ave. Unused Each	Fine Used Each	Ave. Used Each
1912. PARCEL POST DUE STAMPS (N-H ADD 70%)						
☐ JQ1 1¢ Dark Green						
	280.00	210.00	12.00	6.00	4.00	2.80
☐ JQ2 2¢ Dark Green						
	400.00	300.00	75.00	40.00	16.00	9.00
☐ JQ3 5¢ Dark Green						
	125.00	75.00	14.00	9.00	5.00	3.50
☐ JQ4 10¢ Dark Green						
	1200.00	900.00	180.00	150.00	40.00	20.00
☐ JQ5 25¢ Dark Green						
	600.00	425.00	100.00	75.00	6.00	4.00
1912–1913. PARCEL POST STAMPS (N-H ADD 60%)						
☐ Q1 1¢ P.O. Clerk						
	72.00	58.00	3.75	2.40	2.00	1.00
☐ Q2 2¢ City Carrier						
	70.00	50.00	3.80	3.00	1.20	.75
☐ Q3 3¢ Railway Clerk						
	125.00	90.00	6.50	6.00	4.50	3.50
☐ Q4 4¢ Rural Carrier						
	550.00	400.00	20.00	14.00	2.75	2.00

Scott No.		Fine Unused Block	Ave. Unused Block	Fine Unused Each	Ave. Unused Each	Fine Used Each	Ave. Used Each
☐Q5	5¢ Mail Train						
		650.00	420.00	30.00	16.00	2.00	1.30
☐Q6	10¢ Steamship						
		310.00	180.00	48.00	30.00	3.00	1.75
☐Q7	15¢ Mail Truck						
		350.00	240.00	60.00	40.00	11.00	7.00
☐Q8	20¢ Airplane						
		420.00	350.00	125.00	70.00	20.00	15.00
☐Q9	25¢ Manufacturing						
		400.00	325.00	60.00	40.00	6.50	4.75
☐Q10	50¢ Dairying						
		1600.00	1250.00	250.00	200.00	36.00	25.10
☐Q11	75¢ Harvesting						
		525.00	400.00	80.00	60.00	30.00	18.00
☐Q12	$1 Fruit Growing						
		1600.00	1000.00	340.00	200.00	30.00	16.00

1925–1929. SPECIAL HANDLING STAMPS (N-H ADD 40%)

Scott No.		Fine Unused Block	Ave. Unused Block	Fine Unused Each	Ave. Unused Each	Fine Used Each	Ave. Used Each
☐QE1	10¢ Yellow Green						
		26.00	18.00	1.70	1.00	1.00	.76
☐QE2	15¢ Yellow Green						
		32.00	24.00	1.70	1.00	.95	.75
☐QE3	20¢ Yellow Green						
		42.00	24.00	3.00	2.00	1.40	1.50
☐QE4	25¢ Yellow Green						
		260.00	145.00	21.00	13.00	7.00	5.00
☐QE4A	25¢ Deep Green						
		320.00	200.00	30.00	16.00	6.00	4.00

1919–1922. U.S. OFFICES IN CHINA ISSUES (N-H ADD 20%) SHANGHAI 2¢ CHINA

Scott No.		Fine Unused Block	Ave. Unused Block	Fine Unused Each	Ave. Unused Each	Fine Used Each	Ave. Used Each
☐K1	2¢ on 1¢ Green						
		25.00	14.00	22.00	12.00	25.00	14.00
☐K2	4¢ on 2¢ Rose						
		25.00	14.00	22.00	12.00	25.00	15.00
☐K3	6¢ on 3¢ Violet						
		50.00	32.00	48.00	24.00	60.00	29.00

Scott No.	Fine Unused Block	Ave. Unused Block	Fine Unused Each	Ave. Unused Each	Fine Used Each	Ave. Used Each
□K4 8¢ on 4¢ Brown						
	70.00	45.00	50.00	30.00	55.00	30.00
□K5 10¢ on 2¢ Blue						
	80.00	46.00	58.00	40.00	60.00	35.00
□K6 12¢ on 6¢ Orange						
	90.00	50.00	70.00	50.00	72.00	42.00
□K7 14¢ on 7¢ Black						
	100.00	50.00	75.00	60.00	90.00	60.00
□K8 16¢ on 8¢ Olive Bistre						
	80.00	40.00	58.00	40.00	60.00	40.00
□K8a 16¢ on 8¢ Olive Green						
	80.00	40.00	54.00	40.00	60.00	40.00
□K9 18¢ on 9¢ Orange Red						
	80.00	41.00	55.00	40.00	70.00	40.00
□K10 20¢ on 10¢ Yellow Orange						
	70.00	41.00	50.00	29.00	60.00	40.00
□K11 24¢ on 12¢ Brown						
	80.00	50.00	60.00	40.00	75.00	40.00
□K11a 24¢ on 12¢ Brown						
	100.00	65.00	85.00	50.00	90.00	50.00
□K12 30¢ on 15¢ Gray						
	100.00	50.00	80.00	50.00	100.00	60.00
□K13 40¢ on 20¢ Ultramarine						
	140.00	90.00	110.00	80.00	150.00	75.00
□K14 60¢ on 30¢ Orange Red						
	130.00	75.00	100.00	80.00	150.00	80.00
□K15 $1 on 50¢ Violet						
	600.00	500.00	500.00	400.00	550.00	300.00
□K16 $2 on $1						
	500.00	350.00	400.00	300.00	500.00	280.00
□K17 2¢ on 1¢ Green						
	120.00	100.00	110.00	80.00	100.00	70.00
□K18 4¢ on 2¢ Carmine						
	110.00	80.00	100.00	70.00	90.00	60.00

Scott No.		Imperforated (a) Fine	Ave.	Part Perforated (b) Fine	Ave.	Perforated (c) Fine	Ave.

1862–1971. U.S. REVENUE STAMPS

Scott No.			Imperforated (a) Fine	Ave.	Part Perforated (b) Fine	Ave.	Perforated (c) Fine	Ave.
☐R1	1¢	Express	50.00	28.00	31.00	18.00	1.00	.65
☐R2	1¢	Play Cards	750.00	425.00	375.00	250.00	80.00	50.00
☐R3	1¢	Proprietary	510.00	260.00	95.00	62.00	.45	.26
☐R4	1¢	Telegraph	300.00	175.00	—	—	7.75	4.00
☐R5	2¢	Bank Ck., Blue	1.00	.75	1.00	.70	.24	.17
☐R6	2¢	Bank Ck., Orange	—	—	70.00	40.00	.23	.17
☐R7	2¢	Certif., Blue	10.50	6.50	—	—	26.00	11.00
☐R8	2¢	Certif., Orange	—	—	—	—	26.00	11.00
☐R9	2¢	Express, Blue	12.00	6.50	15.00	7.50	.32	.17
☐R10	2¢	Express, Orange	—	—	—	—	6.00	3.15
☐R11	2¢	Ply. Cds., Blue	—	—	100.00	60.00	3.00	1.50
☐R12	2¢	Ply. Cds., Orange	—	—	—	—	26.00	15.00
☐R13	2¢	Proprietary, Blue	—	—	95.00	54.00	.35	.24
☐R14	2¢	Proprietary, Orange	—	—	—	—	34.00	18.00
☐R15	2¢	U.S.I.R.	—	—	—	—	.23	.16
☐R16	3¢	Foreign Ex.	—	—	150.00	85.00	2.50	1.25
☐R17	3¢	Playing Cds.	—	—	—	—	95.00	50.00
☐R18	3¢	Proprietary	—	—	170.00	105.00	1.80	1.00
☐R19	3¢	Telegraph	52.00	40.00	23.00	7.60	2.80	1.30
☐R20	4¢	Inland Exch.	—	—	—	—	1.70	.96
☐R21	4¢	Playing Cards	—	—	—	—	350.00	175.00

Scott No.	Imperforated (a) Fine	Ave.	Part Perforated (b) Fine	Ave.	Perforated (c) Fine	Ave.
☐R22 4¢ Proprietary	—	—	175.00	105.00	4.10	2.50
☐R23 5¢ Agreement	—	—	—	—	.30	.17
☐R24 5¢ Certificate	3.00	2.00	8.50	5.00	.22	.17
☐R25 5¢ Express	3.70	3.00	5.00	3.75	.34	.17
☐R26 5¢ Foreign Ex.	—	—	—	—	.36	.22
☐R27 5¢ Inland Exch.	4.00	3.00	3.50	2.00	.26	.17
☐R28 5¢ Playing Cds.	—	—	—	—	12.00	7.00
☐R29 5¢ Proprietary	—	—	—	—	18.00	8.00
☐R30 6¢ Inland Exch.	—	—	—	—	1.25	.70
☐R32 10¢ Bill of Ldg.	42.00	44.00	130.00	78.00	.90	.41
☐R33 10¢ Certificate	95.00	80.00	100.00	65.00	.41	.24
☐R34 10¢ Contract Bill	—	—	90.00	54.00	.30	.20
☐R35 10¢ For Ex. Bill	—	—	—	—	5.00	3.00
☐R36 10¢ Inland Exch.	120.00	60.00	3.00	2.00	.25	.18
☐R37 10¢ Power of Att'y.	350.00	210.00	18.00	11.00	.44	.26
☐R38 10¢ Proprietary	—	—	—	—	13.50	6.80
☐R39 15¢ Foreign Exch.	—	—	—	—	13.00	6.50
☐R40 15¢ Inland Exch.	24.00	14.00	10.00	6.20	1.00	.65
☐R41 20¢ Foreign Exch.	42.00	24.00	—	—	28.00	16.00
☐R42 20¢ Inland Exch.	13.00	7.20	16.00	10.00	.40	.25
☐R43 25¢ Bond	95.00	58.00	6.20	3.40	1.75	1.00

Scott No.	Imperforated (a)		Part Perforated (b)		Perforated (c)	
	Fine	Ave.	Fine	Ave.	Fine	Ave.
☐R44 25¢ Certificate						
	6.50	3.10	5.00	3.00	.21	.18
☐R45 25¢ Entry of Gds.						
	17.00	10.00	28.00	19.00	.62	.30
☐R46 25¢ Insurance						
	9.00	7.00	10.00	6.00	.32	.20
☐R47 25¢ Life Insur.						
	30.00	18.00	100.00	50.00	5.50	3.50
☐R48 25¢ Power of Atty.						
	5.00	3.00	18.00	8.50	.30	.17
☐R49 25¢ Protest						
	22.00	11.00	125.00	90.00	5.00	3.00
☐R50 25¢ Warehouse Rct.						
	36.00	21.00	125.00	75.00	22.00	11.00
☐R51 30¢ Foreign Exch.						
	52.00	25.00	490.00	250.00	32.00	18.00
☐R52 30¢ Inland Exch.						
	40.00	21.00	45.00	24.00	2.50	1.40
☐R53 40¢ Inland Exch.						
	425.00	250.00	6.00	3.00	2.60	1.60
☐R54 50¢ Convey, Blue						
	10.00	7.00	2.10	.80	.25	.17
☐R55 50¢ Entry of Gds.						
	—	—	12.00	6.00	.31	.17
☐R56 50¢ Foreign Exch.						
	36.00	21.00	31.00	20.00	4.20	2.00
☐R57 50¢ Lease						
	22.00	13.00	50.00	31.00	4.75	2.90
☐R58 50¢ Life Insur.						
	28.00	15.60	52.00	29.00	.82	.45
☐R59 50¢ Mortgage						
	9.50	4.50	1.50	1.00	.40	.25
☐R60 50¢ Orig. Process						
	2.50	1.50	—	—	.35	.22
☐R61 50¢ Passage Tkt.						
	65.00	36.00	100.00	56.00	.60	.30
☐R62 50¢ Prob. of Will						
	33.00	17.00	42.00	24.00	16.00	8.00
☐R63 50¢ Sty. Bond, Bl.						
	112.00	60.00	2.60	1.50	.35	.17

Scott No.	Imperforated (a) Fine	Ave.	Part Perforated (b) Fine	Ave.	Perforated (c) Fine	Ave.
☐R64 60¢ Inland Exch.						
	78.00	42.00	42.00	25.00	5.00	2.80
☐R65 70¢ Foreign Exch.						
	300.00	167.00	80.00	50.00	4.50	2.65
☐R66 $1 Conveyance						
	10.00	7.00	240.00	140.00	2.10	1.00
☐R67 $1 Entry of Gds.						
	25.00	15.00	—	—	1.60	.82
☐R68 $1 Foreign Exch.						
	50.00	27.00	—	—	.70	.40
☐R69 $1 Inland Exch.						
	12.00	8.00	200.00	120.00	.60	.30
☐R70 $1 Lease						
	32.00	17.00	—	—	1.30	.85
☐R71 $1 Life Insur.						
	120.00	80.00	—	—	4.50	2.00
☐R72 $1 Manifest						
	49.00	30.00	—	—	21.00	12.00
☐R73 $1 Mortgage						
	16.00	9.00	—	—	128.00	65.00
☐R74 $1 Passage Tkt.						
	150	90.00	—	—	130.00	69.00
☐R75 $1 Power of Atty.						
	60.00	32.00	—	—	1.75	1.00
☐R76 $1 Prob. of Will						
	56.00	29.00	—	—	33.00	17.00
☐R77 $1.30 Foreign Exch.						
	1400.00	1000.00	—	—	44.00	26.00
☐R78 $1.50 Finland Exch.						
	22.00	10.00	—	—	3.00	1.50
☐R79 $1.60 Foreign Exch.						
	600.00	310.00	—	—	86.00	42.00
☐R80 $1.90 Foreign Exch.						
	1800.00	1500.00	—	—	60.00	35.00
☐R81 $2 Conveyance						
	90.00	48.50	870.00	450.00	2.00	1.10
☐R82 $2 Mortgage						
	80.00	40.00	—	—	2.40	1.35
☐R83 $2 Prob. of Will						
	1800.00	1300.00	—	—	40.00	20.00

Scott No.	Imperforated (a)		Part Perforated (b)		Perforated (c)	
	Fine	Ave.	Fine	Ave.	Fine	Ave.
☐R84 $2.50 Inland Exch.						
	900.00	500.00	—	—	3.00	1.50
☐R85 $3 Chart. Pty.						
	90.00	60.00	—	—	3.75	1.85
☐R86 $3 Manifest						
	85.00	50.00	—	—	19.00	11.00
☐R87 $3.50 Inland Exch.						
	900.00	720.00	—	—	45.00	22.00
☐R88 $5 Chtr. Party						
	200.00	110.00	—	—	5.00	2.50
☐R89 $5 Conveyance						
	31.00	16.00	—	—	5.00	2.80
☐R90 $5 Manifest						
	80.00	46.00	—	—	82.00	46.00
☐R91 $5 Mortgage						
	80.00	42.00	—	—	15.00	10.00
☐R92 $5 Prob. of Will						
	360.00	200.00	—	—	15.00	9.00
☐R93 $10 Chrt. Party						
	400.00	210.00	—	—	20.00	11.00
☐R94 $10 Conveyance						
	80.00	48.00	—	—	48.00	28.00
☐R95 $10 Mortgage						
	290.00	160.00	—	—	21.00	10.00
☐R96 $10 Prob. of Will						
	900.00	500.00	—	—	21.00	10.00
☐R97 $15 Mortgage						
	850.00	460.00	—	—	85.00	45.00
☐R98 $20 Conveyance						
	75.00	34.00	—	—	34.00	19.00
☐R99 $20 Prob. of Will						
	856.00	500.00	—	—	810.00	460.00
☐R100 $25 Mortgage						
	700.00	400.00	—	—	84.00	46.00
☐R101 $50 U.S.I.R						
	151.00	100.00	—	—	76.00	44.00
☐R102 $200 U.S.I.R.						
	1000.00	600.00	—	—	520.00	400.00

Scott No.			Fine Used Each	Ave. Used Each

1871. U.S. REVENUE—SECOND ISSUE

☐R103	1¢	Blue & Black	30.00	20.00
☐R104	2¢	Blue & Black	1.25	.75
☐R105	3¢	Blue & Black	12.00	7.50
☐R106	4¢	Blue & Black	42.00	30.00
☐R107	5¢	Blue & Black	1.00	.70
☐R108	6¢	Blue & Black	70.00	40.00
☐R109	10¢	Blue & Black	.82	.50
☐R110	15¢	Blue & Black	19.50	13.00
☐R111	20¢	Blue & Black	5.00	3.00
☐R112	25¢	Blue & Black	.70	.37
☐R113	30¢	Blue & Black	50.00	40.00
☐R114	40¢	Blue & Black	33.00	20.00
☐R115	50¢	Blue & Black	.60	.40
☐R116	60¢	Blue & Black	60.00	34.00
☐R117	70¢	Blue & Black	30.00	20.00
☐R118	$1	Blue & Black	3.25	2.00
☐R119	$1.30	Blue & Black	200.00	150.00
☐R120	$1.50	Blue & Black	12.00	7.00
☐R121	$1.60	Blue & Black	300.00	210.00
☐R122	$1.90	Blue & Black	125.00	.80
☐R123	$2	Blue & Black	11.00	6.00
☐R124	$2.50	Blue & Black	22.00	13.00
☐R125	$3	Blue & Black	30.00	18.00
☐R126	$3.50	Blue & Black	120.00	70.00
☐R127	$5	Blue & Black	16.00	12.00
☐R128	$10	Blue & Black	90.00	60.00
☐R129	$20	Blue & Black	270.00	175.00
☐R130	$25	Blue & Black	267.00	150.00
☐R131	$50	Blue & Black	303.00	200.00

1871–1872. U.S. REVENUE—THIRD ISSUE

☐R134	1¢	Claret & Black	24.00	14.00
☐R135	2¢	Orange & Black	.25	.19
☐R136	4¢	Brown & Black	29.00	18.00
☐R137	5¢	Orange & Black	.30	.19
☐R138	6¢	Orange & Black	28.00	18.00
☐R139	15¢	Brown & Black	10.00	7.00

Scott No.			Fine Used Each	Ave. Used Each
☐R140	30¢	Orange & Black	12.00	8.00
☐R141	40¢	Brown & Black	22.00	15.00
☐R142	60¢	Orange & Black	50.00	32.00
☐R143	70¢	Green & Black	30.00	28.00
☐R144	$1	Green & Black	1.25	.80
☐R145	$2	Vermilion & Black	19.00	15.00
☐R146	$2.50	Claret & Black	31.00	25.00
☐R147	$3	Green & Black	32.50	25.00
☐R148	$5	Vermilion & Black	18.00	12.00
☐R149	$10	Green & Black	70.00	45.00
☐R150	$20	Orange & Black	475.00	300.00

1874. U.S. REVENUE—FOURTH ISSUE

☐R151	2¢	Orange and Black, Green Paper	.25	.20

1875. U.S. REVENUE— FIFTH ISSUE

☐R152a	2¢	Blue, Silk Paper	.26	.19
☐R152b	2¢	Blue, Watermarked	.26	.19
☐R152c	2¢	Blue, Rouletted	30.00	20.00

Scott No.			Fine Unused Each	Ave. Unused Each	Fine Used Each	Ave. Used Each

1898. U.S. REVENUE—POSTAGE AND NEWS-PAPER STAMPS SURCHARGED I.R.

☐R153	1¢	Green, Small I.R.	1.50	.80	1.00	.80
☐R154	1¢	Green, Large I.R.	.30	.26	.23	.17
☐R154a	1¢	Green Inverted Surch.				
			9.00	6.00	6.00	3.10
☐R155	2¢	Carmine, Large I.R.	.26	.21	.62	.30
☐R155a	2¢	Carmine, Inverted Surch.				
			1.30	.75	1.10	.74
☐R159	$5	Blue, Surch. down	200.00	100.00	150.00	90.00
☐R160	$5	Blue, Surch. up	90.00	48.00	58.00	31.00

Scott No.		Fine Unused Each	Ave. Unused Each	Fine Used Each	Ave. Used Each

1898. U.S. REVENUE—DOCUMENTARY "BATTLESHIP" DESIGN

☐R161 ½¢	Orange	3.00	5.00	5.10	3.50
☐R162 ½¢	Dark Gray	.29	.25	.22	.18
☐R163 1¢	Pale Blue	.35	.25	.22	.18
☐R164 2¢	Carmine	.30	.25	.22	.18
☐R165 3¢	Dark Blue	.90	.60	.22	.18
☐R166 4¢	Pale Rose	.40	.26	.22	.18
☐R167 5¢	Lilac	.36	.26	.22	.18
☐R168 10¢	Dark Brown	.75	.30	.22	.18
☐R169 25¢	Purple Brown	1.00	.50	.22	.18
☐R170 40¢	Blue Lilac (cut .25)	62.00	32.00	1.50	.90
☐R171 50¢	Slate Violet	7.00	4.00	.21	.18
☐R172 80¢	Bistre (cut .15)	27.00	18.00	.50	.40
☐R173 $1	Dark Green	5.00	3.00	.21	.16
☐R174 $3	Dark Brown (cut .18)				
		12.00	6.50	.50	.35
☐R175 $5	Orange (cut .25)	11.00	8.00	1.30	.65
☐R176 $10	Black (cut .75)	33.00	25.00	2.60	1.60
☐R177 $30	Red (cut 25.00)	120.00	68.00	90.00	48.00
☐R178 $50	Gray Brown (cut 1.50)				
		56.00	31.00	4.00	2.75

1899. U.S. REVENUE—DOCUMENTARY STAMPS

☐R179 $100 Brown & Black (cut 15.00)					
		—	—	29.00	20.00
☐R180 $500 Lake & Black (cut 190.00)					
		—	—	450.00	300.00
☐R181 $100 Green & Black (cut 120.00)					
		—	—	320.00	280.00

1900. U.S. REVENUE—DOCUMENTARY STAMPS

☐R182 $1 Carmine (cut .15)	8.00	5.00	.55	.40
☐R183 $3 Lake (cut 8.00)	65.00	42.00	44.00	25.00

1900–1902. U.S. REVENUE—DOCUMENTARY STAMPS SURCHARGED

☐R184 $1 Gray (cut .09)	6.00	3.00	.21	.17
☐R185 $2 Gray (cut .09)	6.00	3.00	.21	.17

Scott No.	Fine Un-Used Each	Ave. Un-Used Each	Fine Used Each	Ave. Used Each
☐R186 $3 Gray (cut 1.15)	31.00	17.00	10.00	7.00
☐R187 $5 Gray (cut .40)	25.00	15.00	4.00	3.00
☐R188 $10 Gray (cut 3.25)	41.00	25.00	11.00	6.50
☐R189 $50 Gray (cut 80.00)	500.00	303.00	300.00	175.00
☐R190 $1 Green (cut .35)	10.00	5.00	3.10	1.75
☐R191 $2 Green (cut .30)	10.00	6.50	2.00	1.10
☐R192 $5 Green (cut 1.60)	72.00	40.00	21.00	15.00
☐R193 $10 Green (cut 27.50)	210.00	121.00	138.00	75.00
☐R194 $50 Green (cut 220.00)				
	900.00	600.00	700.00	390.00

1914. U.S. REVENUE—STAMPS DOCUMENTARY SINGLE LINE WATERMARK

☐R195 ½¢ Rose	5.50	4.00	3.10	2.00
☐R196 1¢ Rose	1.15	.60	.22	.17
☐R197 2¢ Rose	1.50	.90	.22	.17
☐R198 3¢ Rose	30.00	17.00	21.00	12.00
☐R199 4¢ Rose	7.50	5.00	1.25	.65
☐R200 5¢ Rose	2.80	1.50	.22	.17
☐R201 10¢ Rose	3.10	1.50	.22	.17
☐R202 25¢ Rose	17.00	8.00	.52	.34
☐R203 40¢ Rose	9.50	5.00	.60	.31
☐R204 50¢ Rose	4.50	3.00	.22	.17
☐R205 80¢ Rose	50.00	27.00	7.00	4.00

1914–1915. U.S. REVENUE—DOCUMENTARY DOUBLE LINE WATERMARK

☐R206 ½¢ Rose	1.10	.50	.51	.34
☐R207 1¢ Rose	.28	.23	.23	.17
☐R208 2¢ Rose	.26	.24	.22	.17
☐R209 3¢ Rose	1.10	.50	.25	.17
☐R210 4¢ Rose	2.50	1.40	.34	.21
☐R211 5¢ Rose	1.30	.60	.21	.17
☐R212 10¢ Rose	.70	.24	.22	.17
☐R213 25¢ Rose	4.00	3.00	.90	.60
☐R214 40¢ Rose (cut .60)	41.00	21.00	8.50	4.90
☐R215 50¢ Rose	7.50	4.75	.22	.17
☐R216 80¢ Rose (cut 1.10)	50.00	29.00	8.50	5.50
☐R217 $1 Green (cut .20)	17.00	10.00	.22	.17

Scott No.	Fine Un-Used Each	Ave. Un-Used Each	Fine Used Each	Ave. Used Each
☐R218 $2 Carmine (cut .20)	26.00	15.00	.22	.17
☐R219 $2 Carmine (cut .25)	38.00	20.00	1.00	.60
☐R220 $5 Blue (cut .65)	32.00	20.00	1.10	.75
☐R221 $10 Orange (cut 1.10)				
	75.00	40.00	4.50	3.00
☐R222 $30 Vermilion (cut 2.35)				
	140.00	85.00	8.50	6.00
☐R223 $50 Violet (cut 210.00)				
	800.00	550.00	625.00	310.00
☐R224 $60 Brown (cut 47.50)				
	—	—	100.00	62.00
☐R225 $100 Green (cut 16.00)	—	—	44.00	24.00
☐R226 $500 Blue (cut 210.00)	—	—	500.00	250.00
☐R227 $1000 Orange (cut 225.00)	—	500.00	250.00	

1917–1933. U.S. REVENUE—DOCUMENTARY STAMPS—PERF. 11

☐R228 1¢ Rose	.30	.26	.24	.18
☐R229 2¢ Rose	.30	.26	.24	.18
☐R230 3¢ Rose	.50	.28	.26	.18
☐R231 4¢ Rose	.35	.22	.21	.18
☐R232 5¢ Rose	.30	.24	.21	.18
☐R233 8¢ Rose	1.20	.95	.21	.18
☐R234 10¢ Rose	.26	.21	.21	.18
☐R235 20¢ Rose	.55	.35	.24	.21
☐R236 25¢ Rose	1.00	.55	.24	.21
☐R237 40¢ Rose	.95	.55	.24	.21
☐R238 50¢ Rose	1.10	.50	.24	.21
☐R239 80¢ Rose	3.25	1.50	.24	.21
☐R240 $1 Green	4.25	2.50	.24	.21
☐R241 $2 Rose	8.00	5.00	.24	.21
☐R242 $3 Violet (cut .15)	23.00	15.00	.60	.28
☐R243 $4 Brown (cut .20)	15.00	9.00	1.20	.64
☐R244 $5 Blue (cut .13)	12.00	5.50	.26	.16
☐R245 $10 Orange (cut .20)	24.00	12.00	1.00	.40

1917. U.S. REVENUE—DOCUMENTARY STAMPS—PERF. 12

☐R246 $30 Vermilion (cut .80)	33.00	20.00	6.50	5.00
☐R247 $60 Brown (cut 1.00)	42.00	25.00	7.00	4.50

Scott No.	Fine Un-Used Each	Ave. Un-Used Each	Fine Used Each	Ave. Used Each
☐R248 $100 Green (cut .45)	22.00	13.00	1.00	.60
☐R249 $500 Blue (cut 9.50)	—	—	30.00	20.00
☐R250 $1000 Orange (cut 3.50)	90.00	60.00	14.00	7.00

1928–1929. U.S. REVENUE—DOCUMENTARY STAMPS—PERF. 10

Scott No.	Fine Un-Used Each	Ave. Un-Used Each	Fine Used Each	Ave. Used Each
☐R251 1¢ Carmine Rose	1.90	1.00	.90	.60
☐R252 2¢ Carmine Rose	.52	.38	.21	.17
☐R253 4¢ Carmine Rose	6.00	3.00	3.50	1.50
☐R254 5¢ Carmine Rose	1.00	.50	.42	.30
☐R255 10¢ Carmine Rose	1.50	1.20	.90	.70
☐R256 20¢ Carmine Rose	5.25	3.00	5.00	3.00
☐R257 $1 Green (cut 1.90)	58.00	36.00	25.00	18.00
☐R258 $2 Rose	22.00	11.00	2.00	1.10
☐R259 $10 Orange (cut 8.00)	81.00	52.00	29.00	18.00

1929–1930. U.S. REVENUE—DOCUMENTARY STAMPS—PERF. 11 x 10

Scott No.	Fine Un-Used Each	Ave. Un-Used Each	Fine Used Each	Ave. Used Each
☐R260 2¢ Carmine Rose	2.50	1.50	2.00	1.30
☐R261 5¢ Carmine Rose	2.00	1.30	1.40	1.00
☐R262 10¢ Carmine Rose	6.00	5.00	6.00	3.50
☐R263 20¢ Carmine Rose	14.00	9.00	7.00	5.00

Scott No.	Fine Used Each	Ave. Used Each	Fine Used Each	Ave. Used Each
	Violet Paper (a)		Green Paper (b)	

1871–1874. U.S. REVENUE—PROPRIETARY STAMPS—PERFORATED 12

Scott No.	Fine Used Each	Ave. Used Each	Fine Used Each	Ave. Used Each
☐RB1 1¢ Green & Black	4.50	2.00	5.00	3.00
☐RB2 2¢ Green & Black	5.00	2.50	13.00	8.50
☐RB3 3¢ Green & Black	12.00	5.80	37.00	20.00
☐RB4 4¢ Green & Black	7.00	4.50	11.00	7.00
☐RB5 4¢ Green & Black	100.00	57.00	100.00	60.00
☐RB6 6¢ Green & Black	29.00	15.00	85.00	45.00
☐RB7 10¢ Green & Black	210.00	100.00	35.00	18.00
☐RB8 50¢ Green & Black	652.50	360.00	890.00	450.00

Scott No.	Silk Paper (a) Fine	Ave.	Watermarked (b) Fine	Ave.	Rouletted (c) Fine	Ave.

1875–1881. U.S. REVENUE—PROPRIETARY STAMPS—NATIONAL BANK NOTE

Scott No.	Fine	Ave.	Fine	Ave.	Fine	Ave.
☐RB11 1¢ Green						
	2.00	1.10	.38	.21	41.00	20.00
☐RB12 2¢ Brown						
	2.00	1.25	1.10	.75	50.00	26.00
☐RB13 3¢ Orange						
	8.50	4.50	2.00	1.50	56.00	32.50
☐RB14 4¢ Red Brown						
	4.60	2.60	4.00	2.10	—	—
☐RB15 4¢ Red						
	—	—	4.10	2.20	60.00	40.00
☐RB16 5¢ Black						
	95.00	60.00	82.00	36.00	475.00	250.00
☐RB17 6¢ Violet Blue						
	20.00	12.00	13.00	7.00	160.00	90.00
☐RB18 6¢ Violet						
	—	—	21.00	14.00	170.00	100.00
☐RB19 10¢ Blue						
	—	—	210.00	115.00	—	—

Scott No.	Fine Un- Used Each	Ave. Un- Used Each	Fine Used Each	Ave. Used Each

1898. U.S. REVENUE—PROPRIETARY STAMPS—BATTLESHIP

Scott No.	Fine Unused	Ave. Unused	Fine Used	Ave. Used
☐RB20 ⅛¢ Yellow Green	.25	.23	.21	.17
☐RB21 ¼¢ Pale Green	.25	.23	.21	.17
☐RB22 ⅜¢ Deep Orange	.26	.23	.21	.17
☐RB23 ⅝¢ Deep Ultramarine	.26	.23	.21	.17
☐RB24 1¢ Dark Green	.50	.25	.26	.20
☐RB25 1¼¢ Violet	.26	.21	.21	.17
☐RB26 1⅞¢ Dull Blue	3.00	2.00	1.00	.50
☐RB27 2¢ Violet Brown	.41	.28	.26	.17
☐RB28 2½¢ Lake	1.50	7.00	.21	.17
☐RB29 3¾¢ Olive Gray	10.00	7.00	6.00	3.00
☐RB30 4¢ Purple	4.00	2.40	.90	.60
☐RB31 5¢ Brown Orange	4.00	2.50	.90	.60

Scott No.	Fine Un-Used Each	Ave. Un-Used Each	Fine Used Each	Ave. Used Each

1914. U.S. REVENUE—BLACK PROPRIETARY STAMPS—WATERMARKED USPS

☐ RB32 ⅛¢ Black	.26	.22	.21	.17
☐ RB33 ¼¢ Black	1.10	.70	.80	.40
☐ RB34 ⅜¢ Black	.28	.22	.21	.17
☐ RB35 ⅝¢ Black	2.10	1.60	1.70	1.00
☐ RB36 1¼¢ Black	1.50	1.20	.75	.50
☐ RB37 1⅞¢ Black	24.00	15.00	14.00	7.00
☐ RB38 2¼¢ Black	4.10	2.60	2.50	1.50
☐ RB39 3⅛¢ Black	66.00	40.00	42.00	27.00
☐ RB40 3¾¢ Black	24.00	16.00	19.00	10.00
☐ RB41 4¢ Black	42.00	25.00	26.50	14.00
☐ RB42 4⅜¢ Black	700.00	620.00	—	—
☐ RB43 5¢ Black	87.50	50.00	45.00	34.00

1914. U.S. REVENUE—PROPRIETARY STAMPS—WATERMARKED USIR

☐ RB44 ⅛¢ Black	.26	.22	.20	.18
☐ RB45 ¼¢ Black	.26	.22	.20	.18
☐ RB46 ⅜¢ Black	.50	.35	.32	.21
☐ RB47 ½¢ Black	3.00	1.80	2.10	1.00
☐ RB48 ⅝¢ Black	.26	.22	.21	.17
☐ RB49 1¢ Black	4.00	2.10	2.50	1.50
☐ RB50 1¼¢ Black	.45	.22	.21	.17
☐ RB51 1½¢ Black	3.00	1.90	2.10	1.15
☐ RB52 1⅞¢ Black	1.50	.60	.55	.32
☐ RB53 2¢ Black	5.00	3.00	3.30	2.00
☐ RB54 2½¢ Black	1.20	.80	.95	.50
☐ RB55 3¢ Black	3.50	1.50	2.30	1.50
☐ RB56 3⅛¢ Black	4.50	2.50	2.75	1.60
☐ RB57 3¾¢ Black	9.00	5.00	7.00	4.00
☐ RB58 4¢ Black	.45	.30	.22	.17
☐ RB59 4⅜¢ Black	12.00	7.00	7.10	4.00
☐ RB60 5¢ Black	2.50	1.40	2.40	1.15
☐ RB61 6¢ Black	45.00	26.00	38.00	20.00
☐ RB62 8¢ Black	12.00	8.00	10.00	6.00
☐ RB63 10¢ Black	9.00	6.00	7.00	4.00
☐ RB64 20¢ Black	16.00	10.00	14.50	9.50

Scott No.	Fine Un-Used Each	Ave. Un-Used Each	Fine Used Each	Ave. Used Each

1919. U.S. REVENUE—PROPRIETARY STAMPS—OFFSET

Scott No.	Fine Un-Used Each	Ave. Un-Used Each	Fine Used Each	Ave. Used Each
☐RB65 1¢ Dark Blue	.30	.24	.18	.16
☐RB66 2¢ Dark Blue	.30	.24	.18	.16
☐RB67 3¢ Dark Blue	1.10	.62	.59	.36
☐RB68 4¢ Dark Blue	1.10	.62	.52	.34
☐RB69 5¢ Dark Blue	1.25	.75	.50	.35
☐RB70 8¢ Dark Blue	11.00	6.00	8.00	5.00
☐RB71 10¢ Dark Blue	3.10	2.50	2.10	1.10
☐RB72 20¢ Dark Blue	5.00	4.00	3.00	1.75
☐RB73 40¢ Dark Blue	25.00	16.00	10.00	5.50

1918–1934. U.S. REVENUE—FUTURE DELIVERY STAMPS—PERFORATED 11&12

Scott No.	Fine Un-Used Each	Ave. Un-Used Each	Fine Used Each	Ave. Used Each
☐RC1 2¢ Carmine Rose	1.75	1.10	.21	.17
☐RC2 3¢ Carmine Rose (cut 7.50)				
	28.00	18.00	20.00	12.00
☐RC3 4¢ Carmine Rose	3.00	1.50	.22	.16
☐RC3a 5¢ Carmine Rose	—	—	3.00	2.10
☐RC4 10¢ Carmine Rose	5.00	3.00	.21	.17
☐RC5 20¢ Carmine Rose	5.00	3.00	.21	.17
☐RC6 25¢ Carmine Rose (cut .10)				
	12.00	8.50	.70	.48
☐RC7 40¢ Carmine Rose (cut .10)				
	13.00	7.00	.75	.40
☐RC8 50¢ Carmine Rose	4.00	2.50	.40	.17
☐RC9 80¢ Carmine Rose (cut 1.00)				
	22.00	15.50	7.00	4.50
☐RC10 $1 Green (cut .10)	—	—	.28	.17
☐RC11 $2 Rose (cut .10)	—	—	.28	.17
☐RC12 $3 Violet (cut .12)	—	—	2.00	.90
☐RC13 $5 Dark Blue (cut .12)	—	—	.50	.28
☐RC14 $10 Orange (cut .20)	—	—	1.00	.50
☐RC15 $20 Olive Bistre (cut .50)	—	—	4.00	2.50
☐RC16 $30 Vermilion (cut .95)	—	—	3.00	1.85
☐RC17 $50 Olive Green (cut .30)	—	—	1.50	.60
☐RC18 $60 Brown (cut .55)	—	—	2.00	1.25
☐RC19 $100 Yellow Green (cut 5.50)				
	—	26.50	24.00	16.00

Scott No.	Fine Un-Used Each	Ave. Un-Used Each	Fine Used Each	Ave. Used Each
☐RC20 $500 Blue (cut 3.00)	—	—	10.00	6.00
☐RC21 $1000 Orange (cut 1.60)	—	1.50	6.00	3.00
☐RC22 1¢ Carmine Rose Narrow Overprint				
	1.15	.65	.21	.17
☐RC23 80¢ Narrow Overprint (cut .30)				
	—	—	2.50	1.60
☐RC25 $1 Serif Overprint (cut .08)				
	7.00	4.50	.70	.42
☐RC26 $10 Serif Overprint (cut 5.00)				
	—	—	15.00	11.00

1918–1928. U.S. REVENUE—STOCK TRANSFER STAMPS—PERFORATED 11 OR 12

Scott No.	Fine Un-Used Each	Ave. Un-Used Each	Fine Used Each	Ave. Used Each
☐RD1 1¢ Carmine Rose, Perf. 11				
	.65	.42	.22	.17
☐RD2 1¢ Carmine Rose, Perf. 11				
	.30	.23	.22	.17
☐RD3 4¢ Carmine Rose, Perf. 11				
	.42	.25	.22	.17
☐RD4 5¢ Carmine Rose, Perf. 11				
	.40	.25	.22	.17
☐RD5 10¢ Carmine Rose, Perf. 11				
	.40	.25	.22	.17
☐RD6 20¢ Carmine Rose, Perf. 11				
	.40	.26	.22	.17
☐RD7 25¢ Carmine Rose, Perf. 12 (cut .07)				
	.60	.60	.22	.17
☐RD8 40¢ Carmine Rose, Perf. 11				
	.60	.60	.22	.17
☐RD9 50¢ Carmine Rose, Perf. 11				
	.50	.40	.22	.17
☐RD10 80¢ Carmine Rose, Perf. 11 (cut .07)				
	1.10	.75	.24	.17
☐RD11 $1 Green, Perf. 11, Red Ovpt. (cut .40)				
	32.00	22.00	9.00	4.50
☐RD12 $1 Green, Perf. 11, Black Ovpt				
	1.50	.75	.22	.17
☐RD13 $2 Rose, Perf. 11	1.50	.75	.22	.17
☐RD14 $3 Violet, Perf. 11 (cut .17)				
	10.00	4.50	3.00	.90

Scott No.	Fine Un-Used Each	Ave. Un-Used Each	Fine Used Each	Ave. Used Each
☐RD15 $4 Y. Brown, Perf. 11 (cut .07)				
	5.00	2.50	.26	.17
☐RD16 $5 Blue, Perf. 11 (cut .07)				
	4.00	2.10	.26	.17
☐RD17 $10 Orange, Perf. 11 (cut .07)				
	8.00	4.60	.26	.17
☐RD18 $20 Bistre, Perf. 11 (cut 4.25)				
	60.00	32.00	20.00	11.00
☐RD19 $30 Vermilion (cut 1.05)				
	15.00	11.00	4.00	2.40
☐RD20 $50 Olive Green (cut 9.75)				
	80.00	50.00	42.00	36.00
☐RD21 $60 Brown (cut 4.60)				
	76.00	45.00	20.00	12.00
☐RD22 $100 Green (cut 1.10)				
	19.00	11.00	5.50	4.40
☐RD23 $500 Blue (cut 38.00)	—	—	115.00	75.00
☐RD24 $1000 Strange (cut 10.00)				
	—	—	80.00	52.00
☐RD25 2¢ Carmine Rose, Perf. 10				
	.80	.60	.26	.17
☐RD26 4¢ Carmine Rose, Perf. 10				
	.70	.60	.26	.17
☐RD27 10¢ Carmine Rose, Perf. 10				
	.70	.60	.26	.17
☐RD28 20¢ Carmine Rose, Perf. 10				
	2.00	1.00	.26	.17
☐RD29 50¢ Carmine Rose, Perf. 10				
	1.50	1.00	.26	.17
☐RD30 $1 Green, Perf. 10	12.00	9.00	.26	.17
☐RD31 $2 Carmine Rose, Perf. 10				
	12.00	9.00	.21	.17
☐RD32 $10 Orange, Perf. 10 (cut .07)				
	12.00	9.00	.21	.17
☐RD33 2¢ Carmine Rose, Perf. 11				
	4.00	2.10	.65	.30
☐RD34 10¢ Carmine Rose, Perf. 11				
	.95	.40	.21	.17
☐RD35 20¢ Carmine Rose, Perf. 11				
	.95	.40	.22	.17

Scott No.	Fine Un- Used Each	Ave. Un- Used Each	Fine Used Each	Ave. Used Each
☐RD36 50¢ Carmine Rose, Perf. 11				
	2.00	.75	.30	.17
☐RD37 $1 Green, Perf. 11 (cut .11)				
	13.00	8.50	6.40	4.00
☐RD38 $2 Rose, Perf, 11 (cut .12)				
	10.00	7.50	6.50	3.50
☐RD39 2¢ Rose, Perf. 11 (cut .12)				
	3.10	2.00	.42	.17
☐RD40 10¢ Carmine Rose, Perf. 10				
	1.15	.85	.30	.17
☐RD41 20¢ Carmine Rose, Perf. 10				
	1.20	.80	.30	.17

Scott No.	Fine Unused Block	Ave. Unused Block	Fine Unused Each	Ave. Unused Each	Fine Used Each	Ave. Used Each

1861–1862. CONFEDERATE STATES OF AMERICA STAMPS (N-H ADD 40%)

Scott No.		Fine Unused Block	Ave. Unused Block	Fine Unused Each	Ave. Unused Each	Fine Used Each	Ave. Used Each
☐1	5¢ Jefferson Davis, Green						
		—	1300.00	140.00	100.00	110.00	65.00
☐2	10¢ Thomas Jefferson, Blue						
		—	1300.00	210.00	120.00	155.00	90.00
☐3	2¢ Andrew Jackson, Green						
		—	—	430.00	250.00	460.00	325.00
☐4	5¢ Jefferson Davis, Blue						
		700.00	550.00	110.00	60.00	80.00	50.00
☐5	10¢ Thomas Jefferson, Rose						
		—	—	740.00	450.00	500.00	250.00
☐6	5¢ Jefferson Davis, London Print						
		100.00	110.00	19.00	9.00	7.50	6.00
☐7	5¢ Jefferson Davis, Local Print						
		135.00	110.00	13.00	6.50	10.00	6.50

1863.

Scott No.		Fine Unused Block	Ave. Unused Block	Fine Unused Each	Ave. Unused Each	Fine Used Each	Ave. Used Each
☐8	2¢ Andrew Jackson, Brown Red						
		400.00	300.00	52.00	26.00	260.00	170.00
☐9	10¢ Jefferson Davis (ten)						
		—	—	700.00	450.00	460.00	280.00
☐10	10¢ Jefferson Davis (with frame line.)						
		—	—	2400.00	1800.00	1000.00	750.00

Scott No.		Fine Unused Block	Ave. Unused Block	Fine Unused Each	Ave. Unused Each	Fine Used Each	Ave. Used Each
☐11	10¢ Jefferson Davis (no frame.)						
		75.00	60.00	8.50	7.50	8.10	7.00
☐12	10¢ Jefferson Davis (filled corner)						
		89.00	80.00	8.50	7.50	8.10	7.00
☐13	20¢ George Washington						
		365.00	300.00	350.00	240.00	35.00	24.00

1862.

☐14	1¢ John.C. Calhoun						
		800.00	610.00	72.00	50.00	—	—

FEDERAL DUCK STAMPS

Courtesy of Sam Houston Duck Company
P. O. Box 820087, Houston TX 77282
(Specialized Duck Catalog
$3.00 Refundable with Purchase)

JUST WHAT ARE DUCK STAMPS?

The federal duck stamp was created through a wetlands conservation program. President Herbert Hoover signed the Migratory Bird Conservation Act in 1929 to authorize the acquisition and preservation of wetlands as waterfowl habitat.

The law, however, did not provide a permanent source of money to buy and preserve the wetlands. On March 16, 1934, Congress passed, and President Franklin Roosevelt signed, the Migratory Bird Hunting Stamp Act. Popularly known as the Duck Stamp Act, the bill's whole purpose was to generate revenue designated for only one use: acquiring wetlands for what is now known as the National Refuge System.

It has been proven that sales of duck stamps increase when the public has been informed of how the revenue generated through stamp sales is used.

Jay N. "Ding" Darling, a conservationist and Pulitzer Prize–winning political cartoonist, was appointed the head of the Duck Stamp Program. Darling's pencil sketch of mallards alighting was used on the first duck stamp. The same design was reproduced on Scott 2092, a commemorative marking the 50th anniversary of the Migratory Bird Hunting Stamp Act.

In reality, a "duck stamp" is a permit to hunt, basically a receipt for payment of fees collected. Funds generated are used for the preservation and conservation of wetlands.

The term "duck stamp" is a shortened term for the message "Migratory Bird Hunting and Conservation Stamp," which appears on the federal duck stamp.

In fact, use of the word "duck" is inaccurate, since all waterfowl, *including geese, swans, brants, and more*, are intended to benefit from the sale of duck stamps.

WHO ISSUES DUCK STAMPS?

Federal duck stamps are now issued by the U.S. Fish and Wildlife Service, Department of Interior United States Government and have been issued by all states. Currently, 43 states issue duck stamps.

Many foreign countries, including Canada and Provinces, Australia, Russia, Iceland, the United Kingdom, Costa Rica, Venezuela, Italy, Argentina, Mexico, Ireland, Spain, Israel, Croatia, and New Zealand also issue duck stamps.

The issuing authorities within the various governments that release duck stamps are usually conservation and wildlife departments. These programs must be created by some form of legislation for the resulting stamps to be accepted as a valid governmental issue.

Labels featuring ducks are also issued by various special interest groups, such as Ducks Unlimited, the National Fish and Wildlife Foundation, and the National Wildlife Federation. Their issues are referred to as "society stamps." These items technically are not duck stamps, because the fee structure and disposition of funds are not legislated. However, society stamps are very collectible and often appreciate in value. Funds raised by these organizations are also used for waterfowl and conservation efforts.

Valid organizations and societies of this type perform a major service to conservation by their donations and efforts, and they merit public support.

WHEN ARE DUCK STAMPS ISSUED?

Duck stamps are issued once a year. In most states, hunters are required to purchase both a federal and state stamp before hunting waterfowl.

Waterfowl hunting seasons vary, but most begin in September or October, so naturally, stamps are needed prior to opening day of the hunting season.

Currently, the federal stamp and more than half of the state stamps are issued in July. Some are issued on the first day of the new year, and a few at the last minute in September or early October.

THE COST OF DUCK STAMPS

The annual federal duck stamp had a face value of $1 in 1934, jumped to $2 in 1949, and to $3 in 1959. In 1972 the price increased to $5, then up to $7.50 in 1979, $10 in 1987, $12.50 in 1989, and to $15 beginning in 1991.

For every $15 stamp sold, the federal government retains $14.70 for wetlands acquisition and conservation, so very little gets lost in the system for overhead.

Most state conservation stamps have a face value of $5. Maine has the lowest price at $2.50 and Louisiana's non-resident at $25.00.

Funds generated from state stamps are designated for wetlands restoration and preservation, much like the federal funds, but with a more localized purpose.

Most state agencies sell their stamps at face value. However, some also charge a premium to collectors buying single stamps, to help cover overhead costs. Some states also produce special limited editions for collectors.

FORMAT OF STAMPS

The federal stamp is presently issued in panes of 30 stamps. Originally, the stamps were issued in panes of 28, but because of a change in the printing method (and to make stamps easier to count) the 20-stamp format was adopted in 1959. Then switched to 30 in 2000.

Beginning in 1998, the department of the Interior will also issue a single-sheet, self-adhesive Federal stamp used in ATM machines and to ease handling in sporting good stores.

Most states and foreign governments follow the federal format. Many states issue a ten-stamp pane for ease of handling and mailing to field offices.

TYPES OF STAMPS

Currently, about 20 states issue two types of stamps, one for collectors and another for hunter use.

Collector stamps are usually in panes of 10 or 30 without tabs. *Hunter-type stamps* are usually issued in panes of five or 10, many with tabs attached. Hunters use the tabs to list their name, address, age, and other data. Some states use only serial numbers to designate their hunter-type stamp.

State stamps are therefore referred to as either collector stamps or hunter-type stamps. Most dealers will distinguish between these types on their price lists. Separate albums exist for both types and are available from most dealers.

Plate blocks or control number blocks are designations given to a block of stamps, usually four, with a plate or control number present on the selvage. Such a block is usually located in one or all four corners of a pane. Federal stamps prior to 1959 plus the 1964 issue are collected in blocks of six and must have selvage on two sides.

Governors' Editions have been issued by several state agencies as a means of raising additional income. These stamps are printed in small quantities, most fewer than 1,000. They have a face value of approximately $50, and are imprinted with the name of the state governor.

Governors also hand-sign a limited number of stamps. These are usually available at a premium, generally twice the price of normal singles. Hand-signed or autographed stamps are issued in very small quantities and are scarce to rare.

Governors' Editions are valid for hunting by all issuing states thus far. Obviously none would be used for that purpose, however, as it would destroy the mint condition and lower the value of the stamp.

Artist-Signed Stamps are mint examples of duck stamps autographed by the artist responsible for the artwork on the stamp. Such stamps are rapidly gaining popularity with collectors, and most can be purchased for a small premium over mint examples.

Early federal stamps are particularly valuable and difficult to acquire. Signed stamps by artists now deceased also command a substantial premium.

Printed Text Stamps are another popular collectible. Generally, these preceded the later pictorial issues. The term is applied to stamps required for duck hunting that contain only writing but no waterfowl illustration.

Certain American Indian reservations and tribes also issue waterfowl hunting stamps. The stamps of these sovereign Indian nations allow holders to hunt on that reservation when a federal stamp also is purchased. Reservation stamps are becoming increasingly popular with collectors as more people discover their existence.

ERRORS

With the printing of such a large number of stamps year after year by many different states and printing agencies, errors do occur, but are seldom found. A few federal stamps are known to exist with major errors, but only a few, namely on the 1934, 1946, 1955, 1957, 1959, 1962, 1982, 1986, 1990, 1991, and 1993 issues.

Stamps without perforations, with missing or incorrect color, missing or inverted writing on the reverse are all major errors. Smaller flaws, such as color shifts, misplaced perforations, hickeys (or donuts), and other such anomalies are termed *freaks*, rather than errors. These, too, are collectible and have value, but they do not command the same attention as major errors. Major errors are extremely rare and exist in small numbers. All errors and freaks on duck stamps are very desirable and add a great deal of interest and value to a collection.

HOW TO COLLECT DUCK STAMPS

The first basic rule is to remember that stamp collecting is very personal. *You can make your own rules.*

Most collectors prefer to collect mint condition duck stamps. Others prefer collecting stamps on licenses, autographed stamps, plate blocks, stamps signed by hunters, art prints, souvenir cards, first day covers, or a combination. The bottom line, however, is to collect what interests you.

Quality is a very important factor in a stamp collection. This applies not only to duck stamps, but all types. Preserving the mint condition of a stamp is crucial for determining value. A perfectly centered stamp will usually sell for a substantial premium over a stamp with normal centering. Fine to very fine is the norm in stamp collecting, and is the condition priced by Scott.

Care should be taken not to damage a stamp, including the gum. The mint state of a stamp includes the freshness and original gum, so stamp mounts should be utilized when placing a stamp in your album. When a stamp has never been hinged, the abbreviation "NH" is used by dealers.

COLLECTORS ORGANIZATION

The National Duck Stamp Collectors Society exists for the benefit of those who collect duck stamps. Dues are $20 a year and are tax exempt. The NDSCS issues a quarterly newsletter and provides a membership card and lapel pin. Send your $20 directly to the NDSCS, Membership Chairman, P.O. Box 43, Harleysville, PA 19438.

Bob Dumaine is a recognized expert in duck stamps, founder of the National Duck Stamp Collectors Society, writer for *Linn's Stamp News*, publisher of *The Duck Report*, a past judge in the Federal Duck Stamp Contest, and serves on the expertizing committee of Professional Stamp Experts. Dumaine is the owner of Sam Houston Duck Co., a firm that specializes in duck stamps and related material.

Request your copy of our award-winning Duck Stamp Catalog—100 illustrated pages jam-packed with information on federal and state duck stamps, artist-signed stamps, prints, conservation issues and much more. Catalog $2, refundable with first order. Or send $5 and we'll send our catalog along with $35 *(catalog value)* of duck and conservation stamps!

Sam Houston Duck Company, P.O. Box 820087, Houston, TX 77282; 1-800-231-5926; Fax 1-281-496-1445. Visit our Web site at www.shduck.com.

FEDERAL DUCK STAMP DUCKLINGS

The Junior Duck Stamp Program, a recently created nonprofit organization to promote interest among young people, recently unveiled the design of its first federal junior duck stamp. The program also includes a conservation education curriculum that helps students of all ages. It focuses on wildlife conservation and management, wildlife art, and philately. As an outgrowth, the Junior Duck Stamp Design Competition was developed during 1993.

The resulting stamp, unlike the federal issue, is not valid as a revenue, but emulates the federal program in terms of art selection, creation of stamps, prints and other items for sale. All proceeds from the junior duck stamp go to the United States Fish and Wildlife Foundation to further its efforts.

The winning design for the first junior duck stamp was submitted by 16-year-old Jason Parsons of Canton, Ill. Parsons attends Canton High School. His highly realistic colored-pencil rendition of a male redhead duck was selected from 1,045 entries in Illinois, then competed nationally. He was honored by a special trip to Washington, D.C., along with one parent and his art teacher, Scott Snowman. There Parsons was guest at a special reception where the second and third place winners also were honored. The winning artwork is on display at the U.S. Department of the Interior and at festivals, art galleries, and state fairs nationwide. Various products will be available bearing Parsons' winning design.

Participation in the program has grown steadily. From eight states in 1992, the young program expanded to 22 in 1993. The program is now in effect nationwide and in U.S. possessions.

DUCK STAMP AGENCIES

Courtesy of Sam Houston Duck Co.
P.O. Box 820087   Houston, TX 77282
1-800-231-5926   281-493-6386
www.shduck.com

(APPROXIMATE ISSUE MONTH FOLLOWS STATE NAME)

Alabama, (8) Accounting Section, Duck Stamp, Dept. of Conservation & Natural Resources, 64 N. Union, Montgomery, AL 36130, (334)242-3469.

Alaska, (7) State of Alaska, Dept. of Fish & Game, Licensing Section, P.O. Box 25525, Juneau, AK 99802-5525, (907)465-2376.

Arizona, (7) Game & Fish Dept., 2222 W. Greenway Rd., Phoenix, AZ 85023, (602)942-3000.

Arkansas, (7) Game & Fish Commission, Collector Stamps, 2 Natural Resources Dr., Little Rock, AR 72205, (501)223-6300.

California, (9) Dept. of Fish & Game, License Section, 3211 S. St., Sacramento, CA 95816, (916)227-2278.

Colorado, (7) Division of Wildlife, 3824 La Mesa Dr., Ft. Collins, CO 80524, (970)484-2836.

Connecticut, (9) Wildlife Bureau, 79 Elm St., Hartford, CT 06106, (860)424-3011.

Delaware, (7) Divison of Fish & Wildlife, Box 1401, Dover, DE 19903, (302)739-5296.

Florida, (7) Game & Fish Comm, Finance, Sect., 620 S. Meridian St., Tallahassee, FL 32399-1600, (850)488-3831.

Georgia, (-) Dept. of Natural Resources, 2189 North Lake Pkwy. Bldg. 10 Ste. 108, Tucker, GA 30084, (770)414-3333. *(Last stamp issued 1999.)*

Hawaii, (9) Division of Forestry & Wildlife, 1151 Punch Bowl St., Honolulu, HI 96813, (808)587-4187.

Idaho, (-) Collector Stamps, Idaho Dept. of Fish & Game, Box 25, Boise, ID 83707, (208)334-3717. *(Last stamp issued 1998.)*

Illinois, (3) Illinois Dept. of Natural Resources, P.O. Box 19459, Springfield, IL 62794-9459, (217)785-0972.

Indiana, (12) Indiana Division of Fish & Wildlife, License Section (Stamp). 402 W. Washington Rm. W273, Indianapolis, IN 46204-2267, (317)232-4080.

Iowa, (12) Dept. of Natural Resources, Wallace State Office Building, Des Moines, IA 50319, (515)281-5145.

Kansas, (3) Fish & Game, Pratt Headquarters, 512 SE 25th Ave., Pratt, KS 67124, (316)672-0735.

Kentucky, (9) Dept. of Fish & Wildlife Resources, Arnold L. Mitchell Bldg., 1 Game Farm Rd., Frankfort, KY 40601, (502)564-7863.

Louisiana, (6) Dept. of Wildlife & Fisheries, P.O. Box 98000, ATTN: Licensing Section, Baton Rouge, LA 70898-9000, (225)765-2347.

Maine, (8) Dept. of Inland Fisheries & Wildlife, 284 State St., State House Station 41, Augusta, ME 04333, (207)287-8000.

Maryland, (8) Dept. of Natural Resources, Licensing & Registration Services, Box 1869, Annapolis, MD 21404, (410)260-8205.

Massachusetts, (12) Division of Fisheries & Game, License Section, 251 Causeway St., Suite 400, Boston, MA 02114-2104 (617)626-1590.

Michigan, (4) Dept. of Natural Resources, P.O. Box 30181, Lansing, MI 48909, (517)373-3272.

Minnesota, (3) Dept. of Natural Resources, 500 License Bureau, Lafayette Rd., St. Paul, MN 55155-4026, (612)296-0701.

Mississippi, (7) Dept. of Wildlife, Fish & Parks, License Dept., Box 451, Jackson, MS 39205-0451, (601)432-2400.

Missouri, (-) Dept. of Conservation, Fiscal Section, Box 180, Jefferson, MO 65105, (573)751-4115. *(Last stamp issued in 1996.)*

Montana, (4) Dept. of Fish, Wildlife & Parks, P.O. Box 200701, Helena, MT 59620-0701, (406)444-2612

Nebraska, (-) Game & Parks Commission, P.O. Box 30370, Lincoln, NE 68503, (402)471-5478. *(Last stamp issued in 1995.)*

Nevada, (10) Div. of Wildlife, ATTN: License Office, Stamp Sales, 1100 Valley Rd., Reno, NV 89512, (775)688-1500.

New Hampshire, (8) Fish & Game Dept., 2 Hazen Dr., Concord, NH 03301, (603)271-6832.

New Jersey, (7) Division of Fish, Game & Wildlife, Waterfowl Stamp, P.O. Box 400, Trenton, NJ 08625-0400, (609)292-9480.

New Mexico, (-) Dept. of Game & Fish, State Capitol, Villagra Bldg., Santa Fe, NM 87503, (505)827-7920. *(Last stamp issued in 1994.)*

New York, (10) Division of Fish & Wildlife, 50 Wolf Rd., Room 562, Albany, NY 12233-4754, (518)457-4480.

North Carolina, (7) Wildlife Resources Commission, License Section, P.O. Box 29565, Raleigh, NC 27626, (919)773-2881.

North Dakota, (7) Game & Fish Dept., Collector Stamps 100 N. Bismark Expressway, Bismark, ND 58501, (701)328-6334.

Ohio, (8) Division of Wildlife, License Section, 1840 Belcher Rd., Columbus, OH 43224-1329, (614)265-6300.

Oklahoma, (8) Dept. of Wildlife Conservation, P.O. Box 53465, Oklahoma City, OK 73152, (405)521-4629.

Oregon, (11) Dept. of Fish & Wildlife, Box 59, Portland, OR 97207, (503)872-5720 ext 5461.

Pennsylvania, (3) Game Commission, License Section, 2001 Elmerton Ave., Harrisburg, PA 17110-9797, (717)787-6286.

Rhode Island, (9) Rhode Island Fish & Wildlife, Division of Fish & Wildlife, 4808 Tower Hill Rd., Wakefield, RI 02879-2207, (401)789-3094.

South Carolina, (7) Dept. of Natural Resources, License Section, P.O. Box 11710, Columbia, SC 29211, (803)734-3833.

South Dakota, (1) Game, Fish & Parks, License Division, 412 W. Missouri, Pierre, SD 57501, (605)773-5527.

Tennessee, (5) Wildlife Resources Agency, ATTN.: Wildlife Stamps, Box 40747, Nashville, TN 37204, (615)781-6501.

Texas, (8) Parks & Wildlife Dept., License Office, 4200 Smith School Rd., Austin, TX 78744, (512)389-4822. Stamp orders 1-800-895-4248.

Utah, (-) Division of Wildlife Resources, 1596 W. North Temple, Salt Lake City, UT 84116-3195, (801)538-4841. *(Last stamp issued in 1997.)*

Vermont, (9) Dept. of Fish & Wildlife, Stamp Order, 103 S. Main St., 10 South, Waterbury, VT 05671-0501, (802)241-3700.

Virginia, (10) Game Dept., Box 11104, Richmond, VA 23230-1104, (804)367-9369.

Washington, (7) Dept. of Wildlife, 600 Capitol Way North, Olympia, WA 98501-1091, (360)902-2200.

West Virginia, (-) Dept. of Natural Resources, Waterfowl Stamp Program, Box 67, Elkins, WV 26241, (304)637-0245. *(Last stamp issued in 1996.)*

Wisconsin, (8) Dept. of Natural Resources, Box 7924, Madison, WI 53707, (608)264-6137.

Wyoming, (1) Game & Fish Dept., ATTN. Alternative Enterprises, 5440 Bishop Blvd., Cheyenne, WY 82006, (307)777-4570.

FEDERAL & INTERNATIONAL AGENCIES

U.S. Dept. of Wildlife, (7) 18th & "C" Streets, N.W. Room 2058, Washington, D.C. 20240, (202)208-4354.

Alberta, ( )R.D. Miner Philatelics, 83 Woodgreen Dr., Calgary, Alberta Canada T2W 4G6, (403)251-7500.

Argentina, ( ) National Art Publishing Corp., 11000 Metro Pkwy. Ste #32, Ft. Myers, FL 33912-1293, (941)939-7518. *(Last stamp issued 1996.)*

Australia, (-) Jan Sec Fire Stamps, 4/358 Pacific Hwy., Linfield NSW 2070, Australia - P.O. Box 214. *(Last stamp issued 1996.)*

Canada, (8) Wildlife Habitat Canada, 9 Hinton Ave. North Ste. #200, Ottawa Ontario Canada K1Y 4P1.

Croatia, ( ) Duck Stamp Fulfillment Center, 1015 West Jackson, Sullivan, IL 61951, (217)728-8321. *(Last stamp issued 1997.)*

Denmark, ( ) Duck Stamp Fulfillment Center, 1015 West Jackson, Sullivan, IL 61951, (217)728-8321. *(Last stamp issued 1997.)*

Ireland, ( ) Duck Stamp Fulfillment Center, 1015 West Jackson, Sullivan, IL 61951, (217)728-8321. *(Last stamp issued 1998.)*

Israel, ( ) Fleetwood, #1 Unicover Center, Cheyenne, WY 82008, (307)634-5911. *(Last stamp issued 1998.)*

Italy, ( ) Duck Stamp Fulfillment Center, 1015 West Jackson, Sullivan, IL 61951, (217)728-8321. *(Last stamp issued 1998.)*

Mexico, ( ) Duck Stamp Fulfillment Center, 1015 West Jackson, Sullivan, IL 61951, (217)728-8321. *(Last stamp issued 1997.)*

New Zealand, (9) Duck Stamp Fulfillment Center, 1015 West Jackson, Sullivan, IL 61951, (217)728-8321. *(Last stamp issued 1997.)*

Quebec, (4) Rousseau Inc., 230 Rue St., Vacque St., Vieux Montreal, Quebec H2YIL9, Canada. 1-800-561-9977.

Russia, (4) Fleetwood, #1 Unicover Center, Cheyenne, WY 82008, (307)771-3000.

Spain, ( ) National Art Publishing Corp., 11000 Metro Pkwy. Ste. #32, Ft. Myers, FL 33912-1293 (941)939-7518. *(Last stamp issued 1996.)*

Sweden, ( ) Duck Stamp Fulfillment Center, 1015 West Jackson, Sullivan, IL 61951, (217)728-8321. *(Last stamp issued 1997.)*

United Kingdom, (7) Duck Stamp Fulfillment Center, 1015 West Jackson, Sullivan, IL 61951, (217)728-8321.

Venezuela, ( ) National Art Publishing Corp., 11000 Metro Pkwy. Ste. #32, Ft. Myers, FL 33912-129 (941)939-7518. *(Last stamp issued 1996.)*

All the following have the same contact:
Hines-Proguide, Box 25012, Halifax, Nova Scotia, B3M 4H4 Canada (902)433-1441.

British Columbia (10)
Manitoba (10)
New Brunswick (10)
Newfoundland & Labrador (10)
Nunavet Territory (10)
Nova Scotia (10)
Ontario (10)
Prince Edward Island (10)
Saskatchewan (10)
Yukon Territory (10)

Scott No.	Very Fine Plate Block	Fine Plate Block	Very Fine Unused Each	Fine Unused Each	Very Fine Used Each	Fine Used Each
☐RW1 (1934)$1 Mallards, Blue (J.N. "Ding" Darling)						
	12500.00	8000.00	900.00	525.00	120.00	85.00
☐RW2 (1935)$1 Canvasbacks, Rose Lake (Frank Benson)						
	10000.00	7000.00	700.00	425.00	110.00	85.00
☐RW3 (1936)$1 Canada Geese, Brown Blk (Richard E. Bishop)						
	3300.00	2400.00	300.00	195.00	65.00	45.00
☐RW4 (1937)$1Lt. Scaup, Lt. Green, (J.D. Knap)						
	2500.00	1900.00	275.00	175.00	50.00	35.00
☐RW5 (1938)$1Pintails, Light Violet (Roland Clark)						
	3500.00	2400.00	425.00	175.00	50.00	35.00
☐RW6 (1939)$1 Green-Winged Teal, Chocolate (Lynn B. Hunt)						
	2000.00	1600.00	225.00	150.00	40.00	26.00
☐RW7 (1940)$1 Black Ducks, Sepia (F.L. Jacques)						
	1900.00	1400.00	225.00	150.00	40.00	26.00
☐RW8 (1941)$1 Ruddy Ducks, Brown Carmine (E.R. Kalmbach)						
	1900.00	1400.00	225.00	150.00	40.00	26.00
☐RW9 (1942)$1 Widgeon, Violet Brown (A. L. Ripley)						
	1900.00	1400.00	225.00	150.00	40.00	26.00
☐RW10 (1943)$1 Wood Ducks, Deep Rose (Walter E. Bohl)						
	650.00	450.00	95.00	60.00	30.00	20.00
☐RW11 (1944)$1 White Fronted Geese, Red Orange (Walter A. Weber)						
	650.00	450.00	95.00	60.00	20.00	15.00
☐RW12 (1945)$1 Shovelers, Black (Owen J. Gramme)						
	375.00	240.00	65.00	50.00	17.00	14.00
☐RW13 (1946)$1Redheads, Red Brown (Robert W. Hines)						
	325.00	210.00	55.00	42.00	15.00	12.00
☐RW13a Rose Red Error (5-10 known)						
	—	—	6500.00	—	—	—
☐RW14 (1947) $1 Snow Geese, Black (Jack Murray)						
	325.00	210.00	55.00	42.00	14.00	12.00
☐RW15 (1948)$1 Buffleheads, Bright Blue (Maynard Reece)						
	325.00	210.00	55.00	42.00	14.50	12.00
☐RW16 (1949)$2 Goldeneyes, Bright Green (Roger E. Preuss)						
	375.00	250.00	60.00	45.00	15.00	12.00
☐RW17 (1950)$1 Trumpeter Swans, Violet (Walter A. Weber)						
	500.00	300.00	85.00	50.00	9.00	6.00
☐RW18 (1951)$2 Gadwalls, Gray Black (Maynard Reese)						
	500.00	300.00	85.00	50.00	9.00	6.00
☐RW19 (1952)$2 Harlequins, Ultramarine (John H. Dick)						
	500.00	300.00	85.00	50.00	9.00	6.00

Scott No.	Very Fine Plate Block	Fine Plate Block	Very Fine Unused Each	Fine Unused Each	Very Fine Used Each	Fine Used Each
☐RW20 (1953)$2 Blue-winged Teal, Dark Rose Brown (C. B. Seagers)						
	500.00	300.00	75.00	55.00	9.00	5.00
☐RW21 (1954)$2 Ring-necked Ducks, Black (H.D. Sandstrom)						
	500.00	300.00	75.00	55.00	9.00	5.00
☐RW22 (1955)$2 Blue Geese, Dark Blue (Stanley Stearns)						
	500.00	300.00	75.00	55.00	9.00	5.00
☐RW22a Reversed Inverted						
	—	—	4500.00	—	—	—
☐RW23 (1956)$2 Mergansers, Black (E.J. Bierly)						
	500.00	300.00	75.00	55.00	9.00	5.00
☐RW24 (1957)$2 American Eider, Emerald (J.M. Abbott)						
	500.00	300.00	75.00	55.00	9.00	5.00
☐RW24a Writing Inverted						
	—	—	3500.00	—	—	—
☐RW25 (1958)$2 Canada Geese, Black (Leslie C. Kouba)						
	500.00	300.00	75.00	55.00	9.00	5.00
☐RW26 (1959)$3 Labrador, Blue/Ochre/Black (Maynard Reece)						
	500.00	325.00	95.00	75.00	9.00	5.00
☐RW26a Reversed Inverted						
	—	15000.00				
☐RW27 (1960)$3 Redheads, Red Brown/Blue/Bist (John A. Ruthven)						
	450.00	325.00	75.00	60.00	12.00	8.00
☐RW28 (1961)$3 Mallards, Blue/Bist/Brown (E. A. Morris)						
	450.00	325.00	75.00	60.00	12.00	8.00
☐RW29 (1962)$3 Pintails, Blue/Brown/Black (E.A. Morris)						
	500.00	400.00	100.00	80.00	12.00	8.00
☐RW29a Reversed Writing Omitted						
	—	12500.00		—	—	—
☐RW30 (1963)$3 American Brant, Black/Blue/Yellow/Green (E.J. Bierly)						
	500.00	360.00	85.00	60.00	12.00	8.00
☐RW31 (1964)$3 Nene Geese, Black/Blue//Bist. (Stanley Stearns)						
	2200.00	1600.00	95.00	60.00	12.00	8.00
☐RW32 (1965)$3 Canvasbacks, Green/Black/Brown (Ron Jenkins)						
	475.00	360.00	80.00	60.00	10.00	8.00
☐RW33 (1966)$3 Whistling Swans, Blue/Green/Black (Stanley Stearns)						
	475.00	360.00	80.00	60.00	10.00	8.00
☐RW34 (1967)$3 Oldsquaws, Multicolored (Leslie C. Kouba)						
	525.00	300.00	110.00	60.00	10.00	8.00
☐RW35 (1968)$3 Mergansers, Green/Black/Brown (C.G. Pritchard)						
	275.00	170.00	60.00	38.00	9.00	6.00

Scott No.	Very Fine Plate Block	Fine Plate Block	Very Fine Unused Each	Fine Unused Each	Very Fine Used Each	Fine Used Each
☐RW36 (1969)$3 White-winged Scoters, Multicolored (Maynard Reece)						
	275.00	160.00	60.00	38.00	9.00	6.00
☐RW37 (1970)$3 Ross' Geese, Multicolored (E.J. Bierly)						
	275.00	160.00	60.00	38.00	9.00	6.00
☐RW38 (1971)$3 Cinnamon Teal, Multicolored (Maynard Reece)						
	225.00	130.00	50.00	30.00	9.00	6.00
☐RW39 (1972)$5 Emperor Geese, Multicolored (Arthur M. Cook)						
	100.00	75.00	20.00	18.00	8.00	5.00
☐RW40 (1973)$5 Steller's Eiders, Multicolored (Lee LeBlanc)						
	80.00	60.00	15.00	12.00	8.00	5.00
☐RW41 (1974)$5 Wood Ducks, Multicolored (David A. Maass)						
	75.00	60.00	15.00	12.00	8.00	5.00
☐RW42 (1975)$5 Decoy/Canvasbacks, Multicolored (James P. Fisher)						
	65.00	50.00	14.00	11.00	7.50	5.00
☐RW43 (1976)$5 Canada Geese, Emerald & Black (Aldersen, "Sandy" Magee)						
	65.00	50.00	14.00	11.00	7.50	5.00
☐RW44 (1977)$5 Ross' Geese, Multicolored (Martin R. Murk)						
	70.00	50.00	16.00	13.00	7.50	5.00
☐RW45 (1978)$5 Mergansers, Multicolored (Albert Gilbert)						
	70.00	50.00	15.00	12.00	7.50	5.00
☐RW46 (1979)$7.50 Green-winged Teal, Multicolored (Ken Michaelsen)						
	70.00	50.00	16.00	12.00	7.50	5.00
☐RW47 (1980)$7.50 Mallards, Multicolored (Richard Plasschaert)						
	70.00	50.00	16.00	12.00	7.50	5.00
☐RW48 (1981)$7.50 Ruddy Ducks, Multicolored (John S. Wilson)						
	70.00	50.00	16.00	12.00	7.50	5.00
☐RW49 (1982)$7.50 Canvasbacks, Multicolored (David A. Maass)						
	70.00	50.00	16.00	12.00	7.50	5.00
☐RW49a Black and Orange Omitted						
	7500.00	—	—	—	—	—
☐RW50 (1983)$7.50 Pintails, Multicolored (Phil Scholer)						
	70.00	50.00	16.00	11.00	7.50	5.00
☐RW51 (1984)$7.50 Widgeons, Multicolored (W.C. Morris)						
	70.00	50.00	16.00	11.00	7.50	5.00
☐RW52 (1985)$7.50 Cinnamon Teal, Multicolored (Gerald Moblex)						
	70.00	50.00	16.00	12.00	7.50	5.00
☐RW53 (1986)$7.50 Fulvous Whistling Duck, Multicolored (Burton E. Moore)						
	70.00	50.00	16.00	12.00	7.50	5.00

Scott No.	Very Fine Plate Block	Fine Plate Block	Very Fine Unused Each	Fine Unused Each	Very Fine Used Each	Fine Used Each
□RW53a Black Engraved Omitted						
	—	—	4000.00	—	—	—
□RW54 (1987)$10.00 Redheads, Multicolored (Arthur Anderson)						
	100.00	75.00	22.00	16.00	10.00	8.00
□RW55 (1988)$10.00 Snow Goose, Multicolored (Daniel Smith)						
	100.00	75.00	22.00	16.00	10.00	8.00
□RW56 (1989)$12.50 Lesser Scaup, Multicolored (Neal Anderson)						
	100.00	75.00	22.00	16.00	11.00	9.00
□RW57 (1990)$12.50 Black-bellied Whistling Duck, Multicolored (Jim Hautman)						
	100.00	75.00	22.00	16.00	11.00	9.00
□RW58 (1991)$15.00 King Eider, Multicolored (Nancy Howe)						
	100.00	90.00	25.00	20.00	14.00	9.00
□RW58a Error Black Engraved Omitted						
	—	—$12,500.00		—	—	—
□RW59 (1992)$15.00 Spectacled Eiders, Multicolored (Joe Hautman)						
	110.00	90.00	25.00	20.00	14.00	9.00
□RW60 (1993)$15.00 Canvasbacks, Multicolored (Bruce Miller)						
	110.00	90.00	25.00	20.00	14.00	9.00
□RW60a Error Black Engraved Omitted						
	—	—	$4,000.00	—	—	—
□RW61 (1994)$15.00 Red-breasted Mergansers, Multicolored (Neal Anderson)						
	110.00	90.00	25.00	20.00	14.00	9.00
□RW62 (1995)$15.00 Mallards, Multicolored (Jim Hautman)						
	110.00	90.00	25.00	20.00	14.00	9.00
□RW63 (1996)$15.00 Sun Scoter, Multicolored (Wilhelm Goebel)						
	110.00	90.00	25.00	20.00	14.00	9.00
□RW64 (1997)$15.00 Canada Goose, Multicolored (Robert Hautman)						
	110.00	90.00	25.00	20.00	14.00	9.00
□RW65 (1998)$15.00 Barrow Golden Eyes, Multicolored (Bob Steiner)						
	110.00	90.00	25.00	20.00	14.00	9.00
□RW66 (1999)$15.00 Greater Scaup, Multicolored (Jim Hautman)						
	110.00	90.00	25.00	20.00	14.00	9.00
□RW67 (2000)Mottled duck, Multicolored (Adam Grimm)						
	110.00	90.00	25.00	20.00	14.00	9.00
□RW68 (2001)Pintail, Multicolored (Robert Hautman)						
	110.00	90.00	25.00	20.00	14.00	9.00
□RW69 (2002)Black Scoter, Multicolored (Joe Hautman)						
	110.00	90.00	25.00	20.00	14.00	9.00

Scott No.			Fine Unused Each	Ave. Unused Each	Fine Used Each	Ave. Used Each

HAWAIIAN ISSUES
1851–1952. "MISSIONARIES"

Scott No.			Fine Unused Each	Ave. Unused Each	Fine Used Each	Ave. Used Each
☐1	2¢	Blue	—	450,000.00	—	210,000.00
☐		On Cover				425,000.00
☐2	5¢	Blue	—	55,000.00	—	24,000.00
☐		On Cover				52,000.00
☐3	13¢	Blue	—	22,000.00	—	11,000.00
☐		On Cover				36,000.00
☐4	13¢	Blue	—	52,000.00	—	25,000.00
☐		On Cover				40,000.00

NOTE: Prices on the above classic stamps of Hawaii vary greatly depending on the individual specimen and circumstances of sale.

NOTE: Beware of fake cancels on Hawaiian stamps, when the value is higher used than unused.

1853. KING KAMEHAMEHA III

Scott No.			Fine Unused Each	Ave. Unused Each	Fine Used Each	Ave. Used Each
☐5	5¢	Blue	—	1500.00	—	1000.00
☐6	13¢	Dark Red	—	650.00	—	500.00
☐7	5¢ on 13¢	Dark Red	—	6500.00	—	5500.00

1857.

Scott No.			Fine Unused Each	Ave. Unused Each	Fine Used Each	Ave. Used Each
☐8	5¢	Blue	—	450.00	—	370.00

1861.

Scott No.			Fine Unused Each	Ave. Unused Each	Fine Used Each	Ave. Used Each
☐9	5¢	Blue	—	130.00	—	110.00

1868. RE-ISSUE

Scott No.			Fine Unused Each	Ave. Unused Each	Fine Used Each	Ave. Used Each
☐10	5¢	Blue	—	20.00	—	—
☐11	13¢	Rose	—	150.00	—	—

1869–1862.

Scott No.			Fine Unused Each	Ave. Unused Each	Fine Used Each	Ave. Used Each
☐12	1¢	Light Blue	—	3300.00	—	285.00
☐13	2¢	Light Blue	—	3300.00	—	285.00
☐14	2¢	Black	—	3300.00	—	285.00

1863.

Scott No.			Fine Unused Each	Ave. Unused Each	Fine Used Each	Ave. Used Each
☐15	1¢	Black	—	400.00	—	320.00
☐16	2¢	Black	—	400.00	—	340.00
☐17	2¢	Dark Blue	—	5000.00	—	2500.00
☐18	2¢	Black	—	1200.00	—	1000.00

Scott No.		Fine Unused Each	Ave. Unused Each	Fine Used Each	Ave. Used Each
1864–1865.					
☐19	1¢ Black	—	340.00	—	—
☐20	2¢ Black	—	40.00	—	—
☐21	5¢ Blue	—	400.00	—	—
☐22	5¢ Blue	—	320.00	—	—
1864. LAID PAPER					
☐23	1¢ Black	160.00	110.00	—	—
☐24	2¢ Black	160.00	110.00	—	—
1865. WOVE PAPER					
☐25	1¢ Blue	190.00	110.00	135.00	110.00
☐26	2¢ Blue	160.00	100.00	140.00	90.00
☐27	2¢ Rose	190.00	120.00	140.00	110.00
☐28	2¢ Rose Vert	190.00	120.00	140.00	110.00
1869. ENGRAVED					
☐29	2¢ Red	70.00	40.00	40.00	21.00
1864–1871.					
☐30	1¢ Purple	9.00	5.00	6.40	4.10
☐31	2¢ Vermilion	11.00	6.00	8.00	4.10
☐32	5¢ Blue	—	42.00	16.00	10.00
☐33	6¢ Green	18.50	10.00	7.00	4.10
☐34	18¢ Rose	92.00	60.00	17.00	10.00
1875.					
☐35	2¢ Brown	6.00	3.75	2.50	1.85
☐36	12¢ Black	37.00	24.00	19.00	12.00
☐37	1¢ Blue	6.00	4.50	4.70	3.00
☐38	2¢ Lilac Rose	80.00	48.00	27.00	17.00
☐39	5¢ Ultramarine	15.00	8.00	2.10	2.00
☐40	10¢ Black	29.00	14.00	18.00	10.00
☐41	15¢ Red Brown	46.00	22.00	19.00	13.00

Scott No.		Fine Unused Each	Ave. Unused Each	Fine Used Each	Ave. Used Each
1883–1886.					
☐42	1¢ Green	2.40	1.50	1.50	.85
☐43	2¢ Rose	4.50	3.00	1.00	.70
☐44	10¢ Red Brown	17.50	11.00	7.00	4.00
☐45	10¢ Vermilion	22.00	14.00	11.00	8.50
☐46	12¢ Red Lilac	62.00	33.00	30.00	18.00
☐47	25¢ Dark Violet	82.00	50.00	42.00	26.00
☐48	50¢ Red	125.00	90.00	70.00	45.00
☐49	$1 Rose Red	210.00	120.00	100.00	50.00
☐50	2¢ Orange	125.00	97.00	—	—
☐51	2¢ Carmine	23.00	16.00	—	—
1890–1891.					
☐52	2¢ Dull Violet	6.10	2.50	1.25	.90
☐52c	5¢ Dark Blue	110.00	72.00	91.00	50.00
1893. PROVISIONAL GOVT. RED OVERPRINT					
☐53	1¢ Purple	4.10	2.60	3.50	2.25
☐54	1¢ Blue	4.10	2.50	3.50	2.00
☐55	1¢ Green	1.75	.80	1.10	.75
☐56	2¢ Brown	4.50	2.50	3.50	2.00
☐57	2¢ Dull Violet	2.00	.90	1.20	.90
☐58	5¢ Dark Blue	8.50	5.00	6.00	4.00
☐59	5¢ Ultramarine	6.00	3.00	3.25	2.25
☐60	6¢ Green	10.00	6.00	9.00	5.00
☐61	10¢ Black	8.50	4.00	7.10	3.50
☐62	12¢ Black	8.00	4.00	7.10	3.10
☐63	12¢ Red Lilac	115.00	62.00	115.00	50.00
☐64	25¢ Dark Violet	25.00	12.00	20.00	10.00
BLACK OVERPRINT					
☐65	2¢ Vermilion	50.00	28.00	43.00	26.00
☐66	2¢ Rose	1.50	.95	1.00	.85
☐67	10¢ Vermilion	9.50	7.00	8.00	5.50
☐68	10¢ Red Brown	8.50	5.00	7.10	4.50
☐69	12¢ Red Lilac	215.00	115.00	200.00	105.00
☐70	15¢ Red Brown	17.00	11.00	15.00	10.00
☐71	18¢ Dull Rose	21.00	11.00	20.00	16.00
☐72	50¢ Red	55.00	28.00	42.00	26.00

Scott No.			Fine Unused Each	Ave. Unused Each	Fine Used Each	Ave. Used Each
☐73	$1	Rose Red	100.00	65.00	90.00	52.00
☐74	1¢	Yellow	2.25	1.75	1.60	.82
☐75	2¢	Brown	2.50	2.10	.90	.55
☐76	5¢	Rose Lake	4.10	3.00	1.75	1.15
☐77	10¢	Yellow Green	5.00	4.00	4.50	3.00
☐78	12¢	Blue	10.50	6.50	9.50	5.50
☐79	25¢	Deep Blue	11.00	6.50	9.00	5.50

1899.

☐80	1¢	Dark Green	2.50	1.25	1.50	.90
☐81	2¢	Rose	2.50	1.25	1.50	.90
☐82	5¢	Blue	5.00	4.00	3.40	2.10

1896. OFFICIAL STAMPS

☐O1	2¢	Green	32.00	18.00	17.00	10.00
☐O2	5¢	Dark Brown	32.00	18.00	17.00	10.00
☐O3	6¢	Deep Ultramarine	40.00	18.00	17.00	10.00
☐O4	10¢	Rose	31.00	16.00	17.00	10.00
☐O5	12¢	Orange	60.00	38.00	22.00	10.00
☐O6	25¢	Gray Violet	82.00	42.00	17.00	10.00

AMERICAN FIRST
DAY COVERS

THE AMERICAN FIRST DAY COVER SOCIETY

The FIRST and ONLY not-for-profit, non-commercial, International Society devoted exclusively to First Day Covers and First Day Cover collecting.

FIRST DAYS **IS THE AWARD-WINNING OFFICIAL PUBLICATION OF THE AMERICAN FIRST DAY COVER SOCIETY.** FDC collecting is a hands-on hobby of personal involvement—much more than simple collecting. It encourages the individual collector to fully develop his range of interests so that his collection is a reflection of his personal tastes. FDCs will encourage your creativity to reach full expression by adapting cachets or cancellations or using combinations (related stamps). In this hobby uniqueness is the rule, not the exception.

BUT . . . *FIRST DAYS* **IS AVAILABLE ONLY TO MEMBERS OF THE AFDCS.** It's just ONE of the many benefits of membership. Whether you are interested in topical areas of collecting, working on serious research, or just learning more about the hobby in general, this is the organization for you.

AMERICAN FIRST DAY COVER SOCIETY CHAPTERS

A complete list of all of the chapters of the American First Day Cover Society, along with the chapter representative, is included in *The Official Blackbook Price Guide to United States Postage Stamps*. This list is found after this introduction to First Day Covers collecting and before the Glossary of First Day Cover Terms. If you see a chapter that meets in your area, or one that features the type of cover you collect, do not hesitate to contact the chapter representative for more information.

Discover the Fun in First Day Cover Collecting

Presented by the American First Day Cover Society

Combination FDCs or Combo FDCs can be made for any subject. Some research into a new stamp you like is all you need to do. Find some inexpensive stamps that help to tell the full story of the stamp. Many stamps going all the way back into the 1940s will be inexpensive enough to put on your Combo. The Combo shown here contains four stamps with space topics on a First Day Cover of the $2.40 Express Mail Stamp of 1989.

Visit us on the Web at

HYPERLINK "http://www.AFDCS.org"
www.AFDCS.org.

We offer a free mentor service to answer your questions about FDCs. Our two most popular publications are *Handcrafted Cachets: The Make Your Own Cachet and Envelope Book* (third edition) and *A Handbook for First Day Cover Collectors* (fourth edition). They can help you get started on the rewarding creative and diverse hobby of first day cover collecting. For more information, contact AFDCS Central Office P.O. Box 65960, Tucson, AZ 85728, U.S.A.

Autographs on First Day Covers are very popular. This RDC was autographed on the First Day of the 10¢ Flag Stamp issued on December 8, 1973. It was autographed by the designer of the stamp, the Postmaster of San Francisco, and the Governor of California, Former President Ronald Reagan. For more information on autograph collecting, send a 55¢ self-addressed stamped envelope to the Autograph Chapter of the AFDCS, Box 42, Audubon, NJ 08106.

A Joint Issue First Day Cover has two or more stamps issued by different countries to commemorate the same event, topic, place, or person. The cover shown above has the U.S. and Canadian Year of the Tiger stamps, both cancelled with the First Day of Issue cancel of their own country. In 2000, more than 30 countries issued Chinese New Year stamps, including countries with significant Chinese ethnic groups, like the US, Canada, and Australia.

American First Day Cover Society chapters can be reached through the contact person listed, or you can contact the AFDCS chapter coordinator, Foster E. Miller, III, P.O. Box 44, Annapolis, MD 20701, e-mail: fmiller@pobox.net.

#1. Queen City Stamp & Cover Club: Fred Sprague, 503 King George Rd., Basking Ridge, NJ 07920

#3. Baltimore Philatelic Society, Inc.: Alice M. L. Robinson, 1224 N. Calvert St., Baltimore, MD 21202

#5. Motor City Stamp & Cover Club: Robert Quintero, 22608 Poplar Ct., Hazel Park, MI 48030

#6. Chicago Land FDC Society: Randall Sherman, 1101 W. Columbia Ave. #212, Chicago, IL 60626

#7. W. Suburban Stamp Club of Plymouth: Editor, Newsletter, P.O. Box 700049, Plymouth, MI 48170

#9. Harford County Stamp Club: Arch Handy, P.O. Box 632, Bel Air, MD 21014

#12. Carroll County Philatelic Assoc.: Blair H. Law, 4510 Willow View St., Hampstead, MD 21074

#17. Robert C Graebner Chapter of AFDCS: Foster E. Miller, III, P.O. Box 44, Annapolis Junction, MD 20701

#19. Metropolitan FDC Society: Benjamin Green, 66-15 Thornton Pl, Rego Park, NY 11374

#20. FDC Collectors Club: Stephen Neulander, P.O. Box 25, Deerfield, IL 60015

#25. Coryell's Ferry Stamp Club: Mrs. Frank Davis, P.O. Box 52, Penns Park, PA 18943

#26. Ft. Findlay Stamp Club: Tom Foust, 5578 State Rt. 186, McComb, OH 45858

#27. Hazlet Stamp Club: Oscar Strandberg, 54 Crestview Dr, Middletown, NJ 07748

#34. Columbus Philatelic Club: Paul Gault, 120 West 18th Ave., Columbus, OH 43210

#36. Autograph Chapter of AFDCS: George Haggas, P.O. Box 42, Audubon, NJ 08106

#39. Samuel Gompers Stamp Club: Edwin M. Schmidt, P.O. Box 1233, Springfield, VA 22151

#40. Columbia Philatelic Society: Harold T. Babb, 341 Tram Rd., Columbia, SC 29210

#41. FDC Unit of Clifton Stamp Society: Andrew Boyajian, P.O. Box 229, Hasbrouck Heights, NJ 07604

#43. George Washington Masonic Stamp Club: Stan Longenecker, 930 Wood St., Mount Joy, PA 17552

#44. Hamilton Township Philatelic Society: John Ranto, P.O. Box 8683, Trenton, NJ 06850

#45. Joplin Stamp Club: Fred Roesel, 4225 East 25th St., Joplin, MO 64801

#46. Gulf Coast FDC Group: Mrs. Monte Eiserman, 14359 Chadbourne, Houston, TX 77070

#48. Claude C. Ries Chapter of AFDCS: Rick Whyte, 1175 West Base Line Rd., Claremont, CA 91711

#50. The 7/1/71 Affair: Roy E. Mooney, P.O. Box 2539, Cleveland, GA 30528

#53. Central NY FDC Society: Rick Kase, P.O. Box 10833, Rochester, NY 14610

#54. Journalists, Authors and Poets on Stamps: Lin Collette, 78 Gooding St., Pawtucket, RI 02860

#55. Louisville FDC Society: Arthur S. Buchter, 5410 Cannonwood Ct., Louisville, KY 40229

#56. North Texas Chapter of AFDCS: Fred Sawyer, 3520 Pebble Beach Dr., Farmers Branch, TX 75234

#57. Long Island Cover and Autograph Society: Secretary LIC&AS, Box 2095, Port Washington, NY 11050

#58. American Ceremony Program Society: Michael Litvak, 1866 Loma Vista St., Pasadena, CA 91104

#60. Florida Chapter of AFDCS: George Athens, 3295 Datura Rd., Venice, FL 34293

#61. Ohio Cachetmakers Assoc.: Chris & Denise Lazaroff, 2967 Aylesbury St. NW, N. Canton, OH 44720

#62. Gateway to the West Chpt. of AFDCS: Art Rosenberg, 8686 Delmar Blvd., #2W, St. Louis, MO 63124

#63. Delaware Valley Chpt. of AFDCS: George Mullen, 1566 Rockwell Rd., Abington, PA 19001

#64. Society of Philatelists & Numismatists: Joe R. Ramos, 1929 Millis St., Montebello, CA 90640

#65. Cachetmakers Assoc.: Pam Roberts, 83 North 22nd St., Newark, OH 43055

#67. Maximum Card Study Unit: Gary Denis, P.O. Box 766, Patuxent River, MD 20670

#69. Rochester Philatelic Assoc.: Joe Doles, 105 Lawson Rd., Rochester, NY 14616

#70. Tucson Stamp Club: Alex Lutgendorf, 5260 W. Arroyo Pl, Tucson, AZ 85745

#71. North Carolina Chapter of AFDCS: Eric Wile, 2202 Jane St., Greensboro, NC 27407

#72. Gay and Lesbian History on Stamps: Ed Centeno, P.O. Box 230940, Hartford, CT 06123

#73. Hand-Painted Cover Chapter of AFDCS: Alan Freedman, 48 Kent Rd., Hillsdale, NJ 07642

#74. Multnomah Children's Covers: Tommy Lee, 4572 Catalpa St., Los Angeles, CA 90032

#75. American Indian Philatelic Society: Dean Lilly, 5460 Margie Lane, Oak Forest, IL 60542

#76. Harry C. Ioor Chapter of AFDCS: Patrick Tudor, 920 N. Bolton Ave., Indianapolis, IN 46219

#77. Molly Pitcher Stamp Club: Gary Dubnik, 1489 Canterbury Rd., Lakewood, NJ 08701

#78. National Duck Stamp Collectors Society: John Geiser, P.O. Box 43, Harleysville, PA 19438

#79. Art Cover Exchange (ACE): Gary Chicoine, P.O. Box 31, Hall, NY 14463

#80. Waterbury Stamp Club: Laurent Corriveau, P.O. Box 581, Waterbury, CT 06720

#81. Artcraft Cover Collectors Club: David Sofferman, 5225 Pooks Hill Rd., #520, Bethesda, MD 20814

#82. AFDCS Chapter for Computer Users: Kerry Heffner, P.O. Box 460787, Pappillion, NE 68046

#83. Dayton Stamp Club: Frank Shivly, 415 Far Hills Ave., Dayton, OH 45409

#84. Virtual Stamp Club on Delphi: Lloyd de Vries, Box 561, Paramus, NJ 07653, e-mail: stamps@pobox.com

#85. Norwalk Stamp Club: Richard Hoffman, Box 267, Norwalk, CT 06856

#86. Junior Philatelists of America: Courtney Huff, 646 South Rd., Hopkinton, NH 03229

A GLOSSARY OF FIRST DAY COVER TERMS

Compiled by *FIRST DAYS* Staff

Add-on—A cachet design added to a cover which was originally uncacheted. An add-on cachet should be identified by maker and date so that it is clear that it is not contemporary with the cover. Unfortunately, many add-ons are not so identified.

Aerogramme—Postal stationery characterized by a single sheet which may be folded into an envelope, sealed, and then sent at a rate less than the airmail letter rate. Postage is usually but not always imprinted. Also known as aerogram.

AFDCS—American First Day Cover Society.

All-over cachet—A cachet design that covers most of or the entire face (front) of the envelope, as compared to one that occupies just the left side.

All-purpose cachet—A cachet with a general design that can be used for any stamp subject. It has no specific theme. Also, General Purpose.

Alternate cancel—Any First Day cancellation from the official First Day city, other than the official First Day of Issue postmarks supplied by the USPS. (These are sometimes referred to as semi-officials, or by the specific name of the cancel, such as plug, slogan, show, or ship cancels, etc.)

AMF—Air Mail Field. Found in many postmarks of postal facilities located in airports.

Autographed—An autographed envelope bears one or more signatures of individuals who are usually associated with the stamp. The autograph relationships may be the stamp subject, the designer, the local postmaster, dignitaries present at the dedication ceremony, etc. Authenticity and possible mechanical application of an autograph are significant considerations.

Auxiliary markings—Postal markings which are occasionally found on First Day Covers such as "Registered," "Insured," "Return to Sender," "Postage Due ____¢," etc.

B/4—Block of four stamps. Also B4.

Back stamp—The arrival mark of the destination city which usually appears on the reverse of the cover. Most registered covers are back-stamped on arrival.

Booklet pane—A sheetlet of stamps removed from a stamp booklet which may have one or more such panes. On FDC it is desirable to include the tab which is used to bind the pane into the booklet. This may not be possible with some modern issues.

Bullseye—also, bull's-eye. 1) The dial or circular portion of a postmark used by itself as a cancel. 2) Any circular postmark struck directly on the center of a stamp. (See Socked-on-the-nose.)

Cachet—Any textual or graphic design which has been applied to a cover usually, but not always, on the left side of the envelope. A cachet may be produced by any means—printed, rubber stamped, hand drawn, etc. A First Day cachet should be related specifically to the stamp on the cover.

Cachetmaker—One who designs and/or produces cacheted envelopes. Cachets may be identified by the artist's name, brand name, or manufacturing firm.

Cancel—The portion of a postmark which defaces or "kills" the stamp. Often loosely used interchangeably with "postmark."

CDS—Circular date stamp, ie. the dial or circular portion of the postmark.

Ceremony program—The printed program usually distributed by the Post Office or sponsoring organization at the First Day dedication of a new stamp. These are usually collected with the new stamp affixed and cancelled on the First Day.

Classic—The period prior to 1930 during which few First Day Covers were serviced and cachets were not common.

Coil—Stamps produced in rolls for use in vending machines. They are characterized by two opposite edges being straight or imperforate. A horizontal coil stamp is imperforate top and bottom and a vertical coil is straight-edged at the left and right sides.

Combo—One or more thematically related stamps affixed to a FDC. Also, combination cover.

Commemorative—A stamp, usually of large format, which is issued to salute or honor a person, event, state, organization, place, etc. Typically issued on an anniversary in a multiple of 10, 50, 100 years, etc. and produced in limited quantities. Contrasted with "definitive."

Commercial FDCs—FDCs sponsored by an individual, company, or organization used for promoting a service, product or as a gesture of goodwill.

Contract station—A sub-unit of a larger post office which is contracted to a private individual. Most contract stations are located in private business establishments.

Corner card—The imprint at the upper left corner of a cover which may be the return address or other identification of the sender.

Counterfeit—A stamp, postmark, or cachet created in direct imitation of a genuine item and intended to deceive. It is a Federal offense to counterfeit any postal marking or postal issue.

Cover—An envelope that has seen postal service or has a cancelled stamp on it, usually one with philatelic interest. May exemplify some segment of postal history or simply be a souvenir of an event or a place.

Crash cover—Any cover or FDC salvaged from the crash of a plane or vehicle in which it was carried. Usually bears postal markings explaining its damaged condition.

CXL—Abbreviation for "cancel." Also, cxl.

Definitive—Stamp issued for an indefinite period in an indefinite quantity to meet an ordinary postal rate. Designs do not usually honor a specific time dated event or person; most frequently in small format. Contrasted with "commemorative." Also known as "regular issue."

Designated First Day—The date officially announced by the Post Office for the sale of a new postal issue. Many issues prior to 1922 had no designated First Day. Covers cancelled prior to the designated dates are predates.

Dial—Circular portion of a postmark, usually containing the city, date and time. See bullseye.

Dual cancel—Two related or unrelated cancellations on a cover, each cancelling a stamp. One or both cancels may be for a First Day.

Duplex cancel—A metal handstamp containing both cancel and postmark in a single unit. Often found on FDCs before the mid-1930s.

EDC—Earliest documented cover. The earliest known postmark on a postal issue which had no designated First Day. Used interchangeably with EKU.

EFO—Errors, Freaks, and Oddities, ie. stamps, cachets, cancellations, etc. that contain unintended mistakes or design faults.

EKU—Earliest known use. A designation for the earliest identified postmark on a stamp for which a first day of issue was not designated.

Electric eye (EE)—An electronic device which guides the perforating equipment during stamp manufacture. This is accomplished by heavy ink dashes in the selvage, which are used for detection and alignment. FDCs of EE stamps must have the selvage with dashes attached to the stamps.

Embossing—The process of impressing a design in relief into the paper of an envelope.

Engraved—A method of printing in which the lines of the design are cut into metal, which are recessed to retain the ink. The paper is forced under pressure into these lines to pick up the ink. Hence engraved cachets appear to have the design raised above the paper surface.

Error—A consistent abnormal variety created by a mistake in the production of a stamp or postmark. For example, the name of a city may be misspelled in the First Day cancel. Used in contrast to "freak."

Esoterica—Any item, other than a cover or envelope, that has been First Day cancelled that doesn't fit any of the regular collecting categories.

Event cover—A cacheted cover, not a FDC, prepared as a souvenir of a specific event or an anniversary of an event.

Event program—A list of events or speakers in any program related to the stamp release, such as a stamp show, any function at which a stamp is released, or any event honoring the same event as the stamp.

Fancy cancel—A cancellation which is or includes a design. The term is normally used for 19th-century cancels which were created by local postal officials according to personal whim. Also, see pictorial.

Favor cancel—Any postal marking supplied as a favor or accommodation for a stamp collector.

FD—First Day.

FDC—First Day Cover. (FDCs—plural)

FDOI—First Day Of Issue. The slogan found in most First Day cancellations since Sc. 795, released in 1937.

FFC—First flight cover, ie. a cover flown on the inaugural flight of a new air route.

Filler—A stiff piece of paper, cardboard, or plastic found inside a First Day Cover. It provides necessary stiffness for a clearer cancellation. It also protects the cover from bending when it travels through the mail stream. Fillers, also termed stuffers, occasionally are imprinted with an advertising message or information pertaining to the stamp or cachet on the cover.

First cachet—The initial cachet commercially produced by a cachetmaker.

First Day—The day on which a stamp for the first time is officially sold by the Post Office.

First Day cover—Cover with a new stamp(s) or postal indicia, cancelled on the First Day.

Flag cancel—A cancellation used during the early 20th century incorporating a flag design. The stripes of the flag are the killer bars. Also, any more recent cancel with a similar design.

Flocked—A cachet production method in which powdered cloth is adhered to the envelope in the desired design.

Forgery—A fraudulently produced or altered philatelic item intended to deceive the collector.

Frank—A stamp, mark, or signature that shows payment of postage on a piece of mail. (A signature, with no stamp or paid marking, is called a Free Frank. Free as available to Congress and the President.)

Freak—An abnormal variety created by an unusual circumstance and not repeated with regularity. For example, a FDC may bear only a portion of a postmark because the cover was misfed into the cancelling machine. Used in contrast to "error."

General purpose (GP)—A cachet with a general design that is non-specific and may be used with any stamp subject. Also, All-purpose.

Hand cancel (HC)—A canceller which is applied to stamps individually and by hand. May be manufactured of plastic, rubber, or steel and is similar to a rubber stamp.

Hand-drawn (H/D)—A cachet applied to a cover by hand with pen, pencil, brush, chalk, or other art media. Each cachet is made individually and is an original.

Handmade (H/M)—A cachet applied to a cover by hand by adding seals, pasteups, collage, or similar materials. Each cachet is made individually and is an original.

Hand-painted (H/P) or Hand-colored (H/C)—A printed, hand-drawn or handmade cachet to which hand painting or hand coloring has been added.

HC, H/C, H/D, H/M, H/P—See preceding definitions.

HPO—Highway Post Office. The Post Office sorted mail on special motor vehicles in transit between cities. This system was in use from the late 1930s through the mid-1970s. FDCs were occasionally cancelled with HPO markings.

IA—Ink addressed. Refers to the method of addressing a cover.

Inaugural cover—A cover cancelled on the day that a president is sworn into office. Since 1957 the words INAUGURATION DAY have been incorporated into the cancel. The site was usually Washington, D.C., although other locations, like the President's city of birth, are now being designated. (In 1957 and 1985 the inauguration date fell on a Sunday. In both cases, covers of January 20, the private swearing-in ceremony, and January 21, the date of the public ceremony, both exist, and both are considered collectible.)

Indicia—An imprint on postal stationery indicating prepayment of postage. The plural is also "indicia."

Joint issue—Two or more stamps issued by different countries to commemorate the same event, topic, place, or person. Officially sanctioned joint issues are intentionally issued with the cooperation of the postal services of the countries involved.

Killer bars—The horizontal lines of a postmark which cancel the stamp. Since 1937 the FIRST DAY OF ISSUE slogan has appeared between the bars of most First Day cancels.

LA—Label addressed. Refers to the addressing method on a cover.

LSASE—A legal-sized, stamped, self-addressed envelope. See SASE.

Last Day—The final day of a postal rate, post office operation, or similar occurrence. A cover cancelled on this day is referred to as a last day cover.

Lithography, or litho—A common method of printing stamps and cachets in which the design is transferred from a smooth plate by selective inks which wet only the design portion of the printing plate.

LL—Lower left. Refers to the plate number or marginal marking position on a sheet of stamps.

LR—Lower right. Refers to the marginal marking position.

Luminescent—The condition of a stamp or postal stationery which has been treated with chemicals which are sensitive to and glow under ultraviolet (UV) light. This permits automatic cancelling equipment to detect the position of the postage on the cover and to orient it for rapid mechanical cancelling.

Machine cancel (MC)—A cancellation applied by an automatic cancelling device or machine.

Maximum card—A picture (post)card with a reproduction of the stamp or related subject from which the stamp was derived. Maximum card specialists prefer that the card and the stamp be as directly related as possible, but not be reproduced. The attempt is to achieve maximum agreement or concordance between the stamp subject and postcard. The stamp and cancel are usually placed on the illustrated side. This may be cancelled on the First Day of the stamp. See "Souvenir card."

Mellone catalog—A series of cachet catalogs for various time periods. They feature cachet illustrations with assigned code numbers for identification.

Mylar—Dupont's trademark for a durable plastic (polyester) film often recommended for storing stamps or covers because of its excellent chemical stability and the protection offered.

Nondenominated—Stamp or postal stationery without denomination or value in the design. These were created by the Post Office in anticipation of postal rate change when the exact rates could not be determined in advance.

Obliterator—Another term for the cancel portion of a postmark which defaces or obliterates the stamp.

OE—An abbreviation which indicates that a cover has been opened at the end or side.

Official—1) Of or related to the Federal government. USPS postmarks are official markings. 2) Stamps or stationery issued for use by government departments in the course of official business.

Official cachet—1) A cachet produced and applied by or for postal administrations. Official cachets are rare on U.S. FDCs but are common for many other countries. 2) Loosely used to refer to cachets authorized or sponsored by an organization closely associated with the issuance of a stamp, more properly called a sponsored cachet. The word "official" is abused by some cachetmakers.

Official FDC—Any First Day Cover with an official government postmark. This term is often misused for covers with sponsored cachets.

Offset—A printing method in which the design is transferred by ink from the image to another surface and then applied to the paper.

OT—An abbreviation indicating that a cover has been opened at the top.

PA—Pencil addressed. Refers to the method of cover addressing.

Patriotic or patriotic cachet—Design with patriotic or nationalistic theme, most often used to bolster public spirit during periods of war or national stress.

PB—Plate block. A group of stamps with the plate number in the selvage. May contain four or more stamps depending on the configuration of the printed numbers.

Peelable label—A self-stick label that can be easily removed from a cover without leaving adhesive or blemish. Used for addressing covers—later removed to create unaddressed covers.

Philatelic center—A post office window or station where most currently available stamps may be purchased by collectors. Created for the convenience of stamp collectors. Also postique.

Photocachet—A cachet consisting in part or entirely of a photograph.

Pictorial—A cancellation incorporating a pictorial design. Pictorial First Day cancels were used by the United States from 1958 to 1962 and are becoming more widespread on FDC issues of the 1980s and '90s. Many postiques each have a unique pictorial cancel. Many non-FD pictorial cancels are available nationwide, and are used for a limited time at special public or philatelic events.

Planty Catalogue—Catalog of U.S. cachets, for various year periods in individual volumes, assembled by Prof. Earl Planty. Planty identification designations are referred to as Planty Numbers.

Plug cancel—Colloquial name for a round, double circle marking, officially known as a validator stamp. The plug is chiefly used on postal receipts and registered envelopes. Also called a registry cancel or round-dater.

PNC—1) Plate Number Coil, ie. a coil stamp with a plate number thereon. 2) Philatelic-numismatic cover, ie. a cover with a cancelled stamp and a visible coin on the front, both thematically related. May be a FDC for the stamp.

POD—Post Office Department, the predecessor of the USPS. Also USPOD.

Polysleeve—Any of a variety of generally clear plastic sleeves, usually closed on two or three sides, to contain covers so they may be handled without soiling or damage.

Postage due—Stamps issued to indicate a penalty for insufficient postage. Postage due stamps are not used to pay postage, yet some issues are known on FDCs. These FDCs were cancelled inadvertently or by favor.

Postal card—A government produced postcard with an indicia indicating prepayment of postage.

Postal stationery—Postal cards, aerogrammes, and envelopes on which postage has been imprinted. Created as a convenience for the public so postage need not be applied.

Post-cancelled (post-dated, back-dated)—A cover which has been cancelled on a date later than that indicated on the postmark.

Postcard—A privately produced card usually bearing an illustration on one side and spaces for message, address, and postage on the other.

Postique—A special station or location at a post office where collectors may obtain currently available stamps. Each office usually has its own pictorial cancellation.

Postmark—A postal marking which indicates the time and point of origin of the mail to which it is applied. Often loosely used interchangeably with "Cancel."

Precancel—Stamps or stationery issued by the Post Office with words or lines printed thereon which prevent further use of the stamp. Precancelled stamps need not be cancelled again during mail handling. The standard First Day postmarks, however, are applied to FDCs of precancels.

Predate—A cover with a stamp cancelled earlier than the officially designated First Day of sale. Predates usually are created when stamps are sold prior to the official release date, contrary to postal regulations. Predates can exist only for issues with a designated First Day date.

Presentation album—Album containing a pane of a new stamp which is distributed to each dignitary at a First Day dedication ceremony. The album may have the recipient's name engraved on it. The first album is always for the President of the United States.

Presidentials—The 1938 series of definitive stamps featuring the Presidents of the United States.

Prexy—An information alternative term to designate the Presidential series of definitives.

PR—Pair of stamps.

Printed cachets—A cachet design type that is produced by printing, using any one of many methods.

Program—See Ceremony program.

Rag content—Pertains to the use of cotton fiber rather than wood pulp in the manufacture of envelopes. High rag content or 100 percent rag envelopes resist the ravages of time much better than do wood fiber covers, which contain processing chemicals that eventually discolor the paper and make the envelope more brittle.

Regular issue—Stamp issued for an indefinite period and quantity for ordinary postal use. See definitive.

RPO—Railway post office. A system once used by the POD to process mail in railroad cars enroute between cities. A distinctive cancel was used and FDCs exist with RPO postmarks.

Registry cancel—See plug.

RSA—Rubber-stamp addressed. A cover addressing method.

RSC—Rubber-stamp cachet.

Rubber stamps (R/S) cachet—A cachet applied to a cover using a rubber stamp. This method or device was very popular in the 1930s.

SASE—Self-addressed stamped envelope or *SAE*—self-addressed envelope. See also "LSASE."

Scott—Philatelic Publishing Company which produces Scott catalogs. A Scott (Sc.) number refers to a Scott catalog number to identify a stamp—a widely accepted practice.

Second-Day cover—A cover postmarked on the day following the First Day Of Issue. These were popular in the 1940s when the stamps were available at the Philatelic Agency in Washington, DC, on the second day.

Self-adhesive—A pre-gummed postage stamp on a peelable backing which requires no moisture for affixing to an envelope.

Selvage—The edges of a stamp pane beyond the perforations—including the portions that contain marginal markings as plate numbers, copyright notice, and other symbols/text. The plain selvage is usually removed from stamps when preparing FDCs, except for plate numbers and other collectible markings. Also spelled "selvedge."

Service—The act of affixing a stamp to and having it cancelled on a cover.

Servicer—One who performs the act of servicing. Frequently a person who does so on a commercial and large volume basis.

SGL—Single stamp. Also "sgl."

Ship cancel—A cancellation applied aboard a vessel—most frequently U.S. Navy although there are others. Ship cancels are fairly common but such strikes on FDCs are considered unusual because they represent a special effort in order to be obtained.

Show cancel—Special Post Office cancellation designed for and applied at a philatelic show or exhibition station.

Silk cachet—A cachet type with a pictorial design printed on a piece of fabric with a silky finish.

Slogan cancel—A cancellation with a message incorporated, such as—"Mail Early Before Christmas" or "Fight Tuberculosis."

Socked-on-the-nose (SOTN)—Designation for a stamp where the circle of the postmark falls exactly on the center. Another designation for "bullseye."

Souvenir card—A commemorative card, usually with reproductions of previously issued stamps and an inscription, issued by postal authorities in conjunction with a special philatelic event. The card or stamp units cannot be used for postal purposes but are often enhanced by collectors with an actual stamp and cancel.

Souvenir program—See ceremony program.

Sponsor (cachet)—Individual or organization that has commissioned an established cachetmaker to prepare a special design in addition to the regular cachet for a particular issue. The term is sometimes used interchangeably with "cachetmaker."

Sponsored cachet—A cachet authorized or sponsored by an organization closely associated with the issuance of a stamp. See also "Official cachet," No. 2.

Station cancel—A cancellation applied at a temporary postal station established for a convention, exhibition, or other special event.

Stuffer—See filler.

Tagged—Stamp or postal stationery which has had the postage area treated with a material sensitive to ultraviolet (UV) light, so that the cover can be mechanically oriented for canceling. Also luminescent.

Thermography—A printing method for producing raised designs by use of a special powder and heat. Often called, "poor man's embossing."

Tied—The cancellation overlaps the stamp, falling on both the postage and the cover thus affirming that the stamp was affixed prior to the postmarking. Also may be applied to non-postal labels or adhesives to show contemporaneous usage.

Toning—A deleterious condition of a cover resembling darkening or discoloration caused by excess gum at the edge of the stamp or a stain from the gum of the envelope flap. May also result from chemicals used in the production of inexpensive envelopes.

Trade name—A name or identification assigned to a cachet line by the producer. Example: Washington Press produces Artcraft Cachets.

UA—Unaddressed. A cover which does not have an address.

UL—Upper left. Refers to the position of stamp marginal markings.

Unaddressed (UA)—A cover which has no address.

Uncacheted—A cover which has no cachet design.

Unofficial cancel—A private, non-postal marking, usually resembling an official postmark, applied to a stamp or cover.

Unofficial FDC (UO)—A FDC cancelled with other than the official FIRST DAY OF ISSUE slogan cancel or official First Day pictorial cancelled supplied by the USPS for the First Day. For FDCs before the initial use of the FDOI slogan, this term refers to any city other than that which was officially designated. (There is much controversy among specialists and purists about this definition. Some dislike the use of the word "unofficial" as all postmarks are official cancellations of the USPS. Some would like to make a further distinction between stamps purchased in the official FD city, versus stamps sold in error on or before the FD in cities other than the FD city. Both of these are points well taken, but basically UOs are any FDC serviced in the city of issue or another location with any cancel other than the official FD cancel supplied by the USPS. A UO FDC must have the correct First Day date.)

UO—Unofficial First Day cover.

UR—Upper right. Refers to the position of the marginal markings on stamp selvage.

USPS—United States Postal Service, established in 1971.

Validator—See plug.

Please Note: DC indicates Washington, D.C., as the official city and date of issue. Other cities with significantly different values are also listed. When no city is indicated, the number of cities the stamps were issued in is indicated.

Scott No.			Single	Block Of 4

FIRST DAY COVER ISSUES
UNCACHETED

			Single	Block Of 4
☐551	½¢	Hale (DC & New Haven, CT, 4/4/25)	19.00	24.00
☐552	1¢	Franklin (DC, 1/17/23)	22.50	35.00
☐552	1¢	Franklin (Philadelphia, PA)	40.00	55.00
☐553	1½¢	Harding (DC, 3/19/25)	26.00	32.00
☐554	2¢	Washington (DC, 1/15/23)	40.00	50.00
☐555	3¢	Lincoln (DC, 2/12/23)	37.00	50.00
☐555	3¢	Lincoln (Hodgenville, KY)	250.00	400.00
☐556	4¢	Martha Washington (DC, 1/15/23)	65.00	100.00
☐557	5¢	Roosevelt (DC, 10/27/22)	125.00	175.00
☐557	5¢	Roosevelt (New York, NY)	240.00	400.00
☐557	5¢	Roosevelt (Oyster Bay, NY)	1300.00	—
☐558	6¢	Garfield (DC, 11/20/22)	200.00	260.00
☐559	7¢	McKinley (DC, 5/1/23)	150.00	175.00
☐559	7¢	McKinley (Niles, OH)	200.00	—
☐560	8¢	Grant (DC, 5/1/23)	170.00	200.00
☐561	9¢	Jefferson (DC, 1/15/23)	170.00	200.00
☐562	10¢	Monroe (DC, 1/15/23)	170.00	200.00
☐563	11¢	Hayes (DC, 10/4/22)	900.00	3500.00
☐563	11¢	Hayes (Fremont, OH)	2200.00	—
☐564	12¢	Cleveland (DC, Boston, MA, Caldwell, NJ, 3/20/23)	210.00	325.00
☐565	14¢	Indian (DC, 5/1/23)	400.00	500.00
☐565	14¢	Indian (Muskogee, OK)	2000.00	5000.00
☐566	15¢	Statue of Liberty (DC, 11/11/22)	525.00	850.00
☐567	20¢	Golden Gate (5/1/23)	650.00	925.00
☐567	20¢	Golden Gate (San Francisco)	3000.00	—
☐568	25¢	Niagara Falls (DC, 11/11/22)	650.00	900.00
☐569	30¢	Bison (DC, 3/20/23)	800.00	1100.00
☐570	50¢	Arlington (DC, 11/11/22)	1525.00	—
☐571	$1	Lincoln Memorial (DC, Springfield, IL 2/12/23)	5500.00	15,000.00
☐572	$2	U.S. Capitol (DC, 3/20/23)	18,000.00	—
☐573	$5	America (DC, 3/20/23)	30,000.00	—

Scott No.			Single	Block Of 4
☐576	1½¢	Harding (DC, 4/4/25)	42.00	48.00
☐581	1¢	Franklin (DC, 10/17/23)	6000.00	—
☐582	1½¢	Harding (DC, 3/19/25)	40.00	50.00
☐583a	2¢	Washington (Booklet Pane, DC, 8/27/26)	1300.00	—
☐584	3¢	Lincoln (DC, 8/1/25)	56.00	80.00
☐585	4¢	Martha Washington (DC, 4/4/25)	56.00	80.00
☐586	5¢	Roosevelt (DC, 4/4/25)	56.00	80.00
☐587	6¢	Garfield (DC, 4/4/25)	56.00	80.00
☐588	7¢	McKinley (DC, 5/29/26)	65.00	82.00
☐589	8¢	Grant (DC, 5/29/26)	65.00	82.00
☐590	9¢	Jefferson (DC, 5/29/26)	65.00	82.00
☐591	10¢	Monroe (DC, 6/8/25)	95.00	120.00
☐597	1¢	Franklin (coil, DC, 7/18/23)	600.00	—
☐598	1½¢	Harding (coil, DC, 3/19/25)	42.00	—
☐599	2¢	Washington (coil, DC, 1/15/23)	2500.00	—
☐600	3¢	Lincoln (coil, DC, 5/10/24)	110.00	—
☐602	5¢	Roosevelt (coil, DC, 3/5/24)	110.00	—
☐603	10¢	Monroe (coil, DC, 2/1/24)	110.00	—
☐604	1¢	Franklin (coil, DC, 7/19/24)	80.00	—
☐605	1½¢	Harding (coil, DC, 5/9/25)	45.00	—
☐606	2¢	Washington (coil, DC, 12/31/23)	135.00	—
☐610	2¢	Harding (DC, Marion, OH 9/1/25)	25.00	42.00
☐611	2¢	Harding (imperf., DC, 11/15/23)	90.00	120.00
☐612	2¢	Harding (perf. 10, DC, 9/12/23)	110.00	130.00
☐614–16		Huguenot-Walloon, set on one cover 5/1/24 were issued in eleven cities: Albany, NY, Allentown, PA, Charleston, SC, Jacksonville, FL, Lancaster, PA, Mayport, FL, New Rochelle, NY, New York, NY, Philadelphia, PA, Reading, PA, and Washington, D.C.	160.00	—
☐614	1¢	Huguenot-Walloon (5/1/24)	35.00	48.00
☐615	2¢	Huguenot-Walloon (5/1/24)	40.00	50.00
☐616	5¢	Huguenot-Walloon (5/1/24)	65.00	100.00
☐617–19		Lexington-Concord, set on one cover 4/4/25 were issued in six cities: prices are for Boston, MA, Cambridge, MA, Concord, MA, Lexington, MA, and Washington, D.C., Concord, MA sells for 25% more.	150.00	—

Scott No.			Single	Block Of 4
☐617	1¢	Lexington-Concord (4/4/25)	35.00	42.00
☐618	2¢	Lexington-Concord (4/4/25)	36.00	45.00
☐619	5¢	Lexington-Concord (4/4/25)	80.00	112.00
☐620	2¢	Norse-American (5/18/25)	24.00	37.00
☐620–21		Norse-American, set on one cover 5/18/25 were issued in seven cities: Angola, IN, Benson, MN, Decoran, IA, Minneapolis, MN, Northfield, MN, St. Paul, MN, and Washington, D.C.	65.00	100.00
☐621	5¢	Norse-American (5/18/25)	30.00	48.00
☐622	13¢	Harrison	20.00	30.00
☐622	13¢	Harrison (Indianapolis, IN, 1/11/26)	40.00	50.00
☐622	13¢	Harrison (North Bend, OH, 1/11/26)	200.00	400.00
☐623	17¢	Wilson (New York, NY, Princeton, NJ, Staunton, VA, Washington, D.C., 12/28/25)	22.00	32.00
☐627	2¢	Sesquicentennial (Boston, MA, Philadelphia, PA, D.C., 5/10/26)	10.00	15.00
☐628	5¢	Erikson (Chicago, IL, Minneapolis, MN, New York, NY, D.C. 5/29/26)	20.00	30.00
☐629	2¢	White Plains (White Plains, NY, New York, NY, Philadelphia, PA Expo 10/18/26)	7.00	11.00
☐630	2¢	White Plains (complete sheet, 10/18/26)	2000.00	—
☐631	1¹/₂¢	Harding (DC, 8/27/26)	40.00	50.00
☐632	1¢	Franklin (DC, 6/10/27)	45.00	62.00
☐632a	1¢	Franklin booklet of 6 (DC 11/2/27)	3000.00	
☐633	1¹/₂¢	Harding (DC, 5/17/27)	45.00	62.00
☐634	2¢	Washington (DC, 12/10/26)	45.00	52.00
☐635	3¢	Lincoln (DC, 2/3/27)	45.00	60.00
☐635a	3¢	Bright Violet (DC, 2/7/34)	26.00	40.00
☐636	4¢	Martha Washington (DC, 5/17/27)	50.00	62.00
☐637	5¢	Roosevelt (DC, 3/24/27)	50.00	62.00
☐638	6¢	Garfield (DC, 7/27/27)	55.00	65.00
☐639	7¢	McKinley (D.C., 3/24/27)	55.00	65.00
☐640	8¢	Grant (D.C., 6/10/27)	65.00	85.00
☐641	9¢	Jefferson (D.C., 5/17/27)	72.00	100.00
☐642	10¢	Monroe (D.C., 2/3/27)	80.00	110.00
☐643	2¢	Vermont (Burlington, VT, D.C., 8/3/27)	5.50	8.00

Scott No.			Single	Block Of 4
☐644	2¢	Burgoyne	11.00	16.00
☐		(Albany, NY, Rome, NY, Syracuse, NY, Utica, NY, and D.C., 8/3/27)		
☐645	2¢	Valley Forge	4.50	8.00
☐		(Cleveland Phil Sta., OH, Lancaster, PA, Norriston, PA, Philadelphia, PA, Valley Forge, PA, West Chester, PA, and D.C., 5/26/28)		
☐646	2¢	Molly Pitcher	15.00	20.00
☐		(Freehold, NJ, Red Bank, NJ, D.C., 10/20/18)		
☐647	2¢	Hawaii (Honolulu, HI, D.C., 8/13/28)	15.00	20.00
☐647–48		Hawaiian set on one cover (8/13/28)	35.00	76.00
☐648	5¢	Hawaii (Honolulu, HI, D.C., 8/13/28)	20.00	27.00
☐649	2¢	Aero Conf. (D.C., 12/12/28)	7.00	12.00
☐649–50		Areo Conf. set on one cover (12/12/18)	12.00	20.00
☐650	5¢	Aero Conf. (D.C., 12/12/28)	10.00	12.00
☐651	2¢	Clark (Vincennes, IN, 2/25/29)	5.00	8.00
☐653	½¢	Hale (D.C., 5/25/29)	—	30.00
☐654	2¢	Electric Light (Menlopark, NJ, 6/5/29)	8.00	12.00
☐655	2¢	Electric Light (D.C., 6/11/29)	80.00	110.00
☐656	2¢	Electric Light (coil, 6/11/29)	95.00	—
☐657	2¢	Sullivan (16 different New York cities, D.C., 6/17/29)	3.50	6.00
☐658	1¢	Kansas (D.C., 5/1/29)	30.00	41.00
☐658–68		Kansas set on one cover, D.C., 5/1/29	1000.00	—
☐659	1½¢	Kansas (D.C., 5/1/29)	40.00	52.00
☐660	2¢	Kansas (D.C., 5/1/29)	40.00	52.00
☐661	3¢	Kansas (D.C., 5/1/29)	45.00	60.00
☐662	4¢	Kansas (D.C., 5/1/29)	50.00	80.00
☐663	5¢	Kansas (D.C., 5/1/29)	60.00	80.00
☐664	6¢	Kansas (D.C., 5/1/29)	75.00	120.00
☐665	7¢	Kansas (D.C., 5/1/29)	95.00	180.00
☐666	8¢	Kansas (D.C., 5/1/29)	95.00	220.00
☐667	9¢	Kansas (D.C., 5/1/29)	90.00	150.00
☐668	10¢	Kansas (D.C., 5/1/29)	120.00	160.00
☐669	1¢	Nebraska (D.C., 5/1/29)	35.00	50.00
☐659–669		Nebraska set on one cover, D.C., 5/1/29	1100.00	—
☐670	1½¢	Nebraska (D.C., 5/1/29)	40.00	55.00

Scott No.			Single	Block Of 4
☐671	2¢	Nebraska (D.C., 5/1/29)	40.00	52.00
☐672	3¢	Nebraska (D.C., 5/1/29)	45.00	60.00
☐673	4¢	Nebraska (D.C., 5/1/29)	55.00	76.00
☐674	5¢	Nebraska (D.C., 5/1/29)	55.00	76.00
☐675	6¢	Nebraska (D.C., 5/1/29)	75.00	95.00
☐676	7¢	Nebraska (D.C., 5/1/29)	90.00	130.00
☐677	8¢	Nebraska (D.C., 5/1/29)	95.00	145.00
☐678	9¢	Nebraska (D.C., 5/1/29)	900.00	145.00
☐679	10¢	Nebraska (D.C., 5/1/29)	120.00	200.00
☐670–679		Kansas set on one cover (D.C., 5/1/29)	1100.00	—
☐680	2¢	Fallen Timbers (5 cities 9/14/29)	3.25	6.00
☐681	2¢	Ohio River (7 cities 10/19/29)	3.25	6.00
☐682	2¢	Massachusetts Bay Colony (2 cities 4/8/30)	3.25	6.00
☐683	2¢	Carolina-Charleston (4/10/30)	3.25	6.00
☐684	1½¢	Harding Marion, OH(12/1/30)	4.25	5.50
☐685	4¢	Taft Cinncinnati, OH (6/4/30)	5.50	8.00
☐686	1½¢	Harding Marion, OH (coil, 12/1/30)	4.25	6.00
☐687	4¢	Taft (coil, D.C., 9/18/30)	32.00	—
☐688	2¢	Braddock (7/9/30)	4.00	6.00
☐689	2¢	Von Steuben	4.00	6.00
☐690	2¢	Pulaski (12 cities, 1/16/31)	3.75	5.00
☐692	11¢	Hayes (D.C., 9/4/31)	115.00	145.00
☐693	12¢	Cleveland (D.C., 8/25/31)	115.00	145.00
☐694	13¢	Harrison (D.C., 9/4/31)	115.00	145.00
☐695	14¢	Indian (D.C., 9/8/31)	115.00	145.00
☐696	15¢	Liberty (D.C., 8/27/31)	140.00	180.00
☐697	17¢	Wilson (D.C., 7/27/31)	325.00	460.00
☐698	20¢	Golden Gate (D.C., 9/8/31)	300.00	450.00
☐699	25¢	Niagara Falls (D.C., 7/27/31)	375.00	450.00
☐700	30¢	Bison (D.C., 9/8/31)	350.00	500.00
☐701	50¢	Arlington (D.C., 9/4/31)	425.00	550.00
☐702	2¢	Red Cross (2 cities 5/21/31)	3.25	5.00
☐703	2¢	Yorktown (2 cities, 10/19/31)	3.25	6.00
☐704	½¢	Olive Brown (D.C., 1/1/32)	—	3.00
☐704–15		set on one cover	40.00	—
☐705	1¢	Green (D.C., 1/1/32)	3.00	4.00
☐706	1½¢	Brown (D.C., 1/1/32)	3.00	4.00
☐707	2¢	Carmine Rose (D.C., 1/1/32)	3.00	3.75
☐708	3¢	Deep Violet (D.C., 1/1/32)	3.00	3.75
☐709	4¢	Light Brown (D.C., 1/1/32)	3.00	3.75

Scott No.			Single	Block Of 4
☐710	5¢	Blue (D.C., 1/1/32)	3.00	4.00
☐711	6¢	Red Orange (D.C., 1/1/32)	3.00	4.00
☐712	7¢	Black (D.C., 1/1/32)	3.00	4.00
☐713	8¢	Olive Bistre (D.C., 1/1/32)	3.25	4.50
☐714	9¢	Pale Red (D.C., 1/1/32)	3.25	4.50
☐715	10¢	Orange Yellow (D.C., 1/1/32)	3.25	4.50
☐716	2¢	Olympic Winter Games (1/25/32)	3.00	4.10
☐717	2¢	Arbor Day (4/22/32)	2.25	4.00
☐718	3¢	Olympic Summer Games (6/15/32)	3.00	4.00
☐718–19		Olympic Summer Games set on one cover	5.00	7.00
☐719	5¢	Olympic Summer Games (6/15/32)	4.00	5.00
☐720	3¢	Washington (D.C., 6/16/32)	3.25	4.50
☐720b	3¢	Washington (booklet of 6, D.C., 7/25/32)	40.00	—
☐721	3¢	Washington (coil, D.C., 6/24/32)	4.50	—
☐722	3¢	Washington (coil, D.C., 10/12/32)	4.50	—
☐723	6¢	Garfield (coil, 8/18/32)	4.50	—
☐724	3¢	William Penn (3 cities, 10/24/32)	3.00	4.00
☐725	3¢	Daniel Webster (3 cities, 10/24/32)	3.00	4.00
☐726	3¢	Gen. Oglethorpe (2/12/32)	3.00	4.00
☐727	3¢	Peace Proclamation (4/19/32)	3.00	4.00
☐728	1¢	Century of Progress (5/25/32)	2.00	3.00
☐728–29		Century of Progress set on one cover	3.25	5.00
☐729	3¢	Century of Progress (5/25/32)	2.50	4.00
☐730	1¢	American Philatelic Society (full sheet on cover)	60.00	—
☐730a	1¢	American Philatelic Society (8/25/33)	2.75	4.00
☐731	3¢	American Philatelic Society (full sheet)	68.00	—
☐731a	3¢	American Philatelic Society (8/25/33)	2.75	4.00
☐732	3¢	National Recovery Administration (D.C., 8/15/33)	2.75	4.00
☐733	3¢	Byrd Antarctic (D.C., 10/9/33)	4.50	6.25
☐734	5¢	Kosciuszko (6 cities, 10/13/33)	4.50	6.25
☐734		Kosciuszko (Pittsburg, PA)	18.00	24.00
☐735	3¢	National Exhibition (full sheet)	34.00	—
☐735a	3¢	National Exhibition (2/10/34)	5.00	8.00
☐736	3¢	Maryland Tercentenary (3/23/34)	2.50	4.00
☐737	3¢	Mothers of America (D.C., 5/2/34)	2.50	4.00

Scott No.			Single	Block Of 4
☐738	3¢	Mothers of America (flatplate, D.C., 5/2/34)	3.00	5.00
☐739	3¢	Wisconsin (7/9/34)	2.50	3.50
☐740	1¢	Parks, Yosemite (2 cities, 7/16/34)	2.25	4.00
☐741	2¢	Parks, Grand Canyon (2 cities, 7/24/34)	2.25	4.00
☐742	3¢	Parks, Mt. Rainier (2 cities, 8/3/34)	2.25	4.00
☐743	4¢	Parks, Mesa Verde (2 cities, 9/25/34)	2.25	4.00
☐744	5¢	Parks, Yellowstone (2 cities, 7/30/34)	2.50	4.25
☐745	6¢	Parks, Crater Lake (2 cities, 9/5/34)	2.50	4.25
☐746	7¢	Parks, Acadia (2 cities, 10/2/34)	2.50	5.25
☐747	8¢	Parks, Zion (2 cities, 9/18/34)	4.25	6.50
☐748	9¢	Parks, Glacier Park (2 cities, 8/27/34)	4.25	6.50
☐749	10¢	Parks, Smoky Mountains (2 cities, 10/8/34)	4.25	6.50
☐750	3¢	American Philatelic Society (full sheet on cover)	34.00	—
☐750a	3¢	American Philatelic Society (8/28/34)	4.00	—
☐751	1¢	Trans-Mississippi Philatelic Expo, (full sheet on cover)	21.00	—
☐751a	1¢	Trans-Mississippi Philatelic Expo. (10/10/34)	3.00	—
☐752	3¢	Peace Commemoration (D.C., 3/15/35)	5.25	7.30
☐753	3¢	Byrd (D.C., 3/15/35)	6.00	7.50
☐754	3¢	Mothers of America (D.C., 3/15/35)	5.25	7.50
☐755	3¢	Wisconsin (D.C., 3/15/35)	5.25	7.50
☐756	1¢	Parks, Yosemite (D.C., 3/15/35)	5.25	7.50
☐757	2¢	Parks, Grand Canyon (D.C., 3/15/35)	5.25	7.50
☐758	3¢	Parks, Mount Ranier (D.C., 3/15/35)	5.25	7.50
☐759	4¢	Parks, Mesa Verde (D.C., 3/15/35)	5.25	7.50
☐760	5¢	Parks, Yellowstone (D.C., 3/15/35)	5.25	8.00
☐761	6¢	Parks, Crater Lake (D.C., 3/15/35)	6.50	9.00
☐762	7¢	Parks, Acadia (D.C., 3/15/35)	6.50	9.00
☐763	8¢	Parks, Zion (D.C., 3/15/35)	6.50	9.00
☐764	9¢	Parks, Glacier Park (D.C., 3/15/35)	6.50	9.00
☐765	10¢	Parks, Smoky Mountains (D.C., 3/15/35)	7.00	15.00
☐766a	1¢	Century of Progress (D.C., 3/15/35)	5.00	8.00
☐767a	3¢	Century of Progress (D.C., 3/15/35)	5.00	1.00
☐768a	3¢	Byrd (D.C., 3/15/35)	6.50	15.00

Scott No.			Single	Block Of 4
☐769a	1¢	Parks, Yosemite (D.C., 3/15/35)	5.00	7.50
☐770a	3¢	Parks, Mount Ranier (D.C., 3/15/35)	7.00	15.00
☐771	16¢	Airmail, special delivery (D.C., 3/15/35)	7.00	15.00

FIRST DAY COVER ISSUES CACHETED
(FOR DATES SEE UNCACHETED STAMPS)

☐610	2¢	Harding	1000.00	—
☐617	1¢	Lexington-Concord	150.00	—
☐618	2¢	Lexington-Concord	150.00	—
☐619	5¢	Lexington-Concord	190.00	—
☐620–21		Norse American set on one cover	175.00	
☐623	17¢	Wilson	295.00	—
☐627	2¢	Sesquicentennial	75.00	—
☐628	5¢	Erikson	475.00	—
☐629	2¢	White Plains	60.00	—
☐630	2¢	White Plains (sheet) single	65.00	—
☐635a	3¢	Bright Violet	40.00	—
☐643	2¢	Vermont	50.00	90.00
☐644	2¢	Burgoyne	52.00	85.00
☐645	2¢	Valley Forge	46.00	65.00
☐646	2¢	Molly Pitcher	90.00	—
☐647	2¢	Hawaii	65.00	80.00
☐647–48		Hawaii set on one cover	140.00	—
☐648	5¢	Hawaii	75.00	85.00
☐649	2¢	Aero Conf.	48.00	62.00
☐649–50		Aero Conf. set on one cover	60.00	—
☐650	5¢	Aero Conf.	50.00	65.00
☐651	2¢	Clark	30.00	43.00
☐654	2¢	Electric Light	30.00	43.00
☐655	2¢	Electric Light	170.00	—
☐656	2¢	Electric Light (coil)	250.00	—
☐657	2¢	Sullivan, Auburn N.Y.	30.00	45.00
☐680	2¢	Fallen Timbers	30.00	45.00
☐681	2¢	Ohio River	30.00	45.00
☐682	2¢	Massachusetts Bay Colony	32.00	46.00
☐683	2¢	California-Charleston	32.00	46.00
☐684	1½¢	Harding	32.00	46.00
☐685	4¢	Taft	48.00	60.00
☐686	1½¢	Harding (coil)	48.00	62.00
☐687	4¢	Taft (coil)	80.00	90.00
☐688	2¢	Braddock	30.00	45.00

Scott No.			Single	Block Of 4
☐689	2¢	Von Steuben	31.00	45.00
☐690	2¢	Pulaski	31.00	45.00
☐702	2¢	Red Cross	31.00	45.00
☐703	2¢	Yorktown	42.00	60.00
☐704	½¢	Olive Brown	16.00	23.00
☐705	1¢	Green	16.00	23.00
☐706	1½¢	Brown	16.00	23.00
☐707	2¢	Carmine Rose	16.00	23.00
☐708	3¢	Deep Violet	16.00	23.00
☐709	4¢	Light Brown	16.00	23.00
☐710	5¢	Blue	16.00	23.00
☐711	6¢	Red Orange	16.00	23.00
☐712	7¢	Black	16.00	23.00
☐713	8¢	Olive Bistre	18.00	25.00
☐714	9¢	Pale Red	18.00	25.00
☐715	10¢	Orange Yellow	20.00	25.00
☐704–15		Set on one cover	150.00	—
☐716	2¢	Olympic Winter Games	22.00	32.00
☐717	2¢	Arbor Day	17.00	28.00
☐718	3¢	Olympic Summer Games	22.00	30.00
☐719	5¢	Olympic Summer Games	22.00	30.00
☐718–19		Set on one cover	30.00	40.00
☐720	3¢	Washington	35.00	45.00
☐720b	3¢	Booklet pane of 6	180.00	—
☐721	3¢	Washington (coil)	51.00	—
☐722	3¢	Washington (coil)	51.00	—
☐723	6¢	Garfield (coil)	51.00	—
☐724	3¢	William Penn	18.00	23.00
☐725	3¢	Daniel Webster	18.00	23.00
☐726	3¢	Gen. Oglethorpe	18.00	23.00
☐727	3¢	Peace Proclamation	18.00	23.00
☐728	1¢	Century of Progress	12.00	18.00
☐729	3¢	Century of Progress	16.00	23.00
☐730	1¢	American Philatelic Society, full sheet on cover	170.00	—
☐730a	1¢	American Philatelic Society (single)	15.00	24.00
☐731	3¢	American Philatelic Society	170.00	—
☐731a	3¢	American Philatelic Society (single)	15.00	24.00
☐732	3¢	National Recovery Administration	16.00	22.00
☐733	3¢	Byrd Antarctic	26.00	38.00
☐734	5¢	Kosciuszko	21.00	29.00
☐734b	5¢	Kosciuszko (Pittsburgh, PA)	50.00	72.00

Scott No.			Single	Block Of 4
☐735	3¢	National Exhibition (full sheet)	56.00	—
☐735a	3¢	National Exhibition (single)	16.00	—
☐736	3¢	Maryland Tercentenary	17.00	22.00
☐737	3¢	Mothers of America	11.00	17.00
☐738	3¢	Mothers of America	11.00	17.00
☐739	2¢	Wisconsin	11.00	17.00
☐740	1¢	Parks, Yosemite	11.00	17.00
☐741	2¢	Parks, Grand Canyon	11.00	17.00
☐742	3¢	Parks, Mt. Ranier	11.00	17.00
☐743	4¢	Parks, Mesa Verde	11.00	17.00
☐744	5¢	Parks, Yellowstone	11.00	17.00
☐745	6¢	Parks, Crater Lake	12.00	16.50
☐746	7¢	Parks, Acadia	12.00	16.50
☐747	8¢	Parks, Zion	12.00	16.50
☐748	9¢	Parks, Glacier Park	12.00	16.50
☐749	10¢	Parks, Smoky Mountains	12.00	16.50
☐750	3¢	American Philatelic Society, full sheet on cover	60.00	—
☐750a	3¢	American Philatelic Society (single)	14.00	19.00
☐751	1¢	Trans-Mississippi Philatelic Expo., full sheet on cover	55.00	—
☐751a	1¢	Trans-Mississippi Philatelic Expo. (single)	12.00	17.00
☐752	3¢	Peace Commemoration	36.00	42.00
☐753	3¢	Byrd	40.00	44.00
☐754	3¢	Mothers of America	36.00	42.00
☐755	3¢	Wisconsin Tercentenary	34.00	40.00
☐756	1¢	Parks, Yosemite	28.00	35.00
☐757	2¢	Parks, Grand Canyon	28.00	35.00
☐758	3¢	Parks, Mount Rainier	28.00	35.00
☐759	4¢	Parks, Mesa Verde	28.00	35.00
☐760	5¢	Parks, Yellowstone	28.00	35.00
☐761	6¢	Parks, Crater Lake	28.00	35.00
☐762	7¢	Parks, Acadia	28.00	35.00
☐763	8¢	Parks, Zion	28.00	35.00
☐764	9¢	Parks, Glacier Park	28.00	35.00
☐765	10¢	Parks, Smoky Mountains	28.00	35.00
☐766a	1¢	Century of Progress	42.00	62.00
☐767a	3¢	Century of Progress	42.00	62.00
☐768a	3¢	Byrd	42.00	62.00

Scott No.			Single	Block Of 4
☐769a	1¢	Parks, Yosemite	42.00	62.00
☐770a	3¢	Parks, Mount Rainier	42.00	62.00
☐771	16¢	Airmail, special delivery	45.00	62.00

Scott No.			Single	Block	Plate Block
☐772	3¢	Connecticut Tercentenary	7.50	9.00	17.00
☐773	3¢	California Exposition	7.50	9.00	17.00
☐774	3¢	Boulder Dam	9.50	11.00	19.00
☐775	3¢	Michigan Centenary	8.00	9.00	16.00
☐776	3¢	Texas Centennial	12.00	15.00	23.00
☐777	3¢	Rhode Island Tercentenary	7.50	9.00	17.00
☐778	3¢	TIPEX	5.50	16.50	—
☐782	3¢	Arkansas Centennial	8.00	10.00	16.00
☐783	3¢	Oregon Territory	8.00	10.00	16.00
☐784	3¢	Susan B. Anthony	8.00	10.00	16.00
☐785	1¢	Army	4.50	6.00	13.00
☐786	2¢	Army	5.50	7.00	13.00
☐787	3¢	Army	5.50	7.00	13.00
☐788	4¢	Army	5.50	7.00	13.00
☐789	5¢	Army	5.50	7.00	13.00
☐790	1¢	Navy	5.00	6.50	13.00
☐791	2¢	Navy	5.50	7.00	13.00
☐792	3¢	Navy	5.50	7.00	13.00
☐793	4¢	Navy	5.50	7.00	13.00
☐794	5¢	Navy	5.50	7.00	13.00

Note: Beginning with number 795, First Day Covers have a cancellation "First Day Issue."

☐795	3¢	Ordinance of 1787	6.00	7.50	15.00
☐796	5¢	Virginia Dare	6.00	7.50	15.00
☐797	10¢	Souvenir Sheet	7.00	—	—
☐798	3¢	Constitution	7.50	9.00	15.00
☐799	3¢	Hawaii	7.50	9.00	15.00
☐800	3¢	Alaska	7.50	9.00	15.00
☐801	3¢	Puerto Rico	7.50	9.00	15.00
☐802	3¢	Virgin Islands	7.50	9.00	15.00
☐803	½¢	Franklin	4.00	4.50	8.50
☐804	1¢	Washington	4.00	4.50	8.50
☐805	1½¢	Martha Washington	4.00	4.50	8.50
☐806	2¢	Adams	4.00	4.50	8.50

Scott No.			Single	Block	Plate Block
☐807	3¢	Jefferson	3.60	4.50	8.75
☐808	4¢	Madison	3.60	4.50	8.75
☐809	4½¢	White House	3.60	4.50	8.75
☐810	5¢	Monroe	3.60	4.50	8.75
☐811	6¢	Adams	3.60	4.50	8.75
☐812	7¢	Jackson	3.60	4.50	8.75
☐813	8¢	VanBuren	3.60	4.50	8.75
☐814	9¢	Harrison	3.60	4.50	8.75
☐815	10¢	Tyler	3.60	4.50	9.00
☐816	11¢	Polk	4.50	6.00	9.00
☐817	12¢	Taylor	4.50	6.00	9.00
☐818	13¢	Fillmore	4.50	6.00	9.00
☐819	14¢	Pierce	4.50	6.00	9.00
☐820	15¢	Buchanan	4.50	6.00	9.00
☐821	16¢	Lincoln	6.00	7.00	10.00
☐822	17¢	Johnson	5.00	6.50	7.50
☐823	18¢	Grant	4.50	6.50	9.00
☐824	19¢	Hayes	4.50	6.50	9.00
☐825	20¢	Garfield	5.50	6.50	9.00
☐826	21¢	Arthur	5.50	6.50	10.00
☐827	22¢	Cleveland	5.50	6.50	10.00
☐828	24¢	Harrison	5.50	6.50	10.00
☐829	25¢	McKinley	5.50	6.50	12.00
☐830	30¢	Roosevelt	7.50	10.00	14.00
☐831	50¢	Taft	14.00	18.00	26.00
☐832	$1	Wilson	60.00	75.00	125.00
☐832c	$1	Wilson	22.00	30.00	62.00
☐833	$2	Harding	130.00	190.00	280.00
☐834	$5	Coolidge	210.00	275.00	525.00
☐835	3¢	Constitution	6.00	9.00	12.00
☐836	3¢	Swedes and Finns	6.00	9.00	12.00
☐837	3¢	Northwest Sesquicentennial	6.00	9.00	12.00
☐838	3¢	Iowa	6.00	9.00	12.00
☐852	3¢	Golden Gate Expo	6.00	9.00	12.00
☐853	3¢	N.Y. World's Fair	6.00	9.00	12.00
☐854	3¢	Washington Inauguration	6.00	9.00	12.00
☐855	3¢	Baseball Centennial	30.00	40.00	62.00
☐856	3¢	Panama Canal	6.00	9.00	11.50
☐857	3¢	Printing Tercentenary	6.00	9.00	11.50
☐858	3¢	50th Statehood Anniversary	6.00	8.00	12.00
☐859	1¢	Washington Irving	3.00	4.00	6.00

Scott No.			Single	Block	Plate Block
☐860	2¢	James Fenimore Cooper	3.00	4.00	6.00
☐861	3¢	Ralph Waldo Emerson	3.00	4.00	6.00
☐862	5¢	Louisa May Alcott	3.75	7.50	11.00
☐863	10¢	Samuel L. Clemens	6.00	10.00	30.00
☐864	1¢	Henry W. Longfellow	3.00	4.00	8.00
☐865	2¢	John Greenleaf Whittier	3.00	4.00	8.00
☐866	3¢	James Russell Lowell	3.00	4.00	8.00
☐867	5¢	Walt Whitman	3.75	8.00	12.00
☐868	10¢	James Whitcomb Riley	6.00	8.50	30.00
☐869	1¢	Horace Mann	3.00	4.00	7.00
☐870	2¢	Mark Hopkins	3.00	4.00	7.00
☐871	3¢	Charles W. Eliot	3.00	4.00	7.00
☐872	5¢	Frances E. Willard	3.75	7.00	12.00
☐873	10¢	Booker T. Washington	7.50	13.00	30.00
☐874	1¢	John James Audubon	3.50	4.00	7.00
☐875	2¢	Dr. Crawford W. Long	3.50	4.00	7.00
☐876	3¢	Luther Burbank	3.50	4.00	7.00
☐877	5¢	Dr. Walter Reed	4.00	6.00	10.00
☐878	10¢	Jane Addams	6.00	8.50	30.00
☐879	1¢	Stephen Collins Foster	3.00	4.50	6.50
☐880	2¢	John Philip Sousa	3.00	4.50	6.50
☐881	3¢	Victor Herbert	3.00	4.50	6.50
☐882	5¢	Edward A. MacDowell	4.00	6.00	15.00
☐883	10¢	Ethelbert Nevin	6.00	8.00	40.00
☐884	1¢	Gilbert Charles Stuart	3.00	4.00	5.50
☐885	2¢	James A. McNeill Whistler	3.00	4.00	5.50
☐886	3¢	Augustus Saint-Gaudens	3.00	4.00	5.50
☐887	5¢	Daniel Chester French	4.00	7.50	15.00
☐888	10¢	Frederic Remington	6.00	8.00	40.00
☐889	1¢	Eli Whitney	3.25	4.50	7.50
☐890	2¢	Samuel F.B. Morse	3.25	4.50	7.50
☐891	3¢	Cyrus Hall McCormick	3.25	4.50	7.50
☐892	5¢	Elias Howe	3.75	8.00	25.00
☐893	10¢	Alexander Graham Bell	6.25	10.00	50.00
☐894	3¢	Pony Express	6.25	8.00	10.00
☐895	3¢	Pan American Union	5.00	7.50	11.00
☐896	3¢	Idaho Statehood	5.00	7.50	11.00
☐897	3¢	Wyoming Statehood	5.00	7.50	11.00
☐898	3¢	Coronado Expedition	5.00	7.50	11.00
☐899	1¢	Defense	5.00	7.50	11.00

Scott No.		Single	Block	Plate Block
☐899–901	Defense set on one cover	6.00	8.00	—
☐900	2¢ Defense	5.00	7.50	12.00
☐901	3¢ Defense	5.00	7.50	12.00
☐902	3¢ Thirteenth Amendment	7.00	8.50	12.00
☐903	3¢ Vermont Statehood	7.00	8.50	12.00
☐904	3¢ Kentucky Statehood	3.50	4.75	8.00
☐905	3¢ "Win the War"	3.50	7.50	11.00
☐906	5¢ Chinese Commemorative	7.50	10.00	15.00
☐907	2¢ United Nations	3.75	6.00	8.50
☐908	1¢ Four Freedoms	4.50	7.50	10.00
☐909	5¢ Poland	4.50	7.50	11.00
☐910	5¢ Czechoslovakia	4.00	7.00	9.50
☐911	5¢ Norway	4.00	7.00	9.50
☐912	5¢ Luxembourg	4.00	7.00	9.50
☐913	5¢ Netherlands	4.00	7.00	9.50
☐914	5¢ Belgium	4.00	7.00	9.50
☐915	5¢ France	4.00	5.25	9.50
☐916	5¢ Greece	4.00	5.25	10.00
☐917	5¢ Yugoslavia	4.00	5.25	10.00
☐918	5¢ Albany	4.00	5.25	10.00
☐919	5¢ Austria	4.00	5.25	10.00
☐920	5¢ Denmark	4.00	5.25	10.00
☐921	5¢ Korea	4.00	5.25	10.00
☐922	3¢ Railroad	5.00	7.50	10.00
☐923	3¢ Steamship	4.25	5.10	8.00
☐924	3¢ Telegraph	4.25	5.10	8.00
☐925	3¢ Philippines	4.25	5.10	8.00
☐926	3¢ Motion Picture	4.25	5.10	8.00
☐927	3¢ Florida	4.25	5.10	8.00
☐928	5¢ United Nations Conference	4.25	5.10	8.00
☐929	3¢ Iwo Jima	11.00	13.00	16.00
☐929, 934–36	Set on one cover		9.00	—
☐930	1¢ Roosevelt	3.25	4.50	7.00
☐930–33	Roosevelt set on one cover		9.00	7.00
☐931	2¢ Roosevelt	3.25	4.50	7.00
☐932	3¢ Roosevelt	3.25	4.50	7.00
☐933	3¢ Roosevelt	3.25	4.50	7.00
☐934	3¢ Army	4.25	5.50	6.75
☐935	3¢ Navy	4.25	5.50	6.75
☐936	3¢ Coast Guard	4.25	5.50	7.25

Scott No.			Single	Block	Plate Block
☐937	3¢	Alfred E. Smith	3.50	4.50	7.00
☐938	3¢	Texas	4.75	5.25	7.50
☐939	3¢	Merchant Marine	4.75	5.25	7.50
☐940	3¢	Honorable Discharge	4.75	5.25	7.50
☐941	3¢	Tennessee	3.00	4.40	7.00
☐942	3¢	Iowa	3.00	4.40	7.00
☐943	3¢	Smithsonian	3.00	4.40	7.00
☐944	3¢	Santa Fe	3.00	4.40	7.00
☐945	3¢	Thomas A. Edison	3.00	4.40	7.00
☐946	3¢	Joseph Pulitzer	3.00	4.40	7.00
☐947	3¢	Stamp Centenary	3.00	4.40	7.00
☐948	5¢, 10¢	Centenary Exhibition Sheet	3.50	—	—
☐949	3¢	Doctors	4.00	5.00	7.00
☐950	3¢	Utah	3.00	4.50	7.00
☐951	3¢	"Constitution"	3.50	4.50	7.00
☐952	3¢	Everglades Park	3.00	4.50	7.00
☐953	3¢	Carver	3.00	4.50	7.00
☐954	3¢	California Gold	2.50	4.00	5.00
☐955	3¢	Mississippi Territory	2.50	4.00	5.00
☐956	3¢	Four Chaplains	2.50	4.00	5.00
☐957	3¢	Wisconsin Centennial	2.50	4.00	5.00
☐958	5¢	Swedish Pioneers	2.50	4.00	5.00
☐959	3¢	Women's Progress	2.50	4.00	5.00
☐960	3¢	William Allen White	2.50	4.00	5.00
☐961	3¢	U.S.-Canada Friendship	2.50	4.00	5.00
☐962	3¢	Francis Scott Key	2.50	4.00	5.00
☐963	3¢	Salute to Youth	2.50	4.00	5.00
☐964	3¢	Oregon Territory	2.50	4.00	5.00
☐965	3¢	Harlan Fiske Stone	2.50	4.00	5.00
☐966	3¢	Palomar Observatory	2.50	4.00	5.00
☐967	3¢	Clara Barton	2.50	4.00	5.50
☐968	3¢	Poultry Industry	2.50	4.25	5.00
☐969	3¢	Gold Star Mothers	2.50	4.25	5.00
☐970	3¢	Volunteer Fireman	4.00	5.00	7.00
☐971	3¢	Ft. Kearney, Nebraska	2.60	4.25	5.00
☐972	3¢	Indian Centennial	2.60	4.25	5.00
☐973	3¢	Rough Riders	2.60	4.25	5.00
☐974	3¢	Juliette Low	3.50	4.50	7.50
☐975	3¢	Will Rogers	2.60	4.25	5.00

Scott No.		Single	Block	Plate Block
☐976	3¢ Fort Bliss	3.00	4.75	6.50
☐977	3¢ Moina Michael	2.50	4.00	6.50
☐978	3¢ Gettysburg Address	3.00	7.00	7.50
☐979	3¢ American Turners Society	2.25	4.00	6.00
☐980	3¢ Joel Chandler Harris	2.25	4.00	6.00
☐981	3¢ Minnesota Territory	2.25	4.00	6.00
☐982	3¢ Washington and Lee University	2.25	4.00	6.00
☐983	3¢ Puerto Rico Election	2.25	4.00	6.00
☐984	3¢ Annapolis, Md.	2.25	4.00	6.00
☐985	3¢ G.A.R.	2.25	4.00	6.00
☐986	3¢ Edgar Allan Poe	2.25	4.00	5.50
☐987	3¢ American Bankers Association	2.25	4.25	6.50
☐988	3¢ Samuel Gompers	2.25	4.25	6.50
☐989	3¢ Freedom Statue	2.25	4.25	6.50
☐989–992	Nat. Capital Sesquicentennial set on one cover	4.00	—	—
☐990	3¢ Nat. Capital Sesqui. (Executive)	2.25	4.25	6.50
☐991	3¢ Nat. Capital Sesqui. (Judicial)	2.25	4.25	6.50
☐992	3¢ Nat. Capital Sesqui. (Legislative)	2.10	4.25	6.50
☐993	3¢ Railroad Engineers	2.10	4.25	6.50
☐994	3¢ Kansas City Centenary	2.10	4.25	6.50
☐995	3¢ Boy Scout	3.75	7.50	8.50
☐996	3¢ Indiana Ter. Sesquicentennial	2.10	4.00	5.00
☐997	3¢ California Statehood	2.10	4.00	5.00
☐998	3¢ United Confederate Veterans	2.10	4.00	5.00
☐999	3¢ Nevada Centennial	2.10	4.00	5.00
☐1000	3¢ Landing of Cadillac	2.10	4.00	5.00
☐1001	3¢ Colorado Statehood	2.10	4.00	5.00
☐1002	3¢ American Chemical Society	2.10	4.00	5.00
☐1003	3¢ Battle of Brooklyn	2.10	4.00	5.00
☐1004	3¢ Betsy Ross	2.10	4.00	5.00
☐1005	3¢ 4-H Clubs	2.10	4.00	5.00
☐1006	3¢ B & O Railroad	2.10	4.00	5.00
☐1007	3¢ American Automobile Assoc.	2.10	4.00	5.00
☐1008	3¢ NATO	2.10	4.00	5.00
☐1009	3¢ Grand Coulee Dam	2.10	4.00	5.00
☐1010	3¢ Lafayette	2.10	4.00	5.00

Scott No.	Single	Block	Plate Block
☐1011 3¢ Mt. Rushmore Memorial	2.10	4.00	5.50
☐1012 3¢ Civil Engineers	2.10	4.00	5.50
☐1013 3¢ Service Women	2.10	4.00	5.50
☐1014 3¢ Gutenberg Bible	2.10	4.00	5.50
☐1015 3¢ Newspaper Boys	2.10	4.00	5.50
☐1016 3¢ Red Cross	2.10	4.00	5.50
☐1017 3¢ National Guard	2.10	4.00	5.50
☐1018 3¢ Ohio Sesquicentennial	2.10	4.00	5.50
☐1019 3¢ Washington Territory	2.10	4.00	5.50
☐1020 3¢ Louisiana Purchase	2.10	4.00	5.50
☐1021 5¢ Opening of Japan	2.10	4.00	5.50
☐1022 3¢ American Bar Association	2.10	4.00	5.50
☐1023 3¢ Sagamore Hill	2.10	4.00	5.50
☐1024 3¢ Future Farmers	2.10	4.00	5.50
☐1025 3¢ Trucking Industry	2.10	4.00	5.50
☐1026 3¢ Gen. G.S. Patton, Jr.	2.10	4.00	5.50
☐1027 3¢ New York City	2.10	4.00	5.50
☐1028 3¢ Gadsden Purchase	2.10	4.00	5.50
☐1029 3¢ Columbia University	2.10	4.00	3.50
☐1030 ½¢ Franklin	—	2.10	3.50
☐1031 1¢ Washington	—	2.10	3.50
☐1031a 1¼¢ Palace	—	2.10	4.00
☐1032 1½¢ Mount Vernon	—	2.10	4.00
☐1033 2¢ Jefferson	—	2.10	4.00
☐1034 2½¢ Bunker Hill	—	2.10	4.00
☐1035 3¢ Statue of Liberty	2.00	4.00	5.00
☐1036 4¢ Lincoln	2.00	4.00	5.00
☐1037 4½¢ Hermitage	2.00	4.00	5.00
☐1038 5¢ Monroe	2.00	4.00	5.00
☐1039 6¢ Roosevelt	2.00	4.00	5.00
☐1040 7¢ Wilson	2.00	4.00	5.00
☐1041 8¢ Statue of Liberty	2.00	4.00	5.00
☐1042 8¢ Statue of Liberty	2.00	4.00	5.00
☐1042a 8¢ Pershing	2.50	5.00	7.00
☐1043 9¢ The Alamo	2.10	4.15	5.50
☐1044 10¢ Independence Hall	2.10	4.15	5.50
☐1045 12¢ Harrison	2.10	4.15	5.50
☐1046 15¢ John Jay	2.10	4.15	5.50
☐1047 20¢ Monticello	2.10	4.15	5.50
☐1048 25¢ Paul Revere	2.10	4.15	5.50

Scott No.	Single	Block	Plate Block
☐1049 30¢ Robert E. Lee	4.00	5.50	8.00
☐1050 40¢ John Marshall	4.50	7.00	8.50
☐1051 50¢ Susan Anthony	5.50	9.00	15.00
☐1052 $1 Patrick Henry	9.50	15.00	22.00
☐1053 $5 Alexander Hamilton	50.00	80.00	110.00
☐1054 1¢ Washington (coil)	1.90	—	—
☐1055 2¢ Jefferson (coil)	1.90	—	—
☐1056 2¹/₂¢ Bunker Hill (coil)	1.90	—	—
☐1057 3¢ Statue of Liberty (coil)	1.90	—	—
☐1058 4¢ Lincoln (coil)	1.90	—	—
☐1059 4¹/₂¢ The Hermitage (coil)	1.90	—	—
☐1059a 25¢ Paul Revere (coil)	2.25	—	—
☐1060 3¢ Nebraska Territory	2.00	4.00	5.00
☐1061 3¢ Kansas Territory	2.00	4.00	5.00
☐1062 3¢ George Eastman	2.00	4.00	5.00
☐1063 3¢ Lewis & Clark	2.00	4.00	5.00
☐1064 3¢ Pennsylvania Academy of the Fine Arts	2.00	4.00	5.00
☐1065 3¢ Land Grant Colleges	2.60	4.50	6.50
☐1066 8¢ Rotary International	2.90	4.50	6.50
☐1067 3¢ Armed Forces Reserve	2.10	4.50	6.50
☐1068 3¢ New Hampshire	2.00	4.00	5.00
☐1069 3¢ Soo Locks	2.00	4.00	5.00
☐1070 3¢ Atoms for Peace	2.00	4.00	5.00
☐1071 3¢ Fort Ticonderoga	2.00	4.00	5.00
☐1072 3¢ Andrew W. Mellon	2.00	4.00	5.00
☐1073 3¢ Benjamin Franklin	2.00	4.00	5.00
☐1074 3¢ Booker T. Washington	2.00	4.00	5.00
☐1075 3¢, 8¢ FIPEX Souvenir Sheet	5.75	—	—
☐1076 3¢ FIPEX	2.65	3.50	4.50
☐1077 3¢ Wildlife (Turkey)	2.10	3.50	4.50
☐1078 3¢ Wildlife (Antelope)	2.10	3.50	4.50
☐1079 3¢ Wildlife (Salmon)	2.00	3.50	4.50
☐1080 3¢ Pure Food and Drug Laws	2.00	3.50	4.50
☐1081 3¢ Wheatland	2.00	3.50	4.50
☐1082 3¢ Labor Day	2.00	3.50	4.50
☐1083 3¢ Nassau Hall	2.00	3.50	4.50
☐1084 3¢ Devil's Tower	2.00	3.50	4.50
☐1085 3¢ Children	2.00	3.50	4.50
☐1086 3¢ Alexander Hamilton	2.00	3.50	4.50

Scott No.		Single	Block	Plate Block
☐1087 3¢	Polio	2.10	3.75	5.50
☐1088 3¢	Coast & Geodetic Survey	2.00	3.50	5.20
☐1089 3¢	Architects	2.00	3.50	5.20
☐1090 3¢	Steel Industry	2.00	3.50	5.20
☐1091 3¢	Naval Review	2.00	3.50	5.20
☐1092 3¢	Oklahoma Statehood	2.00	3.50	5.20
☐1093 3¢	School Teachers	2.00	3.50	5.20
☐1094 4¢	Flag	2.00	3.50	5.20
☐1095 3¢	Shipbuilding	2.00	3.50	4.50
☐1096 8¢	Ramon Magsaysay	2.00	3.50	4.50
☐1097 3¢	Lafayette Bicentenary	2.00	3.50	4.50
☐1098 3¢	Wildlife (Whooping Crane)	2.00	3.50	4.50
☐1099 3¢	Religious Freedom	2.00	3.50	4.50
☐1100 3¢	Gardening Horticulture	2.00	3.50	4.50
☐1104 3¢	Brussels Exhibition	2.00	3.50	4.50
☐1105 3¢	James Monroe	2.00	3.50	4.50
☐1106 3¢	Minnesota Statehood	2.00	3.50	4.50
☐1107 3¢	International Geophysical Year	2.00	3.50	4.50
☐1108 3¢	Gunston Hall	2.00	3.50	4.50
☐1109 3¢	Mackinac Bridge	2.00	3.50	4.50
☐1110 4¢	Simon Bolivar	2.00	3.50	4.50
☐1110–1	Simon Bolivar set on one cover	3.50	—	—
☐1111 8¢	Simon Bolivar	2.00	3.50	4.50
☐1112 4¢	Atlantic Cable	2.00	3.50	4.50
☐1113 1¢	Lincoln Sesquicentennial	2.00	3.50	4.50
☐1113–16	Lincoln Sesquicentennial set on one cover	8.00	—	—
☐1114 3¢	Lincoln Sesquicentennial	2.00	3.50	4.50
☐1115 4¢	Lincoln-Douglas Debates	2.00	3.50	4.50
☐1116 4¢	Lincoln Sesquicentennial	2.00	3.50	4.50
☐1117 4¢	Lajos Kossuth	2.00	3.50	4.50
☐1117–18	Lajos Kossuth set on one cover	2.75	—	—
☐1118 8¢	Lajos Kossuth	2.00	3.50	4.50
☐1119 4¢	Freedom of Press	2.00	3.50	4.50
☐1120 4¢	Overland Mail	2.00	3.50	4.50
☐1121 4¢	Noah Webster	2.00	3.50	4.50
☐1122 4¢	Forest Conservation	2.00	3.50	4.50

Scott No.			Single	Block	Plate Block
☐1123	4¢	Fort Duquesne	2.00	3.50	4.75
☐1124	4¢	Oregon Statehood	2.00	3.50	4.75
☐1125	4¢	San Martin	2.00	3.50	4.75
☐1125–26		San Martin set on one cover	2.75	—	—
☐1126	8¢	San Martin	2.00	3.50	4.75
☐1127	4¢	NATO	2.00	3.50	4.75
☐1128	4¢	Arctic Explorations	2.00	3.50	4.75
☐1129	8¢	World Trade	2.00	3.50	4.75
☐1130	4¢	Silver Centennial	2.00	3.50	4.75
☐1131	4¢	St. Lawrence Seaway	2.00	3.50	4.75
☐1132	4¢	Flag	2.00	3.50	4.75
☐1133	4¢	Soil Conservation	2.00	3.50	4.75
☐1134	4¢	Petroleum Industry	2.50	4.00	5.00
☐1135	4¢	Dental Health	2.50	4.00	5.00
☐1136	4¢	Reuter	2.00	3.50	4.60
☐1136–37		Reuter set on one cover	2.75	—	—
☐1137	8¢	Reuter	2.00	3.50	4.60
☐1138	4¢	Dr. Ephraim McDowell	2.00	3.50	4.60
☐1139	4¢	Washington "Credo"	2.00	3.50	4.60
☐1140	4¢	Franklin "Credo"	2.00	3.50	4.60
☐1141	4¢	Jefferson "Credo"	2.00	3.50	4.60
☐1142	4¢	Francis Scott Key "Credo"	2.00	3.50	4.60
☐1143	4¢	Lincoln "Credo"	2.00	3.50	4.60
☐1144	4¢	Patrick Henry "Credo"	2.00	3.50	4.60
☐1145	4¢	Boy Scouts	3.00	4.00	5.00
☐1146	4¢	Olympic Winter Games	2.00	3.50	4.50
☐1147	4¢	Masaryk	2.00	3.50	4.50
☐1147–48		Masaryk set on one cover	2.75	—	—
☐1148	8¢	Masaryk	2.00	3.50	4.50
☐1149	4¢	World Refugee Year	2.00	3.50	4.50
☐1150	4¢	Water Conservation	2.00	3.50	4.50
☐1151	4¢	SEATO	2.00	3.50	4.50
☐1152	4¢	American Woman	2.00	3.50	4.50
☐1153	4¢	50-Star Flag	2.00	3.50	4.50
☐1154	4¢	Pony Express Centennial	2.10	3.75	5.00
☐1155	4¢	Employ the Handicapped	2.00	3.00	4.50
☐1156	4¢	World Forestry Congress	2.00	3.00	4.50

Scott No.		Single	Block	Plate Block
☐1157	4¢ Mexican Independence	2.00	3.00	5.00
☐1158	4¢ U.S. Japan Treaty	2.00	3.00	5.00
☐1159	4¢ Paderewski	2.00	3.00	5.00
☐1159–60	Paderewski set on one cover	2.75	—	—
☐1160	8¢ Paderewski	2.00	3.00	5.00
☐1161	4¢ Robert A. Taft	2.00	3.00	5.00
☐1162	4¢ Wheels of Freedom	2.00	3.00	5.00
☐1163	4¢ Boys' Clubs	2.00	3.00	5.00
☐1164	4¢ Automated P.O.	2.00	3.00	5.00
☐1165	4¢ Mannerheim	2.00	3.00	5.00
☐1165–66	Mannerheim set on one cover	2.75	—	—
☐1166	8¢ Mannerheim	2.00	3.00	5.00
☐1167	4¢ Camp Fire Girls	2.00	3.00	5.00
☐1168	4¢ Garibaldi	2.00	3.00	5.00
☐1168–69	Garibaldi set on one cover	2.75	—	—
☐1169	8¢ Garibaldi	2.00	3.00	5.00
☐1170	4¢ Senator George	2.00	3.00	5.00
☐1171	4¢ Andrew Carnegie	2.00	3.00	5.00
☐1172	4¢ John Foster Dulles	2.00	3.00	5.00
☐1173	4¢ Echo I	2.00	3.00	5.00
☐1174	4¢ Gandhi	2.00	3.00	5.00
☐1174–75	Gandhi set on one cover	2.75	—	—
☐1175	8¢ Gandhi	2.00	3.00	5.00
☐1176	4¢ Range Conservation	2.00	3.00	5.00
☐1177	4¢ Horace Greeley	2.00	3.00	5.00
☐1178	4¢ Fort Sumter	3.10	4.10	5.00
☐1179	4¢ Battle of Shiloh	3.10	4.10	5.00
☐1179–82	Set on one cover	10.00	—	—
☐1180	5¢ Battle of Gettysburg	3.10	4.10	5.00
☐1181	5¢ Battle of Wilderness	3.10	4.10	5.00
☐1182	5¢ Appomattox	3.10	4.10	5.00
☐1183	4¢ Kansas Statehood	3.10	4.10	5.00
☐1184	4¢ Senator Norris	1.90	3.50	5.00
☐1185	4¢ Naval Aviation	1.90	3.00	5.00
☐1186	4¢ Workmen's Compensation	1.90	3.00	5.00
☐1187	4¢ Frederic Remington	2.10	3.00	5.10

Scott No.		Single	Block	Plate Block
☐1188 4¢	China Republic	4.50	5.50	7.00
☐1189 4¢	Naismith	7.00	8.00	9.00
☐1190 4¢	Nursing	11.00	12.50	14.00
☐1191 4¢	New Mexico Statehood	2.00	3.00	4.50
☐1192 4¢	Arizona Statehood	2.00	3.00	4.50
☐1193 4¢	Project Mercury	3.10	5.00	7.00
☐1194 4¢	Malaria Eradication	2.00	3.00	4.50
☐1195 4¢	Charles Evans Hughes	2.00	3.00	4.50
☐1196 4¢	Seattle World's Fair	2.00	3.00	4.50
☐1197 4¢	Louisiana Statehood	2.00	3.00	4.50
☐1198 4¢	Homestead Act	2.00	3.00	4.50
☐1199 4¢	Girl Scouts	4.00	4.75	6.00
☐1200 4¢	Brien McMahon	2.00	3.10	5.00
☐1201 4¢	Apprenticeship	2.00	3.10	5.00
☐1202 4¢	Sam Rayburn	2.00	3.10	5.00
☐1203 4¢	Dag Hammarskjold	2.00	3.10	5.00
☐1204 4¢	Hammarskjold "Error"	4.50	7.50	11.00
☐1205 4¢	Christmas	2.10	3.00	4.50
☐1206 4¢	Higher Education	2.10	3.00	4.50
☐1207 4¢	Winslow Homer	2.10	3.00	4.50
☐1208 4¢	Flag	2.00	2.80	4.50
☐1209 1¢	Jackson	2.00	3.00	4.50
☐1213 5¢	Washington	2.00	3.00	4.50
☐1225 1¢	Jackson (coil)	2.00	—	—
☐1229 5¢	Washington (coil)	2.00	—	—
☐1230 5¢	Carolina Charter	2.00	3.00	4.50
☐1231 5¢	Food for Peace	2.00	3.00	4.50
☐1232 5¢	West Virginia Statehood	2.00	3.00	4.50
☐1233 5¢	Emancipation Proclamation	2.00	3.00	4.50
☐1234 5¢	Alliance for Progress	2.00	3.00	4.50
☐1235 5¢	Cordell Hull	2.00	3.00	4.50
☐1236 5¢	Eleanor Roosevelt	2.00	3.00	4.50
☐1237 5¢	Science	2.00	3.00	4.50
☐1238 5¢	City Mail Delivery	2.00	3.00	4.50
☐1239 5¢	Red Cross	2.00	3.00	4.50
☐1240 5¢	Christmas	2.00	3.00	4.50
☐1241 5¢	Audubon	2.00	3.00	4.50
☐1242 5¢	Sam Houston	2.00	3.00	4.50
☐1243 5¢	Charles Russell	2.00	3.25	5.00
☐1244 5¢	N.Y. World's Fair	2.00	3.00	4.50

Scott No.		Single	Block	Plate Block
☐1245 5¢ John Muir		2.00	3.00	4.50
☐1246 5¢ John F. Kennedy		2.75	3.50	5.00
☐1247 5¢ New Jersey Tercentenary		2.00	3.00	4.50
☐1248 5¢ Nevada Statehood		2.00	3.00	4.50
☐1249 5¢ Register & Vote		2.00	3.00	4.50
☐1250 5¢ Shakespeare		2.10	3.50	5.00
☐1251 5¢ Drs. Mayo		4.00	5.00	7.00
☐1252 5¢ American Music		2.75	3.75	5.50
☐1253 5¢ Homemakers		2.00	3.00	4.00
☐1254–57 5¢ Christmas		2.00	5.00	10.00
☐1258 5¢ Verrazano-Narrows Bridge		2.00	3.10	4.50
☐1259 5¢ Fine Arts		2.00	3.10	4.50
☐1260 5¢ Amateur Radio		2.60	3.10	4.50
☐1261 5¢ Battle of New Orleans		2.00	3.10	4.50
☐1262 5¢ Physical Fitness		2.00	3.10	4.50
☐1263 5¢ Cancer Crusade		3.00	5.00	7.00
☐1264 5¢ Churchill		2.00	3.40	5.00
☐1265 5¢ Magna Carta		2.00	3.40	5.00
☐1266 5¢ Int'l. Cooperation Year		2.00	3.40	5.00
☐1267 5¢ Salvation Army		2.00	3.40	5.00
☐1268 5¢ Dante		2.00	3.40	5.00
☐1269 5¢ Herbert Hoover		2.00	3.40	5.00
☐1270 5¢ Robert Fulton		2.00	3.40	5.00
☐1271 5¢ Florida Settlement		2.00	3.40	5.00
☐1272 5¢ Traffic Safety		2.00	3.40	5.00
☐1273 5¢ Copley		2.00	3.40	5.00
☐1274 11¢ Int'l. Telecommunication Union		2.00	3.40	5.00
☐1275 5¢ Adlai Stevenson		2.00	3.40	5.00
☐1276 5¢ Christmas		1.90	3.40	5.00
☐1278 1¢ Jefferson		1.90	3.40	5.00
☐1279 1¼¢ Gallatin		1.90	3.40	5.00
☐1280 2¢ Wright		1.90	3.40	6.00
☐1281 3¢ Parkman		1.90	3.40	5.00
☐1282 4¢ Lincoln		1.90	3.40	5.00
☐1283 5¢ Washington		1.90	3.40	5.00
☐1283b 5¢ Washington		1.90	3.40	5.00
☐1284 6¢ Roosevelt		1.90	3.40	5.00
☐1285 8¢ Einstein		2.10	3.40	5.00
☐1286 10¢ Jackson		1.90	3.10	4.50

Scott No.	Single	Block	Plate Block
☐1286a 12¢ Ford	1.90	3.10	5.00
☐1287 13¢ Kennedy	2.50	5.00	7.00
☐1288 15¢ Holmes	2.00	3.50	4.50
☐1289 20¢ Marshall	2.25	4.00	7.00
☐1290 25¢ Douglas	2.25	4.00	7.00
☐1291 30¢ Dewey	2.50	5.00	7.00
☐1292 40¢ Paine	3.25	6.00	8.00
☐1293 50¢ Stone	4.00	7.00	9.00
☐1294 $1 O'Neill	6.50	8.00	12.00
☐1295 $5 Moore	47.00	90.00	115.00
☐1304 5¢ Washington (coil)	—	pr. 1.60	lp. 3.25
☐1305 6¢ Roosevelt (coil)	—	pr. 1.60	lp. 3.25
☐1305c $1 O'Neill (coil)	—	pr. 1.60	lp. 3.25
☐1306 5¢ Migratory Bird Treaty	3.00	4.00	5.50
☐1307 5¢ Humane Treatment of Animals	2.25	3.00	4.00
☐1308 5¢ Indiana Statehood	1.90	3.00	4.00
☐1309 5¢ Circus	3.00	4.00	6.00
☐1310 5¢ SIPEX	1.90	3.10	4.00
☐1311 5¢ SIPEX (sheet)	2.10	3.10	4.00
☐1312 5¢ Bill of Rights	1.90	3.10	4.00
☐1313 5¢ Polish Millennium	1.90	3.10	4.00
☐1314 5¢ National Park Service	1.90	3.10	4.00
☐1315 5¢ Marine Corps Reserve	2.00	3.25	5.00
☐1316 5¢ Gen'l. Fed. of Women's Clubs	2.10	3.50	5.50
☐1317 5¢ Johnny Appleseed	1.90	3.00	4.00
☐1318 5¢ Beautification of America	1.90	3.00	4.00
☐1319 5¢ Great River Road	1.90	3.00	4.00
☐1320 5¢ Savings Bonds	1.90	3.00	6.00
☐1321 5¢ Christmas	1.90	3.00	6.00
☐1322 5¢ Mary Cassatt	2.10	3.10	5.50
☐1323 5¢ National Grange	1.90	3.00	5.00
☐1324 5¢ Canada Centenary	1.90	3.00	5.00
☐1325 5¢ Erie Canal	1.90	3.00	5.00
☐1326 5¢ Search for Peace	1.90	3.00	5.00
☐1327 5¢ Thoreau	1.90	3.00	5.00
☐1328 5¢ Nebraska Statehood	1.90	3.00	5.00
☐1329 5¢ Voice of America	1.90	3.00	5.00
☐1330 5¢ Davy Crockett	1.90	3.10	5.50

Scott No.	Single	Block	Plate Block
☐1331–1332 5¢ Space Accomplishments			
	12.00	pr. 20.00	24.00
☐1333 5¢ Urban Planning	1.90	3.10	5.00
☐1334 5¢ Finland Independence	1.90	3.10	5.00
☐1335 5¢ Thomas Eakins	1.90	3.10	5.00
☐1336 5¢ Christmas	1.90	3.10	5.00
☐1337 5¢ Mississippi Statehood	1.90	3.10	5.00
☐1338 6¢ Flag	1.90	3.10	5.00
☐1339 6¢ Illinois Statehood	1.90	3.10	5.00
☐1340 6¢ Hemis Fair '68	1.90	3.10	5.00
☐1341 $1 Airlift	8.00	12.00	17.00
☐1342 6¢ Youth-Elks	1.90	3.10	5.00
☐1343 6¢ Law and Order	3.10	4.50	7.50
☐1344 6¢ Register and Vote	2.75	3.10	5.00
☐1345–1354 6¢ Historic Flag series of 10, all on one cover	8.00	—	15.00
☐1345–54 Set on 10 covers	30.00	—	—
☐1355 6¢ Disney	12.00	15.00	20.00
☐1356 6¢ Marquette	1.90	3.10	5.00
☐1357 6¢ Daniel Boone	1.90	3.10	5.00
☐1358 6¢ Arkansas River	1.90	3.10	5.00
☐1359 6¢ Leif Erikson	1.90	3.10	5.00
☐1360 6¢ Cherokee Strip	1.90	3.10	5.00
☐1361 6¢ John Trumbull	2.25	4.00	5.50
☐1362 6¢ Waterfowl Conservation	2.25	4.00	5.50
☐1363 6¢ Christmas	2.25	4.00	5.50
☐1364 6¢ American Indian	1.90	3.10	5.00
☐1365–1368 6¢ Beautification of America	2.00	7.00	11.00
☐1369 6¢ American Legion	1.90	3.10	5.00
☐1370 6¢ Grandma Moses	2.10	3.50	5.00
☐1371 6¢ Apollo 8	3.10	6.00	8.50

NOTE: From number 1372 to date, most First Day Covers have a value of $1.75 to $2.00 for single stamps, $2.75 to $4.00 for blocks of four and $4.00 to $5.00 for plate blocks of four.

Start your U.S. collection with

SCOTT

Stars and Stripes Album
48-page looseleaf album featuring stamps of the last 25 years. Pages can be integrated to the next level album, the Pony Express.

$8.95

Pony Express Album
Housed in a padded leatherette binder, this 200-page album features spaces for thousands of stamps. Each space includes a brief story about the stamp.

$24.95

Minuteman Album
The classic American stamp album. All spaces identified with famous Scott Catalogue numbers. Pages feature brief story about stamps, providing a complete history of the U.S.

$42.50

Available at your local dealer or direct from
Scott Publishing Co., P.O. Box 828, Sidney, OH 45365

MEMBERSHIP IN THE ANA COULD BE YOUR BEST INVESTMENT THIS YEAR.

As a rare coin collector or hobbyist, you continually deal with a variety of questions. How can you know that the coin you're about to purchase is not counterfeit? How can you find the detailed, current information you need to build your collection? There is no authority to help you solve all these problems. Unless you belong to the American Numismatic Association.

Coin Certification and Grading. ANA experts examine rare coins for authenticity to help safeguard against counterfeiting and misrepresentation. ANA now offers the ANACS Grading Service—third party expert opinions as to the condition of U.S. coins submitted for examination, and will issue certificates of authenticity.

Library Service. The largest circulating numismatic library in the world is maintained by the ANA. Its sole purpose is to provide you with free access to invaluable information that can't be found anywhere else.

The Numismatist. The Association's fully illustrated magazine, considered *the* outstanding publication devoted exclusively to all phases of numismatics, is mailed free to all members.

And there are more benefits available through the ANA. Like coin insurance, special seminars, free booklets and photographic services. You can't find benefits like these anywhere else. Don't you owe it to yourself to join?

I want some recognition!
Make me an ANA Member.

Check One:

☐ Regular $26 plus $6 first-year processing fee
☐ Junior $11 (age 17 or younger)
☐ Senior $22 plus $6 first-year processing fee (age 65 or older)

☐ 5-year $120
☐ Life $750
☐ Foreign $28 plus $6 first-year processing fee

☐ Mr. ☐ Mrs. ☐ Ms.

Name _____
Please Print
Street _____

City _____ State _____ Zip _____

Birthdate _____/_____/_____

I agree to abide by the American Numismatic Association's bylaws and Code of Ethics which require the publication of each applicant's name and state.

_____   _____
Signature of Applicant   Signature of Parent or Guardian
                                            (required for Junior applicant)

☐ Check here if you DO NOT want your name and address forwarded to an ANA Club Representative in your area.

☐ Check here if you want your name provided to numismatic-related companies.

☐ Check
☐ MasterCard
☐ AmExpress

☐ Money Order
☐ VISA

_____   Expiration Date _____
Credit Card Account No.

_____
Signature of Cardholder (required)

SPONSOR_____   ANA No._____
(optional)

Foreign applications must be accompanied by U.S. Funds drawn on a U.S. bank.
OR JOIN BY PHONE: Use your VISA, MasterCard or American Express Card.
Call 719-632-2646

**Return application with payment to:
American Numismatic Association
818 N. Cascade Ave.
Colorado Springs, CO 80903-3279**

The Blackbooks!

0-676-60174-X
$7.99 (Canada: $11.99)

0-609-80948-2
$6.99 (Canada: $10.99)

0-676-60177-4
$7.99 (Canada: $11.99)

The leading authorities on U.S. coins, U.S. paper money, and world coins!

All national bestsellers, these dynamic books are the *proven* annual guides for collectors in these fields!

- **Coins**—Every U.S. coin evaluated . . . features the American Numismatic Association Official Grading System

- **Paper Money**—Every government-issued note covered

- **World Coins**—Features the most popular and collectible foreign coins from forty-eight countries around the world

BUY IT ● USE IT ● BECOME AN EXPERT™

Available from House of Collectibles in bookstores everywhere!

Collecting Coins Has Never Been More Fun!

There are fifty reasons to collect coins, and **The Official Guidebook to America's State Quarters** tells you why!

The new commemorative state quarters have become America's latest collecting craze, and this exciting book is packed with valuable information:

- How to identify mint errors and value your collection
- Learn the design process and how to be a part of it in future issues
- Find out when your state's coin will be released

Written by David L. Ganz, the driving force behind the fifty-state program, **The Official Guidebook to America's State Quarters** is a record of American history that will stand for all time.

0-609-80770-6 / $6.99 (Canada: $10.99)